ENVIRONMENT AND DEVELOPMENT

Published for

Lal Bahadur Shastri National Academy of Administration, Government of India, Mussoorie, India.

Sustainable Development Foundation, New Delhi, India; and The South-North Centre for International Policy Studies, School of Oriental and African Studies, University of London, London, U.K.

AMITAVA MUKHERJEE after a distinguished academic career, obtained his first class B.A. (Honours) degree (1972) and his first class Master's Degree (1976) in Economics, from Ranchi University. He secured his Master's Degree in Administrative Science and Managerial Economics from the William Mars Rice University, Houston (1978); studied Comparative Economic and Political Systems at Washington and obtained his Ph.D. degree for his treatise on the 'Behaviour of Firms', (1983); carried out his post-doctorate research at Rice (1985) and at the University of South Florida, Tampa (1987). He held a joint Visiting Appointment at the Department of Economics and the Graduate School of Business, Stanford University, Stanford, USA (1991). He was a visiting Academician to the University of London (1992). Dr. Mukherjee has numerous papers and seventeen books to his credit. His contribution to decentralised planning is internationally recognised.

He is recepient of many awards and honours, including Bihar Governor's Cup for the Best Scholar of the Year (1971), Vivekananda Centenary Endowment Gold Medal (1972), Hem Nalini De Memorial Gold Medal (1973), Rotary Foundation International Fellowship (1977-78), Brown Research Study Grant (1985) and Commonwealth Fellowship (1993), which enabled him to travel, study and research almost worldwide.

He is a life member of the Indian Econometric Society and of the Regional Science Association, a member of the Indian Economic Association, and of the Royal Economic Society, England.

Dr. Mukherjee is currently Professor of Economics and Planning and Faculty Coordinator, Academy of Administration, Mussoorie, prior to which he was advisor and Project Head of the Planning Commission Project on decentralised planning at the Lal Bahadur Shastri National Academy of Administration, Mussoorie. He is the National Project Co-ordinator for the Project of the Food and Agriculture Organisation of the United Nations, Rome.

V.K. AGNIHOTRI is an IAS Officer of the 1968 batch belonging to Andhra Pradesh Cadre. Born on 25th, August, 1945, he obtained his Masters degrees in English Literature and Political Science from the University of Allahabad, Allahabad. Before joining the IAS, he served on the Faculty of the Department of English, in the University of Allahabad. He has held several positions with the State and the Central Governments and his last substantive assignment being Development Commissioner for Handlooms in the Ministry of Textiles, Government of India, prior to his joining the Lal Bahadur Shastri National Academy of Administration, Mussoorie, as its Joint Director. He has been a visiting fellow to the Queen Elizabeth House, University of Oxford, Oxford in 1991-92. He has extensive experience in development administration. His current area of research is public policy analysis.

ENVIRONMENT AND DEVELOPMENT

(Views from the East & the West)

AMITAVA MUKHERJEE
Prof. & Faculty Co-ordinator
Centre for Micro-Planning and Regional Studies
L.B.S. National Academy of Administration
(Government of India)
Mussoorie

and

Edited by
V.K. AGNIHOTRI
Joint Director
L.B.S. National Academy of Administration
(Government of India)
Mussoorie

CONCEPT PUBLISHING COMPANY, NEW DELHI 110059

The views and/or opinions expressed in the various papers of this volume are of the respective authors and in no way reflect the views and/or opinions either of the editors or of the organisations to which they belong.

ISBN 81-7022-788-8

First Published 1993

Published and Printed by
Ashok Kumar Mittal
Concept Publishing Company
A/15-16, Commercial Block, Mohan Garden
NEW DELHI-110059 (India)

Lasertypeset by
Printing Express
H-13, Bali Nagar
NEW DELHI-110015

TO

THE PEOPLE OF

OUR HILLS WHO CAN SAY IN WAR

AND IN PEACE

"FOR YOUR TOMORROW

WE GAVE OUR TODAY"

CONTENTS

List of Tables 11
List of Figures 14
List of Contributors 17
Acknowledgements 20
From the Editor's Desk 21

PART-I
CHANGING PERCEPTION OF DEVELOPMENT

1. Sustainable Development: Concept and Application Case of Developing Countries
   – **Srikumar Chattopadhyay** 39
2. Perspectives on Environment and Development
   – **M. Shafi** 59
3. The Emerging New Development Paradigm: Issues, Considerations and Research Agenda
   – **K.V. Sundaram** 69

PART-II
ENVIRONMENTAL ISSUES (ENERGY, WATER AND LAND POLLUTION)

4. Land Transformation and Environmental Degradation in Jaipur Urban Complex
   – **H.S. Sharma** and **M.S. Nathawat** 91
5. Some Environmental Challenges of Industrialisation in Agricultural Areas : A Case Study from the Upper Ganga Plain, India
   – **D.S. Rawat** 107

6. Landuse Change, Agroforestry and Sustainable Development in North-West India
– **R.B. Singh** 129
7. Dynamics of Rural Energy System and State of Environment: A Study of Rashmi Region
– **R.N. Vyas** 139

PART-III
ANALYSIS OF NATURAL RESOURCES MANAGEMENT SYSTEMS

8. Safeguarding the Land: The Importance of Quaternary Geomorphology to an Understanding of Land Stability in the Tropics
– **Michael F. Thomas** 161
9. Contrasts in the Development of Similar Tropical Environments : Origins and Significance
– **W.T.W. Morgan** 181
10. The State and the Ecology Management Through the People : Some Lessons from the Sukhomajri Experience
– **Gopal Krishan** and **Mehar Singh** 197

PART-IV
RIVER BASIN/VALLEY AND ENVIRONMENT

11. The Koyna Catchment : The Environment Problems Due to Displacement and Rehabilitation
– **K. Sita, V.S. Phadke** and **K.V.S. Rao** 209
12. Environmental Myth as International Politics: The Problems of the Bengal Delta
– **Graham P. Chapman** 223
13. Environmental Implications of River Valley Development: A Micro-Level Study
– **R. Ram Mohan Rao** and **N. Ram Kishan Rao** 257

PART-V
CULTURE AND ENVIRONMENT

14. Environmental Values: Western, Eastern or Global
– **Philip Sarre** 279
15. The Present State of the Hungarian Environment: Attitudes Towards Practical Environmental Provision
– **Alison D. Reeves** 291
16. The Dialectics of Environment and Culture : Kimilsungism and the North Korean Landscape
– **P.J. Atkins** 309
17. Romances of Remoteness in British Culture: The Place of the Highlands and Islands in Imagination and Practice
– **Pamela Shurmer-Smith** 333

PART-VI
SUSTAINABLE DEVELOPMENT

18. Environment and Development Theme : Sustainable Development
– **Andrew Blowers** 349
19. Shifting Cultivation and Sustainable Development in Nagaland
– **Majid Husain** 377
20. Meaning of Development: The Common Man's Concern: A Reflection through Participatory Rural Appraisal Methods
– **Amitava Mukherjee** 387
21. Eco-Development: A Case Study of Haryana
– **Nina Singh** 431

PART-VII
ENVIRONMENTAL POLICIES (GLOBAL AND NATIONAL)-I

22. Urbanisation, Poverty and Environmental Considerations: A Micro-Level Perspective
– **Pushpa Pathak** 449
23. Urbanisation, Rural Environmental Degradation and Resilience in Africa
– **H.A.C. Main** 469
24. Sustainable Urban Environments
– **Alice Coleman** 487

PART-VIII
ENVIRONMENTAL POLICIES (GLOBAL AND NATIONAL)-II

25. Urban Community Development in the Third World: Lessons from Visakhapatnam, India
– **Sheena Asthana** 505
26. The State, Business Diplomacy and the Environment
– **Chandra Pal Singh** 525
27. Urban Environmental Management for a Sustainable Quality of Life in the Metropolis of Developing Countries – A Case Study of Madurai Metropolitan, India
– **K.S. Gopalakrishnan** 541
28. Ethical Foundations of Environmental and Development Education
– **R.P. Misra** 567

Index 579

LIST OF TABLES

1.1 Environmental Appraisal (The procedure for synthesis) **45**
1.2 Themes of Maps **49**
1.3A Details to be Collected/Mapped by the Volunteers **50**
1.3B Parameters to be Investigated for Land and Water Resource (for mapping by the Scientific and Technical personnel) **51**
1.4 Kalliasseri Panchayat : Some sample data **53**
1.5 Intervention Programme **54**
1.6 Panchayat Development Society, its Composition, Task and Goal **55**
3.1 The Agenda for Research Areas Needing Attention **83**
4.1 Population Growth Trends and Projection in Jaipur 1901-91 **97**
4.2 Area Under Different Landuse/Landcover in and Around Jaipur **98**
5.1 Muzaffarnagar District: Industrial Growth 1930-1980 **110**
5.2 Muzaffarnagar District: Distribution of Industrial Units, 1981 **111**
5.3 Meerut Road of Muzaffarnagar City: Industrial Structure, 1993 **112**
5.4 Meerut Road of Muzaffarnagar City: Industrywise ratio of the number of chimneys with the number of industrial units, 1993 **114**
6.1 Characteristics of Forestry and Agriculture **136**
6.2 Forest Species and their Salt Tolerance **137**
7.1 Total Energy Use by Land Holding Classes **143**
7.2 Sectoral End Uses of Total Energy by Landholding Classes **145**
7.3 Estimates of Energy Use Models of the Total System **150**
8.1 Tentative Chronology of Late Quaternary Environmental Change **163**
8.2 Common Allochthonous Surface Deposits in the Tropics **165**

11.1 The Koyna Catchment: Area Categorised on the Basis of Slope and Average Height **212**
12.1 Losses Due to Flooding in Bangladesh, 1987 and 1988 **238**
12.2 Cereal Production in Bangladesh, 1986-88 **240**
12.3 Use of Ganges Water Flow at Farakka **241**
13.1 Soils: Range of Soil Depth **261**
13.2 Crops and Effective Root Zone **262**
13.3 Soil Erosion and Crop Suitability **262**
13.4 Percentage of Area Unfit for Cultivation Due to Excessive Salinity **263**
13.5 Depth of Water Level **264**
13.6 Incidence of Malaria in Mogulpet Village **268**
13.7 Cropping Pattern **271**
13.8 Rice Equivalents Based on APC **272**
13.9 Changes in Yield and Potential Yield of Important Crops **273**
13.10 Crop Productivity and Crop Yields **273**
13.11 Comparative Production of Crops Irrigated to Different Intensities **274**
15.1 Hungarian People's Republic Geographical, Economic and Demographic Information (1992) **293**
16.1 Crop Yields in the DPRK **318**
16.2 FAO Estimates of Crop Production in the DPRK, 1988 **319**
19.1 Nagaland: Selected Villages **378**
19.2 Nagaland: Area under *Jhum* in Selected Villages **381**
19.3 Nagaland: Rotation of Crops: Sema Tribe **382**
19.4 Nagaland: *Jhum* Cycle, Period of Occupancy and Duration of Fallowing **383**
20.1 PRA Tool-Kit **392**
20.2 Eleventh Schedule (Of the Constitution Seventy Second Amendment Bill, 1991) **420**
20.3 Secondary Data About Villages **420**
21.1 Haryana: Shallow Ground Water Quality Zones by Their Areal Extent **434**
21.2 Haryana: Salt Affected Soils **439**
21.3 Haryana: Forests as Per Cent of Total Area **443**
21.4 Haryana: Planwise Expenditure on Environmental Parameters **445**
22.1 Population of Delhi and Trivandrum **453**
22.2 Area and Density of Population **454**

22.3 Access to Safe Water and Sanitation Urban Areas of Delhi U.T. and Kerala **454**
22.4 Service Level of Water Supply, Delhi and Trivandrum **454**
22.5 Salient Features: Selected Slums and Squatter Settlements Delhi and Trivandrum, 1990 **456**
22.6 Access to Water **460**
22.7 Access to Sanitation Facilities **463**
24.1 The Influential Design Variables (slightly simplified) **493**
27.1 Urbanization in India **542**
27.2 Distribution of Class I Centres India - 1991 **545**
27.3 Growth of Population (1901-1991) **548**

LIST OF FIGURES

1.1 Uloor Panchayat: Environmental Appraisal for Landuse Planning **46**

1.2 Panchayat Level Resource Mapping: Activities and Linkages **48**

1.3 Kalliasserri Panchayat Action Plan **52**

3.1 Changes in the Structure and Orientation of Development Planning **78**

4.1 Urban Sprawl: Jaipur City **92**

4.2 Land Transformation: Jaipur City (1975) **96**

4.3 Land Transformation: Jaipur City (1986) **103**

4.4 Land Transformation: Jaipur City (1991) **104**

5.1 Industries in (A) Muzaffarnagar District of the Upper Ganga Plain (B) and along Meerut Road of Muzaffarnagar City (1993) **110**

5.2 Meerut Road of Muzaffarnagar City: Geographic Spread of Industrial Pollutants 1993 **113**

5.3 Meerut Road of Muzaffarnagar City: Industrial Effluents of Ten Selected Industries, 1993 **117**

8.1 The Landscape of *Hollows* and *Rampas* **170**

9.1 Tropical Zones **183**

9.2 Vegetation Types and Different Pattern with Agriculture **184**

10.1 Village Sukhomajri in its Regional Setting **199**

11.1 Koyna Catchment: Location and Space Relations **211**

11.2 Koyna Catchment: Status of Forest Cover (1951-87) **214**

11.3 Kusapur: A Schematic Section **216**

11.4 Munavale: A Transect **218**

11.5 Nivakane: A Cross Profile **219**

12.1 The Myths of Nature **227**

12.2 Mixture of Gravels, Sand and Clay **230**

12.3 Late Quarternary Sea Level Changes in Bengal **231**

12.4 Landforms of Bengal **235**

12.5 Changes in River Courses in Bengal **236**

12.6 Crop Losses due to Floods in Bengal (Bangladesh) **239**

12.7 Area Flooded **245**
12.8 India and Bangladesh's Plans for Water Control in Bengal **246**
12.9 World Bank Proposals **247**
12.10 Saline Incursion in Bengal **251**
12.11 Cyclone Trache in Bengal **252**
15.1 Hungarian People's Republic 1992 **296**
16.1 South Pyongyang Irrigation Scheme **322**
20.1 Transect Through Time. Illustration of Landuse Trend in Mohamadpur Barkali – A Semi-Forest Village in Doiwala Block **396**
20.2 Transact Through Mohmadpur Barkali **397**
20.3 Transect Through Time. Illustration of Landuse Trend in Bagi Village in Doiwala Block **399**
20.4 Transect of Bagi Village **400**
20.5 Transect Through Time. Illustration of Landuse Trend in Majrigrant Village in Doiwala Block **402**
20.6 Transect of Majri Grant Village **403**
20.7 Transect Through Time. Illustration of Landuse Trend in Harrawala Village in Block Doiwala **405**
20.8 The Problems and Solution of Village Harrawala **406**
20.9 Transect Through Time. Illustration of Landuse Trend in Nagal Jwalapur Village in Block Doiwala **408**
20.10 Problems and Solutions of Nagal Jawalapur Village **409**
20.11 Transect Through Time. Illustration of Landuse Trend in Khadari Kharak Maph Village in Block Doiwala **410**
20.12 Problems and Solutions of Khadari Kharak Maph Village **412**
20.13 Transect Through Time. Illustration of Landuse Trend in Balawala Village in Doiwala Block **413**
20.14 The Transect of Balawala Village **414**
20.15 Transect Through Time. Illustration of Landuse Trend in Ranipokhari Village in Doiwala Block **416**
20.16 Problems and Solutions of Ranipokhari Village **417**
21.1 Haryana: Watertable and Soil Problems **437**
23.1 The Kano Region **476**
23.2 Major Sources of Fuelwood for Kano, Mid-1980s **478**
23.3 Water Resource Development in the Kano Region, Mid-1980s **479**
27.1 Madurai City: Study Area **546**
27.2 Madurai City: Population Density **550**

27.3 Madurai City: Distribution of Slums 1988 **554**
27.4 Madurai City: Distribution of Residential Houses **555**
27.5 Madurai City: Number of Persons per Residential House **557**
27.6 Madurai City: Households per 1000 Residential Houses **558**
27.7 Madurai City: Number of Persons per Household **559**
27.8 Madurai City: Level of Education Sample Household **560**
27.9 Madurai City: Level of Income Sample Household **562**
27.10 Madurai City: Residential Environmental Quality **563**

LIST OF CONTRIBUTORS

Sheena Asthana
Department of Geography, University of Exeter, Amory Building, Rennes Drive, Exeter, EX4 4RJ, UK.

P.J. Atkins
Department of Geography, University of Durham, Durham DH1 3LE, United Kingdom.

Andrew Blowers
Open University, UK.

Graham P. Chapman
Professor of Geography, School of Oriental and African Studies, University of London, London, UK.

Srikumar Chattopadhyay
Centre for Earth Science Studies, Trivandrum, India.

Alice Coleman
Professor, King's College, University of London, London, UK.

K.S. Gopalakrishnan
Professor and Head, Department of Geography, Madurai Kamaraj University, Madurai (Tamil Nadu), India.

Majid Husain
Professor and Head, Department of Geography. Jamia Millia Islamia, New Delhi, India.

Gopal Krishan
Professor of Geography, Panjab University, Chandigarh, India.

H.A.C. Main
Division of Geography, Staffordhshire University, Leek Road, Stoke-on-Trent ST4 2DF, Britain.

R.P. Misra
Professor-Director, Gandhi Bhavan, New Delhi and President Sustainable Development Foundation, New Delhi, India.

W.T.W. Morgan
Department of Geography, University of Durham, UK.

Amitava Mukherjee
Professor of Economics and Planning, Centre for Micro Planning

and Regional Studies, LBS National Academy of Administration Mussoorie, India.

M.S. Nathawat

Scientist, B.M. Birla Institute of Science and Technology, Jaipur, India.

Pushpa Pathak

Research Fellow (Urban and Regional Planning), National Institute of Urban Affairs, New Delhi, India.

V.S. Phadke

Department of Geography, University of Bombay, Bombay, India.

K.V.S. Rao

Department of Geography, University of Bombay, Bombay, India.

N. Ram Kishan Rao

Research Associate, Department of Geography, Osmania University Hyderabad, India.

R. Ram Mohan Rao

Professor and Head, Department of Geography, Osmania University Hyderabad, India.

D.S. Rawat

Department of Geography, S.D. College, Meerut University Muzaffarnagar (U.P), India.

Alison D. Reeves

Department of Geography, University of Dundeee, Dundee, DD1 4HN, UK.

M. Shafi

Professor Emeritus, Department of Geography, Aligarh Muslim University, Aligarh, India.

Philip Sarre

Open University, UK.

H.S. Sharma

Associate Professor, Department of Geography, University of Rajasthan, Jaipur, India.

K.V. Sundaram

Development Planner and Consultant to F.A.O., Rome.

Chandra Pal Singh

Department of Geography, Delhi School of Economics, University of Delhi, Delhi, India.

Mehar Singh

Department of Geography, Panjab University, Chandigarh, Punjab, India.

R.B. Singh
Department of Geography, Delhi School of Economics, University of Delhi, Delhi, India.

K. Sita
Formerly of Department of Geography, University of Bombay, Bombay, India.

Nina Singh
Reader and Head, Department of Geography, M.D. University, Rohtak, Haryana, India.

Pamela Shurmer-Smith
Department of Geography, University of Portsmouth, U.K.

Michael F. Thomas
Department of Geography, University of Stirling, Scotland, U.K.

R.N. Vyas
Associate Professor, Department of Geography, M. L. Sukhadia University, Udaipur, India.

ACKNOWLEDGEMENTS

Our best thanks are due to Dr. R.P. Misra, Professor-Director, Gandhi Bhawan, New Delhi and President Sustainable Development Foundation, New Delhi and to Professor Graham Chapman, Professor-Director, South-North Centre for Environmental Policy, School of Oriental and African Studies, University of London, London both of whom conceived this "Indo-British dialogue" and set the ball rolling. We thank Dr. H.N. Misra, Head, Department of Geography, Himachal Pradesh University, Shimla who did all the necessary ground work towards making the "dialogue" a success.

We are most grateful to all the participants, both from India and the U.K., who contributed immensely in making this dialogue fruitful. The support received from the different Universities and Institutes in India and U.K. is sincerely acknowledged.

We are beholden to the Government of India, in the Ministry of Environment, New Delhi and to the Planning Commission, Government of India, New Delhi for their support. Thanks are due to British Council Division of the British High Commission, Delhi and the Commonwealth Human Ecology Foundation, London, for their financial support to the Sustainable Development Foundation, New Delhi to co-sponsor this fifth Indo-British Seminar.

The support, assistance and active participation of the Faculty, Staff and Officer-Trainees of the LBS National Academy of Administration, Mussoorie, and in particular of its Centre for Micro-Planning and Regional Studies, are thankfully acknowledged.

Finally, we thank our publishers M/s Concept Publishing Company, New Delhi, for their co-operation and help in several ways.

FROM THE EDITORS' DESK
(Environment and Development: The Differing Perspectives)

I. Introduction

The debate on Environment and Development has assumed phenomenal importance at the global, national and local levels. The texture and tone of the debate have, however, undergone substantial change with the flux of time. The Cartesian view of man being the controller of nature had generated an economic system, whether Capitalist or Socialist, which exploits nature to produce more and more goods (and services) to meet the material needs of homo sapiens. The pursuit of this approach to development led to exploitation of nature to a point where survival of human race was jeopardised. During the initial years, therefore, the question asked and solution sought revolved around the issue of whether to have development and ignore environment, or preserve environment and foreclose development.

It was soon realised that the drama of man's march from barbarianism to civilisation is the drama of development and growth, and there was no basis in logic and no great probability in practice, to stop that march of development. Progress of development was inevitable; preserving environment, ecology and bio-diversity at a "warranted" level was also crucial. The debate thus transformed itself into how best to have development without further injury to environment. From this crucible emerged two approaches to tackling the problems of environmental degradation and prospects of development from two polarised perspectives: the Northern and the Southern perspective.

II. The Common Grounds

There is a virtual unanimity that economic development and sound environmental management complement each other, given that on one side, development itself contributes to environmental regeneration and rejuvenation, and that, on the other, a healthy environment is a necessary condition for sustainable development. There is widespread realisation of the depressing phenomenon that over one billion people around the world are in abject poverty, and the next generation will see the world's population rising to 3.5 billion, even if the campaign to reduced population growth round the world accelerates. What is most fearsome is that most of these births will be in poorer families, which makes alleviating poverty not only a moral responsibility of the current generation but also a necessary condition for environmental sustainability of this earth and for leaving intact the very basis of future generations' welfare.

It is noted that no country has so far won the war against poverty without economic growth, but economic growth has itself often caused serious environmental damage, threatening the present and the future quality of life, though such disquietening influences of income growth are all avoidable. The response of current day problems of poverty and environment need not be in producing less but be in producing differently. There is no sphere of economic endeavour that cannot be made more sustainable.

Economic growth is essential for progress in developing countries but where growth is achieved at the cost of polluting air and water, destroying forests and depleting natural resources, growth in the real sense of the term could be lower than what the figures reveal *per se* and such growth does not have welfare effect. Measuring the welfare costs of these environmental impacts is essential both for assessing human progress and for effective policy-making. Policies and institutions required are those that encourage more efficient use of resources, that lead to a substitution of scarce resources by the more abundant and renewable ones and that support adoption of technologies and emphasizes practices which are harmless to environment need to be promoted.

From here the divergence between the Northern and Southern view of environmental problems and development perspective starts.

III. The Northern View

It is pointed out by the North that setting environmental priorities inevitably involves choices by developing countries of the South in giving priority to addressing risks to health and economic productivity, associated with dirty water, inadequate sanitation, air pollution, and land degradation, all of which are hazardous to human health. It is specifically mentioned that in poor countries:

(a) Diarrhoeal diseases resulting from contaminated water kill over 3 million children per annum, and cause about 900 million cases of illness each year;
(b) Indoor air pollution from burning wood, charcoal, or animal dung endangers the health of 400-700 million people worldwide;
(c) Dust and soot in city air causes between 300,000 and 700,000 premature deaths per annum;
(d) Soil erosion can cause annual economic losses ranging from 0.5 per cent to 1.5 per cent of GNP;
(e) Twenty-five per cent of all irrigated land suffers from salination; and
(f) Tropical forests, the primary source of livelihood for about 140 million people are being lost at the rate of 0.9 per cent per annum.

The concern over Ozone depletion continues to grow, and though the consequences of loss of bio-diversity and greenhouse warming are less certain, nevertheless they are likely to increase far into the future and would in all probability be nearly irreversible.

For improved environmental management, the North feels, corporations, households, farmers and Government of the developing countries in the South, will have to mend their behavioural patterns. Two sets of policies are seen as critically necessary. For one, policies should be directed towards harnessing the positive links between development and environment; policies that are not concurrently both growth and the environment friendly should be eliminated; subsidies to energy, pesticides, water and logging should be cut out; rights to manage and own lands, forests and fisheries should be clarified; and public enterprises have to be made accountable. It is noted that liberalising trade and investment, promoting macro-economic stability and improving the access of the poor to health, education and family planning will facilitate environmental protection. For the other, targetted policies to ensure that environmental values are properly reflected in the economic activity both of the public and the private sector, need to be operationalised. The interventions that work best are those that combine incentive and regulatory policies, recognise administrative constraints and are tailored to specific problems.

One component of the debate under reference revolves around "information, institutions and participation improving the policy process". It is held by the North that sound environmental policy is not an anathema to development objectives, nevertheless wise policies are the exceptions than the rule, because principally such policies often involve removing well-entrenched "rights" to pollute or use resources that tend to benefit the wealthy and the influential, often at the expense of the poorer sections of society. Incomplete information, uncertainty and weak regulatory powers are contributory factors in weakening public action.

The North argues that Governments in the developing parts of the world, must conserve their scarce resources and administrative capacity to implement change. For this to fructify, improved information base and analytical capability to inform priority setting and policy design; and responsive and effective institutions must be developed. It is plausible that different countries will use different machinery to perform the essential roles of Government, depending upon their administrative traditions, but all governments must foster local level participation in policy-making, monitoring and enforcement.

The North maintains that in developing countries of the South water supply, sanitation and solid wastes are amongst the most important of all environmental issues, given that (as we mentioned earlier) an estimated 3 million people die each year from the diarrohea alone. This is avoidable only if people had reasonable water and sanitation services. A large number of economic costs incurred in trying to compensate for poor quality services could be avoided. It is argued that gains in environment quality, health, equity and direct economic returns, are possible by adopting an approach which comprises four key elements, viz., *one*, management of water resources taking account of economic efficiency and environmental sustainability; *two*, provisioning, at full cost, those private services for which people want and are willing to pay, including water supply and the collection of human excreta, waste water and solid waste; *three*, utilisation of scarce public funds only for those services (specifically the treatment and disposal of human excreta, waste water and solid waste) which provide benefits to the community as a whole, and *finally*, development of a flexible, institutional mechanism for providing these services, with community organisations and private sector having a larger role to play.

The next strand of discussion appertains to "Energy and Industry" We are reminded by the North that unless policies are altered, emissions from fossil fuel power generation will rise ten times in the next forty years; fuel used by vehicles would rise over five times; and industrial emissions and wastes will also go up over five hundred per cent as demand for manufactures rises steeply. Low waste and clean technologies and practices are capable of reducing national pollution levels as output expands. To encourage the adoption of technologies, that are capable of reducing country specific pollution levels with expansion in output, and for opting to reduce carbon emission in the long run, governments the South in must pursue policies which improve the efficiency in energy use. For example, the elimination of subsidies to the power sector, and in many developing countries, for vehicle fuels and coal, will increase efficiency in energy-use and, at once, help to reduce pollution while raising a country's economic output. Policies to reduce pollution directly, using economic incentives, laws and regulations are also advocated.

Rural Environmental Policy is an area of major concern for the North. Given the rate of growth in world's population in the South, over the next few decades, demands for food, fuel and fiber will rise enormously which will make more intensive, and extensive, exploitation of natural resources, like agricultural lands, forests, water bodies and minerals, inescapable. Only if yields are increased by careful and sustainable management of those resources that are already cultivated, will it be easier to resist pressure to draw down even more new resources like draining of wetland, clearing of forests, encroaching upon natural habitats.

Three obstacles that are commonly conceived as standing in the way of sensible resource management by the South are: *one,* failure to recognise scarcity in the natural world, *two*, failure to ensure that the institutions managing natural resources are accountable, and *three*, failure to mobilise knowledge for environmental management. To overcome these obstacles, incentives to individuals to ensure that their activities do not impose costs on others, a clear legal framework and supporting services for common property resources and devolution of the responsibility for managing some resources to individuals and communities, and fiscal accountable utilities, are indispensable. Governments in developing countries of the South need to make use of the system of markets and prices to allocate some resources for protecting property rights, and for supporting the dissemination of knowledge of sound environmental practices.

Not unnaturally, the North is quick in projecting International Environmental concerns. International environment problems are more complicated to solve than national ones because, no single authority can lay down and enforce appropriate policies, and because solutions must accommodate large variations in the balance of benefits and costs to different countries. Some countries with more pressing local problems but less money to solve them, are not likely to act fast enough and to do enough.

Given the likely effects of global warming, it is indicated by the North that a wise policy would include, but be not restricted to, measures to reduce emissions and improve economic performance, such as, elimination of subsidies for fossil fuel consumption and deforestation, investments in more information to avoid the risk of costly over or under reaction; precautionary measures for reducing emissions now at modest costs and bring down the costs of doing so in the future, and financial transfers to help the developing countries to broaden their technological options. A call for a pragmatic international action to protect earth's bio-diversity is clearly and loudly heard. Individual countries can do more to manage these resources in their own interests, but it is not easily realised by the North that additional transfers from the rich to the poorer countries will be needed to ensure as much conservation as the rest of the world would like.

No discussion is complete without reference to "Environmental Protection". It appears, at first sight, that investments in this area have to be large but on closer examination, the North quickly points out, such investments must and can be afforded when judged against the backdrop of the facts that costs are modest in comparison to the potential gains from improved efficiency and economic growth, and that more investments will pay for themselves. Increased international support will nonetheless be essential. The North argues that domestic environmental concerns need to be better embedded in official assistance programmes to developing countries of the South and the fact of close links between environmental quality and poverty reduction warranting additional aid is not understood in the right perspective. Concessional fundings for global problems is required, in addition to aid budgets. Providing the poorer countries with greater access to industrial country trade and capital markets, will be essential for a sustainable future for the globe which the North is seemingly not ready to reflect in its thoughts and deeds.

The debate on Environment and Development as it has evolved in the North thus explores the relationship between development and environment from two perspectives: *first*, environmental quality itself being a part of the improvement in welfare which development in the last analysis attempts at, and, *second*, damage to environment can undermine present and future growth in productivity, which again development seeks out. It is in this context that the complementarity between policies directed to improve and preserve environment, and toward achieving development, are focussed.

The North has correctly recognised that sound development policies will need to be supplemented by strong public institutions and policies, for environment to have any change. By pointing out that though the system of markets and prices provides the best mechanism for growth yet environment is one area in which public action is needed, the North has re-emphasized the element of externalities of environment. This has two implications: *one*, it takes winds off the sails of those who argue that conserving environment should over-ride developmental considerations, and *second*, at a time when public action is looked upon as unfashionable, it gives a call for a reasonable State intervention in an area which we cannot afford to play around with.

The North, as we have mentioned above, identifies unhealthy water, inadequate sanitation, soil depletion, indoor smoke from cooking fires and outdoor smoke from coal burning as the life threatening and most pressing environmental problems of the less developed countries of the South. And for the developed countries, the North is of the view that carbon dioxide emissions, stratospheric ozone depletion, nitrous oxide, hazardous and municipal waste are the areas of major concern. Though there could be much debate about the Northern view on the identification of the major environmental problem sets of the developing and the developed world (including the reasons for which water and sanitation have been put as the top of the line environmental problems of the less developed countries), yet it is correct in establishing that the two sets of problem are interwoven. One cannot be solved without solving the other on a sustainable basis. This enables environmentalists in the South to make a good case for assistance from the developed North to the under-developed South. To that extent it has correctly reflected on the contentious issue of sharing cost of environmental conservation that has plagued the Earth Summit at Rio de Janeiro, held in June 1992.

Though the World Commission on Environment and Development had brought forth the fact that the borderline between development and environment, in policy-making and action, has been progressively blurred, nevertheless the recognition of the inter-linkages between environment and development by the North is an important step forward and this helps to strengthen the case made out for financing of environmental regeneration in the less developed world of the South by the developed countries in the North.

IV. The Southern View

The debate, as articulated in the North, has succeeded in identifying some of the key elements of the growing debate on environment and development, but according to the Southern view there are important gaps that have been left unguarded. First it is pointed out, there is a failure in the sense that much of the blame for environmental problems, current and potential, has been laid at the door step of population growth. There can hardly be any debate that population growth has vital links with environment, via the "consumption function" and the "welfare function", but there is an inadequate understanding in the North about two important dimensions of population growth, viz., *one*, the bearing that the "locale" of the population growth has on the issues at hand and *two*, about the fact that all the environmental problems currently identified as being due to population pressure is not based on irrefutable arguments. We will have to discuss these two issues briefly before proceeding further, as they are crucial to the contemporaneous debate on environment.

The locale of population growth in the coming decades needs to be examined to begin with. The assumption that the impact of per unit growth in population across the board is uniform, is unconvincing. There has to be a "differential approach". The environmental impact of one unit of population growth in the high-income developed countries of the North far outstrips the impact of one unit of population growth in the low income developing countries of the South. To equate them is to miss the woods for the forests. "Nine thousand out of every ten thousand births in the world would occur in the next decade in the developing countries, but every thousand baby born in the developed industrialised world consume three to four times as much of the earths resources as 9000 born in the developing world".[1] That is, every 1000 babies born in the developed countries in the North impose on the earth's carrying capacity a burden equivalent to that imposed by 36000 babies born in the developing countries of the South. The North should take note of this huge disparity in the consumption of resources as being incompatible with sustainable development. According to Benton Musslewhite, an eminent environmentalist, the United States is the world's worst polluter besides consuming the most resources and giving out 21 per cent of the CFCs in the atmosphere. It is, therefore, argued by the South that the containment of consumption by the developed countries of the North within "sustainable limits" is an important as the deceleration in population growth of the less developed countries of the South. Arguably asking the Southern countries to mend their ways without the developed countries of the North themselves making an attempt to behave responsibly, is to offer the world, not bread, but stone.

It is held by the South that attributing all environmental problems to population growth is not necessarily based on irrefutable evidence. For instance, the case of tropical deforestation which has been agitating the developed North visibly for quite some time now, including at the Rio Earth Summit, is cited by the South. There are an increasing number of researchers who are examining the elements germane to tropical deforestation and agricultural frontier extension. A study by Capistrano,[2] and one by Capistrano and Kiker[3] examined the impact of international and domestic macro-economic factors on tropical deforestation, taking changes in timber production forest area as proxy for total deforestation. They found high agricultural export prices and domestic adjustment policies, such as exchange rate devaluation and debt servicing ratios, as important factors inducing agricultural expansion and forest clearing. These studies may be of limited use in the context of deforestation of tropical timber forests but not to overall tropical deforestation. Comparative analysis of 24 Latin American countries highlights an indirect relationship between population pressure and frontier expansion, in that an increasing number of urban consumers raise the demand for domestic production and hence agricultural land.[4] A statistical study covering all tropical forest countries indicates that frontier agricultural expansion (denoted by index of food crop and meat production) and debt servicing has adverse impact on tropical deforestation.[5] Increase in domestic roundwood and per capita GNP had smaller positive impacts and population had a negative impact on deforestation.[6] Thus it is apparent, argues the South, that to relate population growth in unequivocal terms to deforestation is not correct. "Clearly, further work needs to be undertaken to examine the explicit relationship between population growth, population density and deforestation."[7]

Indeed according to the Southern view there are a plethora of both endogenous and exgenous variables that operate upon tropical forests for food and cultivation: climatic factors, lack of affordable low-input technology for improving productivity of traditional varieties, increased concentration of the poor on marginal lands, pressures of livestock, patterns of land ownership, access to on-farm and off-farm employment, level of skills and education, cultural and ethnic origin, economic roles of women and children and so forth, all have bearing on frontier expansion. The interface of all these variables, or some combination thereof, can force poor people to go in for immediate economic benefits at the cost of long run livelihood entitlement. This interface being complex, it does not admit of singling out any one variable as being more operative than others. Thus, the South forcefully puts forth the argument that though it is true that population growth and uneven distribution in some area complicates natural resource management, it is as much true that "population pressures on resources usually reflect the extremely skewed distribution of resources. When farmers encroach on tropical forests or cultivate erodible hillsides, population pressure is blamed, but the pressure typically stems from the concentration of land in large holdings."[8] The debate in the North on environment and development when seen from this side of the globe appears not to have been apparently fine tuned to capture the effects of these elements in the picture.

The North has rightly identified the nexus between poverty and environment, and has therefore, included prescriptions for tackling both the problems of poverty and environmental protection and damage repair. Control of population in the developing countries of the South is the cornerstone of the arch of its prescription for concurrently tackling the threats of poverty and environmental degradation. To that extent it has served a useful purpose well, but in the process it has ended up emphasizing cures more for the symptoms than for the causes.

There is Nurksean style vicious circle of population and poverty: a country is poor because its control on population growth is poor; a country's control on population growth is poor because it is poor. To break this circular constellation of forces requires more than cosmetic treatment of the problems at hand. The problems of poverty cannot be tackled by addressing problem of population alone, because population is the manifestation of poverty perpetrated upon the developing countries of the South by the North. It appears to the South that this the North has often sadly missed. Prosperity, it is said, is the best form of contraceptive. For population control to be sustainable "cash not contraceptives" is the answer.

The experts from the South believe that the two basic causes, amongst others, which perpetrates poverty in the developing countries, namely international trade and international debt have largely eluded the debate as it has intensified in the North. That the North should be seemingly unconcerned about the inequities that persists in international trade, does not appear acceptable to the poorer nations of the South. From the U.N. Secretary General's Report to the informal meeting of the Committee on African Recovery in September 1991, it is evident that the continuing depressed state of so many commodity prices in the world market and the lack of adequate compensatory and other safeguards "have made the whole process of poverty reduction and environmental improvement" in the countries of the South so much more difficult, particularly so in the face of continued escalation of the price of oil and of Northern exports, virtually without exception. The environmental impacts and consumption of natural resources stemming from the production of goods are rarely fully accounted for in the goods' market price. In effect, the least developed countries who use primary resources for 73 per cent of their export earnings are working against their own selves and "underselling" themselves. The North often fails to take account of the fact that increasing output of commodity for export has had a marked effect on land use, inasmuch as between 1974 and 1984, the total land under export crops expanded by 8 million hectares.[9] This increased use of land for exports has extended agriculture to environmentally unsustainable land, which has been further exacerbated by the collapse in commodity prices over the last decade we mentioned elsewhere. The North would have exhibited courage of conviction if its own prescriptions could have sought ways and means for the ordering of world trade that meets global needs and ensured trading strategies that are environmentally sound and sustainable on a worldwide scale.

Debt is the other major factor that perpetrates poverty and is far from environment friendly. The burden of debt is a fundamental obstacle to human development.[10] It leaves one wondering if the global view of the North by being silent on the debt issue, has at one stroke relegates to the background the relationship between debt, development and environment. This silence, it may be mentioned in passing, will additionally boost criticism that Northern Government's have often used tax payer's money to help developing countries repay debts to Northern Banks (the real beneficiaries of the debt crisis) who enjoy the patronage of the Bretton Woods institutions.

The Southern countries are reluctant to believe that the North, the primary purveyors of the third world debts, should have exhibited supposed unawareness of the phenomenon that third world countries contribute 300 per cent more financially (alone) to the North through debt repayments than what they were receiving through aid, and of the resultant environmental implications. The bulk of these repayments on the original loans, now up to 400 per cent higher than what they were when they were originally contracted. There was a reasonable expectation that the North would do well to have these issues examined in the perspective of poverty and environment, at the Rio Summit, but that was not to be.

The contribution of huge foreign debts to environmental plunder, "ethocide" and the widespread impoverishment can hardly be denied. A full scale discussion will be out of context here, but there is no gainsaying the fact that the North and its instruments, like the WB-IMF combine, had sponsored ecological calamities currently being perpetrated in various countries like Brazil and Indonesia. We would illustrate our point by looking at the case of Brazil because it was the home of the first ever World Summit on saving the globe's environment. The famous (infamous?) Polonoreste Project in Rondonia and the Grande Carajasa Iron-Ore Project in Brazil, said to the largest single development scheme in the world (the Tucurui Dam is part of it and was designed to generate power), entail deforestation of areas twice the size of Britain and the area equal to that of France taken together. Similarly the Grande Carajas Project, will cost an estimated $62 billion and entail deforestation of an area equal to France and Great Britain taken together. One can go on multiplying examples of financing provided by the North that are not environment friendly but the essential point to note is that the North has so far failed to explain the "inside story" and to ward off fears expressed since quite sometime now that "the availability of loans from the North and Northern Financial Institutions" may actually encourage deforestation in the poor countries,... that they can gain in the short term twice over, first by selling their forests, and then by getting loans to reforest and repair the environmental-damages, to pay for which they can cut more forests, while the Banks and the lending countries acquire interest payments, export orders and political and economic power."[11]

The question of transfer of "clean technology" from the rich North to the poorer South is a contentious issue which needs to be sorted out. The NBAER has come out with the figure that something of the order of U.S. $5000 per capita income has to be reached by a country before it can undertaken a "cleaning up" job. This is admittedly a far cry for the developing countries. What happens in between? Business as usual with the multinational corporations continuing to export "dirty industries" to the South with impunity? In terms of the Indian Social System this could be described as the "Schedule Caste Syndrome" whereby the society (national or global) while exploiting the economic weakness of one of its segments to perform unclean jobs, also blames it for being unclean. A classic case of catch 22. There seems to be no answer to these questions, which have become particularly important for there is a growing advocacy in the North, abundantly exemplified by The World Bank's Chief Economist Lawrence Summer's internal note that there is no harm done if the relatively unpolluted areas of the globe, meaning the South are polluted till they reach the limits of their pollutable capacity, which bears repetition here:

"(1) The measurement of the costs of health impairing pollution depends on the foregone earnings from increased morbidity and mortality. From this point of view, a given amount of health impairing pollution should be done in the country with the lowest wages . . . the economic logic behind dumping a load of toxic waste in the lowest-wage country is impeccable.

(2) The costs of pollution are likely to be non-linear . . . underpopulated countries in Africa are vastly underpolluted. Only the lamentable facts that so much pollution is generated by non-tradeable industries (transport, electric generation) and that the unit transport costs of solid waste are so high, prevent 'world-welfare' enhancing trade in air pollution and waste.

(3) The demand for a clean environment for aesthetic and health reasons is likely to have very high income-elasticity. . . . Clearly trade in goods that embody aesthetic pollution concerns would be welfare-enhancing. While production is mobile, the consumption of pretty air is non-tradeable".[12]

The more rigorous criticism of the Northern view would include a mention that the discussions pertaining to the problem of global warming and the forseeable consequences of carbon dioxide and other emissions produced by burning of fossil fuel has been kept at a low key (understandably so). From this it automatically follows that the "sink" function of environment has been "way laid" in the Northern view of the debate. Some of the major environmental dangers, precipitated by mining of the earth, nuclear testing by the North, mismanagement of Radio-Active Wastes by the developed countries, dismantling of the military apparatus of the East European Countries, continued military spending, even if reduced, and the expanding reach of Transnational Corporations, which are capable of inflicting environmental injury, that in one night kill 2000 people and cause permanent disability including total blindness to 200,000 men, women and children, such as the one by Union Carbide in Bhopal in 1986,[13] in the developing countries have found scant respect in the North. And then what constitutes the boundary conditions for defining a natural resource as "common property" (like Tropical Forests) for all the nations of the Globe as the North is often keen to suggest. And a clear answer to who should pay and how much for maintaining the earth's bio-diversity does not emerge from the North.

Finally all said and done, the bottom line remains that to the poor of the South, who are too busy to ensure their daily survival, it does not really matter whether their problems are due to depletion of the ozone layer or the distinct possibility of exhaustion of natural resources in their surroundings. They are also naturally not aware that the controversy regarding depletion of ozone layer could be attributed to two plausible causes, namely, the emission of green house gases by human activities on the earth or the explosion of a *supernova* in the vicinity of our solar system millions of years ago.

V. The Resolution

Thus the views of the two parts of the World have more differences than there exists commonality. A reconciliation and, an understanding of each other's views are critically important elements, if we are to survive in this globe. A resolution is necessary and possible, particularly so when the problems of environment, poverty and population can be resolved only through a dialogue between North and South, the dialogue which aims at cutting conspicuous consumption and waste and at promoting rapid development of the South to meet basic needs of the people without further damage to earth's environment, ecology and bio-diversity. In real life situation, it is perhaps easy to remove poverty in the South than to persuade the North to reduce their consumption. The dialogue should aim at a new life style which ensures continuing cultural development of all and limiting material growth within the boundary conditions set by ecology, environment and resources.

The Fifth Indo-British Seminar on Environment and Development held from 6-12 April, 1993 at Lal Bahadur Shastri National Academy of Administration, Mussoorie (India) involving experts from U.K. and India is a part of this continuing dialogue. U.K. represents a mature industrial economy whose fossil fuel resources are of moderate quantity, which is an important member of EEC and which has wide ranging global experiences. It is quite sensitive to the emerging environmental problems. India represents the South in more than one way. The population growth rate is high; it has one of the largest population in the world; its fossil fuel resources are limited; its other biotic and mineral resources when seen on per capita basis are not even modest; and it is making serious efforts to industrialise itself to improve the quality of life of the people. Thus the dialogue between the experts of the U.K. and India was a dialogue between two cultures which face the problems of ecology, environment and development differently. It is hoped that such a dialogue abundantly reflected in this volume, will help in understanding the perceptions of each other on these issues better.

1st May, 1993
Mussorie

AMITAVA MUKHERJEE
V.K. AGNIHOTRI

NOTES

1. Lewis, Julian (1992). "Brundtland Commission Urges New Global Partnership", Perspective, No. 8, Spring, p. 16.
2. Capistrano, A.D. (1991). Macro-economic influences on tropical Forest Depletion: A Cross-Country Analysis, unpublished Ph.D. Dissertation, University of Florida, at Miami, Department of Food and Resource Economics Department.
3. Capistrano, A.D. and Kiker, C.F. (1991). Global Economic Influences on Tropical Closed Broadleaved Forest Depletion, 1967-85 (Miami: University of Florida, Food and Resource Economics Department) Mimeograph.
4. Southgate, D. (1991). Tropical Deforestation and Agricultural Development in Latin America (London: London Environmental Economics Centre, University

College, University of London) LEEC Discussion Paper No. 90-91.
5. Burgess, J.C. (1991). Economic Analysis of Frontier Agricultural Expansion and Tropical Deforestation (London: University College London, Department of Economics) unpublished M.Sc. dissertation.
6. *Ibid.*
7. Barbier, Edwards (1991). *Environmental Management and Development in the South: Prerequisites for Sustainable Development* (London: International Institute for Environment and Development and UCL London Environmental Economics Centre) p. 26.
8. Repetto, R. (1986). *World Enough and Time: Successful Strategies for Resource Management* (new-Haven: Yale University Press) p. 45.
9. This is one estimate There are various other views on this issue as well.
10. United Nations Development Programme (1991). Human Development Report 1991 (New York: UNDP and Oxford University Press).
11. Guppy, Nicholas (1984). "Tropical Deforestation: A Global View", *Foreign Affairs*, Vol. 62, No. 4, Spring, pp. 942-43.
12. As reported in *Economist*, 8th February, 1992.
13. The World Commission on Environment and Development (1987). *Our Common Future* (New York: Oxford University Press) paperback edition, p. 3.

PART-I

CHANGING PERCEPTION OF DEVELOPMENT

1

SUSTAINABLE DEVELOPMENT : Concept and Application Case of Developing Countries

SRIKUMAR CHATTOPADHYAY

Introduction

The earth summit held at Rio in 1992 re-emphasised the need for sustainable development, a term perhaps first used at the time of Cocoyoc declaration in 1970 and gained popular currency through IUCN Report (1980, 1990) and WCED Report (1987) — Our Common Future.

The term "sustainability" and its corollary "sustainable development" is being widely used in government policy pronouncements, scientific articles, publication of international aid agencies, professional literatures, seminar, symposia and popular media.

While unsustainability of the ongoing development processes is well manifested through environmental problems, declining productivity and such other indicators, how sustainability can be achieved is not very clear. Moreover, there is little unanimity in comprehending this term also. It conveys different meaning to different people. In global context, view point of the developing countries differ considerably from that of the developed countries as evidernced in the Rio summit.

The developing countries are mainly concerned to tackle the immediate economic problems and to eliminate poverty, whereas the developed countries' thrust is to combat industry related pollution and to maintain the attained economic level. Various research reports suggest that the developed countries consume resources at a disproportionately high rate in terms of their resource base. It is well documented that growth of many national economies can be sustained only by continuous resource imports from elsewhere.

This paper considers sustainable development in the context of developing countries only, which depend on the land and water resources.

What is really meant by sustainable development and how to apply this concept in operational terms are the points of discussion in this paper.

Sustainable Development (S D): The Concept

Since 1980's, particularly after publication of the report – Our Common Future – a good many literatures are devoted to deal with the concept of sustainable development and its possible application (Barbier, 1987; Brown et al, 1988; Daly, 1989; Lele, 1989; Pezzy, 1989; Redclift, 1987; Rees, 1989 among others). The present author has listed as many as 33 definitions by scanning available literatures published during 1987-1989 (Chattopadhyay and Carpenter, 1990) Brown et al, (1987), Rees (1988) and Lele (1989) summarized the essential elements covered in various deliberations. In broad terms these essential elements or objectives and premises cover the following aspects.

1. Survival of human beings
2. Survival of all other life forms
3. Satisfaction of basic human needs
4. Maintenance of bio-physical productivity
5. Economic efficiency and growth
6. Preservation of environmental quality and ecosystem
7. Inter- and intra-generational equity
8. Social justice
9. Self-reliance and people's participation
10. Stabilization of human population
11. Promotion of values and ethics

There are also attempts to cover a good many of these aspects into a single framework. As a result, instead of being precise, the definition tends to be vague and subjected to misinterpretation. So great is the confusion, that, even this vagueness is justified to be its strength by some authors (Daly, 1989) and some others (Lele, 1989) opined that this lack of precision in definition leads to the faultering of SD in operational terms.

Without going into the merits and demerits of this problem, what is significant in this wide ranging debate is that there is a growing realization about:

1. Excessive stress on bio-physical environment for short-term gain is ultimately counter productive, i.e. there is a limit to which productivity can be raised.
2. Human survival can only be ensured by preserving the basic resource base.
3. Even the renewable resources are not perpetual unless prudent management praxis is followed.
4. Conventional economics does not necessarily indicate the actual status of resource utilisation.

The matter of social justice and equity are prime objectives of any form of development so far conceived. Quite naturally they are also professed goals of SD.

Considering all the above mentioned aspects, SD at the conceptual level can be assumed to maximise three goals — Biophysical, Economic and Social. From other angle SD can be described as a process of development that should operate within a framework, bounded by the Biophysical, Economic and Social coordinates. To operate within these three coordinates it is necessary to resort to a process of trade-offs, primarily to recognise that there are certain limits within which the development process has to be functional. These limits can be broadly identified as Biophysical and Ethico-social limits (Daly, 1989). The bio-physical limit, which actually controls the resource availability, resources use and economic viability, is due to : (i) finitude, (ii) entropy, (iii) complex ecological interdependence (CEI) and (iv) resilience - self ameleorating capacity.

The ethico-social limit has more to do with the philosophical back drop of a society including its legal, executional and policy-making authorities. Therefore, subsequent discussion will be principally on the bio-physical aspects.

Biophysical condition varies regionally and even locally, hence it warrants utmost attention in adopting management practices. Another point to note is that, although when the bio-physical limit is exceeded can be detected from the degraded condition of land, information is quite inadequate to anticipate the triggering of degradation. This is one of the serious problems in natural resource management. In one hand intervention leads to deterioration on the other hand intervention is required because the basal productivity is perceptibly low to support today's population. The next point merits clarification is that it is the development (rather than environment or a particular ecosystem or a particular economy) which is to be sustained. Thus the resource management has to be viewed in its totality considering all the available uses and then the issue will be not the sustainability of any individual project or sector but of the entire production system.

Summarising this discussion on conceptual frame the following points emerge.

1. Development must be sustainable to meet basic human needs of present and future generations as advocated by the WCED (1987).
2. In operational terms SD is a production management system in which inputs do not adversely affect the bio-physical potentiality of the system including its resilience limit.
3. The approach for achieving SD is necessarily interventionist.
4. System approach is to be followed
5. S D has to be conceived based on renewable resources.

Towards Application

The conceptual frame discussed above provides certain clues along which SD can be operationalised. The renewable resources particularly land and water are the mainstay of development in the developing countries. Moreover, due to very biological nature man has to depend on land and water for his sustainance. Forest resource has not been considered separately as it is an integral part of land and water system.

Land and water are not uniformly distributed even at the micro-level. Type of land and its quality vary from one place to other as in the case of water. There is also a startling cross correlation between availability of usable water, geology, landscape, soil fertility and climate, Considered in totality as a matrix or package, the diversity of Indian natural regions can ensure a highly diversified production array (Sinha, 1990). According to the natural principles every parcel of land has a productivity of its own and a corresponding resilience limit — capacity to withstand tampering. Neither all the lands can be put to the same use, nor a particular land can be brought under all sorts of uses.

The governing principle of production potential of each unit of land need to be understood and acted upon. Landuse has to be planned to conform to the bio-physical variabilities. Hence sustainable landuse development requires a proactive planning approach in which ecological integrity is the governing factor and the permissible level of economic activity is the dependent variable (Rees, 1988). Intervention must adhere to this natural principle of spatially differentiated production potential of bio-physical system. Perhaps the basic task in sustainable development planning is "to learn the nature's law" and to master the art of "applying them correctly" (Engles, 1875). This requires data at the base level, covering all aspects. Baseline data helps establishing the current state of the ecosystem, to understand the trend and to assess the load. In this context only the concept of Carrying Capacity (CC) has been advocated by various authors in pursuing sustainable development planning (Rees, 1988; Foy and Daly, 1889). Although it (carrying capacity) conveys the meaning, its assessment is extremely difficult. Carrying capacity is not static. It can be increased by investment and technology and decreased by consumption of capital. How can the CC be determined and what is the optimum limit to which CC can be expanded are two intriguing questions not clearly dealt with. In this situation an assessment like approach — Environmental Appraisal — has been advocated here with specific examples from Kerala. This method is perhaps one of those that can be used till an acceptable method of carrying capacity determination is evolved in the realm of land and water management.

Environmental Appraisal

Environmental appraisal is an assessment of the existing condition, based on which a desirable landuse can be formulated. The assessment is done by considering the total biophysical condition. It helps to understand the current state, problems associated with ensuing activities *vis-a-vis* the potentiality and the possible way to improve the condition. By regressing existing landuse against potentiality the viability of existing practices can be weighed. The entire approach is diagnostic in nature and allows information flow without any rigidity. In this method problems provide the key to alteration.The mitigating measures and/or complete change in ongoing practices can be more convincingly demonstrated to the users.

An environmental appraisal map is worked out by synthesising all the relevant information pertaining to land and water. The approach is landscape based and hence data are assimilated in terms of landscape unit. The procedure for synthesising data into environmental appraisal map is given in the Table 1.1. A model work was done in the Panchayat of Ulloor in the district of Trivandrum, Kerala (Chattopadhyay and Mathai, 1992). The environmental appraisal map (Fig. 1.1) prepared for this model and the legend are provided here. This map forms the base for action plan preparation.

It may be noted that desirable landuse has been worked out by considering the appropriate use practised by some users within a given Integrated Mapping Unit (IMU). The plot of land having this appropriate landuse is considered to be the level to which landuse of all other plots of the same IMU will be raised. Once productivity of all the land units is raised to the set-level then a higher goal can be fixed. This helps users to strive for the modest goal, already achieved by some of his community members. Thus the task is easily comprehensible and not a distant utopian concept. Each IMU is unique in character and has its own resilience limit. Landuse and productivity of these IMUs are different. In effect these IMUs are landscape ecological units. Recognition of their differential production potential is the first step towards sustainable landuse planning.

Local Level Planning

Sustainable development is essentially a planning processes with definite goals and priorities. The scale of operation is an important as the methodology itself. The "trickles down" approach adopted in various planning activities has not produced desired results. Moreover, there is also a serious lacuna in understanding the "Complex ecological interdependence" resulting in lack of integrated approach covering land and soil; groundwater and surface water; forestry, agriculture and pastoral development; urban and rural development, etc.

In the case of sustainable development it is considered both pragmatic and rational to shift to the Local Level Planning — the Panchayat, the lowest administrative unit in India.

It is a fact that environmental degradation and socio-economic problems are expressed mostly at the local level (Carpenter and Harper, 1889), so aggregate statistics can help very little. Barbier (1987) pointed out that the importance of regional and local variations and stressed that individual economic-environmental system may have to

TABLE 1.1: Environmental Appraisal (The procedure for synthesis)

---

1. Mark landform unit with descriptions including slope.
2. Prepare a surface material map describing texture and genesis.
3. Combine Landform and Surface material map in a single map through superimposition. The units merged in this process may be termed as Integrated Mapping Unit (IMU) or Terrain Mapping Unit (TMU).
4. It is necessary to work out the following parameters for each of these IMUs:

   (i) Erosion,
   (ii) Water availability,
   (iii) Existing landuse,
   (iv) Conservational requirement to arrest degradation,
   (v) Desirable landuse or choice of landuse; and
   (vi) Suggestion/Remarks including restrictions of use.

The last three items may be put together as Environmental Evaluation. It is proposed that desirable landuse should be worked out in consultation with local people/panchayat functionaries and Govt. officials involved in planning.

However, a model landuse suitable to the specific terrain condition need to be worked out by the survey team to form the base for discussion. A well managed plot within the panchayat or in other panchayat with similar terrain condition can be considered for this purpose. Hence, it is important to have detail documentation of landuse *vis-a-vis* Bio-Physical condition.

It is essential to have the following information (which are collected during fieldwork in an appropriate data format) to design the Environmental Appraisal map:

(i) Slope parameter - Length degree and direction;
(ii) Local relief;
(iii) Erosion - Type and degree;
(iv) Drainage condition;
(v) Degree of weathering;
(vi) Soil - depth, material, texture, drainage and colour;
(vii) Depth to bedrock;
(viii) Present landuse, management practices; and
(ix) Socio-economic condition (Data collected through detailed survey in structured data format.

Conservational requirement: Area of conservation type of conservation practices and reasons should be specified.

Diserable landuse: All types of scientifically viable landuse should be indicated from which diserable landuse can be arrived at after discussion with the local people and considering socio-economic data. This in effect leads to applying Ecological filter and Socio-economic filter for landuse planning.

Suggestion: Suggestion should be specific, indicating restriction of use for each of the IMUs.

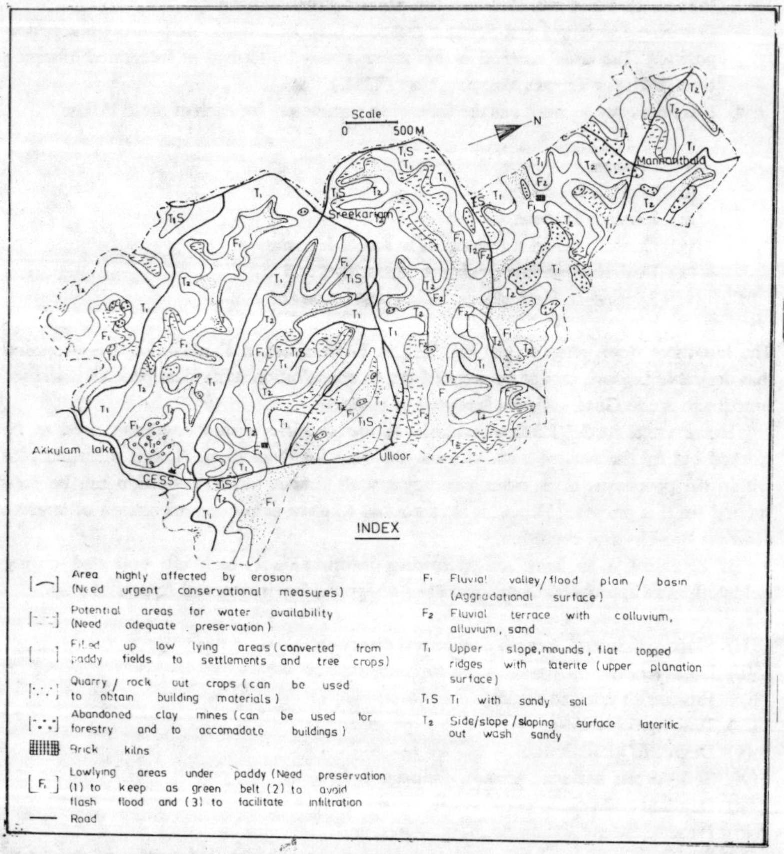

FIG. 1.1: Uloor Panchayat: Environmental Appraisal for Landuse Planning

be assessed for sustainable development. As the problems are manifested at the lowest level it has to be tackled there itself. Naturally involvement of the local communities, actual users, must be ensured in redeeming the situation. It may be recalled that the individual user used to take decisions at the farm level, marginally influenced by the community and policy-makers. With the changed political-economic situation in the last couple of decades the individual divisions are overwhelmingly dominated by the policy-makers. In some extreme cases this has completely alienated the local people and self-reliance of the community became a thing of the past.

The approach advocated here attempts to indicate a way to rectify the situation. Therefore, involvement of the people is considered to be the integral part of the entire planning process. Sustainable development which is need based and attempts to maximise the use of local resources calls for full participation of local people.
This is due to:

1. A local user inheriting traditional wisdom is most aware about the problems and potentialities of his land.
2. Actual users must be made aware about the draw back of the current practices and the positive relationship between environment and development.
3. Local people should be made aware that they need to know the actual status of their resources to take decision.
4. The Panchayat as the local institution should chalk out their own development plans, and lastly.
5. Local level planning is not just devolution of political and economic power to the local bodies, Panchayat in the case of India. Decision-making and programme implementation are integral part of this planning process.

Once we talk about local level planning and people's participation the question automatically raised is how to proceed? The Kerala model described below perhaps answers the question.

The Kerala Model

The salient features of the Kerala experiment are presented here. Those interested in details may refer Centre for Earth Science Studies, 1991 and Chattopadhyay et al, 1991. The Kerala experiment initiated by the

Centre for Earth Science Studies (CESS), Kerala State Landuse Board (KSLUB) and Integrated Rural Technology Centre (IRTC) with financial support from the Department of Science and Technology (DST), Government of india is a demonstrative example of initiating a panchayat level planning process leading to Sustainable Development. Activities and linkages of Panchayat Resource Mapping (caption of this programme in the CESS) are depicted in the Fig. 1.2.

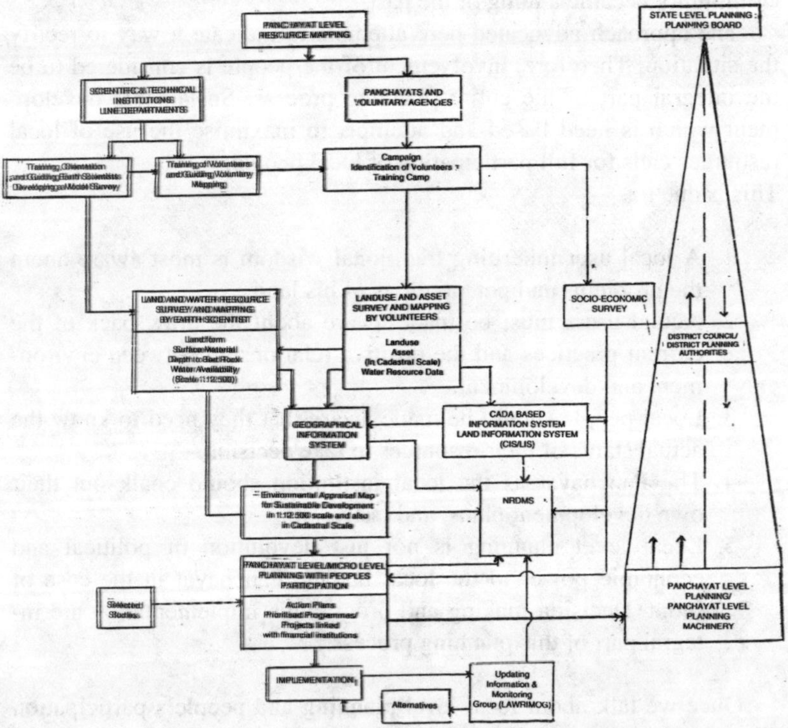

FIG. 1.2: Panchayat Level Resource Mapping : Activities and Linkages

1. This programme envisages:

(i) Integrated resource survey and mapping at the panchayat level by involving volunteers (trained for the purpose) panchayat functionaries and earth scientists. While landuse and asset mapping and monitoring depth of water table in the open well are done by the volunteers, organised by the IRTC/voluntary organisation or panchayat. The inferential details (landform surface materials, geology, groundwater, etc.) are documented by the specialists;
(ii) Geo-environmental appraisal of every plot of land;
(iii) Blending traditional wisdom with appropriate technology for intervention plans;
(iv) To build up a Land and Water Resources Inventory and Monitoring Group (LAWRIMOG) at the panchayat level to ensure continued people's participation; and
(v) To develop Cadastral-based Information System (CIS) and introduce Geographical Information System (GIS) for micro-level planning and development.

2. The voluntary organisation organises volunteers who are trained by the specialists to undertake this job. A prolonged awareness campaign was arranged in the panchayats for initiating this programme.
3. Once the resource mapping and data collection in a panchayat are completed the data are synthesised by the scientific personnel and the following maps (Table 1.2) are prepared.

TABLE 1.2: Themes of Maps

Themes	Scale of presentation
1. Landform and erosion	1: 12,500/1:15000
2. Surface material	do
3. Thickness of the weathered mantle	do
4. Potential area for water availability	do
5. Landuse	1:3960/1:7920/1:5000 (Cadestral scale)
6. Asset	do
7. Environmental appraisal	1:12,500/1:15000 and in cadestral scale

This is considered to be the minimum input model. Data elements are provided in the Tables 1.3A and 1.3B.

4. These maps are presented in the panchayat and discussed in detail with the local people and panchayat functionaries. Following this a short training on conducting socio-economic survey is organised for the volunteers.

5. Subsequently socio-economic survey is conducted by the volunteers and the data are assimilated at the ward (panchayat segment) level and also at IMU level. An example is provided for Kalliasseri panchayat (Table 1.4).

TABLE 1.3A: Details to be Collected/Mapped by the Volunteers

Boundaries	:	Panchayat, village, ward and forest
Transport	:	Road, railways, waterways including stations
Communication	:	Post and telecommunication
Health service	:	Hospital, primary health centre, dispensary etc.
Educational	:	School, college, technical school etc.
Social/Religious	:	Community hall, temple, church, mosque etc.
Recreational	:	Library, cinema hall, theatre, play ground etc.
Commercial/ Co-operatives	:	Market, shopping complex, rationshop, bank etc.
Other services	:	Police Station, court, government office etc.
Mining and Industry	:	Types
Power	:	Power station, H.T.line/transformer
Water related	:	River, canal, pond, well, spring and its use
Landuse/landcover	:	Agriculture - seasonal, annual, tree crop and plantation Irrigation facility Barren lands/wastelands Marsh, swamp and water bodies Forest, scrub, grassland etc. Rock outcrop, sandy patch, laterite, surface etc.

6. *Action plan preparation*: This is the most important part of this programme. Success of this programme lies in devising a viable action plan that can be implemented and results desirably.

In order to draw up an action plan the first step is to collate the environmental appraisal map with other socio-economic and attribute data. Considering the pervasiveness of the problems priorities are fixed and tentative plans are chalked out. The diary written by the volunteers during field investigation helps in this task. A map showing the action plan and all other maps are once again presented in the Panchayats and a detailed discussion is held there to finalize the Action/Intervention plans. Officials from the Line departments and Financial organisations also take part in the deliberations. A sample action plan map showing immediate intervention is presented here (Fig. 1.3).

TABLE 1.3B: Parameters to be Investigated for Land and Water Resource (for mapping by the Scientific and Technical personnel)

Landscape aspect:

Landform — type, local relief, elevation and dissection
Slope — gradient, direction and length
Erosion — degree and type
Drainage condition etc.

Geology:

Lithology, structure, degree of weathering, depth to bed rock, thickness of the loose/unconsolidated material, laterite thickness etc.

Surface material:

Type of material, textural class, thickness of soil, stoniness, colour, soil drainage etc.

Water: Pond/Tank:

Lined/unlined, public/private, area, depth to water table, depth to bottom, present use, energised/non-energised, management, requirement, ownership and descriptions etc.

Water: Wells

Depth to water table, well depth, fluctuation of water table, perenniality, use, energised/non-energised, approximate yield, water bearing formation quality and ownership.

Landuse:

Agricultural use — crop type, stage, intensity, rotation
Irrigation — type and source
Plantation, annual crop
Broad settlement stretch, agglomeration
Land management particulars
Forest, scrubland, grassland
Wetland, wasteland, afforestation

Environmental concern:

Flooding, landslides, slump, slope failure etc.
Drought prone area, waterlogging, salinity/alkalinity
Habitat destruction, land reclamation/conversion status, waste dump, deforestation, beach erosion, river sand mining, mining, Pollution etc.

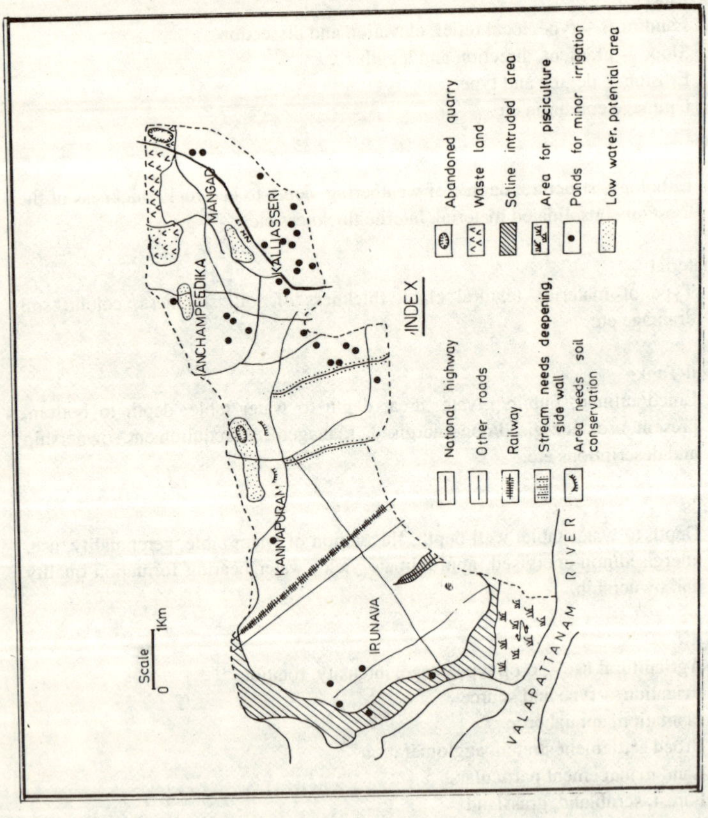

FIG. 1.3: Kalliasseri Panchayat: Action Plan

TABLE 1.4: Kalliasseri Panchayat : Some sample data

Element/Ward	I	II	III	IV	V	VI	VII	VIII	IX	X
L M & US (783)	—	—	—	—	—	73	102	28	40	110
S S (706)	—	—	—	—	—	23	106	87	45	16
V (357)	—	—	—	—	—	18	22	45	39	19
C P (3098)	170	165	209	133	217	58	15	04	02	—
M (48)	—	06	02	—	—	—	04	—	—	—

L M & US = Lateritic mesa and Upper slope; S S = Side slope; V = Valley;
C P = Coastal Plain; M = Marsh.

Note : Figures in the bracket are No. of survey plots. Other figures are area in hectares.

Element/Ward	I	II	III	IV	V	VI	VII	VIII	IX	X
Primary labour	1943	2032	1295	1392	2037	1171	852	1765	910	1723
Job seekers	299	322	270	101	368	306	284	207	150	225

Note : All data are based on primary survey conducted in 1991-92.

Action plans are conceived for short-term, medium-term and long-term intervention. A list of these intervention programme, being conceptualized in the case of some panchayats, are given in the Table 1.5. An intensive CAMPAIGN proceeds all intervention programme. In fact campaigning itself can be considered as the first intervention.

Prioritisation and phasing of this intervention plan have to be done in such a way that each year's programme fits in the total framework of sustainable development planning. Once a perspective plan is prepared action plan for each year can be identified and a proportionate target is fixed. Information about the ongoing and immediately forthcoming programmes are collected for every Panchayat. These programmes should be considered in depth while finalising the action plan of a Panchayat. Whereever possible existing institutional arrangements have to be more efficiently used and the new programmes are gradually internalised. Another point to note is that some of the programmes can be taken up by the individual Panchayat but it may be needed to involve more than one Panchayat for taking up some other programmes. These inter Panchayat programmes can be taken up under the District level planning

TABLE 1.5: Intervention Programme

Short-Term (within 1 to 2 years)
1. Pond rejuvenation for water harvesting, minor irrigation and inland fisheries.
2. Drinking water and sanitation
3. Biological soil conservation
4. Infiltration gallery, terracing
5. Reactivating drainage canals/channels
6. Introduction of vegetable cultivation on experimental basis
7. Road repairing
8. School building and public property maintenance
9. Afforestation and pond catchment management
Medium-term (2 to 5 years)
1. Pisci culture
2. Sericulture
3. Poultry and animal husbandry as household units
4. Health care and sanitation
5. Road construction
6. Minor irrigation
7. School education — Removing illiteracy of the literates
9. Micro watershed management
Long-term (5 years and above)
1. Increasing land productivity using Bio-fertiliser
2. Irrigation
3. Small scale industry
4. Higher educational facilities
5. Marketing network
6. Drinking water scheme
7. Sanitation scheme
8. Watershed management

7. Mobilisation of local resources, labour, material and finance, are to be ensured by the Panchayats for implementation. Panchayat must play a pivotal role in bringing together all concerned department including financial institutions.

In one of the panchayats where the work is at an advanced stage and intervention is being contemplated the panchayat proposed to set up a sub-committees for coordinating and execution of the programmes covering Agriculture, Fishery, Health, Education, Animal husbandry Small scale industry, Road, and drainage/irrigation. Each sub-committee has a specific duty, a definite time frame and a work plan. Work starts with awareness campaign, presentation of maps and other facts acquired through survey (Anonymous, 1992).

It is envisaged that in the long run a Panchayat Development Society (PDS) will be the overall coordinator under the aegis of the Panchayat. Apart from the panchayat members local technical personnel, village elders and NGO representatives will constitute this PDS. The composition of PDS, its task and ultimate goal are provided in the Table 1.6. The Panchayats have to take initiative for this programme. Dependence on the external sources should be kept to the bare minimum. Finally, PDS should be registered as a development society capable of arranging its own finance.

8. Around 40 Panchayats have already been covered for survey. Action plan has also been prepared for some Panchayats. It is expected that intervention plans will be executed in one Panchayat-Kalliasseri-very shortly.

TABLE 1.6: Panchayat Development Society, its Composition, Task and Goal

Composition	:	Elected members (Representing all Parties)
		Village elders
		Local technical personnel
		NGO representatives
		A trained earth scientist with exposure in micro-planning
Task	:	To take decisions and manage local resources
		To implement plan programme
		To manage finance
		To coordinate all activities
		Liaison with the Govt.
		To operationalise "Lawrimog"
Goal	:	To promote people's democracy (Swaraj of Gandhiji)

Conclusion

Initial results, so far obtained are quite encouraging. It is observed that there is enough scope to increase productivity both for Human resources and Natural resources. It is also possible to demonstrate the land and water problems due to inappropriate use at the micro level. This experiment also shows a way, perhaps for the first time, to involve local people for resource management and planning. The sense of belongingness, active participation and level of confidence generated through this programme are unprecedented.

By involving volunteers, it is possible to collect enormous amount of data, which is other ways could not have been possible. It is observed that 500 man days are required to cover a panchayat of 20 sq. km. for landuse and asset mapping. Another 150 man-days are needed for socio-economic survey and data processing. To complete land and water resource survey by the specialists 40 man-days are required for the panchayat of 20 sq. km. Another 40 man-days have to be put for finalising the maps. As the voluntary component is without much of an expenditure the cost of this programme till action plan preparation is around Rs. 1500 per sq. km. at the maximum. Incidentally, it may be maintained here that the Government of Kerala has come forward with a special Government order to cover all the panchayats in the state following this module. The model is also accepted by the Central Government and other State Governments.

Developing countries with limited financial resources but having huge manpower can initiate this programme. It does not require high investment, at the same time it generates invaluable data, extremely useful for any planning operation. The information generated at the plot level (CIS) can be aggregated at the Panchayat level (PIS) which can again be synthesised at the District level (DIS) and at the State level (SIS) and finally at the National level (NIC).

[CIS — PIS — DIS — SIS — NIC]

Therefore, the action plan worked out at the panchayat level can be successfully integrated at the Regional and National level.

It has to be borne in mind that SD can not be achieved over night. It is a process that too a long drawn one. The action programme contemplated at the lowest level must be the base for planning at the successive level and also a step forward towards achieving sustainable development. When people, being involved in every stages, will proclaim that they have done it themselves, then only this programme will be successful and development will be sustainable by meeting ecologic, economic and social aspirations of the society.

REFERENCES

Anonymous, (1992). Kalliasseri Panchayat : A leap forward in rural development. (in Malayalam). Kalliasseri Panchayat Office, Cannanore, Kerala .

Barbier, E.B. (1987). The concept of sustainable development, *Environmental Conservation*, 14 (2) 101-110

Brown, B.J., Hanson, M.E., Liverman, D.M. and Merideth, R.W. (Jr), (1987). Global sustainability : Towards definition, *Environmental Management*, 11 (6) 713-719.

Carpenter, R.A. and Harper, D.E., (1989). Towards a science of sustainable upland management in developing countries. *Environmental Management*, 13 (1) 43-54.

Centre for Earth Science Studies, (1991). Panchayat Level Resource Mapping : An Approach paper — A model for microlevel resource survey with people's participation. pp 38. Trivandrum

Chattopadhyay, S. and Carpenter, R.A., (1990). A theoretical framework for sustainable development planning in the context of a river basin. Unpublished report, Environment and Policy Institute, East west Centre, Hawaii, USA.

Chattopadhyay, S. and others, (1991). Micro/village level resource survey with people's participation for sustainable development. Paper presented in the IGU working group seminar held at the Department of Geography. Delhi University, Delhi.

Chattopadhyay, S. and Mathai, J., (1992). Micro level resource survey for sustainable development—a model with case study on Ulloor Panchayat. C.J. Ramachandran ed. *Proceedings*, IV Kerala Science Congress, STED, Trivandrum.

Daly, H.E., (1989). Sustainable development : from concept and theory towards operational principles. Population and Development Review, Washington.

Foy, G. and Daly, H., (1989). Allocation, distribution and scale as determinants of environmental degradation : Case studies of Haiti, El Salvador and Costa Rica. The World Bank report, Paper no. 19.

International Union for Conservation of Nature (IUCN), (1980). World conservation strategy: Living resources conservation for sustainable development. IUCN, UNEP WWF in collaboration with FAO and UNESCO, Switzerland.

Lele, S.M., (1989). Sustainable development—a critical review. Unpublished report. EAPI, Hawaii, USA.

Pezzey, J., (1989). Economic analysis of sustainable growth and sustainable development. W P No. 15, Environment Department, The World Bank.

Rees, W.E., (1988). A role for environmental assessment in achieving sustainable development. *Environmental Impact Assessment Review*, 8 (4) 273-291.

Redclift, M., (1987). *Sustainable development : Exploring the contradiction.* Methuen and Co., London.

Sinha, S., (1990). The environmental scenario, development and the earth scientist. *Geographical Review of India*, 52 (1) 51-58.

WCED, (1987). *Our Common Future*. Oxford University Press.

Acknowledgement

This paper reports about the Panchayat Resource Mapping programme at present being implemented by the Centre for Earth Science Studies as a nodal agency. The author is grateful to the Director, CESS, Trivandrum for his Kind permission to prepare this paper. Contribution of other CESS scientists, Project scientists and KSSP volunteers and functionaries involved in this work are thankfully acknowledged volunteers and functionaries.

[illegible]

Brown, [illegible] (1988): [illegible] *Environmental management* [illegible]

[illegible] *Environmental Management* [illegible]

[illegible] An Ap[illegible] participatory [illegible]

[illegible] (1991): A theoretical framework for sustainable development [illegible] integrated [illegible]

[illegible] *Papers and Policy* [illegible]

[illegible] *Working* [illegible] Delhi University, Delhi.

[illegible] sustainable development [illegible]

[illegible]

International Union for Conservation of Nature (IUCN) [illegible]

[illegible]

[illegible]

[illegible] Economic [illegible] growth [illegible]

[illegible]

[illegible] development [illegible]

[illegible]

[illegible] *Environmental* [illegible] development [illegible]

[illegible]

Acknowledgement

[illegible]

2

PERSPECTIVES ON ENVIRONMENT AND DEVELOPMENT

M. SHAFI

The ink of the 27 resolutions of the Rio Conference on 'Environment and Development' held in June last had not even dried up and some people might still be mapping or scratching their heads or raising their eyebrows about the implementation of the massive resolutions, when the Department of Geography of Himachal Pradesh University took time by the forelock and started a dialogue between the highly industrialized society on the one hand and the developing society on the other. The problems of the two societies in respect of development are the same, one believing in the investment of more capital and earn more profit, while the developing nations, in order to improve their standards of living, invest more to produce greater amount of food to feed their teeming millions adequately. The import of the two societies on environment are slightly different – one is much more concerned with the air pollution, acid rain, depletion of ozone and the green house effect. The other is much more concerned with the land degradation and water pollution – only a question of priorities of the two societies. It is highly in the fitness of things that an international seminar has been organised between geographers of the two societies, UK and India, to interact on this problem: Environment and Development.

The United Nations Environment Programme in its treatise *Choosing the Options* (1980) has pointed out that the sustained economic and social development of growing population requires an ever expanding utilization of natural resources and the environment. It is, therefore, of utmost importance to understand the interactive physical, chemical and biological processes that regulate the total earth system, the unique environment that it provides for life, the changes that are occurring in this system and the manner in which they are influenced by human activities. It should be noted that the functions of the environment can be impaired or enhanced by society and may, therefore, constitute a constraint or a potential for the achievement of the basic goals of development. Hence the mutually dependent relationship between environment and development be fully and explicitly taken into account in any development strategy.

The rising level of production and consumption of the developed countries, as well as the evolution of their high technology and lifestyles, have led to the demand for raw materials with an increasing reliance on imports from the third world. Developed countries have begun to experience an increasingly serious process of degradation of the environment with negative effects on the quality of life, and their production and consumption pattern is posing major threat to the biosphere. These threats to the environment and living conditions have not been confined to national boundaries but have been extended to other developed as well as developing countries and the world as a whole.

The Scenario of the developing countries in respect of their natural resources is that they depend on the developed countries and export to them their primary commodities. Minerals, oil and products of many industrial crops are imported by the developed countries. In this connection, the practices, technologies and investment in the resource based industries have a close bearing on environment as well as on development of these countries. Again the know-how, forms of organization, acquisition of technology, the creation of new transportation, communication, marketing, industrialization and financial systems, are all parts of the development process. Increasing food production by applying new technologies, in view of the rising population, is an important development process of the developing countries. All the processes that have been mentioned, have their effect on environment.

The dynamics of the developed countries is based on intensive technological innovation and is highly capital and energy intensive.

It will thus be seen that the development process in developing countries is born out of great necessity in view of the high rate of population growth, unemployment and under-employment and the general poverty scenario. In the process of quick development, the environment comes under stress and gives rise to problems of land, water and air pollution. The life style of the developed countries, the massive consumption pattern brings the environment under stress giving rise to green house effect, acid rain and ozone depletion.

The developing countries in the process of growth and development through their primary export activities are subjected to the depletion of the higher grade and best located non-renewable natural resources and the deterioration of renewable resources such as forests and marine resources. The process of modernization of agriculture and other activities, industrialization, transportation and urbanization lead to the rural-urban environmental consequences. The additional pressure of population generates the push and pull factors, creating slums and severely affecting the quality of life. The Rio call is sustainability of resources in the process of development. Sustainability refers to the utilization of resources in order to meet the needs and aspirations of the present generation without compromising the needs of the future generations.

The World Commission on Environment and Development (1987) in its treatise, *Our Common Future*, points out that the scale of our interventions in nature is increasing and the physical effects of our decisions will spill across the national frontiers. Economics and ecology bind us in our tightening networks. Today many regions face risks of irreversible damage to the human environment that threatens the basis of human progress.

The position of the developing countries in respect of sustainability of resources in relation to development is much more difficult compared to the developed countries. The developed countries have to adjust lifestyles to a more rational use of resources with particular emphasis on the present and future resource and environmental needs of the large majority of humanity constituted by the poor people of the developing countries.

There is a genuine fear about global warming. The Intergovernmental Panel on Climate Change (IPCC), basing its reports on mathematical modelling and projections derived from fastest computers, points out the climate impact of increases in the concentration of atmospheric greenhouse gases, which absorb infra-red radiation emitted by earth and suggests the degree of global warming that will occur in the next 50 years. Predictions range from an increase of 1.5°C to 4.5°C of global warming. The volume of Co_2 entering the atmosphere has increased by 25 per cent in the last century. A major source of the increased Co_2 since 1850 has been and is the burning of fossil fuel M. Stuiver has estimated the total release of Co_2 to the atmosphere between 1850 and 1950 as 1.2 billion tonnes per year. The result according to Stuiver is that the Co_2 content increased from 268 ppm to 316 ppm by 1950 – about 18 per cent. More recent studies put the level at 344 ppm in 1979. Another possible source is that released by the destruction of forests and oxidation of humus. According to FAO,

113,000 km^2 of forests were cut down or burnt in tropical countries in 1980 while in 1988 it rose to 245,000 km^2. The tropical forest is disappearing at the rate of 2 acres per second. The total human made emission of Co_2 in the atmosphere as estimated by V.A. Mohnen, et al, is 22.4 billion metric tonnes per year.

The unknown factor however is the extent to which the ocean can continue to act as a sink for the extra carbon inserted into the atmosphere. The National Academy of Science (USA) has projected that a doubling of atmospheric Co_2 will result in a global warming of 1.5 to 4.5°C and at the present rate, Co_2 in the atmosphere will double by 2030 A.D.

The effect of warming would be an increase in the drought prone areas in North America and Central Asia, rise in sea level and a potential danger to all coastal towns. The remedy lies in preventing the increase of Co_2, *Co*, So_2, from the industrial establishments, from the tail pipes of the automobiles and secondly to develop on a commercial scale renewable sources of energy: solar, wind, geo-thermal and tidal. The developed countries can play a major role in controlling the toxic fumes and also in developing renewable sources of energy.

India is making appreciable efforts to develop two important sources of renewable energy: solar energy and biogas areas, where low grade thermal energy is needed, have already become commercial. These include cooking, water heating, water desalination and space heating. A large number of photovoltaic pumps have been installed in the rural areas providing water for drinking and irrigation purposes. Solar photovoltaic street lighting systems have been provided in more than 8000 villages where electricity would have never reached in normal course. The development however touches the tip of the requirements.

Biogas is the most important component of renewable energy supplies in rural areas. As a by-product, biogas plant produces enriched manure also. It provides easy, smokeless and efficient cooking. India has installed over 1.5 million biogas plants which gave a saving of 4.5 mission tonnes of fuel in 1990-91, besides they generated manure of about 2.5 million tonnes. There are over 500 institutional community biogas plants in the country for village community as a whole.

Urban pollution is fast increasing in India and in the metropolitan towns the position has become critical and the major source of pollution is the automobiles. The transport system in Delhi is bursting at the seams and the situation has become chaotic. In 1992 the number of vehicles was about 2 million, and the automobile exhaust accounted for

60 per cent of the total air pollution according to the Director, Centre for Research in Environmental and Biological Sciences. According to one estimate Delhi is one of the most polluted cities in the world with a total of 2000 tonnes of air pollutants per day being let out. The major causes of pollution in Delhi are the toxic gases, sulphur dioxide, nitrogen dioxide and carbon monoxide, but the major irritant is the suspended particulate matter (SPM). The industrial power stations contribute the major portion of these pollutants.

In case of Bombay, the daily pollutants let out into the air is about 3000 tonnes of which half comes from automobiles, and the other half from industries which have sprung up around the city.

The automobiles and domestic cooking by coal have conspired to make Calcutta's environment highly polluted. The quality of urban life in the cities of India particularly in the Metropolitan towns is fast deteriorating because of the great rush to the towns, either because of unemployment in the rural areas and/or better facilities in the towns. The population of Bombay city has crossed 10 million, while that of Delhi today is almost 10 million (9.3 million according to 1991 census). Calcutta, originally planned to accommodate one million people, has about five million with a density of about 22 thousand person per sq. km., while the population density in four wards in north Calcutta is about 175,000 per sq.km. and all measures of the physical quality of life index have failed here.

Water pollution is no less serious than air pollution. Fourteen major rivers in India carry 85 per cent of the surface run-off, and 85 per cent of the country lies within their drainage basin and about 85 per cent of the population lives in their drainage basins. The picture of water pollution is rather gloomy. Even The Ganga, one of largest and holiest rivers of India is heavily polluted and the major source of pollution is the discharge of community wastes from human settlements. The industrial waste waters go straight into water courses making them unfit for use. The domestic discharge is at the rate of 873 million litres a day while the industrial effluent, including toxic waste is about 260 million litres a day. The Central Water Pollution Control Board (CWPCB) has found, on the basis of a detailed survey, that the tradition of throwing away dead bodies into the river in Varanasi and other places is yet another cause of pollution. While it is possible to intercept the other pollutants and treat the river water, it is highly difficult to contain the damage being caused. Further, by another tradition, hundreds of thousands of persons in villages and slum dwellers have the habit of defecation along the river line.

The Central Ganga Authority (CGA) which was set up in 1985 had its main objective to divert the sewage flowing into the river to other locations for treatment and concert into a valuable energy source. The CGA also took up problems of industrial pollution load on the river. However, the pace of work has been rather slow. There has been a marginal improvement in the quality of river water in Patna, but in other sectors the improvement is not significant particularly round the industrial city of Kanpur.

A word must be said about land degradation. The degradation is of various types: (a) waterlogged lands, (b) lands affected by salinity and alkalinity, (c) ravines. The indiscriminate cutting of forest trees and overgrazing upset the ecological balance and lead to soil erosion and land deterioration. Then there are the waterlogged lands where the watertable rises to an extent that the soil pores in the root zone of a crop become saturated and result in the restriction of the normal circulation of air. Supply of oxygen is almost cut-off and the level of Co_2 increases and the crop withers. The waterlogged area in the country is estimated at 6 m. hectare. As a result of inadequate drainage associated with canal irrigation, the saline and alkaline soils are estimated at 7 million hectares. Thus a total of 13 million hectares are waterlogged, saline and alkaline lands. The area under ravines is estimated at 4 million hectares. The ravines are gradually spreading into cultivated lands. According to the reports of the National Commission on Indian Agriculture,700 hectares of good table land is degenerating into ravines every year. This deterioration has affected not only the agricultural land but also habitations, road, railway and other public properties.

It will thus be seen that the total environment – air, water and land – is under great stress. In the developing countries, increasing population and accompanying poverty stand in the centre of the problem. To feed the growing population, the New Agriculture Technology has been ushered in, production of foodgrains in India has almost increased by three and a half times during the last forty years, but the side effects are alarming. Large scale irrigation and massive doses of fertilization have led to waterlogging and upsetting the nitrogen and carbon cycle. In order to catch up with the industrialized world and improve the quality of life, the burning of fossil-fuel on a massive scale, and deforestation to obtain fuel for cooking purposes, and acquiring marginal land for food production have all led to land degradation.

The excessive consumption pattern of the developed countries, and the massive exploitation of resources to earn more profit are the major cause of environmental degradation.

The Government of India established a Ministry of Environment, Forest and Wild Life in 1985 for environmental promotion. National Eco-Development Boards were set up in 1981 to demonstrate feasibility of economic development without ecological imbalance. Planning and implementing programmes to arrest further damage to degraded eco-system, undertaking programmes for their speedy restoration and creating an awareness in youths, are important measures of conservation. Eco-development task forces have been developed for eco-restoration through afforestation and soil conservation. Eco-camps are organised with participation and involvement of people.

From the view point of a geographer, the issue in question should take different lines. In India, the most important step to save the land from degradation is to stem the tide of people rushing from rural to urban areas and prevent the encroachment of first class agricultural lands. In order to achieve these objectives, the village should be taken as a unit, and with the help of remote sensing, aerial photographers and ground surveys, a scientific mapping of existing land use, cropping pattern and a complete inventory of the local resources should be prepared. Land should be devoted to crops in keeping with the eco-system. A network of growth poles and growth centres should be established with adequate facilities of marketing. Small scale industries should be established in the rural areas on the Japanese pattern enhancing the purchasing power of the rural people.

Bio-gas plants should be established in rural areas on a massive scale. Bio-fertilizers should be produced on a large scale to minimize the use of chemical fertilizers and all possible steps should be taken to prevent the industrial and community wastes to be dumped in the rivers.

Automobiles, emitting toxic gases from their tail pipes should be delicensed. These measures need to be taken without delay for the protection of the environment.

At the Global scale, environmental changes may be divided into two types of processes: those that take place *throughout a global system* including the modifications of the climate system as a result of the build up of *greenhouse gasses* and the *depletion of the ozone layer,* and those that take place across the globe such as loss of agricultural land through desertification, *loss of biodiversity* and increase in *acid deposition.*

Mention should be made of IGBP (International Geosphere Biosphere Programme) an independent body established by ICSU to study the interactive physical, chemical and biological processes that regulate the total earth system, the changes that are occurring in this system and the manner in which they are influenced by human activities. Then there is the International Social Science Council to examine the human dimensions of global change.

The Rio Conference on Environment and Development apart from discussing 'greenhouse' effect, ozone depletion, acid rain, discussed in some detail "Biodiversity". Biological diversity means all the ecosystem, of which they are part. The discussion centered round the intellectual property rights on research and products from areas that are rich in biological diversity. It is estimated that between 5 and 30 million species exist on the earth. Apart from ecosystem and species diversity there is also genetic diversity which describes genetic information at different scales. A single organism may have about 1000 to over 400,000 genes. Loss of biodiversity is the process whereby ecosystems, species and genes become extinct. One example occurs when new organism are introduced to Islands or even continents, where they out compete indigenous organisms which are reduced in number or even die out often causing irreversible change in ecosystems.

The message of Rio Conference 'Environment and Development' is clear and needs prompt action.

For sustainable development we have to combat poverty, change the consumption pattern (developed countries), bring down the growth rate of population (developing countries), conservation and management of resources on development, combat deforestation and desertification, protect the atmosphere from toxic gases, conserve biological diversity and sustainable rural and mountain development. These measures will lead to a glorious habitable earth not only for the present generation but also for posterity.

REFERENCES

Bolin, B. et al (eds), (1986). The Greenhouse Effect, Climatic Change and Ecosystem, Scope Report 29, New York.

Braybrooke, D. and G. Paquet (1987). Human Dimensions of Global Change: The Challenge to the Humanities and the Social Sciences. *Transactions of the Royal Society of Canada,* V (11).

Brundtland, G.H. (1989). Global Change and our Common Future, *Environment*, Vol.31, No.5.

Central Arid Zone Research Institute, Jodhpur (1985). *Combating Desertification,* Jodhpur.

Clark, W.C. (ed.), (1982). *Carbon Dioxide Review,* Oxford University Press.

Delwiche, C.C. (1970). The Nitrogen Cycle, *Scientific American,* Vol.225.

F.A.O. (1985). Intensive Multiple Use: Forest Management in the Tropics, *Forestry Paper 55,* Rome.

Government of India, Ministry of Information (1990). India, New Delhi.

Gutierrez, Carlos, B. (1992). Ethics, Politics and Economics on an Amazon Safari in *Eco-Decision,* Montreal.

Hansen, J.D., Johnson, A. Lacis, S. Leleedeff, P. Lee, D. Rind, and G. Russell, (1981). Climate Impact of Increasing Atmospheric Carbon Dioxide, *Science* 213.

Houghton, J.T., Jenkins, C.J. and Ephraums, J.J. (1990). Climate Change: The IPCC Scientific Assessment, *Report of the United Nations Environment Programme, Intergovernmental Panel on Climate Change* (IPCC), New York, 1990.

Houghton, John (1992). Global Warming: A 1992 Update in Elizabeth Camphell Page: *Eco-Decision* Montreal, June 1992.

International Geosphere ! Biosphere Programme (IGBP) (1989). A Study of Global Change, Paris.

International Social Science Council (1990). *A Framework for Research on the Human Dimensions of Global Environment Change,* Paris.

Johnson, W. and W.A. Steere (eds.) (1974). The *Environmental Challenge,* New York.

Kormondy, E.J. (1989). *Concepts of Ecology,* New Delhi.

Labostille, A. (1981). Acid Rain: How Great a Menace? *National Geographic Magazine* 160 (5).

Likens, G.E., R.F. Wright, J.N. Galloway and T.J. Butler (1979). Acid Rain, *Scientific American,* New york.

Manners, Ian R. and Mikesell, Marvin, W. (1974). *Perspectives on Environment,* U.S.A.

Massachusetts Institute of Technology (1970). *Man's Impact on the Global Environment Assessment and Recommendations for Action,* Cambridge, MIT Press.

Miller, J.R., J.T. (1981). *Living in the Environment Concepts, Problems and Alternatives,* 2nd ed. Belmont, CA:Wordsworth Publishing Company.

Ministry of Environment and Forests, Government of India (1989). *Developing India's Wastelands,* New Delhi.

Mitchell, J.K. (1991). *Global Environmental Change: Human and Policy Dimensions,* Vol.1, No.2, New Brunswich, USA.

Renner, M. (1989). National Security: The Economic and Environmental Dimensions, *Worldwatch, Paper 89,* Worldwatch Institute, Washington, D.C.

Report of the National Commission on Agriculture, Government of India, New Delhi (1976). *Resource Development,* Part V, IX and XIII, New Delhi.

Schneider, S.H. (1991). The Global Warming Debate Heats Up: Analysis and Perspective, *Bulletin of the American Meteorological Society,* Vol.71, No.9.

Smil, V. (1987). *A Perspective on Global Environmental Crises.*

United Nations Environment Programme (1980). *Choosing the Options: Alternative Life Styles and Development Patterns,* Nairobi.

Volker, A. Mohnen, et al (1991). The Conflict over Global Warming in Mitchel, J.K. *Global Environmental Change,* Vol.I, No.2, Oxford, U.K.

Watt Kennath (1968). *Ecology and Resource Management,* New York .

Wilson, C.M. and W.H. Mathews (1970). *Mans Impact on the Global Environment,* Cambridge, Mass, MIT Press.

World Commission on Environment and Development, (1987). *Our Common Future.*

3

THE EMERGING NEW DEVELOPMENT PARADIGM: Issues, Consideration and Research Agenda

K.V.SUNDARAM

Introduction

The concern about "Development", particularly as it relates to the developing countries, came to be voiced around the 1940's. Since then, the meaning of this term has shifted from time to time in keeping with certain major political, administrative, economic, social and technological changes as well as certain perceptions relating to income and regional disparities in the developing countries.

The major changes witnessed during the 1950's and 1960's included decolonisaton (in a number of countries in Asia and Africa), central control of government functions following independence and ushering in a massive effort directed towards national reconstruction and development based on country-specific needs and priorities. These changes have been followed during the 1970's, 1980's and the 1990's by a succession of far reaching shifts in development orientation, characterised by new thrusts and strategies appropriate to the 'developing countries'. These have been referred to in planning literature as "shift in the development paradigm".

Development as Economic Growth

Initially development as interpreted by economists, was regarded as synonymous to economic development. Also economic development, for quite some time, was confused with "economic growth", that is, of increase in gross national product (GDP) and income per capita. Sometimes, the two terms 'development' and 'growth' were used interchangeably. When this philosophy of development was mechanically foisted on the developing countries, it resulted in the well known phenomenon of a "dual economy", characterised by a growing export sector, distinguished in space as an 'enclave economy', and a stagnant traditional sector covering most territories of rural space, thus exacerbating rural poverty, and spatial disparities in development. In some quarters, this was seen as "economic colonialism".

This economic growth game also implied industrialisation and modernisation, as it was through this route that the West European and American styles of development emerged. In the developing countries, while industrialisation led to tremendous spatial inequalities in development, indigenous societies with their negative side-effects.

The 'Trickle Down Process' of Development

Thus the "economic growth game", as envisaged above aimed at the accumulation of capital through increase in per capita incomes and the investment of this capital in selected areas of growth, in industrialisation, modernisation and urbanisation through a "top-down process" of planning and control. It was expected that as economic growth snowballed, a "trickle down process" of development will ensue, leading to spread and multiplier effects of the benefit of development.

However, by the end of the 1960's it become clear that neither development as economic growth nor as modernisation could bring about a wide ranging effect on the standards and conditions of living of the majority of individuals in many Third World Countries. The "trickle down process" did not certainly operate. If anything, the relative position of the masses of poor people worsened *vis-a-vis* that of the relatively rich. Widespread poverty and destitution became visible, tangible and compelling. Viewing these developments, many thinkers began to perceive the "growth" dimension of development, in its exclusive pursuit towards the production of material things, as naive, superficial and unrealistic. In a penetrating analysis on the meaning of development, Dudley Seers characterised it as a mere "web of fantasy".[1]

Growth with Equity Considerations

Following this disenchantment with development, the idea of distributive justice or redistribution with growth was vigorously advocated. As a sequel, a host of issues — poverty, unemployment, inequality (in terms of income distribution, regional disparities, and social inequality) and quality of life came to be regarded as the critical issues to be tackled directly and frontally. The question of satisfying certain "basic needs" — nutrition, health, water supply, shelter, sanitation and education and alleviating poverty through mobilising government and aid spending rather than relying on market forces were considered the major priorities in the context of the developing countries.

Following these ideas, new programmatic approaches emerged among which the Basic Minimum Needs Approach (BMN), Poverty Alleviation and Employment Generation Programmes for the Rural Poor, Target and Target Group Area (Backward Areas) Programmes, Integrated Rural Development Programmes in different combinations and Development Programme for Women may be specifically cited.

The Concern for the Environment

The seventies were thus characterised by governments in the various developing countries experimenting with different policy and programmatic approaches, guided by the shifting emphasis of development thought by the planners. This period also coincided with a sense of concern and anxiety experienced by the advanced industrial countries about environmental pollution and the fear of a rapidly depletion of global natural resources. The United Nation Conference on the Human Environment held at Stockholm in 1972 raised the first warning signal about the negative aspects of the prevailing development strategies.

Limits of Growth

In 1979, the United Nations Symposium on "Interrelations Among Resources, Environment, Population and Development,[2] identified the question of consumption problems and lifestyles as one of the most basic sources of conflict in the world. Hence, it stressed the urgent need, both in the North and in the South, for exploring alternative patterns of consumption and development that are environmentally sound, socially responsible and less wasteful. This implied limiting the reckless "mining" of natural capital, practicing austerity in consumption, reducing wants and caring for long-term prosperity. The Club of Rome talked about "limits to growth". In a further elaboration of the "limits" idea, both an 'upper limit' and a 'lower limit' (i.e. minimum and maximum) to economic growth were stressed, implying resource exploitation based on considerations of sustainable resource use, avoidance of environmental degradation in any form and maintenance of an ecological balance at the desired level of quality of life. It was advocated that all countries should specify their growth rates of national product both in terms of a minimum as well as maximum (Sundaram, Chandrashekhara).[3,4] It has been argued that there are certain viable and attractive technologies, economic structures and lifestyles to which the developed countries and the Third World could move.

These alternatives imply the acceptance of simple material living standards; abandoning the quest for endless economic growth; maximising regional economic self-sufficiency; employing alternative and intermediate technologies; and adopting cooperative ways of working, wherever possible. "These alternatives constitute a third way. They involve the rejection of the capitalist way with its emphasis on the limitless increases in consumption and waste, its disregard for the poor, and its indifference to any concept of appropriate development."[5]

Sustainable Development

The Bruntland Commission's Report in April 1987 *Our Common Future*[6] became a landmark in developing thinking and added further impetus to the governments in the developing as well as developed countries to address environmental issues in their practical country programmes. Sustainable development became the key word, which was defined by the World Commission on Environment and Development as "development which meets the needs of the present without compromising the ability of future generations to meet their own needs". Such sustainable development may mean different things to different countries. To the rich nations, sustainable development may imply preserving for posterity, and already high standards of life achieved in their countries. To the poor nations, it may seem a pathway of economic development which can help to meet the minimum needs of the people without harm to the environmental capital stocks. Initially, the debate on sustainable development came to be centred on issues relating to growth versus environmental conservation, which implied a basic contradiction in thinking. A more exhaustive study of the problem by the Brundtland Commission led to the conclusion that the relationship between sustainable development and the environment is really one of complementarity and interdependence. "What is required is a new approach in which all nations aim at a type of development that integrates production with resource conservation and enhancement and that links both to the provision for all of an adequate livelihood and equitable access to resources".[7] Since poverty is both a major cause and effect of global environment problems, a world in which poverty is endemic will always be prone to ecological and other catastrophes. Thus, economic growth, poverty alleviation and proper management of natural resources are all the mutually interdependent facets of the ultimate development goal and what is called for today is the achievement of a better balance and closer integration among these objectives. This then is the philosophy of the new development paradigm — that of growth with equity, stability and sustainability. The major concern, of the developing and developed countries today is how to incorporate the environmental dimensions into their plans, so that they are informed by all the four considerations of growth, stability, equity and sustainability. What this implies is that sustainability has to be explicitly recognised in every aspect of any planning and development problems.

The Growing Environmental Awareness

The new development paradigm has now led to the environmental dimension becoming a recognisable element in our development agenda. Project documents prepared by bilateral and multilateral agencies during the 70's and 80's barely made mention of the environment. Similarly, project appraisal manuals did not include it in their content. The speed with which the issues of the environment broke the surface of development thinking may be gauged by the fact that the World Bank did not mention environmental issues *per se* in its 1984 annual report, yet in the 1985 report, it warned that the destruction of environmental systems was assuming "massive proportions in many developing countries, particularly in Africa".[8]

During the last twenty years or so, there is no doubt that there have been considerable advancements in environmental awareness, ecological research and the application of neoclassical economic principles to environmental issues. The publication of a document by the International Union for Conservation of Native and Natural Resources (IUCN) in 1980 titled "World Conservation Strategy" was a landmark and provided decision-makers with an overall blueprint for sustainable development of their environments. There is now a growing preoccupation in the developed world with the collection of environmental data in support of policies for environmental protection and natural resource utilisation through both regulatory and market mechanisms. This has been encouraged by the growing body of economic literature expounding welfare economics in support of principles such as "polluter pays and user pays".

In the developing countries also, awareness of environmental issues has grown considerably in recent years. Most bilateral as well as multilateral development agencies have also been striving to incorporate environment appraisal, monitoring and evaluation into their aid policies, programmes and projects.

Experiences with Introducing Environmental Considerations

Although environmental awareness has grown, the actual task of introducing explicit environmental considerations into development planning and activities and thus "planning environmentally" on a scientific basis is only emerging in slow steps. Analytical tools and practical programmes have only begun to catch up with environmental planning and for taking account of environmental destruction into national economic record-keeping. These attempts are yet to go a long way towards perfection, though some beginnings have been made.

Until recently, developing countries have generally regarded environmental protection as a luxury that only rich countries could afford. In the context of planning for development, environmental considerations were kept as an "externality" or "additive" to a development plan and were not woven integrally into it. This meant that environmental considerations were given only marginal significance. During the plan implementation stage, these were, in many instances, hardly taken into consideration. Thus, the "additive approach"' which saw environmental or resource management issues as a "technical fix"' did not really succeed in solving environmental problems.

Since 1984, however, donor agencies like the World Bank, the Asian Development Bank etc. have been insisting on a more systematic appraisal of the environmental implications. This consisted of evolving a method of building into the project cycle environmental concerns, particularly during the project identification, project preparation, Appraisal and Evaluation stages. The Asian Development Bank, for instance, adopts the following approach:

I. *During project identification phase*

(i) Preparation of Environmental and Natural Resources profiles.
(ii) Division of projects into three broad impact categories.

Category A. Projects rarely having significant adverse environmental impacts.

Category B. Projects generally having significant adverse impacts, but which can be readily identified and quantified and for which remedial measures can be prescribed.

Category C. Projects which invariably have significant adverse impacts, requiring detailed environmental analysis.

II. *During project preparation phase*
Conducting Initial Environmental Examination (IEE) on Bank missions.

III. *During Pre-Appraisal/Appraisal phase*
Environmental Impact Assessment (EIA) and proposed mitigation measures.

IV. *During Post-Evaluation phase*
Evaluate whether project met the proposed environmental requirements and whether any anticipated effects were caused by the project.

The World Bank also followed a method in which the approach to environmental management came to be based on Environmental Impact Assessment (EIA's) of individual projects and on investment in programmes such as pollution abatement, afforestation or water management. Assuming that some protection and conservation achievement have been possible by incorporating some environmental dimensions into individual project exercises, it cannot be overemphasised that a more comprehensive approach conceived in a larger spatial setting is needed to achieve the full impact of such measures.

The experience with all the above approaches showed that despite the use of environmental impact assessment and other techniques, major economic development projects have caused unacceptable environment degradation. It is now abundantly clear that these approaches address only symptoms, not root causes. The wisdom has dawned that the ecological dimension of development has regional and local characteristics, which demand not merely its perception in individual projects and programmes, but also its integration into well-conceived local regional and national strategies for managing the environmental and natural resources on a sustainable basis.

One important lesson that stands out from all these experiences is that the development of natural resources should not be perceived in terms of restraints on development only. Rather, we must regard environment as a valid sector of development, or as an overarching sector that addresses the dynamic interactions, among other sectors. Furthermore, the key question is no longer: How can we best safeguard the environment? Rather, the question is: How can we reconcile development with environment? It is really the problem of having the cake without eating it. If we have to adopt such an approach, we need to understand the process of environmental degradation as an integral part of economic development. In future, our methods of tackling environmental concerns must therefore be linked with the economy-wide models of economic development.

Environmental Orientation to Planning at Different Spatial Levels

The new planning paradigm must be addressed at the levels of plans, programmes and projects. At the level of plans, the planning system should incorporate regional environmental protection/conservation needs into economic development planning at several different planning levels, along with linkages established among and between these levels. At the national, regional and local levels, the following will be the major tasks/functions with environmental orientation.

National — Resource Inventory and Environmental profiles; country strategy studies; sectoral reviews outlining appropriate strategies and priorities; Providing Environmental guidelines to sectoral and sub-national levels.

Regional – Resource Inventory and Environmental profiles; Regional sectoral reviews with strategies and priorities for sustainable development; Identification of ecosystems and problems; Landuse planning with focus on land degradation problems, afforestation, watershed development and wasteland development.

Local – Village Eco-development with focus on the "bottom-up" approach to environmental development; management of common property resources and community involvement; use of appropriate technology.

While at the national level, planning will be macroscopic and policy-oriented, at the regional and local levels, it will be area specific and local resources-oriented with the focus on the integration of environmental-dimensions into the regional and local economic development plan. At the latter area levels, it should be noted that it would not simply be a mechanical addition and compilation of economic and environmental plans. The accent would be on the linkages between economic development, resource use, production of residuals, impacts on environmental quality and communities. Thus, environmental dimensions will get totally enmeshed into the economic development plans at the various spatial level like warp and woof in a tapestry.

As may be seen from the above discussion indicating the tasks at the different levels, the major tasks will revolve around:

1. Resource Inventorying;
2. Preparation of Environmental profile;
3. Identification of ecosystems and problems;
4. Integration of plans, programmes and projects; and
5. Community involvement.

Changes in the Organisational Structure of Development Planning

As changes in the orientation of Development Planning were taking place, they also necessitated certain concomitant changes in the organisational and administrative structure in each country. The compulsions for such changes were dictated by political, administrative and development considerations.

These changes led to a range of socio-politico-administrative reforms hinging on the concept of Centralisation-Decentralisation Continuum. In a number of Third World Countries, where such changes took place, the actual form of decentralisation depended on the specific needs, aspirations and socio-political circumstances of each country. The structural changes, in each case, depended on the extent of Centralisation, Deconcentration, Decentralisation, or Local Self-reliance.

The changes in the orientation and structure of development planning are summed up in Fig. 3.1.

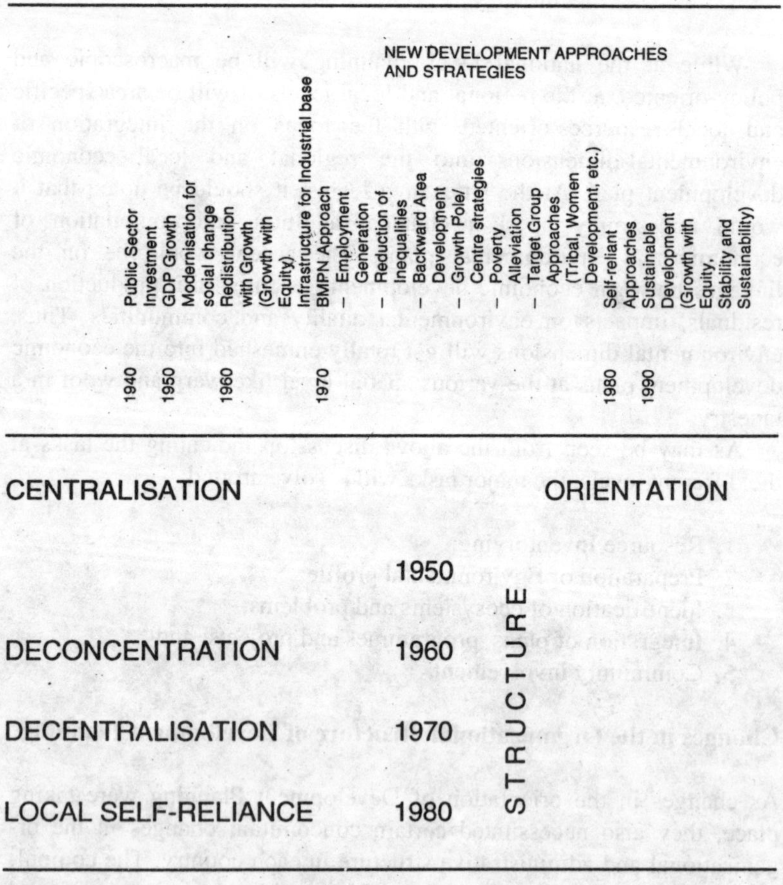

FIG. 3.1: Changes in the Structure and Orientation of Development Planning

Paradigm Shifts

From the foregoing account, it may be seen that development thought has gone through many vicissitudes of change. With our developmental experience in the various countries, new perceptions have grown and these new perceptions have continually imparted new orientations to planning. Countries have accordingly tried to incorporate these new orientations into their numerous policies and programmes. It has always been a search for newer, more dynamic, more comprehensive, more relevant and more specific forms of development addressed to a multiplicity of objectives. With the benefit of hindsight, we may view all these changes with the various emphases placed on development as so many shifts in the Development Paradigm. Our concern here is on the latest or the new development paradigm that has emerged and how to operationalise it at the sub-national levels in a country. Inevitably, it is an innovative endeavour and poses extraordinary challenges to the planner.

Towards Operationalising the New Development Paradigm

The new development paradigm has, no doubt, increased the awareness of the need to arrest the grave environmental damage that has been and is being done in many parts of the world and to promote environmentally sound forms of natural resource management. International and national agencies are aware that the achievement of sustainable development poses a major challenge, which has to be met through concrete action in a number of areas. In this context, a wide-range of policy and research activities are being undertaken all over the world. The question of integrating environmental concerns into the mainstream of a country's economic policies and development plans is receiving increasing attention. The World Bank has identified five priority environmental problems that require special attention. These are: destruction of natural habitats; land degradation; degradation and degradation of fresh water resources, urban, industrial and agricultural pollution; and depletion of the "global commons". The developing countries assisted by external agencies have to address themselves to all these problems. The basic need is to incorporate in their perspective, five year and annual plans, various programmes intended to achieve the objective of economic growth. At the macro level (i.e. national level), these will take the form of environmental policy.

analysis and incorporation of environmental dimensions into sectoral plans. At the sub-national levels (i.e. Regional and local levels), these have to be given an operational focus involving action by governments, other development agencies, relevant NGO's and the community. For all these to happen, the planning methodologies which are being followed in the developing countries must be seen as a dynamic phenomenon, responding to the shifts in the paradigm of development.

Major Issues

In this context, a number of issues arise. The major issue is that of Sustainable Natural Resource Management. In the first place, sustainability has to be imparted its operational meaning for each resource to be managed in its specific ecosystem spatial context. The core of the sustainability issue is a careful balancing of the intra-generational and inter-generational aspects of development. Here the problems arising from the futuristic nature of the phenomenon and associated uncertainties demand a serious consideration of the ecosystem spatial context. The operational definition for sustainability must be specified for each type of ecosystem and resource use, case by case. General definitions of sustainability abound in a lot of literature that has appeared in recent years. These, no doubt, highlight some broadly common elements, but do not indicate the operational meaning. The operational meaning becomes clear only when related to specific situations. Jodha defines sustainability as "the ability of a system (e.g. Mountain Agriculture) to maintain a certain well-defined level of performance (output) over time, and if required, to enhance the same, including through linkages with other systems without damaging the essential ecological integrity of the system".[9] The long-term productivity and health of a natural resource base is, in turn, affected by the pattern and intensity of its use. Thus, the sustainability/unsustainability is an outcome of match/mismatch between: (1) basic characteristics of the natural resource components, and (2) patterns and methods of their utilisation. The latter can change (with the changing needs or perceptions of the community), but the former is normally difficult to change, unless the whole resource base is transformed.

Sustainability has to be inferred through the unsustainability conditions or negative changes that have emerged. The following are some examples of such negative changes in the mountain areas. (Jodha et. al, 1992).[10]

- The higher extent and severity of landslides;
- the lower water flow in traditional community irrigation systems;
- the general decline in yields of major crops (except in highly patronised pockets);
- the reduced diversity of mountain agriculture;
- the longer inter-seasonal hunger gap (food deficit period);
- the longer time spent by villagers for collection of fodder and fuel from neighbouring uncultivated areas or common property lands;
- the negative changes in the botanical composition of species in forests and pastures; and
- the increase in the extent of poverty, unemployment, and out-migration of the hill people.

The above kind of negative changes must be treated as indicators of unsustainability. They may relate to (1) resource base (e.g. land degradation), (2) production flows (e.g. persistent decline in crop yields), and (3) resource management/use systems, (increased unfeasibility of annual perennial based intercropping or specific crop rotations). Some of the negative changes are directly visible (e.g. landslides). Some are concealed (and one has to labour hard to detect them) owing to people's adjustments to negative changes (e.g. the substitution of shallow-rooted crops for deep-rooted crops following erosion of top soil). A third category of negative change is inherent in development initiatives with potentially negative consequences. (e.g. a farm technology that increases mountain agriculture's crucial dependence on external inputs, like fertiliser for instance, as against the locally renewable input resource).

Thus, one set of the major issues lies in the identification or detection of negative changes or factors that have caused unsustainability conditions. This is to be perceived in an ecosystems perspective and taking note of each area and each resource dealt with.

A second set of major issue is with the understanding of the causes and effects of the negative changes referred to above. This is a difficult process, as many of the impacts of environmental degradation often occur externally to any market system and involve complex processes of ecological-economic interaction. Several studies have identified the market failures and government policies as being at the centre of many environmental degradation problems facing developing countries.

Market failure exists when markets fail to reflect fully environmental values. The presence of open access resource exploitation, public environmental goods, externalities, incomplete information and markets, and imperfect competition all contribute to market failure. Policy failure occurs when the public policies required to correct a problem are inadequate or when government decisions or policies themselves lead to negative changes (environmental degradation). All these call for redirecting public policies for sustainable development. This is seen to be a major challenge facing planners and environmental economists. This calls for improved analysis of both the impacts and the causes underlying environmental degradation.

A third set of issues concerns the exploring of the various avenues for alternative frameworks and solutions. Here again, the context with its configuration of peculiar problem situations, matters a good deal. Broadly, it is an attempt to balance the dilemmas posed by natural preservation, cultural preservation and rural development. The problem is quite a complex one because of the nexus of environmental conservation with the problem of poverty, which is pervasive in all the third world countries. The alleviation of poverty demands intensive resource to achieve growth, while at the same time it is imperative to protect the earth's environmental integrity and biodiversity. Since both socio-economic development and biological conservation are to become sustainable, a balance has to be found towards a pragmatic and responsible course of action. The problem however, defies easy solution, particularly in areas where man and nature are closely and spatially juxtaposed, with the latter providing the life support systems to the former.

To sum up, the three major sets of issues that are posed by the new development paradigms are:

(i) identifying the negative changes or factors that are causing unsustainability conditions in various ecosystems;
(ii) diagnosing the causes and effects of these negative changes; and
(iii) finding viable solutions or alternative frameworks of development and strategies that will balance growth with equity, stability and sustainability objectives.

Broadly these issues will be subsumed under the three major activity phases in the development planning context. These are:

1. the identification phase;
2. the diagnoses phase; and
3. the planning phase

The Agenda for Research

The identification of the major issues lends clues to an agenda for research. We, therefore, set out in a somewhat disjointed and tentative way, what we consider to be important research areas for attention. In the Table 3.1, an attempt has been made to set out some research areas.

TABLE 3.1: The Agenda for Research Areas Needing Attention

Activity		Research areas needing attention
Identification	(1)	Identification of Ecosystems and sub-systems
	(2)	Ecosystem specificities (dominant elements)
	(3)	Natural process linkages between/among ecosystems
	(4)	Negative changes — Evidence of nature and extent
	(5)	Indicators of unsustainability
	(6)	Identification of problems and constraints (Macro-Meso-Micro levels)
Diagnosis (causes and effects)	(1)	Resource inventory characteristics and resources survey integration — Ecosystem and sub-ecosystemwise
	(2)	Population — natural resource base relationships. (Carrying capacity models)
	(3)	Patterns of symbiosis between human use of resources and biodiversity
	(4)	Poverty levels, population growth, employment generation and environmental degradation
	(5)	Social factors/deprived groups/position of women
	(6)	Indigenous cultural practices (valuable traditional components)
	(7)	Human interventions — type, scale, technology
	(8)	Nature — Man interactions: conflict areas
	(9)	Environmental profile — Nature and intensity of environmental degradation, Reversibility — irreversibility status (state of environment)
	(10)	Institutional constraints

(*Contd.*)

TABLE 3.1 *Contd.*

Activity		Research areas needing attention
Problem-Solving and Solution-Finding (Planning and Development at Macro, Meso and Micro levels)	(1)	Setting of Objectives, Policies, Strategies and Priorities
	(2)	Planning at the level of administrative areas in an eco-systems Perspective-Methods and Procedures
	(3)	Political dimensions and administrative fiat
	(4)	Environmental Data Base — Methods of data collection for environmental resources and establishing the baseline (bench mark)
	(5)	Evolving norms and standards for area development — Resources and Ecosystem-wise
	(6)	Threshold limits for — carrying capacity (Human, livestock) — Grazing — Energy (biomass) consumption
	(7)	Strategies and technological options for sustainable development in: (a) high resources potential areas (b) low resource potential areas
	(8)	Resource Management issues: — renewable resources — non-renewable resources — common property resources — cultural resources — social impact assessment, conflict management and co-management issues
	(9)	Alternatives for integrated area management and development of natural and cultural resources
	(10)	Ecodevelopment based on sustained yield with built-in participatory action approaches — Macro, Meso and Micro levels
	(11)	The institutional mechanisms for Resource Management and social change
	(12)	Action research (e.g. Forestry-Farming linkages; Ecosystems interactions; Replicable patterns of participatory development etc.
	(13)	Most appropriate innovative planning models and approaches
	(14)	Monitoring of environmental change
	(15)	Evaluation: Learning from successes and failures
	(16)	Environmental accounting

The above Table 3.1 represents in broad outline a set of research issues that must be addressed in the context of sustainable development. It is illustrative and not comprehensive. Many of these research issues cannot be dealt with in isolation by a single discipline. They could be realistically addressed only through a multi-disciplinary analysis, with many disciplines – ranging from anthropology to zoology – contributing valuable insights and outputs.

It must be emphasised that the research agenda set forth here only provides abroad indication of the research areas. They need to be spelt out in more specific terms when grappling with specific area/ecosystem contexts. For example, when a low resource potential area fails in a dry area, research needs to be focussed on dry farming practices and the innovations needed in this context. Similarly, in the buffer zone adjacent to protected forest areas, the research must be focussed on the resident peoples and their needs *vis-a-vis* protection measures to conserve the forest. In fragile mountain systems, for instance, it is necessary to investigate into the environmental cost implications of alternative development interventions e.g. implementing capital intensive projects *vis-a-vis* small projects using appropriate technologies.

Improved analysis of both the impacts and the causes underlying environmental degradation will become crucial in the years ahead. Substantial policy distortions and market failures affecting natural resource management do exist in the developing countries. In this context, research on some of these issues becomes crucial, as it is necessary to reorient public policies in the best informed manner, to correct for these distortions as best as possible. At the macro-level, there is a need for substantive and extensive analysis of the implications of various macro-economic, trade and sectoral policies for management of the natural resource base. Alternative policy options that explicitly take into account the resource constraints of the most vulnerable economic groups also need to be properly formulated and analysed. At the meso level, regional economic development-cum-environmental planning must be operationalised to identify areas of comparative advantage as well as "problem zones", to recommend alternative landuse patterns and to set the limits for growth. At the micro level, ecodevelopment planning with participatory action is strongly advocated. At this level, there is need for intensive analysis (a) of the economic costs of environmental impacts; (b) of natural resource allocation decisions at the village or farmer level; and (c) of the monitoring of the impacts of policy decisions and investment programmes. When all is said and done, the problem at the village-farm level is the one of increased use intensity of land resources (for higher productivity). What is most relevant in the context of sustainable development is application - oriented basic research from the village upwards with people's active participation and the interlinking of such investigation with research at higher scales or levels (meso and macro), which usually concentrate on harnessing the achievements of science and technology to production-oriented activities.

Priorities for Geographical Research

In any research agenda, the thematic coverage is bound to be wide, cutting across many disciplines and several spatial scales. Here some prioritisation is indicated not merely in the light of development urgencies, but also in the context of specific disciplines. The question, therefore, of the scope and content of geographical research becomes a relevant issue. Geography as a discipline is traditionally concerned with investigating Earth-Man relationships and human responses to earth specificities. It is also concerned with Place-Work-Folk interrelationships in specific natural regions, which correspond, by and large, to the ecosystems and sub-systems. It is therefore, suggested that this road investigational area should be cut out for innovating research contributions by geographers. Within this larger 'research realm', if one is to further prioritise, it is research at the micro-level that should claim priority attention. Here the author is perhaps biased in favour of his own field of specialisation i.e. regional and local area development. Nevertheless, it can be argued that attention to the elements of land, water and vegetation at the grass roots level constitutes the basic foundation for any meaningful research aiming at sustainable development. It is at this level that man-nature interfaces are close and critical. The proper decisions taken at this level are bound to influence the whole range of decisions across the entire spectrum of planning levels. If these are valid arguments, then the following research themes may perhaps be particularly relevant for geographical research on an priority basis. It should be noted that even when the focus is narrowed down in this manner to a few specific themes at the regional and local levels, they constitute a sufficiently wide range of research issues that are relevant to sustainable development. These priority research areas may be summed up as follows:

1. Natural Resources inventorying and analysis using modern

scientific methods for updation and survey integration in an Ecosystems Framework.

2. Building environmental profile at regional and local levels including the identification of the severity of environmental problems (the degree of stress) and the correctives needed for restoration, preservation and management with limited use and conservation in the natural state.
3. Estimation of threshold limits for carrying capacity, biomass energy consumption, livestock population and fodder consumption, and biomass renewal–Case studies at Regional and local levels.
4. Potential, problems and constraints for sustainable agriculture development in –

   (a) High potential, and
   (b) Low potential agricultural areas–Case studies

5. Man-Nature interaction in (a) Forest buffer zone areas; (b) Hill-Plain interface areas; (c) Areas susceptible to natural hazards (e.g. flood plains)
6. Village Ecodevelopment for integrated agriculture and forestry development.
7. Traditional farming systems and practices and their potentials for sustainable agricultural development.

REFERENCES

1. Dudley Seers (1969). "The meaning of development", *International Development Review* No. 4, Dec.
2. United Nations Symposium on Interrelations among Resources, Environment, Population and Development" (1979). Stockholm.
3. K.V. Sundaram (1988). "Rural Development and Environmental Conservation" (Keynote Address) in *Proceedings of* International Symposium on The Development of Regional Agriculture and Environmental Conservation in South-east Asian Countries; Kyoto, March 15-17.
4. C.S. Chandrasekhara (1985). Environmental Planning and Management for Local and Regional Development — A Conceptual Framework' — Paper to the International Workshop on Environmental Management for Local and Regional Development, 9-13 June, Nogaya (Japan), sponsored by the United Nation's Centre for Regional Development.

5. Ignacy Sachs: "Developing in Harmony with Nature" in *Ecodevelopment, Concepts, Projects and Strategies* (ed.) (1984). Bernhard Glaesar, Pergamon Press, Oxford.
6. World Commission on Environment and Development (WCED) (1987). *Our Common Future*, London, Oxford University Press.
7. WCED — *Ibid.*
8. Quoted in Jonathan M. Blackwell, Roger N. Goodwillie and Richard Webb (1991). "Environment and Development in Africa — selected case studies" EDI Development Policy case series, No. 6.
9. N.S. Jodha "Mountain Perspective and Sustainability: A Framework for Development Strategies" in Jodha N.S. et al., (Eds.) (1992). *Sustainable Mountain Agriculture – Perspectives and Issues,* Vol. 1, Oxford & IBH Publishing Co. Pvt. Ltd., New Delhi.
10. Jodha et al. (1992). *Ibid.*

PART-II

ENVIRONMENTAL ISSUES (ENERGY, WATER AND LAND POLLUTION)

4

LAND TRANSFORMATION AND ENVIRONMENTAL DEGRADATION IN JAIPUR URBAN COMPLEX

H.S. SHARMA and M.S. NATHAWAT

Introduction

Jaipur city is distinct and unique from most of other urban complexes of the country in its historical development and fame as the 'Pink City' of India. It is one of the few planned cities of the eighteenth century of Pre-British India. The walled city of Jaipur was founded in 1727 A.D. by the then Maharaja Sawai Jai Singh II who was said to have studied Shilpa Shastra and commissioned Vidyadhar Bhattacharya to prepare a plan for the new city. The planner involved a grid iron plan with the main roads running east-west along the sandy ridge in the core of the city plan. The construction was started in 1728 A.D. A masonry crenelated wall about 3.5 metres and 2.5 metres thick entirely encloses the city. There are seven fortified gateways in all directions. The walled city is having an area of 6 square kilometres and is regularly laid cut in rectangular blocks. The main street is 33 metres wide and runs 3.2 kilometres in a straight line from Surajpole in the east to Chandpole in the west. There are two other main streets running north-south at right angles to the main street. The city is further divided into *Chokaris* or blocks and the blocks into *Mohallas*. In all there are 407 *Mohallas*.

Jaipur city is located on a sandy triangular plain 'conjectured to be on a bed of dried up lake' (*Imperial Gazetteer,* 1908). This sandy plain is enclosed on three sides by ranges of hills (Fig. 4.1). The eastern and north-western portions of this sandy plain are undulating and dissected into many rain-fed *nallahs*. The hills form a north-eastern continuation of the Aravallis – belonging to the oldest orogeny. The average height of these hills is about 500 metres above mean sea level.

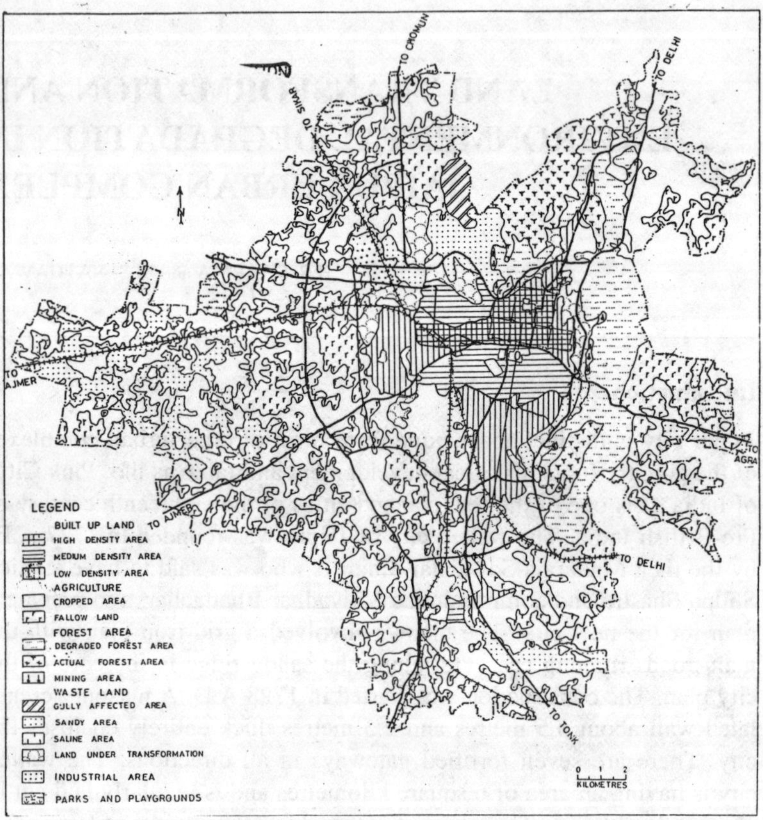

FIG. 4.1: Urban Sprawl: Jaipur City

Jaipur 250 Years Ago – Developed on Ecological Principles

The walled city was planned ideally taking all environmental and ecological factors into consideration. It was on relatively high ground with gentle slopes so that water could easily drain away from the town. The entire supply of water to the town was through well distributed wells. The groundwater was plentiful since the site is located between hills. The hills then must have been rich in vegetation. The forest would have allowed clear water to seep through the old consolidated dunes. Thus the choice of the site was appropriately made to ensure that the city had high sloping ground, had enough groundwater, and also other necessary supplies such as forests, pasture land, agricultural land, etc. If we forget the vast sprawling city of today, old Jaipur must have been nestling cosily and comfortably, sheltered by the hills.

It is surprising to note that in the history of human settlements perhaps Jaipur is the only example where human settlements more than one lakh of people could live in harmony with the natural surroundings for a period of nearly 22 years. The presence of wild life within municipal limits as late as 1940 suggests that a proper ecological balance was maintained.

The sudden increase in population of Jaipur, unplanned growth, rapid industrialization and continuous land transformation[1] has disturbed this ecological balance and has created many environmental problems such as land degradation, depletion of resources, over crowding, waste disposal, inadequate water supply, sanitation, pollution, etc.

The present study deals with land transformation and environmental degradation due to man's interference in the fragile ecosystem of Jaipur and its environs.

The Objectives of the Study

The objectives of the study are:

(a) to monitor urban landuse pattern resulting due to land transformation in Jaipur city and its environs;

(b) to examine the applicability of the remote sensing products in the extraction of information in the process of urban and regional study;

(c) to study the changes and direction of urban expansion from satellite data products;

(d) to study and identify various environmental hazards in area under study and to suggest suitable rational measures for improved landuse planning of the city.

Methodology

It has been demonstrated in India and many other countries that remotely sensed data can be used to identify the problem of any area, map and monitor the changes on the land surface over a period of time. The detection of abrupt changes is possible using satellite images in many cases where the changes produce an extreme visual contrast between the old and the new. Satellite remote sensing data have been used since 1980 for studying urban growth. In the present study remote sensing data, obtained from different satellite have been used. Systematically geocoded false colour composite images are used in order to extract information about landuse/land cover and land transformation.

The methodology is based on monoscopic visual interpretation of IRS. (LISS-II) and MSS and TM (Landsat). Standard False Colour Composite (FCC) generated on 1:1,000,000 scale for identification of different landuse/land cover classes, based on the image characteristics like tone, size, shape, pattern, texture, location, association etc. have been used. A broad image interpretation key.has been developed, based on such image characteristics so as to enable interpretation of satellite images for landuse/land cover mapping.

The multi-date imagery of three time data (1975, 1986 and 1991) were interpreted to identify and map the details of landuse, land under transformation, fallows lands. Ancillary data like topographical maps and other thematic maps, the skill and the local knowledge of the interpreter, also supports interpretation and mapping of landuse/land cover. Based on the ground verification, the boundaries of the different landuse/land cover units were finalised. The corrected details were transferred to the base map prepared from the topographical maps. Wherever it was required to correct the differences in the scale between the imagery and base map, the Optical Reflecting Projector (ORP) and Optical Pantographs were used for transferring the interpreted details onto the base map. The geographical area under different landuse/land cover categories were calculated by planimeter. The areas of each landuse/land cover class were calculated to square kilometres and expressed in simple percentage to the total geographical area.

Based on the monoscopic visual interpretation techniques, various landuse changes have been delineated and mapped, wherever, it has not been possible to differentiate different landuse details, because of similar spectral response, such droughtful areas have been verified on the ground. The final corrected details have been transferred on to the base map prepared on 1:50,000 scale. The changing landuse patterns are shown on maps and the areas under different landuse for respective years of 1975, 1986 and 1991 are shown in Table 4.2. A generalised system of classification has been considered to obtain better reliability and to avoid problems of compatibility. After preliminary scanning and identification of the physical characteristics of the image, 8 main first level classes and 10 second level sub-classes have been formed. The landuse/land cover classes and their changes are being discussed in the following pages.

History of Development of Jaipur City

The old Jaipur was confined to the walled city (Fig. 4.1). With the influx of immigrants after the partition in 1947 and natural growth rate of population, the city started expanding outside the wall (Fig. 4.2). With the installation of the Railways, importance of the city of Jaipur was increased. In 1900, the population within the city walls was 1,16,563, whereas outside the walls, it was 21,324. The rise in population was steady upto 1941 with a minor declining trend between 1901 and 1921 which was due to large number of deaths by plague, cholera, etc. There was a steep rise from 1.75 to 6.15 lacs between 1941 and 1971, due to refugee influx after partition, shifting of state capital to this city in 1949, rapid industrialisation, etc. The population reached 16.54 lacks by 1991 (Table 4.1).

The Table 4.1 indicates that population shows a steady rise from 1921 to 1941 and sudden increase from 1941 to 1991 i.e. about 10 fold rise in a span of 50 years.

Due to the pressure of population, the city has grown aboundingly in the areal extension. The multi-function characteristics of Jaipur which has developed lately have also made it an unplanned city today. Its areal growth in all directions, with an utter disregard to the inhabitants.

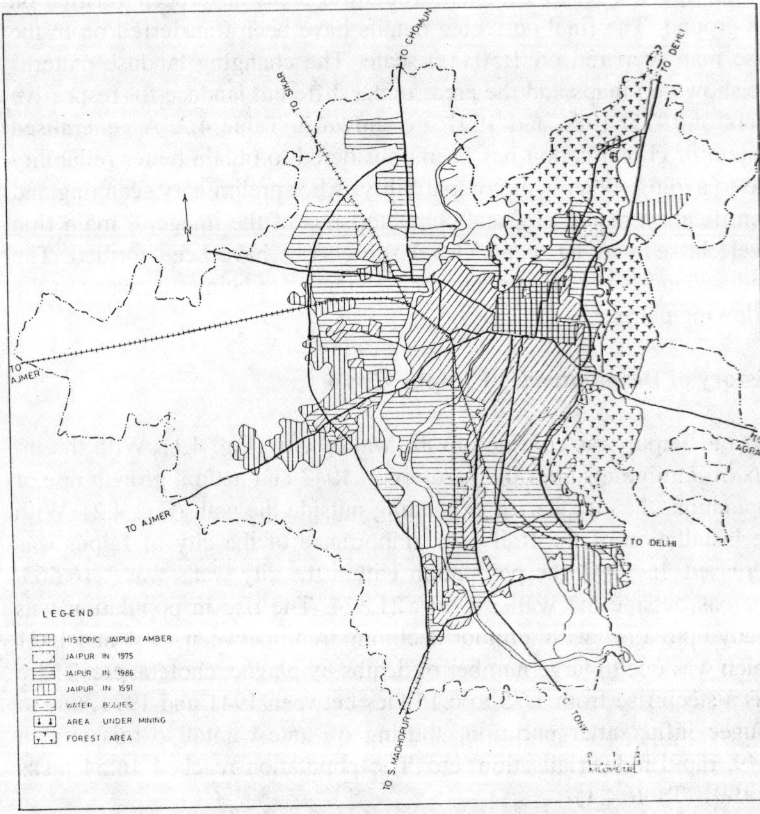

FIG. 4.2: Land Transformation: Jaipur City (1975)

TABLE 4.1: Population Growth Trends and Projection in Jaipur 1901-91

Year	Population	Growth rate percentage variation	Density person/ha (JDA Region — 1077 square miles)
1901	1,60,167	—	108
1911	1,37,098	– 14.40	92
1921	1,28,207	– 12.32	86
1931	1,44,179	+ 19.94	97
1941	1,80,940	+ 25.50	122
1951	3,04,380	+ 68.22	206
1961	4,10,376	+ 34.82	277
1971	6,36,768	+ 55.17	431
1981	10,15,160	+ 59.48	687
1991	15,18,235	+ 48.56	1120

Source : Census of India and TPO Projection.

The original city built on 6 square kilometres of land has today assumed the gigantic size of more than 200 square kilometres. Thus a sizeable part of its hinterland which abounded with forests and cultivated fields in ancient times has now been engulfed by the city. The green belt has either totally disappeared or exists in much degraded form.

The increase in population directly results in expansion of the area growth in physical terms. Historically Jaipur started bursting out of the city walls in the year 1881 to accommodate the growing population. In 220 years (from 1727 to 1947) the built up area of Jaipur city increased to only 4 square kilometres and 70 square kilometres of built up area was further added by the year 1971, which has been increased to 85 square kilometres in 1985. 1991 IRS LISS II data reveals that a total of 39.66 square kilometres area has been further added till 1991.

Land Cover/Land Transformation

The Table 4.2 reveals the area under different landuse/cover and land transformation. The detailed analysis is being given in the following pages.

A. *Built up Land*

It was quite possible to interpret and delineate the different density of built-up areas according to its intensity of development. Therefore, sub-classes of first class built up land were further grouped into three classes, such as high density, medium density and low density. In all the images the walled city remained high density regions and the density of built up area increases as 9.27 square kilometres (1975), 14.79 square kilometres (1986) and 45.42 square kilometres (1991) respectively. Area under medium and low density was 16.86 square kilometres and 16.41 square kilometres in 1975, 37.81 square kilometres and 29.46 square kilometres in 1986, and 38.20 square kilometres and 37.81 square kilometers in 1991.

TABLE 4.2: Area Under Different Landuse/Landcover in and Around Jaipur

(In square kilometres)

Sl. No.	Landuse/Landcover	1975	%	1986	%	1991	%
A.	Builtup land						
	1. High	9.27	1.92	14.49	2.99	45.42	9.36
	2. Medium	16.86	3.48	37.81	7.79	38.20	7.88
	3. Low	16.41	3.38	29.46	6.08	37.81	7.80
B.	Forest Land						
	1. Degraded	29.81	6.15	44.63	9.21	56.6	11.47
	2. Actual Forest	15.09	3.11	10.87	2.25	3.9	0.80
C.	Agricultural Land						
	1. Cropped Area	222.71	45.93	238.68	49.21	186.28	38.41
	2. Fallow	99.60	20.54	37.81	7.79	338.37	7.91
D.	Waste Lands						
	1. Gully Affected	2.89	0.59	4.39	0.90	4.77	0.99
	2. Saline Area	1.92	0.39	1.60	0.33	1.80	0.37
	3. Sand Sheet/dunes	40.24	.15	11.10	2.28	2.77	0.57
E.	Industrial Area	3.09	0.64	7.38	1.52	9.43	1.94
F.	Land under transformation	14.08	2.90	42.02	8.66	50.77	10.47
G.	Water Body	1.44	0.296	1.24	0.26	1.37	0.28
H.	Mining Area	1.46	0.30	1.80	0.37	6.41	1.32
I.	Parks and Play Ground	1.13	0.23	1.72	0.35	2.10	.43
	Total	485	100.00	485	100.00	485	100.00

B. *Forest Area*

The area under forest has been reduced not only due to degradation of forest but also due to stone quarrying at Jhalana, Amagarh, Nahargarh and Harmara. This is also divided into two sub-classes, viz. forest area and degraded forest area which are 15.09 square kilometres and 29.81 square kilometres in 1975 and 10.87 square kilometres and 44.63 square kilometres in 1986 and 3.9 square kilometres and 55.6 square kilometres in 1991.

C. *Agriculture*

The Table 4.2 indicates 186.28 square kilometre land under agriculture use in 1991 which shows a decrease of 36.43 square kilometres from 1975. This could be due to the slow and steady encroachment for residential and industrial areas due to increasing population pressure and the constraints of the hill ranges towards the east and the north. Future expansion of the city shall necessarily have to be towards the south-west and north-west, which is on good agricultural land. This class is divided into two sub-classes, viz. crop land, which include all the standing crops present at the time of imagery and fallow land, which includes land lying fallow at that time. The area under crop land is 222.7 square kilometres, 238.68 square kilometres and 186.28 square kilometres in 1975, 1986 and 1991, shows à decrease because more agricultural land was engulfed by urban sprawl. Same is the case with fallow land which is 9960 square kilometres, 37.81 square kilometres and 38.37 square kilometres at the same time.

D. *Wasteland*

Wasteland may be defined as the lands which presently lying unutilized of not being used to its optimum potential due to various constraints. This class is further sub-divided into three classes. The areal extent and change are shown in Table 4.2. By proper treatment and plan the land can be brought under green belt for the city.

E. *Industrial Area*

There were only two major industrial areas in 1975 whereas they have increased to 4 in number by 1991. A large patch of land is transformed under this category. Large extent degradation of land surface has taken place due to brick making activities in Agra Road. Manufacturers have converted a 15.6 square kilometres of land into wasteland because the upper fertile layer has been removed by the activity of mining.

F. *Land under Transformation*

Under this class vacant land under constructional sites were selected and an increase in this class is observed viz. 114.08 square kilometres, 42.02 square kilometres and 50.77 square kilometres in 1975, 1986 and 1991 respectively. From the maps it is clear that agricultural land shows (crop and fallow land) a decreasing trend. This is because of the increase of the demand for residential land and for other urban requirements.

G. *Water Bodies*

The area under water bodies has also shown a decreasing trend from 1.44 square kilometres in 1975 to 1.37 square kilometres in 1991.

H. *Mining Area*

Due to population pressure quarrying for building stone has created an unprecedented situation. Quarrying on the Jhalana, Amagarh, Goetor and Nahargarh hills have totally defaced the hill slopes which appear like scare on the once lush-green hills. These base rocks also enhance heat radiation in summers, thereby increasing the city's temperature.

I. *Parks and Playgrounds*

According to Master Plan, about 3 per cent of the total urban land should be under this category but looking to the total urban area of Jaipur 121.43 square kilometres only on 1.75 per cent of land parks and playgrounds exist.

Analysis

Land Transformation Changes between 1975-86

The urban area of Jaipur has started outward expansion, which has been increased by three times whereas land under agriculture has shown a decreasing trend. It has been observed from the present study, that in 1975 the total area under mining, built up area and land transformation was 58.09 square kilometres (Table 4.2). Further between 1975 and 1986 (more than a decade), the demand for land for various constructional purpose in Jaipur has resulted in the encroachment upon good agriculture land, especially in the south and south-western part of the city (Figs. 4.3 and 4.4).

Land Transformation Changes between 1986 and 1991

Substantial changes in landuse were observed between 1986 and 1991 in a span of five years (Figs. 4.4 and 4.5). There has been a considerable decrease in the total area under agriculture. The area which was still in the process of development have been classified as land under transformation, which has been increased by 10 square kilometres over 1986.

From the analysis presented in Table 4.2 and maps it is evident that the land transformation is in progress in the following areas:

(i) Agricultural to urbanisation;
(ii) Sand dunes to agricultural and urbanisation; and
(iii) Hill area to quarry area.

It is also evident that the land transformation particularly agricultural to urban area has taken place drastically after 1975. Prior to this most of the urbanisation and industrialisation was confined to open spaces/sand dunes/sheet area only.

Conclusions and Recommendations

The continuous change in the structure of a city is the utmost concern of urban planners and decision-makers. The rapid increase of urban population and the transforming urban economy lead to an ever increasing demand on the urban environment in terms of urban capture in the fringe areas and change in the internal structure of the city. This type of unregulated development on the peripheral areas become a liability when they become part of the city in so far as provision of infrastructural facilities and specific amenities are concerned. Moreover, it is expected that nearly 10 million hectares of productive agricultural land will be lost by the year 2001 due to unplanned growth. It is, therefore, desirable to plan for the city and peripheral areas in an integrated manner so that in due course, as the city grows the periphery can emerge into the whole. In doing so, a lot of productive agricultural land can be saved in the peripherals of the city. The Remote Sensing data being repetitive, is useful in providing information on physical growth pattern, development and trend of urban areas, changes in landuse pattern etc., which will help the planners and administrators in formulating development plans, guidelines for maintaining the environment and the quality of life.

The green belt district encompassing an area of 59,000 acres envisages to be developed around the periphery of Jaipur is still aforlorn cry. The Master Plan had also proposed the development of certain rural settlements as 'urban villages' to strengthen the economy of rural population but it has yet to take shape even after 20 years of planned development. Instead a maze of irregular residential colonies have cropped up in the fringe area of the city providing it a rurban character.

The area under the residential-cum-commercial purposes has increased more than 50 per cent within the period 1975 to 1991. The land transformation particularly agricultural to the urban has taken place drastically after 1975.

The city is expanding towards south, west and south-west direction because of the physical barriers in the north, east and north-eastern sides.

The geo-ecological problems have thus multiplied enormously on every front. Only 51.5 per cent of the city area was set apart for residential colonies but now we find that the actual area under this category exceeds the limits. The target of using 3 per cent of the city area for the parks and recreation activities has also not been achieved. Due to degradation in the living conditions the quality of life has deteriorated and remedial measures are not yet in sight.

Rectificatory measures will be necessary in all sectors for prevention of further degradation through modification of the plan for further development. Due and proper consideration of the natural characteristics and 'carrying capacity' of the various zones for different landuses is of paramount importance.

To avoid the misuse of land and in the interest of preserving the environmental balance the following steps ought to be taken:

1. The dune areas stretching in the epidemic zone of the hills of Jhalana, Amagarh, Nahargarh, etc. should be immediately planted.
2. Areas susceptible to large scale gully erosion should be conserved by proper methods of soil conservation.

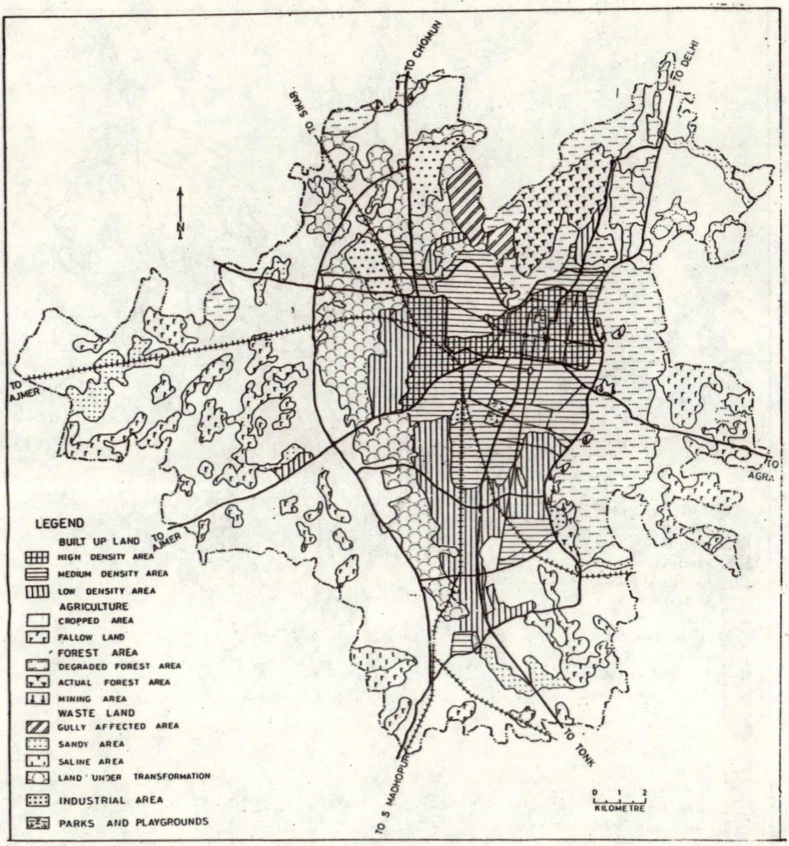

FIG. 4.3: Land Transformation: Jaipur City (1986)

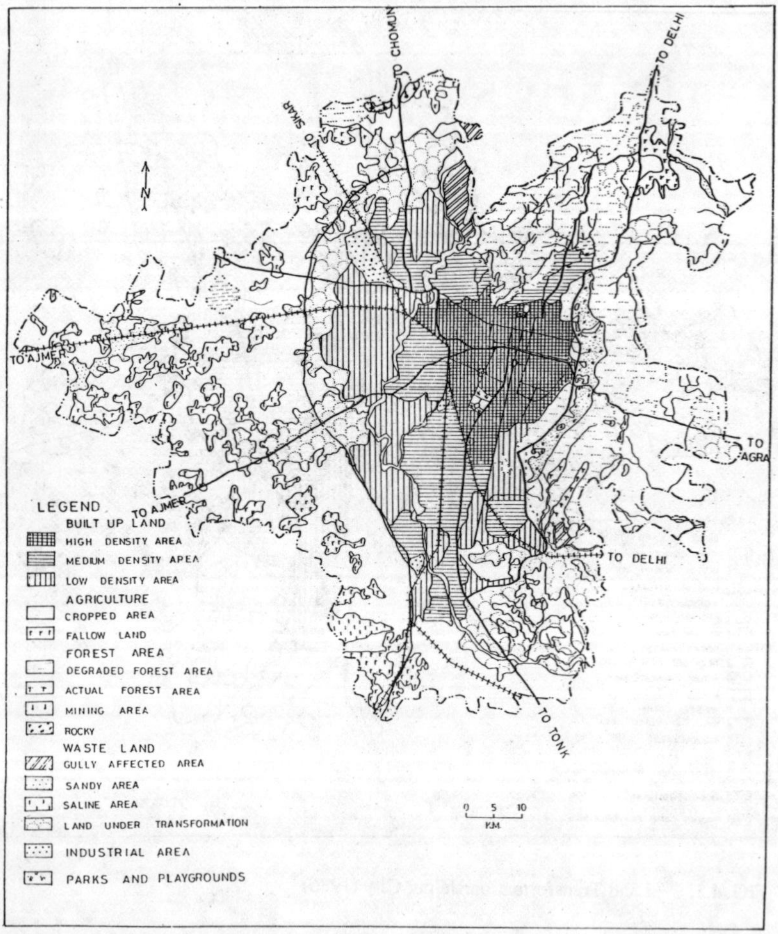

FIG. 4.4: Land Transformation: Jaipur City (1991)

3. The lateral drainage along the Jhalana hills and the Nahargarh hills, which has now been plugged and stopped by the construction of residential colonies and encroachment by slums, should once again be regulated and preserved with necessary skills and methods of engineering.
4. Quarrying of building stones near Jhalana hills, Amagarh hills and Nahargarh hills should be stopped. This activity has not only defaced the mountains on the side of the city but has also made them susceptible to more erosion. As alternative sites, the Harmara hills on the Sikar road can be leased for quarrying.
5. The useful agricultural land, south and west of Jaipur, has depleted the agricultural hinter land of the city. Residential colonies should as far as possible be constructed on wasteland and developments of satellite towns should be emphasised.

In the present study efforts have been made to present the use of Remote Sensing Technology to monitor land transformation. As the limited land resources in the city get used up due to unprecedented population explosion the pressure mounts bringing into force economics of scarcity. There is, therefore, an increasing demand on urban land and services. This result in a spirally outward development from the urban boundary so as agriculture land gets converted into urban use. Since, most of the landuse and zoning plans are limited to the extent of municipal area or designated urban area, therefore, fringe areas have grown haphazardly with a chaotic mix of landuses and unrecorded. In such time data vacuum the planner or the administrator, is forced to take policy-decision concerning vital urban plan development policies without sufficient and reliable information regarding landuse, type of development, growth etc. At this juncture, Remote Sensing has a great role to play.

NOTE

1. Land transformation is defined as changes in physical, chemical, physio-chemical and biological characteristics of land which may be permanent, or semi-permanent, due to impact of natural and anthropogenic factors.

5

SOME ENVIRONMENTAL CHALLENGES OF INDUSTRIALISATION IN AGRICULTURAL AREAS: A Case Study from the Upper Ganga Plain, India

D.S. RAWAT

Introduction

At the threshold of the twenty-first century, there is a perceptible realisation that man has built a suicidal living system out of his world. This has given rise to a new direction to thought with regard to man-environment relationship which is no more confined to geography. Now many more disciplines are paying attention to this issue. At present, there is an increasing belief that the relationship is not in a good shape. The marred relationship seems to have originated from perceiving man as independent of nature and also from man's intelligence, which has unfortunately been subservient largely to the negative urge of human nature. Besides human greed, the absence of an acceptable definition of a reasonably good quality of human life; prominence of materialism, individualism and egoism; ruthless use and misuse of nature and irresponsible attitude of the affluent few seem to have spoilt the relationship.

Obviously, there is need of a philosophy of life based on symbiosis instead of the Darwinian survival of the fittest. Human world has been, and should in future remain, full of natural and human diversity. All intelligent thinking and research has now to be linked to the ultimate fate of man of this beautiful living planet. It is from these deeper foundations that this small contribution has risen.

Purpose and the Case Study Area

The purpose of this study is to present some glimpses of what is happening in agriculturally advanced areas of contemporary India in respect of industrialisation and eventual environmental consequences. This also proposes a low-cost and simple Link Road Plan for recently industrialising cities to make them receptive of the onslaught of industrialisation. Finally it tries to make the point that the ultimate solution of all environmental problems lies in the transformation of a materialistic human society into a humanistic society. While the nature of embryonic industrialisation has been studied with the help of Muzaffarnagar district's case, environmental consequences are assessed by reconnaissance of a 12 kilometre Meerut road industrial corridor and it 10 selected industrial units. The idea of Link Road Plan has been conceived from the nature of industrialisation in the district and from the trend of accelerating concentration of modern industries around its head city.

The case study area of Muzaffarnagar district is considered fairly representative of India which has many things in common with other countries of the South, especially in respect of industrialisation. Situated in the Upper Ganga Plain, the district is a 90 kilometre long and 50 kilometre wide land with an area of about 4200 km^2 (Fig. 5.1). It is a gently south-sloping plain between the Ganga and the Yamuna with rich surface and groundwater resources, fertile soils and hard working people sensitive to agricultural innovations. This has been a purely agricultural area without forests and minerals, a richly cultivated land with 42 per cent of net sown area under wheat and 38 per cent under sugarcane. The area is also the heartland of India's northern sugarcane growing region. This crop forms its economic foundation. District's 80 per cent of net sown area is irrigated and under the impact of Green Revolution. In the middle of this land and on the eastern bank of the Kali river is situated its head city of Muzaffarnagar. It is about 120 kilometres northeast from Delhi by road and railway, both running close to each other. It is one of the numerous such Indian cities as are recently experiencing industrialisation.

Industrialisation

On the basis of empirical evidences, this section tries to build the proposition that consequent upon agricultural advances, increasing

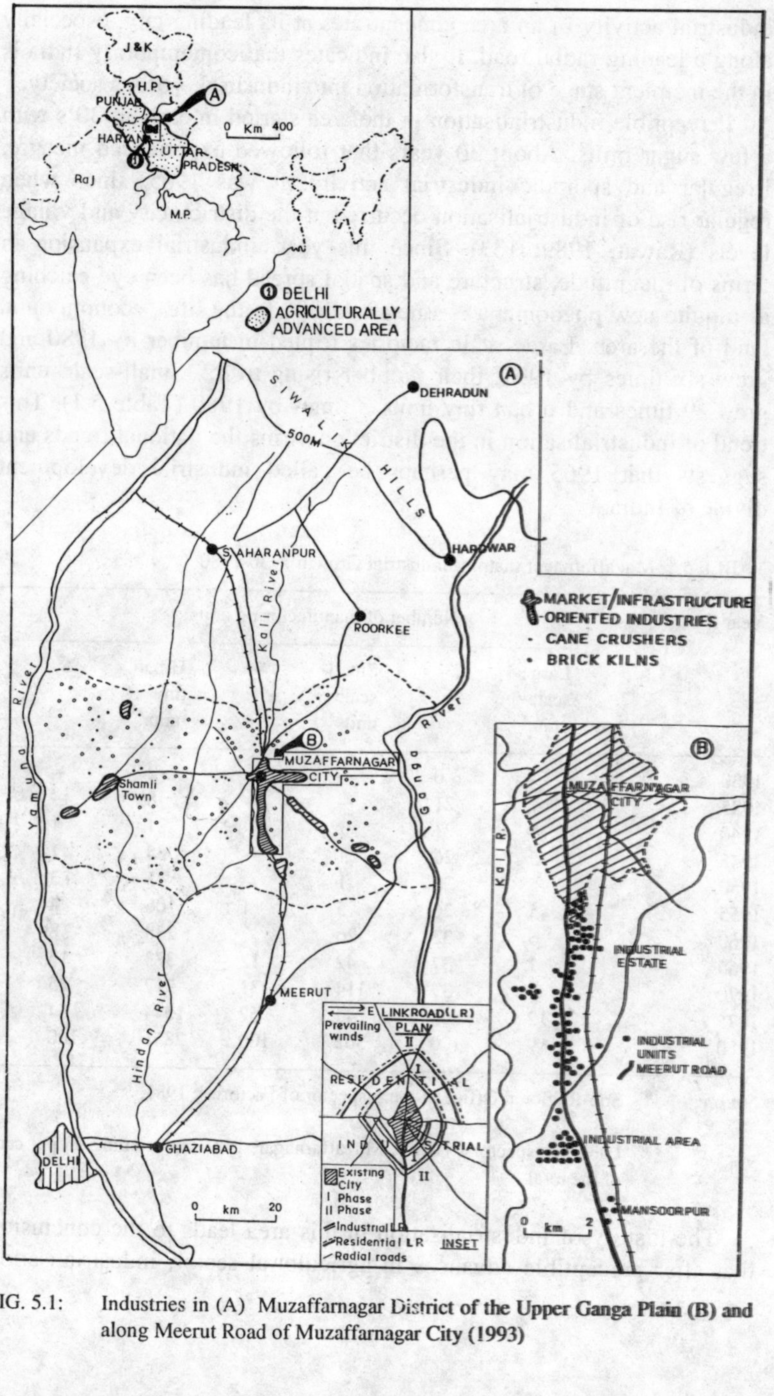

FIG. 5.1: Industries in (A) Muzaffarnagar District of the Upper Ganga Plain (B) and along Meerut Road of Muzaffarnagar City (1993)

industrial activity in an area concentrates at its leading city, especially along a leading radial road. It also indicates that contemporary India is in the incipient stage of transformation into industrial – urban society.

Perceptible industrialisation in the area started in early 1930's with a few sugar mills. About 30 years that followed experienced meagre, irregular and sporadic industrial activity. It was 1965, since when regular rise of industrialisation occurred at the district, city and village levels (Rawat, 1989; 133). Since this year, industrial expansion in terms of magnitude, structure and spatial spread has been eye-catching as a quite new phenomena – a new addition to the life , economy and land of the area. Large-scale factories tripled in number by 1980 and grew six times by 1991, their number rising to 42. Small-scale units grew 9 times and urban tiny units 8 times by 1980 (Table 5.1). This trend of industrialisation in the district confirms the national trends and suggests that 1965 may perhaps be called industrial development divide of India.

TABLE 5.1: Muzaffarnagar district: Industrial Growth 1930-1980

Year	Number of manufacturing units					
	Large-scale units*	%	Small-scale units*	%	Urban tiny units**	%
1930	—	0	—	—	2	—
1935	4	21	—	—	8	—
1940	4	21	1	—	21	1
1945	5	26	1	—	35	1
1950	5	26	1	—	75	3
1955	5	26	5	1	106	4
1960	6	32	26	7	238	8
1965	7	37	42	12	373	13
1970	7	37	114	31	717	25
1975	12	63	244	67	1544	54
1980	19	100	362	100	2851	100

Source: * Sub-Regional Office of the Inspector of Factories; 1981;

** Labour Inspector's Office, Muzaffarnagar, 1981 representing 33 per cent of the total.

The history of industrialisation in this area leads to the conclusion that after perceptible advances in agricultural sector, industrialisation evolves significantly. Agricultural development prepares the area for the germination of industrialisation. After such germination, the evolution of industrialisation is a complex process evolving wide ranging changes in many aspects of human life and work.

Spatial fallout of this industrialisation process is found highly concentrated at and around the leading city of the area. This is more true in case of modern industries which are not based on agricultural raw materials and which are indicative for industrial advancement and diversification. The observation is further supported by a recent structural shift in small-scale sector in favour of non-cane crushing units, their ratio increasing from 30 per cent in 1981 to 50 per cent in 1991. Most of them are located at the leading city. This is substantiated by the locational distribution of all factories and quite large number of tiny industrial units in unorganised sector (Table 5.2). Of the three locational classes of industries observed in the district in their developmental sequence, almost half of their magnitude belongs to urban industries. These classes are: (1) Widely scattered village industries including brick kilns and tiny processing units catering for the poor rural markets, (2) Lineally located cane crushers along country roads, and (3) Nodally agglomerating footloose industries at urban places. Large units are found along outer section of radial roads, small factories along inner radial routes and tiny units are located within the city. Tentative measurement of the magnitude of industries belonging to these three locational kinds has revealed that 50 per cent of the total magnitude is located at urban places, 40 per cent is widely scattered in rural areas and 10 per cent along country roads.

TABLE 5.2: Muzaffarnagar District: Distribution of Industrial Units, 1981

Class of Industries	Muzaffarnagar city %	Rest of the district %	Total units
1. Large-scale factories	80	20	20
2. Small-scale factories	25	75	360
1. Non-cane crushing units	70	30	110
2. Cane-crushers	00	100	250
3. Urban tiny units	30	70	8700
4. Rural tiny units	00	100	14600

Source: Compiled from the offic of the Inspector of Factories, Meerut, Labour Inspector's Office, Muzaftarnagar and Private Sample Surveys for rural tiny sector, 1981.

However, only a few radial roads of the leading city emerge as industrial corridors. One road may surpass all of them, as Meerut road in the present case has done. It is a 12 kilometre industrial corridor from Muzaffarnagar to Mansoorpur. Almost all large-scale and many new kinds of small-scale factories have agglomerated here (Table 5.3).

TABLE 5.3: Meerut Road of Muzaffarnagar City: Industrial Structure, 1993

Industry	Number of industrial units	%
1. Iron, steel and rolling	112	47
2. Chemicals and fertilizers	31	13
3. Engineering	20	8
4. Plastic and rubber	15	6
5. Paper	13	5
6. Refractories	9	4
7. Flour	8	3
8. Animal and vegetable fats	7	3
9. Cement	7	3
10. Bricks	6	3
11. Textiles and fibres	4	2
12. Cold storage	3	1
13. Sugarcane processing	5	2
Total	240	100

Source: Private survey, January 1993.

Industrialisation, it may thus be inferred, follows advances in agricultural sector and, starting from widely scattered patterns, tends to agglomerate heavily at leading radial road of the leading city of an agricultural area.

Environmental Consequences of Industrialisation

The most industrialised 12 kilometre Meerut road industrial corridor of the district was observed for assessing the environmental consequences of industrialisation. Besides a general survey of the corridor, a careful reconnaissance of its three industrial agglomerations and 10 selected industrial units was undertaken. The three agglomerations are (1) Industrial Estate, Sujroo at the southern boundary of the city, (2) Industrial Area, Begrajpur at about 10 kilometres and (3) mansoorpur at 12 kilometres from the city. Ten representative case industries include

1. sugar mill 2. cane-crusher 3. tiny village cane-crusher 4. distillery 5. paper mill 6. edible oil mills 7. brick kiln 8. iron and steel factory 9. chemicals factory and 10. lime factory (Fig. 5.2).

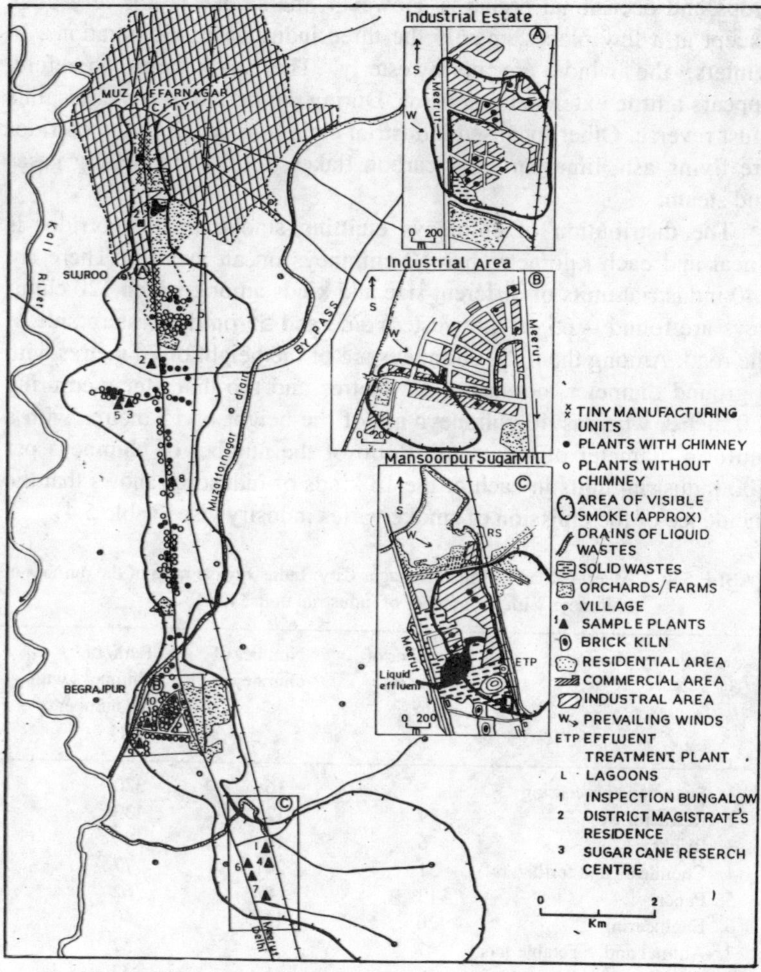

FIG. 5.2: Meerut Road of Muzaffanagar City: Geographic Spread of Industrial Pollutants 1993

From the general survey, the area of smoke along the corridor is identified. Visible smoke area is a 1 to 5 kilometre-wide belt. This belt widens near industrial agglomerations. The maximum width is observed near a sugar mill. The land beneath this smoke-area is under crops and occasional orchards. However, the smoke is not very thick except at a few places, mainly the three industrial agglomerations. In winters, the winds are northwesterly. The smoke-area, therefore, appears a little extended eastwards. During the period of easterlies, this must reverse. Other localised industrial emissions found in the corridor are flying ash, lime particles, carbon flakes, soot, bad smelling gases and steam.

The distribution of chimneys emitting smoke in the corridor is lineal and each kilometre has 10 chimneys on an average. There are 240 industrial units of different size and kinds among which 120 chimneys are found – 65 on the western side and 55 on the eastern side of the road. Among them, 80 chimneys are of the height of 26 metres with a ground diameter measuring 2.2 metres and top diameter measuring 1.0 metre, whereas 40 chimneys are of the height of 15 metres with a uniform diameter of 0.3 metre. Ratio of the number of chimneys per 100 industrial units in each of the 13 kinds of industries shows that the incidence of the emission of smoke varies industrywise (Table 5.4).

TABLE 5.4: Meerut Road of Muzaffarnagar City: Industrywise ratio of the number of chimneys with the number of industrial units, 1993

Industry	Number of industrial units	Number of chimneys	Ratio of chimneys with the number of units %
1. Sugarcane processing	5	16	320
2. Refractories	9	12	133
3. Bricks	6	6	100
4. Chemicals and fertilizers	31	24	77
5. Paper	13	8	62
6. Engineering	20	12	60
7. Animal and vegetable fats	7	4	57
8. Plastic and rubber	15	5	33
9. Iron, steel and rolling	112	32	29
10. Cement	7	1	14
11. Flour	8	0	0
12. Textiles and fibres	4	0	0
13. Cold storage	3	0	0

Source: Private survey, January 1993.

Four groups of industries emerge. The highest ratio is that of sugarcane processing, refractories and brick kilns. These industries comprise quite large part of the total industrial activity of the district, though they are not concentrated along Meerut road. Second group of lower ratio comprises of chemicals, fertilizers, paper, engineering and animal and vegetable fats. Industries of these two groups are highly polluting. Third group of cleaner industries consists of plastic, rubber, iron, steel, steel rolling and cement. The cleanest industries, so far as smoke is concerned, comprise of flour mills, textiles, fibres and cold storage.

Liquid effluents terminate locally after flowing along roads and occasionally into small irrigation channels. This is when the effluent is in small quantity. If it is considered harmless for crops, it is used for irrigation. However, larger quantities and harmful effluents flow into Muzaffarnagar drain through smaller drains. This is the largest natural drain carrying different kinds of effluents. It carries black and highly polluted liquid effluents. These are discharged into the Kali river and ultimately into the Yamuna through the Hindan river.

Survey of three industrial agglomerations on the Meerut road industrial corridor reveals that the environmental consequences of their industries are of varying degree. Mansoorpur, the location of a group of 4 large-scale factories demonstrates considerable geographic spread of environmental impact, both on the land and the air. Here smoke-area is the most widespread. This place gives rise to a large quantity of polluted water carried by a 3.0 metre wide and 1.0 metre deep drain. About 20 acres of land is under spread-water and dumping ash. Second cluster of industrial units is at the Industrial Estate. This is affected by air and noise pollution but land bears very little industrial waste due to the kinds of industries. The spread of smoke area is relatively limited to about 2 kilometres in the leewardside. Newly planned Industrial Area near Begrajpur village started attracting industrial units since mid-1980's. Though this is still an open industrial agglomeration, its southern part with a few chemical and lime factories, has already introduced people to quite serious environmental impacts.

As the agglomerated industrial growth occurs along radial roads of Muzaffarnagar city, pollutants like liquid effluents, smoke, gases, flying particles and solid dumping wastes are on the increases year after year. These find refuse either on the land of an individual factory owned for the purpose, or on public lands along roads. This has harmed roadside trees and new plants. Nevertheless, pollutants may spill over into or be carried to the private lands by such natural agents as flowing rainwaters or winds. However, some solid wastes are being used in industries and others for filling in the city. Liquid effluents reách rivers after flowing along roads or railway lines and natural drains.

A description of the selected industries gives some exposure to the nature of environmental consequences of different industries (Fig. 5.3).

1. The sugar mill selected uses 25000 quintals of sugarcane per day and large quantity of bagasse and paddy husk (as fuels). It gives out waste materials as well as byproducts. Sugar output is 12 per cent of the sugarcane inputs. Molasses comprises 4 per cent. Remaining of this input is the waste. Bagasse accounts for 30 per cent and cane juice impurities for 4 per cent. Thus about 50 per cent should be liquid effluent and vapour.

Molasses is used in an adjoining distillery which gives out highly polluted liquid waste. Effluent treatment plant and 8 brick lined lagoons for its safe disposal are not yet under use. Consequently, this harmful effluent finds its may to public land along the railway line and partly spills over into an adjoining sugarcane field. This has dried up the sugarcane stands in its contact. The extent of its effect is extremely limited but the severity is clearly indicated.

Huge quantities of bagasse are largely taken away by paper mills daily. The remaining part is used as fuel alongwith paddy husk. Their burning emits carbon flakes from a low chimney. These are observed lying on the top of the plants of various crops and the soil upto 5 kilometres on the leewardside. The precipitation of carbon flakes has become a major problem for last 3 years when the chimney height was reduced to about 18.3 metres, probably to save expenses on its replacement.

In its oval-shaped area of precipitation these flakes often settle into the eyes, causing eye-irritation. Working in the fields becomes unpleasant and difficult because carbon flakes blacken workers' head and clothes. Agricultural labourers refuse working in the fields. Besides, villagers can not sleep in the open, dry up washed clothes in the sun and keep water open. Vegetative part of sugarcane is spoiled by the flakes as domestic animals do not eat this stapple green fodder. Other green fodder crops are not grown for the same reason. Farmers also feel that more irrigation is needed on the affected land. Mango output in a neighbouring orchard has drastically declined. However, agricultural output is not yet affected.

Thick solution of impurities removed from sugarcane juice, after drying up, is used in brick kilns as brick – reddener. This makes bricks appear well-baked. Among other solid wastes, dumping ash is a major

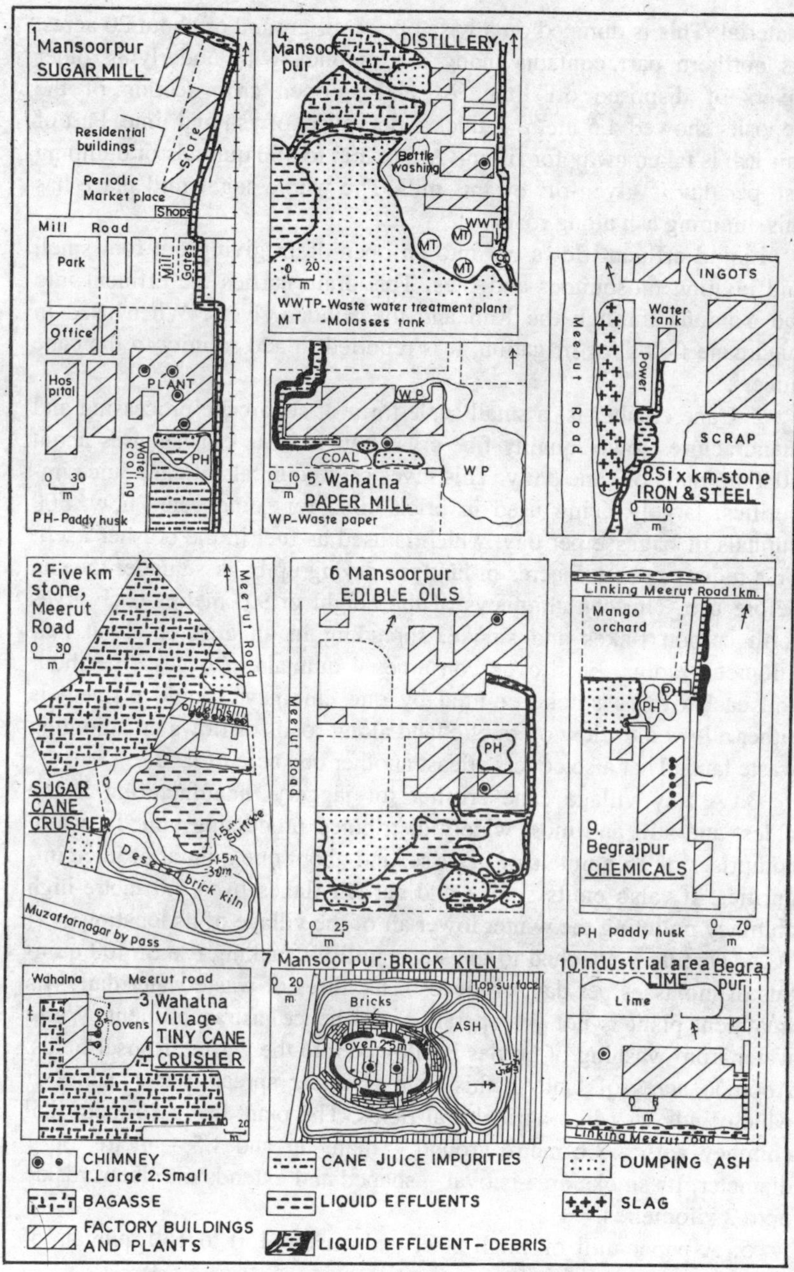

FIG 5.3: Meerut Road of Muzaffanagar City: Industrial Effluents of Ten Selected Industries, 1993

material. This is dumped on a wise open mill ground of about 20 acres. Its northern part contains many ash mounds with underlying older layers of disposed off lime. At places, open cross-section of the deposits showed 4.5 metre – thick older layers of ash and lime. Part of this ash is taken away for filling. About 300 to 400 quintals of dumping ash per day is given off by this mill. The whole sugar mill place has this dumping ash along roads.

Liquid effluent flows out into an open drain giving out foul smell and inviting mosquitoes and flies. This drain carries the effluent into the Yamuna through the Kali and the Hindan rivers. When used in sugarcane fields for irrigation, it is reported to add salinity to the cane juice.

2. Cane crusher is a small-scale form of sugarcane processing and manufactures lower quality fine-crystal sugar. The crusher uses about 4000 quintals of cane daily. This gives of 20 quintals of cane juice impurities, largely being used in brick kilns for some years now, 500 quintals of bagasse per day, which is used as fuel in the crusher itself. This requires about 5 acres of land for drying up bagasse under the sun before use. Thirteen chimneys of the height of 9.0 metres each gives forth carbon flakes and smoke, spreading in an area of about half kilometre-radius. Each oven consumes 4 quintals of bagasse per hour and each oven's smoke emitted by one chimney. Liquid effluent is either allowed to flow on public land along roads or flows on adjoining waste land. That also covers atleast another one acre of land.

3. A tiny village cane crusher for jaggery manufacturing is the oldest and still and most widely distributed processing unit. Its waste comprises of 15 quintals of bagasse, and about one quintal of juice impurities. It also emits smoke and carbon flakes by a 3.0 metre-high chimney polluting the winter lower air of the village of its location.

4. Distillery attached to the sugar mill for making use of 400 quintals of molasses per day, produces 4 lac litres of waste water daily. Its treatment plant is not yet operative and hence, astray effluent. Waste water from washing of bottles is allowed into the waste disposal fields. About 5 acres of land in this field is under spread–water, some of which finds way into agricultural fields. The plant has a 46-metre tall chimney with a 3.6 metre ground – diameter and 1.5 – metre top – diameter. Its smoke area is oval – shaped and extends into leewardside upto 2 kilometres.

5. A paper mill of small size, daily using 150 to 160 quintals of

waste paper, brought largely from Delhi is another major kind of emerging industry and produces packaging paper and paper board. It also gives off 30 to 40 quintals of refuse per day in the form of thick solution which is dumped around plants site and along roads to dry up before it is carried to the brick kilns for reddening bricks. It also gives forth liquid waste containing chemicals and wastes. The use of 100 quintals of coal per day causes emission of 40 to 60 quintals of dumping ash, besides smoke. These wastes also cause foul smell in the area of their dumping or flow.

6. Two edible oil mills mainly gives forth dumping ash. They use about 250 quintals of coal, 220 quintals of bagasse and 150 quintals of paddy husk per month. One of them uses 250 quintals of raw material daily. Only 8 per cent of this material is the waste. At refined oil factory, the percentage of waste to the materials is 5 per cent. Smoke, waste water and flying ash are the main pollutants. Waste water flows into a common 5 acre land kept for waste disposal.

7. Brick kilns are widely scattered in the district. Smoke and flying ash are their main pollutants. Heavier ash is used again in the kiln. But the loss of soil and land that they use around the kiln is an irreparable loss. The earth is dug for brick-making upto a depth of 1.5 metres. This land is turned useless for agriculture. It is also liable to be filled in by rainwaters. A deserted brick kiln presents a badland – like view. A piece of land about 10 acres in area, is rendered useless for many kinds of human uses by only one brick kiln and their total number in the district is about 450.

8. Iron and steel industry, using the Delhi scrap, is relatively cleaner. But is causes noise pollution. Only one per cent of the raw material is the waste as slag which lies dumped along roads, occasionally to be carried for filling. The industry is clean in respect of smoke and waste water.

9. Chemicals factory is dangerously polluting its environs. Besides the emission of unpleasant and harmful gases and smoke, some of them are found causing skin diseases like eczema, ringworm, and cold-cracks among their workers. A chemical factory producing calcium carbonate emits smoke, lime-mixed water, flying ash and dumping ash. Flying ash and lime particles precipitate on agricultural land around the factory in a half-kilometre radius, while smoke spreads upto 3 kilometres in the leewardside. These fields, as is experienced by the farmers, need more irrigation now.

10. A lime factory emits smoke and large quantities of flying lime

particles, precipitating in an area of one-kilometre radius. The whole area is covered by white powder of these particles. This whitens the landscape. Out of 140 quintals of ash emitted by the plant daily, 50 quintals is flying ash. The ash and lime adversely affect the eyes of the factory workers. The plant also causes noise pollution in the calm of the night which affects the people of an adjoining village and the workers. The waste water flows into Muzaffarnagar drain. All these factories are only 2-3 years old and their fully-blown effects are yet to appear.

From the survey of the Meerut road industrial corridor, it may be concluded that the environmental consequences of industrialisation may not be said to be alarming at present. This is due to the early stage of industrialisation in which the scale and spread of industrial units is limited. However, the intensity and gravity of their effects is by no means small. The dangers of the impact of different kinds of industries on air, water, land, soil, plants, crops, orchards and people is sufficiently indicated. But the impact is not widespread at present. Nevertheless, the consequences appear to pose serious challenges for environment in the near future, given the current rate of industrialisation, acceleration of this rate by recent liberalisation policy and the intensity of environmental impact.

Skies of the industrial corridor are still relatively clean. One has to make efforts to identify the spread of visible smoke except at a few places of industrial agglomeration. The scale and spread of atmospheric pollution by industries is very little. Solid wastes and liquid effluents affect land and water only to a limited extent. But once the process of industrialisation accelerates, the epic scale of the problem cannot be ruled out. The problem causes more concern because society and government appear to be very little sensitive to it. One immediate measure to face this problem may be to make newly industrialising cities receptive of the rush of factories by Link Road Plan.

Link Road Plan of Recently Industrialising Cities

The need of the proposed plan lies in the fact that there is a class of cities which are recently industrialising with unprecedented rapidity, and which should eventually face increasing level of air pollution. This is suggested by the study of recent industrialisation in Muzaffarnagar district and its head city. The plan is founded on the trends of industrialisation observed in the district and around the district place. As industrialisation in India and the South must find one major manifestation in urbanisation with pollution, affecting very large part of humanity in the near future, this may be considered as an immediate short-term measure to meet the environmental challenges of industrialisation in the developing of the globe.

The major goal of this plan is to direct the prospective industrial part of the city to automatically grow segregated from the remaining part, which is largely residential, in such a way that prevailing winds do not carry atmospheric pollutants to the residential part. It is observed that residential colonies may not come up in the industrialising parts of a city, but industries may venture into or near residential parts. The plan, therefore, aims at diverting all prospective industries into a chosen part of the city, a result which the inbuilt forces of this plan would automatically effect.

The number of such cities as are rapidly industrialising at present or shall reach this stage in near future, must be quite large in the South. This plan is to prepare them to receive the onslaught of industrial enterprises in such a way that the air of the residential parts of the cities remains cleaner. Besides, the industrial part of the city would evolve more compactly and scattering of industrial units in the city would be avoided. This will save agricultural land and provide economical sites to industries.

Appropriateness of this plan for resource – poor developing countries like India lies in its very low-costs, as the monetary needs of the plan in the initial stages are low and further needs are only in phases; in simplicity of the execution of its planning procedure not needing high skills; in its postulated effect of cleaner industrial cities; in saving agricultural lands and crops from industrial expansion and in its being dynamic in nature, requiring planning procedure with the growth of the city and with intermediate pauses.

The conceptual bases of the plan are derived from the temporal and spatial locational behaviour of industrial units in agricultural areas. It is found that agricultural development in an area is followed by evolutionary industrialisation. As has been revealed earlier, the heaviest fallout of the industrialisation process is experienced by the head city of an area, followed by others in order of their size. Cities having the largest market potential and development level of infrastructure naturally have a strong attraction for modern footloose industries. But the plant locations in and around a city are decided by individual profit maximisation which is often in conflict with general welfare. There are harmful locations of industries not only for citizens in general, but later for efficient functioning of the plants themselves.

Four locational tendencies of plants around a city are used as the bases for desired effects :

1. The tendency of industrial units to reach close to the city.
2. Their tendency to agglomerate along roads for outward spatial interactions.
3. Their tendency to prefer a radial road leading to a bigger city in the vicinity, so that their locations extend to places far away from the city on this road.
4. Preference of entrepreneurs to choose a location in the already industrialising part of the city.

To these tendencies is added the use of prevailing winds over the city and thus the plan would not be a success if a city experiences frequently varying wind-directions. The plan also presumes that the residential part of a city expands more rapidly than the industrial part.

The Link Road Plan (LRP) comprises of link roads transversely joining radial roads emanating from a city. Proposed Link Roads should be wide and without sharp bends or turns to enable fast and through flow of traffic on them. Such roads encircling the city at decided distances, are to be constructed in phases and in specific fashion (Fig. 5.1, Inset).

The procedure of planning comprises of the following :

1. First of all, a road passing through the city – centre and running in the direction of prevailing winds is to be identified as dividing-line of a city into two halves. In case of Muzaffarnagar, Shamli Road and Bhopa Road together from such a line.
2. Of these two halves, the one through which a radial road with the heaviest industrialisation enters the city, as Meerut road in case of Muzaffarnagar, is to be identified as the industrial half of the city, the other half being residential.
3. The first link road around the city is to be so constructed as to keep it closer in the industrial half and at a greater distances in the residential half, so that all prospective entrepreneurs are allured along the link road of the industrial half for the reasons already mentioned. Continuity of this link road would be disjoining at dividing-line separating industrial and residential

halves, identified in the inception. This is all for the first phase.

4. Second phase would start, only when it is needed. It will be required when the near - total occupation of space by industries along the first industrial link road is reached.
5. In this phase, another link road around the city is to be so constructed as to keep its spacing from the first link road atleast double in the residential half as compared to that in the industrial part. Thus inter-link road spacing in the industrial part shall be half the spacing in the residential part. This is postulated to divert all industries into the industrial part, residential part being chosen by none of them due to greater distance from the city.
6. Distances of these link roads from the city-centre have to be worked out by further quick surveys as they may vary from city to city, atleast in the case of first link road. Other variations from this model may also be worked out and the model adapted accordingly.
7. This process shall be repeated in subsequent shapes and shall continue with the growth of the city.

The Moment for a Pause and Choosing New Direction

If the case studies presented above are any indications, two deductions can be made. First, countries of the South like India are at the threshold of massive and accelerated industrialisation. Secondly, environmental consequences of this industrialisation are likely to be similar to or even worse than those of the North.

What is likely to follow this state of today appears good to none in the world.

But the massive South with their huge population size may be forced, out of necessity, to become a colossal grinding machines of materials for manufacturing things. This has to be crude technology-based due to poverty and would mean a far earlier collapse of natural environment system. Man seems to be stretching his life-base system of natural environment by positive feedbacks, leading to the point of breaking by continual suppression of negative feedback (Meadows, 1972). Artificially stimulated development process has temporarily enlarged the living-base for larger population and has sapped natural productive efficiency of the natural environment. This has only postponed devastation. Negative feedbacks cannot be deferred indefinitely and they must occur. But then it should be a sudden and a colossal process of bringing about equilibrium. It may be devastating for human beings. The danger looms large until man changes his course of living and working on the earth. There is need for a pause and choosing a new direction.

Human civilization has now reached such a point as raises certain fundamental questions with regard to man's use of the natural environment : Is there really a need of complicating and inflating human needs? Should all learning, science and technology be developed for exploiting nature? Is development of modern times fulfilling its objectives? Why should there be affluence and hunger side by side on the earth? Why should the present kind of development, bulk of whose fruits reach only a few, concern man? Should a few people destroy environment for personal gains? Is man able to do some introspection when there is need of so doing?

Man must perhaps make a new beginning from correcting his perception of nature and also of man's place in it. Nature is neutral, calm and passive. There are no meanings of good or bad in a purely natural world. Man qualifies it with meanings according to his own need and convenience. Man is only an element of nature despite of his intelligence. Nature is not conscious as man is. If the whole earth becomes a desert, it is still nature with the only difference that many men would not live on it. It is, therefore man, his nature and behaviour that need be studied because there is nothing wrong with nature. Elements of human nature such as greed, for example, are major factors of degradation of natural environment.

Secondly, man has come to believe in materialism and this belief needs be examined. The belief has done more harm than benefit to the quality of human life. It is no less than a psychological disease which man has failed to avoid. On the contrary, more and more people are falling prey to it. Even science and technology have been made subservient to a crude materialism devoid of ethical touch. There is obviously a need of moving from materialism to humanism, from permissiveness to restraint, from abundance to conscious and deliberate paucity, from negative needs of greed to positive ones, from consumerism to austerity, from focusing attention on external nature to inner human nature, from selfishness to benevolence and charity, from emphasis on production to emphasis on distribution and from massive poverty and selective affluence to reasonably good quality of life for all. Above all, there is need to build a widespread belief that such a need is relevant and significant.

Further, there is a need of redefining reasonably good quality of human life and also of what development should be like in a human world. Man now needs to learn how to come back to nature, a value which could be held in high esteem. Or in case of a reduced resource-base, there is probability of suicidal armed conflict for possessing the limited resources. Development itself shall have to be redefined in keeping with the purpose of life, avoiding its such associates as over-work and stress, yawning gaps between the poor and rich and bar-renisation of the earth.

It has got to be realised that environment is a common human heritage. As man depends on it, he owes a fundamental duty towards it, especially in those societies which industrialise. It has got to be realised that the industrialisation course of the North was a maiden ex-perience which, if followed, by the yet-to-industrialise part of the world, would give rise to the environmental consequences of epic scale. This calls forth the curbing of human greed, evolving social sys-tem providing work for all and distributive justice. However, these goals can not be achieved with selfishness and individualism at family, kin, social, regional and national levels.

A new value system that holds nature and natural ways of existence in very high esteem is the need of the time. Man needs be uncovered from his shell of artificiality evolved with great care and effort. Man needs be put stark bare in nature without a separating cover. Artificial should mean anti-nature and therefore, anti-human. Man has got to learn and muster the courage to ride the ebb of development and gradually recede to the ocean of nature to remain its integral part as man really is. Man can live more contented with fewer things. Let there be a general scarcity of things. Let man slow down the killer rush for materials. Now the time is ripe when value addition to things has to be made by their paucity - an exercise in conquering human nature and not the external nature. It is time to return from the course deviated from natural path on which man seems to have come far, recently realising its futility. This is time to pause and choose a new course based on a right philosophy of living.

All religious thoughts on human living on the earth have many identical philosophical bases. All of them concentrate their attention on man whose divine responsibility of making choices is intertwined with righteousness. Thus the Gods and philosopher – saints perhaps started their research from where the modern research ends. It is obvious by now that the modern course has failed humanity in respect of secular problems. This has, no doubt, given temporary solutions. One important role of modern sciences, therefore, would be to help man increasingly realise that the core of all problems lies in the inner world of man and then seek their secular solutions.

India has a rich treasure of concepts, theories and philosophies of human existence from her longer experience of civilised life and these, as well as others from different parts of the world could perhaps be a starting point to a new direction. These ideas are available in the most ancient works of intelligent man in *Vedas,* messages of her history, in her culture, customs, traditions, beliefs of her people, popular sayings, folk arts and ways of life. Most of them indicate man - nature symbiosis. These educate man to recognise the right place of every organism in the nature by such human qualities as kindness towards all forms of life, a simple fact underlying modern need of biodiversity.

India's present stage of development is also a good starting point for building a new direction. She may start from building an organic-base of industrialisation in which sustaining nature would become essential out of need. Development would then spring from enrichment of natural environment and not from its destruction beyond natural replenishment. In so doing, India like many other developing countries, also has the responsibility of striking a balance between three equally important aspects of development - rapidity, equity and environment.

Common man has to be entrusted the responsibility of what is happening to the environment, especially in developing countries, where people's ignorance is often sustained for easy rule by the political parties. Governments in such countries may not be sincerely interested in environment. It is only the common man who can and must care for environment as they shall be the earliest victims of a depleted environment. Science should also reach the people by the endeavour of scientists themselves. Indian philosopher–saints saw to it that their findings reach the common man for application, so that piety was attached to mountains, rivers and trees and five fundamental elements of life were considered deities (Mahadev, 1992.

REFERENCES

Mahadev, P.D. (1992). Sustaining Our Heritage, *Presidential Address*, XIV Indian Geography Congress, Jaipur.

Meadows, D.H., et al. (1972). *Limits to Growth*, London:Earth Island.

Rawat, D.S. (1989). *District Planning for Industrial Development*. New Delhi: Commonwealth Publishers.

Acknowledgement

The author is thankful to Mr. Anil Kumar, Research Fellow, Aligarh Environment Project, Geography Department, Aligarh Muslim University, Aligarh, U.P. who, alongwith the author and three postgraduate students of geography department of S.S. College, Muzaffarnagar, U.P., namely Sanjay, Manoj and Purushottam, is mainly responsible for collecting information and drawing rough sketches of industrial corridor of Meerut road and its 10 industrial enterprises.

6

LANDUSE CHANGE, AGROFORESTRY AND SUSTAINABLE DEVELOPMENT IN NORTH-WEST INDIA

R.B. SINGH

Introduction

Landuse of humanized form of earth surface synthesizing physical, chemical biological system and process together with socio-economic transformation and behaviour in space and time. The monitoring of this complex system form includes the diagnosis and prognosis of changes in man land interaction in a holistic manner at various levels. Landuse change may be examined by considering conversion of forest to crop and rangeland, loss of productive land through various factors; conversion of wetlands to agriculture and urban use; and conversion of other types of land to various human uses, etc. The per capita availability of land in India decreased from 0.9 ha in 1951 to 0.5 ha in 1980-81; of course the situation of cultivated land is even more critical. The per capita availability of such land had declined from 0.48 ha in 1951 to 0.20 ha in 1981. This is likely to decrease further to 0.15 ha by C.E. 2000. About 85 mill. ha of agricultural land and 37 mill. ha of forest land are degraded to varying degrees out of the total land of 143 mill. ha and 67 mill. ha respectively (NLUCB, 1988). In recent years, various sustainable landuse initiatives are being taken at national and global level under Tropical Forestry Action Plan, World Food Programme and UNCED initiated forest principles and Agenda 21. The Government of India has initiated Agro-forestry programme as an integrated sustainable landuse management system. On 2nd June 1992, the government announced National Conservation Plan in order to tackle such multi-dimensional problems, the nation is facing today.

Agriculture has undergone drastic changes from mid 1960s through the introduction and application of various newly developed techniques in agro-sciences such as crop and water management practices. Emphasis has been given on the integrated system approach in crop production. It is essential to plan and implement rational policies to minimize the regional imbalances of agricultural production. The present growth in crop production has to be sustained with an aim to form a balance between ecological order and economic needs, emphasizing the existing as well as emerging frontiers to enhance agricultural growth on sustainable basis. The understanding of agro-climatic relationship through crop-weather conditions, soil fertility, water use efficiency, rain water management, appropriate cropping patterns based on regional resources potential must be emphasized at priority level. Further emphasis on agro-forestry, integrated crop management, bio-technology and utilization of renewable energy should be considered for use in environmentally harmonious agriculture. Training of farmers has to be essentially adopted to the changing technological environment.

The forest affects soil and water in many ways. Leaves and branches decrease wind strength, alter the absorption of solar radiation, and increase the surface area for evaporation. The root growth and the decomposition of plant organic matter, by soil fauna and microbes, modify soil texture and structure, thus affecting water penetration and drainage, changes in vegetation cover can therefore have a significant influence on the hydrological cycle and climatic system (IGBP, 1992).

The study area consists of the states of Punjab, Haryana, Himachal Pradesh and Jammu & Kashmir. On the basis of physiography and soil resources, this region is clearly divisible into two sub-zones, viz. the plains of Punjab and Haryana, and the Highlands. Based on altitude, soil types, geology, rainfall, each of these two sub-zones may further be sub-divided. Major source of water in the region, in additional to rainfall and rivers are, water in the lakes, water in the ice caps of glacier, and underground water. Underground water is largely concentrated in the plains of Punjab and Haryana. The region covers a varied landuse from highly intensive monocultures, through rotational and intercropping to grazed rangeland and near natural forests.

Landuse Change

The analysis of landuse for the last forty years in the four states suggests that Punjab and Haryana have reached to absolute limit of expansion of area under cultivation with almost 84 per cent of geographical area being cultivated. Six to 8 per cent of the area in these states is under urban uses. Another 5 per cent is under forests (mainly strip forests) and the remaining 2-3 per cent are roads, canals and other infrastructural and industrial uses. Cultivable wastes, as a category, has virtually disappeared in these two states. Such intensive landuse for agriculture is sustainable only with increasing and continued high doses of balanced nutrients and other inputs like chemical fertilizers and insecticides. The proportion of area available for cultivation in Himachal Pradesh and Jammu & Kashmir because of topography and physiography is rather small and cannot be expanded without major private and public investments; this in return will result in major ecological demures and should be avoided.

The cropping pattern in the region has undergone a substantial change with wheat and rice emerging as a major crop rotation in Punjab and half of Haryana. Its expansion in Himachal Pradesh and Jammu & Kashmir has been moderate. Crops which have been replaced by wheat, rice, gram, bajra, barely, millets and pulses. Area under cotton has increased in Haryana. In the absence of expansion of sugar industry, area under sugarcane has remained static. The cropping pattern of the region has unnecessarily become energy intensive and is affecting the static balance of the underground water resources in the plains of Punjab and Haryana. The growth of infrastructure, irrigation, and other technological factors are responsible for major shift in cropping pattern in favour of wheat and rice in the states of Punjab and Haryana.

A number of policy steps to encourage farmers to switch from rice, a water and fertilizer intensive crop in the region to crops which are relatively less water consuming is a social imperative. This can be achieved through prices policy, research and development efforts and establishment of agro-processing industries so as to make sustainable alternatives more attractive to the individual farmers.

Without supplementary organic manure, intensive agriculture leads to deplete soil fertility. Ludhiana, a district in the green revolution state of Punjab recording the highest yields of many crops now also records the highest deficiencies of plant micro-nutrients extensive use of organic manure is the only way to overcome to the micro-nutrient problem. In Punjab, about five million tonnes of rice straw are being burnt every year during October to December. If crop residues will be ploughed back into the soil, the rate of micro-nutrient depletion would be substantially reduced (CSE, 1982).

Since 1965 when canal water from the Bhakra canal was brought to the farm, rise of water table also becomes a serious phenomenon. During last 16 years, the rate of rise in water table has been above one metre annually. Patches of salinity have started appearing at the farm level. The situation is worse in higher rainfall areas where water-logging follows seriously shortly after. Apart from affecting agricultural crops, high water table causes floods even during slight spells because of the reduced moisture storage capacity of the soil. In Hissar, the bearing strength of soil has declined to less than 50 per cent in 50 years.

Diversification of Agriculture

Under diversification of agriculture, the area under oil seeds and pulses should be encouraged. Sun-flower cultivation is becoming prominent amongst all the oil seeds. Although, the sugarcane area has been substantially increased yet has not reduced pressure on ground water. The ground water position got disturbed due to tremendous increase in the food production specially wheat and rice (199.2 lac tonnes. In the year 1980-81 to 192.14 lac tonnes in the year 1992-93).

The ravineous and undulating areas of Kandi tract could be developed for the use of horticulture by spending less on reclamation. The land development firstly for agriculture, followed by diversion for horticulture is not the appropriate method. The requirement of water is also less in case of horticulture as compared to intensive cropping.

More area under cotton should be brought because this crop can compete with the replacement of area under paddy from the angle of per ha return. The rotation of crop which is a fertilizing process, should be promoted in a holistic manner. About 7 to 8 per cent area should be cultivated under fruit trees alongwith marketing facilities.

Potential for Diversification of Agriculture

The economy of Jammu & Kashmir and Himachal Pradesh records large forestry and horticulture sub-sectors. Forest and forestry development areas under forests in both of these states is quite substantial. Growth of different types of forests for different years during the last two decades has been uneven. Area under forests in Punjab and Haryana is less than 5 per cent but it is slowly growing. There is not much scope for the growth of block-forests in these states. Most of the growth has been in strip forest on the banks of the canals, etc.

Despite major data problems for a temporal analysis of forest cover in the study area, it is found that as per official records, 33 per cent of geographical area of Himachal Pradesh, 9 9 per cent of Jammu & Kashmir, 5.6 per cent of Punjab and 3.8 per cent of Haryana were under forest cover in 1986-87. On per capita basis the lowest forest cover is recorded in Haryana and the highest in Himachal Pradesh. In absolute terms, total tree covered area is 20,000 km^2 in Jammu & Kashmir, 12,882 km^2 in Himachal Pradesh, 766 km^2 in Punjab and 644 km^2 in Haryana. The regeneration status of forest in Himachal Pradesh needs to be monitored more carefully. Returns per hectare of various forest types in combination with horticulture, pastoral system, etc. suggests that there is a wide variation in expected returns per year per hectare, i.e. above the crop husbandry. Returns to farm forestry also seem to be more attractive than crop husbandry provided marketing is taken care of.

The region needs establishment of agro-forest processing industry on a regional basis rather than states basis. The problem of marketing of forest products, particularly of wood, in the absence of such industries within the region is emerging as an important stress discouraging individual producers from undertaking this activity.

Integration of Horticulture with Agriculture

Area under horticulture in all the four states have been growing fast since 1970-71 with the fastest rate in Himachal Pradesh and Jammu & Kashmir record a significantly by growing horticulture sub-sector which is emerging as a major component of agricultural sector. Marketing and agro-processing facilities are some of the important problems of this sector.

Himachal Pradesh and Jammu & Kashmir are rightly considered the fruit baskets of the region because of favourable climatic and topographic condition. Of course in Punjab and Haryana, area under horticulture is small (less than 1 per cent) however it is constantly increasing. Some illustrative exercises at measuring rates of return from horticulture suggests returns ranging between 30 and 40 per cent. However, the experience of marketing, particularly of apple, suggests that expanding wood demand for packing of fruits is creating serious stress on the forests especially silver fir and spruce. This has already been noted by the Government of Himachal Pradesh and Jammu & Kashmir. Remedial steps in terms of subsidized card-board boxes are being experimented with.

Considering the climatic condition along with the rugged terrain, fruit production is the only enterprise that is of high profit, where crop growing is not of much utility. Moreover, horticulture assist the cohesiveness of the soil, preventing soil erosion.

With increase in demand for fruits, the National Commission on agriculture has recommended to increase the production accordingly. To achieve this aspect, farmers ought to be induced to grow more fruit trees. Induction of farmers is possible, once a complete understanding of soil economics is achieved.

The following potentialities are favourable to horticultural activities in the zone.

1. Agro-climatic and topographic conditions favour horticulture as an excellent source of income per unit of land area.
2. Horticulture helps in utilizing the land more efficiently than crops, and conserve the soil which is highly susceptible to erosion in case of cultivation.
3. Permits the maximum, utilization of natural resources by adopting the negative propagation.

The actual impact of horticulture on environment rises from the need for packing-cases. Supply of wood for packing fruits has greatly increased the burden on the forest wealth, leading to extensive deforestation. Forests are depleting annually.

The standard boxes for packing apple, though vary regionally, can contain between 9 to 18 kgs. However, one tone of the fruit is supposed to be contained in 55 standard boxes. In the process of wastage of wood during exploitation and manufacturing the required standing boxes 25 per cent of the wood is further wasted on manufacture of logs and billets, 10 per cent on saw dust and 15 per cent on cut-off rejection. Thus, one-third of the standing volume go to waste. About 65 packing cases of standard size are obtained from one cubic metre of the silver fir and spruce forest. The trend indicates that annually 10.8 sq.

km. of forests is lost while 6 sq. km is planted i.e. loss of about 3000 trees. The nursery stock takes about 5 years to be raised while about 100 to 120 years is needed for trees to be able to be exploited, therefore, a head pressure is displayed against the forest – finally leading to deforestation. Deforestation in turn leads to land degradation, resulting to soil erosion. To curb the problem and have an economically feasible and environmentally compatible horticulture, there is an urgent need to (a) design for alternatives sized of packing cases (b) use of other materials for packing, and (c) use of wood in other forms.

The Himalaya is now under tremendous transformation that are accelerated with enormous speed. Most of the original lush green natural vegetation is presently replaced by shrubs, savannas, grass accompanied with gullies, ravines, eroded and scarped landscape. The major use of forests presently is through the demand for industrial wood which is needed in a greater quantity, a larger part of which is used for packing horticultural products. Native plant cover normally provides good erosion control, hence sustenance of natural resources base for economic growth and development compatible with environment. Problems arise, when an area is deforested and converted into cropland and led to increase soil erosion. The resulting soil loss reduces soil productivity and modifies environment.

Agriculture and Forestry: Mutual Co-existence and Complementarity

Integrated development of agriculture and forestry should be developed in the form of farm-forestry and agro-forestry under which crop productivity and fertility of soil and environment improve. Both sectors are ecologically and economically, inseparable. An enquiry of the two field indicates major difference (Table 6.1). However, ecosystem approach and the crop management approach are complementary, giving base for more productive agroforestry systems derived by farmers and rural people. It is desirable to grow or more species together, a combination of species can be complementary. This is the basis of silviculture systems where crops are grow with commercial species for intercropping potential on rotation basis.

Agroforestry System

Various traditional and modern agroforestry techniques are being utilized by farmers in different geosystems. The systems are:

1. Agro silvicultural (Taungya system)
2. Farm and grove system
3. Tree planting among agricultural crops
4. Silvopastural combined tree, shrub and animal production
5. Home garden systems (Agrosilvopastural)
6. Alley cropping (wood, green foliage or green manure for food crops).

TABLE 6.1: Characteristics of Forestry and Agriculture

Forestry	Agriculture
Perennial woody plants	Annual or biennial plants
Focus on vegetative growth	Focus on reproductive growth
Thousands of species	Tens or hundreds of species
Mixed culture frequent	Monoculture frequent
Multiple products and value	Single or few production goals
Extensive, low-cost cultivation	Intensive, high-cost cultivation
Positive wildlife values	Negative wildlife values
Negative domestic animal value	Positive domestic animal values

Source: Gordon and Bentley, (1990).

Agroforestry: Issues and Opportunities

Around the settlements, a sizeable rural population, particularly the small and marginal farmers and landless labourers, depend on the common property resources (CPR) for their sustenance and also other day to day social amenities. CPR generally consists of village/common lands which can be brought under suitable forest species and to raise seedlings for plantation. Such land should be allocated to landless population and small/marginal farmers for raising suitable forest/agroforestry to meet the various requirements. Subsequently, conservation forestry is emerging as an important sustainable method for taking balance production from the natural areas. This takes optimum production of fuelwood and timber from land and gives bulk soil humus and fertility. The cultivation of wastelands particularly on salt affected soils, require choice of suitable hardly crops. Based on experiment of salt tolerance limit, the fruit crops have been classified as follows.

1. High tolerance	:	Detapalam, *Ber, Imli* and *Lasoda*
2. Medium tolerance	:	Anola, Phalsa, Pomegrante, Karonda, Fig., Annanas, Jamun, Basbades, Cherry, and Sapota.
3. Low tolerance	:	Guava, Mango, Grape, and Bael.
4. Susceptible	:	Banana, Papaya, Pine apple, Jack fruit and temerate fruits.

In wastelands particularly salt affected lands, the selection of plant species should be restricted to have salt tolerance, deep root system, some degree of drought tolerance, ameliorative effect on soil properties and relatively fast growing. Various fruits and forest species which have some degree of salt tolerance and have been found most suitable wastelands in Table 6.2.

TABLE 6.2: Forest Species and their Salt Tolerance

Species	Salt Tolerance (ph.)
1. Casuarina equisettifolics	9.5
2. Dalbergia sisso	9.5
3. Leucalha leucocephala	9.0
4. Eucalyptus tereticorris	9.0

Agroforestry system may be evolved along with compatible livestock management both of land and water and prepared integrated land and water development plans for various biomass production, regeneration of land resource base and increasing employment and income. The development of non-forest areas for their sustainable use would call for regenerating or recreating an integrated interdependent land management system. This would require people's initiatives and obtaining continuous participation of people through NGOs/VAs. More inputs from science and technology will be required in order to get maximum benefit.

Integrated and Sustainable Land and Forest Development Initiatives: Suggested Measures

1. Development of Land Information Systems (LIS) and Soil Mapping on Scale of 1:15,000 and 1:15,000.
2. Preparation of human/livestock carrying capacity based on

geoecological principles.

3. Land capability and irrigability classification.
4. Giving priority to critical land sensitivity and regions.
5. Understanding landuse and forestry response.
6. Integrated strategy for surface water, ground water and rain water through water harvesting pond.
7. Diversification of agriculture through agro-forestry, horticulture, oilseeds (sunflower), sugarcane and fruit, vegetable around urban areas.
8. Natural principles of agriculture through crop combination and integrated fertility management.
9. Development of four tier forestry systems, i.e. block forest along river, strip forest along roads, railway and CPR, stray plantation along bunds, wells and farm houses, agroforestry on croplands.
10. Focussing livelihood security of people in integrated land management system.
11. Involving people's indigenous knowledge for management strategy.

REFERENCES

Centre for Science and Environment (1982). *State of India's Environment-1982*, New Delhi.

Chaudhuri, D.P., Singh, R.B., Deb, S. and Pirazizy, A.A. (1991). *Land Use, Sustainability and Agricultural Development in the North-West India (1951-88)*, Report Prepared for Ministry of Agriculture, Govt. of India.

International Geosphere-Biosphere Programme (1992). *Global Change-Reducing Uncertainties*, Stockholm.

Gordon, John C. and Bentley, W.R. (1990). *A Handbook on the Management of Agroforestry Research*, Winrock Int.

National Land Use and Conservation Board (1988). *National Land Use Policy Outline and Action Points*, Ministry of Agriculture, Govt. of India, New Delhi.

Singh, R. B. ed. (1990). *Environmental Geography*, Heritage Pub., New Delhi.

Singh, R.B. ed. (1992). *Dynamics of Mountain Geosystems*, Ashish Pub., New Delhi.

7

DYNAMICS OF RURAL ENERGY SYSTEM AND STATE OF ENVIRONMENT : A Study of Rashmi Region

R.N. VYAS

Introduction

Issues pertaining to production and utilisation of energy resources are central to the concept of eco-friendly as well as sustainable development. The situation is all the more critical and full of contradictions in areas hitherto remained unaffected by intensive energy using technologies. Rural areas of relatively less developed regions are typical examples of such scenarios.

Different cultural groups, in different physico-climatic settings, processes of socio-cultural accomplishments and *modus operandi* of economic development have evolved their own energy system with definite linkages and compositions. As a part and parcel of the total system and having ramifications in all aspects of contemporary human society, energy studies have assumed a very significant position in social science investigations.

The large majority of developing countries are facing energy crisis. That too when these countries with 77.27 per cent population in 1990 consumed a small share (27 per cent) of the world's commercial energy (World Bank, 1992). The rising trend in consumption of commercial energy in developing countries must be seen as a crucial challenge for both of their economies and environment. The situation, within these developing nations is highly disturbing. People in rural areas have restricted access to certain energy sources either due to limited purchasing capacities or because of technological base at their command.

Thus, the rural system largely depends on locally available and produced animate and biomass energy sources. There is an increasing pressure on forest cover which is primarily of tropical and subtropical type and take longer duration to regenerate. The depleting forest cover culminates into new problems like soil erosion paucity of fodder and fuel and adverse micro-climatic changes.

Use of labour intensive and less energy efficient technologies not only restrain the production capabilities but also keep the rural produces at disadvantageous position *vis-a-vis* non-rural produce. Lower strata of the rural society in general and their women in particular are worst sufferers of this situation because of poor resource base. In order to meet basic needs of energy from the natural base people have started degenerating or degrading the basic sources of their food, fuel and fodder.

Objectives

The present work concerned with rural energy system is an attempt to examine the structural attributes of the system and then to analyse its dynamics of relationship with other systems. Major objectives of the paper are :

1. To interpret the patterns and flow of energy use;
2. To analyse the functional relations between energy use and its environs; and
3. To examine the implications of energy scenario for the state of environment.

Data Base

The study based on intensive field work has been conducted in 25 sample villages of the total 75 villages of Rashmi Tehsil during the period 1987-89. In aggregate one third of the total villages have been chosen for sample study with a variable proportion of 25, 50 and 100 per cent from the three size classes of villages. At the second stage; households from sample villages have been selected with stratified sampling in terms of social groups and size of land-holdings. With a fixed proportion of 2.5 per cent and a minimum of four sample households. In all 190 households were chosen for the intensive investigation.

Methodology

Data pertaining to different energy sources are analysed by aggregating them in terms of their heat content of calorific values. Animate energy i.e. human and animal labour have been converted into calorific value according to their food intake. Conversion factors are derived by getting the averages of various experiments and studies (NCAER, 1978; TERI, 1983; Davidson, 1985; Shankar and Rao, 1987; Sharma and Bhatia, 1988, Agrawal; 1981; and Gopalan et al, 1971 and CTAE, 1990).

The study includes all principal types of energy including human, animal, biomass, fossil fuels and electricity. Energy use in household, animal husbandry, agriculture and in other trades are discussed for the present work.

Grouping of sample households for certain variables have been done with the help of non-hierarchical clustering method (Mather, 1976). Dynamics of energy use or the explanations of the variations in energy use are explained by stepwise multiple regression analysis and zero order correlation matrices.

The Region

The study region, Rashmi Tehsil of Chittaurgarh district, a small homogenous regions with seventy-five villages inhabited by 65,769 (1991) persons provide an ideal humanized landscape of rural society of South Central Rajasthan. The region with 449 sq. km area may not be a perfect geographic region, but as an administrative and development unit since the beginning of this century, has acquired a status of functional region. Almost plain in topographic features the region is divided into two parts by the Banas river. The general gradient along the course of the river is only 0.11 per cent. Overwhelming Rural characteristics and familiarity as well as understanding of the region prompted to chose the tehsil for the present exercise.

Pattern of Energy use

Sectoral and subsectoral use of energy sources by economic stratification are discussed in the present section.

The aggregate use of energy is an important component of the total energy system. Table 7.1 depicts the pattern of total energy use by land ownership size classes in the region. It is revealed that the average per capita use of all types of energy is 2820.9 mcal per year. The major source of energy is biomass which fulfils 55.5 per cent needs of the people. The biomass in the form of firewood, crop residue and dungcakes are obtained from the immediate neighbourhood. The animate power of human labour (14.9 per cent) and animal labour (24.5 per cent) together provide 39.4 per cent of the total energy used by the people of this region. Thus a significant portion (94.90 per cent) of the energy component of the system originates within itself. Fossil fuels and electricity are two major sources of energy which are brought into the system. The relative contribution of electricity is 2.9 per cent and that of diesel is 2.2 per cent.

Total energy use by size class of holdings reveals significant faces. The per capita use of energy increases significantly as the size of holding increases (Table 7.1). The per capita use of energy in the case of large holding class is more than double of the landless class. The use of all types of energy sources increases with the size of holding. However, there are few exceptions of landless and marginal holding classes in which due to some other occupation the use of electricity is more than the expected level. The same is the case of small holding class in the use of fossil fuels. The relative pattern of energy uses in different forms presents different scenario. The proportional use of human energy and biomass decreases with the size of holdings, whereas there is positive association between the percentage use of animal energy and size of holdings. These trends of relationship further suggest that the agricultural system of the region is highly dependent on animate energy system which is an integral part of the rural system in general and of agricultural sub-system in particular.

Sectoral Flow of Energy

The strength of relations within a system is determined by the causal interconnections and interdependence of its elements as well as by relative magnitude of the flow of substances or energies among different segments of the system. Analysis of flow within a system is an essential part of system modelling. Accounting of the state and the changes three in are of state is done on the basis of intercompartmental flows.

TABLE 7.1: Total Energy Use by Land Holding Classes

Land holding (ha)	Land holding (%)	Population (%)	Human	Animal	Total animate	Biomass	Fossil fuels	Electricity	Total inanimate	Total
Nil	0.0	0.9	311.7 (18.5)	0.0 (0.0)	311.7 (18.5)	1050.5 (62.5)	19.2 (1.1)	299.9 (17.8)	1369.6 (81.5)	1681.3 (100.0)
Less than 1	3.6	14.4	342.3 (15.3)	374.7 (16.7)	717.0 (32.0)	1431.0 (63.9)	27.1 (1.2)	65.7 (2.9)	1523.9 (68.0)	2240.9 (100.0)
1-2	6.7	14.2	388.3 (15.2)	448.2 (17.5)	836.5 (32.6)	1583.2 (61.8)	109.1 (4.3)	33.8 (1.3)	1726.1 (67.4)	2562.6 (100.00)
2-4	20.4	25.4	406.8 (15.2)	668.8 (25.0)	1075.7 (40.3)	1495.1 (56.0)	32.0 (1.2)	68.6 (2.6)	1595.8 (59.7)	2671.4 (100.0)
4-10	41.0	32.7	444.9 (14.4)	867.9 (28.1)	1312.8 (42.5)	1623.4 (52.6)	57.4 (1.9)	95.5 (3.1)	1776.3 (57.5)	3089.2 (100.0)
10 & above	28.4	12.3	525.0 (15.1)	973.8 (28.0)	1498.8 (43.1)	1741.3 (50.1)	117.9 (3.4)	120.9 (3.5)	1980.1 (56.9)	3478.9 (100.0)
Average	100.0	100.0	421.0 (14.9)	691.6 (24.5)	1112.7 (39.4)	1566.6 (55.5)	61.0 (2.2)	80.7 (2.9)	1708.2 (60.6)	2820.9 (100.0)

Note: Figures in parentheses are percentage to row total.

The flow and its accounting provide methods for keeping track of all system components (Wilson, 1961). The dynamics of energy use cannot be followed without understanding the inter-compartmental flows. Soddy's remark that the flow of energy should be the primary concern of economics (Soddy, 1933) no longer limits the purview of energy systems. All concerned with energy, have to study the flow of energy resources.

Wilson (1981) elaborates various techniques of accounting of flow pertaining to economic and ecological systems. In this connection, Patten (1971) provides necessary base to understand the ecological modelling of flow. Extended approaches to input-output analysis are presented by Macgill (1977).

The flow of energy in anthropoecosystem is associated with the cycle of matter (Ramade, 1981). At macro level it has been the central point of concern for ecologist. Odum (1971) systematized the method to study the flow of energy within an ecosystem. It is further strengthened by Cook (1976), Cripps et al (1974), Ramade (1981) and others. Likewise the dynamics of energy flow at micro level has also been studies in detail.

The comprehensive analysis of the flow of energy within the system is constrained by the scope of the study. As the present study is limited to work, fuel and power resources, the complete flow of energy in the system cannot be assessed. Like the pattern of energy use, the flow has also been analysed according to size class of land holdings.

Though it is very difficult to aggregate different energy sources providing power and fuels, as none of them is an absolute substitute in the total energy system. Even if some sources are substitutional to each other, these can not be replaced by one another due to certain binding characteristics of the wider system environs of the people and the region. However, the aggregation has to be done to understand the system linkages and importance of each sector in the system. Since the analysis pertains to both work and fuel resources, these are aggregated on the basis of their heat equivalents. The total energy use also includes the human and animal energy hired out by households (Table 7.2).

The annual per capita use of total energy among all types of households is 2908 mcal (Table 7.2). It is significantly revealed that important energy using sector is household sector which alone consumed 58.25 per cent of the total energy. The average share of agriculture is 31.88 per cent and that of animal husbandry and other trades is

4.78 and 2.07 per cent respectively. The proportion of energy hired out is 3.02 per cent. It suggests that the energy system is dominated by household and agricultural sectors and the share of other sectors is very low. These conditions define the nature of the system that it is primarily a rural system in which linkages between land and people are stronger.

TABLE 7.2: Sectoral End Uses of Total Energy by Landholding Classes

(*Per cent to total use*)

Holding Size (ha)	Per capita use (mcal)	House-hold	Animal husbandry	Agricul-tural	Other traders	Hired out	Total
Nil	1764	67.80	4.31	0.00	23.22	4.67	100.00
< 1	2364	65.52	4.76	20.76	3.73	5.23	100.00
1-2	2672	65.01	5.05	23.24	2.59	4.11	100.00
2-4	2784	57.15	5.01	31.57	2.21	4.06	100.00
4-10	3154	55.74	4.38	36.05	1.77	2.07	100.00
> 10	3507	53.98	5.19	40.01	0.00	0.82	100.00
Average	2908	58.25	4.78	31.88	2.07	3.02	100.00

Table 7.2 shows that the per capita total use of all kinks of energy increases with the size of holding. The per capita use of energy among large households is twice of that among landless households. It is mainly due to agricultural operations. The percentage of energy used in agricultural sector increases significantly with the size of holding. It is 20.76 per cent in the marginal land-holding class, whereas it is more than 40 per cent in large land-owning class. The percentage of energy flow towards household sector shows a reverse trend. It decreases with the size of land-holdings. However, the percentage of energy used in livestock rearing remains around 4.78 per cent. The share of energy diverted towards other trades and hired out decreases as the size of land owned increases. Among landless households 23.22 per cent energy is used for other trades, whereas, it is less than 4 per cent in the remaining classes of households. The proportion of hired out energy is high among semi-medium and all other smaller holding classes and low in medium and large holdings.

The above analysis suggests that the rural economic system is highly agrarian in nature. In such systems the demand for energy is governed by the size of holdings, techno-economic and social systems through which the process of development culminates into a more complex and highly inter-linked overall system.

Dynamics of Energy Use

Energy use pattern not only varies according to social groups and holding size class but also varies according to various socio-economic and spatial characteristics of the individual household and the space where these households are living and working. Thus, the energy use is a reflection of man's responses to his cultural and natural environment which lead to sustenance, growth and development of civilisation. The understanding of the system of energy use demands a multidimensional probe to define the direction and intensity of causal relationships among different elements of the system. Though the dynamic systems theory is concerned with the way in which system changes through time (Wilson, 1981; p. 179) it can also be applied to understand the state of causal relationships among various elements. The examination of such causal relationship requires the use of multivariate analysis.

In this section the rural energy system has been examined as a multivariate problem. This section deals with the specification of the model variables and the results. The analytical and predictive model of multiple regression has been applied to analyse the behaviour of the rural energy system.

The Generalized Energy Model

Different forms of energy sources and their combinations are regressed separately to measure the behaviour of the energy use in the context of physico-cultural system of the region and its people. The following form of linear regression model has been applied for each source of energy and their combinations:

$$Y_i = b_o + b_1X_{i1} + b_2X_{i2} + b_3X_{i3} \ldots + b_k X_{ik} + u_i$$
$$(i = 1,2,\ldots, n)$$

where

Y_i = per capita use of energy in megacalories by $_i th$ household;

b_o = intercept of regression, constant;

$b_1, b_2, b_3, \ldots, b_k$ = partial regression coefficients of each explanatory variables;

X_{ik} = value of ${}_k th$ explanatory variable pertaining to the ${}_i th$ household;

u_i = Disturbance term

Dependent Variables

The above mentioned regression model is applied for the following forms of energy sources:

Human (h), animal (a), animate (1), biomass (b), fossil fuels (f), electricity (e), commercial i.e. fossil fuels and electricity together (c), and total of all forms (t).

Explanatory Variables

The energy use variation among households and establishments is a function of varied physico-cultural characteristics of the system. These characteristics can be alluded and measured by different kinds of indicators. Though no indicator is perfect replica to represent the reality explicitly but a rationally constructed indicator may explain the behaviour of the element of the system to a significant extent for which it has been selected. To overcome the problem of selection of appropriate indicators varied indices have been computed to elucidate the characteristics of the system on the basis of (1) a priori reasoning, (2) earlier studies mentioned in the review, and (3) field observations. Though initially 35 variables were considered for the analysis on the basis of their power of explanation and examination of multicollinearity, only 21 variables are retained as regressors in different energy use models. These selected explanatory variables are grouped as locational, institutional, economic and technological.

System's component behaviour under various sectors represent the total system, but cannot provide the holistic view of the relationship between energy use and its explanatory variables. Thus, the sectoral aggregation of different energy sources is important to study the energy system efficiently. In order to enable the analysis of feedback relations in system, certain energy uses have also been regressed with the inclusion of substitute energy sources in the model. Energy use in the total system has been standardised in terms of per capita use to make it comparable among households of different sizes.

Hypotheses

The behaviour of energy use system is quite complex and not easy to comprehend perfectly. However, a significant part of the whole gamut of relationship can be postulated and examined in the form of following hypotheses;

1. Resource endowment of the natural setting reduces the effort space and thereby demand of energy is also reduced.
2. With the increasing interiority, use of animate energy sources increases, whereas, those of commercial energy sources decreases.
3. The per capita use of energy sources increases with the caste hierarchy.
4. Economies of scale associated with the size of family reduces the per capita use of energy.
5. Labour supply enhances the use of human energy but restricts the use of non-human energy sources.
6. As literacy level rises the use of human energy decreases and that of commercial energy increases.
7. The horizontal as well as vertical expansion of the economic base intensify the energy use in the system.
8. The energy use increases with the rise in income levels.
9. Traditional technologies are basically animate energy intensive.
10. Relations in the energy system are both serial as well as of feed-back type.

The Model

In the context of above mentioned hypotheses, following regression model is formed :

$$T_i = b_0 + b_1 Ns_1 + b_2 Ns_2 + b_3 Dk + b_4 So + b_5 Fs + b_6 Wp + b_7 Aw + b_8 Lt + b_9 Lf + b_{10} Lp + b_{11} Lt + b_{12} Ap + b_{13} Ep + b_{14} Ch + b_{15} T_i + u$$

where,

T_i = per capita use of ${}_i th$ energy in the total system in mcal;
Ns_1 = type of natural setting of land, $i = 1$ and 2;
Dk = distance from the nearest central place in km;

So	=	social hierarchy
Fs	=	family size;
Wp	=	percentage of workers;
Aw	=	percentage of workers engaged in agriculture and livestock rearing;
Lt	=	percentage of total literates;
Lf	=	percentage of female literates;
Lp	=	per capita ownership of cultivated land in hectares;
Lt	=	ratio of intensity of irrigation;
Ap	=	per capita animal units;
Ep	=	per capita non-food expenditures in Rs.;
Ch	=	irrigation by charas;
T_i^*	=	per capita use of $_ith$ energy in the system as a substitute in mcal; and
u	=	sample residuals.

Results

Regression estimates of different energy use models of the total system are presented in Table 7.3. A comprehensive overview of the results reveals that regression estimates of the aggregate energy use are more significant in comparison to sectoral results. It shows that aggregation has improved the explanatory power of the regressors, since both the sets of dependent and independent variables are closer to the totality of the system than to individual component.

All the relationships shown in Table 7.3 are significant and better estimates of the population with 99 per cent and more level of confidence. The adjusted coefficient of multiple determinations ($\bar{R}_2$) suggest that about 55 to 77 per cent variations in animate energy use are explained by the regressors included in the model. The behaviour of human energy use is best estimated ($\bar{R}_2$ = 0.769) than that of animal energy ($\bar{R}_2$ = 0.547). The inclusion of commercial energy use in the models of animal as well as total animate energy use as a substitute regressor improved explanatory power of the equation by 2.7 and 2.0 per cent respectively.

Though the inanimate energy use models are also good fits, these have lower explanatory power. The R_2 of these models are limited to 0.25 to 0.36. It suggests a significant proportion of the total variations in energy use has to be sought in the context of other variables. However, it is significant to note that the lower R_2 is associated with

TABLE 7.3: Estimates of Energy Use Models of the Total System

N = 178

	Models	Inter-cept	Regression Estimates											Substi-tute		
			Ns_1	*Dk*	*Fs*	*Wp*	*Aw*	*Lt*	*Lf*	*Lp*	*It*	*Ap*	*Ep*	*Ch*	*Ti*	R^2
1.	*Th*	204.51	-42.08 (29.37)	—	-10.29 (29.37)	1.09 (6.34)	—	—	-0.72 (3.91)	211.07 (47.34)	17.21 (36.86)	74.96 (90.34)	0.06 (12.71)	—	—	0.769 (74.84)
2.	*Ta*	26.75	-208.59 (4.86)	36.55 (7.03)	—	-3.46* (2.73)	—	—	-4.24 (5.15)	1092.32 (50.41)	554.43 (13.70)	95.28 (5.75)	0.18* (3.79)	336.49 (17.19)	—	0.547 (24.78)
3.	*Ta*[1]	-178.15	-211.65 (5.32)	27.69 (4.15)	—	—	—	—	-2.84* (2.70)	1208.59 (63.00)	58.40 (17.81)	82.32 (4.76)	0.32 (11.92)	267.87 (11.24)	-0.616[2] (13.47)	0.574 (27.51)
4.	*Tl*	-0.12	-247.65 (5.70)	33.65 (4.95)	—	—	—	—	-4.54 (5.42)	1322.17 (61.37)	67.30 (18.76)	157.79 (13.68)	0.25 (6.72)	351.75 (15.73)	—	0.625 (37.87)
5.	*Tl*[1]	29.90	-257.92 (6.51)	25.16* (2.83)	—	—	—	—	-4.11 (4.66)	1429.45 (72.65)	73.23 (23.08)	158.29 (14.52)	0.38 (13.54)	297.46 (11.43)	-0.593[2] (10.27)	(36.65)
6.	*Tb*	1596.95	—	—	-47.81 (27.20)	—	—	—	—	—	—	217.42 (41.60)	0.20 (5.67)	—	—	0.324 (29.30)
7.	*Tf*	18.84	-41.91* (2.82)	—	—	—	—	—	—	—	—	—	0.17 (52.48)	-40.16* (3.15)	—	0.246 (20.24)
8.	*Tf*[1]	1.32	-42.82* (2.97)	—	—	—	—	—	—	77.26* (2.67)	—	—	0.17 (47.85)	—	-0.04[3] (5.41)	0.252 (15.90)
9.	*Te*	93.43	—	-15.65 (11.79)	—	—	-0.80* (2.48)	0.85* (2.34)	—	204.25 (21.77)	13.90 (10.14)	—	—	-45.62 (2.72)	—	0.256 (11.16)
10.	*Te*[1]	-4.37	—	-13.37 (8.79)	—	—	—	0.98* (3.19)	—	255.99 (21.72)	16.89 (15.17)	—	0.06* (3.46)	—	-0.08[3] (11.29)	0.291 (13.09)
11.	*Tc*	62.23	—	-14.61 (6.47)	—	—	—	—	—	165.94 (8.02)	8.18* (2.27)	—	0.22 (34.67)	-91.15 (6.55)	—	0.360 (20.90)
12.	*Tc*[1]	28.21	—	-8.78* (2.31)	—	—	—	—	—	314.55 (20.25)	14.53 (6.92)	—	0.24 (42.90	-52.76* (2.15)	-0.112[3] (13.16)	0.402 (20.84)
13.	*Tt*	1753.39	-255.04* (2.91)	40.17* (3.81)	-66.73 (21.33)	—	—	—	—	1607.33 (46.66)	105.12 (22.70)	359.35 (34.29)	0.58 (18.33)	—	—	0.657 (49.50)

1. Model includes the substitute.
2. *Tc* as substitute.
3. *Ta* as substitute.

Note: Figures in parentheses are F-values. All coefficients are significant at 95 per cent level and above except marked with esterisks, which are significant between 85 to 95 per cent level.

the fact that the use of these energy resources is much limited except that of biomass (Tb) and their variations are more random. Poor results can also be attributed to the distorted responses to create a pseudo image of the household. The substitute variable of animal energy use has improved the fitness of the models pertaining to fossil-fuels, electricity and total commercial energy sources by 0.6, 3.5 and 4.2 per cent respectively.

The total energy use model of the total system, the most aggregated model of the study is significant at one per cent. Its R^2 is 0.657 which suggests that about two-third of the variation in the total energy use can be explained in conjunction with the set of elements representing the rural energy system and its environs. Principal deductions based on significant regression coefficients; pertaining to these models are as follows :

1. The significant negative coefficient of type one setting, i.e., fertile natural setting in all the equations except electricity and commercial energy sources proves the hypothesis that the man's interactions with nature are less toilsome in the regions of plenitude. Since the resource copiousness reduces the effort-space and thereby reducing the demand of energy to overcome the effort distances. However, it holds true with a critical assumption that other components are operating at the same level, particularly in institutional and technological spheres.
2. The physical distances in the geographical space can be covered only by putting more energy in the means of transportation and thus the use of energy increases with the increasing distances from the central places. However, physical distances also increase inaccessibility to neoterism resulting in the lesser use of commercial sources of energy. These hypotheses are proved by the positive regression coefficients of *Dk* with animate energy sources and negative with electricity and total commercial energy sources.
3. The insignificant coefficient of *So* suggest that the role of social hierarchy, in itself, is not significant in explaining the behaviour of energy use. It is to be noted that *So* has not entered as significant regressor in any of the models. It signifies that either the affects of caste system are over taken by other socio-economic factors and/or it is less significant variable in comparison to other institutional factors in explaining the variations

in energy use in the region.

4. The role of family size as an indicator of scale of operation is significant only in the case of human and biomass energy use. It is also significant in the model of total energy. The negative coefficient approves the hypothesis that as the size of family increases, the per capita use of energy sources decrease due to economies of scale. The advantage of economies of scale has created a false impression among poor rural households that larger families are beneficial to them as they provide greater amount of labour force.
5. The positive regression coefficient of percentage of workers with human energy model suggests that easy supply of labour enhances the use of human energy. Contrary to it, the negative coefficients of *Wp* and *Aw* with animal energy use and electricity respectively prove the hypothesis that greater supply of human energy delimits the use of non-human energy. This suggests that in rural areas where unemployment is very higher the pressure of workers on land is high, first priority is given to the cheaper and easily available human labour.
6. Results prove that female literacy is a more decisive factor than the total literacy in the use of animate energy sources. The negative coefficient of female literacy in all the equations related with animate energy sources indicate that the social development reduces the dependence on animate energy sources in the total system. However, the sectoral results have shown that the demand of human energy increases with literacy levels in household sector. These results are not contradictory but impart strength to the hypothesis that social development leads to greater awareness of social welfare and thus human energy from non-household sectors is shifted towards household sector. There, it is replaced by commercial energy sources. The positive coefficient of *Lt* with electricity and total commercial energy use also support the above deduction.
7. The principal components of the economic base of the rural areas are land, animal and irrigation. The expansion and development of these resources will increase the demand of energy sources significantly as evident from the positive regression coefficients of per capita land, intensity of irrigation and per hectare animal units. Of all the factors, these three are most significant with very high magnitude of the coefficients.

However, the growth in land and irrigation increases the use of all energy resources but for biomass which is not used in agriculture. The animal sectors growth will increase the use of animate as well as biomass energy sources.

8. The hypothesis that economic development will increase the use of energy is also proved with positive coefficients of per capita non-food expenditure in all the energy use models. It also supports the earlier hypothesis explaining the relationship between energy use and economic base as non-food expenditure is a better proxy variable of household income.
9. The positive coefficients of *Ch* in animate energy use models and negative in commercial energy models prove the hypothesis that the traditional technology is basically developed to utilize animate energy sources. It also indicates that traditional technologies have given impetus to self-reliant energy systems. As much of the energy needs for supporting animate energy sources are produced from the agricultural and animal husbandry sectors and which they produce with the power of animate energy sources only.
10. The feedback relations in energy system are evident by the significant coefficients of substitute. The negative coefficients indicate that animate energy sources are substituted by commercial sources *vis-a-vis* commercial energy sources by animate energy sources. However, the higher coefficient values of commercial substitutional energy suggest that commercial energy sources are better substitute of animal energy than *vice versa.*

The dynamics of energy use behaviour reveals significant details regarding the rural energy systems. It allowed us to peep into the complex relations between energy utilizations and the environs of the space and people. It is evident from the analysis that energy use is not an isolated issue. It provides a comprehensive knowledge of the intricate components of the space, people and technology in transforming the rural systems from primitivity to modernity, from animate energy uses to inanimate energy uses and from self-reliant system to an open system.

Policy Implications

As an element of the total anthropoecosystem, energy system is closely associated with the problems, implications and solutions of other systems. Hence, energy use issues have wider implications in the fields of social transformations, economic development, techno-cultural advancement as well as environmental amelioration. Therefore, no planning or strategy for the improvement of human or ecological systems can afford to avoid energy problems. However, due to variations in the nature and availability of different energy sources, implications of the use vary significantly.

Human energy, as evident from the study, is used more because of its easy availability in the household. The excess supply of human labour results in greater pressure on land. This leads to low labour productivity and creates stronger ties between land and people only to hold the society at subsistence level and thus the process of development and growth is restrained.

The problem of excess supply of human energy can be solved by effective measures of family welfare, but these are long range solutions. Results shows that children's education and techno-economic know-how for shifting to non-agricultural activities can reduce the human pressure on land. The withdrawal of labour force from agriculture can than be facilitated by making use of inanimate energy sources so that both land and labour productivity is increased. At regional level, a better infrastructure for general education as well as for skill enhancing technological centres are to be developed to diffuse the scientific knowledge and technology for transforming the muscular human energy into techno-friendly human energy.

Animals, are the second most important energy converters in rural areas, but the desired growth and diversification of the economic system, can not be achieved if it is powered by bullocks. It is evident from the gradual induction of inanimate power sources like fossil fuels and electricity in the areas of agriculture, transport and other trades. However, the reduction of drought animals is slow and thus, there is a surplus of animal energy in the region. The animal energy use is also less productive. It is persisting and will continue to dominate the energy systems, since it is the most easily accessible form of energy source in terms of technology, capital investment and operational costs. The continuation of its use results in the perpetuation of less productive traditional and to some extent obsolete technology.

It is, therefore, obligatory to reduce the size of drought animals with the introduction of inaminate energy sources. The problems of minimum number of bullocks required and its time specific use may not permit households to ignore the animal energy completely, particularly when the investment and operation costs of alternatives are very high. Therefore, alternative or non-agricultural uses of animal energy is to be explored. The use of animal energy should also be supported by improved devices and machines so that the losses in converting muscular energy into mechanical of other types of energy are minimum.

The basic thing about problem of biomasses is this that these are the only renewable energy sources used by rural households. The supply of wood, a primary source of fuel, is fast declining and thus can not be considered as renewable energy source in the strict sense. The use of inferior quality unconventional firewoods and other crop residues shows that there is a shortage of fuels for cooking and other purposes. The shortage of fuel has resulted in excessive and destructive use of commons. The use of non-heat efficient fuels takes more human hours in cooking and the emitted smoke is harmful to the health of women. The worst affected to the shortage of fuels are the poor or landless and marginal households.

The problem of scarcity of fuel does not exist for all households. It is associated with the distribution of land. Therefore, the problem of fuel crisis can be solved with effective land reforms. The development of the farm-forest by individual household can increase the wood production in the region. A significant proportion of land lies as commons but due to non-accountability of its productivity, it is lying idle and producing very little biomasses in relation to private lands. Thus the proper management of these common lands is necessary for the production of biomass energy sources.

The efficient use of energy or the efficient conversion of energy amounts to production of additional energy. The future solutions of fuel problems lie with the efficient use of biomasses like crop residue and dung. Improved variety of cooking stoves are needed to minimize the energy losses, but the efficient use of crop residue, dung and other dry and green biomasses is possible only through its gasification process. The conversion of biomass into fuel gases give double advantage to the user. The gas can be used as fuel for cooking and the slurry is used as manure. It is observed that the dried slurry is more productive than the common dung manure. These innovative propositions, either at individual or at community levels, can be achieved only when the proper know-how, subventions and maintenance facilities are provided to household at their door steps.

Commercial fuels and power sources are becoming popular because these energy sources can move the wheel with greater speed and consistency. The problem of their use is more of economic nature. These are productive but require greater capital investments. Thus the distribution is more uneven than any other source of energy. The supply of certain power resources like electricity is restricted due to preferential supply to urban centres over rural countryside.

The use of commercial energy sources is thus, essential for economic development and to preserve the natural vegetation. The popularization of these energy sources and associated technologies depends upon the diversification of the economic base and development of agrobased industries in the region.

It is significant to note that the ultimate solution of poor people does not lie in the accelerated use of energy resources but with the efficient, egalitarian and eco-friendly employment of energy to ease the human ordeals.

REFERENCES

Agrawal, S.C. (1981). Rural energy system in two regions of Uttar Pradesh; First Phase Report, State Planning Institute, Uttar Pradesh, Lucknow.

CTAE, (1990). Annual Report 1989-90: Technical Back up on Improved *Chulha*, Renewable Energy Centre, CTAE Udaipur.

Cook, E. (1976). *Man Energy and Society,* W.H. Freeman and Company, San Francisco.

Cripps, E.L. et al. (1974). Energy and materials flows in the urban space economy, *Transportation Research,* 8, 293-305.

Davidson, Ogundade R. (1985). *Energy Use Patterns - Sierra Lione,* The International Development Research Centre, Ottawa.

Gopalan, C. et al., (1971). *Nutritive Value of Indian Foods,* National Institute of Nutrition, ICMR, Hyderabad.

Odum, H.T. (1971). *Environment, Power and Society,* John Wiley & Sons, Chichester.

Macgill, S.M. (1977). Rectangular input-output tables — Multiplier analysis and entropy maximizing principles : A new methodology, *Regional Science and Urban Economics,* 8, 355-370.

Mather, P.M. (1976). Computational Methods of Multivariate Analysis in Physical Geography, John Wiley & Sons, London.

NCAER (1978). *Survey of Rural Energy Consumption in Northern India,* National Council of Applied Economic Research, New Delhi.

Patten, B.C. (1971). *Systems Analysis and Simulation in Ecology,* Academic Press, New York.

Ramade, Francois (1984). *Ecology of Natural Resources,* John Wiley Sons, Cheshester.

Shanker, T.L. and Rao, U.S. (1987). Rural Energy Consumption Survey : Godavari Delta Region, Institute of Public Enterprise, Hyderabad.

Sharma, R. and Bhatia, R. (1986). *India : Meeting Basic Energy Needs of the Poor,* International Labour Organisation, New Delhi.

Soddy, Frederick, (1933). *Wealth, Virtual Wealth and Debt,* 2nd ed., Dutton, New York.

TERI, 1983, International Workshop on National Energy Data Systems; Background Papers, Tata Energy Research Institute, New Delhi.

Wilson, A.G. (1981). *Geography and the Environment - Systems Analytical Methods,* John Wiley and Sons, Chichester.

World Bank (1992). *World Development Report, Development and the Environment,* Oxford University Press, Oxford.

PART-III

ANALYSIS OF NATURAL RESOURCES MANAGEMENT SYSTEMS

8

SAFEGUARDING THE LAND: The Importance of Quaternary Geomorphology to an Understanding of Land Stability in the Tropics

MICHAEL F. THOMAS

Introduction

The understanding of soil erosion in different conditions of landform and climate and under a variety of plant cover types has been greatly advanced by research over several decades. Much of this work has been directed towards the measurement of rainfall erosivity and soil erodibility, and almost all of the findings concern the sediment yield (soil loss) from experimental plots or small drainage basins. By contrast, the subsoil conditions, and the potential for deep gullying or landsliding have only been sporadically investigated by those concerned with rural landuse; much of the work which has been accomplished coming from engineering investigations.

The fact that the distribution and distinctive properties of superficial deposits in the tropics are seldom given more than passing mention in soil studies or in land evaluation is seen as a potentially dangerous gap in our knowledge and understanding of tropical landsurfaces, their processes and histories of formation. It will be argued here that these unconsolidated materials have a potential for instability and rapid change in response to ecological disturbance. Such disturbance may arise from deforestation or other changes to patterns of landuse and practice, but it can also result from extreme weather events which may either form a part of the normal variability of climate or reflect longer term changes in climate. The instability that results can lead, not only to the loss of surface soil, but to the irreversible loss of the land itself. Although initially localised, such land loss can profoundly alter the potential of the land resource, by lowering water-tables, increasing hydraulic gradients and reinforcing positive feedback mechanisms leading to further instability.

Emphasis is commonly given to the long and continuous pre-weathering of tropical soil materials and to their intensive homogenisation (Ollier, 1959; Stoops, 1989). Stoops (1989, p.96) has gone so far as to assert that : 'most soils of the humid tropics contain few indications of past environmental changes. Almost no information exists on relict properties or features recognized in tropical soils, except for studies of stone lines and lateritic gravel.' However, unconsolidated surface deposits in tropical areas are usually inherited from late Quaternary or early Holocene environments and are potentially unstable within present-day environmental systems. This instability can be triggered by ecological disturbance arising from changes in land cover or can be due to extreme weather events.

In southern Africa, Dardis et al. (1988, p.191) claimed that, 'the nature of the host materials is probably the single most important parameter influencing soil erosion type', and that much of the erosion occurs in deposits less than 25,000 years old and which, 'may have formed under a unique set of circumstances', associated with late Pleistocene climatic change. This observation is equally applicable to the humid tropics, where Quaternary environmental changes were also profound.

Events of the Late Quaternary Period

During the last glacial advance in high latitudes which lasted from around 22/20,000 yr BP until 13/12,000 yr BP, most tropical areas were cooler (by 4–6°C) and drier (by 30->50%) than today. Forests gave way to grassland savanna or open deciduous woodland, while in areas of present-day savanna, conditions were semi-arid to arid, with strong evidence for the decay of integrated drainage systems and the development of pans and even sand dunes. After 12,500 yr BP abrupt changes to the patterns of rainfall led to wetter conditions throughout the tropics in the early Holocene, but evidence from south America and west Africa suggests that the rainforest did not re-colonise to its present limits until around 9000-8500 yr BP (Absy et al. 1989; Talbot et al., 1984). The increasing precipitation, therefore, fell on open vegetation communities, and is thought to have led to high rates of erosion and sedimentation on tropical landscapes (Hall et al., 1985; see also Knox, 1972).

Huge floods occurred in the Nile Valley after 12,500 yr BP (Rossignol-Strick, 1982; Paulissen, 1989), while the sediment loads of the Amazon, Niger and Congo rivers rose abruptly at this time, with an increase in the proportion kaolinitic clays (Damuth & Fairbridge, 1970; Pastouret et al., 1978). Smaller rivers in west Africa that had been inactive for several thousand years discharged floods capable of carving bedrock channels, while coarse sediments were deposited during the falling stages of these floods (Thomas & Thorp, 1980). It is clear that major changes to the dynamics of the entire landscape occurred throughout the tropics during this period.

Notwithstanding the occurrence of very much older deposits on tropical landscapes, a majority of unconsolidated, transported materials belong to this late Quaternary period. The long dry phase from post 22,000 yr BP until around 12,500 yr BP was the most important episode, but Holocene oscillations of climate were also dramatic, with cooling and aridity persisting for perhaps 500-1000 years around 11,000 yr BP (Allerod), and again post 4500 yr BP (see Table 8.1).

TABLE 8.1: Tentative Chronology of Late Quaternary Environmental Change

Radiocarbon Yr BP	Probable environmental conditions (recorded examples in brackets)
60,000 (?) – Ca 52,000 yr BP	Scattered records of sedimentation suggest rapid warming at end of isotopic zone 3 – dating insecure (Venezuela, Brazil, Kalimantan)
Ca 40,000 yr BP	Cooling of upland climates evident, possibly becoming drier (Amazonia, Uganda)
(these two stages and dates are very tentative)	
>32,000 – 22,000/20,000	Cooler, probably humid to sub-humid (Ghana, Sierra Leone, Uganda, Brazil)
Post 22,000 – 13,000/12,000	Becoming cold in uplands and dry in most lowlands; by 18,000 tree-line depressed 1000 m, rainfalls possibly reduced by 50% (most sites ion tropical south America, Africa and Asia)

(Contd.)

TABLE 8.1: *(Contd.)*

Radiocarbon Yr BP	Probable environmental conditions (recorded examples in brackets)
12,500 – ca 11,000	Rapid warming with unstable climates and prolonged heavy rains in tropical Africa, very high lake levels (world-wide)
11,000 – 10,500	Dry interval in many areas; low lake levels.
10,500 – 4,500	Second humid period with high lake levels and discharges; re-establishment of forest by 9000-8500, with reduced river discharges in West Africa after 7000 yr BP (Ghana, Brazil)
4,500 – 3,000	Mid Holocene dry phase, probably quite severe. (West Africa)
Post 3,000	Increased humidity in forested tropics with rising discharges, but concomitant with deforestation and human occupation.

Sources: Absy et al. (1989); Adamson et al. (1980); Butzer (1980); Schubert (1988); Street & Grove (1979); Talbot et al. (1984); Thomas & Thorp (1989, 1985); Thorp et al. (1990).

Landscape Dynamics and Climate Change

The increased sedimentation in river valleys was matched by changes on hill slopes which became subject to enhanced mass movement and colluviation as well as accelerated surface erosion. Evidence for these changes is partly derived from hill slope deposits. However, interpretation of these must recognize that depositional events may have been responses to individual, high magnitude rainfall events and are not always the results of long term climatic change. It is also possible for a complex response to result from internal re-adjustments within the denudation system as thresholds are exceeded for erosion or deposition within a catchment. Nevertheless, confirmatory evidence of vegetation changes from pollen studies, justifies the view that most hillslope sediments have resulted from important and longer-term changes to the external environment.

The Importance of Superficial Deposits in the Tropics

Watson et al. (1983) observed widespread colluviation throughout the southern African savannas, where rainfalls range between 600-800 mm yr^{-1}, and attributed much of this colluvium to the effects of late Pleistocene aridity. Hill & Rackham (1978) called attention to the importance of colluvial/alluvial deposition of the Jos Plateau of Nigeria, where rainfall is 1000->1200 mm yr^{-1}. Detailed studies in Cameroon (Hori, 1977; Kadomura, 1986) have also established the importance of colluvial deposits in the forested tropics (1500->2000 mm yr^{-1}). Similar observations come from south America and other tropical landmasses. A broad classification of surface deposits, their landscape associations and probable conditions of formation are indicated in Table 8.2. To this list must be added the residual mantle of saprolite which is also susceptible to instability and erosion. Much of the fine-grained material is a largely unsorted, loamy sand (3->5 m deep), to which the term 'colluvium' tends to be applied. Yet we do not have a clear idea of its formation. It is likely that ephemeral water flows on open hill slopes moved sediment in waves on to the piedmont, often as a series of small mudflows. But in some cases sediment was sorted into sand or clay beds and resulted from suspended sediment transport in overland flows.

TABLE 8.2: Common Allochthonous Surface Deposits in the Tropics

---

A. Interfluve and plateau deposits

1) Duricrusts
— massive ferricrete containing allochthonous elements (H-A)
— silcrete cappings, often impregnating sediments (A/h)
— (bauxites in these situations are usually residual)

2) Gravel layers
— duricrust (petroplinthite) fragments (H/a)
— stone-line gravels containing rolled and unrolled quartz (A)

3) Sand cover
— aeolian sand sheets, including dunes (A)
— 'white sands', eluvial, alluvial and colluvial (H-A)

B. Hillslope deposits

4) Landslide debris
— boulder accumulations from rock falls or slides (H/A)
— earthflow debris from slumps and translational slides (H)
— debrisflow and mudflow sediments, often channelised (A, A-H)

5) Coarse talus/fan deposits
— coarse, clast-supported debris fans and talus fans (A)

(Contd.)

(Contd.)

— debris flows similar to 1) above (H/a)
— earthflows associated with rotational slides (H)
— braided channel sediments, often very coarse (A/h)

C. Hillslope-piedmont zone deposits

6) Colluvium ('colluvium-alluvium')
— mudflow deposits, sometimes as gully-fills (A)
— sheetflood sediments — laminated sands and silts (A, A-H)
— shallow, quazi-alluvial fan and channel sediments (A/h)
— unstratified colluvium (process obscure) (A or A-H)

7) Ferricrete benches
— Fe cementation of mainly colluvial and alluvial deposits

D. Piedmont zone and valley deposits

8) Alluvium
— alluvial fan facies, frequently fine-grained (A/h)
— sheetflood sandy sediments ('pedisediment') (A)
— deep channel fills; flood sediments, fining upwards (A-H)
— shallow braided valley sediments (A, A-H)
— clay fills in *dambo* valleys; clay pans (A)
— floodplain facies from meandering streams (H)

H = humid; A = semi-arid; A-H = arid to humid transition — upper case, prominent; lower case, less common)

Saprolite Profiles

Whereas bauxitised residues are thought to form over 10^6-10^7 yr, partial alteration of crystalline rocks to depths of tens of metres may be achieved in 10^4-10^5 yr, in humid tropical climates, placing such profiles within the Quaternary. Calculations and estimates for the rate of weathering penetration into crystalline rocks range from ca 2m Ma^{-1} – 50m Ma^{-1} in the Appalachian Piedmont (sub-tropical - 36°-39° N) (Pavich, 1986, 1989; Velbel, 1985, 1986). For the humid tropics, where rainfall may be 3x and soil temperatures 2-3x those of the SE USA, much higher rates of alteration are likely beneath well drained sites. This suggests that rates of at least 50-100m Ma^{-1} may apply.

There is also strong evidence for the periodic stripping of saprolites from steep slopes in the humid tropics, as a consequence of prolonged, and intense rainfalls. Several studies of catastrophic landslides in eastern Brazil make this point (Jones, 1973; De Ploey & Cruz, 1979), while observations in Sierra Leone (Thomas, 1983) and Puerto Rico (Jibson, 1990) confirm that such slides from a major and recurrent process in hillslope formation. Although slides may be triggered on the same sites at infrequent intervals, the landslide scars are spatially frequent on steep slopes above 28°. According to Deere & Patton (1971, p99/100); (1) landslides are a common and perhaps the predominant method of slope development in areas of deep residual soils; (2) they are associated with characteristics of the weathering profile; (3) they are especially common during periods of heavy rainfall and/or earthquakes; (4) Shallow slides are the most common on the steeper slopes but deeper slides which incorporate weathered rock and both shallow and deep layers of colluvium are also frequently encountered; (5) rapid erosion is common on slopes where the silty sands and sandy silts of the saprolite . . .become exposed'.

Relict discontinuities present in the saprolite fabric can predispose cut faces to collapse, sometimes by toppling failures, where blocks of less weathered rock are embedded in a saprolite matrix. Irfan & Wood (1988) considered these discontinuities to be one of the most significant factors in generating landslides in deep saprolites (most of the microstructures discussed above occur in the upper residual soil layer). Water ingress occurs into relict joints opened by stress release, and along other relict shear surfaces, leading to the deposition of clay. Where movement has previously occurred along such planes, polished slickensided surfaces with clay coatings contribute to a greatly reduced shear strengths. Clay infills may also act as groundwater dams, building high pore water pressures in the upslope saprolite. It can readily be foreseen that heavy rainfall can lead to premature failure of such slopes, the mass strength of which may have been greatly weakened. The combined effects of the rise in pore water pressures after heavy rainfall and rapid movement along the relict discontinuities, can result in complex and rapid landslide failures.

If most of the mantle is stripped by a single event then a period of slope 'maturation' will be necessary before further slides of the same kind will recur. Slope failures in thick saprolites are commonly deep seated and included rotational slumps. Subsequent failure along relict shear surfaces is common in these. Where thick saprolite mantles have been dissected into 'half orange' hills (*Fr. demi orange, Port. meias laranjas*), these may exhibit steep marginal slopes which become subject to repeated landsliding and gullying.

The relationship of landsliding to vegetal cover is less certain. In Atlantic Brazil, De Ploey & Cruz (1979) found that the root mat is generally confined to a depth of 3m, with roots of larger trees penetrating to 5m. This root mat has the function of increasing infiltration and throughflow. These processes can increase the likelihood of slope failure by promoting a rise in pore water pressure and a consequent decrease in cohesion; they also induce a downslope, seepage stress. Shear stress strengths also appear to decrease towards the base of the slope and these authors argued for more attention to be paid to the initiation of landsliding at this position. This is in contrast to most debris slides/flows which start high on the slope, close to the interfluve or in hollows, and are often initiated by runoff. These can be favoured by lack of forest cover, and many originate in pre-existing water courses or hollows (Dietrich et al., 1987; Reneau & Dietrich, 1987).

Hillslope Colluvium and Pedisediment

Studies from the Pacific NW of the USA have demonstrated the importan of colluvium-filled hollows as sites for shallow landslides. After prolonged rainfall rapid debris flows are generated within the colluvium and scour 1st and 2nd order stream channels downslope. Not all of these events scour to the bedrock interface, and pollen analysis of charcoal samples from the basal sediments in many hollows have been dated to the latest Pleistocene period (typically 14,500-9000 yr BP) which led Reneau et al. (1986) to suggest that rapid climate change at the end of the last glacial period may have triggered a large number of the more deep seated slides. Shallow slides, however, can be triggered by rainfall events within the present-day climate, and Dietrich et al. (1987) have suggested that on steep slopes (>50°) on pumice and ash, the recurrence interval may be only 20-30 years. This probably rises to about 1000 years on 20°-40° slopes on granite. In a study by Ellen et al. (1988) 80 per cent of 4600 documented flows occurred on slopes >27.5°; 50 per cent originated in amphitheatres above drainage heads, and 26 per cent were contiguous with previous landslide scars.

The system of hollows functions by concentrating water and sediment flows into concavities on hillsides, and failure occurs only after the build-up of sediment in the hollow has reached a critical thickness. This depth will vary with slope steepness and vegetation cover, but the forms under discussion are all quite small, averaging 7-10 m in width, 10-20m in length and 0.7-1.1m in depth of flow, although some larger slides >2.5 m depth accounted for 21 per cent of the volume in the central Californian Coast Ranges (Reneau & Dietrich, 1987). According to Dietrich and Dunne (1978), as soils thicken, root penetration to bedrock becomes progressively more difficult until this stabilisation mechanism is eliminated.

The importance of colluvium in the humid tropical landscape can be gauged by the figure of 50 per cent for the proportion of land in Sao Paulo State (Brazil) covered by these sediments (Ferreira & Monteiro, 1985). In Hong Kong, where great emphasis have been placed upon the nature of granite weathering profiles, it is nevertheless the case that many slopes which fail are underlain by colluvium, which is extensive and may exceed 30m in thickness (Brand et al., 1985). In the Lower Himalayas, Fookes & Marsh (1981) have also demonstrated the importance of colluvium and taluvium in the course of engineering studies.

Studies from eastern Brazil have revealed widespread mass movement, and colluviation contributing to what are described as *rampa complexes*. These comprise amphitheatre–like hollows and associated glacis, that may be both colluvial and alluvial in origin. The deposits are complex and a tentative chronostratigraphy has been advanced (De Meis & Monteiro, 1979; De Meis et al., 1984; Modenesi, 1988), from locations that vary in altitude from <500->2000m asl; each displaying a characteristically steep, multi-convex topography incised 50-100m below an older planate surface. Hollows have often been formed by deep seated slump-slides in thick saprolite, though some have been extended by slope retreat into the regolith, producing *glacis d'erosion* or *erosional rampas* (De Meis & Monteiro, 1979). The landscape of *hollows* and *rampas* is one of dominantly conclave elements cut into the multi-convex relief, the distal ends of the rampas merging and interfingering with the alluvial deposits of the valley floors (De Oliveira, 1990, and Figure 8.1).

In mountainous terrain, exceptional thicknesses of colluvium may be encountered. Murray & Olsen (1990) described a 200 m thick colluvial accumulation derived from a fluidised slide arising from the catastrophic failure of a ridge in Daria limestone at the *Ok* Menga hydroelectric scheme, near Tabubil in Papua New Guinea. The authors suggested that a *lower colluvium* at the site is a result of a continuous process of weathering and colluviation that was interrupted (*c* 8000 RC yr BP) by the *upper colluvium* event.

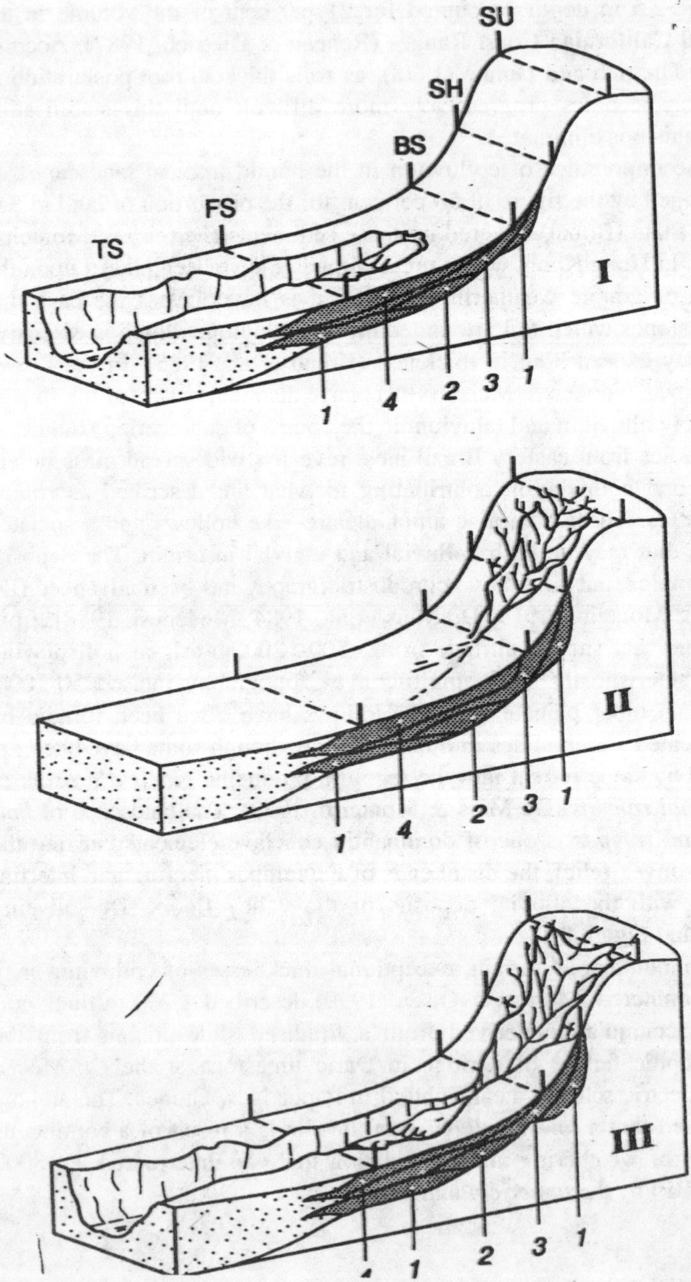

FIG. 8.1: The Landscape of *Hollows* and *Rampas*

Source: After Teixera De Oliveira (1990)

The upper colluvium is non-plastic, has a low (<10%) water content, and virtually no clay. Its bulk density is around 2.0 and angles of shearing resistance reach 39 to 43°. However, the lower colluvium, has a plastic limit of 17 to 25 per cent, with a water content of 20 to 30 per cent and variable clay. It is a stiff silty clay containing rafted limestone blocks. The upper material tends to break away by slab failure on the upper slopes, probably by stress release but assisted by high rainfalls, while the lower colluvium, is subject to shallow slides turning into mudflows after rain.

Complex slope sequences of weathered volcanics and derived colluvium have been identified widely in Java, wherever road traces have been made (Heath & Saroso, 1988). Landslides and groundwater releases are common and creep failure resulting from saturation of the lowest deposits is widespread. It has been calculated that there are 1.4 slope failures for every one km of road in Java (Brand, 1985). In these circumstances, the role of impermeable layers causing a build-up of groundwater and saturated conditions during heavy rain is crucial. Most of the material is porous, with voids ratios of 0.8 - 1.2, and also contains fissures and pipes creating a high permeability. The more permeable deposits receive almost continuous groundwater flows from the higher volcanic mountains, and, when 24 hour rainfalls approach or exceed 100 mm, the collapse of fissures and pipes quickly leads to translational slides that develop into mudflows towards the base of the slopes, where groundwater flow has become obstructed. Along many road sections the removal of support has led to rotational slumping.

Stone-line Complexes

The extensive, colluvial layer present on most humid tropical hillslopes, is typically underlain by a stone-line or stone layer that is often interpreted as a lag or pediment gravel (Folster, 1969; Rohdenburg, 1970, 1983; Hori, 1977 and Embrechts & De Dapper, 1987; De Dapper, 1989). These authors agreed that shallow pedimentation cycles have contributed to the combination of half-orange hills associated with slope pediments cut into the saprolite and mantled by pedisediment. At the base of this pedisediment is a coarse stone-line, encountered at the boundary with the saprolite and containing large clasts, mainly from quartz veins. Superimposed on this is a finer stone-layer (mainly gravel >2mm), which can attain 3-4m depth on gently sloping lower ground. A fine hillswash covers the pediment gravel. The presence of secondary, nodular petroplinthite (ferricrete) in the gravel indicates the occurrence of earlier pedimentation cycles.

Stone-lines have generated a lot of discussion and they are clearly not all of a single type. The concentration of stone-lines as a result of *biological pedoturbation* has been claimed by several authors (see Johnson & Watson-Stegner, 1990), and the particular role of termites has long been emphasised in the seasonal tropics (Nye, 1955; Soyer, 1989; Watson, 1974). In another model coarse clasts from quartz veins, accumulate as weathering penetrates the subjacent rock and fine materials are removed by wash, throughflow or by dissolution. This process requires no environmental crisis and is considered as an integral component of landsurface downwasting or *etching* (Aleva, 1983; Thomas, 1989; McFarlane & Pollard, 1989). However, a majority of examples have been explained by invoking an environmental crisis capable of producing sheet flows that effectively remove fine particles downslope, to produce a surface gravel which is later covered by redeposition of fines or by termite activity (bioturbation). In certain instances stone-lines are associated with gully-fills, and Stocking (1978) has described repeated gully erosion, accompanied by colluvial sedimentation, in the headwaters of the Umsweswe River basin in Zimbabwe. He considered that the sediments are probably the result of climatic fluctuations, and the present gullying due more to natural system changes than to anthropogenic interference. Some stone-line materials are clearly of fluvial origin and represent degraded terrace gravels.

It seems likely that most stone-lines progress through several stages:

(1) Residual accumulation resulting from dissolution and removal of weatherable and finer material under humid conditions;
(2) Redistribution and concentration of gravel by surface water flows and related colluvial activity, associated with dry climates; and
(3) Modification and burial by bioturbation, soil creep, tree throw, and possibly of anthropogenic activity.

Stone-lines can affect the soil environment in fundamental ways. If they are exposed at the surface or are found at 20-30 cm depth, they clearly form a stony phase, promoting infiltration, but having little water holding capacity. This probably occurs only locally, over quartz-rich igneous and metamorphic rocks or in conglomeratic sediments. Stone-lines at greater depth will form discontinuities in the profile and preferential pathways for the movement of water and leachates. The presence of large, open voids also promotes oxidation of Fe^{2+}, and the formation of ferricrete incorporating stone-line gravels is quite common.

Floodplain and other Valley Sediments

In landscapes widely mantled by deep saprolite, there is a major store of fine-grained materials that can erode to become sediments in transfer towards river channels. These materials are temporarily stored on hillslopes, in hollows, on pediments and glacis and in valley floors, where they may accumulate to form valley fills. In highly seasonal climates, river flows may have great amplitude in water levels and leave large quantities of fine sediment as overbank deposits. Bedload is mainly sand. When these materials are abandoned as terraces, they can become subject to rapid gullying, and a series of cut-and-fill episodes may diversify the terrace deposit.

Shallow headwater valleys, typical of the plateau uplands of Africa and South America, often exhibit channelless reaches described as *dambos* (Thomas & Goudie, 1985). These features commonly contain an infill of clay and sand, that buries a former linear stream channel (Meadows, 1985; Thomas, 1986). The clays of the dambo floors accumulate cations and retain moisture, and tend to form vertisols or sodic soils. Degradation and gullying of dembos in Zimbabwe have been recorded by Whitlow (1988), and they appear to be a typical instance of sediments occupying former extensions of the stream network, and potentially liable to rapid evacuation. A different interpretation has, however, recently been offered by McFarlane & Whitlow (1992), who claim that leachates from the interfluves have been reconstituted as smectite clays, without significant colluvial/ alluvial transfer into the dambo floor. These are contributory processes, but evidence from other areas for colluvial/alluvial infills is overwhelming, and it is clear that channelless stream valleys are similar to the 'zero order basins' forming hillslope hollows in more accidented terrain analysed by Reneau et al. (1986) and Dietrich et al. (1987).

White Sand Formations

Materials appearing in the landscape as *white sands* were described by

Duchaufour (1982) as *tropical hydromorphic podzols*; they are characteristic of the sandy coastal plains of the per-humid, equatorial regions, and they are also found on the surfaces of ancient cratonic plateaus in Africa and south America, in areas that are now savanna. According to Lucas et al. (1989) and other French workers, these tropical podzols can result from the destabilisation of ferrallitic profiles as a result of *lessivage.* The *humicrete* (Bh horizon) often found beneath the leached horizon (Daniels et al. 1976; Holzhey et al., 1976; and see also Righi & Chauvel, 1989), appears often to be associated with beds or lenses of fine silty sand and clay.

The materials with which they are most commonly associated are unconsolidated, thick sandy Quaternary sediments in coastal plain of riverine situations. These have subsequently become subject to hydromorphic conditions and strong lateral flows of water that has leached most of the iron and removed much of the interstitial clay. Ab'Saber (1982) considered such sediments in the Amazon basin to have been deposited in a savanna environment, and this also is the case in western Kalimantan (Thorp et al., 1990). But as noted by Fairbridge & Finkl (1984), white sands are common on the old landsurfaces of elevated plateaus, where they have formed by the loss of clay from ferrallitic profiles. These soil materials are some of the most impoverished in the world and tend to support at most a species poor, 'heath' or *Kerangas* forest, used for fuelwood.

Quaternary Deposits and Landsurface Stability

The widespread re-working of tropical soils and subsoil materials is indisputable, but the complexity and episodic nature of that re-working have not always been acknowledged. Quaternary climatic changes have repeatedly driven the denudation systems towards instability, and the record of the past 40,000 years, although incomplete, demonstrates the importance of these oscillations.

These deposits represent sediment stores in landscape positions that can become subject to rapid readjustment by landsliding or by incisions, as a consequence of ecosystem disturbance. Such disturbance may come from natural events, such as large storms, prolonged droughts, or major fires, but will also be a function of land development, whether for forestry, agricultural or urban uses. Sustainable land development presupposes that the land resource will be stable. This cannot be taken for granted and land evaluators should give serious attention to the correct identification and recording of sensitive soil parent materials. These can include a wide range of deep, residual and transported materials, not always recognized in soil or land surveys.

The principal conclusions from this survey are that,

(i) superficial deposits are widespread, almost always relict and were often formed in a different environment;

(ii) such materials are potentially unstable within the present-day environmental systems;

(iii) instability in the forms of landsliding or accelerated erosion and sedimentation can be triggered by changes in landuse practice or by construction; and

(iv) most colluvium occurs in predictable associations in the tropical landscape and can therefore be anticipated in land evaluation procedures.

Not all tropical areas will exhibit the same features, and some have been subject to more severe climatic changes in the Quaternary than others. The legacy of late Quaternary dry climates is particularly important in the present context, and this takes the form of superficial sediment stores in the landscape. Correct identification of these materials should be possible in the course of soil and geomorphological investigations for land evaluation, and it is important that physical geographers take a wider view than is sometimes evident from important, but often repetitive and imitative, process studies.

Awareness of these deposits and of the areas which they occupy is important for the avoidance of land instability and land erosion in conservation and development programmes today, and could become a more serious issue if the direction of climate change in the future leads the changes in the patterns of rainfall and plant cover.

REFERENCES

Ab'Saber A.N. (1982). The paleoclimate and paleoecology of Brazilian Amazonia. *Biological Diversification in the Tropics* (ed. by G.T. Prance), pp. 1-59. columbia, New York.

Absy, M.L., Van Der Hammen, T., Soubies, F, Suguio, K., Martin, L., Fournier, M., Turcq, B. (1989). Data on the history of vegetation and climate in Carajas, eastern Amazonia. *International Symposium on Global Change in South America During the Quaternary,* Sao Paulo, 1989, Special Publication, 1, 129-131.

Adamson, D.A., Gasse, F., Street, F.A. & Williams, M.A. J. (1980). Late Quaternary history of the Nile. *Nature,* 287, 50-55.

Brand, E.W. (1985). Landslides in Southeast Asia: a state of the art report. *IV International Symposium on Landslides,* Toronto 1984, Vol 1, 17-59.

Butzer, K.W. (1980). Pleistocene history of the Nile Valley in Egypt and Lower Nubia. *The Sahara and the Nile* (ed. by M.A.J. Williams and H. Faure, Balkema, Rotterdam, pp253-280.

Damuth, J.E. & Fairbridge, R.W. (1970). Equatorial Atlantic deep-sea arkosic sands and Ice-age aridity in tropical South America. *Bulletin of the Geological Society of America,* 81, 189-206.

Daniels, R.B., Gamble, E.E. & Holzhey (1975). Thick Bh horizons in the North Carolina coastal plain: I. Morphology and relation to texture and soil groundwater. *Soil Science Society of America,* Proceedings, 39, 1177-1181.

Dardis, G.F. , Beckedahl, H.R., Bowyer-Bower, T.A.S., & Hanvey, P.M. (1988). Soil erosion forms in southern Africa. In G.F. Dardis & B.P. Moon (eds) *Geomorphological Studies in Southern Africa,* Balkema, Rotterdam, 187-213.

De Dapper, M. (1989). Pedisediments and stone-line complexes in Peninsular Malaysia. *Stone-Lines. Journee d' Etude, Bruxelles, 24 mar.* 1987 (Ed by Alexandre, J. & Sympoens, J.J.) *Academie Royale des Sciences D' Outre-Mer, Geo-Eco-Trop,* 11, 37-59.

Deere, D.U. & Patton, F.D. (1971). Slope stability in residual soils. *Proceedings of the 4th Panamerican Conference on Soil Mechanics and Foundation engineering,* Puerto Rico, June 1971, 1, 87-170, American Society of Civil, Engineers, New York.

De Meis, M.R.M. & De Moura, J. R. da Silva (1984). Upper Quaternary sedimentation and hillslope evolution: southeastern Brazilian plateau. *American Journal of Science,* 284, 241-254.

De Meis, M.R.M. & Monteiro, A.M.F. (1979). Upper Quaternary "rampas": Doce river valley, Southeastern Brazilian plateau. *Zeitschrift fur Geomorphology N.F.,* 23, 132-151.

De Oliveira, M.A.T. (1990). Slope geometry and gully erosion development : Bananal, Sao Paulo, Brazil. *Zeitschrift fur Geomorphology N.F.,* 34, 423-434.

De Ploey, J . & Cruz, O. (1979). Landslides in the Serra do Mar, Brazil. *Catena,* 6, 111-122.

Dietrich, W.E. & Dunne, T. (1978). Sediment budget for a small catchment in mountainous terrain. *Zeitschrift fur Geomorphologie, N.F. Supplementband,* 29, 196-206.

Dietrich, W.E., Reneau, S.L. & Wilson , C.J. (1987). Overview: "zero order basins" and problems of drainage density, sediment transport and hillslope morphology. In R.L. Beschta, T. Blinn, C.E. Grant, F.J. Swanson & G.G. Ice (eds), *Erosion and Sedimentation in the Pacific Rim,* IAHS Publication No 165, 27-37.

Duchaufour, P. (1982). *Pedology, Pedogenesis and Classification* (English Edtn. Trans. T.R. Paton), George Allen and Unwin, London.

Embrechts, J. & De Dapper, M. (1987). Morphology and genesis of hillslope pediments in the Febe area (South-Cameroon). *Catena,* 14, 31-43.

Fairbridge, R.W. & Finkl, C.W. Jr. (1984). Tropical stone lines and podzolised sand plains as palaeoclimatic indicators for weathered cratons. *Quaternary Science Reviews,* 3, 41-72.

Ferreira, R.C. & Monteiro, L.B. (1985). Identification and evaluation of collapsibility of colluvial soils that occur in the Sao Raulo State. *First International Conference on Geomechanics in Tropical Lateritic and Saprolitic Soils,* Brazilia, 1985, Volume 1,

269-280.

Folster, H. (1969). Slope development in SW Nigeria during the late Pleistocene and Holocene. *Gottinger Bodenkundliche Berichte,* 10, 3-56.

Fookes, P.G. & Marsh, A.H. (1981). Some characteristics of construction materials in the low to moderate metamorphic grade rocks of the Lower Himalayas of East Nepal. 1: Occurrence and geological features. *Proceedings Institution of Civil Engineers,* Part 1, 70, 123-138.

Hall, A.M. Thomas, M.F. & Thorp, M.B. (1985). Late Quaternary alluvial placer development in the humid tropics: the case of the Birim Diamond Placer, Ghana. *Journal of The Geological Society,* 142, 777-787.

Heath, W. & Saroso, B.S. (1988). Natural slope problems related to roads in Java, Indonesia. *Geomechanics in Tropical Soils,* Proceedings of the Second International Conference on Geomechanics in Tropical Soils, Singapore, 1988, Volume 1, 259-266, Balkema, Rotterdam.

Hill, I.D. & Rackham, I.J. (1978). Indications of mass movement on the Jos Plateau, Nigeria. *Zeitschrift fur Geomorphologie N.F.* 22, 258-274.

Holzhey, C.S. Daniels, R.B. & Gamble, E.E. (1975). Thick Bh horizons in the North Carolina coastal plain: II. Physical and chemical properties and rates of organic additions from surface sources. *Soil Science Society of America, Proceedings,* 39, 1182-1187.

Hori, N. (1977). Weathering and cuirasses in the Yaounde area and geographical variation of weathering profile and superficial deposits. In *Geomorphological studies in the forest and savanna areas of Cameroon* (Ed. by H. Kadomura), 61-71

Irfan, Y.Y. & Woods, N.W. (1988). The influence of relict discontinuities on slope stability in saprolitic soils. *Geomechanics in Tropical Soils,* Proceedings of the Second International Conference on Geomechanics in Tropical Soils, Singapore, 1988, Volume 1, 267-276, Balkema, Rotterdam.

Jibson, R.W. (1989). Debris flows in southern Puerto Rico. In *Landslide Processes of the Eastern United States and Puerto Rico* (Ed. by A. P. Schultz & R.W. Jibson), Geological Society of America, Special paper 236, 29-55.

Johnson, D.L. & Watson-Stegner, D. (1990). The soil-evolution model as a framework for evaluating pedoturbation in archaeological site formation. *Geological Society of America,* Centennial Special volume, 4, 541-560.

Jones, F.O. (1973). Landslides of Rio de Janeiro and the Serra das Araras Escarpment, Brazil. *US Geological Survey Professional Paper,* 697, pp 42.

Kadomura, H. (1986). Late glacial-early Holocene environmental changes in tropical Africa: a comparative analysis with deglaciation history. *Geographical Reports, Tokyo Metropolitan University,* 21, 1-21.

Knox, J.C. (1972). Valley alleviation in southwestern Wisconsin. *Annals of the Association of American Geographers,* 62, 401-410.

Lucas, Y., Boulet, R., Chauvel, A., and Veillon, L. (1989). Systemes sols ferrallitiques - podzols en region Amazonienne. *Podzols et Podzolisation* (ed by D. Right & A. Chauvel), Comptes Rendus de la Table Ronde Internationale, 53-65, Association francaise pour l 'Etude du sol, ORSTOM/INRA.

McFarlane, M.J. & Pollard, S. (1989). Some aspects of stone-lines and dissolution fronts associated with regolith and dambo profiles in parts of Malawai and Zimbabwe. Alexandre, J. & Symoens, J.J. (Eds.). *Stone-Lines. Journee D'Etude, Bruxelles, 24 mars 1987. Academie Royale des Sciences D'Outre-Mer, Geo-Eco-Trop,* 11, 23-35.

McFarlane, M.J. & Whitlow, R. (1990). Key factors affecting the initiation and progress of gullying in dambos in parts of Zimbabwe and Malawi. *Land Degradation and Rehabilitation*, 2, 215-235.

Meadows, M.E. (1985). Dambos and environmental change in Malawi, central Africa. In Thomas, M.F. & Goudie, A.S. (Editors), *Dambos: Small channelless valleys in the tropics. Zeitschrift fur Geomorphologie Supplementband*, 52, 147-169.

Modenesi, M.C. (1988). Quaternary mass movements in a tropical plateau (Campos do Jordao, Sao Paulo, Brazil). *Zeitschrift fur Geomorphologie N.F.*, 32-440.

Murray, L.M. & Olsen, M.T. (1990). Colluvial slopes – A geotechnical and climatic study. *Geomechanics in Tropical soils*, Proceedings of the Second International Conference on Geomechanics in Tropical Soils, Singapore, 1988, Volume 2, 573-579, Balkema, Rotterdam.

Pastouret, L., Chamley, H., Delibrias, G., Duplessy, J.C., & Theide, J. (1978). Late Quaternary climatic changes in western tropical Africa deduced from deep-sea sedimentation off the Niger delta. *Oceanologica Acta*, 1, 217-232.

Paulissen, E. (1989). The inundations of the Saharan Nile around 12,500 BP: unique catastrophic floods of an exotic river. *Abstracts of Papers, Second International Conference on Geomorphology, Frankfurt/Main*, 1989. Geoko-plus, 1, 216.

Pavich, M.J. (1986). Processes and rates of saprolite production and erosion on a foliated granitic rock of the Virginia Piedmont. *Rates of Chemical Weathering of Rocks and Minerals* (Eds Colman S.M. & Detheir, D.P.), pp 552-590. Academic Press, New York,

Pavich, M.J. (1989). Regolith residence time and the concept of surface age of the Piedmont 'peneplain'. *Geomorphology*, 2, 181-196.

Pflug, R. (1969). Quaternary lakes of eastern Brazil. *Photogrammetria*, 24, ,29-35.

Reneau, S.L. & Dietrich, W.E. (1987). Size and location of colluvial landslides in a steep forested landscape. In R. L. Beschta, T. Blinn, C.E. Grant, F.J. Swanson & G.G. Ice (eds), *Erosion and Sedimentation in the Pacific Rim*, IAHS Publication No 165, 39-48.

Reneau, S.L., Dietrich, W.E., Dorn, R.I., Berger, C.R., & Rubin, M. (1986). Geomorphic and paleoclimatic implications of latest Pleistocene radiocarbon dates from colluvium-mantle hollows, California. *Geology*, 14, 655-658.

Rohdenburg, H. (1970). Hangpedimentation und Klimawechsel als wichstigste Faktoren der Flachen und Stufenbildung in den wechselfeuchten Tropen and Beispielen aus Westafrika, besonders aus dem Schichtstufenland Sudost-Nigerias. *Zeitschrift fur Geomorphologie, N.F.*, 14, 58-78.

Rohdenburg, H. (1983). Geomorphologisch-bodenstratigraphischer Vergleich zwischen dem Nordostbrazilianischen Treckengebeit und immerfeucht-tropischen Gebeiten Sudbraziliens mit Ausfurungen zum Problemkereis der Pediplain-Pediment-Terrassentreppen. *Catena*, Suppl. 2, 74-122.

Rossignol-Strick, M., Nesteroff, W., Olive, P. and Vergnaud-Grazzini, C. (1982). After the deluge: Mediterranean stagnation and sapropel formation. *Nature*, 295, 105-110.

Schubert, C. (1988). Climatic changes during the last glacial maximum in northern south America and the Caribbean: a review. *Interciencia*, 13, 128-137.

Soyer, J. (1989). Role des termites dans la formation du complexe de la stone-line. *Stone-Lines. Journee d'Etude, Bruxelles, 24 mar. 1987* (Ed by Alexandre J. & Symoens, J.J.) *Academic Royale des Sciences D' outre-Mer, Geo-Eco-Trop*, 11, 97-108.

Stocking, M.A. (1978). Interpretation of stone-lines. *The South African Geographical Journal,* 60, 121-134.

Stoops, G. (1989). Relict properties in soils of humid tropical regions with special reference to central Africa. *Paleopedology* (eds) A. Bronger & J.A. Catt. *Catena Supplement,* 16, 95-106.

Street, F.A. & Grove, A.T. (1979). Global maps of lake level fluctuations since 30000 BP. *Quaternary Research,* 12, 83-118.

Talbot, M.R., Livingstone, D.A., Palmer, P.G., Maley, J., Melack, J.M., Delibrias, G. & Gulliksen, S. (1984). Preliminary results from sediment cores from lake Bosumtwi, Ghana. *Palaeoecology of Africa,* 16, 173-192.

Thomas, M.F. (1983). Contemporary denudation systems and the effects of climatic change in the humid tropics - some problems from Sierra leone. *Studies in Quaternary Geomorphology* (ed. by D.J. Briggs & P.R. Waters), pp. 195-214. Geo Books, Norwich.

Thomas, M.F. (1986). Savanna. *Handbook of Engineering Geomorphology* (ed. by P.GH. Fookes & P.R. Vaughan), Surrey Univ. Press, Guildford, pp. 125-136.

Thomas, M.F. (1989). The role of etch processes in landform development I. Etching concepts and their applications. *Zeitschrift fur Geomorphologie N.F.*, 33, 129-142.

Thomas, M.F. & Goudie, A.S.(eds) (1985). Dambos: Small channelless valleys in the tropics. *Zeitschrift fur Geomorphologie, Supplementband,* 52, pp. 222.

Thomas, M.F. & Thorp, M.B. (1980). Some aspects of the geomorphological interpretation of Quaternary alluvial sediments in Sierra Leone. *Zeitschrift fur Geomorphologies, N.F., Suppl. -Bd.* 36, 140-161.

Thomas, M.F. & Thorp, M.B. (1985). Environmental change and episodic etchplanation in the humid tropics of Sierra Leone: the Koidu etchplain. *Environmental Change and Tropical Geomorphology* (Ed. I. Douglas & T. Spencer), Allen and Unwin, London, pp. 239-267.

Thomas, M.F. & Thorp, M.B. (1992). Landscape dynamics and surface deposits arising from late Quaternary fluctuations in the forest-savanna boundary. In P.A. Furley, J. Proctor & J.A. Ratter (eds.) *Nature and Dynamics of Forest-Savanna Boundaries,* Chapman & Hall, London, 215-253.

Thorp, M.B., Thomas, M.F., Martin, T. & Whalley, W.B. (1990). Late Pleistocene sedimentation and landform development in western Kalimanatan (Indonesian Borneo). *Geologie en Mijnbouw,* 69, 133-150.

Velbel, M.A. (1985). Geochemical mass balances and weathering rates in forested watersheds of the southern Blue Ridge. *American Journal of Science,* 285, 904-930.

Velbel, M.A. (1986). The mathematical basis for determining rates of geochemical and geomorphic processes in small forested watersheds by mass balance: examples and implications. *Rates of Chemical weathering of Rocks and Minerals* (ed. by Coleman S.M. & Dethier, D.P.), Academic Press, New York, pp. 431-451.

Watson, J.P. (1974). Termites in relation to soil formation, groundwater, and geochemical prospecting. *Soils & Fertilisers,* 37, 111-114.

Watson, A, Price-Williams, D. & Goudie, A.S. (1983). Palaeoenvironmental interpretation of colluvial sediments and palaeosols of the Late Pleistocene hypothermal in southern Africa. Palaeogeography, *Palaeoclimatology and Paleoecology,* 45, 225-250.

Whitlow, J.R. (1988). *Land degradation in Zimbabwe: A geographical study,* Natural Resources Board, Harare.

9

CONTRASTS IN THE DEVELOPMENT OF SIMILAR TROPICAL ENVIRONMENTS : Origins and Significance

W.T.W. Morgan

Why are lands in different parts of the world, but with closely comparable environments, used very differently by their inhabitants? A brief response could be: why not? Similar environments do not offer only one opportunity but a range of options. The question must therefore be rephrased to ask why in some places one option has been taken up and in another place an alternative? In attempting an answer we can hope first to learn something about the complexity of the human-land relationship and from this something of the origins and significance of cultures. For this we will compare Eastern Tanzania and Tamil Nadu in southern India. Secondly, and in a more practical way, we can consider the value of transferring one technique used in one region to another region with apparently similar or resource endowment, a process known by development practitioners as searching for the "best practice". We will briefly consider Nigeria and the North East of Brazil. Finally we can take an even wider view point and ask for one eco-type across the world, what differences do we see, how did they originate and where are they tending? For this audacious enterprise, we shall compare some of the uplands within the tropical zone (Fig. 9.1).

Tanzania and Tamil Nadu

At first sight, Eastern Tanzania and Tamilnad (Tamil Nadu) appear completely different worlds. It is only a closer and more objective examination that reveals that the original physical endowment of the two regions was closely comparable and the contrasts evident today derives from the different use made of the landscape over a long period of time. This has been detailed elsewhere (Morgan, 1988) so only the broad argument will be presented here.

The physiographic similarities of the two regions derive from similar geographical histories. As portions of the ancient land man of Gondwana land, they share landscape of peneplains cut across areas of crystalline. Precambrian rocks with much younger near-horizontal sedimentary strata towards their eastern, coastal, margins where major rivers have created discontinuous alluvial plains bordering their estuaries or deltas. Diversified by faulting, especially in Tanzania, the most common landscape features of both areas include inselbergs, rising from lateritic surfaces, patterned with shallow valleys (in Tanzania, "mbugas" or "vleis"). The two regions are on opposite sides of the equator across which sweep the great movements of pressure and air flow which bring a sequence of dry and wet seasons. The range of parallel ecological zones and niches is occupied, where untransformed by human interference, by similar vegetation types. The physiological similarity, with some shared genera, is obscured by differences in terminology but in the classification Dry Evergreen Forest, South Indian Dry Forest and Southern Thorn Forest, botanists of Tamilnad (Champion, 1936 and Pondichery, 1962-66) were describing natural vegetation similar to the Coastal Mosaic, the Miombo Woodland and the Deciduous Bushland and Thicket of Tanzania (White, 1983).

This similarity of the natural or *intrinsic* landscapes is not reflected in the achieved landscapes (Morgan, 1983 p. xix) we see today. Most of Tamilnad presents an intensively domesticated aspect with irrigated fields separated by heavily utilized interfluves with the indigenous vegetation largely eliminated and replaced by field crops and useful tree or palm species. If we were to look at a piece of identical topography in Tanzania, we would see a very different pattern with cultivation concentrated upon the more extensive rainfed agriculture between the largely undrained valleys with a much greater proportion of residual woodland or bush (Fig. 9.2). There are still extensive areas with few inhabitants, including game reserves. The population density of Tamilnad is around twenty times that of Eastern Tanzania and includes a closer network of towns and villages.

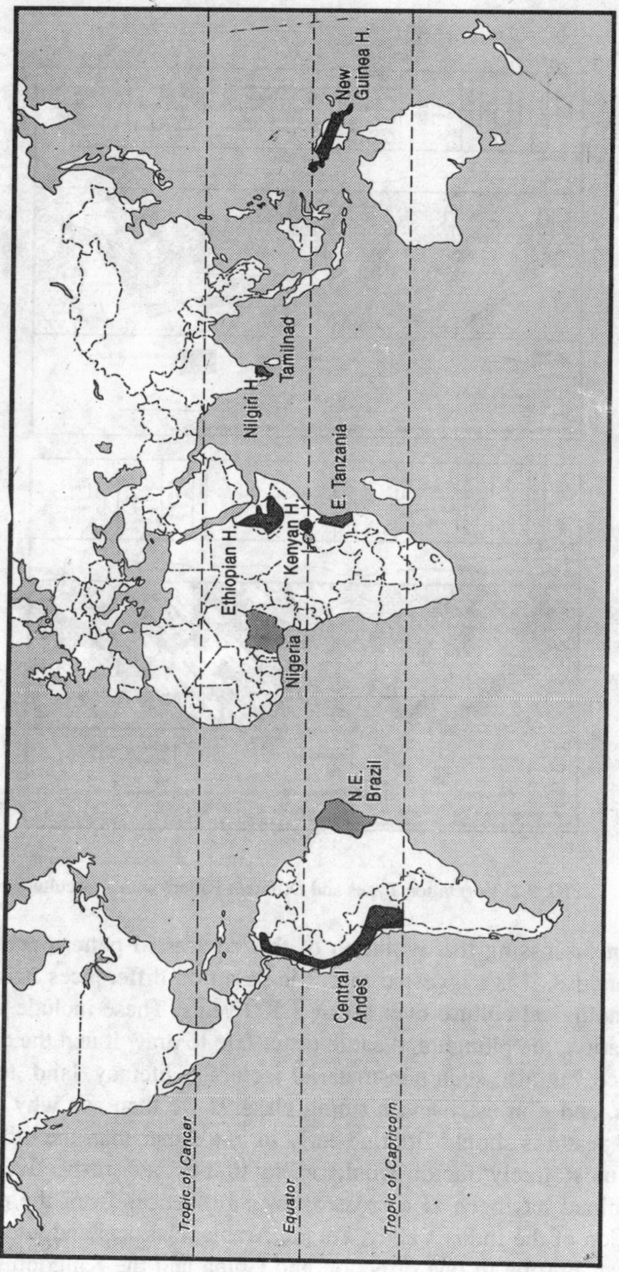

FIG. 9.1: Tropical Zones

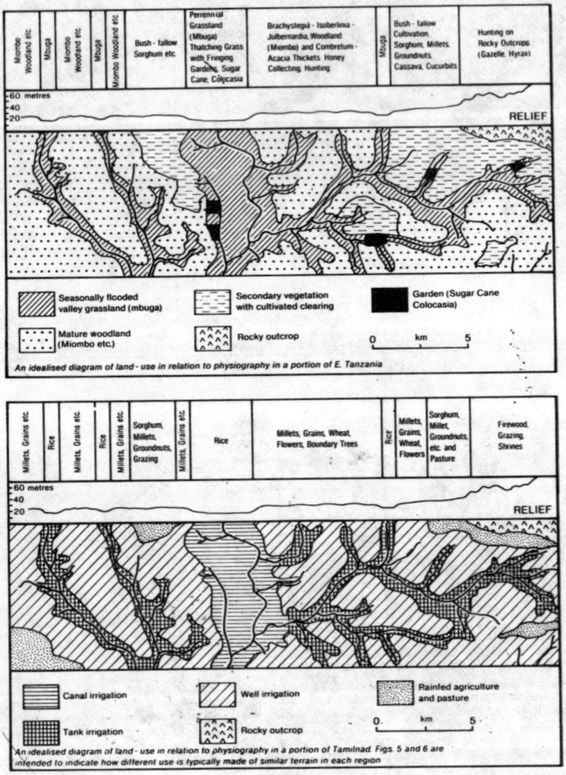

FIG. 9.2: Vegetation Types and Different Pattern with Agriculture

In discussing the evolution of this contrasted pattern and intensity of landuse, it is suggested that it is based on differences in social and technological culture over about 2,500 years. These include the use of irrigation, the plough and cattle or buffalo to draw it and the cultivation of rice, but also such non-material factors as literacy, land tenure systems, and a priestly and a ruling class. If we then ask why these cultural features should flourish early in one rather than the other region, the most likely factor would seem to be their respective location. Tamilnad has been at a crossroads of influences from the early civilization of the Indus Valley, Persia, Arabia, classical and later Mediterranean Europe in one direction and China and the Kingdoms of south east Asia on the other. A land link between these maritime route lay through the Palghat gap right across Tamilnad, marked by finds of ancient coins. By comparison, Eastern Tanzania was along a cul-de-sac beyond which lay only the wastes of the southern ocean and Antarctica. This was not changed until the arrival of Vasco da Gama put it on the sea-route between western Europe and India and the East in 1498.

With the opening of the Suez Canal in 1869, the significance of location was again modified but in recent years an equivalent factor has been the attitude of governments to external influences. Following periods of alien rule, both India and Tanzania were cautious of overseas commercial and other links but their value as avenues for innovation is receiving increasing recognition.

Nigeria and North East Brazil

If we take another pair of regions we find the comparison throws up a different range of contrasts for which alternative explanations must be sought and their significance will be different. We will now take Nigeria and the North East of Brazil (the Nordeste), selecting aspects of their differential development which raise questions relevant to present and future policies.[1]

Again we suggest that the physical environment of each region are sufficiently alike to make comparisons meaningful. In the geological past they were adjacent portions of Gondwana land and, balanced on either side of the equator they experience a tropical range of temperatures with average rainfall regimes varying between 2000mm received in ten months to 400mm mostly received within 4-5 months of the year. There are limited semi-montane areas over 1000m in both and each contains one particularly large river valley, of the Niger-Benue and the Rio São Francisco.

The impact of the west upon these two regions was the greatest factor leading to the present differences in the way in which the land is used. For nearly three centuries following the arrival of Portuguese ships along the Nigerian coast in 1472, European intervention was largely restricted to seaborne trade. On land the traffic in slaves and other commodities was in the hands of the indigenous people and it was not until the nineteenth century that European traders and missionaries began to penetrate the interior. Colonial administration extended slowly from Lagos in 1861 until the creation of Nigeria approximately within its present boundaries became effective by 1903, with independence arriving in 1960. Nigeria was not a colony of settlement and official policy was against the establishment of foreign-owned plantations. The consequence was that most changes following contact were by accretion rather than by replacement of endogenous systems of landuse which had been worked out over a thousand years or more. Indigenous Technical Knowledge (ITK) was retained. Events in Brazil were very different. From the Portuguese arrival in the Nordeste in 1535, Brazil was regarded as a colony to be settled with the land under direct management of the Europeans and as the local labour supply became inadequate, slaves from Africa, including Nigeria, were imported. Both management and labour were exogenous. The process was the one of replacement of the pre-existing system rather than an accretion and although indigenous crops such as maize and manioc were used, much ITK must have been lost or disregarded. The consequences of these different histories are seen in the differing agricultural system in use in comparable environments. We will identify some of these and ask whether such differences still have validity today or whether some practices could usefully be transplanted. These are put forward as possible fields for research rather than as conclusions.

The marked difference in the use made of the rain forest zone is largely related to the land tenure systems, derived from historical circumstances. Landholding in Nigeria is dominated by small scale proprietors often based on traditional rights of usage. In Brazil holdings tend to be bigger with a large proportion of the land held in units of 500 to 1000 hectares and over with more secure, tradeable, title by contract. This makes easier the holding of agricultural land for speculation which appears to be factor in land utilisation, a feature, much less common in Nigeria where it is more restricted to urban areas. Subsistence is a more prominent feature of cultivation among the peasant households of Nigeria and it is here that the preservation of ITK and the large number of crop types grown is significant. In south east Nigeria as many as 43 kinds of indigenous vegetables were identified in local markets (Epenhuijsen, 1974) in addition to a full range of exotics from Europe and South America. Although discouraged by the colonial government, foreign-owned plantations exist and although large scale plantings have increased since independence much of the commercial production (including cocoa and palm oil) for domestic or export markets derives from smallholders. This small scale multi-crop agriculture of the Nigerian forest zone is in sharp contrast to that in

Brazil. Large areas are held in estates producing sugarcane or cocoa serving local factories processing sugar, alcohol and chocolate. All the labour is hired and in recent years has mostly moved from labour-lines on the estates to the towns from where they travel for employment by the day("boya fria"). Reflecting these differences each region has its characteristic problems as well as favourable features. Nigeria might benefit by larger production units able to raise the capital needed for modern farming, sufficient acreage to justify mechanisation and specialisation developing new improved varieties and techniques and to achieve the lowered costs of bulk handling. Brazil might benefit from less dependence on one crop which has seen booms followed by slumps and profitability dependent not only on market forces but also potentially fickle political policies (e.g. the alcool programme). The welfare of landless labourers is not enviable under either system. Monoculture tends to be harder on the soil and is more dependent upon inputs.

Both countries use cattle to graze their savanna interiors and both solve the problem of seasonality of grazing and of cattle disease by moving herds between the dry and wet season. The difference in the method however is striking. In Nigeria large numbers of the distinctive white cattle are managed by the Fulani community by a system of normadic pastoralism. They own little or no land of their own but as the rains spread northwards they drive their herds in that direction to graze the fresh grass and forbs and avoid the seasonal outbreak of insect-borne diseases (especially from the tsetse fly) in the more moist south. As the dry season sets in, they migrate southwards to graze their cattle which eat the crop residues and manure the land of the sedentry Hausa and other farmers. With increasing intensification and sophistication of farming methods, this seasonal visitation is becoming less welcome to farmers and there is less fallow and water land for the pastoralists to use. The system is becoming outdated. In Brazil, same problem of seasonal change in the pattern of grazing occurs and is met by movement but it takes place within a system more dependent upon ownership of both wet and dry season grazing. Large scale ranches also own crop lands in the hills and the more rainy areas which are let out subject to rights to graze on the residues. Some fodder is also grown, notably the palma cactus and sown grasses are cultivated, especially in the São Francisco valley for use in the dry season and for fattening (Andrade, 1980). In facing up to their changing circumstances, the Fulani might benefit from a consideration of the Brazilian system.

Cultivating techniques in the Savanna of Nigeria and the Sertão of Brazil could also be compared. African sorghum has been introduced into the Açu valley of Rio Grande do Norte and there may be other, perhaps currently minor, crops which could be usefully transferred in either direction. Agro-forestry also has potential. Nigeria has traditionally made much use of farm trees with endemic species according to the ecology such as the Shea Butter tree (*Butyrospermum paradoxum*), the Locust Bean tree (*Parkia clappertoniana*), *Acacia albida* and others. Colonial officers were enthusiastic in spreading useful introductions including the mango, citrus and for firewood or shade, neem (*Azadirachta indica*) and Eucalyptus spp. The exotics, but not the African indigenous trees, are also found in Brazil and the local Carnauba palm is valued for its wax. The value of *Prosopis juliflora* (algaroba) is being tested in the Nordeste and the evidence could be relevant to Nigeria. Both regions make special use of the moist riverine lands (fadama in Nigeria, vazante in Brazil) and for these, a comparison of the systems used could be extended to consider the tank cultivation of similar sites in southern India.

Tropical Uplands

In a broader perspective, it is particularly instructive to observe differences and similarities in the use of the various upland areas within the tropics. Empirical observation points towards a zone of distinctive landuse between the altitudes of approximately 1500m and 3000m. These altitudes are significant in the application of the long established, frequently criticized, but continuingly useful climatic classification of V.P. Köppen (Trewartha, 1954). His boundary between the tropical and the warm temperate climates (A and C) is defined by a coolest month with the mean temperature below 18°C. Because of the reduction of temperature with altitude, this is found at about 1500m at the equator. The boundary of the polar tundra climate (ET) is given as a warmest month of 10°C which, flowing the same calculation, occurs at 2800m. Köppen's boundaries were based on selecting values that would correspond as closely as possible to categories of vegetation, so the biological relevance of these boundaries is not surprising. It is at about 1500m and above that forests tend to be classified as "montane" in Africa including *Podocarpus* and *Juniperus* spp. By 3000m a distinctive flora, often described as "Afro-Alpine", begins to appear marked by giant forms of *Lobelia* and *Seneccio.* The same tendency to giantism at high altitudes is found in other continents, but involving completely different genera, providing a striking visual indicator of similar environmental factors at work. The cool temperatures and the occurrence of related species suggests the label of "Afro-Alpine" but the intra-tropical similarities of montane climate and vegetation are greater than those with the middle latitudes such that this ecological zone would be better described by the South American term "paramos". The major climatic singularity is the much larger diurnal than seasonal range in temperature. The abrupt drop in temperature at sunset brings "summer every day and winter every night".

For human settlement, the paramos tend to be marginal marsh land beyond the limit for many crops and largely limited to unimproved grazing. The lower zone, to 1500m, is a much more favourable human habitat. The seasonal range is reduced so that "winter never comes" but temperatures remain high enough for strong plant growth throughout the year. Relief-induced rainfall and reduced evapo-transpiration means that humidity is unlikely to be too low. With increasing altitude some tropical crops drop out but others, including some from temperate latitudes, enter. The incidence of tropical pests and diseases, notably malaria and bilharzia is greatly reduced.

The climatic type outlined above endows upland regions across the tropical zone with sufficient comparability that the observed differences in their landuse raises questions of their origins and significance. In considering these we shall refer to the upland regions of the Central Andes, Ethiopia, Kenya, New Guinea and the Nilgiri Highlands of southern India. (Fig. 9.1). Their distinctive utilisation developed over the long period before their inhabitants were aware of each other following the explorations of the fifteenth and sixteenth centuries which led to "the closing of the ecumene". It was during this time that scale and degree of isolation were dominating factors.

Early Development

The Central Andes is the largest of these tropical uplands extending some 4500km from Venezuela to the tropic of Capricorn in northern Chile, beyond which the southern Andes continues uninterrupted, deep into the southern temperate zone. To the north the highland connection is less complete but the biological and cultural link appears to have been equally or even more important. Here developed a fully fledged agricultural system and societies with a range of adoptions to the tropical upland environment. The most important cultigens were the root crops: potato, ulloca and others, with which were developed the freeze-dried method of storage and, in some cases, improvement (chũno). The meat of domestic and wild animals and birds was also freeze-dried ("charqui"), making use of the diurnal temperature range. Llamas and alpacas were the livestock developed suited to the altitude but where animal manure was not developed, long fallows and the use of nitrogen-fixing lupins maintained soil fertility. These pre-Columbian cultures were largely coterminous with the highlands, being replaced by others at lower altitudes. Within their highlands they made use of the potential of different attitudes by grouping several ecological belts in one administrative unit, with exchange of products and seasonal movements of labour in a system described as the "control of verticality" (Murra, 1975).

The Ethiopian highlands are another very extensive area of uplands within the tropics of some 1500 km by 1000 km. They have no continuous altitudinal link with the temperate zone but biological and cultural links are evident. There is an important indigenous cultigen in teff (*Eragrostis abyssinica*) but Ethiopia is also within the zone of ancient Middle Eastern cereal cultivation growing barley, wheat and finger millet at appropriate altitudes and using the plough, absent from pre-Columbian South America. Other more or less localised crops included the narcotic, Chat (*Catha edulis*), coffee and, at lower altitudes, ensete (*Ensete edule*). There are no domesticated endemic livestock species but horses, donkeys and cattle are long established and the combination of endemic crops and of crops and livestock derived from middle latitudes, provided Ethiopia with a broad assemblage of domesticated plants and animals suited to a range of altitudes. Perhaps the best known consequence of the link with the Middle East is the early establishment of Christianity with its survival, despite attempts at conversion by Islamic forces, assisted by its highland location (Pankhurst, 1961).

In contrast to Ethiopia, the Kenya highlands are smaller (450 km × 350 km) and more isolated. They appear to have originated no crops or livestock adapted to higher altitudes and not to have gained any from elsewhere. Neither teff from Ethiopia nor "hungry rice" (*Digitaria exilis*) from West Africa penetrated this far. Instead, tropical crops such as sorghum, millet and yams were grown at altitudes up to a point where the returns were not worth the effort with higher levels being used for seasonal grazing during the dry season or when there were droughts at lower altitudes. Settlement at high altitudes was a sparse and although remains exist to attract archaeological investigation, there were no cultures comparable with Axum and subsequent kingdom of Ethiopia or the Incas and their predecessors in the Andes (Morgan, 1973).

The narrow cordillera of New Guinea (Papua New Guinea with Irian Barat) extends over 2300 km but its inhabitants appear to have been as equally isolated from contacts with temperate or other highland areas as the Kenya highlands. Again the tropical suited of food crops was grown towards the upper limit of their viability (sago, bananas, taro) but some indigenous domestication, of a root crop and the nuts of *Pandanus* seems also to have taken place (Brookfield, 1989).

The previous examples of tropical uplands have all been large enough to develop at least a partially self-contained socio-economic system or systems. The Nilgiri hills are representative of a class of much smaller uplands whose significance is in large measure due to their difference from their surroundings and their relationship with them. They are only 12,500 km² in extent and remained unvisited by the British administration until 1812 although there are records from a visit by Father Jacomo Finicio in 1603. The handful of indigenous inhabitants appear to have occupied separate niches as hunter gatherers, slash and burn cultivators and buffalo-keeping pastoralists, the polyandrous habits of the latter sharply distinguishing them from the Hindu culture of the lowlands and emphasising the isolation and refuge nature of the highlands. Further refugee agriculturalists arrived from Mysore during the *c.* 12 to 16th centuries. Small as they are, the Nilgiris are at a biogeographic cross-roads sustaining *Rhododendron* and *Pieris* spp. typical of the Himalayas and a giant *Lobelia sp.* characteristic of the tropical 'afro-alpine' flora (von Lengerke, 1984).

In reviewing the use made of these tropical uplands before "the closing of the ecumene" we can see a sort of balance between the influence of scale and of accessibility. Ethiopia had a large area and population within which to develop an indigenous basic food crop (teff) suited to its distinctive ecology but it was also accessible to the technological culture of the Middle East so the crop was a cereal cultivated with a plough. Non-indigenous crops (barley, wheat) were also imported from the middle latitudes. The central Andes were even more extensive and also developed indigenous crops (potatoes, etc. and the extension of the cordillera gave it access to maize from the presumed Mexican hearth. The Kenya highlands are smaller than both but the absence of an indigenous high-altitude crop probably has more to do with lack of contact with other highlands or temperate lands. The role of population pressure in the history of these three highlands must remain pure speculation in the absence of evidence. New Guinea has a very long, although narrow, belt of central highland. Indigenous species appear to have been used but not to the extent of a basic foodstuff. Although the area involved is so large in total, its mountainous nature makes communication between populations relatively restricted compared to the Andes or in Ethiopia as demonstrated by the great number of individual language. Isolation from both without, and between valleys within, the mountain mass would appear to have been a major influence upon culture. By comparison, using the Nilgiris as one example among many, small isolated uplands, if they are inhabited at all, owe any distinctiveness in landuse and culture to a role as a refuge.

In drawing attention to these features of scale and accessibility, there is an obvious comparison with the commonly used metaphor of isolated highland masses as "islands" bearing a distinctive ecology among a sea of a more extensive type (MacArthur, 1967). Biogeographers do refer to the size and extent of isolation of oceanic islands as influences upon the number of species and the presence of endemics but the cultural component, as well as the limited sample size, make any comparison with human geography inappropriate.

Modern Developments

For the long period while the tropical uplands were exploited by communities isolated from each other, it is appropriate to consider their development separately. Once exchange between them had become possible, we can treat them as a group subject to a number of common influences and we can compare the consequences.

The most appropriate exchange has been the translocation of crops between the similar ecosystems, between the uplands themselves. This might be described as the adoption of the "best practice". From the Andes, the potato and the sweet potato have spread widely into the upper and the lower zones respectively of tropical uplands. In New Guinea the sweet potato (*Ipomea batatas*) has become the staple diet of the highlands, its introduction apparently dating from after the arrival of Portuguese at the coast but before the inland penetration by Europeans. Arabica coffee has similarly spread widely from Ethiopia and Yemen but *Chinchona*, or "Peruvian bark" had a more limited introduction into the Nilgiris as a government measure to provide a treatment for Malaria in India. Tea might be described as subtropical rather than tropical in origin but it is now largely associated with tropical uplands. Among the Columbian exchange, which has been so important, it is striking that no livestock were involved, the Llama and other camelids have not spread.

The middle latitude "temperate" zone is less precisely comparable with the climate of the tropical uplands but it has provided a much larger range of crops and livestock which have been adopted for use in the tropical upland. Barley was long established in Ethiopia but has spread further as also have wheat and even oats. A wide range of green and root vegetables are now widespread of which cabbage and carrot seem frequently to have become an essential component of modern urban diet. Pyrethrum from the Balkans has become a specialist product of tropical high altitudes. Temperate trees have been a most useful introduction. The Australian *Eucalyptus* spp. have dispersed within both lowland and upland tropics according to species and provenance but their contribution for firewood in the cool uplands has been particularly valued. Their introduction to Ethiopia in the late 19th century is reputed to have enabled Addis Ababa to become established as the capital. For constructional timber and pulp wood such conifers as *Pinus, Cupressus*, and *Araucaria* are grown in plantations. European livestock have been particularly successful in tropical uplands including European breeds of cattle and sheep. They can have entered by a circuitous route as with corriedale sheep from Australia into the Kenya Highlands.

The importance of introductions from the northern temperate zone can be cited as another example of the impact of the European colonial powers. The episode of the so called 'White Highlands' policy in Kenya is a classic instance of the comprehensive translocation of a temperate system of technology, economy and society into a tropical upland (Morgan, 1963, 1968). The altitude of five thousand feet became of critical, political and landuse significance.[2] Some of the first introductions, however, were before the establishment of territorial control and were the result of trade or a spontaneous migration among a subsistence peasantry. The question remains, over translocations both from the temperate zone and between tropical uplands, whether sufficient work has been done to adapt the crop to its new setting and whether there are other underutilised species, or varieties which could be introduced or improved with profit.

Since tropical uplands are growing crops not easily grown in the surrounding lowlands, servicing this local market has become of major importance. The towns and irrigation settlements of the arid coastal plain of Peru are a market for Andean farmers and the Kenya highlands has a large market in the tourist resorts of the coast and gameparks, the holiday industry benefiting from the local availability of vegetables and dairy product familiar to its European clientele. Small areas of upland are well placed in relation to their proportionately larger adjacent lowlands and temperate vegetables from the Nilgiris or the Cameron Highlands (Malaya) or Bandung (Java) find a ready market. Since most of the Ethiopian population is in the highlands, the lowland market is less significant and to some extent this true of New Guinea.

Another very important service to their encircling lowlands has been the furtherance of health, comfort and leisure in the form of the traditional hill station. These are thought of as having had a hey-day during the colonial period when they provided refuge from heat, monsoons and tropical diseases for administrators, traders, missionaries and their families when evacuation to Europe was costly, slow, impractical and often too late. In fact, their attraction is not confined to alien communities and many continue to thrive with hotels, holiday cottage and as places for retirement. The popularity of hill stations such as Ootacamund in the Nilgiris threatens to spoil the very ambience which has attracted an excess of population.

With improvements in transport, tropical uplands have been able to extend their operations further and supply fresh temperate produce to the middle latitudes during their winter, competitive with greenhouse production but with the warmth provided for free by nature. An early example was Kenya where colonial settlers made use of a temporary glut of air cargo capacity in Britannia turbo-prop aircraft following are typical exports.

Future Problems

Tropical uplands today often appear as more favourably endowed parts of the tropics, supporting concentrations of population and enterprise. Some of the relative advantages, however, could diminish in the near future. With the increasing scale and reduction in costs of air transport, suppliers of the winter markets of the north hemisphere could begin to face competition from large agricultural exporters from south of the Equator where Chile and South Africa are already active. The hill station is no longer resorted to for health reasons since curative drugs, prophylaxis and environmental management provide a cheaper, quicker and morer reliable alternative. Together with air conditioning, these factors have changed the relative advantages of upland and lowland. It is a part of a general re-assessment of the value of the lowland tropics as a producing system and as a place to live healthily and comfortably. In contrast, there are reported indications of reductions in settlement at the very highest altitudes in the Andes and Papua New Guinea.

NOTES

1. Nigeria : 924,000 sq km. population (1992) 88.5 million, density 96 p.sq. km ., Nordeste: 1,549,000 sq. km., population estimate 40 million, density 26 p.sq. km. The Nordeste includes the states of Maranhão, Piaui, Ceará, Rio Grande de Norte, Paraiba, Pernambuso, Alagoas and Bahia.
2. "In Kenya the climatic conditions which have in the past generally been regarded as favourable to European settlement have usually been encountered at about 5,000 feet and upwards." Report of the Kenya Land Commission. Nairobi, 1933, para. 1951. See also: Morgan, W.T.W. 'The White Highlands' of Kenya," *Geographical Journal*, 129 (1963), pp.140-155.

REFERENCES

American Anthropologist (1964). Vol. 66, Special pub. No. 4, part 2, New Guinea, the Central Highlands.

Andrade, M.C. de (1980). *The land and people of north east Brazil.* Albuquerque : University of New Mexico Press.

Australia, Commonwealth Scientific and Industrial Research Organization, Canberra (1975). *Land Research Series* no. 15, Lands of the Arabag-Tari Area, Papua New Guinea.

——— (1970). *Land Research Series* no. 27, Lands of the Goroka-Mount Hagen Area, Papua New Guinea.

Brookfield, H., (1989). Frost and drought through time and space III: what were conditions like when the high valleys were first settled? *Mountain Research and Development,* 9.3., 306-321. (Special number on New Guinea).

Brookfield, H. and Allen, B. (1989). High altitude occupation and environment. *Mountain Research and Development*, 9.3. 201-209. (Special number on New Guinea).

Brush, S.B. (1982). The natural and human environment of the central Andes. *Mountain Research and Development*, 2.1. 19-38.

Dollfus, O. (1982). Development of land-use patterns in the central Andes. *Mountain Research and Development*, 2.1. 39-48.

Epenhuijsen, C.W. van (1974). *Growing nature vegetables in Nigeria.* Rome : FAO

Folke, Steen, (1966). Evolution of plantations, migration and population growth in Nilgiris and Coorg (South India) *Geografisk Tidsskrift* 65.2, 198-239.

Mabogunje, A.L. and Gleave, M.B. (1964). Changing agricultural landscape in southern Nigeria — the example of Egba Division, 1850-1950. *Nigerian Geographical Journal*, 7, 1-15.

MacArthur, R.H. and Wilson, E.O. (1967). *The theory of island biogeography*, Princeton University Press.

Mitchell, N. (1922). The Indian hill station: Kodaikanal, *University Chicago Dept. Geography Research Paper* no. 141.

Morgan, W.T.W. (1963). The 'White Highlands of Kenya. *Geographical Journal* 129, 140-155.

Morgan, W.T.W. (1968). The role of temperate crops in the Kenya Highlands. *Acta Geographica* 20, 273-278.

Morgan, W.T.W. (1973). *East Africa.* Harlow : Longman.

Morgan, W.T.W. (1977). Altitude and crop zones : A transect in the Kenya Highlands. *Die Erde*, 108, 124-128.

Morgan, W.T.W. 1983. *Nigeria*, Harlow, Longman.

Morgan, W.T.W. (1988). Tamilnad and Eastern Tanzania : Comparative regional geography and the historical development process. *Geographical Journal* 154, 69-86.

Mountain Research and Development (1988). Special numbers on African mountains and highlands vol. 8 nos. 2, 3 and 4.

Murra, J.V. (1956). *The Economic Organization of the Inca State,* Ph.D. Dissertation, University of Chicago, Chicago, U.S.A.

Murra, J.V. (1975). *Formaciones economicas y politicas del mundo andino*, Lima: Instituto de Estudios Peruanos.

Noble, W.A. (1971). Settlement patterns and migrations among Nilgiri herders, south India. *J. Tropical Geography*, 33, 57-70.

Pankhurst, R. (1961). *An Introduction to the Economic History of Ethiopia from early times to 1800*. London: Sidgwick and Jackson.

Pullan, R.A. (1974). Farmed parkland in West Africa. *Savanna*, 3, 119-51.

Sillitoe, P. (1983). *Roots of the Earth: crops in the highlands of Papua New Guinea.* Manchester: University Press.

Spencer, J.E. and Thomas, W.L. (1948). Hill stations and summer resorts of the orient. *Geographical Review* 38, 637-651.

Taylor, K.S. (1978). *Sugar and the Underdevelopment of Northeastern Brazil.* Gainsville : University of Florida Press.

Trewortha, G.T. (1954). *An Introduction to Climate*, 3rd ed. McGraw Hill, Appendix A.

Udo, R.K. (1970). *Geographical Regions of Nigeria*. London : Heinemann.

von Lengerke, Hans J. (1984). Mountain settlement and development in south India: environmental perception and change. *Applied Geography and Development* vol. 23, 79-93

Waddell, E. (1972). The Mound Builders: Agricultural practices, environment and society in the central highlands of New Guinea. *American Ethnological Society Monograph* 53, Seattle: U. Washington press.

White, F. (1983). *The Vegetation of Africa*. Paris : UNESCO.

Williams, D. (1962). Clement Robert Markham and the introduction of the chinchona tree into British India. *Geographical Journal* 128. 431-42.

10

THE STATE AND THE ECOLOGY MANAGEMENT THROUGH THE PEOPLE:

Some Lessons from the Sukhomajri Experience

GOPAL KRISHAN and MEHAR SINGH

The development-ecology debate is raging. It started with a concern for the damage to ecology that modern development has caused. Eco-fundamentalists insist on moderating the pace of development. Increasing human demands are seen as damaging the natural resource base-land, water and air, upon which all life depends (United Nations Population Fund, 1988).

There was a natural reaction from the developmentalists. They pointed out that development alone builds a capacity for improving the quality of ecology. Hence the development process is not to be halted in the interest of both economy and ecology.

A golden mean between the two extreme positions is represented by the concept of sustainable development. Its basic message is that the wheel of development must move on but it should advance within the supportive capacity of the ecosystem. The present needs are to be met without compromising the ability of future generations to meet theirs (World Commission on Environment and Development, 1987).

The World Development Report, 1992 stresses that any policy package must aim an accelerated development and better environmental management. It believes that sound environmental policies complement and reinforce development in the long run. These are rated as of special value to the poor who are the direct victim of any ecological damage.

It is observed that some ecological problems decline as the

development process proceeds. This refers to public health and sanitation in particular. Some problems initially worsen but then take a turn for the better. A phase of scientific afforestation may follow an earlier one of deforestation. Some problems may regularly aggravate with development. Air pollution caused by emission from cars, thermal plants and industry, is one such case. Obviously, the development-ecology compound is just not one single commodity.

Indeed the basic issue is not of containing development to save ecology but of managing ecology to promote development. So far a distorted view has prevailed which led to an anti-development bias. The truth is that 'what is good for development is equally good for ecology'.

This viewpoint deserves some elaboration. Any desired development must have the ingredients of efficiency, equity and democracy. Efficiency stands for an optimal utilization of resources, including their conservation. Equity takes care of the disadvantaged which is possible when the production base of the poor is protected. Democracy, in an operational sense, involves people in the development process at the grass-roots level. And when this is done, the people tend to take ecology-friendly decisions.

We intend to test the validity of these ideas through a case study of the Sukhomajri project. The experiment has earned a worldwide acclaim as a success in economic transformation through ecology management. Our purpose is not to join the eulogy chorus but to have a rather critical evaluation of the exercise. This is done by way of raising some basic issues in respect of dynamic sustainability, necessary transmutability, financial viability and spatial replicability of such projects. A comparative assessment of the government's role and peoples' involvement is also made. Some meaningful morals have been drawn from the story. But let us first see what the whole thing was about.

The Sukhomajri Project

Hardly two decades ago, Sukhomajri was a little known, ecologically degraded small village at the foot of Siwalik hills (Map 10.1). It found a location at a crow flight distance of hardly 15 kms to the northeast of Chandigarh. Its inhabitants were traditionally graziers, Gujjars by caste. Most families additionally had small landholdings, less than two hectares each, on which they carried rainfed subsistence agriculture in maize, wheat and pulses.

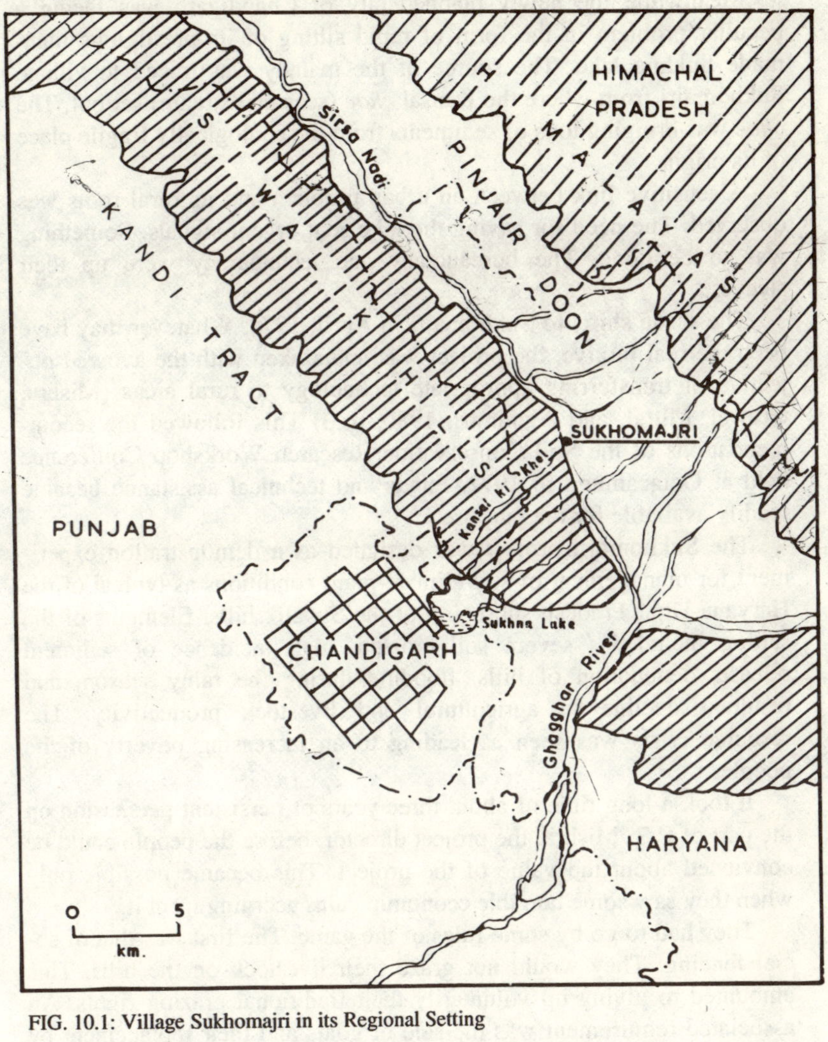

FIG. 10.1: Village Sukhomajri in its Regional Setting

A gradual increase in population impelled an extension of the cultivated land to hill slopes. Grazing was also spread to any available pasture nearby. The water retention capacity of the land was getting reduced, soil cover was getting eroded, and overall ecology was getting degraded. The village was finding it difficult to support a population of just 455 with 411 heads of livestock in mid-seventies.

Meanwhile the newly planned city of Chandigarh was facing a peculiar problem in the form of rapid silting of its prestigious man-made Sukhna lake. The source of the malady was traced to village Sukhomajri from where the Kansal *choe* (seasonal stream) set out. The *choe* was bringing tons of sediments from the ecologically fragile place of its origin.

A sensitive link between an urban problem and its rural roots was observed. The need for saving the lake sent urgent signals. Something was to be done. The bureaucracy and technocracy were up their sleeves.

The scene shifts to Sukhomajri in April, 1975. Whatever may have been the real motive, the project was undertaken with the avowed objective of transferring appropriate technology to rural areas (Mishra, Grewal, Mittal, and Agnihotri, 1980, p. 3) This followed the recommendations of the Soil Conservation Research Workshop Conference held at Ootacamund in 1972. Funds and technical assistance became readily available for the purpose.

The Sukhomajri project was designed as a demonstration experiment for management of soil-climate-plant conditions as typical of the Haryana-Uttar Pradesh subregion of the Siwalik hills. Elements of the setting included : severe soil erosion, high incidence of sediment release, denudation of hills, flooding during the rainy season, and resultant decline in agricultural and livestock productivity. The resource crisis was seen as leading to an increasing poverty of the people.

It took a long time of about three years of persistent persuasion on the part of P.R. Mishra, the project director, before the people could be convinced about the value of the project. This became possible only when they saw some tangible economic gains accruing from it.

They had to go by some rules of the game. The first was that of social fencing. They would not graze their livestock on the hills. This amounted to giving up voluntarily their traditional grazing rights. An associated requirement was the sale of goats and their replacement by cattle. The former were seen as doing a serious damage to the hills by way of causing extensive erosion. Eventually there was more natural grass in pastures and more fodder in irrigated fields. Cattle could be raised in a large number. Milk was produced on a grand commercial scale.

The second rule of the game followed the tenet of equity. A major component of the project was the construction of three dams across the local seasonal streams to harvest the rain water. This was meant to provide an irrigation base to the village's agriculture and thereby raise its productivity. A problem arose in respect of distribution of water. There was eventually a consensus in favour of its equitable distribution to every family, whether or not it owned agricultural land. Landless families could sell their share of water to others. Water was, thus, distributed amongst people and not on agricultural land directly.

There was a third rule of the game too. It laid down that all welfare activities of the village will be carried out through the 'local society'. In particular, the government decided to contract out the sale of the natural grass here to villagers rather than to outsiders. The benefit was made available only to a formally constituted 'local society' and not to any individual. The profit accruing from the sale of the grass was to be spent on the village as a whole. The villagers readily agreed to this.

Meanwhile regular assistance was provided not only by the Forest Department of Haryana but also by the Central Soil and Water Conservation Research and Training Institute, Chandigarh, the Ford Foundation, and some Chandigarh-based social activists. Much came in by way of advice, technical support and funding. The estimated financial input was to the tune of Rs. 10,000 per hectare of land.

The dividends were rich. Major among these were as follows :

(i) Milk production increased ninefold during the nine year period of 1978-87;
(ii) Average crop yields were enhanced by four to five times;
(iii) All houses were transformed from their previous *kutcha* state to *pucca*;
(iv) The sediment flow was reduced to one over-fifteenth of its previous level;
(v) A large fund became available with the local society for undertaking a variety of development activities; and
(vi) Above all, people learnt the art of managing ecology on cooperative basis.

In brief, the village was metamorphosed from a state of *sukha majri* (dry village) to *sukho majri* (prosperous village). Notably the various agencies involved described the project in different ways. The govenment initially started it as a 'technology transfer' scheme. The technical personnel looked at it as a 'watershed development for sediment, drought and flood control' operation. The International Institute of

Environment and Development titled it as 'social security through social fencing'. The local village society chose to change its name from the original 'soil and water conservation society' to 'hill resource management society'. This was perhaps the most appropriate.

A Critical Appraisal

The Sukhomajri project is popularly described as a success story. It took off primarily because the members of the implementing agency from the government side were highly committed. People could be motivated for a collective action because they visualised direct economic gains accruing within short time. Things were kept in momentum because consistent institutional, technical and financial support was made available by both government and international agencies.

But there is the other side of the picture too. Let us examine it point by point.

First, the primary purpose of the project was to check silting of the Sukhna Lake at Chandigarh. This was largely achieved. The measures included construction of check dams, plantation of trees, and stabilisation of slopes through trenching along contours. But efforts at controlling the headward extension of gullies on to the agricultural land were not that effective. The problem persists in the upper western part of the village.

Secondly, the main component of the project was the building of three reservoirs through harvesting of rain water for irrigation. But then the available water was far too inadequate. It could not serve even a half of the cultivated land. The task of supplementing irrigation through tubewells was not taken up by the government. This job was left to private initiative.

Thirdly, an important aspect of the project was the provision of fodder grass on a big scale. This helped raising of diary cattle in a large number. Production of milk got a boost. Sale of milk brought in money for the people. Again no arrangement was made for procurement and marketing of milk on organised lines. People are selling their milk to local vendors at a rate which is just two-thirds of what they could get if the middle men were dispensed with.

Fourthly, while a conscious attempt was made to sustain the project through the activities of the 'village society' yet few plans existed for its transmutability. The thrust remained on irrigated agriculture and milch cattle raising. It was not much realised that the capacity of the village even for these two sectors was limited. Several persons had to look for any available job in nearly urban places, such as Pinjore, Kalka, Surajpur and Chandigarh. It was desirable to make new beginnings in pomiculture, poultry and milk processing for which a great scope exists. Likewise, installation of *gobar gas* plants could have saved precious manure from being used as fuel.

Fifthly, there was a peculiar fall out of this ecology preservation project. The newly planted forest, the natural grass and the water reservoirs provided an ideal locale for wild life, including deer, boars and blue bulls. They became a menace for the crops grown. Night time vigil has become necessary for the villagers. Despite all this, frequent crop losses are reported.

Finally, enthused by the Sukhomajri success, the experiment was extended to some one hundred odd villages. Many of the newly covered villages are large in population size, multi-caste in demographic composition and diverse in occupational background with conflicting interests. There are serious constraints in bringing the people on a common platform. Economic cost involved is also heavy. The task is proving formidable. No wonder that hardly 20 per cent of such villages have made some beginning in this direction (Dhar, Gupta and Sarin, 1989, p. 7).

Morals of the Story

Here we propose to draw the most salient inferences from the context, conceptualization and methodology of a fairly successful experiment in micro-level management of ecology for development. First, it is evident that the degradation of environment can be caused at times by the local people, as was the case with Sukhomajri, and often by outsiders with a commercial motive, as has been the case with most of the deforestation on the Siwalik hills. An intervention by the government is essential in both situations but with differing styles. At the local level, the efforts should be in the form of a well conceived project; at the regional level, the thrust should be on policies which are protective and promotive of ecology.

Secondly, the local people will extend their cooperation to a project only when they see some tangible economic gain which is not only quick in its realisation but also equitable in its distribution. As economic returns often take time to materialise, financial support by way of government funding becomes essential.

Thirdly, the micro-level projects, like the Sukhomajri, have limited diffusion effect without government intervention and financial support. Hardly any neighbouring village picked up a similar project on its own. It was left to the government to undertake such projects at other places.

Fourthly, the indirect influence of these projects, however, cannot be underestimated. This may occur in three ways : (i) the people may be sensitised to approach the government for covering their villages also; (ii) the government may be tempted to extend its activities to many more villages, if necessary cooperation of the local people is forthcoming; and (iii) the government may design comprehensive watershed management projects at the regional level on the basis of experience gained from projects like Sukhomajri. The Kandi Area Development Project in the neighbouring state of Punjab can be cited as an illustration. Macro-level ecology projects should normally be preferred to the micro-level ones for reasons of greater financial viability.

Fifthly, the present case study emphatically brings out the role of the government even for ensuring peoples' participation in local projects. This does not conform to the current thinking which recommends that government should perform only a supporting role by way of being a facilitator and enabler. The ground reality in Sukhomajri was that the activities of the project virtually came to a halt whenever the government withdraw its active attention. In developing countries, the people look to the government not only as a provider of advice, technical assistance and funds but also as a resolver of their local conflicts. As an agency whose power is duly acknowledged, it is seen as more objective than the rival parties in a given situation.

Finally, many of the inadequacies of the project would have been taken care of if it had been visualised as a comprehensive village development project. In its present form, it remained a water and soil management project and became the sole responsibility of the Forest Department. The need was for involving other government departments also. A punch lesson emerges here. The government should not merely seek the cooperation and participation of the people but also ensure the coordination in functioning of its own various departments. Indeed projects like Sukhomajri require new kinds of institutional arrangements to replicate themselves on to new locations (Dhar and Sarin, 1987, p. 30).

REFERENCES

Dhar, S.K., J.R. Gupta and Madhu Sarin (1989). *Sustainable Forest Management,* Ford Foundation, New Delhi.

Mishra, P.R., S.S. Grewal, S.P. Mittal and Y. Agnihotri (1980). *Operational Research Project on Watershed Development for Sediment, Drought and Flood Control* : Sukhomajri, Central Soil and Water Conservation Research and Training Institute, Chandigarh.

Mishra, P.R. and Madhu Sarin (1987). *Social Security through Social Fencing,* International Institute of Environment and Development, London.

United Nations Population Fund (1988). *The State of World Population*, New York.

World Bank (1992). *World Development Report : Development and Environment,* Oxford University Press, Oxford.

World Commission on Environment and Development (1987). *Our Common Future,* Oxford University Press, Oxford.

PART-IV

RIVER BASIN/VALLEY AND ENVIRONMENT

11

THE KOYNA CATCHMENT :
The Environmental Problems Due to Displacement and Rehabilitation

K. SITA, V.S. PHADKE and K.V.S. RAO

Introduction

Dams and their associated reservoirs which represent large infrastructural investments naturally cause changes in the pre-existing environment, physical as well as human. Some of the consequential impacts are positive while others are negative (Dixon et al. 1989; Goodland, 1985). The most important economic benefits are their role in providing assured water and power-supply as well as ensuring flood control. Hence, dams such as Hirakud, Bhakra etc. were considered to be symbols of economic progress and were hailed as "the Temples of Modern India".

However, there is growing concern about the cost of dams in terms of their indirect environmental and social effects which had not been adequately taken into account in Environmental Impact Assessment in the early years (Bandyopadhyay, 1990; Dogra, 1990). Inundation of upstream areas and consequent displacement of people, rehabilitation of persons in marginal lands, siltation of dams, danger of seismicity and absence of good water management practices in command areas are some of the problems that have been highlighted in numerous studies. The increasing awareness of ecological factors has resulted in differences of opinion between development technologists and environmentalists.

A part of the dissatisfaction also stems from the fact that big dams have extracted a heavy price from the persons who have been displaced by the dam and who have therefore developed a deep sense of alienation from the mainstream development process. There is an increasing awareness regarding the unequal sharing of costs and benefits, socially and spatially (Amte, 1990; Singh, 1990). Hence the objections to large dams are partly on grounds of social justice, equity and right of access to national resources (Pant and Dharmadhikari, 1989). Some people take the extreme view that all large dams are bad.

A more balanced approach is that decisions should be based on merits of individual cases rather than simply criticizing big dams per se. Each watershed has to be studied in the context of its specific characteristics to evolve the most appropriate planning programmes. The present paper, relating to the Koyna Catchment, focuses on the environmental problems that have come to the fore due to the displacement and subsequent rehabilitation of persons as a consequence of the Koyna Project; it is based on a research project sponsored by the Ministry of Environment and Forests, Government of India. The duration of the project was from December 1987 to March 1991.

Characteristics of the Study Area

The Koyna is one of the upper level tributaries of the Krishna river and rises on the Mahabaleshwar Plateau at Kshetra Mahabaleshwar. The river descends from the plateau through a steep gorge – like valley and initially flows in a general north-south direction through a fault valley. Beyond Helwak the river takes a major right angle turn and flows eastward upto its confluence with the Krishna at Karad (Fig. 11.1). The basin is bounded by the Sahyadris on the west while on the remaining three sides the limits follow the crestline of high tablelands, ridges and hill ranges. The height and continuity of the eastern ridge have effectively cut-off communication between the Koyna basin and areas further east.

Most of the basin area, except the south-eastern riverine plains, exhibits a rugged topography. It consists of flat topped ridges and plateaus bordered by steep slopes tending to be scarps in some places and narrow, elongated valley floors. Mahabaleshwar plateau in the north is the highest of the tablelands rising to over 4500' (1372 m.). The narrow valleys have resulted in limited areas with a height less than 2000′. The construction of the dam near Helwak for impounding the water of the Koyna has resulted in the submergence of areas below 2150′ on the upstream side. The form of the valley has resulted in the reservoir having a narrow elongated shape.

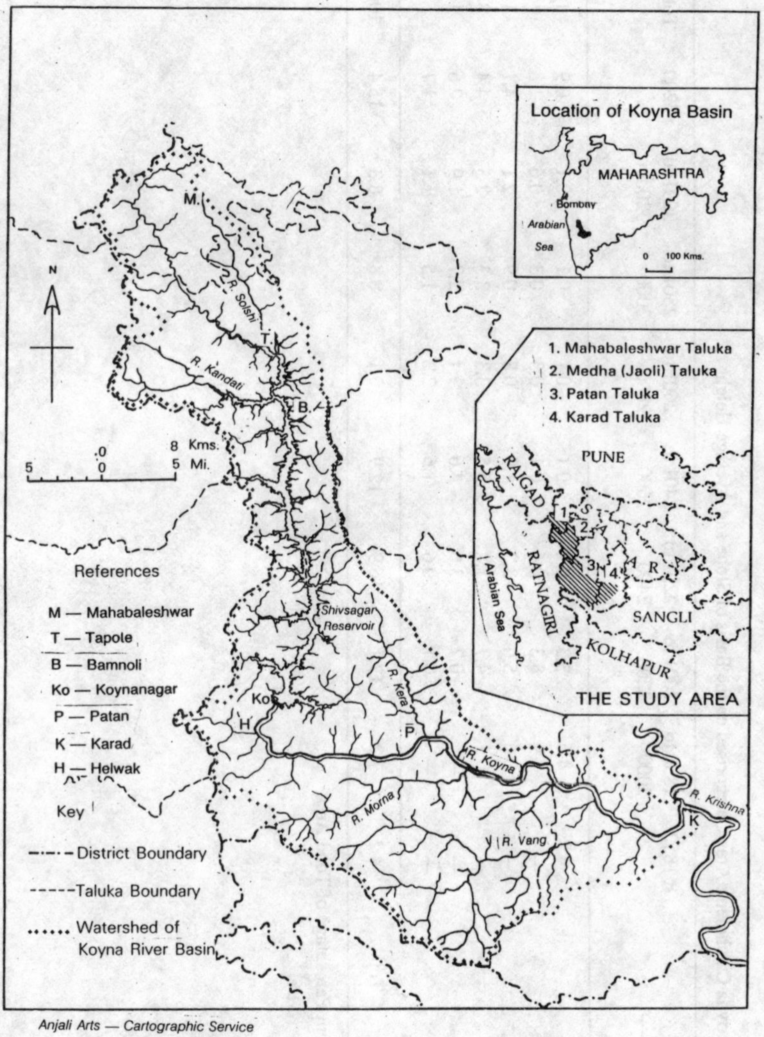

FIG. 11.1: Koyna Catchment: Location and Space Relations

TABLE 11.1: The Koyna Catchment: Area Categorised on the Basis of Slope and Average Height

Average height in Ft. / Slope in Degrees	< 1850	1850 to 2000	2001 to 2200	2201 to 2400	2401 to 2600	2601 to 2800	2801 to 3000	3001 to 3200	>3200	Total
Less than 1.0	4.2	4.6	3.3	0.2	0.1	0.1	0.1	0.1	0.9	13.6
1.0 – 2.9	–	1.9	3.3	0.6	0.1	0.3	0.3	0.6	1.8	8.9
3.0 – 5.9	–	0.6	5.0	3.2	1.0	0.8	0.9	2.1	4.1	17.7
6.0 – 10.9	–	0.1	4.7	7.8	5.5	3.3	3.3	2.5	4.4	31.6
11.0 – 17.9	–	–	0.7	3.6	4.6	3.4	2.7	1.9	2.6	19.4
18.0 & above	–	–	0.1	0.6	1.6	2.2	1.5	1.1	1.7	8.8
Total	4.2	7.2	17.1	16.9	12.9	10.1	8.8	8.3	15.4	100.0

Note: Figures Represent Percentage of Total Area.

The main valley floor being almost level has a slope of less than one degree; hence the relatively flat areas are predominantly concentrated in the height range of 1800-2200′ with a significant proportion at heights of over 3200′ corresponding to some plateau tops (Table 11.1). The foothill belt is characterised by moderate slopes and the slope increases abruptly to over 12 degrees at higher elevations. Slopes exceeding 18 degrees are localised and scattered coinciding with the scarp slope near the plateau edges. In most of the settlements, 50 per cent and over the total area is occupied by moderate and steep slopes. The soils are predominantly lateritic and thin, coarse and infertile.

A large part of the area is thus marginal in terms of suitability to agriculture due to steep slopes and thin soil cover. However, there are significant intra-regional contrasts, especially between the catchment and command areas. These have been accentuated after the construction of the dam.

Land alienation on the upstream side has been caused by submergence of the limited level land by the reservoir. On the downstream side the availability of land for cultivation has been augmented due to irrigation. The assured water supply has also changed the cropping patterns.

An analysis of the forest cover indicated that it comprised 22.6 per cent of the total area – a low figure for an upland drainage basin. Of this, stable forest accounted for 14.8 per cent and areas of afforestation for 7.8 per cent. There is evidence to indicate that 5.6 per cent of the area has suffered deforestation in the last 3 decades. The location of areas which have suffered deforestation indicates the causative factor to be encroachment of cultivation in the neighbourhood of the settled area aggravated by half-hearted rehabilitation measures (Fig. 11.2).

In terms of demographic characteristics a clear-cut difference emerges between the upper, middle and lower parts of the catchment. The upper catchment due to the hilly, rugged terrain has mainly small settlements of less than 500 population size, with the exception of Mahabaleshwar, the tourist centre. However, due to the small areal extent of the settlements, population densities are moderate. The impact of Mahabaleshwar is visible in the case of settlements in its immediate vicinity. The middle catchment stands out in terms of small settlements, many of which became uninhabited in 1971 due to displacement of population. Low levels of literacy characterise the area and most of the workforce is engaged as cultivators. The lower

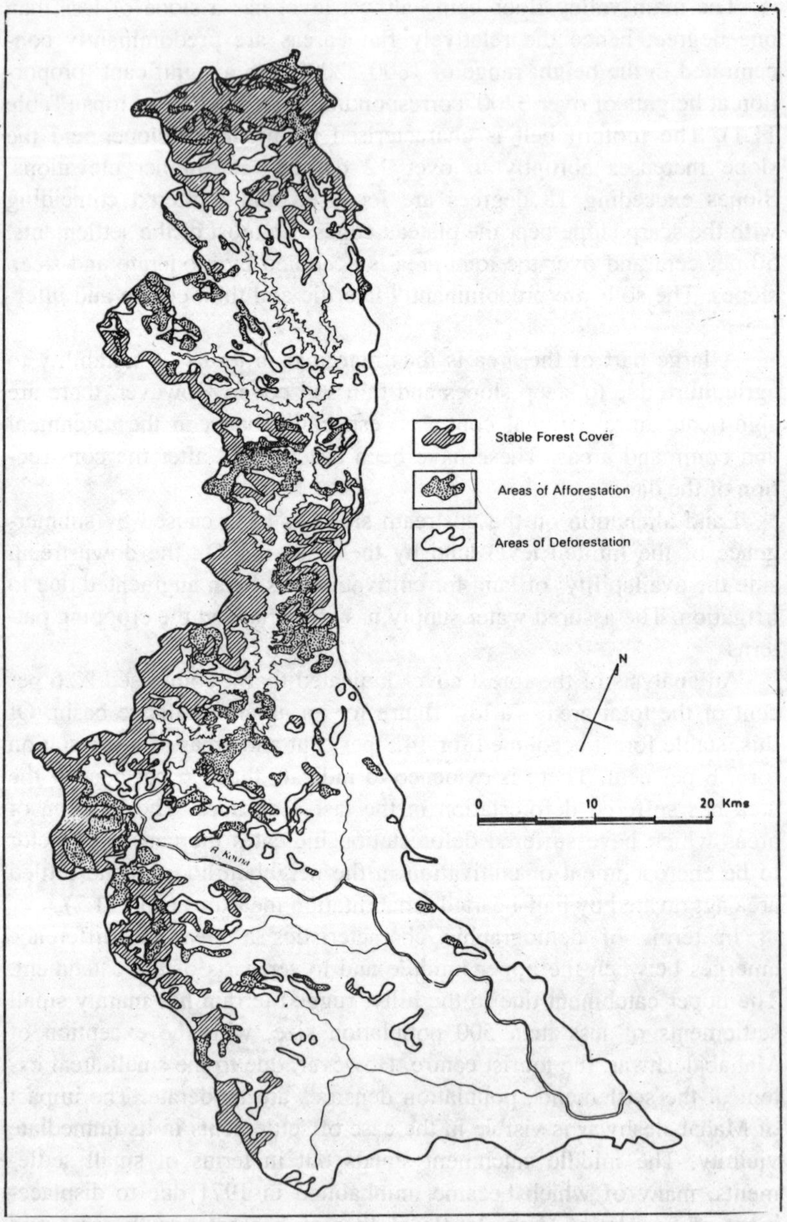

FIG. 11.2: Koyna Catchment: Status of Forest Cover 1951-87

catchment is characterised by larger settlements, many of which registered a significant growth in recent years. The advantage of being located on the downstream side of the reservoir in the riverine belt together with proximity to Karad, a major urban centre, has affected the demographic characteristics of this region. Higher density of population, higher levels of literacy and a significant proportion of agricultural labourers are the manifestations of a high degree of commercialization of agriculture.

The landuse has been considerably affected by the physical factors with slope emerging as a key element in differentiating areas of cultivation and forest cover. The catchment-command contrast is also noteworthy. However, though the project has resulted in increases in net irrigated and net sown areas the increase is not very appreciable due to the nature of the project. Within the catchment area the contrast is evident between the upper and middle catchment as in the former, the presence of the tourist centre of Mahabaleshwar has affected the landuse.

Environmental Problems due to Displacement and Rehabilitation of Persons

The problems due to displacement and rehabilitation of population as a consequence of the construction of the reservoir were found to be critical in the middle catchment. Some of the environmental problems that have come to the fore can be illustrated by some case studies.

Kusapur is an example of the failure of formal attempts at rehabilitation. It is a small hamlet located on the right bank of the Kandati river which now forms an arm of the reservoir in its upper reaches. The original site of the village was submerged and the villagers were formally rehabilitated in a far-off place in Bhiwandi taluka in Thane district and given a meagre compensation. At the new location the villagers could not get assimilated in the mainstream and consequently some of the uprooted families decided to return to their native village. They built their houses on a tiny patch of flat land at the foot-hills, almost a kilometer upslope from the original site and the present gaothan is backed by a steep scarp (Fig. 11.3). Since the land is marginal in terms of soils they were forced to resort to shifting cultivation. They cannot supplement their resources through the collection of forest produce due to government restriction and this has caused further pressure on marginal lands.

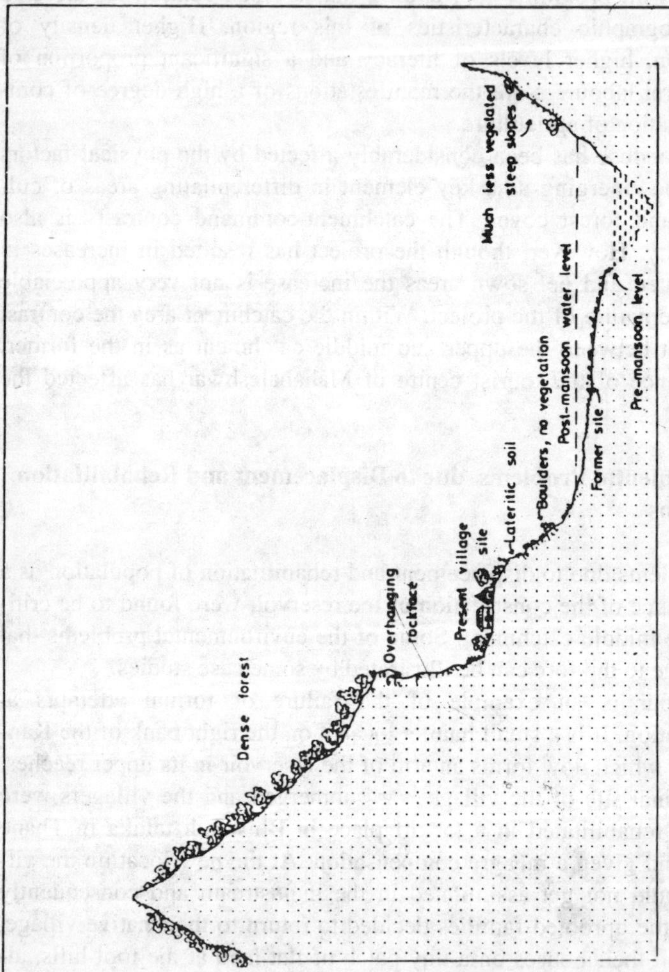

FIG. 11.3: Kusapur: A Schematic Section

Munavale, another settlement is a case of half-hearted rehabilitation. It was submerged and the villagers were resettled on higher land. They were provided with forest land in order to compensate for the lost agricultural land. The new land could not obviously qualitatively match the land originally possessed by the villagers. This has resulted in the need for shifting cultivation and slopes upto 17 degrees have been brought under cultivation (Fig. 11.4).

In Nivakane, one comes across an attempt at resettlement by displaced persons. The villagers from Aral, a submerged village, purchased a small hill from the local landlord and established a colony of their own; they named it Aral after their home village. The name does not appear in census listings as it is in reality a part of Nivakane. The settlement consists of 20 rehabilitated families and 4 native resident families. The displaced families claim to have been compensated very marginally and had to migrate to the location almost at their own cost. Most of the land purchased by them is steeply sloping and covered with loose, partially laterised red sandy soils; hence it has a low productivity. Lower gentle slopes are used with terracing for paddy cultivation, moderate middle slopes with crude terraces for maize and bajra while steep upper slopes are unterraced and cannot support stable cultivation (Fig. 11.5). This forces the farmer to practice shifting cultivation. The native families, in contrast, own land near the river and can grow 3 crops a year.

In Manari, a village in the lower part of the middle catchment, encroachment of cultivation on upper slopes due to population pressure was accentuated by rehabilitation. The rehabilitated families had been pushed into marginal lands and hence could not cultivate the area continuously. In this village the maximum period for which the upper slopes could be cultivated was 3 years while they had to be left for 10 years.

These four case studies illustrate that the issue of rehabilitation which is of critical importance in this area has not been accorded proper attention. The displaced persons, who were originally farmers, have been rehabilitated or pushed into marginal lands. This has forced them to resort to shifting cultivation. The encroachment of cultivation on steep upper slopes has led to rapid deforestation. These slopes are getting denuded of their vegetal cover so that bald hills are a common feature. It has also given rise to geomorphic hazards such as land slides, slumps and rock-falls as the processes of erosion and mass-wasting have gained momentum. The coarse material washed down is

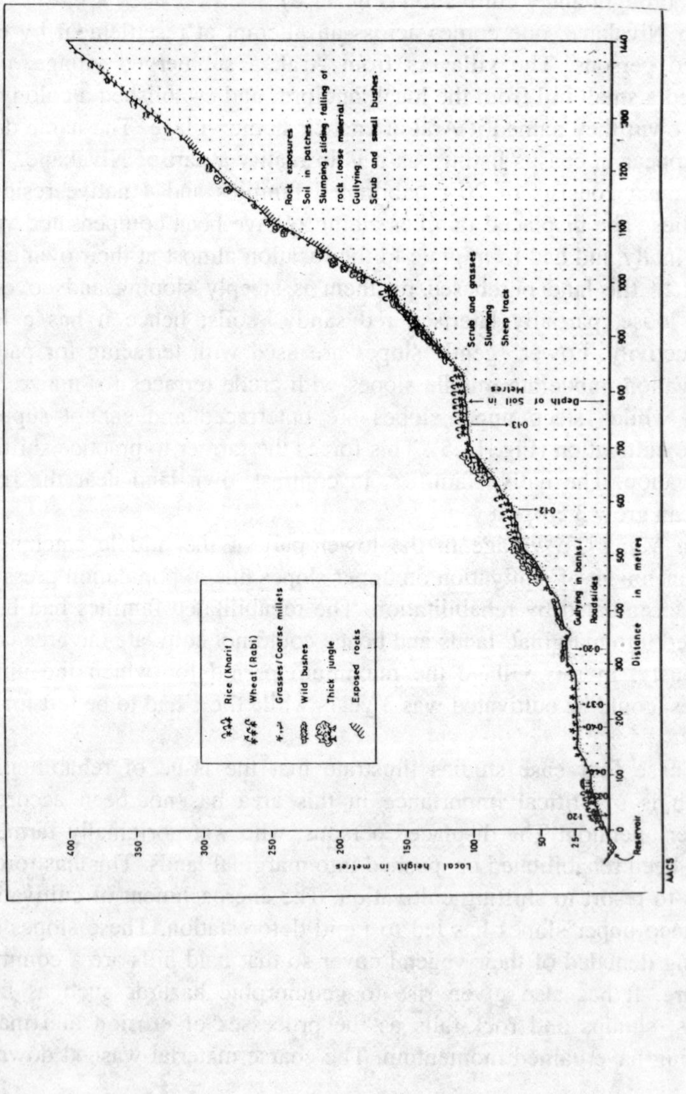

FIG. 11.4: Munavale: A Transect

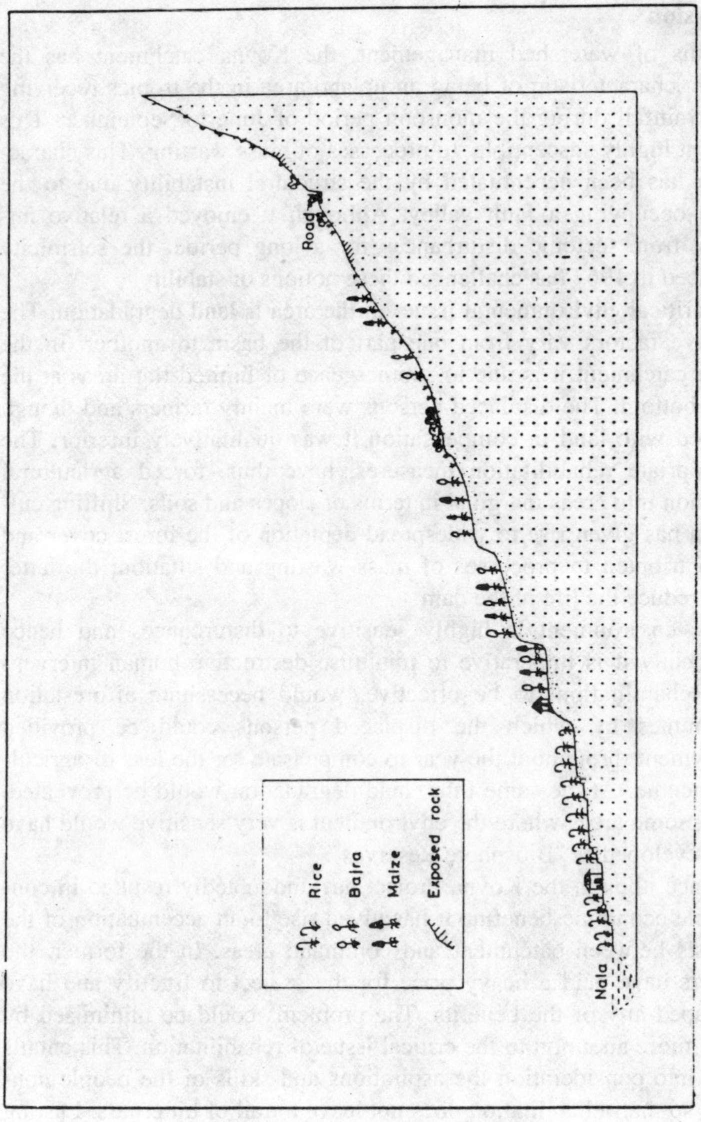

FIG. 11.5: Nivakane: A Cross Profile

deposited lower down resulting in textural and colour changes of the soil in addition to reduction in their moisture retentivity.

Discussion

In terms of watershed management, the Koyna catchment has the specific characteristic of being an upland area in the tropics receiving heavy rainfall during the monsoon period of June to September. This makes it highly susceptible to processes of mass wasting. This characteristic has been accentuated by the structural instability due to the stream occupying a fault valley. Although it enjoyed a relative immunity from tectonic disturbances for a long period, the seismicity evidenced in 1967 has challenged these notions of stability.

A critical environmental issue in the area is land degradation. The causative factors vary from one part of the basin to another. In the middle catchment it is due to submergence of limited flat areas at the valley bottom. The displaced persons were mainly farmers and though provided with land in compensation it was qualitatively inferior. The inappropriate rehabilitation measures, have thus, forced agricultural expansion into areas marginal in terms of slopes and soils. Shifting cultivation has given rise to widespread depletion of the forest cover and has contributed to processes of mass wasting and siltation; the latter would reduce the life of the dam.

The environment is highly sensitive to disturbances and hence ecologically it is imperative to minimise destructive human intervention. Rehabilitation, to be effective, would necessitate afforestation programmes by which the displaced persons could be provided employment throughout the year to compensate for the loss of agricultural income. At the same time, land degradation would be prevented. In fact, some areas where the environment is very sensitive would have to be developed as "Biosphere Reserves".

Hence, though the Koyna Project has undoubtedly resulted in considerable economic benefits, it has given rise to an accentuation of the contrasts between catchment and command areas. In the former, the villagers have paid a heavy price for the project to fructify and have not reaped any of the benefits. The problems could be minimised by paying more attention to the critical issue of rehabilitation. This entails taking into consideration the aspirations and skills of the people concerned so that rehabilitation does not leave a trail of bitterness. Lasting solutions which would result in sustainable development are rooted as much in social and economic reforms as in effective technologies.

REFERENCES

Amte, B. (1990). "Narmada Project: The Case Against and an Alternative Perspective", *Economic and Political Weekly*, 25(16), 817-18.

Bandyopadhyay, J. (1990). "Tehri Dam: Challenge before NF Government", *Economic and Political Weekly*, 25(5), 243-44.

Dixon, J.A. et al. (1989). " Dams and the Environment", World Bank Technical Paper 110. (The World Bank, Washington DC).

Dogra, B. (1990). "Tehri Dam: What do Experts Say?" *Economic and Political Weekly*, 25(1), 540.

Goodland, R. (1985). "Environmental Aspects of Hydroelectric Power and Water Storage Projects", Paper presented to International Seminar EIA of Water Resources Project, University of Roorkee.

Pant, C. & Dharmadhikari, S., (1989). "Mounting Antagonism towards Big Dams: Discussion", *Economic and Political Weekly*, 24(35 & 36) 2035-36.

Singh, S.K. (1990). "Evaluating Large Dams in India", *Economic and Political Weekly*, 25(11), 561-74.

12

ENVIRONMENTAL MYTH AS INTERNATIONAL POLITICS : The Problems of the Bengal Delta

GRAHAM P. CHAPMAN

Introduction

Popular Explanation and Recent Floods in Bengal

In 1987 and 1988 Bangladesh suffered from two widespread and damaging floods, some of the worst of those for which reasonable records exist. The popular press was quick to build on anxiety (expressed in such publications as Eckholm's (1976) book *Losing Ground*), about deforestation in the Himalayas because of fuelwood scarcity and the farmers' land hunger, consequent excessive run-off and high silt loads leading to deposition on the plains and increased flooding. That such a simplistic view could cause great damage by warping political relations and changing development priorities was noted by Ives (1989) and by Ives and Messerli (1989), and yet it is still widely current.

In a recent paper entitled "Indo-Bangladesh common rivers: the impact on Bangladesh" published in a new and serious journal *Contemporary South Asia*, Dr. Nahid Islam (1992) has highlighted what he perceives as the deleterious consequences that follow from the fact that India and Bangladesh share so many rivers (57 are recognised). The list of evils which he notes is widened as follows (p.215).

> "The consequences of hydrological change [*note: on which of the shared rivers is not specified*] because of upstream diversion are as

follows:

(i) siltation and rise of river beds leading to flood, demolition of river embankment and changed river course;
(ii) decreased soil moisture and increased salinity leading to desertification;
(iii) decreased water level leading to problems in agriculture, industry, navigation, fishery and domestic use; and
(iv) decreasing upstream flow leading to saline intrusion in the coastal area and damage to mangrove forest."

As if that was not enough Islam also notes armed clashes between Indian and Bangladesh border forces over border demarcation in area where the rivers are shifting their courses.

This generalised list includes charges relating to flood and also to the lack of water and desertification. It is a list which has been derived from observation of present problems only–with no sense of the history of environmental change in Bengal. Further, the culprit is seen in singular terms as upstream management-meaning in this context India. Now, there are indeed many environmental problems in Bangladesh, many of which have upstream elements within their complex set of causes, most of these elements being natural and few man made. But to group all these problems together, and then attribute them in such a singular way without a proper investigation of their causes is not intellectually sound.

Why should this happen? At one level it is easy to say that there is a simple political motivation to embarrass India: but I do not doubt the sincerity of the authors who write like this, and such an answer does not really address the issue that the claims are seen to be real by the people that make them. The problem is partly that it is in the nature of the man-environment interface that there are many complex causes, and many resultant effects, making it difficult to disentangle natural from anthropogenic changes. But it is also more than that: our ideas of cause and effect in science are heavily biased towards experiment and replication, and the derivation of general principles, which are valid for all places and all times. Such an approach undercuts the value of historical and uniquist explanation.

One strand of this paper is therefore to consider some of the environmental problems of Bangladesh. But another and equally important strand is a consideration of Environmental Claims Making.

Environmental Claims Making

This is the subject of research in Europe by Burgess and Harrison (1993), and Burgess. From this work it is quite clear that there is a relationship between popular understanding of the environment, the media's need to process these issues as news stories, and wider political responses. Given the limited factual basis to knowledge of most environmental issues, and given the enormous scope for collision between conflicting value systems – such as conservation versus development – it is often not the issue itself which steers the debate, but the preconceptions that proponents bring to it. Of the controversy over Himalayan deforestation Thompson (1993) observes:

> "Facts, therefore, are seldom clear-cut and self-evident truths. More often than not they are "smeared out" a bit, and it is up to us to pull them together. That people (a) do succeed in pulling them together, and (b) do not all pull them together in the same way, suggests that they are guided in their choice of facts by the values they hold."

> And:

> "The extensive deforestation that is seen as the root cause of the environmental degradation of the entire Himalayan region is conceptualized as a vicious circle: the forest is being used faster than it grows. There have been many attempts to measure these two rates, and it is an easy matter to tabulate and compare them. This exercise reveals that estimates of the per capita fuelwood consumption rate vary by a factor of 67 and that estimates of sustainable yield from forest production vary by a factor of at least 150. Far from giving us a precise, quantitative description of the vicious cycle of degradation, these results tell us that (if the most pessimistic estimates are correct) the Himalaya will be as bald as a coot overnight and that (if the most optimistic estimates are correct) they will shortly sink beneath the greatest accumulation of biomass the world has ever seen."

Figure 12.1 from Schwarz and Thompson (1990) summarises the kinds of models that guide people's reactions. In the bottom left, nature is benign and equilibrial disturbances will be accommodated, and man need not worry unduely. At the bottom right, nature is precarious: any intervention is likely to lead to catastrophic change. At the top right, nature is benign if kept within limits. This model appeals most to hierarchical organizations which need to demonstrate that they have an effective managerial role to play. In the Himalayan case it is the model which FAO follows. FAO dismisses as not credible those estimates of forest change which show either (a) there is a problem beyond control, or (b) the problem is so minimal it needs no control. It can therefore, conclude both that there is a problem, and that it is needed to avoid negative effects.

I wish next to introduce a separate idea (but not yet properly researched), namely that the expectation that 'urban western man' has of the concept of "knowledge". Because of the legacy of Baconian science, knowledge is intimately tied up with the idea of controlled experiment, of management, and of technical hardware solutions. In such an approach knowledge derived from experiment can be replicated. It is thus essentially an *a historical* approach to knowing, since laws are held to be universal in time and space. It is also an approach which tends to trivialise the complex specificities of place–whether in ecological or cultural terms. This approach to the definition of knowledge is worldwide – it has also been implanted in most officials and educationalists of the developing countries too.

What distinguishes the environmental concerns that underlay the 1992 United Nations Conference on Environment and Development at Rio is that academics and politicians are alerted to possible long-term feedback relationships such as those underlying the thesis of Global Warming. But these concern are now projected on a public whose understanding *and expectation* of "knowing" lacks historical depth. The result is somewhat perverse. A single year of drought in Britain is evidence in the newspapers of global warming. A single cold wet winter evidence that the thesis is a sham. With respect to Bengal, undoubtedly there are many changes occurring now in the delta. But there always have been. Thus what perhaps is different now is the perception of those changes, that they necessarily have an anthropogenic cause – implying that man has caused a disruption of a natural equilibrium. What distresses me about Islam's paper on the Common Rivers is both the lack of any (geo)historical depth and the willingness to appeal to pseudo-universals (i.e. 'desertification').

The next section of this paper tries cursorily to fill in some of the geo-historical background to Bengal's problems, and, for reasons which will become apparent later, to include some recorded details of the impacts of seismic forces on the delta.

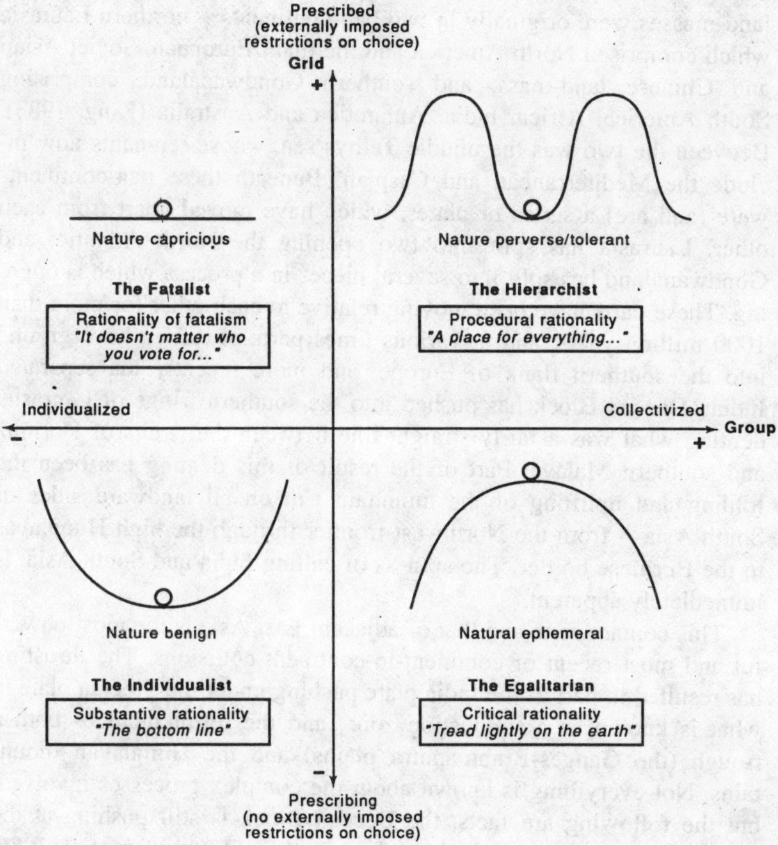

FIG. 12.1: The Myths of Nature

(*Source:* Schwarz and Thompson (1990)

Formation of the Bengal Delta

Continental Collision and Current Activity Rate

Current knowledge is fairly conclusive about the fact that the earth's land-masses were originally in two pan-continents – northern Laurasia which comprised North America and the main European, Soviet Asian and Chinese land-mass; and southern Gondwanaland, comprising South America, Africa, India, Antarctica and Australia (King, 1983). Between the two was the middle Tethys sea, whose remnants now include the Mediterranean and Caspian. Beneath these pan-continents were (and are) a series of plates, which have moved apart from each other. Laurasia has split into two opening the North Atlantic; and Gondwanaland has split into several pieces in a process which is ongoing. These parts have been moving relative to each other for more than 1000 million years, and at various times parts of Africa have ground into the southern flank of Europe, and more recently the separated Indian Deccan Block has pushed into the southern fringe of Laurasia, denting what was a fairly straight line between the straits of Hormuz and southern Malaya. Part of the result of this denting has been the folding and uplifting of the mountain rim on all landward sides of South Asia – from the Northwest frontier through the high Himalayas to the Burmese border. The aptness of calling India and South Asia, is immediately apparent.

This contact zone and that of adjacent East Asia is the most powerful and most recent of continent-to-continent collisions. The thrusting has resulted in part of the India plate pushing under the Tibetan plate in what is known as a subduction zone, and the result includes both a trough (the Ganges-Brahmaputra plains) and the Himalayan mountains. Not everything is known about the complex processes involved, but the following are facts: the Deccan Block is still pushing at the Tibetan plateau at a rate of about 5 cms a year (Tarponnier et al. 1986, p. 116); the Himalayas are uplifting at the rates of between 1 and 9 cms a year (Ives and Messerli, 1989, p. 98); and inevitably this is a very active zone both for seismic (earthquake) and tectonic (mass land-displacement) activity. The earliest stages of Himalayan uplift are dated at about 70 m years Bp, some of the more recent uplifting of Tibet and the Himalayas towards current heights is within the last 600,000 yrs Bp, therefore, within the Pleistocene, and the uplifting of the fore ranges such as the *Mahabharat* began 200,000 years ago – so recently in terms of earth history, that if the earth has existed for one year, this event started in the last 23 minutes.

Given that this has happened in an area of extremely high rainfall, that some of the rock lifted and exposed has been comparatively young sediment from the Tethys sea bad, it is not surprising that the Himalayas are suspected of having the highest natural denudation rate in the world (Ives and Messerli, 1989, p96 f). It is of course this denudation that has deposited the great alluvial plains, in places on top of marine sediments, which are quoted as being 5000m thick (Ives and Messerli, 1989, p. 21) and more than a mile deep (Michael, 1967, p. 30, with respect to the Indus basin). The sediment pouring into the Bay of Bengal has built the current visible delta, but sedimentation from the Ganges-Brahmaputra continues into the Bay for a further 2,000 nautical miles (King, 1983, p119): the current delta is a little like the proverbial ice-berg, 9/10ths hidden, and the actual point at which land crawls out of the sea almost arbitrary.

During the height of the last pleistocene glaciation sea level was of course much lower than now. The rivers (proto-Ganges-Brahmaputra) incised their course into whatever form the proto-delta took. During the retreat of the ice-caps and the rapid rise in sea levels the river discharges from the Himalayas were presumably much higher than now, and the sediment certainly of a different nature — being more sandy/gravelly and less silty. The cross-section of the lower delta in Figure 12.2 shows in mixture of gravels, sands and clays: which, is partly a function of distance from main channels, since floods deposit fine alluvium far from the river channels, whereas bedloads are coarser sands.

The relative sea-level is thus a function of several variables; including the eustatic postglacial changes (accounting for much of the change in Figure 12.3), tectonic uplift or depression of different areas, rates of silt deposition, and rates of silt compaction. The Figure suggests that there is no reason to expect complete stability in an indefinite future.

The landforms of the whole Ganges-Brahmaputra plains are still highly dynamic. The inland equivalents of the delta are the alluvial fans at the foot of the mountains, across which the rivers migrate as they drop their loads. The Kosi has migrated 100 kms West in 250 years (Ives and Messerli, 1989 p.140), the Tista has behaved similarly (see below): the Beas (Indus basin) was captured by the Chenab in 1790 (Buckley quoted in Michel, 1967, p. 48). Below, further information is given on the movement of rivers with Bangladesh. Figure 12.4

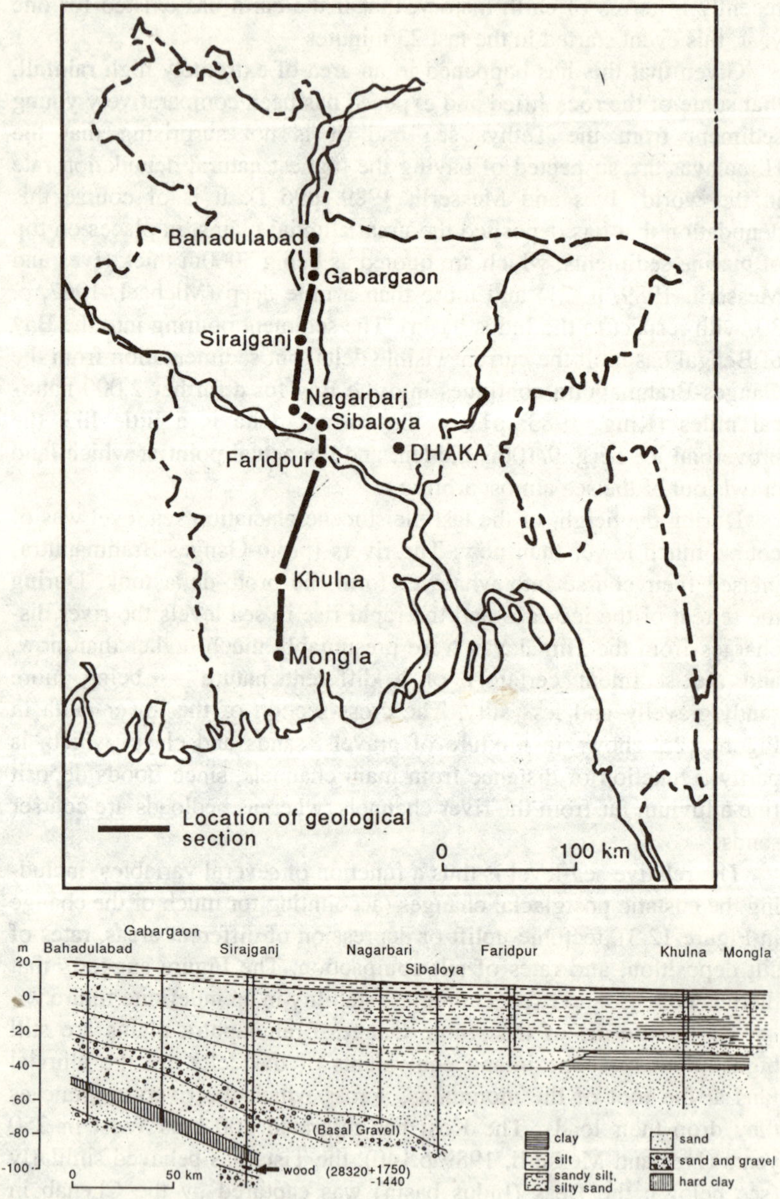

FIG. 12.2: Mixture of Gravels, Sand and Clay

(*Source*: UMITSU (1987)

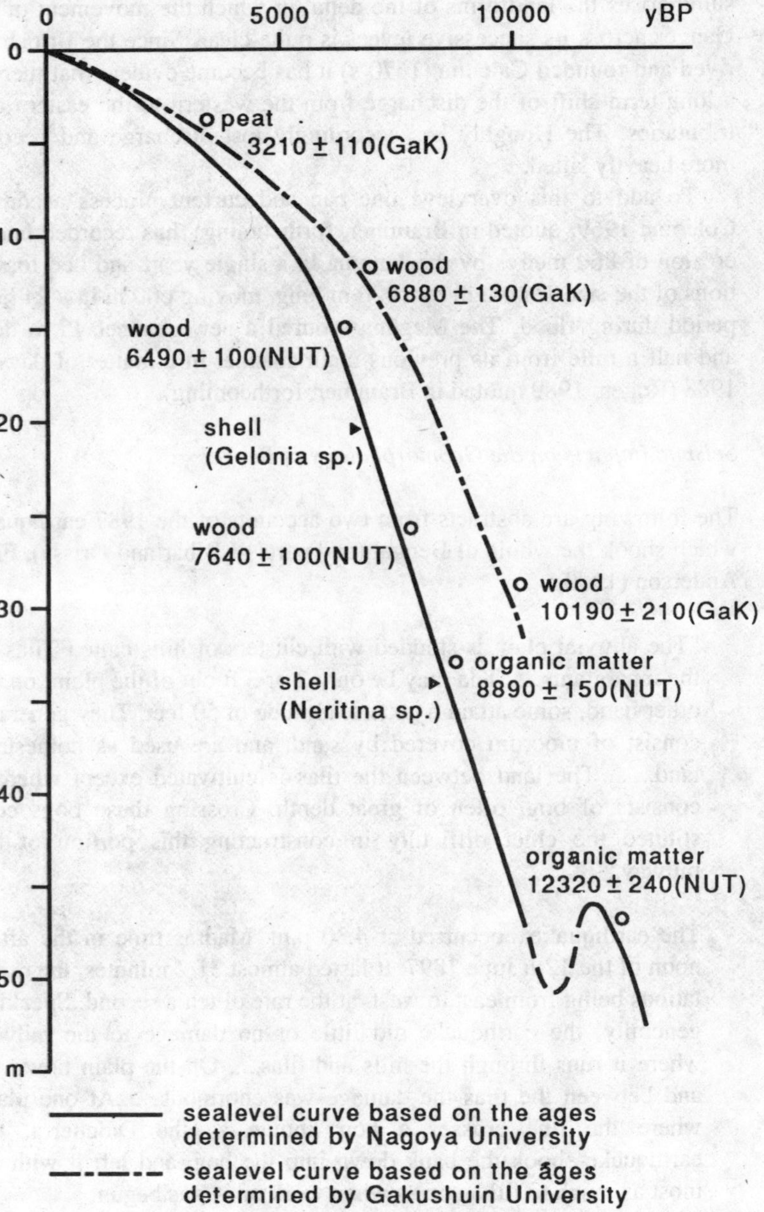

FIG. 12.3: Late Quarternary Sea Level Changes in Bengal

(*Source*: UMITSU (1987)

summarises the landforms of the delta, in which the movement of the Ganges across its successive levees is quite clear. Since the British arrived and founded Calcutta (1670's) it has become evident that there is a long term shift of the discharge from the western to the eastern distributaries. The Hooghly has accordingly lost discharge and become more heavily silted.

To add to this overview, one can add current process accounts. Coleman 1969, quoted in Brammer, forthcoming), has recorded lateral erosion of 860 metres by the Jamuna in a single year, and bed formations of the size 15m high by 1000 m long, moving 600 m in a 24 hour period during flood. The Meghna scoured a new channel 45 m deep and half a mile from its previous main channel in a matter of days in 1988 (Rogers 1989 quoted in Brammer, forthcoming).

Seismic Impacts on the Geomorphology of Bengal

The following are abstracts from two accounts of the 1987 earthquake which shook the whole of Bengal (and parts of Bihar and Orissa). First Anderson (1900):

> "The alluvial plain is studded with clusters of hills called Tilas by the inhabitants. A Tila may be only 2 or 3 ft out of the plain; on the other hand, some attain a general altitude of 50 feet. They generally consist of moorum covered by sand, and are used as homestead land....... The land between the tilas is cultivated except where it consists of bog, often of great depth. Crossing these bogs constituted the chief difficulty in constructing this portion of the railway......
>
> The earthquake....occurred at 4.30 p.m. Madras time in the afternoon of the 12th June 1897. It lasted almost 31/2 minutes, the oscillations being from east to west at the rate of ten a second. Speaking generally, the earthquake did little or no damage to the railway where it runs through the hills and tilas..... On the plain however, and between the tilas the damage was enormous. ....At one place where the line crosses a bog known as the Dulcherra, the earthquake shook the bank down into the bog, and left it with almost as much to fill again as when work on it was begun.
>
> ....Near the Khawai [river] the bank opened out in great

fissures...... on the ordinary ground level mud and sand welled out of the fissures and did much damage to the crops. One of the most extraordinary effects of the earthquake occurred at a point 11/2 miles east of the Khawai. Here the whole road, bank, rails and bridges for a length of over a mile was shifted about 6 to 8 feet northwards. At Daragaon 5 miles a length of over a mile was shifted about 6 to 8 feet northwards. At Daragaon 5 miles east of Shaistaganj, the west end of the station yard, for its whole width of 4 chains, sank two to three feet into the ground; as the ground sank, water welled up, and nothing could be more terrifying to behold than the manner in which the very ground seemed to dissolve in welling water........

To restore the line to a condition fit for running would have been easier had the earthquake occurred in any of the earlier months of the year: the ordinary labour in Sylhet, the district through which this part of the railway runs, is all imported from countries west of Calcutta, and it is the custom of the labourers to return to their homes at the beginning of the rains.

The second account is from the Rangpur District Gazetteer (from current northwest Bangladesh) it observes :

[the earthquake] "was heralded by a loud rumbling noise from the east, followed by instantly yarning fissures, east to west in direction, from which torrents of sand and water poured over the surrounding country. ......Large tracts of cultivated land were covered with a thick layer of sand, causing much damage to cultivated crops and rendering many lands unculturable. The earthquake wrecked or damaged most of the public and private masonry buildings, the railways, all sources of water supply, and almost all the roads and bridges.

....The earthquake made great changes in the drainage of the country. The beds of many rivers were upheaved and also contracted by the slipping of their banks.....Both the Tista and the Ghaghat were reported to have suddenly become fordable in places. The latter river, an important drainage channel in the district was since 1897 a shallow sluggish stream with a weak current and strong tendency to silt and be choked with aquatic vegetation.

Upheaval in some place was accompanied by subsidence in others. On the whole, the effect of the earthquake was to raise the level of the district. The conversion of considerable arable areas, especially in the Gaibanda subdivision, into uncultivable marshes and swamps would seem to indicate the contrary. This is account for by the fact that, in the process of upheaval the country had assumed in places a cup-shaped formation, allowing little or no outlet for accumulated rainfall. Vast new *beels* formed, and the rivers became marshes."

It is suspected that seismic activity played a large part in the change of the Brahmaputra's course (Fig. 12.5) from east side of the Madhopur tract to the west side starting in 1830 (Umitsu, 1985, p. 157). The earthquakes of Assam between 1951 and 1956 have been attributed with releasing greatly increased sediment loads (Ives and Messerli, 1989 p. 137), that have contributed to the formation of new islands at the river mouths. Much of the delta itself is sinking, as the sediments compress. The Tista (also noted above) shifted its course suddenly in 1787 during an exceptional flood, only to change it again after the earthquake in 1897 (Johnson, 1975, p. 10).

Hazards in Bengal

Cyclones at the Land-sea Interface

On October 5th, 1864 a massive cyclone struck west Bengal, causing death and destruction far inland. The number of dead from the initial storm damage is unknown, but certainly many more died in the outbreak of disease and starvation that followed. In Calcutta itself there was extensive damage to buildings, and two steamers, the Leviathans of the age, were among the 200 boats reported sunk. More recently the parts of Bengal that lie in Bangladesh have been subjected to the terrible storms of November 1970 which probably killed as many as half a million people, and the recent disaster of May 1991 near Chittagong.

These storms are a part of the 'normal hazards' of the Bay of Bengal as a whole — Andhra Pradesh in India has suffered badly in recent years too. But they have a particular impact on the northern coast of the bay, because the tidal waves are here funnelled towards that small part of the delta (ice-berg like, much of it is under water) which creeps imperceptibly out of the sea, offering no natural barriers to steam the onrush of the waves.

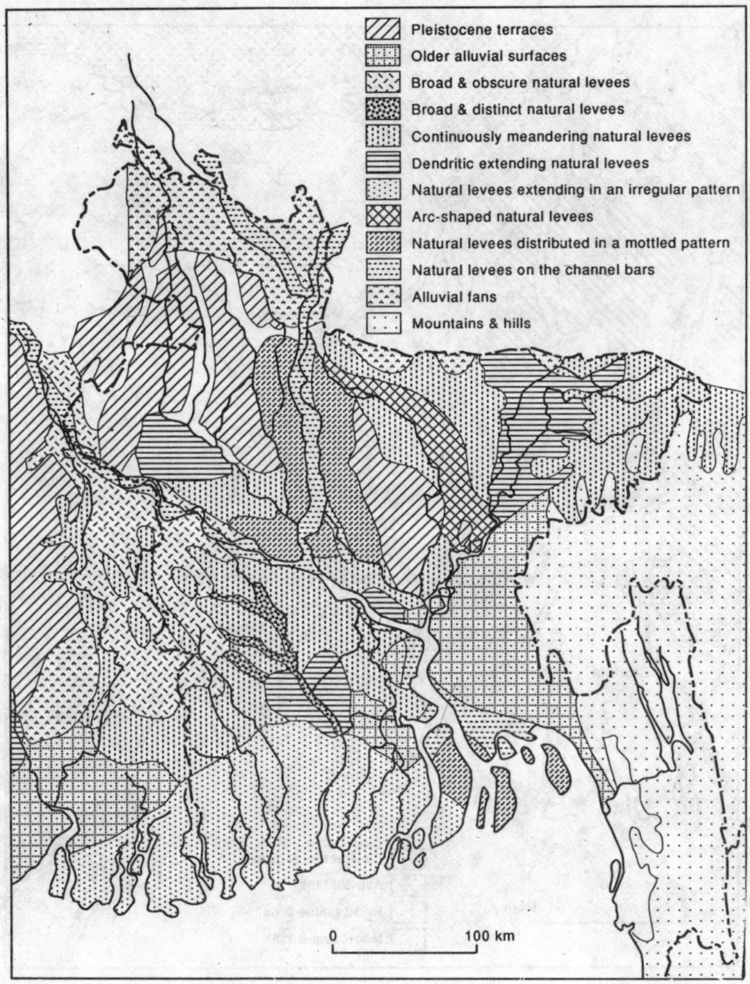

FIG. 12.4: Landforms of Bengal

(*Source*: UMITSU (1985)

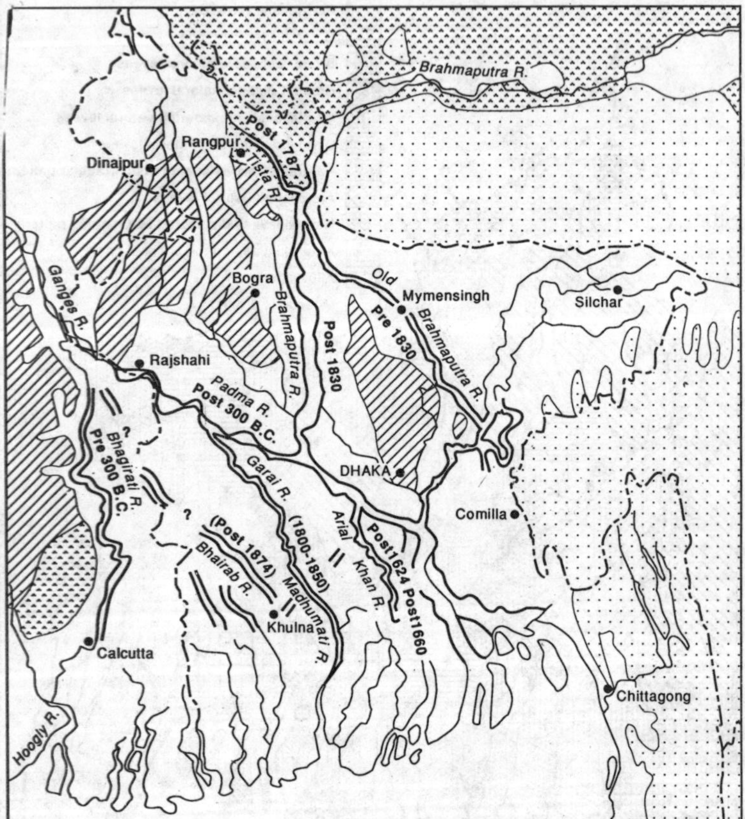

FIG. 12.5: Changes in River Courses in Bengal

(*Source:* UMITSU 1985)

But also, as with the floods described in the next section, escalating population pressure plays its part in turning adverse conditions into disaster. The population doubling time in Bangladesh is now only 32 years. More people now live in higher exposed coastal sites than ever before.

Floods in Bengal

There are three types of flooding in Bengal, which can happen independently, or, (a true calamity) simultaneously. These are flash-floods from adjacent higher ground, usually around the edges of some of the Pleistocene terraces. They come fast and go fast. The second is river flooding when the major exotic rivers over-top their banks. Thirdly there is rain-water flooding, common everywhere, when the monsoon rains falls faster than it is drained. This is usual in most of the *bhils* (*beels*) and other back-swamps, and the whole of the Meghna/Sylhet depression routinely turns into a lake during the monsoon.

None of this is necessarily too much water. The impact of the floods depends on the extent to which there is a 'normal' expectation of them and adjustment to them. Agriculture is finely tuned: flooded swamp land is planted as waters recede. In deep-water areas (predominantly in Bangladesh) there are long strawed rice types that can grown up to 12" in 24 hours (Farmer, 1979), and ultimately to 12' high, to keep abreast of rising floods waters. But throughout history there have been major floods, often when rainfall floods are back-up by coincident river floods, which have caused major damage. On these occasions crops may be inundated long enough (total submergence for more than 4 days is usually fatal) to be killed off: human lives may be lost: drought animals may be lost with consequently impacts on the next land preparation: capital equipment (ploughs, byres, houses) may be lost. In addition roads and railways may be damaged.

Flood protection levees have therefore been built in various places, some big, some small, some totally enclosing polders, to give some insurance against such losses. The problem is that the rivers shift their courses, and barriers built far back may even then find themselves under attack. If such barriers work for some years, then are breached, the result can be worse than if they had never been built. Given the staggering and ever-increasing population pressure in Bangladesh, people start to live in lower areas which appear safer from risk after a barrier has been built, and hence these people are, almost literally, sitting ducks in the event of a breach of the defences.

The 1987 floods (Fig. 12.6) (a map of the actual floods is not possible since there were no cloud-free days for satellite or aerial photography) were predominantly local flashfloods and rainfall floods, whose drainage was impeded by exceptionally high river levels, particularly in the Ganges. The floods of 1988 were predominantly river floods caused by exceptionally heavy rainfall in the Himalayas and the Shillong block. The Brahmaputra (Jamuna in Bangladesh) effectively became a river 60 kms wide (Brammer, 1990).

Production losses due to the floods in addition to capital losses were very high (see Table 12.1). But, the actual yearly production totals were not so bad (Table 12.2). Some farmers were able to resow after the floods subsided, but in general greater emphasis was put on the second season (the rabi) crop, when soil moisture was much higher than usual, and the farmers' efforts were rewarded by higher prices.

TABLE 12.1: Losses Due to Flooding in Bangladesh. 1987 and 1988

	1987	1988
Area flooded	57000 km2	82000 km2
Cattle, Goats lost	64700	17200
Rice production lost	3.5m tonnes	2 m tonnes
Trunk roads damaged	1523 km	3000 km
Rural hand tubewells flooded	n.a.	24000

Source: Brammer, 1990.

Partly this also reflects the growing emphasis on rabi wheat crops, and on irrigated boro rice (both outside the monsoon season) which is happening anyway, as cropping intensity rises. Indeed, controlled water from pumpsets in the dry season (from tubewells or rivers) is also seen as offering the best support to new seed types in both wheat and rice.

The Problems of Too Little Water in the Dry Season

West Bengal is home to India's largest city, the ex-imperial capital of Calcutta (population in 1981 was 9.2 m), for long India's largest and most important port and manufacturing centre. It is still overwhelmingly the most important port for the whole of east and northeast India.

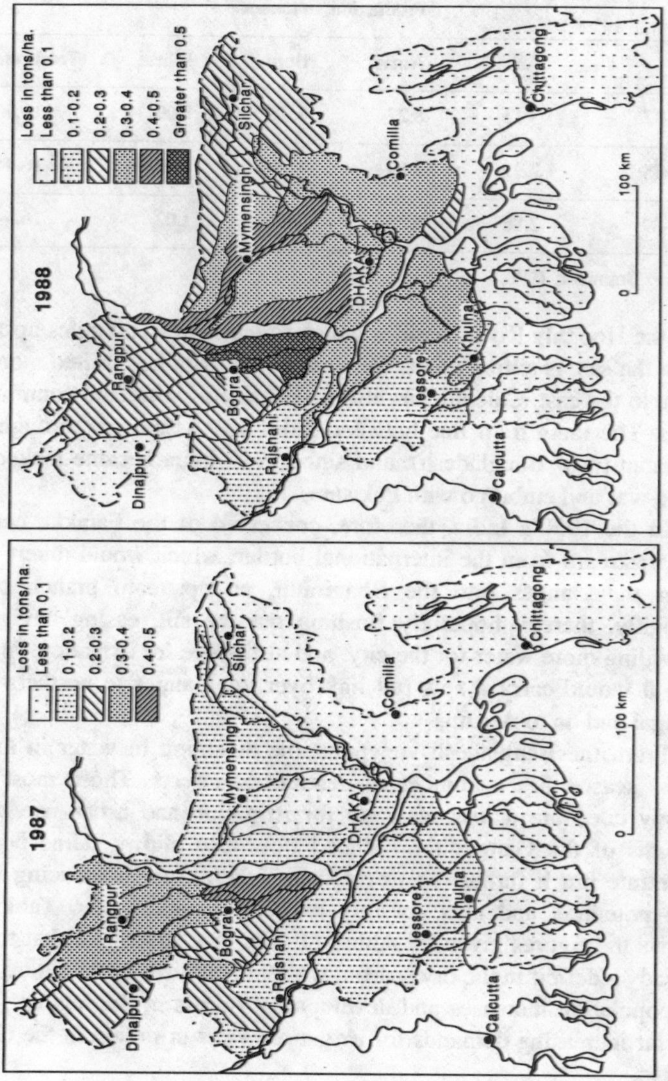

FIG. 12.6: **Crop Losses Due to Floods in Bengal (Bangladesh)**

(*Source*: Brammer (1990)

TABLE 12.2: Cereal Production in Bangladesh, 1986-88

Year	Production, m tonnes				
	Aus	Aman	Boro	Wheat	Total cereals
1986-87	3.13	8.27	4.01	1.09	16.50
1987-88	2.99	7.69	4.73	1.05	16.46
1988-89	2.86	6.86	5.80	1.02	16.54

Source: Brammer, 1990.

But the Hooghly River, besides which Calcutta lies 100 miles upstream from the sea, is silting up, as the flow in the delta has shifted more and more to the east. Calcutta has also had problems with land communications. The main train line between India and Assam ran through East Pakistan (now Bangladesh), and since 1949 India became locked in a trade-war and embargo with Pakistan.

In the 1950's India, therefore, conceived of the Farakka barrage, just upstream from the international border, which would divert water from the Ganges into the Bhagirathi, an upstream branch of the Hooghly, thereby hopefully flushing out the silt, easing navigation, providing more water for the city, and also some for irrigation. In addition it would carry a new rail link over the Ganges to northern West Bengal and on to Assam.

From the Bangladesh viewpoint the diversion of water in the dry (low) season has a number of deleterious effects. Those most commonly cited are a loss of water for irrigation and urban use. In the mouths of the Ganges the reduced flow also allows saline bores to penetrate much further upstream than hitherto, again reducing irrigation potential, and also possibly harming ground water. Table 12.3 shows the figures given by Abbas (1982), to demonstrate that there is already a deficit in the dry season, without counting on the future needs as population increases and development occurs in the region, in particular increasing demands for irrigation water upstream in the Ganges plains.

India's attitude to Bangladesh's protests has given the impression that as the upstream state, she has is inclined to believe she has prior to do with the water as she wishes. This attitude, if correctly identified, can be linked conceptually to the dispute between India and Pakistan over the sharing of the Indus waters — a difficult issue which was resolved in the Indus Waters Treaty of 1960 only with the help of massive investment from the World Bank underwritten by the USA, and

TABLE 12.3: Use of Ganges Water Flow at Farakka

(*in millions of acre-feet*)

	Dry Season (November to May)	Wet Season	Total
	50	322	372
Requirements			
Bangladesh	42	6	48
India	17	12	30
Nepal	**	**	30
Excess/deficit	-9	304	264

**not calculated
Source: Abbas (1982)

which allocated all the water of the three eastern rivers of the Punjab to India, and the waters of the western rivers to Pakistan. This meant that Pakistan had to re-supply canals cut off from their original source (Michel, 1967). In 1956 during the confrontation between the two states India unilaterally abrogated her adherence to the Barcelona Convention, to which she had been a signatory in 1921, which forbade a state to alter natural conditions to the detriment of neighbouring states.

The Farakka dispute post-dates the Indus dispute: and it can be said that India has proved a tough negotiator in this case too, though some of the arguments, such as the fact that very little of the flow into Bengal originated in Bangladesh are not normal grounds for indifference to a downstream state. But is also true that to some extent history caught India out, in that the building of Farakka began in the Pakistan days, and India did have at that time serious foreign policy problems in relation to Pakistan as a whole – most notably over Kashmir. But now sovereign Bangladesh has inherited the problems over Farakka, despite the fact that she is now much more of a candidate for

Indian cooperation and concern, and is less linked to extraneous foreign policy complications.

Crow and Lundquist (1990) divide the history of negotiation into 4 phases. From 1951 to 1971 the project was discussed and planned. From 1971 to 1977 the barrage was built and implemented, without international agreement. In 1977 a short-term agreement was signed between India and Bangladesh over the allocation of low season flows, running for five years. During this time it was imagined that the negotiation of a full-scale treaty settling the principles for the development of the Ganges-Brahmaputra basin would be completed, and implementation would follow in 1982. In the event there has been serious difficulty in reaching an agreement, hence there have been a number of *ad-hoc* extensions of the 1977 agreement pending a new 'final' solution.

Part of the problem is that there is an ever changing and more complex understanding of what exactly constitutes 'the problem.' Initial concern focusses on the division of the available dry season flow at Farakka. But increasingly other issues have grown in significance. Firstly there is the possibility of augmenting the dry-season flow, by upstream storage dams. Next there are many other shared rivers which should also be the subject of agreement — for example there are new Indian barrages on the Teesta and Gumti. So should there not be a regional rather than individual river approach? Next, whereas there is high demand for Ganges water, but not enough of it, there is little demand for Brahmaputra water, and much of it. (This is a mirror image of the Indus/Punjab situation, in which the eastern areas of greatest demand were in the commands of the smallest rivers — so in the end a regional water transfer was devised, followed by a myriad of subsequent developments.)

Figure 12.8 broadly summarises the conflicting strategies of India and Bangladesh in the early 1980's. Bangladesh wanted many storage dams in the Ganges, the biggest on the Nepalese border, to augment the low season flow. (It would also allow a new navigation canal to link the new port of Mongla with Nepal, though crossing a neck of Indian land). At various stages Bangladesh attempted to initiate trilateral talks with all three countries, although India resisted, insisting that it would be the vehicle through which the downstream-upstream issues could be discussed (Crow and Lundquist, 1990). Effectively the suggestion has been subjected to diplomatic strangulation.

The Indian proposal was to augment the flow at Farakka by diverting flow from the Brahmaputra. This would involve a canal half a mile wide right across Bangladeshi territory, with both of the significant control points in Indian hands.

Because these two approaches are clearly radically different, one can imagine how the talks could drag on without resolution.

The current situation is that Bangladesh seems to be developing a 'New Line', something akin to the original Indian proposal and close to a variant of it proposed by India, but with different political implications. The engineering basis is for a Brahmaputra-Ganges link, but wholly within Bangladeshi territory. But Bangladesh not unnaturally does not wish to commit itself to such a solution without an agreement on the actual figures for sharing of the waters both in the Brahmaputra and the Ganges. This is extremely difficult to achieve, not least because there is a major disagreement between the two sides over what are the correct figures for the Brahmaputra's discharge.

The essence of the dispute at the moment has been summarised by Crow and Lundquist (1990) as: India will not consider sharing (of the Ganges and others) without augmentation from the Brahmaputra, and Bangladesh will not consider augmentation from the Brahmaputra without a guaranteed share of the principal joint rivers.

The irony is that in the end it is possible that a solution might be to allocate all (low season) discharge of the Brahmaputra to Bangladesh, and all (low season) discharge of the Ganges to India, compensating for the division by engineering works — all highly reminiscent of the vivisection achieved in Punjab. It should also be noted that there the absolute division of the rives in Punjab required a detailed ten year transition with allocation of water flows season by season, and very considerable argument over costs — who was going to pay for replacement and facilitating works in whose territory? Would India pay for Bangladesh's engineering works to get more Ganges low season flow?

Towards the end Crow and Lundquist (1990) account mentions that the floods of 1987 and 1988 have had a very limited impact on the progress of the negotiations. The floods are seen as a separate issue, because the only major works upstream that could mitigate them (and then only some of them) would be the colossal storage, dams which would have to be managed tri-laterally by India, Nepal and Bangladesh (and conceivably by China and Bhutan too). And the reason why Bangladesh has recently begun to shift its negotiating stance is that is beginning to concede that the dams might be too big, too costly, too far off in the future, and too unreliable in terms of operational performance (much of the rainfall that causes flooding would occur downstream of the storage sites anyway.) Some agreement has been reached between India and Bangladesh about levées on smaller rivers which cross the border. Mostly, however, current G7 and World Bank proposals are for work to get going on project within Bangladesh as soon as possible.

One aspect of the new link canal that I have not seen discussed is its possible impact on flooding. Such canals impede drainage, not only be seepage loss and changing local groundwater levées, but also because their embankments impede drainage lines, and borrow pits become new swamps. The railways of Bangladesh and the Ganges plains and such an impact that they were attributed by some aiding an increase in malaria. Consider the position of the link canal (Fig. 12.8) in relation to the area flooded in 1988 (Fig. 12.7).

The Human Response to Floods

There has always been a human response and adaptation to the vagaries of this environment. Historically this has been small-scale, but in recent decades the proposed responses have escalated, as international involvement in 'development' has escalated, and the assumption that governments can effect change at larger scales has grown stronger in the public mind. Governments have sought refuge in part in the seductive promises of modern earthmoving machinery and modern engineering methods.

Several countries and country groups became involved in planning to obviate as far as possible repeats of Bangladesh's flood disasters, or at least to alleviate their worst affects. The G7 group of developed industrial countries have involved themselves in attempting to devise 'a solution' to the floods problem (Brammer, forthcoming), and French and Japanese proposals were also forthcoming for different embankment schemes. The World Bank then became involved in producing a coordinate Flood Action Plan with the Government of Bangladesh, publishing the first overview and proposals in late 1989 (World Bank, 1989) (Fig. 12.9).

The proposals cover many different aspects of the problem. They include studies of the engineering and siting of embankments, the development of compartmentalised polders, river training, and approaches to improving the management of water control, flood warning and flood preparedness, and enhancing flood refuges. The compartmentalised polders would allow selective flooding of land in the

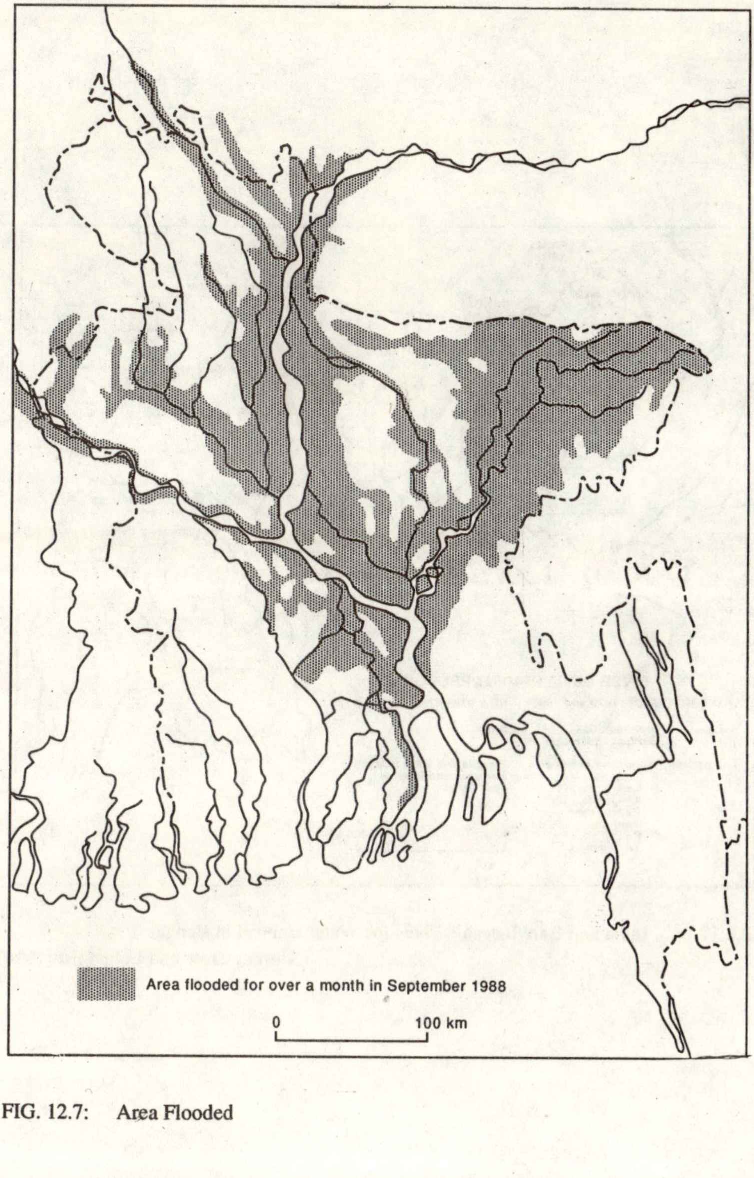

FIG. 12.7: Area Flooded

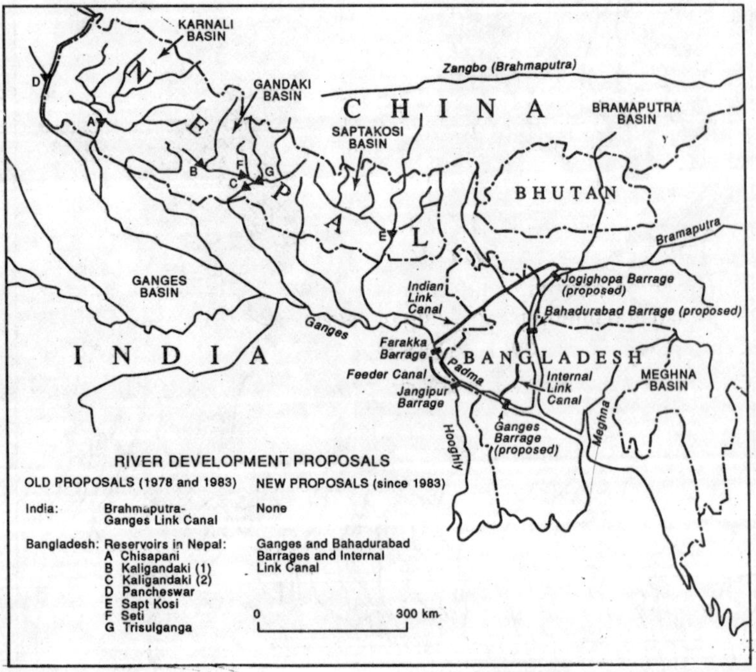

FIG. 12.8: India and Bangladesh's Plans for Water Control in Bengal

(*Source*: Crow and Lundquist (1990)

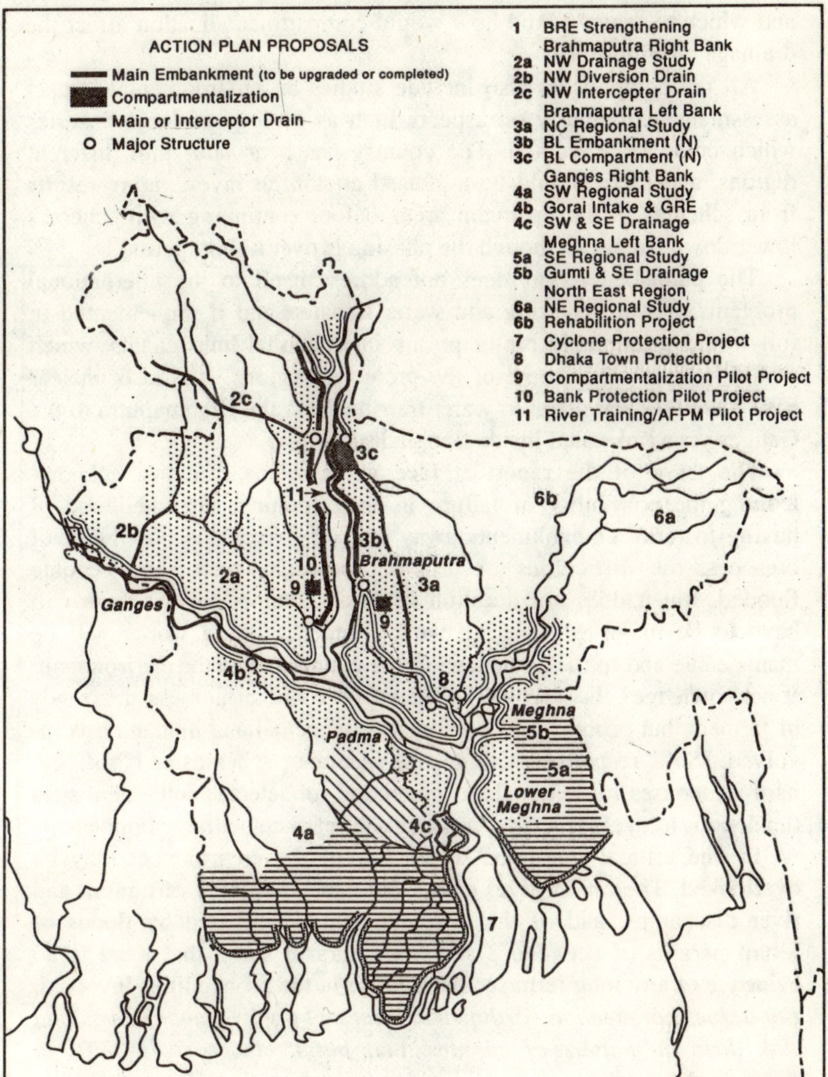

FIG. 12.9: World Bank Proposals

(*Source*: World Bank (1989)

even of extreme flood events. Who would choose which land to flood and which to "save"? And how would compartmentalization affect the drainage of rainwater?

All the components also include studies on environmental impact assessment, particularly on aspects such as ecology of local fisheries which could be disrupted. The country has been split into different regions, and there should be a phased attempt at investigating results from schemes in the upstream areas before continuing with schemes lower down stream — though the phasing is over a short period.

The published report does not address itself to the international problems of water sharing and water transfer, and if implemented in full would presumably pre-empt any international links canals, which would have to cross some of the protected regions. It is also unclear how it would even relate to water transfer from the Brahmaputra to the Ganges via a link canal inside Bangladesh.

The tenor of the report at face value seems cautions, acknowledging the possibility of failure in river training, the likelihood of having to retire embankments away from the river, the possibility of breaches, the difficulties of draining polders which have become flooded. But it does not question its basic assumption that there will have to be major engineering works, and that these works will be manageable and to the advantage of the economy and the environment. It acknowledges that the works themselves will dispossess thousands of farmers, but probably underestimates the actual and human costs involved. "Soft" responses such as crop insurance schemes and "soft and hard" responses for better flood protection for selected settlement sites (analogous to cyclone shelters) get only brief and ancillary comment.

In one critical sense the dynamism of the environment may be overlooked. The report gives evidence of the variability of rainfall and river discharges, and of the different damage inflicted by floods of return periods of between 2 and 500 years. It states that there is no evidence of any long-term secular change in the probabilities involved. *But it does not mention earthquakes, that can liquify embankments and sink them in matters of minutes, and initiate large scale shifts in drainage patterns.*

The flooding in Bangladesh has so far been identified as simply of 3 types: flash, river, and rainfall. But there are many who believe the major cause is the aggrading of the river beds which has been caused by excessive silt deposition, and which becomes part of a positive feed-back system, since aggrading river beds will drop more load, causing further aggradaton. This is the line of argument then leads to popular concern over deforestation in the Himalayas and increased erosion and deposition. Ives and Messerli (1989) show that there is very little evidence that there is currently extensive deforestation, that there is no evidence of increasing flood frequencies, that there is no evidence of enhanced erosion rates caused by man's activity (natural processes seem quite capable of producing the current effects), and that in any event if there is increased erosion the most likely immediate impact is in Nepal at border dams, or on the Indian plains.

From a more local viewpoint, Farakka is somehow supposedly implicated in both increasing siltation in the lower Ganges, and also in causing flood releases. Islam several times mentions that India takes only silt-free water and pushes the silt into Bangladesh. Several mass marches across the border by thousands of Bangladeshis have been planned from time to time — a convenient way of externalising internal discontent. But according to Crow and Lundquist (1990) these views should not be given much credence.

Conclusions

Simplistically, one normally proceeds on the basis that there is a problem, that one can find a set of solutions, and that one can choose and implement the best solution.

In practice problem-solving is an iterative process — that can involve at the least the following three steps, starting at any one of them, and then progressing through the whole loop more than once. After a few iterations, the problem(s) might not be the problem one first thought one had.

(1) Finding the solution to a problem depends in the first place on agreement on the nature of the problem.

(2) Secondly, it depends upon a proper assessment of the causes, even when 'proper' means confessing to a present and likely continuing state of ignorance or uncertainty. Lack of proof to the contrary should not be a licence for a half-baked theory to masquerade as fact.

(3) Thirdly, solutions have to be tested for feasibility, which means testing the assumptions on which they lie. There is no point in pursuing impossible solutions, feasible only in an ideal world (usually that of physical engineering bereft of political and so-

cial engineering).

My starting point is that the problem of Bengal is development: how to improve the lives of the rapidly increasing millions in the population. (In this light perhaps the best anti-flood device would be an immediate halt to all population growth. But that has to be dismissed as an unreal-world engineering scenario.) The biggest problem the population faces is that of uncertainty — over the timing and extent of possible losses to crops, property and even land (Fig. 12.10).

The back-drop to this is Continents-In-Collision, and the dynamic and ever-changing delta region, the most active surface reminder of the activity of the plates beneath. The active superficial geomorphology is a major source of uncertainty on a sub-continental scale. This uncertainty is not subject to elimination. (It may get worse because of climatic change. Interestingly, Brammer (1989a) considers the possible effects of sea-level change, and considers that deposition — often deliberately 'harvested' — may match sea-level rise: there could also be reductions or increases in rainfall, which would of course lead to major changes in sedimentation in the lower basin.)

The major constraint on action at larger scales is the difficulty of coordinating governments which are individually responsible to their own citizens, not to the population of the basin. Crow and Lundquist (1990) begin their illuminating reports with the observations that 500 million people live the Ganges-Brahmaputra basins: that 30 per cent of the world's 800 million poorest people live here. But the most significant fact is concealed by these aggregated figures — that they are partitioned into separate sovereign states. To relax this constraint the concepts of responsibility and sovereignty would have to be modified by a basin-wide Common Environment. Not only is this unlikely in the short term, the very fact that there have been and may been major political realignments suggests that no long-term and expensive technological fix should presume continuity of current political form. (The British assumption of a continuing hegemony in the Indus is to the development of an integrated scheme which was dis-integrated after 1947 at great cost.)

An idiosyncratic and unconventional proposal is to presume that the problem is not one of droughts or floods or cyclones. It is of risk which small farmers and the poor face at the micro-scale, such that for many there are inducements to have large families (although there are also strong cultural impulsions as well). Interestingly in a way, most of

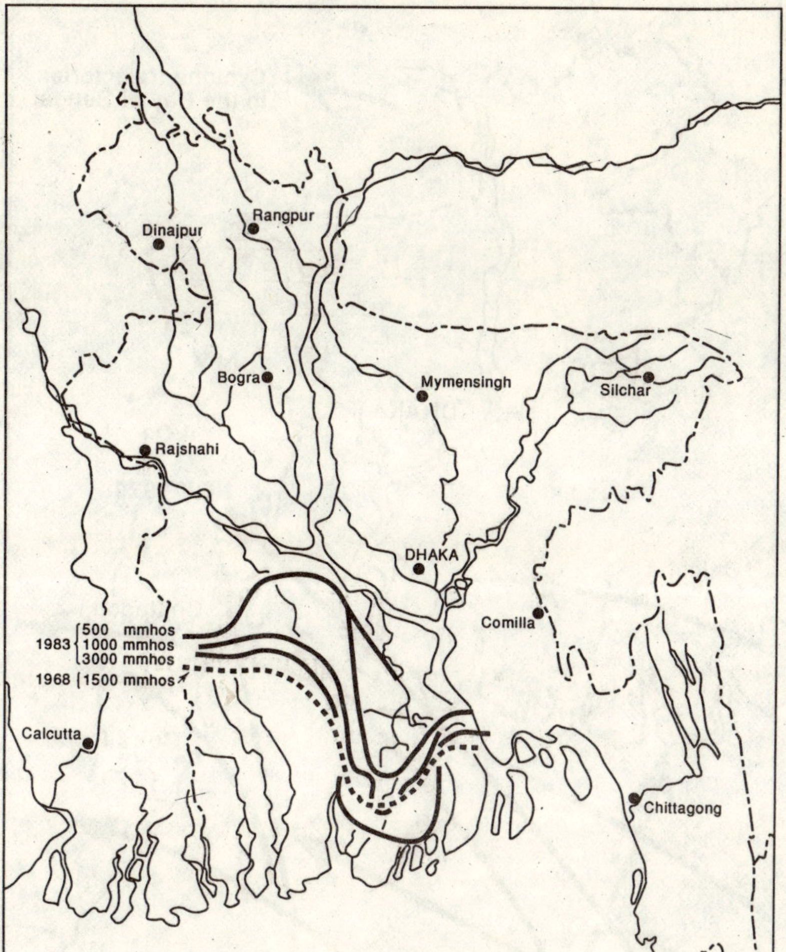

FIG. 12.10: Saline Incursion in Bengal

(*Source:* Islam (1992)

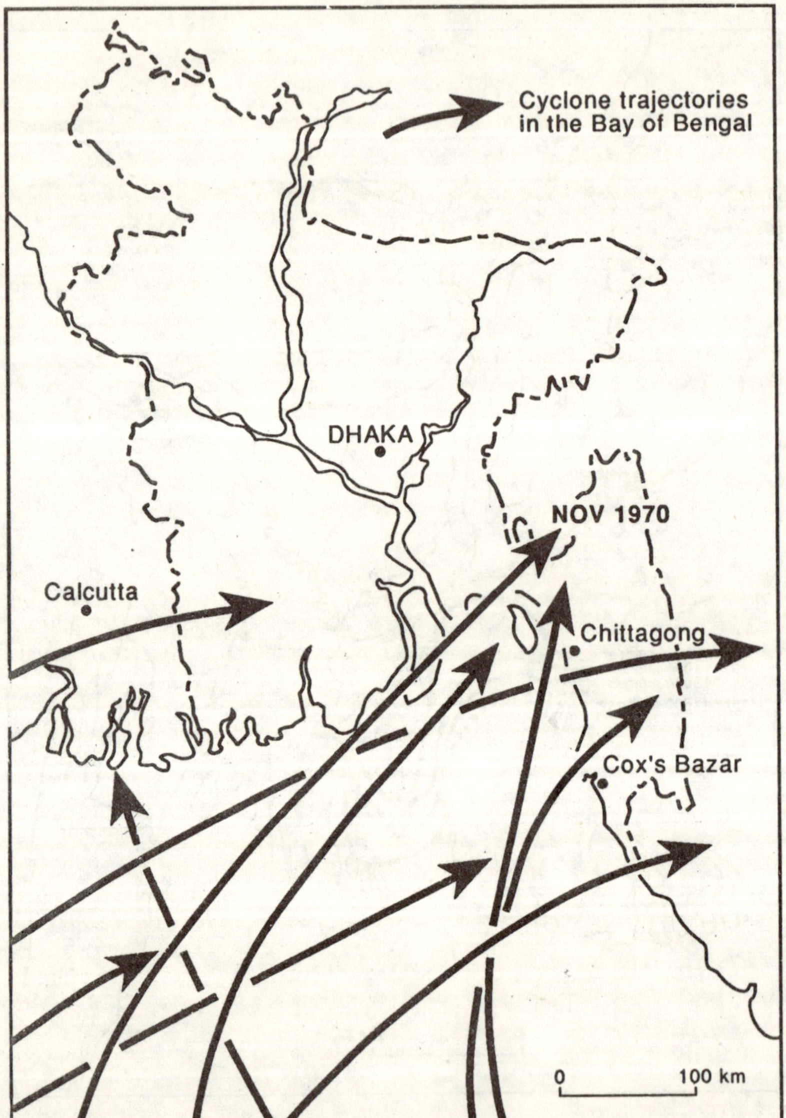

FIG.12.11: Cyclone Trache in Bengal

(*Source*: Johnson (1975)

the current agricultural improvements are occurring at the micro-scale – through the use of small scale irrigation in the dry season. The link between micro and macro scale does not have to be through embankments and river training. And there are strong suspicious that many of these schemes will be costly, transitory, and ecologically disruptive (Fig. 12.11).

Brammer (1990) has shown that at the national-scale even in bad years Bangladesh has not done as badly as at first feared (Table 12.2). If at the macro-scale risk even in bad years is not so high, there could theoretically be a means to redistribute risk. (This was one of the benefits that the railways are thought to have brought to India in the 19th century.) Therefore, as a thought experiment, let us assume that there are donors around who might be prepared to sink billions of dollars into vast engineering schemes, but then ask them to re-consider, instead to lend the same money to an institutional innovation — a national crop insurance scheme run at local levels (and an urban-regional plan to concentrate the more expensive capital investments of urbanization on Pleistocene terraces, or other sites selected by astute geomorphologists). This means doing what the local farmers have done for millenia: accepting the vagaries of the environment and having a flexible response, but this time with an added institutional extra layer that the flexible response is local but plugged into a national framework. Bangladesh is probing this path: by building village safety mounds — local earth encampments surrounded by borrow pits — and by trial crop insurance schemes (Bangladesh Minister for Information, personal communication, May 1990). Such a proposal is actually presaged now by the volte-face which has occurred in the UK this year over the management of coastal erosion. The south of Britain is sinking, and major amounts of money have been poured into coastal defences, often of land of lowish value. Sometimes defences in one place change the movement of sediment, and result in erosion in other places. The defences have continually been damaged and breached. Now the government has decided that managed retreat is better: the sea should be allowed to have its own way, and new salt marshes encouraged to develop, and for farmers and other land users suitable economic help should be provided for the adjustments they make. This is a historically sensitive and place specific approach. But such a soft approach is not yet part of the paradigm of Bengali Development International Ltd.

I do not pretend that such a soft approach will answer all the problems. Farakka still exists; the investment in Calcutta is fixed in a way that the rivers are not since ironically in Bengal the speed of economic and social locational change is slower than that of environmental change; the demands on the Ganges low season flow will escalate. With hindsight, it might have been best if this flow had not been interfered with at all, and all upstream development made dependent on extraction from the massive groundwater reserves (which however is energetically expensive). But of course the current state of affairs has to be accepted as the reality, and hence in this respect at least if Bangladesh does want to augment the Ganges low season flow, than a physical link with the Brahmaputra seems likely. However, even here there is a caveat. Looking at the current proposal it seems that a great deal of digging will shift the confluence (for some of the waters) only a small way up-stream, so that a new Ganges barrage will become necessary as well. One wonders how long a life such a project would have.

My final conclusion is that simplified myth-propagation will not anyone. That India and Bangladesh have a problem over Farakka and that this barrage affects dry-season flows cannot be denied. But to generalise from the one tangible case to make India a scapegoat for all other environmental ills is not useful. Quite clearly, the manifold problems of Bengal cannot be blamed simply and only on India's and Nepal's upstream behaviour.

REFERENCES

Abbas, B.M. (1982). *The Ganges Water Dispute*, New Delhi.

Anderson, Francis Philip (1900). "The Effects of the Earthquake in 1897 on the Shaistaganj Division of the Assam-Bengal Railway". *Proceedings of the Inst. of Civil Engineers,* Vol 141, No. 3, pp 258-61.

Brammer, H. (1990). "Floods in Bangladesh: Geographical Background to the 1987 and 1988 floods". *The Geographical Journal,* Vol. 156, No.1, pp. 12-22

Brammer, H. (forthcoming). "Floods in Bangladesh: Flood Mitigation and Environmental Aspects". *The Geographical Journal.*

Brammer, H. (1989). "Flood in the Agro-ecology of Bangladesh". Paper presented at, International Seminar on Bangladesh Floods: Regional and Global Environmental Perspectives. Dhaka.

Brammer, H. (1989). "Monitoring the Evidence of the Greenhouse Effect and its Impact on Bangladesh" Paper presented at: The International Conference on the Greenhouse Effect and Coastal Area of Bangladesh. Coastal Area Resource Development Management Association (CORDMA), Dhaka.

Burgess, J. (1985). "News from nowhere: The Press, the Riots, and the Myth of the Inner City" in Burgess, J. and Godl, J. (eds.) *Geography, the Media and Popular Culture.* Croom Helm.

Burgess, J. and Harrison, C. (1993). "The Circulation of Claims in the Cultural Politics of Environmental Change". in A. Hansen (ed.) *Environmental Issues and the Mass Media*, Leicester University Press.

Chapman, G.P. *One into Three: the Geopolitics of South Asia from British Raj to India, Pakistan and Bangladesh.* Book MSS, forthcoming.

Crow, Ben and Lundquist, Alan. (1990). "Development of the Rivers Ganges and Brahmaputra: The Difficulty of Developing a New Line". *Development Policy and Practice Working Paper No 19*, The Open University, Walton Hall, Milton Keynes.

Eckholm, E. (1976). *Losing Ground*, Worldwatch Institute, USA.

Farmer, B.H. (1979). "The Green Revolution' in South Asian Ricefields: Environment and Production". *Journal of Development Studies*, 15. pp 304-319.

Islam, N. (1992). Indo-Bangladesh Common Rivers: The Impact on Bangladesh", *Contemporary South Asia* Vol. 1, No. 2, pp 203-225.

Ives, Jack D. (1989). "Deforestation in the Himalayas: The cause of increased flooding in Bangladesh and Northern India?" *Land Use Policy.* No. 6(3). pp 187-193.

Ives, Jack D., Messerli, Bruno (1989). *The Himalayan Dilemma: Reconciling Development and Conservation*, The United Nation University and Routledge, London and New York, pp 295.

Johnson, B.L.C. (1975). *Bangladesh*, Heineman, London, pp 104.

King, Lester C. (1983). *Wandering Continents and Spreading Sea Floors on an Expanding Earth*, John Wiley, Chichester, pp 232.

Michel, A.A. (1967). *The Indus Rivers: A study in the effects of Partition*, Yale University Press, New Haven and London, pp. 595.

Shwarz, M. and Thompson, M. (1990). *Divided we stand: Redefining Politics, Technology and Social Choice*, Harvester Wheatsheaf, New York.

Tapponnier, P., Peltser, G. and Armijo, R. (1986). "On the mechanics of the collision between India and Asia" pp. 115-157 in *Collision Tectonics* (Geological Society Special Publication No 19), Coward, M.P. and Ries, Alison C. (eds.) Blackwell Scientific, Oxford.

Thompson, M. (1993). "Policy Making in the Face of Uncertainty" in Chapman, G.P. and Thompson, M. (eds.) *Environmental Problems in the Ganges Brahmaputra Basin.*

World Bank (1989). *Bangladesh Action Plan for Flood Control*, Washington, D.C.

Umitsu, Masatomo (1985). "Natural Levées and Landform Evolution in the Bengal Lowland" *Geographical Review of Japan*, Vol. 58 (Ser. B). No. 2, pp. 149-164.

Umitsu, Masatomo (1987). "Late quaternary Sedimentary Environmental and Landform Evolution in the Bengal Lowland". *Geographical Review of Japan*, Vol. 60 (Ser. B), No. 2, pp. 164-178.

13

ENVIRONMENTAL IMPLICATIONS OF RIVER VALLEY DEVELOPMENT : A Micro-Level Study

R. RAM MOHAN RAO and N.RAM KISHAN RAO

Major structural changes in the agricultural production system is the essence of agricultural development for most of the third world countries. In order to meet the growing needs of food for teeming millions in the third world countries, one of the measures taken by the concerned governments has been the accelerated development of modern agricultural practices based on irrigation and use of fertilizers. Great emphasis on the creation of irrigation potential in India under the aegis of planned development has been laid since the beginning of planning era with a view to attain self-sufficiency in agricultural production and to reduce dependence on erratic rainfall for ensuring reliable production. Irrigation is a critical part for growth of agriculture. It is not only a key factor in raising agricultural production but also in minimising instability attributable to uncertain and irregular rainfall.

Indian farmers are long accustomed to irrigation. In the pre-independence era, the development of surface irrigation accelerated the renovation of several existing canals, and early in the 19th century, and later, with the construction of several major irrigation works. The earliest form of irrigation was flood or *Sailab* irrigation mostly in the flood plains of rivers of north India and deltaic tracts of central and south India. In the middle of last century the British rulers with great foresight executed large irrigation projects, such as the Cauvery Delta System, Godavari Delta System, and Krishna Delta System under the stewardship of Sir Arthur Cotton. But major irrigation, whether termed 'protective' or productive, was designed to provide some protection from long breaks in the monsoon by adding river water through canals over long tracks of land during monsoon period. The emphasis on the drought insurance aspect of irrigation has since undergone a change and irrigation is being viewed as a means of stability and raising productivity in the agricultural sector. Rapid strides have been made since the beginning of first five year plan, and since, then an irrigation potential of 60 million hectares has been created so far. Of this vast irrigated area, an overwhelming proportion is saved by canals systems of major and medium sized irrigation projects. This large scale modern agricultural irrigation has made it possible to turn vast areas of dry, uncultivated land into fertile crop land.

Modern canal irrigation is closely connected with and directly related to environmental factors. Construction of huge dams across a natural river course and the laying of canal network and consequent transformation are apt to interfere in, and even seriously alter, existing ecosystems — affecting vegetation, water-balance, soil characteristics and biotic resources. Therefore, irrigation development in the river valleys cannot and should not be regarded as merely an agricultural matter since it may have far-reaching influence on environment and consequently on human welfare. Failure to recognise this vital concept and giving emphasis only for crop raising aspect has led to disastrous environmental crop raising aspect has led to disastrous environmental results. Unfortunately, the environmental aspects have too often been overlooked in the development of modern irrigation programme.

It is true that man has always been making a living out of nature. By learning about the laws of nature and working in the direction of exercising more control over nature to reduce his vulnerability to its vagaries, man has started to disturb the ecosystem. Vegetation, soil, climate and water replenish themselves over cycles to make this earth a suitable habitat. However, if cycles are disturbed by man's activities the very source of living is then under threat of extinction. Therefore, advancing technologies like large scale canal irrigation farming in river valleys have an obligation to ensure that man's exploitation of natural resources does not drastically disturb and destroy the environmental balance.

In order to fully comprehend the role of irrigation in changing environment, it is necessary to emphasise that water is only one of the inputs to agricultural production. The other are soil, seeds, fertilizers, labour, technology and solar radiation etc. It is for this surrounding of irrigation system can be identified by several integrating complex sub-system.

Environmental problems associated with development of river valley with the means of canal irrigation constitute some of the most complex problems of a third world country like India which is located in one of ecologically vulnerable areas of the world. These environmental problems come hand in hand with change. Traditional agricultural systems tend generally to exist in a dynamic balance with environment, so that ecological vulnerability is minimized. Environmental analysis for development involves understanding the role of environmental factors in the dynamic evolution of the agricultural system inducted by the development process.

Environmental impact of canal irrigation in river valley is felt both on biotic and abiotic components of environment. Impact of irrigation on environment, though, mostly manifests on physical environment, changes in social and economic environments, are also discernible. Many studies have been made in India and other countries about the extent of environmental impact of irrigation on such aspects as soil degradation, waterlogging, deforestation, landuse, cropping pattern, health, etc. However, these problems have been studied only at macro level and not many attempts have been made to study the environmental impact of irrigation at grass root level. We are aware of the problems only in a general sense, but there is a gap in knowledge with regard to the impact of irrigation at village level and at farmers' level. Farmer's perception is not that well documented and researched so far. This study aims at filling up this gap in knowledge by attempting an analysis of the information obtained at micro-level. Thus the objective of the study is to examine the extent and nature of environmental impact of irrigation at village/farm/farmer level. The positive and negative effects of environmental change are investigated. An analysis of what the farmer and members of the village community perceive of their altered environment is also attempted. Finally a set of recommendations are made to over come the problems.

Before proceeding further, it is necessary to state the limitations within which the study is made. The study related only to a village and its community and can not be described as a comprehensive statistically valid sample study. It can be described as a pilot study which can be a precursor for a more elaborate analysis of environmental impact in the entire command area of the irrigation project. The generalisation made in the course of analysis may not necessarily be universally valid for the irrigated areas or even for the command area in which the village is located. This is for the simple reason that type of vegetation, soils and other components of environment would naturally be different in other areas.

Information collected from the field at village level and household level forms the basis of the present study. A survey of the farming households was made on census basis. Data base also consists of village records, landuse and cropping pattern figures obtained from the concerned authorities. Method of collection of data for different physical attributes is explained in the respective sections.

Study Area

The study area is Mogulpet village which is located in the irrigated tract of Sriramsagar Command Area. Sriramsagar is a state sector major irrigation project in Telangana Region of Andhra Pradesh State. The Masonry dam built across river Godavari is located at Pochampad village upstream of Son bridge on Hyderabad — Nagpur National highway, 200 km north of Hyderabad. The length of Godavari river from source, Triambak in Maharashtra, to Bay of Bengal is 940 kms. The project is to be completed in two phases. The project command area in the first phase covers 2.90 lakh hectares and the second phase encompasses an area of 3.61 lakhs. The first phase has already been completed. Work on the second phase is in progress. At present, the project has acquired a storage of 112 TMC ft of water.

The village Mogulpet is situated ten kilometres away from the taluk headquarters of Metpalli and twelve kilometres from the dam site. It is two kilometres away from river Godavari. The village has been selected for study after a very careful reconnaisance survey of the entire command area. Authors extensive knowledge of command area helped in selecting the village. It formed part of the sample survey made in 1981. (Rao & Simhadri, 1989). The main reason for selection of Mogulpet for the survey is that it typifies the areas with environment impact caused by irrigation. The physical conditions such as soils, hydrology etc. are similar to many other parts of the command area, and as such the village can be considered as representative of the entire command area to a great extent. The societal structure such as caste composition, proportion of different classes of farmers etc. is near similar to that of command area. So is the economy. Another reason for selecting the village is the fact that the village is one of the first villages which received canal waters way back in 1977, and as such, has experienced the positive and negative impact of provision of canal irrigation. The following analysis of impact of irrigation on environment relates to, not only physical environment, but some of the social and economic aspects as well. It has to be said in this context that the physical, social and economic facets are all interrelated and cannot be studied in isolation disregarding their mutual interdependence.

Impact of Irrigation on Soil Conditions

In order to study the impact of irrigation on soil conditions in the command area of major irrigation projects, soils have to be examined in relation to their fertility, water retention capacity, qualities of permeability, soils variability, salinity and alkalinity and depth of soils.

Soils depth refers to soil thickness over hardrock below which roots cannot pass on to a permanently saturated zone, in which roots cannot survive due to unfavourable conditions. Soil depth is directly related to development of root system, moisture storage, nutrient availability etc.

The soils of the village are predominantly red. The red soils occur mostly in higher reaches and black soils in the lower reaches of topography. Soils are mostly shallow to moderately deep. The percentage occurrence is as follow.

TABLE 13.1: Soils: Range of Soil Depth

Soils type	Range of soil depth in cms				Total
	< & 22.5	22.5-45	45-90	90 & >	
Red soil	15.5	58.2	10.5	5.8	100
Black soils	1.2	2.8	14.5	82.5	100

A shallow soil of less than 22.5cm depth has limited moisture holding capacity, restricted feeding zones and root growth and would need frequent irrigation. Interviews with farmers and field observations revealed that there have been only a few cases of change in the range of soil depth. However, some problems had arisen because of provision of irrigation as to the crop to be grown during rabi season. As most of the village farms have soils depths upto 50 cms or so, no other crop except rice could economically be grown which is not possible due to limited supply of water during Rabi season. This has led to anamalous situation where by the farmers are not in a position to get full benefit out of irrigation facility. Cultivation of wet-cum-dry crops requires deep soils which are found only in certain pockets of the village cropped area. As a result of which, the yield of the crops, forced to be grown despite their being not suitable, are not high.

TABLE 13.2: Crops and Effective Root Zone

Crop	Effective Root Zone in cms
Groundnut	45
Wheat	60
Castor	90
Tobacco	90
Maize	120
Cotton	120
Sorghum	120
Sugarcane	180

Soil Erosion

Soil erosion is associated with loss of useful top soil, reduction of soil depth, loss of nutrients and decline in fertility. The data obtained from field survey of the village revealed the following.

TABLE 13.3: Soil Erosion and Crop Suitability

Erosion Class	Erosion Intensity	Crop suitability	Per cent Net cropped area
I	Less than 25% of surface horizon lost	Wet & dry Irr	85%
II	Moderate erosion 50-70% of surface horizon lost	same as above	8%
III	Severe erosion (complete surface horizon is lost)	wet & I.D. (groundnut & wheat)	5%
IV	Very severe erosion (entire surface horizon & 25-75% horizon B) lost	Not suitable for cropping	2%

It is evident that erosion in 85 per cent of the area can be termed as slight, and as such, soil erosion cannot considered as a big problem in the village. In fact, the farmers opined that the intensity of soil erosion has lessened after the release of water due to construction of field channels and bunds necessary for irrigated farming. Whatever, erosion that occurs, is found in the elevated areas of the village where the irrigation facility could not be provided.

Soil Salinity

All soils contain salts which originated from rocks as they weather into soil. Salts are leached downwards with the percolating water where they are deposited into the soil. It is generally observed that salinity increases with the provision of canal irrigation. This is attributed to extensive seepage which occurs from water flowing in canals resulting in the rise of groundwater table. The project report of Sriramsagar project (Anonymous, 1964) revealed that the soils of command area have low salt content. Field investigations revealed that no field has been rendered not culturable due to land becoming salty. The proportion of area unfit for cultivation has remained nearly the same during two time periods as is revealed by the following table.

TABLE 13.4: Percentage of Area Unfit for Cultivation Due to Excessive Salinity

1. Mogulpet Village	(1993) 0.82 (1981) 0.80
2. Sriramsagar Command Area	(1981) 0.79
3. Nagarjunasagar Command Area	(1981) 0.99
4. Krishna Delta	(1981) 2.40
5. Godavari Delta	(1981) 0.17

Waterlogging

Setback to agricultural development in the areas of surface irrigation due to waterlogging is well recorded in the world history of canal irrigation. It is a major challenge to human ingenuity to practice irrigated farming in arid and semi-arid regions. The problem of waterlogging in the command areas of major irrigation projects was noticed and reported by many researchers especially in the arid and semi-arid regions where it is found to be higher. However, attempts to identify and diagnose were scant.

The waterlogging is defined as occupation of pore spaces of soil profile by water, such that, for lack of aeration, the root system of most of the crops fail to perform their function for proper crop growth during different seasons. The areas with water-table depth ranging between 0-3m is considered to be waterlogged. Two types of waterlogging conditions are recognised. The first type is on account of irrigation water neither being able to drain through the soils, nor, getting drained as run-off. The second type is on account of general rise in ground water levels. The construction of a surface drainage system and programme for optimal utilization is essential to avoid waterlogging.

Waterlogging in the Village

The topography of the village comprises of prominent ridges here and there amidst gently to moderately sloping land. The area can be described as a rolling terrain with slopes ranging from one per cent to three per cent. The plane areas lie between 850 ft. to 1050 ft. and slope in the northern and north eastern direction towards river Godavari. The sandy loam textured soils are found in most of the village area. Undulating topography facilitated good drainage before the onset of canal irrigation.

Around a quarter of the total cropped area is waterlogged during some part of the year and the total number of farmers affected is 45 out of which twenty-two are badly affected ten are affected moderately and the rest are only marginally affected. The water-table has been rising in the village under study right from the year of provision of water from the year 1978 as is evident from the following table.

TABLE 13.5: Depth of Water Level

Year	average depth of water level from the ground	month of recording
1978	28 ft	June
1981	12 ft	December
1985	10.5 ft	March
1990	6 ft	March
1993	5 ft	January

The figures in the table are to be interpreted with caution, since, they were not recorded in the same month of year as it should be for a more meaningful interpretation. Still, enquiries with the farmers revealed that the problem of waterlogging has been increasing year after year and it is the number one problem now. The water-table has been rising at an average rate of 25 cm per annum and has shown some slackening in recent years.

The causes for waterlogging in the village are as follow:

(i) Land shaping, land levelling and flattening in order to facilitate irrigation in the area has abnormally increased the infiltration rate resulting in charging the groundwater at a very high rate;

(ii) Lack of outlets for draining out the water and unsystematic scheduling of release of water into canals and field has also led to waterlogging. Field drains, carrier drains have not been properly maintained;

(iii) Seepage from canals is considerable and as a result of it water percolates down into the ground even when it is not required by the crops;

(iv) As the schedule to release of water is not properly regulated and because of the lack of knowledge of the exact requirements of water for various crops, the farmers in the village tend to over-irrigate their field as a precaution against any delay in the timely release of water by the authorities;

(v) Agricultural fields in the village have become waterlogged as the water from wells, which used to be the sole sources of irrigation before canal irrigation set in, is not being utilised at all. Had the farmers utilised the water from the wells alternatively with canals, water table would have gone down and waterlogging would not have taken place; and

(vi) The embankments of main lines, branch lines and distributaries of canals themselves offer obstruction to the run off of rainfall resulting in water stagnation.

Village survey results reveal that the farmers in the village consider waterlogging as the major problem for which they do not seem to have any solution in sight. This is so because the problem of waterlogging can be tackled by the entire village community and not by individual farmers. The following steps are required to be taken in order to lessen the problem of waterlogging and to maintain natural water table conditions.

(i) Conjuctive use of surface and groundwater from irrigation may considerably ease the situation. This measure will not only take out excess water, but also would help in irrigating more area. The command area authorities should release water into the branch and distributing canals only when the groundwater is found to be insufficient. At present there is no much restriction and farmers of the village complained that the authorities release water even when the water is not required for the fields;

(ii) Lining of canal system with cement of minimise seepage losses in the water conductor system is yet another solution. Technology with regard to lining of canals by a plastic film has also been developed in recent years, but this may be out of reach of the third world countries;

(iii) Proper regulation of field outlets by the farmers themselves to draw water for irrigation within the prescribed requirements and time may also lead to lessen the impact of the problem of waterlogging;

(iv) Tendency to over-irrigate the fields should be stopped;

(v) Improvement and maintenance of surface drainage system is necessary to prevent waterlogging; and

(vi) Waterlogging problem can also be met by growing suitable crops depending upon the degree of waterlogging and availability.

Information collected from individual farmers affected by waterlogging, indicates, that the crop yields of certain wet-cum-dry crops such as sugarcane, maize, jowar which have relatively greater effective root zones of higher than 100 cms have declined considerably. They do not survive well in the waterlogged areas. Even if the survive during certain part of the year, the yield from them is considerably reduced. Yields in waterlogged areas are 25-30 per cent less on an average, than the yields in the non-waterlogged areas. Fall in yields vary from crop to crop. Millet crops are the worst hit of all the crops. It is found that even in case of rice which is a completely wet crop, the yields in the waterlogged and non-waterlogged areas of the village decreased from an average of 2.9 metric tonnes to 2.2 metric tonnes per hectare.

River Valley Development and Health Aspects

Canal irrigation in river valleys is closely connected with and directly related to environment factors. Major irrigation projects are apt to interfere in and seriously alter the existing eco-system affecting its water balance, biotic composition, and in course of time, the health of the people. Irrigation development is therefore to be regarded not only as an agricultural matter, but also as having repercussions on man's health.

A close relationship between water and health of people has been known for a long time but it is only a little over century ago since this relationship began to be understood, and the causes of infection from certain diseases were identified with water. Stern (1988) classified. Infective disease related to water into three groups:

(i) *Water borne*, in which infection is transmitted by water. e.g., typhoid, cholera, Hepatitis, Dysentry etc.;
(ii) *Water-based*, in which infections are transmitted through an aquatic invertebrate e.g. guinea worm; and
(iii) *Water-related*, in which infections are spread by insects which depends on water, examples of which are Malaria and Filaria.

Provision of canal irrigation to semi-arid village like Mogulpet is bound to increase health hazards by providing conditions more favourable to the transmission of diseases related to water. In canal irrigated areas, water is made to stand either in storage in furrows or in pools in the fields. Increase in the incidence of some diseases is an additional harmful effect of dam construction. The construction of huge reservoirs can elevate the sub-soil water in the vicinity with the consequent change in the levels of calcium and trace elements. This changes the nature of flurosis, a crippling bone diseases, in areas where it is already prevalent.

Incidence of Malaria

Information collected on the incidence of malaria since the introduction of irrigation in the village has revealed substantial increase, consequent to multiple cropping. Coupled with increased waterlogging it has resulted in steep rise in the incidence of Malaria. The primary malaria vector identified in the village is 'Anopheles culifacacies'. Available literature on malaria refers to this species occurring frequently in fresh water and as sun loving and favouring moderate shade, all of which conditions exist in the village. According to Jayaraman (1982), who has made a study of malaria impact of surface irrigation project in Gujarat, the rate of growth of larvae depends upon the habitats which are (1). Permanent and semi-permanent standing fresh water such as small ponds, pools and stagnant canals and ditches, standing agricultural water as in rice fields, (2). Transient fresh water pools in cart tracks, and (3). Permanent or semi-permanent fresh water in open streams, canals and distributaries. Based on the data provided by the health authorities and the National Malaria Eradication programme workers, the Annual Parasite Index (API) has been worked out for the village. The API is defined as the number of positive malarial cases detected per thousand population.

TABLE 13.6: Incidence of Malaria in Mogulpet Village

Year	Annual Parasite Index
1970	1.11
1971	1.15
1972	1.02
1973	1.25
1974	1.52
1975	1.32
1976	1.25
1977	1.20
1978	1.40
1979	1.45
1980	2.03
1981	1.92
1982	3.45
1983	5.85
1984	5.72
1985	8.07
1986	10.69
1987	11.22
1988	14.48
1989	13.43
1990	15.60
1991	17.25
1992	16.72

An examination of the above table reveals that the incidence of malaria as more of less stable for six years preceding the onset of canal irrigation and five years after it. However, in the subsequent years, there has been a steady rise in the incidence of malaria with the maximum API recorded in the year 1991. The rising rate of malaria incidence is all the more significant alarming, since, this happened despite the health authorities launching and intensifying the drive against malaria control during this period. The villagers consider malarial fever as the most important health problem. In the early years of canal irrigation, villagers did not consider malaria as a major health problem. Their perception of this health hazard had changed considerably during recent years and instances have come to the notice, of forcing local authorities to adopt anti-malaria measures. The village has a malaria para-medical worker and a clinic having laboratory facilities for testing blood smears and stocking medicines to combat malaria is located in the nearby primary health centre. All these measures have not led to decrease in API. Nevertheless, they helped in containing it at least. But, the people have to learn to live with this health problem caused by impact of irrigation on environment. It has been found that incidence of malaria is more in the agricultural labour class and among marginal farmers than amongst the relatively better off sections of village community.

Other water related diseases suffered by the villagers include stray cases of filaria, some case of encephalaties and the crippling knock-knees (*gen-velgum*) condition. But the person affected by these diseases are not many and the diseases are not endemic in character.

Agro-Economic Setting

River valley development invariably leads to the drastic changes in the agro-economic setting. In this study an attempts has been made to analyse certain agro-economic aspects like cropping pattern, crop productivity and crop yields.

Cropping Pattern

As per the allocation made by the Sriramsagar command area authorities, water is being supplied for wet crop during kharif season, and for irrigated dry crops, during rabi season. Normally, crops like paddy, sugarcane are grown during kharif season (June to December). However, sugarcane is an annual crop and hence grown only by farmers with assured groundwater facilities and in those areas where waterlogging problem is not as acute as to prevent its cultivation. As wet crop season coincides with monsoon period 40 per cent of total cultivated area is devoted for paddy cultivation. In the rabi season (December to April), the cropping pattern is influenced by water availability and the policy of the command area development authorities. The project authorities have been ensuring for the last many years a minimum of two-thirds proportion of cultivated area of the village for irrigated dry crops and water is released to these areas during rabi season.

Cropping may be of two types — single cropping and multiple cropping, single cropping may be either monoculture pattern wherein only one crop is grown year after year and rotational pattern in which crops are rotated. Multiple cropping may be of (i) sequential type with two or more crops grown on the same piece of land in a year, (ii) intercropping type in which two crops or some time more are grown on the same piece of land at the same time.

Single cropping — Monoculture / Rotational

Multiple cropping — Sequential / Intercropping

As one moves from left to right, management of irrigation becomes more complex. In monoculture water can be distributed in proportion to area over the entire village. On the other hand, when multiple crops are grown concurrently, water supply needs to be adjusted to meet respective crop requirements. This is not always possible in canal irrigated areas. In Mogulpet village, a flexible form control is found, where areas are 'localized' for certain crops which respectively have different water requirements. But this is not necessarily followed by individual farmers as is clear from the following analysis of cropping pattern.

In order to fully grasp the impact of irrigation on cropping pattern it is essential to compare the present pattern with that existed in the year before release of waters and some intermediate periods. In order to facilitate this cropping pattern data is collected for 1976-77, 1981-82, 1986-87 and 1991-92. Detailed season-wise cropping pattern is given in Table 13.7.

A perusal of the figures reveals that the area under kharif crop has remained nearly same throughout the study periods with minor variations. But the area under rice cultivation, as expected, went up considerably. This has happened at the cost of all other crops specially jowar and pulses. During rabi season, rice cropped area went up. But

TABLE 13.7: Cropping Pattern

Season	Crop	1991-92		1986-87		1981-82		1976-77	
		area in Ha.	%	area in Ha.	%	area in Ha.	%	area in Ha.	%
Kharif	Rice	512	31.9	510	32.7	432	29.9	290	22.5
	Maize	124	7.7	145	9.14	212	154.7	278	21.60
	Jowar	67	4.18	152	9.58	215	14.9	222	17.20
	Pulses	52	3.24	22	1.38	78	5.41	148	11.03
	Others	50	3.12	44	2.77	152	10.34	102	7.88
	Total	805	50.28	873	55.01	1089	75.57	1040	80.05
Rabi	Rice	105	6.55	72	4.54	52	3.6	44	3.15
	Maize	245	15.30	252	15.89	85	5.89	04	0.32
	Jowar	92	5.74	102	6.43	44	3.0	12	0.94
	Groundnut	109	6.88	68	4.29	21	1.45	00	0.00
	Pulses	28	1.74	15	0.94	12	0.8	13	1.00
	Others	112	0.75	19	1.19	22	1.52	12	0.93
	Total	591	36.41	528	33.3	236	16.37	85	6.59
Two Seasonal	Sugarcane	42	2.62	28	1.76	14	0.97	04	0.31
	Chillies	84	5.24	92	5.8	75	5.2	124	9.6
	Pulses	25	1.56	19	1.19	12	0.83	117	1.31
	Cotton	29	1.81	20	1.26	0	0.00	00	0.00
	Others	25	1.56	25	1.57	15	1.04	18	1.39
	Total	205	12.8	184	11.60	116	8.04	163	12.60
Grand Total		1601	100.00	1585	100.00	1441	100.00	1288	100.00

the area under irrigated dry crops such as maize, jowar, groundnut, also increased significantly. Annual crops such as sugarcane, chillies and pulses, etc. cannot be counted as major crops, since, they are cultivated only in small proportions. Field data revealed that the cropping pattern as of now is not the result of farmer's choice and governments recommendations, but is dictated by environmental conditions. For example, waterlogging even of moderate intensity has forced farmers to opt for rice cultivation during kharif season instead of commercial crops such as maize, pulses, groundnut, etc. which would have proved more economical and profitable for the farmers.

TABLE 13.8: Rice Equivalents Based on APC

Rice	—	1.00
Maize	—	0.66
Jowar	—	0.68
Pulses	—	1.30
Cotton	—	2.00
Groundnut	—	1.60
Chillies Dry weight	—	4.00
Sugarcane	—	0.10

Irrigation and Crop Yield

Apart from changes in cropping pattern one expects an increase in per hectare crop yields as a consequence of extension of irrigation facilities. The present and past yield statistics given below are the averaged figures by farmers. They can not be taken to be very correct since many farmers do not be taken to be very correct since many farmers do not even maintain any count of the production except at the ime of marketing. However, they are the only figures that are available at micro level. The potential yields are the ones given by the command area authorities.

It is evident from the above table that the yields (in rice equivalents) is highesι for sugarcane cultivation and lowest for jowar. It can also be observed that the yields rise considerably during the periods and irrigation can be taken as the causative factor. Under ideal agro-ecological conditions, all the farmers would like to raise only those crops where,returns are high. But this has not happened as the choice of the crop to be raised by the farmer is not in their hands, but is determined by the degree of the adversity of environmental impact of irrigation.

TABLE 13.9: Changes in Yield and Potential Yield of Important Crops

(*kg per hectare*)

Crops	Actual Yields Converted into Rice Equivalents		
	1976-77 q/ha	1991-92 q/ha	Potential q/ha
Rice	8.50	18.05	44.0
Jowar	4.11	9.52	18.2
Groundnut	N.A.	26.21	45.0
Pulses	6.24	8.45	22.4
Sugarcane	N.A.	44.20	62.6

Crop Productivity and Crop Yields

It is worthwhile to study the production augmenting role of irrigation by examining the actual productivity per unit of irrigation water. In the absence of field data on the volume of irrigation water supplied to different farms in the village, information on number of waterings done for an irrigated crop has been gathered from farmers and used as a surrogate for quantum of irrigation water.

TABLE 13.10: Crop Productivity and Crop Yields

		Food grains	Non-food grains
1.	Average yield (Kg/ha)	1805	4817
2.	No. waterings	3.80	8.12
3.	Output per watering	427.60	593.20

Canal irrigation has been found to change both crop pattern and crop yield in the village under study. Yield per hectare, boosted up from a little over 6 quintals to a little over 18 quintals (in terms of rice units). These yields are substantially below the potential of 40-50 quintals per hectare indicated in several agronomical findings in other parts of India. The yield hiatus between promise and performance is mainly due to substantial input gap between the recommended and the actual doses of two leading but complimentary inputs of irrigated farming, namely, chemical fertilizers and irrigation water at the right-time and when needed. Another overpowering reason for the gap is the degradation of soil and/or waterlogging of many areas.

The discussion made in the preceding paras may be summarised as follows:

1. Lightly irrigated crops, like pulses and oilseeds and spices are more productive than heavily irrigated crops, such as, paddy and sugarcane when production is assessed in terms of water units utilised.
2. Productivity of irrigation water is positively related to both chemical fertilizers and volume of water.
3. Conjunctive use of surface and groundwater produces superior output results to those obtaining under surface irrigation alone.
4. Non-food grain crops as a group are more superior to food grain crops.

TABLE 13.11: Comparative Production of Crops Irrigated to Different Intensities

	Area %	Yield kg/ha	No. of waterings	NPK kg/ha	Yield per watering
1. Lightly irrigated crop	12.2	1350	2.72	16	496.32
2. Medium irrigated crop	27.8	3800	2.25	120	1688.89
3. Heavily irrigated crops	60.00	2100	4.25	66	494.12
4. All crops	100.0	2215	4.4	72	503.41

Above Table 13.11 presents a comparative picture of heavily irrigated crops *vis-a-vis* lightly irrigated crops in respect of yield per unit and incremental output per unit of watering. It is clear that productivity per unit of water is inversely related extent of irrigation.

It may be summarised that canal irrigation in the study area has vastly transformed the cropping pattern and helped in increasing the yields of nearly all the crops. The productivity of crops has gone up despite the set backs caused by environmental factors. In order further streamline, the agricultural activity in the village following steps are suggested.

1. Strict implementation of 'warbandi' and 'localisation' schemes.
2. Removal of communication gap between the command area

authorities and the farmers in the village, so that, the farmers may get information as to what crop is beneficial to grow in a particular situation and time. Village farmers are well versed more with dry farming techniques than the irrigated farming as is the position now.

3. To attain full potential of crop yields, farmers need to be provided with the necessary inputs such as fertilisers, pesticides, better seeds etc. Provision of water for irrigation may not be sufficient by itself. This input has to be augmented simultaneously with other inputs.
4. Formation of a political farmers' association in the village will go a long way in evolving a cropping strategy acceptable to all. The association, if formed, can be in a position to force the authorities to take into account the ground realities and frame a workable proposition acceptable to local farmers.

Conclusion

Environment, if not disturbed drastically and indiscriminately, is conducive for all living things-humans, flora and fauna, there is a truth in the old age that, there is enough in the world for everyone's needs but not every one's greed. If our resources are conserved and careful managed, there will be no cause for much concern and environmental impact from development activity will be within the manageable limits. Comprehensive polices and preventive action to avert environmental damage before it occurs are necessary. It has to be said that there can be no stoppage of development activities like commissioning of major irrigation projects etc in the third world countries like India where the requirements food are rising year after year. No government will be in a position to block development activities just because environmental disturbances. This is so for the simple reason that the man's most basic requirement is food and has to be met at any cost. All other things come after this. A starving man or nation does not think of environmental consequences. However, of late situation in some third world countries including India is fast changing. Food is no more a problem of as much intensity as it used to be before Green Revolution. Therefore, it is time to think of the steps that are to be taken to ensure that socio-economic development is carried out with minimal ecological harm. It is all the more necessary as land and water-based occupation, namely, agriculture, animal husbandry, fisheries and forestry constitute the important sources of our renewable wealth. The negative aspects of river valley projects are all often stressed more than necessary.

There are many positive and creative facets of the development of river valley projects. These include besides assured supply of irrigation and flood control in lower reaches, development of tourism and recreation facilities, renewable and pollution free production of hydel power, pessiculture in the reservoir, provision of water transport.

PART-V

CULTURE AND ENVIRONMENT

14

ENVIRONMENTAL VALUES : Western, Eastern or Global?

PHILIP SARRE

Introduction

It is now widely accepted that a range of environmental issues pose serious problems to society. It is also apparent that, at Rio and elsewhere, policy changes have been inadequate even to prevent the problems getting worse. In part, the muted response has resulted from different interpretations and interests, but a major factor has been the plethora of pressure groups and value positions. In parallel with work on scientific, technical and political aspects of environmental issues, I believe that environmentalists need to be more explicit about the values which inspire them. It is simply not good enough to let media debates rest on the dualism 'deep green versus shallow', especially when it is strongly implied that the former are 'wrong but romantic' and the latter 'right but repulsive'.

In seeking out and evaluation environmental value positions, my own prejudice is to look for positions which seem likely to inspire action rather than those which seek analytical precision. As a result, I have been more concerned with religion and politics than with philosophy or economics. I am encouraged in this prejudice by Brennan's (1991) recent argument that neither philosophy nor economics have solved the problems arising from conflicts between the intrinsic value of species or ecosystems and their use values for complex and fragmented societies. I have no doubt that economics will play an important part in future environmental policy, but in spite of the pioneering work of Pearce (1989) I think economics should be the means rather than the end.

Before moving into the detail of the argument, I think I should clarify my own attitude in pursuing these issues. Although I have a long-standing concern about environmental issues, I am a relatively recent recruit to environmental scholarship, having unexpectedly found myself chairing the UK Open University's first interfaculty course on environmental issues from 1989-91. This gave me a crash-course in the science, technology and politics of the environment and raised, but did not solve, questions of environmental values. It made it clear to me that, since many of the problems are global, it would be necessary to move towards values which could inspire global response. So I have had to widen my search beyond the western value systems which are familiar to me and look to other cultures. I regard this conference as an opportunity to put forward my tentative interpretations and learn from people who know much more about eastern value systems than I do. I hope that the final version of the paper will go well beyond what I can do today.

It's time now to consider a range of value positions relevant to the environment, under the subheads 'western', 'eastern' and 'global'. In doing this, I am concerned not just to explore the range of positions which exist but to begin to clarify the criteria which can be used to assess their strengths and weaknesses.

Western Values

The main thrust of western values, encouraged by a selective reading of the Judaeo-Christian tradition, has been towards the domination and exploitation of nature (Passmore, 1978). Just as Max Weber showed Protestantism as ideally fitted to the rise of capitalism, so the tradition of exploitation helped to launch the development of industrial society. Whether guided by the profit motive or by state socialism, industrialisation has brought unprecedented material affluence to a minority of the world's population at the cost of gross inequality between people and of substantial environmental destruction. Paradoxically, advanced industrialisation holds out both the possibility of solving environmental problems and the probability of greatly increased pollution and resource depletion. There are those who argue that industrialisation can be made environmentally sound by taxes which make polluters pay and by changing discount rates to encourage resource conservation. Others argue for more radical changes based on different value systems.

Some of these alternative value systems have very ancient roots (Pepper, 1984). I have long admired the elegance with which Glacken (1967) teased out the different strands of thought in pre-modern Western societies. His themes of the designed earth, the influence of nature on culture and the perfectibility of the creation show that early European societies recognised the multi-stranded relationships between society and nature. Unfortunately he stopped short of pursuing these themes during industrialisation, except for a brief review published just before his death and republished in 1992.

Reactions to nineteenth century industrialisation have been explored by Brown (1990), who also recognised three stands. First was a restatement of another Christian theme : the idea of *stewardship* emphasises that humans are not freehold owners of the earth but tenants, and as such they are irresponsible to keep the property in good order. In the traditional concept, accountability was to God as creator, but this was taken less seriously as the century progressed and society became more secular. One of its rivals was *Utilitarianism,* explicitly designed as a rational and secular doctrine that would guide policy without recourse to religion or metaphysics. The maximisation of pleasure and minimisation of pain may have some value in allocating resources between social groups, but minimised concern for environment as only animal pain could be relevant and even that could be solved by painless elimination. In practice, the difficulty of measuring pleasure or pain led to an emphasis on demand, which made utilitarianism an ally of market economics. Brown's third strand was *Romanticism*, with its stress on individual encounters with nature and its re-evalutation of wild places. This is the value position which goes furthest towards the aesthetic, both the beauty of the settled agricultural landscape and the sublime challenge of the wilderness (Eagleton, 1990). Americans have long felt a more macho relationship to wilderness (Nash, 1982) than is true of most Europeans. Many environmentalists feel initial sympathy with Romanticism, but then find that it is more of a temporary escape from industrial society than confrontation with it. The real confrontation, inspired by Karl Marx, was with socialism but, in spite of efforts by people like Ruskin, Morris and Kropotkin, this was essentially a social movement with the little concern for the environment (Smith, 1991). As practiced in Eastern Europe, socialism had equally negative environmental effects as did capitalism.

They strands recognised by Brown continued into the twentieth century but it is only since about 1970 that self consciously environmentalist rather than conservationist value positions have been articulated and put into practice (Jamison et al, 1990). There seems to be a negative correlation between size of membership and explicitness of value position. Issue based campaigns, from protection of birds to whales or countryside, have recruited millions while deeply considered positions have few adherents. It is hard to see how the drop-out life style of Arne Naess (1973) can solve the problems of urban dwellers in the developed world let alone those of Asia, Africa or Latin America. The social ecology of Murray Bookchin (1982) is carefully thought through at a local level, but like all anarchist prescriptions, sound less convincing at a national scale let alone globally. Perhaps the most alarming a manifestation of environmentalism is that of groups like Earth First! in the USA (Tokar, 1988) of the Animal Liberation Front in the UK. Their advocacy of the rights of trees and animals seems to justify inhuman treatment of people seen as being at fault. This way lies eco-fascism.

Perhaps the crucial test of this range of environmentalist position is that over twenty years of campaigning by pressure groups have managed to persuade most western citizens that there are serious environmental issues to be addressed but not to have convinced them that solving the problems requires a change in values and goals. As voters, they tend to vote for politicians who they hope will deliver more economic growth and higher 'standards of living' as conventionally measured. Some Green Party politicians have been elected, but their influence has been very limited. In the most successful example, the West German green party was torn apart by disputes between factions adopting fundamentalist green values and those willing to compromise to achieve minor policy changes. I think its reasonable to conclude that western environmental values are less than compelling.

Eastern values

My longest acquaintance with eastern views has been through the work of YiFu Tuan (1974). I've always found it enticing but problematic. The range of his ideas and the link between secular and sacred are attractive, but the proliferation of symbols and the remoteness from current concerns made it difficult to see any practical applications. It was quite recently that I began to think about global responses to environmental problems and to realise that non-Western concepts could be vital. I think it's ironic that environmentalists have tended to admit the values of native North Americans, Australian Aborigines and rain-forest dwellers rather than to study the ideas of the old civilisations of Asia. I suppose it is the complexity of Asian ideas about society and nature that makes it hard for us. It is only since attending the pre UNCED conference at Taplow Court (de Silva, 1992) a year ago that I have felt I have been making any progress. Whether or not I've done so is for you to judge.

Even if this conference were not in India, one would have to start with Hinduism because of its great age and its coexistence with other religions. At first my responses were as divided as they had been to Tuan. Some of the basic assumptions about the unity of man and nature, the coexistence of sacredness and lawfulness and of subjectivity and objectivity seemed to promise much more than Western dualisms. But the baffling proliferation of deities and the importance of symbol and ritual (Singh, 1992) make progress difficult for an analytically trained outsider. Knowledge of environmental problems in India and Ravindra and Murry's (1991) judgement that in spite of the appropriate values held by Indian religions "India's record in these matters is not enviable" left me wondering whether and how to go on. Two lines of argument have helped me to make some progress.

Pandeya (1992) alerted me to the cross-cutting of two tines of argument: one that looked at the evolution of Hinduism from pantheism to monotheism and its absorption of varied pre-existing cultures, the other a philosophical principle separating the conscious and the non-conscious. This seemed to begin to make sense of a reverence for nature for its own sake in some views set against a devaluation of nature as merely a product of and pointer to the underlying Brahman. At worst, this seems to lead to an apathy about nature in favour of perfecting the conscious self in its relation to God. At best, as outlined by Balasubramian (1991) Hinduism's realist epistemology seems to have the potential of balancing the knower and the known, the spiritual and the organic, self-improvement and responsible behaviour towards nature.

The origin and significance of these cross-cutting ideas became much clearer to me on reading Gadgil and Guha's (1992) account of the ecological history of India. The encapsulation of pantheistic groups of hunter-gatherers by monotheistic cultivators not only made sense of some of the contradictions between reverence for nature and forest clearance, it also provided a plausible account of the origins of the caste system. Their later discussion of British forest law and administration also made it clear that Indian environmental values were not the prime cause of environmental damage in the sub-continent. However, the continuation of forest exploitation by government and capital after 1947 shows that western values are easily exported. Their discussion also suggested that resistance to deforestation, including the Chipko movement of which we have heard a lot in the west, was more a social protest in which forests were being valued for the use by local communities rather than an ecological protest about the value of trees per se. The variety of Hindu interpretations seems particularly susceptible to this kind of clash between local and wider priorities, and the preference for large scale industrialisation over Gandhi's vision of local craft development suggest that it won't be easy to shift the balance.

Buddhism is increasingly seen as ideally suited to the promotion of environmental ethics (de Silva, 1991). The tension between the value of life and human right to property is resolved through the injunction to lead a sane and simple life. Gadgil and Guha see this as linked to the need of established societies, including both cultivators and gatherers, to stabilise their environmental base and give dignity to low caste groups. However, the later emphasis on the conduct of monks seems to distance Buddhism from the practicalities of food production in favour of emphasising the mystical side of the religion. This, and the adoption of the Buddha as the incarnation of Vishnu may explain the withering of Buddhism in India.

The spread of Buddhism into China would have brought it under the influence of Taosim and Confucianism, hence stressing the value of nature and the need for society to conform with natural law. This seems to have led it towards a more communal response rather than individual free will, but also to accept the even monks should work to produce food.

The third shift of Buddhism, to Japan, involved another superimposition on to a pre-existing religion (Nakamura, 1992). Shinto was another polytheistic village region with a high regard for nature and belief in the sacred character of natural feature like mountains, forest and promontories. A distinctive feature was the link between the sun, the gods and the people, since the imperial family were seen as divine and ancestors took their place as gods. In this context, Zen encouraged people to live naturally–including working to the best of their ability–in harmony with nature and the place in which they lived. It also encouraged the Japanese love of miniaturised forms which distil nature in a single plant or stone. To Western eyes this seems a conformist religious prescription but it was one which was founded in reverence for nature.

The problem, as in India, came from adoption of Western style industrialisation and economics. Although not imposed by imperialism, at least until 1945, Senda (1992) described the adoption of western ideas by Japanese geographers as uncritical and as displacing indigenous traditions. The outcome is the paradoxical position of Japan in relation to global environmental problems–at once vilified for its pollution in the 1950s and regarded as the main eco-predator in the 1980s, especially in relation to tropical forests, and at the same time in the lead in energy, efficiency and domestic environmental policy. (Maull, 1992, Tsumi and Weidner, 1989). Once again, there is a conflict between a traditional value system which seems to encourage harmony with nature and an imported approach which sanctions exploitation and pollution.

My tentative conclusion from this brief survey of Asian religious values is that Hinduism and Buddhism have values which are consistent with environmentalism, but that those attitudes are strongest in stable local communities. They don't seem all that effective in a society pursuing economic growth and technological development. The need seems to be to encourage a more progressive form of conservation which would enhance living standards without damaging the environment: an Asian form of sustainable development.

Global Values

At present it seems to me that there are two approaches which are genuinely global concepts relevant to environmental values. However, one treats values only implicitly and the other is more concerned with development than with environment. They are, as you've no doubt realised, the Gaia hypothesis and sustainable development. I'll start with the latter.

As articulated by the World Commission on Environment and Development (1987), the concept of sustainable development has been very influential in moulding debates about environmental policy. It has certainly influenced political responses before, during and after Rio. I don't want to go too deeply into the pros and cons of the concept as that is being done by my colleague (Blowers, 1993). I just want to highlight what I take to be its crucial strengths and weaknesses. Its key contributions were (a) that it linked environment and development instead of opposing them; (b) that it included social criteria among its imperatives, notably the call for equity between countries; and (c) that in emphasising sustainability of resources for future generations it mobilised the values of stewardship, arguably the most acceptable of the western positions I outlined earlier. These positive features were the reasons for its wide acceptability in principle, but it has two problems which may have reduced its practical effects. First, in spite of huge amounts of detailed work, most people are unclear about what sustainable development means in practice, so may accept the label without really accepting its implications. Second, most of the goals are actually development goals with the environment valued mainly for use rather than in its own right. At worst, sustainable development can be treated as an anthropocentric, pro growth concept, as is the case when British cabinet members talk about achieving sustainable growth', i.e. growth which will go on indefinitely. If a concept is so flexible that politicians can reverse its meaning, its widespread acceptance may be bought at too great a price.

The other global concept, Gaia (Lovelock, 1979, 1988), seems to have had a much more critical reception. This may be more to do with the rhetoric than the reality: most climatologists, geologists and biologists seem to accept that there are feedback mechanisms between physical and biological processes. Goldsmith's distinctive contribution was to insist that these processes make up a super-organic 'being', to name it *Gaia* (the Greek earth goddess) and to suggest that it is self regulating. Many have seen the hypothesis as teleological, though Goldsmith insists that there is no need for conscious purpose to act to keep the biosphere in a state suitable for life. His intention was to stimulate scientific research, but Gaia has been taken up buy environmentalist as a world view which links science to spirituality. My reading of Goldsmith's work suggests that some of the New-Age readings are wide of the mark and that Gaia is primarily a statement of holistic view of the biosphere with more to say about its ability to eliminate mankind than about how environmental policy should be shaped–for example Goldsmith shocks environmentalists by his unwillingness of regard nuclear hazard as apocalyptic. His criticisms of the three C's-cattle, cars and chainsaws – do hint at how planetary health can be achieved. My own conclusion about Gaia is that it is a world view which is consistent with science and also excites reverence, even awe, for nature. It has the potential to inspire environmentalists to value nature for its own sake and not only as a resources base for society. The strength of Gaia does allow change, but beings to suggest what kinds of change are beneficial and what are harmful (Sarre and Smith, 1971).

Conclusion

After this survey of value positions relevant to the environment, I think I am somewhat clearer about the attributes of a desirable environmentalist ethic. While trying to formulate my own ideas, I realised that I was groping towards a division of knowledge and that Kant had formulated what I needed two centuries ago. An effective value system must perform in relation to 'pure reason', practical reason and 'aesthetics'. It needs to be consistent with science, to generate ethical principles and practical policies and to inspire aesthetic responses – both for the quality of everyday life and the challenge of the sublime. If those are the criteria, none of the value systems I have surveyed seem to pass the test.

At a local scale, Buddhism seems to combine a reverence for nature with rules for everyday life, but the emphasis on the self seems to divert attention away from improving society and environment. Social ecology extends the scope of improvement to the community, but needs to link with other communities. At a global scale, a fusing of Gaia with sustainable development is needed to integrate the science of the sublime with the politics of development. But such an integration will take time to work out and time is what we do not have.

It occurs to me that achieving a global response requires a strategy similar to that of Hinduism: absorbing and reorienting the values of different groups rather than eliminating or converting them. But the pressing need is to make the values of the politicians and businesses more environment sensitive. In my view, notwithstanding Beck, 1992, that is a task which can only be done by application of science. The effectiveness of global warming and ozone depletion mobilising politicians could be developed into a more holistic view of the global ecosystem, perhaps based on Gaia, demanding the maintenance of key global systems. A more difficult proposition will be to make those global decision-makers take the environment and development needs of different localities seriously: that seems to contradict most of past experience about political or economic colonialism. Perhaps the key is to require local assent to activities which may damage the environment, and hence to require full compensation for any detriment. A more positive view is to stress economic development aimed at environmental improvement rather than production of consumer goods in spite of environmental damage. This must be a priority in the short to medium term. In the long-term, when all people enjoy a reasonably humane living environment, there would need to be wilderness areas to sustain environmental diversity and offer a challenge to the comfortable.

Whatever the source, I think we need not just to foster reverence for nature, but to emphasise the perfectibility of the world to meet human needs.

REFERENCES

Balasubramian, R. (1991). The Hindu attitude to knowledge and nature' in Ravindra, R. (ed.) *Science and Spirit*, New York, Paragon House, pp.53-81.

Blowers, A. (1993). "Paper to the fifth Indo-British Geographical Seminar".

Brennan, A. (1991). 'Moral pluralism and the environment' *Environmental Values* 1, pp 15-33.

Brown, S. (1990). 'Humans and their environment: Changing attitudes' in Sarre, P. and Silvertown, J. (ed.) *Environment and Society*, Hodder and Stoughton, pp. 238-269.

Beck, V. (1992). 'From industrial society to the risk society: questions of survival, social structure and ecological enlightenment', *Theory, Culture and Society*, Vol.9, pp. 97-123.

Bookchin, M. (1982). *The Ecology of Freedom*, Palo Alto, Cheshire Books.

de Silva, P. (1991). 'Environmentalist Ethics: A Buddhist perspective' in Fu, C.W. and Wawrytko, S.A. (eds.) *Buddhist Ethics in Modern Society*, New York, Greenwood, pp. 173-184.

de Silva, P. (1992). Environmental Ethics in a Pluralist World, Paper presented to the pre UNCED conference held at Taplow Court, 12-15 April.

Eagleton, T. (1990). *The Ideology of the Aesthetic*, Oxford Blackwell.

Gadgil, M. and Guha, R. (1992). *This Fissured Land: An Ecological History of India*, Oxford University Press.

Glacken, C.J. (1967). *Traces on the Rhodian Shore*, Berkeley and Los Angeles, University of California Press.

Glacken, C.J, (1992). 'Reflections on the history of western attitudes towards nature', *Geojournal*, vol. 26, no.2, pp. 103-111.

Jamison, A. et al. (1990). *The Making of the New Environmental Consciousness: A Comparative Study of the Environmental Movements in Sweden, Denmark and the Netherlands*, Edinburgh University Press.

Lovelock, J. (1979). *Gaia: A New Look at Life on Earth*, Oxford University Press

Lovelock, J. (1988). *The Ages of Gaia: A Biography of Our Living Earth.*

Maull, H.W. (1992). 'Japan's global environmental policies' in Hurnell, A. and Kingsbury, B. (eds.) *The International Politics of the Environment*, Oxford, Clarendon Press, pp. 354-372.

Naess, A. (1973). The shallow and the deep: Long range ecology movement. A summary' *Inquiry* 16, pp.95-100.

Nakamura, Ho. (1992). 'The idea of nature in the East in comparison with the West' *Geojournal*, vol. 26, no.2, pp.113-128.

Nash, R.F. (1982). *Wilderness and the American Mind*, New Haven, Yale University Press.

Nash, R.F. (1990). *American Environmentalism: Readings in Conservation History* (third edition), New York, McGraw Hill.

Pandeya, R.C. (1992). 'Indian attitude towards nature' *Geojournal*, vol. 26, no.2, pp.135-138.

Passmore, J. (1978). *Mans Responsibility for Nature: Ecological Problems and Western Traditions*, London, Duckworth.

Pearce, D. et al. (1989). *Blueprint for a Green Economy*, London, Earthscan.

Paper, D. (1984) *The Roots of Modern Environmentalism*, London, Croom Helm.

Ravindra, R. and Murray, P. (1991) in Ravindra, R, (ed.) *Science and Spirit*, New York, Paragon House.

Sarre, P. and Smith, P.(1991). *One World for One Earth*, London, Earthscan.

Senda, M. (1992). 'Japan's traditional view of nature and interpretation of landscape', *Geoforum* vol. 26, no.4, pp.129-134.

Singh, R.P.B. (1992). 'Nature and cosmic integrity: A search in Hindu geographical thought', *Geojournal* vol. 26, no.2, pp.139-147.

Smith, P. (1991). 'Global development issues' in Smith, P. and Warr, K. (eds.) *Global Environmental Problems* London, Hodder and Stoughton, pp.203-242.

Tokar, B. (1988). 'Exploring the new ecologies: Social ecology, deep ecology and the future of green political thought', *Alternatives*, vol. 15, no. 4, pp.31-43.

Tsumi, S, and Weidner, M. (eds.) (1989). *Environmental Policy in Japan*, Berlin, Edition Sigma.

Tuan, Yi-Fu (1974). *Topophilia: A Study of Environmental Perception, Attitudes and Values*, Englewood Cliffs, Prentice Hall.

World Commission on Environment and Development, *Our Common Future*, Oxford University Press.

15

THE PRESENT STATE OF THE HUNGARIAN ENVIRONMENT: Attitudes towards Practical Environmental Provision

ALISON D. REEVES

"An entity like the environment cannot have problems of itself, but we can project ours on to it."

– *Simmons.*

Historical Background

The recent non-violent revolution in Central Eastern Europe has shown that it is indeed possible to transform a repressed system. However, the orderly transition has not yet meant that Hungarians have gained more control over their own lives. Instead, this 'phase' of uncertainty has left people feeling relatively helpless and demoralised. The poorer communities are suffering from a great deal of stress and tension (commonly classified as diseases of the West), lowered immunity, lowered life expectancy and deterioration in housing conditions. On this basis, what real hope is there that the people of Hungary will have the energy to adhere to or the financial means to uphold their Government's new, pro-environment development strategy?

In Hungary, the history of reports on the state of the environment only dates back to 1984. At that time, Government decided to publish annual reports which were submitted by the Environmental Agency (now the Ministry for Environment and Regional Policy). The first issue appeared in 1986 and was assigned 'Top Secret' status. In 1989 it was recognised, that if an environmental report was going to be 'mobilising', then it needed to be freely and widely distributed. It was printed in a daily newspaper with a circulation of 103,000 (Magyar Hirlap: Bulla, 1991)

The existing condition of the native environment has mainly been ascribed to Stalinist and post-Stalinist ideology. Fleischer et al. (1991) described it as 'environmental nihilism': the complete domination of man over nature. The complication of environmental degradation was compacted by a consummate technocratic view point. After it was liberated from German occupation (1945), Hungary became a satellite of Russia and was used as a source of raw materials without consideration for the future.

Certainly since the mid-seventies oil crises, the carrying capacity of the environment has been seriously denuded due to the absence of meaningful management strategy. It was an extremely impoverished nation which, requiring new production systems, had no choice but to accept low-efficiency Soviet technology. The resulting and unquestioned pace of development meant that environmental protection was, once again, entirely overlooked. An over centralised scheme of manufacturing industry emerged, one third of industrial production is now focussed in Budapest. Of the 10 million total, 1 in 5 of the Hungarian populace live in the capital.

During the early 1980s, growth of infrastructure began to lag and, in addition to the production processes requiring higher levels of raw materials, consumption became even more wasteful and pollutant. The shortfall of technological development and the continuous subsidisation of low efficiency companies slowed down the rate of production and innovation. In fact, the progression of heavy industry began to restrict its own expansion due to the shortage of uncontaminated sites. As a result of Soviet domination, Hungary now has to confront an abhorrent legacy of contamination.

Current Problems

The original newspaper statement, concerning environmental adulteration, generated a large and well-based selection of critiques. The present Government (Democratic Forum MDF: Dr. Joseph Antall) openly recognise that radical planning is required to ensure economic reform whilst controlling pollution and the continuing deterioration of the natural resource base.

Documentation from the Ministry for the Environment and

Regional Policy candidly reports on its accumulation of foreign debt (20 billion U.S. dollars) and states that Hungary has borrowed a loan of a least the same magnitude from nature and from future generations. The quantifiable environmental damage amounts to 4 to 5 per cent of GDP each year. The funds spent on environmental protection are decreasing, due to recession, from 1 to 0.5 per cent. It is detailed (Szendrei, 1992) that 1993 will see Hungary's economic revival. The GDP is expected to increase by 0 to 3 per cent in 1993, and by 2 to 4 per cent 1994. The forecast puts the unemployment figure at 800,000 and the rate of inflation at 16 to 19 per cent for 1993. Geographical, economic and demographic information is given in Table 15.1.

TABLE 15.1: Hungarian People's Republic Geographical, Economic and Demographic Information (1992)

Land	
Eastern Europe	
Landlocked	
Area:	93,036 Km^2
Highest point:	Kékes at the rate of 1,015m
Lowest point:	Tisza River Valley at the rate of 79m
Populace	
Population:	10,675,000 (urban 54%)
Capital:	Budapest (population 2,064,000)
Ethnic Groups:	Hungarian 92%; Gypsy 3%; German 3%
Language:	Hungarian
Religion:	Roman Catholic 68%; Calvinist 20%; Lutheran 5%
Life Expectancy:	73 years female; 66 years male
Government	
Hungarian Democratic Party (MDF)	
J. Antall	
Economy	
GNP:	$65,200,000,000
Currency:	Forint (£1 Sterling = 135 Ft)
Imports:	Machinery, fuels, chemicals
Exports:	Agricultural produce, wine, machinery
Main Trade Partners:	Germany, Austria, Commonwealth of Independent States

Before launching an elaborate environmental strategy with a priority to reduce contaminant sources, the environment has to be suitably evaluated. Hungarians are aware that the quality of their surroundings are worsening. With privatisation and new home ownership schemes, this is becoming more poignant and new levels of information are being sought by the public.

More contentious issues such as the Gabcikovo Hydropower Dam Project have not eluded the international media. Discussions in the 1950s between the Hungarian and Czeckslovak Government lead to the eventual construction (1978) of a Danubian hydropower scheme. The upper part, near Dunakiliti, includes a reservoir (200 million cubic meters capacity) and a 25 km canal to divert river flow to the power station at Gabcikovo. The old Danube was to be used as a floodway. The lower part of the scheme at Nagymaros was never completed and is now being dismantled. One of the functions of the second plant was to regulate water level fluctuations caused by the barrier upstream. Nationalistic concerns crippled environmental considerations during construction of the Gabcikovo dam. Now the project has been completed, Budapest is openly predicting environmental disaster, unilaterally altered borders and poisoned drinking water. Unknowingly, the public have given up control of a priceless resource: barely justifiable in the light of new policy statements such as:

> "Everyone shall have the opportunity to become acquainted, especially concerning his/her country, with the basic principles of sustainable development, the protection of nature and the environment, and to participate individually or with others in shaping decisions directly concerning the environment" (Article 3.3: Danube Basin Ecological Convention).[1]

A report submitted by UNDP/WHO in 1976, which targets water quality management, warned that the barrage system would cause 'negative impacts'. The expected water quality problems relate to the trophic state of the Danube. Nutrient loading and algal biomass are expected to increase due to reduced water flow. Quality problems are related to the old Danube bed where the flow is only 50 to 200 cubic metres per second (mean flow of the Danube is 2,000 cumecs). As the course of the Danube has been diverted north of the Hungarian border through Slovakia, groundwater levels are beginning to fall in areas surrounding the dam. Periodic flushing of the region, at the expense of power production, could resolve this problem. Currently, aquifers are not being recharged. The result is that Szigetköz, a region in north-west Hungary, 52 km long and 6 to 8 km wide, is drying out (see Fig. 15.1). It is likely that the area will only receive flood water and not irrigation water due to problems of water regulation and poor water supply procedures. The hydrological state of Szigetköz is essentially determined by the Danube and its tributaries. The flood plain area supports a valuable hardwood forest. There is already evidence that the falling water table will jeopardise the biodiversity of the land and arid march meadow could replace tracts of elm, oak and birch, thus realising conservationists' fears.

Water Quality

National water quality is poor (Varga et al., 1990). A very high proportion (95%) of surface water comes from abroad. Municipal water supply has grown much faster than the rate of sewage collection and sewage treatment. After entering Hungary, the Danube receives most of its pollutant load in the form of domestic and agricultural sewage downstream from the capital. Approximately 65 per cent of the drinking water supply has no protection from sewage contamination. Budapest is not yet totally connected to the sewerage system: 86 per cent of flats are connected (300,000 are not). Up to 2 mission cubic meters of sewage leaks into the Hungarian soil each year. The current rate of untreated sewage discharge to ground and surface water is about 10 billion cubic meters per year. Groundwater resources primarily comprise waters that are stored in the banks of rivers, 75 per cent of this water is stored in the alluvial terraces of the Danube. Normally, 85 per cent of drinking water supply for Budapest is abstracted from the bank filtered resources along this river and the remainder from groundwater wells. The summer of 1992 was unusually hot, maximum daily temperatures of 40°C were recorded for most of August. During drought periods a higher percentage of the drinking water supply comes from groundwater wells. Unfortunately, a high percentage of these sources are contaminated. There are two sewage treatment plants in Pest built in the 1950s and 1960s. The waste-water from Buda enters the Danube completely untreated. Recently there have been tremendous changes in the organisational structure and management system, in the ownership pattern and the control of water management facilities leading to potential privatisation of 49 per cent of the drinking water and sewage purification works.

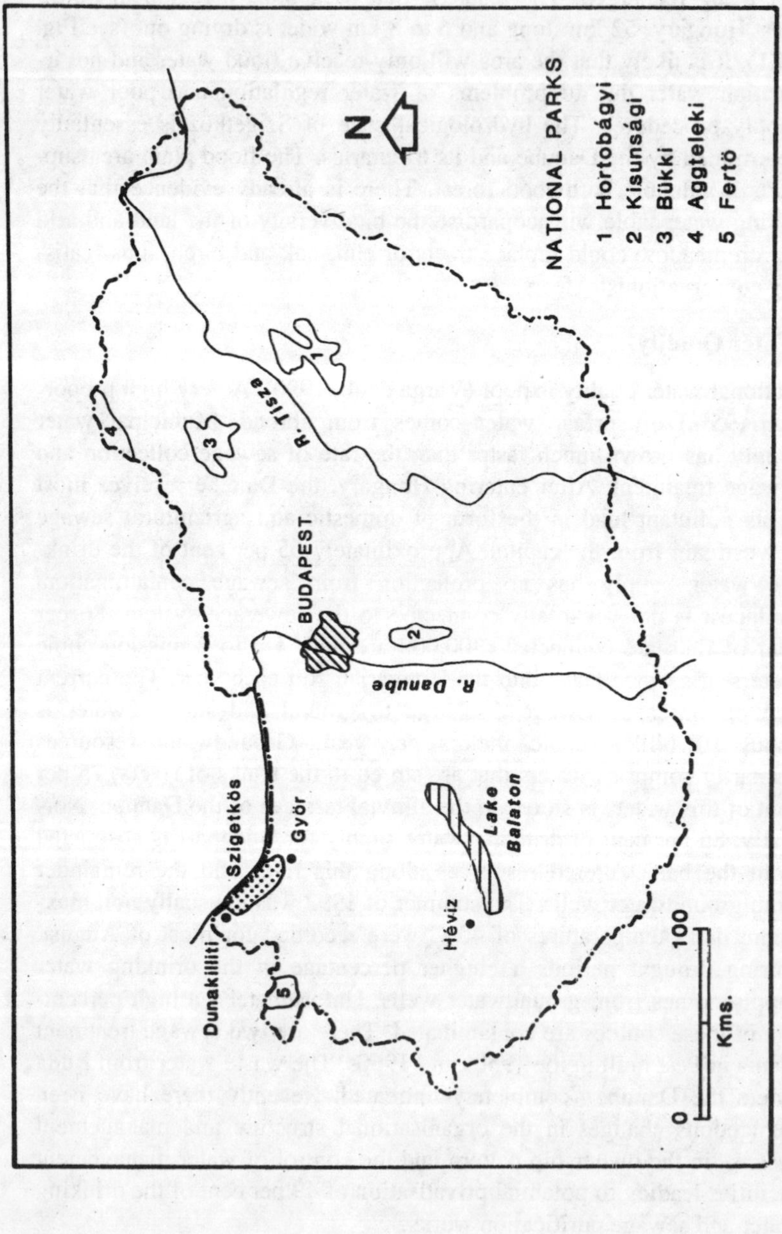

FIG 15.1: Hungarian People's Republic 1992

Political Structure

In 1988 water management and environmental protection were combined in a ministry. This ministry collapsed during the political change of 1989, coinciding with the Gabcikovo-Nagymaros dam controversy. The water management section (responsible for water supply) was split from the environmental protection section and now forms a part of the Ministry of Transport, Communication and Water Management. The Ministry for Environmental Protection and Regional Policy (responsible for water quality) control the National Agency for Nature Conservation, the National Building Agency, Regional Development and Environmental Protection.

New environmental legislation due in 1990 has been delayed. The Ministry for Environment Protection has not found collaboration with other governmental departments very easy. Relations are described as poor (Anderson, 1993). Neither ministry is having great success in persuading parties of the need for environmental impact assessments during the privatisation of state enterprises. E.I.A. is considered obligatory but new corporations do not want to be held responsible for past sins. New land owners are discovering contamination on site after possession. It is expected that Government will create a private agency to provide compensation if companies/individuals take measures to remove the contamination themselves. This problem is stopping foreign investors moving on to old sites. Instead, they are building on previously untouched sites and environmental clean-up is not being promoted. By contrast, in recent years the system of pollution control in the UK has undergone a series of transformations into one integrated approach. Many of the changes are incomplete and are still evolving towards a single regulatory body dealing with all emissions from all processes. Change were driven by environmental concern and pressures from the EC. New directives forced alteration to UK conduct. There was no comparable pressure to force change in Hungary.

In the UK, the main control for ensuring contaminated land is not used for any unsuitable purpose has been through the planning system. Control is put on the use of land for a particular purpose and remedial work is specified as part of the development permission. The major problem is that no (or patchy) records exist of former landuse. Management of the system is not very satisfactory. The introduction of a duty under Section 143 of the Environment Pollution Act. 1990/1 on local authorities to compile registers of land which may have been subject to contaminative use has been badly received. Registers are seen as a compilation of site records and maps identifying land which is being or has been put to a contaminative use and consequently may be contaminated. They are not registers of actual contamination.

In Hungary, polluted soil will present problems for centuries. Mining industries and the Soviet military are refusing to decontaminate old sites. Total restoration of contaminated land to an unpolluted state probably would not be achievable, and may not be completely necessary in all the cases. Remedial action should be planned depending on the areal extent, the type of contamination and the intended usage.

Soil Pollution

Soil is Hungary's most important renewable resource.[2] The proportion of cropland is uniquely high (88% of total land) and 75 per cent of this is under cultivation. During the last 20 years, the area of land utilised by agriculture has decreased due to the expansion of settlement and industry. However, the real danger is not the shrinkage of cropland but its deterioration due to sewage contamination, badly applied fertiliser and the presence of heavy metals from mining activities. Lead, cadmium, zinc and copper poisoning are common place.

Air Pollution

Severe air pollution occurs over 11 per cent of the country, in which 44 per cent if Hungary's population live. The Regional Air Quality Monitoring network, operated by the Public Health and Epidemiological Stations have provided data on atmospheric pollutants since 1974. Annual amounts of pollutants emitted into the atmosphere are typically: 800 kilotons of dust, ash and soot; 300 kilotons of nitrous oxides and 1,300 kilotons of sulphur dioxide. This, combined with the hydrocarbons and lead from road vehicles and from inefficient communal heating systems gives rise to poor air quality. For example, in Budapest, the heightened occurrence of chronic bronchitis and asthma in adults and respiratory abnormalities in children has been directly linked to air borne pollutants (Bulla, 1991). East European cars, in particular Trabants, Ladas and Skodas are generally old and poorly tuned. Recent improvements include engine emission testing after which car owners are presented with a green card which has to be renewed annually. This year (1993) sees the introduction of new standards for industrial emissions of carbon dioxide, sulphur dioxide and the nitrous oxides. Although the charges have not yet been calculated, a system of fines will be operated where emission limits are exceeded.

Future Approaches

What should be done to improve the quality of environment and ensure the rational use of natural resources? The decline in environmental calibre was, in part, due to the lack of a detailed and workable legal framework. Guidelines produced were not consistently enforced. The effectuation of law requires a thorough and honest analysis of cumulative environmental damage. The changes now occurring include the transformation of the legal system and economic structure giving rise to a new and positive agenda; environmental protectionism.

> "Everyone shall have access to means of legal redress either in administrative or in court procedure, according to due process of law if his/her environment has suffered or may suffer from adverse impact" (Article 3.4: Danube Basin Ecological Convention).[1]

There are notable differences between the attitudes to environmental protection in the 'East'. The domination of state ownership resulted in the paradoxical situation where the state was not the owner of the polluting facilities and the authority proceeding against the polluter. The exceedance of applied limits were tolerated and punished simultaneously. The structure of Hungary's economy does not suit either the natural conditions or its production traditions and the technological level reached would not be acceptable in a market system. Continuous wasting of materials, energy and manpower was due to the emulation of Soviet practice. This was environmental suicide for a small country. When establishing an administration, the intention was to achieve an organisation which would cause the smallest possible change to the functioning of the regime. A peculiar method developed for treating environmental problems. 'What is unknown to the people or what cannot be superficially proved, does not exist or is harmless' (Fleischer et al., 1991). According to Commoner (1990), this type of tactic is known as the Humpty Dumpty approach. In *Through the Looking Glass*, Alice gets into an argument with Humpty Dumpty, who claims that the word "glory", means "a nice knock-down argument." When Alice objects to this arbitrary definition, Humpty Dumpty says: "When

I use a word it means just what I choose it to mean."

The environment aside, the victims of pollution are the people of Hungary. During the socialist regime a lot was done to prevent the recognition of adverse impacts. Even if discovered, what could the individual have done? Measuring and monitoring network were never encouraged and the results of environmental analyses were kept secret. All possible information was kept from local officials lest decision be 'disturbed'. Protestations would lead to arrest and conditions of domestic housing meant that a socialist citizen could never move. Individual problems were heightened if working conditions were poor leading to ill health. Stress was always present but only now is it discussed. Although statistics are not readily available, 1985 figures show that Hungary possessed the worlds' highest mortality rate from cardiovascular disease of any of the industrialised countries. The US State Department has recently given a $ 2.1 million grant to form an American-Hungarian medical partnership. Coronary care is approximately 30 years behind western standards. It will take at least 15 years before the upward trend in heart disease suffers is slowed and eventually reversed.

Previous environmental protection efforts have included the instigation of the Law on Environmental Protection 1976. Although passed by Parliament, there was no policing of the law and therefore a lack of efficient regulation. In the 1980s it was hoped that the decline in industrial development would lead to an improvement in pollution levels. This recovery never occurred because, even with slow growth, the same aging and polluting infrastructure was applied. Continued deterioration of the natural environment is testament to insufficient efforts in resource management. Environmental protection was never integrated into the priorities of the economy.

> 'Fundamental changes, the development of an overall ecological strategy are required, which concentrate on prevention instead of the moderation and elimination of harms and deteriorations' Bulla (1989).

The primary task of overcoming the critical state of the environment is a re-appraisal of the worthiness of natural resources, producing a totally new scale of values. The longer term biological and socio-economic requirements have to overtake the shorter term economic expediency. However, the position already exists where unlimited growth and maximum consumption cannot be realised due to limited environmental resources. Polluted environments have lower marketability.

It is sincerely hoped that new environmental policy (e.g. Danube Basin Ecological Convention) will represent the interests of the whole society. The task is to produce a workable structure that not only ensures the rational use of natural resources but also produces a state which guarantees healthy living. Hence, there has to be a break with plans which describe the future in terms of an extrapolation of present trends. There has to be a fundamental alteration in the economic-social environment association. Obviously a transitory phase is required in which the parallel expansion of green economics, damage limitation, regeneration of contaminated land and the elimination/prevention of pollution are encouraged.

Restructuring the economy will be coupled with the introduction and application of environmentally friendly technologies. Sectors in which improvements are needed immediately include; energy policy (renewable and non-polluting energy technologies), agriculture and forestry, promotion of public transport, water quality, waste management and tourism.

Energy Sector

The energy sector is an area where change has already occurred. The privatisation of the Hungarian Electricity Board lead to the formation of the Hungarian Power Company. This outfit provides 98 per cent of the country's power, almost 50 per cent of it comes from Paks nuclear station. Domestic fuel is becoming more expensive. Coal subsidies are being reduced leading to mine closures. Imported natural gas from Western Europe is taking over from the declining supplies from the commonwealth of Independent States. The Ministry of Industry has decided that future energy requirements are to be met by a combination of sources i.e. Paks, imported gas and domestic lignite. An important consideration has been air pollution control. No power plant has yet been fitted with flue-gas desulphurisation (FGS) as this seems unaffordable. The most important tasks to reduce air pollution are firstly, implementation of a 30 per cent reduction in sulphur dioxide emissions to reduce transboundary air pollution (Geneva Convention). To meet the criterion, low sulphur and ash fuels are required. Secondly, the reduction of industrially produced volatile organic carbons, odours and heavy metals. Thirdly, the phasing-out of CFC's in line with the Montreal Protocol. Lastly, a review of vehicle emissions (installation of catalytic converters, urban traffic control, decrease lead content in petrol etc.)

Water Quality Management

An effective institutional system is needed for water-quality management. The aim has to be to protect health. Portable water is scarce so water conservation has to be a priority. The Water Research Centre (VTTUKI) was founded in 1952 to act for the Hungarian National Water Authority undertaking both basic monitoring and applied research. This included studies related to the development, conservation and management of water resources in the country. Vituki was merged with the Hungarian Hydrographic Service (est. 1886) to form a comprehensive research facility. The main areas of investigation are hydrology/hydrogeology; hydraulics; water quality, pollution control and support servicing (e.g. licensing). One of its most important functions is to develop new drinking water directives. Vituki is expanding to include the analysis of trace organic pollutants. This type of facility had not reached a very sophisticated level due to the expense of measuring equipment, though EC money is easing the situation. The measurement of organic compounds is of great importance in the monitoring of sewage contamination and sewage sludge dispersal. This is a good example where an existing system can be upgraded and expanded to meet new demands.

Waste Management

Upgrading of waste management is also required especially for hazardous and nuclear waste. In comparison with other developed countries. The quality of industrial waste produced is high whilst the proportion of waste recycled is low. Recycling programmes do exist for industrial waste but this is an area which has to be dramatically improved. Illegal transportation of waste, compiling inventories of toxic waste and the clean-up of recognised hot spots all need urgent consideration. Since 1988-89 the 12 regional Environmental Authorities have installed 2 high capacity incinerators and 6 landfill sites per region. The landfill sites, for disposal of domestic waste, are all reaching their maximum capacities. Recycling of domestic waste has not yet been established.

Nature Conservation

Aesthetic resources need protecting and reconstructing. Scenic regions and nature conservation areas, including 5 national parks (Hortobágyi; Kiskunsági; Bükki; Aggteleki and Fertö; see Fig. 15.1), have already been designated by the National Authority for Nature Conservation. The latest development is the formation of a trilateral, transfrontier national park between Hungary, Slovakia and Austria, to be opened in 1995. A Danube Fund is being initiated to 'establish and separate' the most valuable areas along the Danube and its tributaries from all detrimental activities (Danube Charta: the declaration on the sustainable development of the Central Danube area).[3] Most of Hungary is lowland (the Great Plain), divided into three sections by the Danube and Tisza rivers. Mountains in the north-east only reach 1,000 metres. The lack of variation in physical features results in an unexpectedly temperate climate. Areas which are protected exhibit the main types of natural vegetation; broad-leaved and coniferous woodland, wetlands, steppe (or puszta) and meadows. The economic importance of the majority of flora and fauna in the country has yet to be assessed. Other protected regions include karst cave systems (all caves are placed under national protection), Lake Balaton and Héviz Spa. These areas are designated at local or national level depending on there importance. The total area under protection at national level is 518,000 hectares in 155 sites. At local level there are 36,000 hectares divided between 791 sites. The emphasis is on conservation which includes research on protection, restoration and management of natural systems. Nature conservation guidelines are seen as critical issues in the formulation of new policy. In the past, areas have been protected simply because they are of no other possible use.

Recent Changes and Future Improvements

The completion and realisation of new environmental policy will take 10 to 20 years. Certain legal and administrative regulations are already in place, these accentuate the polluter pays and user pays principles, passing responsibility on to the contaminators. Even in Western Europe inflictable fines do not motivate industry to behave responsibly. Stricter sanctions are required. A new element would be included, cumulative fines in cases where pollutants are allowed to accumulate. The system of fining already in operation is not satisfactory and generates less money than the cost of damage and restoration. Modernisation should result in a set of uniform principles which facilitate lowered emissions. However, besides sanctioning, methods of motivation are necessary. Standards should progressively change towards EC legislative limits.

We are now able to witness the gradual introduction of economic regulations with the prerequisites of maintainable development, rational economics and resource protection. Industry has to meet the cost of the use of the environment/landscape. The promotion of environmental well-being will be appearing in forms of taxation (carbon tax?). Some reasoning is questionable. In 1992 the price of petrol and diesel was increased by 0.5 forint per litre. This accounts for less than one per cent of the cost but the income is to be applied to road improvement! Business loans will have to support the introduction of eco-industry, promote the idea of 'green' consumerism and embrace the implications of the cradle to grave philosophy. Importation of 'green' goods will also be examined.

Research and technical development has a enormous role in environmental monitoring through identification of appropriate indicators of change, determination of the place of environmental protection in the market economy, evaluation of economic-ecological resources, and generation of a proficient administrative back-up. Allied to this, of course, is access to good education. The whole system of training and public education needs to be changed so that attitudes and opinions can be based on the dissection of 'true' data. The media has a role in activating support, propagating pro-environment interest and reporting accurate information. The most efficient means of changing awareness is by involving people directly so that they can identify with the objectives and practical measures required. Training programmes have been initiated at the Regional Environment Centre for Central Eastern Europe (Budapest). Further education in economics and environmental protection at graduate level is only just starting for example, at Györ College (Györ). In the UK our own experience of the environment is assimilated from a combination of sources (reading, travel and outdoor pursuits, media, market research statistic etc.). The level of individual understanding depends on opportunity, accessibility of information and a willingness/ability to learn. Environmental awareness in Hungary has been considered an issue strictly for politicians. The expertise and knowledge base is available in many environmentally related subjects. However, capabilities are not exploited for solving practical problems

(Somlyódy, 1992). The difference between east and west is the application of problem-solving 'know-how': Education is far too theoretical. The experiences of Western Universities are rarely called upon.

> "Experts are people who gain extensive knowledge in one specialised field. There comes a point where they know everything about nothing." (J. Polger, Pers. Comm. October 1992).

Government views the formulation of policy in terms of social coordination and individual sacrifice. Because of privatisation and the primary accumulation of capital, a class system is developing with entrepreneurs and the political elite at the top of the structure. The new business owners are cautious of a humancentric approach to environmental policy. They want their companies to thrive and decentralise at all costs. It is likely that environmental consultancy companies will be generated to assist with greening of industry and business. In the middle of the class structure are the people who spend their earnings to survive and who have no financial reserves. This group are afraid of change but still present a nationalistic front to outsiders. Then, there are those that are trying to survive below the physical minimum (including black marketeers). It is felt by the Government that the poor and unemployed are easy to influence. It is difficult to see where effective environmental education should fit into such a structure. In the past, intervention by green organisations such as the Danube Circle, Reflex and the Nature Conservation Club has been treated as a nuisance, but now they are being called upon to strengthen schooling. As yet, they have not been involved in any decision-making processes. It is considered that their participation may discourage contamination/damage at community level, assuming people want to learn and/or voice opinion.

Although Hungary is only a companion member of the EC, the need for international support is considerable and has lead to the instigation of a specific programme (PHARE: Pologne-Hongrie Actions pour la Reconversion Economique). This reflects the notion that the Community has a responsibility for the environment that extends beyond its own boundaries.[4] There are signs that the EC is encouraging the regional approach which is regarded as a cooperative attack on both internal and transboundary problems. This could go ahead in the form of a regional action plan for the environment in Central and Eastern Europe (Alcamo, 1992).

Western aid organisations look favourably on this type of litigation because it minimises duplication of remedial work. Money from the PHARE programme is mainly being aimed at the improvement of water treatment plants. Other creditors include the World Bank and the European Development Bank. The problem now arising is the increase in service fees to cover interest on loans. Money from the PHARE programme is also being directed towards the creation of an international park at Lake Fertö (considered to be an internationally important wetland). This joint project with Austria has received ECU 1.4 million.

Besides disarmament and human rights, environmental protection has become a very important issue in international politics. New environmental policy addresses what ought to be done, but gives no indication on how it should be achieved. The establishment of local government in Hungary may help promote the amelioration of domestic problems but joint ventures are required which will encourage the exchange of information, foreign trade, cleaner technology and external funding. The proposed Regional Development Act covers the regional management of crises, transformation of the socio-economic systems, co-operation between zones along state boundaries and regional landscape protection.

If the East is to fully integrate with the West, then it will have to do so within the EC framework. Most European countries have identified areas for action: the need for sustainable lifestyles, to question rapid economic growth as an indicator of effective development and the necessity for individuals, families, communities, corporations and Government to halt environmental destruction.

Initiatives are required that are directly concerned with promoting the understanding of science, economy and the environment. In Hungary, all the normal contradictions between development and conservation are being addressed for the first time. The country has an initiative role in improving East Europe. As for her people, it feels to an outsider as though policy is still forming the public viewpoint rather than the attitudes of the public forming new policy.

> "Strictly speaking, there is no single expert opinion about attitudes toward quality of the environment; there are the opinions each person holds, the opinions he thinks others hold, and the opinions he thinks they should hold. Many public administrators get mixed up about this." (White, 1966)

NOTES

1. Information obtained from the Danube Basin Ecological Convention, Second Draft. Ministry for Environment and Regional Policy. Temporary Secretariat. Budapest, September 1992 and January 1993.
2. Information obtained during discussion with Béla Thurnay, Senior Counsellor, Ministry of Transport, Communication and Water Management, Budapest, 14th October 1992.
3. Extract from the Danube Charta printed at Politishe Okalogie, October 1990. Article Subtitle, Ecological Bricks for our Common House of Europe. ISBN 3-928244-001-9.
4. Report of the Commission of the European Communities to the United Nations Conference on the Environment and Development. Rio de Janeiro, June 1992. Eastern and Central Europe: pp. 107-109.

REFERENCES

Anderson, M. (1993). 'Change is not easy' in *Acid News* (No. 1), February 1993, 2-4.

Alcamo, J. (1992). *Coping with crisis in Eastern Europe's Environment*, Parthenon.

Bulla, M. (1990). 'The necessity of change' in *State of the Environment in Hungary and Environmental Policy*. Presto Ltd. Budapest, 58-61.

Bulla, M. (1991). 'State of our environment' in Ministry for Environment and Regional Policy: Review on the environment, nature conservation, building and regional policy. Budapest, 27-32.

Commoner, B. (1990). *Making Peace with the Planet*. London, Victor Gollancz Ltd.

Fleischer, T., Pomázi I. and Tombácz E. (1991). 'Is there any remedy for the environmental crisis in the socialist countries?' in Ministry for Environment and Regional Policy: Review on the Environment, nature conservation, building and regional policy. Budapest, 16-19.

Simmons, I. (1992). 'Environmental Problems: A phrase to forget' *Geography Review*. September, 12-14.

Somlyódy, L. (1993). 'Water quality management in Hungary: Past experiences and future needs', in Alcamo, J. (ed.) *Coping with crisis in Eastern Europe's Environment*, 143-165.

Szendrei, T. (1992). 'Government projects GDP growth' in *Budapest Week*, October 1-7, p. 2.

UNDP/WHO Project Terminal Report (1976). 'Pilot zones for water quality management in Hungary' HUN/71/505-HUN/PIP001, Budapest.

Varga, P. Abraham, M. and Simor, J. (1990). 'Water quality of the Danube in Hungary and the major determining factors' *Water Science Technology*, 22(5), 113-118.

White, G. (1966). 'Formation and role of public attitudes' in Environmental quality in a growing economy, 105-127 Jarret, H. (ed.), Baltimore: John Hopkins University Press.

16

THE DIALECTICS OF ENVIRONMENT AND CULTURE : Kimilsungism and the North Korean Landscape

P.J. ATKINS

> 'The landscape itself provides material manifestation of the intelligibility of human action, and a means by which historical conditions can be interpreted and understood.
>
> (Kobayashi, 1989, 182)

Introduction

The elation after the end of the Cold War has induced a collective amnesia about the socialist systems which dominated an important part of political space for over 40 years, and also a collective blindness to the rump of communism which stubbornly clings to power. Let us remember that over a fifth of the world's population still lives by the creed of Marxism-Leninism. Apart from China, a coming superpower, we tend to ignore smaller socialist countries such as Cuba, Vietnam and North Korea. My argument here will be that our ignorance of these residual scraps of socialism leads us to neglect important aspects of the relationship between culture and environment.

It is I think a fair criticism of marxist writers that, although they have generated a substantial theoretical literature about they have generated a substantial theoretical literature about the relationships between humans and nature, they have said relatively little about specific socialists material landscapes. There are, of course exceptions, for example Berentson (1992), but a chance was missed after Second

World War, during the flood tide of the soviet empire, to describe their restructuring through explicit ideological principles. My task here will be to suggest provisional interpretations of the landscape of one small socialist state.

In 1991 I was fortunate to visit the Democratic People's Republic of Korea (DPRK) at the invitation of the Korean Social Science Association. I stayed at the campus of the Juche Academy outside Pyongyang and was generously and courteously hosted. I was not allowed to undertake any field work in the normal sense understood by western geographers or social scientists but I was driven around (carefully) pre-selected parts of the country and allowed to take photographs. No data was provided other than that I was able to glean from various conversations. After returning to Durham I read the collected Works of the Great Leader, Kim Il Sung, and found them (surprisingly) informative and at times astonishingly frank. These works, along with the writings of the Dear Leader, Kim Jong Il, and my own limited personal observations, form the texts on which this article is based.

Korea : Nature and Nation

"It is the duty of communists to master and remake nature". Kim Il Sung (quoted in *Korea Today* 7 (1981) 43).

Traditional oriental ideas about the harmony between humans and nature (Nakamura, 1992) have received short shrift in north Korea. The official attitude to the relationship derives more from western philosophy, via Marxism-Leninism and Stalinism, than from Buddhism or Confucianism. We will identify in particular two important sources of thought.

(a) Struggle Firstly, the attitude of the Workers' Party of Korea (WPK) towards its environment must be seen in the context of twentieth century Korean history, which has been a series of momentous struggles. The Japanese colonial phase (1905-45) was a particularly difficult time, with widespread and systematic cruelty, exploitation time, with widespread and systematic resistance was mounted by a variety of groups, but it was not until the end of the Second World War that liberation came. The north was then occupied by Soviet tanks and Kim Il Sung came to power, initially as a client.

The Korean War (1950-53) was an appallingly destructive conflict which achieved very little other than a bloody stalemate. No peace treaty was signed and the armistice has been maintained only by the mutual deterrent of massed forces. Since 1953 the DPRK has not given up the hope and intention of incorporating the south into a broader socialist state, although their rhetoric has recently been in favour of confederation rather than conflict.

North Korea sees itself as an embattled state, in constant struggle against all-comers. The recent collapse of communism in eastern Europe has merely confirmed their suspicions about the poor resolve of their socialist brethren and encouraged even more of a siege mentality.

In this historical context it is not difficult to appreciate that the struggle against nature is seen as merely one among many struggles. The challenge of the environment, with a mountainous topography restricting the amount of arable land, and a hostile climate occasionally manifest in severe floods or droughts, has been taken up and, in the eyes of the government at least, more than matched by a coherent set of policies employed with little change over 40 years.

These policies, part of what came to be known from the 1950s as the juche philosophy, stress the self-reliance of Korea and her need to solve her own problems. Kim Il Sung (1980, 203) was already outlining such ideas in 1946 at the ceremony for starting the Potong River Improvement Project to reduce the risk of flooding in Pyongyang:

> 'No one presents us happiness and prosperity as a gift. They have to be carved out with our own hands and won through struggle. We should start with magnificent nature-remaking projects.......'.

There is an element in this Juche philosophy (Kim Jong Il 1985) of Engels' now unfashionable notion of a dialectic of nature independent of humans, which in turn draws upon Hegel's view of nature as externality (Schmidt 1971, 59). Such a separation legitimates the view of a nature which is subordinate and itself has no meaning of purpose other than as raw material for human action.

> 'Man's [sic] relation with other things in the world is a relation between an independent being and a simply dependent and restricted beings, between a creative being and adapted beings, and between a conscious being and unconscious beings. From this relation proceeds man's domination of the world...And the world knows no other being than human beings which are capable of reshaping other things. From this it follows that the relation between creative

> man and other things is bound to be a relation of domination of the latter by the former...The movement of nature itself has no purpose...The Juche idea convinces us scientifically that man is the only master and transformer of the world and inspires with a firm faith in the victory of the solemn cause of remodelling and altering the world' (Anon. 1986).

This sentiment is echoed by Schmidt (1971, 77):

> 'By releasing the "slumbering powers" of the material of nature, men redeem it: changing the dead in-itself into a living for itself...'.

There are echoes here of the endless struggle between humans and nature in the writings of the Frankfurt school of marxist writers, a struggle which must continue in a socialist society even when other struggles, for instance those between classes have been resolved (Jay, 1973; Leiss, 1974). It is therefore, the 'ultimate' struggle (Smith, 1990).

A logical extension of this view is that humans are not constrained in their ability to modify nature, other than the limits of the technology they are currently employing (Redclift, 1984, 7). Juche Korea has boundless optimism about its powers of intervention and control and relatively less concern about the negative environmental consequences of its actions, unless production is thereby curtailed, for instance where excessive tree clearance has caused soil erosion.

The resulting aggressive anthropocentrism of Kim Jong Il (1991, 2) has a certain chilling quality:

> 'The Juche idea is a man (sic) centred outlook on the world. It has clarified the essential qualities of man as a social being with independence, creativity and consciousness. It has, on this basis, evolved the new philosophical principle that man is the master of everything and decides everything. The Juche idea has established the viewpoint and attitude of dealing with everything in man's interests and approaching all changes and developments on the basis of man's activities'.

For Routley (1980, 240) this

> 'represents an extreme form of placing of man [sic] in the role pre-

viously attributed [by Hegel] to God...the results of the transposition appears to warrant, and even to encourage, unlimited and unconstrained human transformation of the natural world, now in the name of expression rather than domination. And the human hubris which results from this transposition has led to a vast overconfidence and overestimation of human ability to interfere in complex and only partially understood natural systems without ill consequences, a major factor in generating environmental problems'.

Adorno and Horkheimer Contended that

> 'the domination of nature ensued once man's primal embeddedness in nature was transcended and then forgotten. A radical humanism carries with it the latent threat of species imperialism, which ultimately returns to haunt human relations themselves. Indeed, from the first, the domination of nature was intertwined with social hierarchy and control' (Jay 1984, 62).

Some reports suggest that environmental crises have indeed occurred in North Korea. Kim Il Sung has candidly admitted several times that 'soil fertility has deteriorated to a considerable extent' due to poor agricultural practice (Kim Il Sung 1989, 120), and his son was responsible for guiding the terracing of steep hill sides in the late 1970s with allegedly disastrous results for soil erosion and the silting of rivers (Anon 1992a, 57).

(b) Humanized Nature Marx's standpoint was rather different from that articulated above. He argued that nature had already been changed to a greater or lesser extent by the impact of economic forces and it had therefore been reborn as a social product.

> 'Labour is....a process between man [sic] and nature, a process by which man, through his own actions, mediates, regulates and controls the metabolism between himself and nature. He sets in motion the natural forces which belong to his own body, his arms, legs, head and hands, in order to appropriate the materials of nature in a form adapted to his own needs. Through this movement he acts upon external nature and changes it, and in this way he simultaneously changes his own nature' (Marx 1976, 283).

Schmidt (1971, 61) Elaborates Further

> 'Man [sic] forms the connecting link between the instrument of labour and the object of labour. Nature is the subject-object of labour. Its dialectic consists in this: that men change their own nature as they progressively deprive nature of its strangeness and externality, as they mediate nature through themselves, and as they make nature itself work for their own purposes'.

This exceptionally interesting and important conclusion about the humanizing dialectical relationship will be a central theme of this paper.

Korea: Landscape as Political Project

> 'Landscapes are expressions of a persistent desire to make the earth over in the image of some heaven' (Meining 1979, quoting J.B. Jackson).

It is not possible to approach the DPRK with an innocent eye as one might through the glossy pages of a brochure advertising the neutral, de-cultured holiday resorts of the Mediterranean. Selecting a jury to try the case of 'humanity' versus North Korea would reveal a severely limited choice of unbiased observers in Western countries. It may be a 'far away country of which we know little', but that lack of knowledge is not entirely due to the DPRK government's unwillingness to divulge officials data. It is also a consequence of the steady trickle of negative reporting by the western media since the conclusion of the Korean War in 1953 which has inculcated a subconscious hostility, now unchallenged for 40 years. Even President Kim's socialist allies have fallen away in recent years so that we now seems isolated and universally vilified.

North Korea is seen by many (most?) in the West as open prison, or worse: George Orwell's Nineteen Eighty-Four come true. In view of the following quotation, one wonders whether someone in the Pyongyang has a grisly sense of humour:

The Ministry of Truth...was Startlingly Different from any Other

> object in sight. It was an enormous pyramidal structure of glittering

white concrete, soaring up, terrace after terrace, three hundred metres into the air...The Ministry of Truth contained, it was said, three thousand rooms above ground level...' (Orwell 1984, 159).

This is an extraordinarily accurate description of the Ryugyong Hotel in the centre of town, which is pyramid shape, 300 metres tall and has 3000 bedrooms.

One conclusion from out discussion of culture and nature is that the interaction of humans and their physical environment creates a continuously changing humanized landscape in the world and a naturalized landscape of the mind. The importance of this dialectical relationship cannot be over-stressed. The implication is that the humanized, cultural landscape is embossed with the individual and collective consciousness and subconsciousness.

My argument is that the Juche philosophy has been a fundamental factor in shaping the state view of nature, which in turn has 'produced' its environment as a reflection of that society. To borrow a concept from hermeneutics, it is possible to read the environment of North Korea as a text written with the vocabulary, grammar and syntax of the WPK. This is a discourse alien to western sensibilities but one that we must learn to recognize. It bears the indelible traces of communism in its various guises but also displays elements of the collectivism and authoritarianism that are also visible in the Republic of Korea (ROK). Western fears of north Korea are fundamentally a fear of the 'otherness' of the oriental (Said, 1978), compounded by a distance for an increasingly isolated political system which makes it a pariah. Cornered in every sense by a lack of understanding, it is hardly surprising that the DPRK has been driven to a sense of defensive paranoia.

Juche has sought not only to influence people's behaviour through their environment but also to grasp their minds. It is a monolithic philosophy which derives its inspiration from Kim Il Sung as living saviour, his son acting as mere interpreter and elaborator of the sacred text. As a discourse, Juche is holistic, exclusive, hegemonic, and intellectually totalitarian. It brooks no plurality of action or intent, and seeks to eliminate even plurality of interpretation.

> 'In the past the people of some countries that were building socialism wavered in the face of transient difficulties that arose in the course of building socialism and went so far as to yield to the pressure of the imperialists..."Pluralism" can never be tolerated in a

socialist society....The introduction of "pluralism" into socialist society fosters individualism and liberalism that encroach upon the common interests of the society, break the unity and cohesion of the popular masses and produce social disorder and chaos. Permitting liberalism in ideology and a multiparty system in politics in a socialist society is, in the long run, to open a road to counter-revolutionary manoeuvres that are aimed at demolishing the foundation of socialist society and overthrowing the people's government' (Kim Jong Il 1992, 10).

Kim Il Sung has in effect composed the landscape of the DPRK as a retrospective historico-geographical autobiography (Gulley 1961, Baker 1968). The past heroic struggles of soldiers, peasants and workers are a constant theme of state interpretations of present realities and the landscape is used as a key source of evidence for those interpretations. Indeed it constitutes the bulk of Kim Il Sung's Works beyond the 37 published volumes. The DPRK may not have achieved a high standard of material wealth but the impact of its polity upon the landscape has been extraordinary.

Rural Landscapes

'Rice means communism' (Kim Il Sung, 1990, 236).
'The Juche farming method...has been evolved by the Great Leader

Comrade Kim Il Sung....The slightest violation of the principles of this method must be combated without compromise so that it can be implemented to the letter...Strenuous efforts should be made to increase the area of farmland...In our country the area of farmland is limited...a continuous increase in agricultural production will be impossible unless the area of farmland is expanded. The Union's organizations should pay close attention to the reclamation of tidal flats and give strong support to this work so that a wider area of tidal flats is reclaimed; they should also ensure that the reclaimed land is laid out as soon as possible so that it can be used for agriculture. Low hills, tableland and other arable land should also be reclaimed in order to increase the area of cultivated land' (Kim Jong Il 1989, 13).

Although the WPK has given priority to heavy industrialization and urbanization, in an attempt to emulate Soviet economic history, agriculture has not been neglected (Atkins, 1993). Two factors have driven policy since the earliest days. First, the severe shortage of flat, fertile, irrigable arable land has been a major constraint for a culture so reliant upon rice as its staple food. The basic, yet modest aim of the government, to provide its people with rice and meat soup and a tiled roof over their heads, has proved difficult to fulfil. Second, the Juche philosophy of self-reliance has discouraged any notion of an import strategy to balance the nutritional budget.

There has been, therefore, an urgent need to find ways of improving productivity and expanding the cultivated area. An early and successful policy was land reform, a programme of confiscation being implemented in only one month in 1946 (Pak, 1983). Agriculture was then collectivised between 1954 and 1958 (Son, 1986). There are now 990 state farms, 3,000 cooperative farms, 28,000 work teams and 95,000 sub-work teams.

Kim Il Sung seems to have taken a particular interest in matters rural. There are records of scores of on-the-spot guidance visits to villages and farms, especially to model enterprises such as Chongsan-ri (Anon. 1984a). He personally directed agriculture from at least 1973 to 1983 (Kim Il Sung 1991a, 391). In 1964 he published his blueprint for a rural revolution, known as the 'rural theses' (Kim Il Sung 1984a; Kwon et al. 1985-86). These outlined a threefold revolution: ideological, technical and cultural.

Perhaps the most interesting aspect for our present purposes is the technological revolution which has undoubtedly had a major impact on Korean agriculture. By 1980 mechanization had already affected 95 per cent of rice transplanting, and 100 per cent of ploughing, threshing and transport. Ironically, considering the Juche obsession with self-sufficiency, this has left the DPRK very vulnerable because she has to import all of her oil. This was not a problem so long as cheap of bartered oil was readily available from sympathetic socialist trading partners. A crisis has arisen since the collapse of communism, however, because the Russians started insisting on hard currency payments for their goods in 1988 (Kim and Cha, 1992, 2) and the Chinese followed suit in 1993. My own experience of the rice harvest in 1991 indicated a mechanization of no more than 33 per cent. In the late 1980s Iran agreed to barter one million tonnes of oil in exchange for arms, including long-range scud missiles.

Chemicalization was less constrained by imports. From an early date soil analyses were conducted on every ten hectares of cultivable land and fertilizer added accordingly. In the mid-1980s it was claimed that 1.6-2.0 tonnes per hectare were used, (Kwon, 1985; Pang, 1987,

137) very high by world standards. In 1991 recommended doses were 700 kilograms per hectare of nitrogen, 700 kilograms of phosphorus, and a secret amount of potassium, for a rice yield of roughly 7 tonnes per hectare. The secrecy about potassium is simply because the country has yet to develop a manufacturing capability (Kim Il Sung 1991b, 319). The over-use of chemical fertilizers was apparently criticized in a 1991 UNDP report (Foster-Carter, 1992, 16). Ninty-seven per cent of paddy fields were treated with herbicides at one point (Pang, 1987, 137) but it is claimed that these chemicals have now been abandoned on health grounds and replaced by biological control. If the latter does not succeed then the rural planners have a problem because weeding by hand cannot be a viable alternative with the DPRK's perennial labour shortage. Pesticides are still extensively used.

TABLE 16.1: Crop Yields in the DPRK

(*tonnes per hectare*)

Year	Rice	Maize
1944	2.5	0.7
1949	3.0	1.3
1960	3.0	1.2
1974	5.9	5.0
1980	7.2	6.3
1982	7.6	6.5
1990	7.6	6.5

Source: DPRK National Agricultural Exhibition Hall (1991)

There are currently about 700,000 hectares of rice, and 800,000 hectares of other annual crops on flat land (Hong, 1990, 57). In addition there are 300,000 hectares of orchards and 200,000 hectares of (mainly) industrial crops on steep slopes. Despite good yields by third world standards, this amount of land is simply not enough to sustain food self-sufficiency. A curiously heated debate recently in the Bulletin of concerned Asian Scholars (Barkin, 1986; McDonald, 1987; Barkin, 1987) about food supplies in the DPRK ignored the fact that the north Koreans themselves admit to problems. Their rice and maize yields have hardly changed over the last decade and even the Great Leader himself has complained that 'agricultural production has not yet reached the level where food can be supplied according to needs' (Kim Il Sung, 1990, 235).

TABLE 16.2: FAO Estimates of Crop Production in the DPRK, 1988

('000 Tonnes)

Rice (paddy)	5500	Wheat	220
Maize	4400	Barley	150
Potatoes	2100	Oats	60
Sweet potatoes	505	Millet	60
Soya beans	455	Sorghum	15
Pulses	326		

Source: FAO Production Yearbook

In its Production Yearbook the Food and Agriculture Organization of the United Nations makes generous estimates of food output (Table 16.2). South Korea commentators are more sceptical, suggesting for 1992 a grain harvest of only 4.8 million tonnes.

There are four constraints on north Korean agriculture: crop varieties; falling soil fertility; seasonal water shortages; and the shortage of arable land. We will deal with each of these in turn.

(a) The violet bean of Pungsan Kim Il Sung is reported to have conducted experiments on crops in his own back garden and to have made recommendations about varieties to be diffused, such as the violet bean of Pungsan in cooler, hilly areas (Anon. 1988, 24-26). The enforced, and apparently unpopular, change to maize from traditional dry-land crops such as millet was also his decision (Anon. 1988, 59).

This bizarre personal involvement of the country's President in crop breeding symbolizes the regime's commitment to a scientific solution to the food problem and helps to explain north Korea's priority to develop its own improved varieties of rice and other crops from an early date. Her Green Revolution was achieved in the 1960s and 1970s with a claimed 240 per cent increase in the yield of rice per hectare 1960-80. Since then yields have stagnated as the genetic potential of 'miracle' varieties such as Pyongyang 4 has been reached.

(b) Worn out earth in 1980 the Great Leader admitted that the use of chemical fertilizers had not achieved lasting results.

> 'Over recent years crop yields have increased annually in our country without a lot of manure being used. As a result, the soil fertility has deteriorated to a considerable extent' (Kim Il Sung 1989, 120).

Three years later he stated baldly that–

> 'at present the fertility of our fields is very poor...There is even a danger that this year's output of cereals will be lower than that of last year' (Kim Il Sung 1991a, 382-3).

The early 1980s seem to have been a period of particular self doubt and reassessment in agriculture. Several major policies were reformulated at this time. The Korean tradition of 'guest-soil work' was revived and 3-5 cm of new soil, organic matter and silt, were spread. In 1982 paddy fields were made the priority and since 1990 other fields have benefited. (Anon. 1992b) To cope with this new need, humus/compost factories were established, using an unpromising-sounding raw materials source of bushes, grass, peat and rice straw. Cultivation practices were also reviewed, including the possible use of green manure after maize and even fallowing.

(c) Water the wet paddy system of rice cultivation demands careful hydrological management to create a suitable micro-ecosystem. It is the cycle of wet and dry phases which governs the biochemistry which accounts for its extraordinary long-term productivity throughout south and east Asia.

Lansing (1991) has studied the relationship between human culture in Bali and the cultivation of rice. He concludes that the role of water has been a major structuring factor in Balinese rural life through the ritual system associated with 'water temples'. The concept of holy water which enters a farmer's field from a–

> 'weir shrine transforms the weir into the symbol of a specific social unit. It is through this symbolism that farmers acquire concepts for social units more abstract than the immediate face-to-face community of neighbours...In the long run it is the social relationships constructed by water temples, not the mechanics of water flow, that create and sustain the terrace ecosystem' (Lansing, 1991, 130).

Such micro-scale religious subtleties are not present in socialist Korea but we can argue nevertheless that the need of large-scale control of water for rice cultivation has had a major impact on its psyche. The drive for food self-sufficiency has demanded the higher yields available from controlled soil moisture and this in turn has encouraged a reflexive reinforcement of Juche principles.

Perhaps their biggest achievement in remaking nature has been the north Koreans' outstanding record in irrigation. The irrigation of 1.4

million hectares of land has been completed, about 70 per cent of the total. This has been achieved by the planning of a complex system of 1,700 reservoirs fed by 25,800 pumping stations, and 40,000 kilometres of major irrigation canals. The reservoirs are often on high ground and store water pumped up from rivers such as the Taedong, Chongchon, and Amnok. Hydro electric power is generated when these waters are released under gravity flow. The largest schemes include:

- The Amnokgang irrigation scheme which waters the 90,000 hectares of 130 cooperative farms in 8 countries of North Pyongan Province. It employs 10 reservoirs, 700 pumping stations, 20 barrages, and 7,000 canals (Anon. 1984b).
- The Pyongnam irrigation project which serves the 100,000 hectares of over 100 cooperatives and state stock farms in South Pyongan Province. It comprises 10 reservoirs, 1,000 pumping stations, 10,000 canals, and 2,000 kilometres of major waterways (Anon. 1984c).
- The Kiyang irrigation scheme in the south west of South Pyongan Province. This irrigates 65,000 hectares from 1,800 kilometres of canals 30 reservoirs, and 600 pumping stations. HEP stations at the reservoirs generate 7 million kilowatt hours of electricity (Anon. 1984.d).

Especially important in the recent expansion of the irrigated area has been the construction of the West Sea Barrage near Nampo. This stretches 8 kilometres across the mouth of the Taedong River, and ponds back the fresh water of the river to create a large lake. Apart from irrigation, this water is also used for domestic and industrial purposes. The temperature increase of 1.5C in the river is reported to have encouraged fish and changed the micro-climate of riverain farms, but other, negative ecological implications seem to have been ignored.

The barrage itself was a major engineering feat accomplished by 30,000 workers between 1981 and 1986. The cost of $4 billion included very substantial amounts of the country's scarce construction materials: 2 million cubic metres (1.1 million tonnes) of concrete, 16 million cubic metres of aggregate, and 280,000 tonnes of steel. The decision to build was made by the President. The port of Nampo is not cut off: three locks allow ships of up to 50,000 tonnes to pass (Anon. 1990).

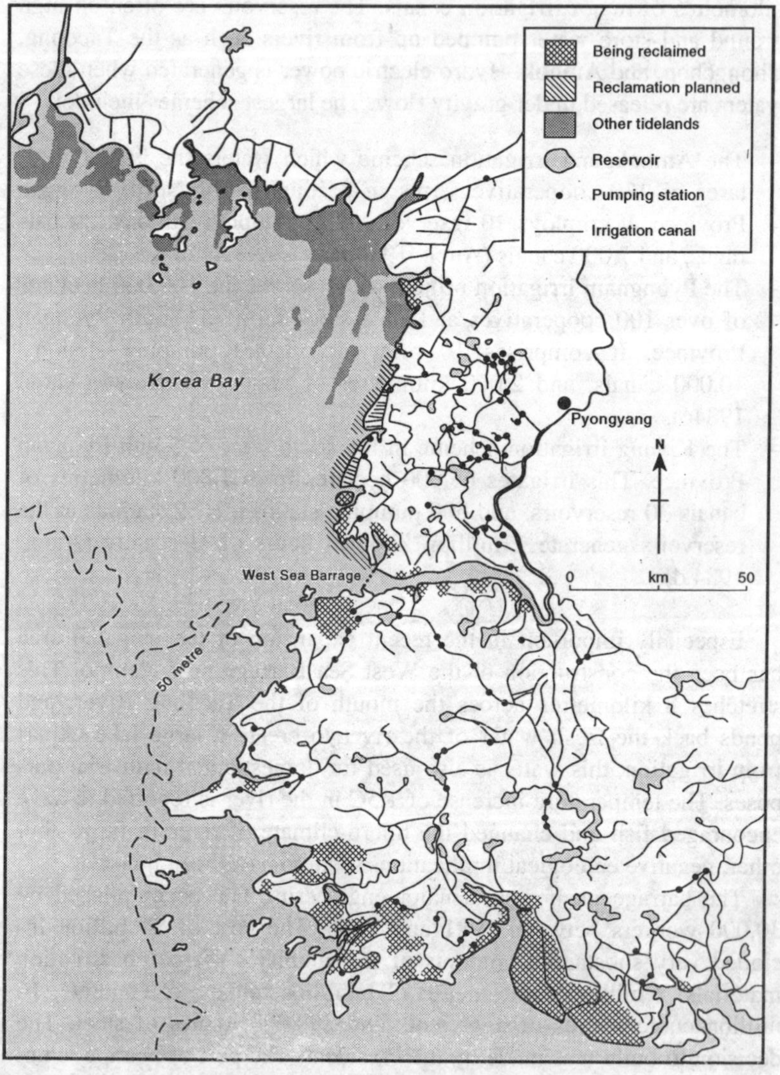

FIG. 16.1: South Pyongyang Irrigation Scheme

Water pumped from the ponded Taedong will be used to irrigate 340,000 hectares via 800 kilometres of canal. Son (1990) reported the completion of a 132 kilometre waterway from the barrage to Sinchon, Kangryong and Ongjin and a change in the hydrological regime of the River Chaeryong which reversed its flow due to the higher level of the R. Taedong, facilitating the movement of water southwards. April 1992 saw the completion of a major trunk canal from the barrage 70 kilometres south westwards to Unryul (irrigating 4,300 hectares of reclaimed tideland) and Yulli Reservoir in Kwail Country.

(d) The rhetoric of reclamation What Cosgrove (1992) calls the 'rhetoric of reclamation' is amply demonstrated in the four nature-remaking projects, as set out at the Fourth Plenary Meeting (1981) of the Sixth Central Committee of the Workers' Party of Korea:

- 300,000 hectares of tideland reclamation;
- 200,000 hectares of new arable land;
- the construction of the Nampo Barrage; and
- the construction of the Taechon Power Station to facilitate water pumping for irrigation (Kim Il Sung 1991c; Anon. 1984e).

The reclamation of marsh, swamp, woodland and sloping land has been a theme of government policy from the 1940s. The First Five Year Plan (1957-1961) set a target of planting 100,000 hectares of orchards in order to boost fruit and mulberry production (Kim Il Sung, 1983a). Orchards were increased from 8,000 to 80,000 hectares, many plantings being on terraced hill sides (Kim Il Sung, 1983b). At the Pukchong Enlarged Meeting of the Presidium of the Central Committee of the WPK in 1961, Kim Il Sung outlined a scheme for a further large-scale expansion of pomiculture. By 1987 orchards had increased to 300,000 hectares (Pang, 1987, 140).

The Great Leader has called for a further 200,000 hectares of reclamation of unused land for sugar beet and oil seeds, for instance the wetlands of Ryanggan Province and other land in North Hamyong Province. He also points to unused land beside railways (Kim Il Sung 1990).

The strongest policy direction towards nature modification, however, has been the frequently restated priority of coastal reclamation. The Gulf of Korea on the west coast is relatively shallow. The 50 metre isobath is 70 kilometres offshore at the mouth of the River Taedong and large areas of 'tideland' are potentially reclaimable for agriculture. Most of this lies in the long arc of coast between Nampo and the River Amnok.

During the Fatherland Liberation War a team of geographers from Kim Il Sung University was given the task of surveying the west coast for potentially reclaimable land (Kim Il Sung 1991a). They reported that 150,000 hectares were available. This figure was later increased by the politicians.

By 1978, 30,899 hectares of tidal flats had been reclaimed (14,000 in South Pyongan Province, 12,000 in North Pyongan, and 4,000 in South Hwanghae), 78 per cent of which were already in use as paddy fields, reed beds, reservoirs, fish farms and salterns (Kim Il Sung, 1985a). The Sixth Congress in 1980 instructed the Agricultural Commission to establish a General Bureau of Tideland Reclamation (GBTR) and set an objective of 300,000 hectares of reclamation in the 1980s (Kim Il Sung, 1990; Cho 1984). In 1983 Kim Il Sung altered these targets to 300,000 hectares by 1987 or 1988 and a further 200 — 300,000 hectares thereafter, making a total of at least 500,000 hectares (Kim Il Sung, 1991b, 324). This compares with the Netherlands' drainage of 165,000 hectares of land in the Zuyderzee between 1927 and 1968.

- In North Pyongan Province a number of islands were to be linked in the estuary of the Amnok River and the sea dammed off up to Chongju, to a total of 110,000 ha (Kim, G.S. 1984).
- In South Pyongan Province a stretch of land up to 16 kilometres out to sea was to be reclaimed from the R. Chongchon to the R. Taedong.
- In South Hwanghae Province all the deeply indented bays were to be dammed.

This was one of the ten major prospective goals of socialist economic construction for the decade, the time limit for which was later extended to the end of the third seven year plan (1987-1993). On a visit in 1991 I was told that 100,000 hectares had so far been reclaimed.

By way of example, the Unryul ore mine (South Hwanghae) was having problems disposing of its waste, mainly overburden excavated from this opencast site. Kim Jong Il is credited of having the idea in 1974 of dumping this in the sea from a long conveyor belt to create a causeway linking several islands to the mainland (Anon. 1983). Eventually this will become a major reclamation project when the embankment is completed. 3,500 hectare have already been reclaimed according to recent reports.

As in all investigations of the DPRK, there is a severe shortage of data, although the government magazine *Korea Today* and newspaper *The Pyongyang Times* reveal perhaps more than they intend, (Chon, 1980; Kwon, 1981; Li, 1983; Choe, 1986; Ro, 1990; Han, 1991; Son, 1992; Yang, 1992) as is also the case with the works of Kim Il Sung.

It seems that the confidence in re-ordering the environment instilled by Juche has not been sufficient. There have been at least six major sources of difficulty. Firstly, the cost of the construction work has been a drain on the national budget, but to an indeterminate extent. The definition of tideland is the sea bed which is either dry of under less than one metre of water at low tide (Kim Il Sung, 1991a, 365). The reclamation process is carried out initially from anchored barges which dump material to make a sea wall. At Ryomho-ri, Kwaksan County, North Pyongan Province, for instance, 2,600 hectares of reclamation required a nine kilometre long, ten metre high, dyke of feldspar and concrete, with a total of 1.6 million cubic metres of rubble.

Astonishingly, Kim Il Sung admitted that –

> 'at present this construction work is executed not in a planned manner but by rule of thumb, and we do not know how much money is spent on the reclamation of one hectare of tideland. . . we have no accurate estimates not only for the construction of a network of facilities in the reclaimed land but also for the general work of tideland reclamation. . . . It is difficult nor for us to trust the figures for tideland areas which the provinces have decided to reclaim because these have been provided without conducting field surveys' (Kim Il Sung 1991a, 380).

Secondly, salty tideland soil has required more fresh water for flushing than the nation can reasonably afford. In 1978 12,000 cubic metres of fresh water per hectare were said to be required to irrigate tidelands, 20 per cent more than ordinary rice fields (Kim Il Sung, 1988, 147), a figure confirmed recently for the November 10th State Youth Farm, 10 kilometres south of Yomju in North Pyongan Province (Ro, 1990).

Thirdly, the coastal work has diverted other scarce resources or suffered because they were not available. Labour has been the most serious problem, mainly because the DPRK keeps a standing army of 1.32 million, the fifth largest in the world. The Great Leader in 1983 identified this as a constraint and suggested that 200,000 able bodied men should be sent to the rural areas in general, 170,000 from factories and 30,000 from the army, or 200,000 from school leavers. He stated that he did not want people to go against their will! (Kim Il Sung, 1991a, 391). On 300,000 hectares of tidelands a simple back-of-an-envelope calculation implies a very large labour requirement.

Each person on the newly created farms will be expected manage three hectares, hence a need for 150,000 people, including auxiliary manpower. The November 10th State Youth Farm comprises 1,000 hectares of paddy on reclaimed land, worked by 200 families (Ro, 1990). Extrapolating this average of five hectares per family, and assuming four persons per family, the situation is even graver, the need rising to 240,000 people plus 50,000 auxiliaries. In a country of 20 million, with a slow growing population, it is difficulty to see how this can possibly be serviced. Experimentation with sowing seed from the air in order to overcome the labour bottleneck suggests desperation.

Other scarce resources are needed as well. At one tractor to each 20 hectares of reclaimed land, a major industry will be required to produce the total of 15,000 tractors (Kim Il Sung, 1990, 243).

Fourthly, there will inevitably be major environmental disturbance as a result of these reclamation works. These will be ecological and geomorphological. There is no evidence that such considerations have played any part in the planning process.

Fifthly, there have been open political tensions about the priority which the tideland projects should receive in the overall economic planning process. The Kims made it one of their ten national goals for the decade of the 1980s but their subordinates clearly did not agree. Kim Il Sung's own speeches are the best source for this conclusion.

'A long time ago I gave the June 3rd Cooperative Farm in Onchon Country, South Pyongan Province, the task of mechanizing farm work and using chemicals widely so that each farmer could tend three hectares of tideland paddy fields. But this task has not yet been implemented. The senior officials of the Sough Pyongan Provincial Party Committee have not even visited the farm. This is a grave error. The chief secretary. . . must be well aware of the task we have given, and must make strenuous efforts to carry it out. But he does not seem concerned about how the task is being implemented. He is putting on airs, cooped up in his office' (Kim Il Sung, 1988, 151-2).

'According to a recent [3 day] on-the-spot study, by the First Vice-Premier of the Administration Council and the Chairman of the State Planning Commission, the reclamation has not been proceeding smoothly, although one and a half years have passed since the Fourth Plenary Meeting of the Sixth Party Central Committee. We have mobilised no small quantities of manpower and equipment for this reclamation but have failed to obtain reliable data from geological surveys or produce well-drawn plans for the reclamation of tidal land.

The failure of the reclamation is ascribed to the fact that the Administration Council has not supervised and directed it properly. Though it has many Vice-Premiers, none of them has visited the reclamation site. Even though they had been told that the problem of tideland reclamation would be discussed at this enlarged meeting of the Political Bureau of the Central Committee, no one attempted to visit the reclamation site to learn the actual situation there. . . . This shows that the senior officials of this council are indifferent to the implementation of the Party's decision. Since reclamation in South Pyongan Province was not satisfactory, I spoke about this on several occasions to the former provincial party chief secretary and to the newly appointed one too, but attention still is not paid to this project' (Kim Il Sung 1991a, 369-370, emphasis added).

'At present some senior officials of the provinces are not greatly interested in the reclamation of tidal flats. Some senior Officials of South Pyongan Province have not even paid a visit to the tidal flat reclamation site simply because the project is the responsibility of the Bureau of Tidal Flat Reclamation. Because they do not demonstrate great interest in the project, the young shock-brigade members working on it are not provided with proper living conditions and they have complained. Not many tidal flats have been reclaimed this year. From next year onwards we must concentrate our efforts on this project' (Kim Il Sung, 1991b, 323).

Finally, the yields achieved on reclaimed sites have been disappointing, only 4-5 tonnes of rice per hectare compared with the national average of 7.6 tonnes (Han, 1991). As already noted, one problem has been the lack of water for irrigation. In order to reduce water use, experiments into underground piped irrigation have been personally guided by the Great Leader (Anon, 1988).

Conclusion

North Korea has developed what Unwin (1992, 191) calls a 'human meaning of landscape'. The authorship and interpretation of that landscape has been single-minded, from a single mind. The resulting landscape of the DPRK is an outcome or a bye-product of socialism but also a key medium through which the society has been transformed. The confrontation with nature has in turn dominated and transformed the Korean version of socialism.

REFERENCES

Anon. (1983). Korean map will be reconstructed, *Korea Today* 5, 97-99.

Anon. (1984a) New looks of Chongsan-ri Pyongyang: Foreign Languages Publishing House.

Anon. (1984b). *Amnokgang irrigation* Pyongyang: The Agriculture Publishing House.

Anon. (1984c). *Pyongnam irrigation* Pyongyang: The Agriculture Publishing House.

Anon. (1984d). *Kiyang irrigation* Pyongyang: The Agriculture Publishing House.

Anon. (1984e). Interview with Li Gyu Il, Director of the Tideland Reclamation General Bureau, *Korea Today* 10, 60-61.

Anon. (1986). Principles of the Juche idea: what is the World we Live in? *Korea Today* 5, 30-31; 6, 18-19; 7, 26-27.

Anon. (1988). *The Peerless Great Man: The song of the Phoenix* (1953-61] Pyongyang: Foreign Languages Publishing House.

Anon. (1990). *The West Sea Barrage* Pyongyang: Korea Pictorial.

Anon. (1992a). Korean unit: The Cost, *Far Eastern Economic Review* 15, 26th March, 54-61.

Anon. (1992b). Interview with Cha Rin Sok, Deputy Director of the Production Guidance Bureau of the State Commission of Agriculture, *Korea Today* 5,37.

Atkins, P.J. (1993). Development North Korean Style, *Geography Review* 6, 3, 39-41.

Baker, A.R.H. (1968). A note on the retrogressive and retrospective approaches in historical geography, *Erdkunde* 22, 243-4.

Barkin, D. (1986). Food Self-Sufficiency in the DPRK, *Bulletin of Concerned Asian Scholars* 18, 4, 20-40.

Barkin, D. (1987). On Scholarship and Understanding, *Bulletin of Concerned Asian Scholars* 19, 2, 70-72.

Berentson, W.H. (1992). The Socialist Dace of the GDR: Eastern Germany's Landscape — Past, Present and Future, *Landscape and Urban Planning* 22, 137-151

Cho, J.R. (1984). Great Plan for Tideland Reclamation, *Korea Today*, 10, 58-9 Choe, C.S. (1986) A Farm has Risen in the Sea, *Korea Today*, 12, 24-25.

Chon, B.H. (1985). Expansion of Arable Land and its Protection and Utilization, *Korea Today* 11, 4-8.

Chon, J.H. (1980). Along the West Coastline (1), *Korea Today* 8, 62-3.

Cosgrove, D.E. (1990). Environmental Thought and Action: Pre-Modern and Post-Modern, *Transactions of the Institute of British Geographers*, new series 15, 344-58

Cosgrove, D.E. (1992). The Palladian Landscape: Geographical Change and its Cultural Representations in Sixteenth Century Italy Leicester: Leicester University Press.

Fitzsimmons, M. (1989). The Matter of Nature, *Antipode* 21, 106-20.

Foster-Carter, A. (1992). Korea's Coming Reunification: Another East Asian Superpower? London: Economist Intelligence Unit.

Glacken, C.J. (1967). Traces on the Rhodian Shore: Nature and Culture in Western Thought from Ancient Times to the End of the Eighteenth Century Berkeley: University of California Press.

Gulley, J.L.M. (1961). The Retrospective Approach in Historical Geography, *Erdkunde* 15, 306-9.

Han, Y.R. (1991). The March 3rd State Farm, *Korea Today* 9, 27.

Hong, S.U. (1990). *Economic Development in the DPRK*, Pyongyang: Foreign Languages Publishing House.

Jay, M. (1973). *The Dialectical Imagination: A History of the Frankfurt School and the Institute of Social Research 1923-1950,* London: Heinemann.

Jay, M. (1984). *Adorno*, London: Fontana.

Jung, H.Y. (1983). "Marxism, Ecology and Technology", *Environmental Ethics* 5, 169-71

Kim, G.S. (1984). A people's asset, *Korea Today*, 10, 62-4.

Kim Il Sung (1980). Encouraging address delivered at the ceremony for starting the Potong River Improvement Project, 1946, pp 202-205 in *Ibid*, Works, Volume 2, Pyongyang: Foreign Languages Publishing House.

Kim Il Sung (1983a). On the tasks of party organizations in South Pyongan Province, 1960, pp 6-47 in *Ibid*, Works, Volume 14, Pyongyang: Foreign Languages Publishing House.

Kim Il Sung (1983b). On Planting Orchards Through an All-People Movement, concluding speech at the Pukchong enlarged meeting of the Presidium of the Central Committee of the Workers' Party of Korea, April 7, 1961, pp 49-60 in *Ibid*, Works, Volume 15, Pyongyang: Foreign Languages Publishing House.

Kim Il Sung (1984a). On the ten major tasks of Pyongyang City, speech delivered at a plenary meeting of Pyongyang City Committee of the Workers' Party of Korea, June 26 1964, pp 295-321 in *Ibid*, Works, Volume 19, Pyongyang: Foreign Languages Publishing House.

Kim Il Sung (1984b). Theses on the Socialist Rural Question in Our Country, 1964, pp 163-212 in *Ibid*, Works Volume 18, Pyongyang: Foreign Languages Publishing House.

Kim Il Sung (1985a). On Some Measures for the Reclamation of Tideland in a Well Defined Framework, pp 60-66 in *Ibid*, Works, Volume 23, Pyongyang: Foreign Languages Publishing House.

Kim Il Sung (1985b). For the Large-Scale Reclamation of Tidelands, pp 74-86 in *Ibid,* Volume 23, Pyongyang: Foreign Languages Publishing House.

Kim Il Sung (1988). On the Wide-Scale Reclamation of Tidal Flats and their Cultivation, speech at a consultative meeting of agricultural officials April 3, 1978, pp 146-58 in *Ibid*, Works, Volume 33, Pyongyang: Foreign Languages Publishing House.

Kim Il Sung (1989). On the Current Problems in this Year's Farming, speech at a consultative meeting of senior officials in charge of agriculture, 1980, pp 114-124 in *Ibid,* Works, Volume 35, Pyongyang: Foreign Languages Publishing House.

Kim Il Sung (1990). Let the entire Party, the whole country and all the people carry out the great project for the transformation of nature to reclaim tidal flats and other new land, speech delivered at the Fourth Plenary Meeting of the Sixth Central Committee of the Workers' Party of Korea, October 5, 1981, pp 233-252 in *Ibid.*, Works, Volume 36, Pyongyang: Foreign Languages Publishing House.

Kim Il Sung (1991a). On Accelerating the Reclamation of Tideland and Increasing the Fertility of Fields, speech delivered at an enlarged meeting of the Political Bureau of the Central Committee of the Workers' Party of Korea, April 2, 1983, pp 368-395 in *Ibid.*, Works, Volume 37, Pyongyang: Foreign Languages Publishing House.

Kim Il Sung (1991b). On Certain Tasks Involved in Improving the Management of Agriculture and Increased Agricultural Production, 1983, pp 305-335 in *Ibid*, Works, Volume 37, Pyongyang: Foreign Languages Publishing House.

Kim Il Sung (1991c). Tasks of the People's Government in Modelling the Whole Country on the Juche Idea, 1982, pp 98-125 in *Ibid*, Works, Volume 37, Pyongyang: Foreign Languages Publishing House.

Kim Il Jong (1985). *On the Juche Idea of Our Party*, Pyongyang: Foreign Languages Publishing House.

Kim Il Jong (1989). *On stepping up the work of the Union of Agricultural Working People,* Pyongyang: Foreign Languages Publishing House.

Kim Il Jong (1991). "Our Socialism Centred on the Masses shall not Perish," talk to the senior officials of the Central Committee of the Workers' Party of Korea, May 5, 1991 Pyongyang: Foreign Languages Publishing House.

Kim Il Jong (1992). "The Historical Lesson in Building Socialism and the General Line of Our Party", *Study of the Juche Idea*, 57, 6-26.

Kim T. & Cha Y.K. (1992). "Prospects for Political Change and Liberalization in North Korea", *The Washington Quarterly* 15, 3, 155-69.

Kobayashi, A. (1989). "A Critique of Dialectical Landscape", pp 164-83 in Kobayashi, A. & Mackenzie, S. (eds.) *Remaking Human Geography,* Boston: Unwin Hyman.

Kwon, J.G. et al. (1985). Implementing Socialist Rural Theses, *Korea Today* 1, 31-2; 2, 34-35; 3, 24; 4 33-34; 5, 23-24; 6, 33-34; 9, 37-38 10, 42; 12, 38-40; 8 (1986) 31-32

Kwon, O.S. (1981). Along the west coastline (11), *Korea Today* 9, 42-4.

Lansing, J.S. (1991). *Priests and Programmers: Technologies of Power in the Engineered Landscape of Bali*, Princeton: Princeton UP.

Lee, D.C. (1980). On the Marxian View of the Relationship Between Man and Nature, *Environmental Ethics*, 2, 3-16.

Leiss, W. (1974). The Domination of Nature Boston: Beacon Press.

LI, J.H. (1983). Tideland into Fertile Fields: a Visit to Tideland Reclamation Site of the West Sea, *Korea Today*, 10, 31-32.

McDonald, A.W. (1987). "On Lies and Lying", *Bulletin of Concerned Asian Scholars* 19, 2, 68-70.

Marx, K. (1976). Capital, Volume 1, Harmondsworth: Penguin.

Meinig, D.W. (1979). Reading the Landscape: An Appreciation of W.G. Hoskins and J.B. Jackson, pp 195-244 in Meinig, D.W. (ed.) *The Interpretation of Ordinary Landscapes: Geographical Essays,* New Haven: Oxford University Press.

Nakamura, H. (1992). The Idea of Nature in the East in Comparison with the West, *Geojournal* 26, 113-128.

O'Connor, H. (1989). Political Economy of Ecology of Socialism and Capitalism, *Capitalism-Nature-Socialism* 3, 93-106

Orwell, G. (1984). *Nineteen Eighty-Four: with a Critical Introduction and Annotations* by *Bernard Crick*, Oxford: Clarendon Press.

Pak, K.H. (1983). Agricultural Policy and Development in North Korea, pp 214-229 in Scalapino, R.A. and Kim, J.Y. (eds.) *North Korea today: Strategic and Domestic Issues,* Berkeley: Centre for Korean Studies, Institute of East Asian Studies, University of California, Berkeley.

Pang, H.J. (1987). *Korean Review*, Pyongyang: Foreign Languages Publishing House.

Peet, R. (1989). New Models of Environment and Resources: Introduction, pp 43-47 in Peet, R. Thrift, N. (Eds) *New Models in Geography: the Political-Economy Perspective,* Volume 1, London: Unwin Hyman.

Redclift, M. (1984). *Development and the Environmental Crisis: Red or Green Alternatives*? London: Methuen.

Redclift, M. (1987). "The Production of Nature and the Reproduction of Species", *Antipode* 18, 212-230.

Rhee, S.W. (1992). "North Korea in 1991: Struggle to Save Juche Amid Signs of Change", *Asian Survey*, 32, 1, 56-63.

Rhodes, C. (1992). A Consideration of the Juche Ideology, unpublished paper presented to the conference on North Korea in the New World Order, London 31st October.

Ro, Y.C. (1990). "The Waves Use to Sweep Here", *Korea Today* 11, 39-40.

Routley, V. (1981). On Karl Marx as an environmental hero, *Environmental Ethics* 3, 237-244.

Said, E.W. (1978). *Orientalism* London: Routledge.

Schmidt, A. (1971). *The Concept of Nature in Marx* London: New Left Books.

Smith, N. (1990). *Uneven Development: Nature, Capital and the Production of Space* 2nd ed. Oxford: Blackwell.

Smith, N. & O'Keefe, P. (1980). "Geography, Marx and the Concept of Nature", *Antipode* 21, 2, 30-39.

Son, J.H. (1986). *Experiences of Agrarian Reform*, Pyongyang: Foreign Languages Publishing House.

Son, S.R. (1991). "A New Waterway", *Korea Today* 3.

Son, Y.G. (1990). "Along the New Waterway of the West Coast Granary", *Korea Today* 9, 23-24; 10, 30.

Son, Y.G. (1992). "Reclaimed Tideland", *Korea Today* 9, 27.

Tolman, C. (1981). "Karl Marx, Alienation and the Mastery of Nature", *Environmental Ethics* 3, 63-74.

Unwin, P.T.H. (1992). *The Place of Geography*, Harlow: Longman.

Yang, R.H. (1992). "How have Tidelands been Reclaimed?" *The Pyongyang Times* 30th May, 4.

17

ROMANCES OF REMOTENESS IN BRITISH CULTURE : The Place of the Highlands and Islands in Imagination and Practice

PAMELA SHURMER-SMITH

In this paper I intend to explore some of the romantic notions which are attached to the idea of the remote in certain strand of British culture and to relate these to conceptualisations of marginality, which is only superficially the same thing. I see remoteness as belonging in the realm of the symbolic, marginality in the economic and political; however, I also assume that these two realms are not watertight compartments but that there is communication between them in the construction of notions of value.

There is a deep vein of ruralism in British urban (particularly, but not exclusively, middle class) culture. This has been particularly well documented by Raymond Williams in his *The Country and the City* which considers the interplay of evaluations of the urban and the rural in English literature and society. Contemporary geographers (notably Nigel Thrift) have demonstrated the ways in which currently rurality has been espoused by the upwardly mobile new service class as it tries to construct an élite identify for itself. At one level this can involve a taste for supposedly rural decor in urban and sub-urban dwellings, whether this be in the "country house" or "cottage" style, but at the other extreme it involves the actual purchase of housing in the countryside, whether for commuting or as a second home. Between these two there is the part-time rural living of tourism and leisure. Complicated notions of "tradition", naturalness and "authenticity" contribute to this idealisation of the countryside, but they mostly congeal around ideas about benign, land-owning lowland rurality, where the urban is sufficiently close as to serve as a known counterpoint.

If the near rural is in fertile communion with its urban, the remote rural is used to signify stark contrast and discontinuity. It is not tamed into the ingredients of any urban "lifestyle", for it is associated with unregulated nature, rather than with a landscape at the service of society. It is as if the one were regarded as a pleasure garden for the city, the other as an alien wilderness.

It is important to stress that I am talking in terms of the metaphorical uses to which the rural is put, rather than the physical "realities" which may be experienced in different rural areas in Britain. The reality is that all parts of Britain are in reasonably easy access of a large city, there is nowhere that is (unwillingly) cut off from modern services, nowhere that is unaffected by social and economic change, including fashion and lifestyle.

The remote rural, then, serves as a signifier of nature outside society and by extension it can represent a whole range of positive and negative a social ideas and values which are not necessarily inherently rural. Human desires and passions may then be projected onto the screen of the remote and contemplated there outside the domain of society and inside the realm of nature; the contemplation of transgression then becomes safe, but exciting.

In this paper I am drawing upon and elaborating Edwin Ardener's use of the concept of remoteness, which contain within it several deliberate logical contradictions. Indeed it is quite overtly not a logic proposition at all, but instead operates as a metaphor. Ardener's remote places are *removed* from mundane places. They need not be far away, other than in the mind, and though the remoteness may be enhanced by distance, mere distance is not enough to confer it. So the Highlands of Scotland are regarded by the South East of England as remote, but New York is not, it is merely far away. Apparent difficulty of access is an important part of a characterisation as remote, but that difficulty is often seen as a challenge and the visitors are *attracted* to remote places, leading to the contradiction that remote places then become very well connected to central places. This connectedness is compounded by the observation that remote places provide migrants to the centre, but these migrants have strong identities, provided by their home place and are lured back. Remote places have a high degree of imageability, become the stuff of literature and music, but also of travelogue; remote places, then, are *known* and being known, they are appropriated into the national culture as symbols, rather than just as localities.

The important point is that the attitude to remote places is *emotional* rather than rational. They become the repository for fantasies about escape, utopian living, heroism, freedom, authenticity, and as such they attract, as incoming residents and tourists (but also as field-classes and research projects) those who would enact their desires. As Ardener points out, they are likely to draw in conservationists, artists, and those who practise "traditional" crafts; people who are enacting a withdrawal from the urban economy and lifestyles associated with it. (It is important to emphasises the word *enacting,* for the ritual element is significant.)

When Ardener first presented his paper on Remote Places it was half in jest. It appeared at a conference on "Anthropology at Home" and, close to the end of his career, Ardener was musing upon the various places he had lived in and been associated with. It was greeted affectionately but as a rather silly paper. However, in time, people began to realise that there was in fact something very illuminating in this conceptualising of the remote as being qualitatively different from the merely distant and the paper gradually built up a reputation in anthropology beyond that of the original joke.

I am aware that it sounds as if I am saying something rather banal, that some places are remote because people think of themes remote, but that to meet the criteria of remoteness a place needs only to be thought of as such. To some extent, this is exactly what I am saying, that remoteness is an endowed, not an inherent characteristic, associated with highly imaged deep rural places. Here I would emphasise the high imageability and stress that the culturally constructed meaning takes precedence over nature as a thing in itself. The remote then becomes something remarkably similar to the sacred, the set aside.

It was, of course, the Romantics, like Wordsworth and Coleridge, who familiarised us with the power of supposedly untamed nature in the experience and communication of overwhelming sentiments, whereas Modernists often turned aside both from a glorification of unbridled passion (castigated as sentimentality rather than sentiment) and from remoteness as a trope. So, for example, in the poetry of Auden, nature is often contemplated, but never with feelings of terror or submission. Nature is little more than a setting for the poet's observations. The arts of the Modernist era more characteristically address the condition of man in society (that "man" was not a phallogogentric slip, it referred to male persons). Nature contained within society became more evident than nature structurally opposed to it and depictions of nature as sublime or awe inspiring came to be seen as clichéd, overblown, melodramatic.

As the structures and narratives of modernism loose their persuasiveness we can witness yet another shift in the human relationship to both nature and society and its representation. The term *postmodern* is fast loosing any power it had, but it is still a usable catch-all for the things which are current but cannot be characterised as modernist in function or intent, so, in spite of its overworking, I shall employ it in this sense. In postmodern culture, nature does not just serve polysemously in the representation of a range of emotions and aspirations, as it did for the Romantics; it enters the discourse as a subject as well as a signifier, but, like all subjects, its position is challengeable. At its most radical this is manifested in the ideological positions of the "deep ecologists", Gaiaists, eco-feminists, where human subjects no longer have a privileged position (either logically or politically) and where the individual, the social, the natural are not perceived as meaningful orders of difference. Radical ecological positions are held only by a tiny minority of people in contemporary "western" society, but that they are tenable at all (without being castigated as complete lunacy) demonstrates a fundamental shift. In less radical forms, variations on these views are fast being accepted as a new orthodoxy, especially by younger people.

What I am trying to say is that within the wide repertoire of meanings which can be attached to the remote countryside in a *postmodern* context is one which sees nature as a player upon the stage. This new meaning does not stand in opposition to pre-existing meanings of nature as a locus for particular types of activity or a vehicle for particular modes of expression, it participates within them and draws upon them.

Many of the popular accounts latch onto the way in which pastiche is a common device in postmodern culture, using this as evidence of the way in which in the postmodern "anything goes", where styles, eras, regional characteristics, registers, moods may be jumbled up together or used "inappropriately" in the name of "play". This is commonly taken as evidence of shallowness and lack of serious intent or sometimes an indication of simple ignorance of appropriate categories. Certainly the employment of vernacular and "historical" styles in certain stands of postmodernist art and architecture has been an excuse for the espousal of neo-traditionalist lifestyles and naive revivalisms in present day British culture, but this is only one stand of the complex fabric of possibilities that make up contemporary life. Less conservatively, postmodernist pastiche offers the means whereby transgressive ideas may be thought and anti-structures envisaged. If one era leaks into another, localities loose their specific locatedness, if élite and popular forms can converse, if age groups and genders are no longer stylistically self-evident, it becomes difficult to be convinced of the absolute necessity for a view of the world as structured. The process of de-differentiation, then, is not just a matter of mixing things up but of breaking structures down.

It is not mere nihilism which seeks to challenge existing structures of thought and action but a consciousness that modernist structure only ever "worked" for a minority of people within the confines of a particular experience of industrial capitalism. As that experience becomes ever more rare there is an awareness not only of a clamour of rival thoughts from previously excluded "Others", but also of the inability of modernist structures to help us theorise post-industrial conditions, with their characteristic flexibility, fluidity, chaos.

Against this backdrop I want to look at the practical and communicative outcomes of contemporary romances of remoteness by focusing upon the Highlands and Islands of Scotland.

If we look at this region in practical terms we can see that it has throughout its history had a marginal status, in terms of economic, political and cultural dependency and its identity has been forged in subordinate relationship to Norsemen, Kings of Ireland, Lowland Scots and the English. With rugged terrain a short growing season, high rainfall the region has long been unable to support itself without emigration and client relationships with the centre. Since long before the industrial revolution and the growth of British towns, the region sent excess population away for significant parts of their adult lives as soldiers, fishermen and fish "wives" and into the colonial service. Later large numbers migrated (some to return on retirement) to the towns of Lowland Scotland and England and abroad. In the 19th century the vicious clearances forced large numbers of families to Canada, the United States, Australia and New Zealand as well as into British towns. Today the pattern of permanent and temporary out-migration continues, particularly of highly educated younger people.

This diaspora population, however, retains strong emotional ties with the region, often over many generations, perpetuating and propagating the regional culture, which in turn absorbs elements from the diaspora experience. Many of the folk songs associated with the region are those which were written by migrants longing for home — perhaps the best known is *The Road to the Isles,* which charts the route from Glasgow to the Isle of Skye, but the songs go on being written up to the present by popular Folk/Rock groups like *Battlefield Band* and *Runrig,* sometimes wistful, but often defiant and resentful of the economic and political conditions which remove so many from a loved home region.

The region traditionally depends upon semi-subsistence agriculture, growing oats and root vegetables, keeping a few animals and fishing, but this has long been supplemented not only by out-migration but also semi-industrial processes, like weaving and kelping. In the eighteenth century the system of land tenure known as crofting emerged (a neo-feudal successor to the clan based systems of usufruct) which saw the emergence of large, often powerful and ruthless, landlords who learned the ways of the English aristocracy just as quickly as they could.

The role of the region during and after the 1745 Rebellion (opposing the Hannoverian succession to the British throne) more than any other single episode in history served to mark the Highlands and Islands of Scotland off from the Lowlands and England. They came to be seen as a rugged landscape harbouring adventurous free spirits. Their use of the Gallic language, their bagpipes, highland dress and military traditions were all used to emphasise the Highlander as a kind of "noble savage" and the territory as harsh but beautiful (the metaphors of people and place are remarkably similar to the way in which Rajasthan is depicted in many Indian films — glamorous but wild.) It is not necessary at this point to go into detail about the extent to which this Highland culture was a contemporary fabrication, but certainly the eighteenth century saw the more or less conscious construction of what we now regard as Highland tradition, a process in which local elites connived with romantic outsiders in the construction of an ethnic identity. (This has been particularly well documented by Hugh Trevor-Roper).

The Highlands and Islands, then, fulfil Ardener's criteria of remoteness — most importantly, they are highly imaged in their *difference.* People who come from the region have (and usually guard) a strong identity; people visit to experience the dramatic landscapes but also to partake, however, vicariously, in the local traditional culture; Highland artifacts are exported world-wide, not just for their instrinsic value but also for their ability to communicate something of the special lifestyle of the region — the malt whiskey, the tweeds summon up something of the "nature's gentleman" that the Highlander is characterised as being.

The Highlands and Islands have drawn visitors since long before the days of mass tourism. Boswell and Johnson are often regarded as the pair who promoted the region as an exciting and alien part of the British Isles with their twin accounts of their tour in 1773. Johnson helped to glorify the role of Flora McDonald in the escape of the prince and who generally depicted his hosts as living surprisingly sophisticated lives in what he perceived to be outlandish settings. For example, he writes of a hazardous journey across wild countryside, necessitating a local guide, to visit Dunvegan Castle, the seat of the MacLeods. without pointing out that the usual way to visit Dunvegan, like practically all of the settlements on the Isle of Skye, would have been by fairly reliable boat service. He deliberately distances the castle from (his view of) civilisation and then, anticipating primitveness, wonders at the refinement of the McCleod's daughters, educated in England and the excellence of the castle's hospitality. His description put me in mind of Jacquemont's 1830 letter to his father "Do you not see Simla on your map? A little to the north of the 31° of latitude and a little to the east of the 77° of longitude, some leagues from the Sutledge. Is it not curious to dine in silk stockings at such a place, and to drink a bottle of hock and another of champagne every evening?" or Emily Eden's 1839 thoughts about ". . . .eating salmon from Scotland and sardines from the mediterranean. . . .and all this in the face of those high hills, some of which have remained untrodden since the creation. . . .and we Europeans being surrounded by at least 3,000 mountaineers, wrapped in their hill-blankets. I sometimes wonder they do not cut all our heads off and say nothing more about it."

Remoteness, wildness and access to the luxuries of Europe; for some people there was little to distinguish Shimla from Dunvegan. This is no sophistry on my part, what these two places have in common (and in common with other romanticized remotenesses) is that their strong identity is department more upon external fantasising than upon local characteristics. They become locations for the projection of outsider desires, from the mundane aspirations of tourists to an artistic reaching for the sublime (with considerable cross fertilisation between the two).

No single person did more to lodge the invented image of the Highlands and the Highlander in Lowland consciousness than Sir Walter

Scott, who peddled his tales of primitive gallantry to finance an extravagant lifestyle. Art met life when Scott, judged to be the expert on Highland culture, was asked to stage a gathering of the Highland chieftains for King George IV, an event which he orchestrated and costumed as if it were a pantomime, but which became the basis for subsequent clan-based rituals. It was Scott's Highlands, elaborated by Stevenson and hundreds of imitators, which became the Scotland of popular consciousness and tourist promotion, a Scotland which is represented on calendar, biscuit-tin and souvenir picture book.

I shall skim over the way in which the Highlands have been appropriated as an upper class symbol, the country-house pursuits, the shooting, the fishing and the balls which continue to attract the socially mobile English. However, the Highlands are perceived by many as aristocratic, an observation which is not missed by the lifestyle magazines of several European countries. For at least two hundred years "new money", whether from industry, finance or rock music has often surfaced in the Highlands, where the purchase of an estate or an island or the construction of a fake castle seems to confer instant nobility on the merely wealthy.

Throughout the period when we can regard Britain as an important industrial nation the population of the Highlands and Islands of Scotland declined, despite optimistic assumptions in the immediate post-war years that the region might take of industrially with the development of hydro-electric power. It was regarded as a depressed region and in 1966 a Labour Government established the Highlands and Islands Development Board in an attempt to foster local employment and turn the tide of out-migration. The board worked through a mixture of propaganda, grants and loans to stimulate business activity and though it was willing to encourage a wide range of activities, its major success was in rejuvenating the tourist industry of the region. Small entrepreneurs were generously aided in upgrading accommodation or providing it from scratch; restaurants, craft workshops, recreational and quasi-educational facilities started up.

My own work has been done on the Isle of Skye in the Inner Hebrides, a place where the population dropped from 23,000 in 1841 to its all-time low of less than 7,500 in 1971 where it remained at the time of the next census in 1981, but by 1986, the stimulated economy had prompted a rise of nearly 17 per cent to 8,685. Disagregated figures for Skye for the 1991 census are not available yet, but Skye and Localsh has shown a substantial increase and is clear that growth is primarily on the island side. It is too simple to lay the whole success at the door of the Highlands and Islands Development Board — the transformation of the island was a part of the economic, social and cultural transformation of Britain as a whole; the transformation which we variously think of as post-industrial and postmodern. Merely providing the facilities for tourists was not sufficient to boost the long-standing tourist trade, especially when we find that many British holiday resorts were loosing trade to warmer and more exotic places abroad. We need to look at the intentions of the provides and consumers of Scottish holidays, and these are often grounded in fantasy and desire.

Overwhelmingly the new tourist provision was in the hands of incoming English people, rather than those born and reared on Skye. The typical enterprise would be run by a professional couple from an urban background, seeking a better, more autonomous, lifestyle. The steady growth in home ownership and rise in house prices through the 1970's and 1980's combined with relatively low cost housing in idyllic rural settings meant that those with town houses to sell could realise considerable capital sums which, combined with grants and loans could finance the establishment of a business. Many of those making this move were taking an early retirement with a pension and as a consequence required only a modest return on their business activities. It is fair to say that for practically all of the incoming business, lifestyle was a more important driving force than profit. Another category of new resident did not seek to earn a living locally but was made up of newly retired people living entirely on pensions and investments. All incomers stimulated the local economy by requiring the services of local trades people, particularly builders. Although native born people were not much involved in the direct growth of tourist activity, the tide of out-migration was partially stemmed by a local stimulation of the demand for a range of services.

The lifestyle aspirations of incomers fed directly off the romantic imaging of the region as a place where sturdy independent souls could flourish away from the moral and physical pollution of urban life, a place which had apparently not compromised its culture to materialist pressures. People used cliches about "getting back to nature", "dropping out of the rat-race" and "being themselves". What was very noticeable was that the majority of the incomers were people who had themselves holidayed in the region; in a sense the move was an attempt to capture the fantasy life we indulge in when we escape routine by going on holiday.

John Urry has been particularly influential in pointing out the ways in which tourism is changing in a transforming western society and coins the term "post-tourist" to cover the range of behaviours of those who do not wish to see themselves as conventional holiday-makers and whose activities are not simply oriented towards pleasure. Some of the people who make up the visiting population of Skye and similar places like to fantasise about the possibility of a more permanent escape, and meeting tourist provisioners who have themselves achieved this only makes the dream seem more possible. The story of the realised escape from the unsatisfying drudgery of urban experience into a more "authentic" lifestyle is willingly told to anyone who will listen and itself becomes a contemporary Hebridean myth. There is, then, less of a discontinuity between the "professionals" and the "punters" in the holiday experience than can be found under mass tourism, the providers are, to some extent, practising a hobby – like activity; the consumers are toying with the idea of making a move. What is provided for the tourists is not escapist luxury but escapist "reality", whether at the level of the country house or the cottage or camping and climbing.

A confrontation with the elements is an important part of a holiday on the island and the appalling weather is not something to discourage these visitors who seek to distance themselves from the plebian pleasures of "sun, sand and sex" in the Mediterranean. Skye tourists are critical of provisions which seem overly "touristic"; night-clubs do not thrive, but dances in village halls do as people try to catch a part of what it is to be an islander. For tourists and incoming residents alike, merging in and being accepted are important (but ultimately unachievable) aspirations. The indigenous population is an important cultural validator, even though it is far less self-consciously "ruralist" in its tastes than the tourist or incomer population. It has, however, learned from the same sources what it is that outsiders value in the Highlands and Islands and there has been a shift not only in practice but in the decoding of local culture.

Much of this may be founded in the realm of make-believe but it matters acutely in practical economic and political terms. The very tangible influx of tourists and settlers is vital to the maintenance of basic services and employment on the island, in a way that the apparently more "authentic" crofting could not. The changes have in fact helped to shore up the "traditional" crofting practices by supplementing meagre incomes with full or part-time waged work. If new local sources of income had not presented themselves, crofting units would have consolidated into economically viable farms of sufficient size to employ modern methods and crofters would have been lost to the mainland towns. As it is, the semi-subsistence practices continue, the landscape is relatively unchanged, the families are less disrupted, but it is an illusion to see this continuation of tradition as being founded on anything other than profound structural change and a new set of urban values.

The Highlands and Islands of Scotland have experienced a changing status of marginality throughout their history; their present role is, I argue, based upon their communicative value rather than upon exploitable material resources and, in embodying a wildness and remoteness, they serve as a counterpoint to urban lifestyles, whilst being securely integrated into the same service based-economy. Their hyperreality becomes at least as important as their reality. Their function, then, shifts to come in line with the pastoral idyll I outlined earlier for the lowland rural, despite such dramatic differences in the form.

With the radical change in British politics which we associated with the 1980's, the community development oriented ethos of the Highlands and Islands Development Board gave way to the commercialism of Highland Enterprise. An aggressive marketing campaign seeks to promote the business potential of the region and a new representation of an old fantasy is pedalled at the same time. The concept of remoteness is integrated into the time/space compression of flexible capital accumulation. The idea of the creative escape is retained but the intervening distance is denied by recourse to telecommunications. Whilst conceptually far from the horrors of a conurbation, the publicity material stresses that flight times from Inverness to world capitals is comparable to those from London. The marginality can dwindle into residential preference as a global scale is invoked.

Familiar themes of individualism, independence, élite rural lifestyles, authenticity are still employed in the new rhetoric, but ideas about localism, ethnicity, lack of change are played down as the Highlands and Islands are represented as a fitting environment for working members of the new service class; a place for escape *within,* not escape *from* the mainstream economy.

At the simplest level, promotional material employs the testimonials of business people who have relocated to the Highlands and Islands and who have experienced both commercial success and personal fulfilment. More sophisticated devices, however, are used to shift the view of the region from one reliant on traditional modes of production to one with high technology potential. Here the romantic notion of the sublime is pressed into service — nature representing human potential, striving, reaching out, mastery; a dawning of a new era in the clean and pure mountains of the North, an implicit belittling of England's South East through the use of creative cartography.

But it is not just the region and its agencies which draws upon Highland imagery for new purposes. Advertisers of products not manufactured in or traditionally associated with the region commonly select Highland settings in order to endow commodities with the complicated range of values generated there. Highland locations for car advertisements are becoming a cliché and one does not need to be particularly skilled to decode them — rugged mountains/rugged performance; subline landscape/sublime experience; escape from a mundane environment/escape from ordinary cars; remote from civilisation (especially garages)/doesn't matter, car won't break down; association with freedom, nobility, independence, tradition, reliability, taste, breeding, solidity ... one is tempted to go on all day. The multiple images of the place enhance the prestige of the product, but the imaging process feeds back into the realm of meanings adhering to the region, this time meanings which are generated out of internationally recognised status goods.

As I draw to a close I want to turn my attention to the gender assumptions implicit in this neo-romantic imaging. It is hard to escape the realisation that the glamour is unambiguously masculine, heroic, masterful, notwithstanding Flora MacDonald, for her actions were those of hero(ine) — a woman acting nobly out of role. Women appear in the Highland drama only in supporting parts, they are not involved in the creation of the great regional myth nor does the landscape serve to personify them or their virtues. In fact, Highland women have long been full participants in society. The system of inheritance of land and other property was traditionally bilateral and by children of both sexes; women as well as men conferred clan membership on their children; women worked the land and went away as migrants in their own right; women were involved in industry and fuel production; they were artistically creative and many of their folk-songs demonstrate that they were far from submissive in either their selection of sexual partners or their relationships with their husbands. But none of this feeds into the construction of the Highland remote or is appropriated by the media or tourism.

Today women who are attracted to the area as residents or tourists are often those who wish to enhance and glorify the position of the nuclear family, whether radically (as an alternative to the external aggressiveness of society) or conservatively. In either case mothering and domestic roles (often craft-based and backward-looking), rather than social ones are emphasised. The romantic imagery of the militant highlander is of little use to this fantasy and one of nurturing based on the cottage, hearth and an inwardness replaces it.

I am left musing whether the concept of remoteness is one which serves only to embody the desires of dominant, but routinised, groups within core regions; whether it is at all serviceable as a fantasy for those who find themselves marginalised?

REFERENCES

Ardener, E. (1987). "Remote Areas: Some Theoretical Considerations" in Jackson, A. (ed.) *Anthropology at Home* ASA Monographs 25. London. Tavistock.

Barr, P. & Desmond, R. (1978). *Simla: A Hill Station in British India,* Delhi: B.R. Publishing.

Champion, A. (1990). *Counter Urbanisation: The Changing Place and Nature of Population Decentralisation.* London: Edward Arnold.

Chapman R.W. (Ed) (1924). *Johnson's Journey to the Western Islands of Scotland and Boswell's Journal of a Tour to the Hebrides with Samuel Johnson,* Oxford: Oxford University Press.

Cohen, A. (1982). *Belonging: Identity and Social Organisation in British Rural Communities,* Manchester: Manchester University Press.

Eden, E. (1983). *Up the Country,* London: Virago.

Featherstone, M. (1991). *Consumer Culture and Postmodernism,* London: Sage.

Giddens, A. (1991). *Modernity and Self Identity: Self and Society in the Late Modern Age,* Oxford: Polity Press.

Harvey, D. (1989). *The Condition of Postmodernity,* Oxford: Blackwell.

Jeans, D.N. (1983). "Wilderness, Nature and Society: Contributions to the History of an Environmental Attitude", *Australian Geographical Studies* 21, pp 170-182.

Lash, S. (1990). *Sociology of Postmodernism,* London: Routledge.

Lash, S. & Urry, J. (1987). *The End of Organised Capital,* Oxford: Polity.

Moore, H. (1990). "Visions of the Good Life Anthropology and the Study of Utopia." *Cambridge Anthropology,* Vol. 14, pp 13-33.

Ricoeur, P. (1978). *The Rule of Metaphor: Multidisciplinary Studies in the Creation of Meaning in Language,* London: Routledge.

Ricoeur, P. (1986). *Lectures on Ideology and Utopia,* New York: Columbia University Press.

Shurmer-Smith, P. (1991). "Ideal Homes: Two Islands in the Construction of Family Identity" in Philo, C. (ed.) *New Words, New Worlds: Reconceptualising Social and Cultural Geography,* Lampeter: IBG, pp 102-113.

Shurmer-Smith, P. (1992). "Social Transformations in the Highlands and Islands of Scotland: A Case Study from the Isle of Skye" in *Geographie Sociale,* 12, pp 367-378.

Squire, S.J. (1988). "Wordsworth and Lake District Tourism: Romantic Reshaping of Landscape", *The Canadian Geographer,* 32, pp 237-47.

Thrift, N. (1989). "Images of Social Change" in Hamnett, McDowell & Sarre (eds.) *The Changing Social Structure*, London: Sage.

Trevor-Roper, H. (1983). "The Invention of Tradition: The Highland Tradition of Scotland", Hobsbawm, E. & Ranger, T. (eds.) (1983). *The Invention of Tradition*, Cambridge University Press.

Turner, V. (1968). *The Ritual Process*, London: Routledge & Kegan Paul.

Turner, V. & Turner, E. (1978). *Image and Pilgrimage in Christian Culture*, Oxford: Blackwell.

Urry, J. 1990). *The Tourist Gaze*, London: Sage.

Urry, J. (1992). "The Tourist Gaze and the 'Environment", *Theory, Culture and Society*, Vol. 9, No. 3, 1-26.

Wagner, R. (1986). *Symbols that Stand for Themselves*, Chicago: University of Chicago Press.

Williams, R. (1973). *The Country and the City*, London: Paladin.

Wright, P. (1985). *On Living in an Old Country : The National Past in Contemporary Britain.* London: Verso.

PART-VI

SUSTAINABLE DEVELOPMENT

18

ENVIRONMENT AND DEVELOPMENT THEME : Sustainable Development

ANDREW BLOWERS

From Chernobyl to Rio

With the catastrophe at Chernobyl in 1986 the world glimpsed the abyss — the destructive potential for global environmental pollution and degradation of modern industrial development. Six years later at Rio de Janeiro in 1992 the Earth Summit presented a programmes for action to avert global environmental disaster based on the underlying principles of sustainable development. These two events mark a period during which the environment was fully established on the agenda of international policy-making. It has been a period of major political change. There has been the ending of the Cold War, the break-up of the former Soviet Empire, the war in the Gulf and conflicts elsewhere and the emergence of an array of new nation-states. The uneasy stability of the superpowers has been replaced by an increasingly unpredictable world. As the vast arsenals of nuclear weapons were destroyed there opened up the prospect of diverting resources into more creative, peaceful purposes. One of these was the environment.

In the advanced western countries public interest in the environment mounted. In eastern Europe and the former USSR the urgency of the problems was underlined by the emerging evidence of grossly degraded and polluted areas. In the developing countries problems of deforestation, desertification and resource depletion were also attracting greater attention. And, the longer term but nonetheless apparently inevitable threats from global warning and ozone depletion underlined the global interest in environmental protection. At national, international and global level environmental policy achieved a higher priority and underwent vigorous development. At all levels the notion of *sustainable development,* the leitmotif of the Brundtland Report in 1987, had become the accepted goal of policy at Rio five years later (World Commission, 1987).

It soon became clear that optimism must necessarily be qualified. Interest in the environment, though sustained, was not always translated into action in the face of more immediate and pressing economic concerns. The dissolution of the soviet economic system, the problems of poverty in the developing world and the deepening recession in the west emphasised the competing priorities and inherent conflicts between environment and development. The eponymous process of balkanisation in areas such as former Yugoslavia (but also in other areas such as the Middle East) threatened to entangle countries in a series of regional conflicts. As the Gulf War had shown such conflicts could do serious harm to sensitive ecosystems (Barnaby, 1991). Over all was the threat of nuclear proliferation more alarming as the soviet nuclear complex was dispersed and which, if not restrained, would pose a far more imminent threat to world survival than the more publicised problems of global warming and Progress, was nonetheless, made. There was, for example, the international agreement to ban mining in Antarctica; the series of agreements (Vienna Convention, 1985, Montreal Protocol, 1987 and London Agreement, 1990) which led to the banning of CFCs to protect the ozone layer and the various agreements designed to restrict the trade in hazardous wastes (Basel Convention, 1989, Bamako Convention, 1991 and related EC Directives).

This process of global negotiation and agreement on environmental problems culminated at the Rio Summit which saw the adoption of 27 principles constituting a Declaration on Environment and Development, the first of which, was 'Human beings are at the centre of concerns for sustainable development'. Over 150 nations signed a Framework Convention on Climate Change to tackle the problem of global warming and also a Convention on Biological Diversity. By consensus the summit endorsed Agenda 21 an 800 page action programme covering every conceivable issue designed to set the programme of follow-up (United Nations, 1992). Although the Summit had been preceded by conflicts especially between North and South over issues of responsibility and resources Rio produced a number of positive features. It was a process engaging more governments than ever before and the participation of 6,500 non-government organisations and 15,000 participants at their Global Forum. The involvement of ngos had begun at the Bergen Conference on Sustainable Development in 1990. Despite the failure to reach agreements on certain issues, notably forests, and the USA's reluctance to enter into binding targets or to sign the Biodiversity Convention, Rio was a global endeavour at cooperation in the interests of mutual security. 'It defined the new international values of equity and environment, linked them inseparably, and dramatised how powerfully they affect North-South relations' (Speth, 1992, p. 145). Rio should also be seen as a stage in a continuous process of developing policy and securing implementation.

Sustainable development has now passed a threshold of public and political concern that makes it fully and permanently established as an issue of high priority on the national and international policy-making agenda. Although the environment is on the agenda, environmental policy-making is fraught with uncertainty and conflict, particularly between North and South.

Environment and Development — Contrasting Perspectives

At Rio the contrasting attitudes to environmental problems between the rich and the poor countries (usually categorises as North and South though this leaves the designation of the former communist bloc somewhat ambiguous) were at the heart of the political conflict over global environmental policy. In the North the emphasis is on environmental problems and there is a tendency to see economic growth and environmental protection as mutually compatible, not contradictory aims of policy (Pearce et al., 1989; Jacobs, 1991). Indeed, environmental protection is now seen as a spur to economic growth. The largest and most technically advanced environment markets, and also environment industries, have developed in those countries with the most comprehensive and effective environmental regulations' (OECD, 1992). In the rich countries environmental quality has become an integral aspect of the quality of life.

In marked contrast the problems in the developing countries stem from underdevelopment and poverty. This was an underlying theme of the Brundtland Report, 'Poverty reduces people's capacity to use resources in a sustainable manner; it intensifies pressure on the environment' (World Commission, 1987, p. 49). The 'poor are forced to forgo the needs of the future to meet the needs of today' (Holmberg et al., 1991, p. 32). Hence the issues that concern the South, poverty, food security, desertification stand in stark contract to the environmental preoccupations of the North. In the poor countries environmental inequality is a direct result of uneven development.

Environmental inequalities are, of course, partly determined by natural factors, it is perfectly obvious that deserts, some dense forests, tundra or mountainous regions are often inhospitable. Beyond the largely unoccupied wilderness areas uneven development can, in part at least, be explained by differences in climate, resource endowments or accessibility resulting from natural and spatial factors. But, environmental determinism, though it cannot be altogether discounted, is often a relatively unimportant explanatory factor. Uneven development is not simply the product of natural factors; it is much more complex involving historical, cultural and economic explanations that are the source of considerable academic debate and controversy (see, for example, Smith, 1991; Open University, 1992). It is, in short, a largely socially determined process.

Uneven development is a major source of conflict and, consequently, a major impediment to the achievement and implementation of environmental policy. It is at the heart of the conflict between North and South which was emerged, perhaps, as the critical political fault line in the contemporary world. Put simply, the North tried to set an agenda to deal with environmental issues of ozone, global warming, deforestation and biodiversity. The North wants the South to tackle population control and to halt the depletion of global assets such as tropical rainforests. By contrast, the South insisted on the linkage between environment and development; identified the North as most implicated in the squandering of global assets; and demanded that resources and technology be transferred in various ways to enable the South to cope with the environmental problems arising from underdevelopment. The South's position was put cogently and uncomprisingly by Dr. Mahatir, Prime Minister of Malaysia.

> 'If the rich North expects the poor to foot the bill for a cleaner environment Rio [will] become an exercise in futility. . . . There will be no development if the poor countries are not allowed to extract their natural wealth. The only way for them to develop and yet avoid damage to the environment is for them to receive substantial material help' (*Independent,* June 5, 1992).

Uneven development also affects the capacity of individual countries to deliver environmental policies. The poorer countries lack the scientific information base, the monitoring capability, and the administrative support essential to implementing agreements. Moreover, abiding by externally induced environmental targets or deadlines is scarcely the highest priority for countries crippled by debt and poverty and, in some cases, river by internal conflicts and lack of social cohesion. Even in a rich region such as the EC there are frequently complaints about the unwillingness or inability of members to adhere to environmental policies. In the wider global context it is difficult enough (as Rio has shown) to gain agreement on policies let alone procedures for detailed implementation. Equity among the participants is the key to success (RIIA, 1991). Successful implementation will require pledge and review processes that are clear as to what is required of participants, significant in terms of the commitment to goals and verifiable through effective monitoring (Greene, 1991). The success or failure of environmental policy will depend, in part, on the quality and interpretation of the evidence, the subject of the next section.

Science and Policy

The Evidence of Environmental Degradation

Within the advanced countries environmental data provide a record of environmental degradation or improvement. Such data has provided a basis for monitoring environmental change within countries and has stimulated conservationist policies. More recently it is the evidence of deterioration at the global level that has done most to force the environment up the international policy-making agenda.

In the past there has been considerable disagreement among scientific experts over trends and their implications. The Club of Rome's Malthusian predictions of global catastrophe were savaged by academics, business people and public officials and quickly sank from sight (Buttel et al. 1990). By contrast the ozone hole and global warming have become universally accepted as palpable threats to the global ecosystem. In the case of ozone the evidence was unmistakable. The Antarctic ozone 'hole' can reach up to four times the size of the United States with depletion rates commonly at 40 to 50 per cent and occasional readings as high as 95 per cent. By 1992 there was evidence of 15-20 per cent depletion in ozone levels in the northern hemisphere. The cause, CFCs and other depleting chemicals such as halons, and the consequences, skin cancers and cataracts, are widely known and have been a spur to action.

In the case of global warming, too, there has been a remarkable scientific consensus. Overall estimates of global warming have been refined by the International Panel on Climate Change to 0.3°C per decade giving a 1°C rise by 2030, a rate believed to be too high for adaptation by plant and animal communities. The implications have been forecast in terms of, for example, potential flooding in England and Wales, (Dept. of Environment, 1992a and b), agricultural change in Europe (Carter et al, 1991), hunger in Africa (Downing, 1991) or water resources in the Middle East (Lonergan and Kavanagh, 1991). The acceptance of the inevitability of global change is, perhaps, striking; 'for a notion that challenges the basis of modern industrialisation, global change has gained extraordinary respectability' (Buttel et al., p. 60). It may be explained by the strength of the scientific consensus and the lack of any real dispute over the general climatic trends and its anthropogenic causes. The prominence of the issue stems from the existence of a scientific 'epistemic community', that is, 'a network of professionals with recognized expertise and competence in a particular domain and an authoritative claim to policy-relevant knowledge within that domain or issue-area' (Haas, 1992, p. 3).

While there can be no doubt that scientific evidence has been instrumental in identifying issues for the environmental agenda, the evidence is often incomplete, provisional or uncertain. As a result science has provided a basis for conflict between interests that impedes progress in policy-making. The evidence is problematic in several ways.

1. *The problem of establishing cause and effect:* For example, it is known that radioactivity causes certain cancers. There is a strong presumption but no conclusive proof that nuclear facilities are responsible for leukaemia clusters (eg. Craft and Openshaw, 1987). The Black Report reached a qualified conclusion after an extensive investigation, noting that although there was an observed statistical relationship the possibility of a causal link was 'not one that can be categorically dismissed, nor, on the other had is it easy to prove' (Black, 1984). Similarly the precise causes and effects of acid rain are difficult to identify. The scientific problem of cause and effect means it is difficult

to establish responsibility for the externalities produced by polluting activities.

2. *The problem of forecasting impacts*: This is notably the case with global warming. While there is broad agreement on the general range of the uplift in average global temperature, there is considerable uncertainty about the incidence, distribution, timing or effects of the process (Idso, 1991; MacCracken, 1991; Schneider, 1991). Thus, although it is a global process the costs and benefits will be unevenly distributed. Some areas may gain a better climate or have the resources to mitigate impacts. For instance, in the United States the costs of extra sea defences might be easily outweighed by improved crop yields from a better climate whereas, in parts of Africa, global warming might exacerbate the already severe problems of drought and food supply. Thus countries who perceived benefits may be unenthusiastic about providing support for countries who must bear the brunt of the harmful effects. This unevenness of the potential impacts could undermine a global approach to the problem such as has been initiated with the Convention signed at Rio. Indeed some commentators, taking a narrow regional view of impacts, have even interpreted the rise in temperatures in such terms as 'the single best thing that could ever happen to the biosphere' (Idso, 1991, p. 181).

3. *Uncertainty over the consequences of present actions and the risks imposed on future generations:* The destruction of habitats is literally depriving the future of its natural assets. Only about one in every 100 plant species has been subject to scientific investigation and the proportion for animals is even less. The potential resources locked up in the earth's ecosystems is simply unknown and can only be realised over a long time span. 'Biological resources constitute a capital asset with great potential for yielding sustainable benefits, with new ways constantly being found in which they can contribute to sustainable development; for example, through new foods, pharmaceuticals and many other products' (UN, 1992, p. 67). If present trends continue it is thought that up to 25 per cent of the world's species could be gone by the middle of the next century (IUCN et al., 1991, p. 28).

The precautionary approach has become widely adopted in principles to protect the future against the harmful actions of the present. At Rio it was declared, 'Where there are threats of serious or irreversible damage, lack of full scientific certainty shall not be used as a reason for postponing cost-effective measures to prevent environmental degradation' (Rio Declaration on Environment and Development, Principle 5). The difficulty is that it is sometimes better not to act for fear of committing irreversible damage at some time in the far distant future. The uncertainty of effects may lead to paralysis of policy or, more dangerously, a tendency to ignore of discount the future risks of present action.

4. *Inadequacy of evidence and the problem of interpretation:* As concern for the environment has grown so more effort has been put into collating evidence showing trends in pollution, habitat degradation or resource depletion and is published in annual reports or monitoring statements (OECD, 1991, Dept. of Envt., 1992a, Brown et al. 1991). Some records have long time spans and are reliable. But, in general, collection of environmental data has been patchy and it is difficult to compare over time of between places. In some crucial areas evidence is almost complete absent. For instance, in Africa south of the Sahara there is only one upper atmosphere ozone measurement station and there are no systematic measurements of greenhouse gases in the African continent. Consequently, in very crucial areas the quantity and quality of data are inadequate.

There is the additional problem that interpretation of evidence is wide open to manipulation by vested interests. It is generally acknowledged that the rich countries of the North are responsible for the major burden of polluting substances that threaten long-term survival. In terms of CO^2 emissions the United States produces 5 tonnes per head per year against in average of 0.2 tonnes in the developing countries. The OECD countries with about a sixth of the world's population consume 11 times more fossil-fuel energy per head than the developing countries; are responsible for half the CO^2 output; produce three-quarters of the industrial wastes' four-fifths of hazardous wastes and have three-quarters of the world's cars which produce a cocktail of noxious emissions and contribute an increasing share of greenhouse gases. Furthermore practically all the anthropogenic ozone depleting substances are produced by the advanced industrialised countries. Not surprisingly the developing countries argue that the rich countries must reduce their disproportionate claims upon the planet's limited resources and the regenerative capacity of its ecosystems.

In their defence the rich countries argue that their share in polluting the planet is diminishing (by 2025 only one-third of CO^2 is forecast to come from OECD countries for instance). The developing countries with their burgeoning populations and demand on resources and energy pose a looming threat which should be tackled now. A dialogue of the deaf has opened up with each side interpreting the evidence in the most favourable light for their own purposes. The United States, for example, has tried to shelter behind the composite index of greenhouse gases prepared by the World Resources Institute (McCully, 1991). By combining the gases in a single index three developing countries (Brazil, India and China) are exposed as major contributors through deforestation, methane production etc. while the USA is shown to have a smaller proportion of total emissions (18%) compared to its share of CO^2 output (over a fifth) with a stable output and therefore declining share by the year 2000. But this composite index nicely masks the fact that stability is achieved by a decline in CFCs while CO^2 output continues to rise. Furthermore the index is favourable to the rich countries in other ways — it underestimates the lingering effect of CFCs, it is based on uncertain and selective data for methane and deforestation, it neglects the feasibility of action which is much higher for gases produced in the richer countries. Finally, by implying a shared responsibility, the index provides the rich countries with an excuse to evade their prime responsibility for the problem and its solutions.

New evidence and interpretation can further complicate the picture. it is now argued that CFCs are less important than was thought since their contribution to global warming as a greenhouse gas is partly offset by their depletion of the ozone layer which promotes cooling. This certainly qualifies if it does not altogether undermine the United States' argument that its contribution to reducing global warming from phasing out CFCs compensates for any increase in CO^2 outputs. This debate over the evidence demonstrates the ample scope for procrastination and conflict between interests which inhibits effective cooperation.

5. *Science and Politics:* In attempting to understand the behaviour of ecosystems science is confronting problems of enormous subtlety and complexity. At a fundamental level there is controversy over the role and potential of natural processes. This debate has a metaphysical as well as scientific dimension. There is the view, most evidently publicised through the Gaia hypothesis, of the earth as a living complex entity with a feedback system which maintains an optimal physical and chemical environment by active control – a process called

'homeostasis' (Lovelock, 1979, 1988). The Gaia hypothesis was originally propounded 'as an alternative to that pessimistic view which sees nature as a primitive force to be subdued and conquered' (1979, p. 12). But, the recuperative powers of the earth in the long-term certainly do not rule out catastrophe for human society in the short-term. As Lovelock puts, it, 'Anything that makes the world uncomfortable to live in tends to induce the evolution of those species that can achieve a new and more comfortable environment. It follows that, if the world is made unfit by what we do, there is the probability of a change in regime to one that will be better for life but not necessarily better for us' (1988, p. 178). Critics of Gaia dispute that the Earth is a self-regulating set of complex systems but is, instead, vulnerable to unanticipated, chaotic and catastrophic changes. But all sides seem to concur that human processes are perfectly capable of rendering the environment unsustainable for the human species.

Science cannot provide definitive answers. 'Science is not knowledge, and never will be, but it is the advancement of knowledge' (Winan, 1991, p. 245). Science depends on interpretation of evidence and judgement as to its significance. In the present state of the available evidence and the techniques of interpretation much of the evidence on environmental processes may be ambiguous and uncertain. Therefore, scientific judgements will be provisional and revocable (Yearley, 1991 a, b). Evidence can be manipulated to serve particular interests. It is, therefore, important to understand the nature, terms and quality of evidence. There is a need to develop interdisciplinary approaches across the natural sciences and between the natural and social sciences to ensure greater understanding of the interaction of natural processes and the implications for social processes. This process has begun with an emphasis on Science for Sustainable Development in Agenda 21 at Rio and, for example, in the major research initiative on Global environmental Change initiated by the UK's Economic and Social Research Council. Greater research and understanding will contribute to greater consensus on policy. But, the political constraints and sustainable development will also have to be confronted and overcome.

Sustainable Development – the Necessary Conditions

The Political Implications of Sustainable Development

Sustainable development has been criticised as a catch-all offering different meanings to different interests. It has been adopted enthusiastically by environmentalists and is now a commonplace in official reports and a slogan for politicians. Business has enthusiastically embraced it to help legitimate its activities (WICEM II, 1991). At an intellectual level Redclift has warned that sustainability obscures 'the contradictions that 'development' implies for the environment'. Instead of bringing intellectual rigour to the discussion of environment and development, we frequently encounter moral convictions as substitutes for thought' (Redclift, 1987, p. 2).

It would be a mistake to dismiss sustainable development as mere platitude or just the fashion of the day soon to disappear like the concern about "limits to growth" of an earlier era. For one thing many of the issues, the depletion of resources, the growth of population, the increase of pollution, the degradation of soil, habitats and species are recurrent themes. They threaten the planet's overall carrying capacity and the ability of its ecosystems to regenerate themselves. By linking development and environment the needs and aspirations of the developing world have been incorporated. It has become apparent that environmental issues cannot be dealt with in isolation – 'they are interdependent parts of a greater whole, and that whole is the overarching and problematic question of the relationship between humans and nature; and between humans and humans' (Dovers and Handmer, 1992). Strenuous efforts are being made to define, interpret and introduce sustainable development at local, national and global levels. Sustainable development is already passing from being just a vague concept (Redclift, 1991, p. 36, Holmberg et al., 1991, p. 6) to becoming a set of objectives and policies requiring implementation.

On the other hand it is by no means clear that the implications of sustainable development are fully recognised. The off-quoted Brundtland definition suggests more than marginal adaptation is needed for survival,

> 'Sustainable development is development that meets the needs of the present without compromising the ability of future generations to meet their own needs' (World Commission, 1987, p. 8)

This involves a wholesale shift from resource exploitation to conservation, a redistribution of wealth from rich to poor in order to meet needs and a withdrawal from those activities which could harm future generations (Blowers, 1992a). This is a very tough set of propositions which have been but dimply grasped by policy-makers engaged on programmes for sustainable development.

It is now widely assumed that the pace of environmental degradation is such that, if it is not arrested, catastrophe will – gradually or suddenly – overwhelm the earth's ecosystems. There has been an unprecedented attempt to grapple with global environmental problems which reached its apotheosis at Rio de Janeiro. Rio demonstrated just how far there was to go in understanding the problems, devising appropriate solutions and in overcoming the conflicts between states and interests that threaten to subvert the implementation process. Sustainable development poses a challenge to the most entrenched bastions of contemporary political and economic organisation. It challenges the nation-state and in particular the notions of sovereignty, the free market and the prevailing inequitable distribution of resources.

The Role of the Nation-State

National Interests in Conflict

The challenge of the nation-state is posed by the transboundary nature of environmental processes. Until relatively recently the negative externalities of industrialisation were localised. The distribution was inequitable falling upon poorer groups within a city or region. As the scale of technology has increased the inequitable distribution occurs between countries. Externalities are exported to other countries in the form of pollution of the Rhine or North Sea or acid rain arising from tall stacks designed to dilute and disperse localised pollution.

Global pollution from greenhouse gases or CFCs is different since it is virtually indiscriminating in its impact. All are threatened and none can ultimately escape.

From a realist perspective it would appear that the predictions of the Tragedy of the Commons are coming true. So long as an individual country continues to gain from a polluting activity it will continue production regardless of the impact on the carrying capacity of the environment. Hardin argues that, under assumptions of a free market, this incentive for individual countries to pollute the global commons continues until well beyond the point when global deterioration sets in and may become irreversible (Hardin, 1968).

Global warming illustrates the point. Its onset is imperceptible but inevitable. It poses a Catch-22 for policy-makers as outlined by Prins, 'when you don't see it, you could still act to prevent it but it is denied status by 'realist' politics so you can't; when you do see it and it is granted status and you could act, you probably can't because natural processes have passed a point of no return' (1990, p. 729). Latterly, as recognition has dawned of the global span of pollution so self-interest has fused with a common interest in environmental protection and has, at last, created the political environment for negotiation and agreement. To avert catastrophe it is necessary to adopt the precautionary principle, that is to act 'where there are good grounds for judging either that action taken promptly at comparatively low cost may avoid more costly damage later, or that irreversible effects may follow if action is delayed' (HMSO, 1990, p. 11). It is the mutual interest in survival that has prompted international agreements on ozone and global warming. While there is clearly conflict between national interests, there is also a genuine and growing transnational interest in environmental conservation and protection.

The nation-state is a universal form of organisation which has the administrative complexity to develop policy, the legitimate government to make binding decisions, the economic resources to carry them out and the coercive power to enforce them (Giddens, 1985). Within its own territory the state can manage the physical environment as it chooses. At the same time the state is capable of creating transboundary pollution that inflicts negative externalities on other states. In a real sense states can invade the sovereign territory of other who may be incapable either of defence or retaliation. Where it is in the mutual interests of states to do so solutions must be found by agreement. In essence it is state interests that are paramount. This is certainly the way political leaders appear to think and speak. For example, President Bush, for once, made his position unequivocally clear on his arrival in Rio, declaring, "I am determined to protect the environment, and I am also determined to protect the American taxpayer. The days of the open cheque book are over" (*Independent*, June 12, 1992).

From a purely realist perspective it follows that the nation state is both the cause and the solution of the world's environmental problems. Agreements need to be forged among the nation states which have the capability to regulate, monitor, verify and enforce. Again, there are grounds for criticising a realist perspective based entirely on the promotion of self-interest. In the first place, it is not always clear where a nation state's real interests lie. Very often the state's interests are difficult to foresee clearly and to calculate. Secondly, states are not simply unitary organisations with a single-minded consensus on interests. They are themselves composed of a congeries of different, frequently conflicting interests. These interests are expressed in terms of class, politics, regions, ethnic groups, cultural affinities and so on. At different times the state's interests will reflect different aspects of its many interests providing different emphases. For example, in environmental policy there is bound to be a shift in the expression of the United State's interests with the change in the Presidency in 1993.

A third reason for qualifying the role of the nation-state is that the capability of states to develop and deliver policies varies considerably. Many states simply lack the resources, the bureaucracy or even the motivation to ensure that policies are implemented. Supranational governmental organisations (e.g. UNCEP, the EC's Environmental Commission) as well as non-governmental organisations have raised awareness and influenced policy-making that extends beyond the boundaries of the nation states. In practice, the developments in environmental policy-making cannot be explained simply as an expression of balancing competing interests, though that is clearly a necessary condition for success. Rather, environmental policy is an outcome of a dynamic and developing process of interaction between a wide diversity of interests not simply confined to the environment. Complicated trade-offs between environmental, security, economic and other policies may be necessary. For instance, it is becoming clear that the United States cannot stand aside from the debate about sustainable development since its fundamental interests are involved. Speth makes the point explicit.

> 'If population growth continues to outpace the creation of new jobs, if pressures on resources mount and growth proves unsustainable, if social and ethnic tensions increase, the effects could be felt in many spheres – from the collapse of governments to the adoption of authoritarian measures, to waves of ecological refugees, to civil unrest and regional conflict' (Speth, 1992, p. 153).

Looked at in this broad sense conflicts over environment are an aspect of more general conflicts, an integral element in an interlocking system of policy-making to ensure economic, environmental and social survival. Sustainable development is therefore not simply an environmental objective but a fundamental principle relevant to all areas of policy at local, national and global levels. Its achievement, in part, on the evaluation of transnational political institutions.

The Challenge of Sovereignty

An interesting development in recent years has been the development of a new framework for environmental policy-making that extends well beyond the frontiers and capability of individual nation states. Transnational political processes have developed that challenge the nation-state. This process may be described as *globalisation.*

Globalisation is characterised by the development of organisational forms which transcend the nation state. These are of three kinds. There are, firstly, the *intergovernmental organisations* (IGOs) which seek to identify common interests between states often on a global scale. For example, the United Nations Environment Programme seeks to develop common environmental strategies and played the key role in promoting the UN Conference on Environment and Development at Rio and in borkering international conventions and agreements. The Global Environmental Facility (GEF) was established in 1991 as a fund managed by the World Bank to support the efforts of developing countries to meet the obligations of the various conventions. Many IGOs affect the environment although the environment is not specifically within their remit. Examples of these are the Food the Agriculture Organisation, the General Agreement on Tariffs and Trade or the International Atomic Energy Agency. The World Bank and multilateral development banks have been much criticised for the adverse environmental impacts of development projects they have funded (Bramble and Porter, 1992). It is clear that IGOs possess considerable power and provide a challenge to the sovereignty of the nation-state.

A second kind of transnational organisation is the *multinational corporation* (MNC) whose operations often have a global reach. They have a major stake in the exploitation of the earth's major economic physical resources of energy (notably oil), minerals, timber and some commercial agricultural products. They can move investment capital around the globe and have a major influence on governments which are, to some extent, dependent upon them (Lindblom, 1977). While they are bound by environmental regulations, they will also indicate clearly to governments what they consider to be the extent of the regulation they will find tolerable. Therefore, MNCs are, in certain respects, beyond the control of individual governments.

Non-governmental organisation (NGOs) constitute a third form of transnational organisation. NGOs encompass an enormous diversity ranging from small, localised NGOs through national bodies up to international NGOs. They cover a wide variety of issues. As well as NGOs directly concerned with the environment there are all kinds of NGOs engaged in such fields as development, human rights, women's concerns, youth etc. which frequently have an indirect bearing on the environment. The Global Forum in Rio was the most visible expression of the multitude of NGOs concerned with the environment. NGOs vary in their orientation, organisation and culture and in their strategies and techniques for achieving influence. In relation to the state NGOs may seek to complement state provision, to reform the state by representing specific interests or they may oppose the state's policies (Clark, 1991). In respect of environmental issues NGOs exhibit all three strategies. They are increasingly significant in drawing attention to problems, mobilising opinion and lobbying for specific policies. Some of the biggest NGOs such as *Friends of the Earth or Greenpeace* have built up global networks, developed counter expertise and displayed skilful use of the media. The attempts to establish development as the key theme on the environmental agenda has been substantially the work of NGOs, especially those speaking for Third World interests.

In different ways IGOs, MNCs and NGOs are components of the process of 'globalisation'. Through complex and dynamic interactions environmental policy-making is mediated at supranational level and, consequently, the sovereignty of individual nation states is compromised. The development of supranational authority in Europe has led to the dramatic debate about *subsidiarity*. This was broadly defined in the Treaty of Maastricht as a process 'in which decisions are taken as closely as possible to the citizen'.

The debate over sovereignty and *subsidiarity* has focused on the power of the nation state. What has been neglected is the sub-national level.

It is at the sub-national level that environmental movements are particularly strong and effective. Local environmental action groups developing as a spontaneous response to external threat have frequently been successful though frequently if unfairly criticised for their self-interested NIMBY motives. Conservation groups, often linking up with established NGOs, have done much to arrest the tide of destruction of landscapes, habitats and species; they have campaigned against polluting and hazardous activities; and they have promoted the case for more sustainable forms of development. A relatively new feature has been the development of coalitions of action groups able to invoke traditional patterns of community and local identification and able to cut across modern class-based social patterns (Blowers and Leroy, 1993). Such coalitions can potentially operate across state frontiers. A good example of this newly emerging form of environmental movement is provided by the protests against nuclear waste repositories (Blowers, et al., 1991).

In the case of environmental policy national sovereignty is challenged both from above and below. The interaction and integration of policy-making from local through to national and up to global level is a feature of environmental issues. Another feature is the extent to which policy-making and implementation has become dependent on the market, the issue to which I turn next.

The Market, the Environment and the Role of Intervention

The Triumph of the Market

At the end of the 1980s it appeared that market capitalism had achieved a universal triumph. In the developed countries of the West the market was hailed as the source of efficiency and economy and, consequently, the prescription for economic growth. In many countries, whatever the orientation of the party in power, the market was encouraged through deregulation, privatisation and the removal of subsidies and barriers to trade. In the UK especially the process has been deeply entrenched through fourteen years of Conservative Government. Large areas of the public sector have been either privatised or invested with regimes of cost accounting, competition and contracting out.

Internationally, the market and free trade have been dominant economic forces over the past decade. As the state centralism imposed by communist regimes disintegrated the market offered a natural – if immediately painful – route to prosperity. The EC became a single internal market in 1993 though some barriers remained. The Uruguay Round of the General Agreement on Tariffs and Trade (GATT), despite conflicts over certain goods, basically espouses the doctrine of international free trade. This is regarded as an unquestioned benefit to all trading partners paving the way through increased growth and resources that will support the environmental improvements that ensure sustainable development. Agenda 21 affirms that 'Trade liberalisation should be pursued across economic sectors so as to contribute to sustainable development' (UN, 1992, p. 24). There appears to be a universal political rhetoric that the development of market forces is a means – indeed, the means – to ensure the ultimate protection of the environment.

As might be expected this view is challenged by Marxist theorists who hold that capitalist economic development is the fountain head of uneven development with its pattern of dominance and development. Capitalism wrecks the environment through flows of trade, investment and aid that encourage the exploitation and waste of resources, pollution and destruction of the ecosystems. The answer for marxists is 'a social, economic and cultural revolution that abolishes the constraints of capitalism and, in so doing, establishes a new relationship between the individual and society and between people and nature. '(Gorz, 1980, p. 4). The rhetoric of revolution is captivating though the pathway to transformation is unclear.

What is interesting is that a critique which accepts that market capitalism is responsible for environmental degradation is now widely shared and beginning to influence political thinking. Economists of various leanings have emphasised the existence of ultimate limits to growth set by the finite stock of non-renewable resources and the capacity of the atmosphere, earth and oceans to absorb the burdens of production and pollution now being imposed upon them. (Pearce et al., 1989; Redclift, 1987; Daly and Cobb, 1989; Jacobs, 1991). Environmental assets should not be regarded as free goods but should be properly valued. GNP is an inadequate measure of development, 'since it treats sustainable and unsustainable production alike and compounds the error by including the costs of unsustainable economic activity on the credit side, while largely ignoring processes of recycling and energy conversion which do not lead to the production of goods or marketable services' (Redclift, 1987, p.16). Some argue that solutions should be sought through the market, that once a proper valuation is secured it will, in principle, be possible to devise means of intervention in the market that will ensure patterns of sustainable development (Pearce et al., 1989). Opponents contend that it would be difficult to value future unknown environmental resources (e.g. forest habitats) or those whose scarcity value increases over time or to recognise the possible changes in the evaluation of resources by different societies over time.

As this thinking develops so governments have begun to examine a wide range of market based economic measures (taxes, incentives, pollution permits, recycling credits and so on) designed to protect resources, prevent pollution and encourage sustainable forms of technology. Business has turned its attention to life cycle analysis of products, use of sustainable resources and new technologies designed to reduce environmental impacts. In both government and industry regulatory instruments are adopted as a necessary complement to market mechanisms. The UK's Conservative government in Britain is comfortable with the idea that regulation is necessary just as, conversely, the Labour Party has accepted the importance of the market in the prosecution of environmental policy (The Labour Party, 1990).

The Case for Intervention

Paradoxically, this convergence in political thinking on the approach to environmental policy may prove detrimental to the cause of environmental protection. In the first place, lack of political conflict and a presumed consensus reduces the political visibility of the environment. The environment is securely on the agenda but it becomes less of a priority than those issues over which there is conflict. This point was certainly evident in the British General Election of 1992 when the environment received little attention compared to the big issues of the economy, the health service and even the constitution (Carter, 1992). In developing countries concern for the environment tends to be subsumed by the problems of poverty and survival. Important though it undoubtedly was for the longer term, the Rio Earth Summit was scarcely recollected in the popular imagination (as reflected by journalists and politicians) as an event of great significance when compared to the world recession, conflicts in Bosnia, the changing Presidency in the United States or the future of the Maastricht Treaty. The urgency about environmental problems undoubtedly felt by some politicians, NGOs and environmentalists has not yet conveyed itself to the wider public audience. The close links between environment and development have scarcely been registered.

The political consensus over environmental management has another unfortunate consequence; it stifles debates over policy options. The pervasive belief in a market solution tempered by necessary regulation denies debate about the need for far more interventionist strategies. The idea and practice of planning as a process of economic and environmental management has suffered a virtual eclipse in recent years. Right Wing ideologies attacked the controls, subsidies and the bureaucratic structures associated with state planning as evidence of waste, inefficiency and inflexibility. The supremacy of the market seemed to be vindicated by the collapse of the Soviet state planning system and the subsequent revelations of appalling environmental catastrophes it spawned. The inadequacies of the market as the primary vehicle for delivering a sustainable environment were ignored.

The major failing of the market, in relation to the environment, is that it is concerned with short-term economic criteria placing an emphasis on growth achieved through comparative advantage. As specialisation develops those areas unable to complete become impoverished, and, elsewhere, the environment becomes degraded through the pollution, waste or resource depletion associated with overexploitation. The market fails to take account of externalities which impose unwanted or unforeseen costs on third parties (individual, communities or countries). Moreover, the market promotes the private interest over the public and ignores or discounts the interests of future generations. Finally, the market values resources in respect to their use in production and does not account for the costs of depletion of non-renewable resources. For these various reasons the market intrinsically cannot deal with the long term conservation of the environment. Intervention becomes necessary to deal with market failure.

Concern for the environment may revive political interest in the merits of planning. It is important to recognise that planning for sustainability 'stands in contrast to the operation of market forces, but it does not preclude the existence of markets' (Jacobs, 1991, p.125). The essential characteristic of planning is that goals or outcomes are specified by the planning authority, be it local, state or international. In order for the desired goal to be achieved a planning process will need to identify targets, specify methods for achieving them and possess the capability for monitoring and evaluating outcomes and, where necessary the sanctions necessary to secure compliance. This process, even if only in a residual form, may be observed in the ozone depleting chemicals supported by financial funds to assist the compliance of poorer countries. In the case of the climate convention, only the first stage, the setting down of targets, has been reached.

An environmental planning system in which the market is subordinate to long-term environmental criteria appears, in the early 1990s, to be a distant possibility. But as environmental factors impinge more and more on economic policy-making so the need for a planned approach to resource conservation and pollution control will become evident. A shift towards greater intervention through what might be termed 'environmental planning' to defend the environment can be predicted over the coming decade. Even in the most ideologically committed market economies environmental constraints will begin to impinge more on policy-making. For example, in the UK the creation of the Environment Agency represents a further step in the direction of integrating environmental protection bodies (DoE, 1991). While remaining chary about the role of regulation, the government is conducting intensive research into the use of economic instruments to ensure that 'environmental costs are taken into account in decision-making in the same way as other costs' (HMSO, 1992, p.34). The rudiments of a more interventionist approach to environmental policy-making, albeit still clothed in market philosophy, are beginning to emerge.

Environmental planning may develop in various ways. In principle it will reflect an emphasis on the longer term through the *precautionary* approach; it will be a *strategic* process dealing with the environmental implications of sectoral policies; it will *integrate* spatial economic planning, landuse planning and environmental protection; and it will *coordinate* policies at different governmental levels through the development, monitoring and implementation of plans at different levels of government from the local through the regional to the national and international level. These plans will set out the goals, time-scales and targets to be achieved. The justification for environmental planning for sustainability and an indication of how it would work in practice has begun to be set out by academics and professional planners (Jacobs, 1991; Blowers 1992b and c).

Equity and the Principle of Compensation

It was argued earlier that environmental policy goals will be difficult to establish, let along achieve, unless fundamental inequalities are tackled. This involves providing compensation to those communities who experience the environmental costs of economic development; preventing over exploitation of resources and environmental deterioration in poorer countries; improving environmental conditions in areas already suffering degradation; preventing or ameliorating transboundary impacts of pollution and risks; and ensuring that the present generation does not rob or imperil the future. These are the preconditions needed to ensure the third principle of the Rio Declaration, *The right to development must be fulfilled so as to equitably meet developmental and environmental needs of present and future generations.*

Environmental risks and degradation have become concentrated in communities that were earlier defined as 'peripheral'. Within the advanced industrial countries hazardous activities are found in what may be called 'pollution havens' such as petrochemical complexes or 'nuclear oases' such as Sellafield or Hanford in the United States (Blowers, et al., 1991; Loeb, 1986; McSorley, 1990). A process of peripheralisation may be perceived, strengthening over time, whereby peripheral communities are created and reinforced by the power of communities to prevent unwanted landuses combined with the powerlessness of peripheral communities to resist them (Blowers and Leroy, 1993). A similar process may be observed at international level where polluting and hazardous industrial activities are found in various developing countries. It must be emphasised that peripheral communities are primarily economically determined. Industries have developed and remain in those locations that have become dependent upon them. Therefore, environmental degradation is a consequence rather than a cause of peripheralisation. There is, though, little evidence to suggest that dirty activities migrate to pollution havens primarily to avoid environmental regulations.

In the developed countries it is becoming increasingly difficult to extend hazardous activities at existing sites and virtually impossible to establish them in new greenfield locations. Compensation in various forms is becoming a political expedient as well as a moral principle. Compensation can take a variety of forms including economic incentives (tax concessions, infrastructure provision, economic development and training programmes), social provision (education, community and health programmes) and participation in decision-making affecting the community. Indeed, research into siting nuclear facilities undertaken in the United States and Canada indicates that shared power and some local control over decisions is regarded as more important for the local community than any other form of compensation or incentive (Solomon and Cameron, 1985; Siting Process Task Force, 1987, 1990). At the international level it is also clear that countries will increasingly resist becoming dumping grounds for industrial and hazardous wastes. The Bamako Convention banning the import of hazardous wastes illustrates the power of collective action among developing countries.

The principle of compensation will be necessary to protect the global environment. Pressures will grow on the rich both to reduce their own excessive demands on the global environment and to provide finance and technology to enable sustainable development in the poor countries. Debt for nature swaps, technology transfer and the Global Environmental Facility are early if modest indications of some redistribution of resources to promote environmental goals.

This process may have to go further. Certain global resources will have to be conserved to protect the environment. But, nations are unlikely to waive their sovereign rights to develop their territory unless they are fully compensated for doing so. Developing countries are clearly unprepared to make unilateral sacrifices to save the global commons. If it is necessary in the common interest to withhold certain global assets such as tropical forests from exploitation then it is equally justifiable to provide greater access to the resources to those areas that are exploited. Resources in both developed and developing worlds are arguably the property of the global community whether exploited now or held in reserve to protect the environment and to pass on to future generations (Luper-Foy, 1992). To put it simply, if Brazil is expected to conserve its rainforest, the United States might equally be expected to share more widely the benefits of exploiting its resources, or, alternatively, to transfer some of its wealth in the interests of sustainable development.

The principle of global property rights argues that sovereignty does not confer on individual countries a right to exploit their territory as they please. It applies equally to the problem of transboundary pollution. There can be no justification for one country inflicting gratuitous damage on its neighbours. Where damage occurs compensation is appropriate, though, in the case of certain hazards such as radioactivity, it is difficult to envisage any appropriate compensation. Some countries are too poor to provide compensation or to prevent transboundary effects without help. For example, it is well known that nuclear reactors of Soviet design in Russia, the Ukraine and Eastern Europe are potentially unsafe. But, if they were shut down power supplies would be cut off over large areas. These countries lack the resources to upgrade their reactors. Therefore, technological and financial assistance from the West may be necessary if the threat of further widespread radioactive leakages is to be averted.

Finally, there is the obligation of the present to future generations, the principle of inter generational equity. This does not mean handing on the environment as it is since much of it is heavily degraded anyway but rather avoiding actions that will deprive the future of environmental assets. In some cases present benefits from technological development (e.g. toxic and radioactive wates) are responsible for inevitable future risks. Where future hazards are unavoidable then we are obliged to mitigate the risks through research and appropriate technology and to provide resources for the future management of hazardous sites. The problem of securing the future while maintaining present development is at the heart of the quest for sustainable development. Neither the present nor the future environment can be sustained unless equity is at the core of policy.

Postscript

Over the past five years or so the environment has become established as a key area of policy-making. Scientific analysis and evidence has had a significant impact on policy. The need for greater integration of environment into all areas of policy-making has been recognised. The environment has assumed greater importance in political debates at all levels. There has been greater public interest. The widespread participation of citizens' groups and NGOs is a trend that is likely to have major influence on setting the environmental agendas over the next decade. Governments at all levels have responded to the growing alarm at the threats posed to health and survival by the gross exploitation of our natural resources. Within the UK the environment has been the subject of comprehensive legislation and a major white paper; in the EC it has been a prominent and, on the whole, successful area of policy-making; and at the international level there has been an impressive series of agreements culminating in the Rio Earth Summit in 1992. Consensus on the importance of the issues reigns.

Though now well established on the policy agenda the environment has not yet secured its place alongside the quotidian preoccupation with economic management. Indeed the interdependence of economy and environment is barely recognised and the practical integration of the environment into all sectors and levels of policy-making is still a distant prospect. The environment remains a somewhat tangential issue, a matter of vague forebodings but, as yet, the social and economic implications of the quest for sustainable development have still to be fully appreciated. When they are the consensus may well dissolve into a conflict over resources as powerful interests and countries seek to acquire or defend a bigger share of resources. The seeds of discord are already sown.

International attention has been focused on the relatively distant dangers of deforestation, global warming, ozone depletion etc. Future security lies in present action. A set of principles, some significant agreements and a programme for future action (Agenda 21) were established at Rio, evidence of the growing sense of urgency and commitment to the desirable if unspecific goal of sustainable development. But, the more immediate threat to global survival posed by nuclear proliferation has excited much less attention.

Herein lies the biggest danger. The prospects of a nuclear exchange did not subside with the end of the Cold War. If anything the danger of nuclear conflict has increased with plutonium accumulating from reprocessing operations notably in the UK, France and Russia; large stockpiles from production and dismantling of nuclear weapons capability in several countries. The problem of proliferation demands the most urgent attention alongside the other global environmental issues. Otherwise the quest for sustainable development may be in vain.

REFERENCES

Barnaby, F. (1991). 'The environmental impact of the Gulf War', *The Ecologist*, Vol. 21, No.4, July/August.

Black, D. (1984). *Investigation of Possible Increased Cancer in West Cumbria*. Report of Independent Advisory Group Chaired by Sir Douglas Black, HMSO: London.

Blowers, A., Lowry, D., Solomon, B. (1991). *The International Politics of Nuclear Waste*, Macmillan: London.

Blowers, A. (1992a). "Sustainable Urban Development: The Political Prospects", in Breheny, M. (ed.) *Sustainable Development and Urban Form*, European Research in Regional Science, London: Pion.

Blowers, A. (1922b). "Planning a Sustainable Future: Problems, Principles and Prospects", *Town and Country Planning,* Vol.61, No.5, May 132-35.

Blowers, A. (1992c). 'Planning for a Sustainable City', *Streetwise*, No. 10, Spring, pp. 3-10.

Blowers, A. and Leroy, P. (1993). "Power, politics and environmental inequality: a theoretical and empirical analysis of the process of peripheralisation", first presented at International Sociological Association Symposium on *Current Developments in Environmental Sociology*, Woudschoten, Netherlands, June 1992.

Bramble, B. and Porter, G. (1992). "NGOs and the making of US policy", in Business Council for a Sustainable Development, *Changing Course: The Global Business Perspective on Development and the Environment*, Cambridge: MIT Press.

Brown, L.R. et al. (1991). *State of the World 1991*, London: Earthscan.

Buttel, F.H., Hawkins, A.P., Power, A.G. (1990). "From limits to growth to global change: constraints and contradictions in the evolution of environmental science and ideology", *Global Environmental Change*, Vol. 1, No. 1, Dec., pp. 57-66.

Carter, N. (1992). "Whatever happened to the environment? The British General Election, 1992", *Environmental Politics,* Vol. 1, No. 3, Autumn, pp. 442-48.

Carter, T.R., Porter, J.H., Pary, M.L. (1991). "Climatic warming and crop potential in Europe: prospects and uncertainties", *Global Environmental Change,* Vol. 1, No. 4, September, pp. 291-312.

Clark, J. (1991). *Democratising Development: The Role of Voluntary Organisation,* London: Earthscan.

Craft, A. and Openshaw, S. (1987). "Children, radiation, cancer and the Sellafield nuclear reprocessing plant", in Blowers, A. and Pepper, D. (eds.) *Nuclear Power in Crisis*, London: Croom Helm.

Daly, H. and Cobb, J. (1989). *For the Common Good,* London: Green Print.

Department of the Environment (1991). *Improving Environmental Quality*, Consultation Paper, HMSO: London.

Department of the Environment (1992b). *Land Use Planning Policy and Climate Change,* HMSO: London, April.

Dovers, S. and Handmer, J. (1992). "Uncertainty, sustainability and change", *Global Environmental Change,* Vol.2, No.4, December, pp. 262-76.

Downing, T.E. (1991). "Vulnerability to hunger in Africa: a climate change perspective", *Global Environmental Change,* Vol. 1, No. 5, December, pp. 365-80.

European Communities (1992). *Treaty on European Union,* Maastricht Treaty, CM1934, HMSO: London.

Giddens, A. (1985). *The Nation-state and Violence,* Cambridge: Polity Press.

Gorz, A. (1980). *Ecology as Politics,* Boston: South End Press.

Greene, O. (1991). "Building a global warming regime: the significance of verification and confidence building measures", Paper to Conference on 'International Arrangements for Reaching environmental Goals, Strathclyde, September.

Haas, P.M. (1992). "Introduction: epistemic communities and international policy coordination", *International Organization*, Vol. 46, No. 1, Winter, pp. 1-36.

Harden, G. (1969). "The tragedy of the commons", *Science*, 162, pp. 1243-48.

HMSO (1990). *This Common Inheritance*, CM 1200, HMSO" London.

Holmberg, J., Bass, S., Timberlake, L. (1991). *Defending the Future: A Guide to Sustainable Development,* London: IIED/Earthscan.

Idso, S.B. (1991). "Carbon dioxide and the fate of Earth", *Global Environmental Change* Vol. 1, No. 3. June, pp. 178-82.

IUCN, UNEP, WWF (1991). *Caring for the Earth: A Strategy for Sustainable Living,* Gland, Switzerland.

Jacobs, M. (1991). *The Green Economy*, London: Pluto Press.

The Labour Party (1990). *An Earthly Chance.*

Lindblom, C.E. (1977). *Politics and Markets: The World's Political-Economic Systems,* New York: Basic Books.

Loeb, P. (1986). *Nuclear Culture*, Philadelphia: New Society Publishers.

Lonergan, S. and Kavanagh, B. (1991). "Climate change, water resources and security in the Middle East", *Global Environmental Change*, Vol. 1, No. 4, September, pp. 272-90.

Lovelock, J. (1979). *Gaia: A New Look at Life on Earth*, Oxford: Oxford University Press.

Lovelock, J. (1988). *The Ages of Gaia: A Biography of our Living Earth*, Oxford: Oxford University Press.

Luper-Foy, S. (1992). 'Justice and natural resources', *Environmental Values*, Vol. 1, No. 1, Spring, pp. 47-64.

MacCracken, M.C. (1991). 'Comment on "Carbon dioxide and the fate of Earth" by Sherwood B. Idso', *Global Environmental Change*, Vol. 1, No. 4, pp. 266-8.

McCully, P. (1991). 'Discord in the greenhouse: how WRI is attempting to shift the blame for global warming'. *The Ecologist*, 21, pp. 157-65.

McSorley, J. (1990). *Living in the Shadow*, London: Pan Books.

Meadows, D. et al (1972). *The Limits to Growth*, London: Earth Island.

Open University (1992). *Third World Development*, Course U208, Milton Keynes.

Pearce, D., Maarkandya, A., Barbier, E. (1989). *Blueprint for a Green Economy*, London: Earthscan.

Popper, F.J. (1985). 'The Environmentalist and the LULU', reprinted in Lake, R. (ed.) (1987). *Resolving Locational Conflict*, New Jersey: Rutgers University.

Prins, G. (1990). 'Politics and the Environment', *International Affairs*, 66, 4, October, pp. 711-30.

Redclift, M. (1987). *Sustainable Development: Exploring the Contradictions*, London: Routledge.

Redclift, M. (1991). 'The multiple dimensions of sustainable development', *Geography*, 76, pp. 36-42.

Royal Institute of International Affairs (RIIA) (1991). *Pledge and Review Processes : Possible Components of a Climate Convention*, Report of a workshop, London, August.

Schneider, S.H. (1991). 'Why global warming should concern us', *Global Environmental Change*, Vol. 1, No. 4, September, pp. 268-71.

Siting Process Task Force (1987). 'Socially responsive impact management: a discussion paper', Report to the Siting Process Task Force on Low-level radioactive waste disposal, Energy, Mines and Resources, Canada, October.

Siting Process Task Force (1990). 'Opting for Cooperation', Report of the Siting Process Task Force on Low-level radioactive waste disposal, Energy Mines and Resources, Canada.

Smith, P. (1991). 'Global Development Issues', in Smith, P. and Warr, K., *Global Environmental Issues*, Open University, Hodder and Stoughton.

Solomon, B. and Cameron, D. (1985). "Nuclear waste repository siting : an alternative approach", *Energy Policy*, Vol. 13, No. 6, December, pp. 564-80.

Speth, J. (1992). 'A post-Rio compact', *Foreign Policy*, No. 88, Fall, 145-61.

United Nations (1992). *The Global Partnership for Environment and Development : A Guide to Agenda 21*, UNCED, Geneva, April.

WICEM II (1991). "Official Report, Second World Industry Conference on Environment and Management", in *Environment Strategy Europe*, London: Campden Publishing, pp. 71-107.

Wiman, Bo L.B. (1991). "Implications of environmental complexity for science and policy: contributions from system theory", *Global Environmental Change*, Vol. 1, No. 3, June, pp. 235-47.

Wolsink, M. (forthcoming). 'Entanglement of interests and motives in facility siting: the not-in-my-backyard theory', draft.

World Commission on Environment and Development (1987). *Our Common Future*, The Brundtland Report, Oxford University Press.

Yearley, S. (1991a). *The Green Case*, London: Routledge.

Yearley, S. (1991b). 'Greens and science: a doomed affair?', *New Scientist*, 13 July, pp. 37-40.

19

SHIFTING CULTIVATION AND SUSTAINABLE DEVELOPMENT IN NAGALAND

MAJID HUSAIN

Living with an immediate environment contact, the indigenous people of Nagaland consist of nineteen major tribes. The cultural landscape of these tribes has evolved by forest clearing for *Jhuming* (shifting cultivation) or the terracing of hillsides for subsistence farming. They not only make use of an enormous variety of plant life, but cultivate *Jhum* fields in a highly organised way. The Konyaks, Lothas, Rengmas, and Semas practice seed selection, and crop rotation and compliment their agriculture with hunting, gathering and fishing. In this way they benefit from a wide range of nourishment while regrowth and replenishment in the forest ensure food for their future. Thus in the Naga societies, the acquisition of food, shelter, and clothing and the overall cultural ethos, depends on the utilization of natural resources of land. Despite the empirical experience and the expertise of shifting cultivators in the utilization of their endowment, the natural environment in Nagaland is increasingly degrading. The present paper is an attempt to examine the *jhuming* scenario with a focus on the agricultural operations, rotation of crops, *Jhum* cycle and the ecological consequences of the existing utilization of soil and forest resources.

There is paucity of data and information about the area, production and rotation of shifting cultivation. The present paper is based mainly on the field work conducted in the sample villages. Primary data was gathered with the help of village headmen and interpreters (school teachers of the respective villages). The major problem, the field investigators confronted in the collection of data was the great variation in the units of linear, areal and weight measurements as they differ from tribe to tribe and region to region. Consequently, to make them comparable was cumbersome and time consuming. The problem was overcome with the help of interpreters. Some of the respondents grasped properly the idea of the questions of the questionnaire and assisted the investigators in the speedy completion of work.

The state of Nagaland has 1096 villages, out of which five villages were selected for the study. These villages are the representatives of the different dominant Naga tribes. The selected villages are: Aliba (Mokokchung district), Jotsoma (Kohima district), Lakhauti (Wokha district), Rungzumi (Phek district) and Tsadanger (Tuensang district). The salient attributes of the sample villages have been given in Table 19.1.

TABLE 19.1: Nagaland: Selected Villages

Village	Altitude in metres	Tribe	Population	
			1981	1991
Aliba	1280	AO	1102	1321
Jotsoma	1224	Angami	1096	1335
Lakhauti	1419	Lotha	1079	1287
Rungzumi	1408	Rengma	875	1051
Tsadanger	1435	Changs	664	798

The state of Nagaland sprawls over 16,579 sq. kms and has a population of 1,215,373 (1991) with an average density of 73 persons per sq. km. About 83 per cent of the total population of the state is dependent on *Jhum*. According to the census of 1991 the total work force was 850,081 out of which 722,514 (85%) were engaged in shifting cultivation. The growth of population in the state is one of the highest in the country as in about two decades it has increased by more than double. In 1971 the total population of the state was 516,449 which rose to 1215,573 in 1991. Consequently, the pressure of population on the highly fragile ecosystems of *Jhum* land has increased stupendously.

Jhuming in Nagaland has been described as an economy of which the main characteristics are: rotation of fields rather than crops; absence of draught animals; use of manual labour; employment of dibble-stick or hoe, short period of occupancy (one or two years) alternating with long fallow periods. In *Jhuming* system, the fields are abandoned after one or two years, the cultivator shifts to another clearing, leaving the old field for natural recuperation. This explains the use of the term shifting cultivation. Clearing of forest land, fully or partially burning of biomass are the other features of shifting cultivation.

Nagaland, with a tropical rain forest climate (Am) has wide tracts under shifting cultivation. In this climate, temperatures at low altitudes (below 100 metres) remain high i.e. about 27°C throughout the year. The summer monsoon is strong which generally lasts from June to October. In such climate conditions the shifting cultivators follow a time schedule for the various operations of agriculture, which has been described briefly in the following:

The usual process demands the selection of a hillside to be brought under cultivation in the subsequent agricultural year. The selection of land is generally made in the months of December and January by the village headman in consultation with the village priest and other elderly persons of the village. Usually, the whole village cultivates in one tract, though in the case of large population village, like Aliba, Jotsoma and Lakhauti, each *khel* (a sub-division of Naga village) may select a different area (hill-side) for cultivation. This gregarious method has several advantages. For example, it is easier to fence a large tract than a lot of small fields, birds are not as destructive to cereals as they would be in small isolated patches in the forest; and friends can conveniently help each other in sowing, planting, hoeing, weeding and harvesting.

Clearing of undergrowth and felling of trees is an arduous task which is generally done by the male work force. This operation is completed in six to ten days, depending on the nature of forest and the infested undergrowth. The month of March is a period of clear skies in which the day temperature reads up to 32°C. The twigs, branches and grasses dry in the bright sun of March. Depending on the prevailing weather conditions, the dried growth as well as the uncut trees standing in the clearance are set on fire. The objective of burning is to add more nitrates to the soil to enhance its fertility and to get rid of weed growths. The *Jhumias* believe that the burnt fields remain weed free for a longer period.

Once the field is burnt, it is allotted to each household of the village. In the process of allotment the size and workforce in the family are taken into consideration. The basic axioms of *Jhumias* life is *from each according to his capacity and to each according to his needs*. Thus in the society of Nagas, the old infirms, women, widows and children have an equal share, and each member of the society plays a role according to his physical and mental abilities. It is interesting and judicious that the old, infirms, and widows are allotted land in the central part of the *Jhum* field, while the young and energetic members share the fields in the periphery. This arrangement guarantees full protection against wild animals to those who are incapable of protecting on their own.

The day of sowing is considered as a ceremonial occasion for the entire village. The male work force reach the field early in the morning and engage themselves in the preparation of digging sticks. The seeds are sown either by broadcast or by dibbling. The dibbling of seeds is generally done by females while the broadcast of rice, maize, cotton, pulses and sesamum is done by men. The seeds sprout after three or four days under the hot and humid conditions of the season (June). After sowing, the most crucial phase of *Jhuming* is the protection of crop for which fencing is done. Huts are constructed on high platforms where young men can sit during the day wátching the crops and women bring cooked food to the fields and spend sometime there to scare birds and weeding the crops.

Some of the vegetables (French beans, turnips, carrots, radish and spinach are harvested/within forty days after their sowing. The main crops of maize, rice, millets, pulses and oilseeds are harvested in the months of September and October. When the main crops are harvested, the *Jhumias* are free from the routine work of agriculture, and they arrange feasts, marriages and celebrate festivals in which the young boys and girls perform traditional dances, folk songs and participate in competitions of games and sports. As the winter season is in its peak, the elderly people start deliberations about the next agricultural calendar and the piece of land to be brought under *Jhuming*. This cycle goes on and so passes the life of Nagas.

Jhum Land

Out of the total reporting area of 13.51 lakh hectares of Nagaland, nearly 6.25 lakh hectares are affected by *Jhuming*. The *Jhum* land available to the people of a particular village depends on its territorial jurisdiction, terrain, slope of territory and the size of population. Reliable data on the land under *Jhum* is not available as the cadestral survey has not been done and the people are not familiar with the units of area measurement. On the basis of information available, the approximate area affected by *Jhuming* in the sample villages have been given in Table 19.2.

TABLE 19.2: Nagaland: Area under *Jhum* in Selected Villages

(*Area in acres*)

	Village	Area affected by *Jhum*	Area under *Jhum* at one point of time	Percentage
1.	Aliba	1900	195	10.0
2.	Jotsoma	2650	260	9.8
3.	Lakhauti	1558	187	12.0
4.	Rungzumi	1835	188	10.2
5.	Tsadanger	2530	216	8.5

Source: Field work by the author.

An analysis of Table 19.2 shows that about 8 to 12 per cent of the total *Jhum* land is brought under cultivation in a particular. The village of Lakhauti which has a large population and more steep slopes has high percentage under sowing in a year, while this percentage is about 9 and 10 in the Tsadanger Jotsoma villages respectively. It has been reported that each year more percentage of *Jhum* land is being brought under cultivation to meet the growing food demand of the rapidly increasing population.

Rotation of Crops

In the *Jhum* lands of Nagaland rotation of crops is practised only in those fields in which the *Jhum* cycle is more than 15 years, the slope of the field is gentle and the field is sown for two or more than two years consecutively. In general, as the fertility declines in the subsequent years, the *jhumias* reduce the number of crops to be mixed for sowing and increasingly concentrate on legumes. Some of the important crops which are rotated have been given in Table 19.3.

Mixture of several soil exhaustive and soil enriching crops is a common feature of cropping pattern in the summer season, while fallowings of land is a universal practice in the winter season (Table 19.3). In the second year rice is generally replaced by small millets and pulses.

TABLE 19.3: Nagaland: Rotation of Crops: Sema Tribe

	First year		Second year	
	Kharif (Summer) Season	Rabi (Winter) Season	Kharif (Summer) Season	Rabi (Winter) Season
1.	Paddy, maize, kachu vegetables, soyabean, oilseeds	—	Short duration paddy, maize, pulses, vegetables	—
2.	Paddy, nagdal, vegetables sesamum, oilseeds, cotton millets	—	Small millets, pulses vegetables	—
3.	Maize, millets, nagdal, vegetables	—	Small millets, pulses	—

Source: Field work by the author.

Jhum Cycle

A peculiar feature of the shifting cultivation is the rotation of fields, known as *Jhum*-cycle. The *Jhum*-cycle is determined by the pressure of the population, biomass of the forest, slope of the field, quality and depth of soil and the quantity and distribution of rainfall in the different months. Areas of sparse population generally have longer *jhum* cycles (15 to 20 years), while areas with high pressure of population on cultivated land have shorter *jhum* cycle. Thus the period of fallowing differs from slope to slope and from village to village. In the past the shifting cultivators had vast areas of forests to move about, but at present the *jhumias* are staked down to smaller areas and they have not got much choice to shift about. His world has become small. Consequently, the *jhum* cycle has shrunk and now it varies from about five years in Ao and Angami tribes of Mokokchung and Kohima districts respectively to twenty years in Chang and Konyak tribes.

The *jhum* cycle, period of occupancy and the duration of fallowing in the selected villages have been given in Table 19.4.

The rapid increase in population and the consequent decrease in the *jhum* cycle has resulted into structural changes of tribal economy. As the *jhum* cycle gets reduced, the quality of land available for cultivation also declines. Owing to shorter cycle of *jhum*, the forest and biomass do not achieve majority and the thick forest cover disappears speedily. The disappearance of forests deprives the tribal population of

TABLE 19.4: Nagaland: *Jhum* Cycle, Period of Occupancy and Duration of Fallowing

Village	Average annual rainfall	Duration of cropping	Fallowing period
Aliba (Ao)	150	one year	5 –10 years
Jotsoma (Angami)	145	one year	5 – 8 years
Lakhauti (Lotha)	145	two years	6 –12 years
Rungzumi (Rungma)	150	two years	8 –10 years
Tsadanger (Changs)	155	two years	8 –15 years

Source. Field work by the author.

a secondary source of food, fuelwood and fodder. A significant impact of short duration of *jhum* cycle appears in the form of change in the mode of utilization of *jhum* land. In the traditional *jhuming* with long fallowing period (over 20 years), the *Jhumias* were able to fulfil their small cash requirements by selling forest products like nuts, fruits, skins, horns of wild animals in the markets of neighbouring towns. With disappearance of forests they are forced to produce some cash crops to be sold in the market to fetch some money from fulfilment of needs such as clothing, tools, kerosene, medicine and social functions. Consequently, the *Jhumias* are compelled to devote more land to crops such as potato, ginger, onion, garlic, pineapple, vegetables and other saleable crops. The change in the cropping patterns brings many structural changes in the traditional simple economy of the shifting cultivators. So long as money incomes depended on the sale of natural forest products, there was limit to its acquisition. But this limit disappeared with the removal of forests. Under the changed conditions an individual may be tempted to have larger amount of money incomes through greater and more intensive utilization of *Jhum* land. Since income is generally personal in character, it has several other serious socio-economic implications. In order to quench the thirst for money one begins to engage labourers and thus the labour class emerges in the communities of shifting cultivators. The traditional well established norms of *Jhuming* are violated, individuals begin to incline towards propriety rights on *jhum* lands, the institutions of mutual co-operation and reciprocal and become weak and finally disappear. The income disparity accentuates, the outmigration of the weaker labourers commences and the pacified tradition bound society comes in the grip of social tension. Moreover, it not only changes the social and economic structure, it inevitably leads to commercialization of shifting cultivation. The intensive use of the highly fragile ecosystems of the hill slopes results into soil erosion and land depletion under the torrential rains of the summer monsoon. From such degraded lands the *jhumias* outmigrate to the neighbouring towns in search of employment where they face many socio-cultural problems in the new cultural environment.

Sustainable Development

The primitive technique of land utilization in *jhuming* leads to many ecological crisis and create many socio-economic problems. This system is increasingly becoming a serious threat to numerous plant and animal species. In the opinion of environmentalists, shifting cultivation is economically unviable and ecologically unsustainable. Despite all these short-comings *jhuming* cannot be stopped completely as the life style and cultural ethos of the tribal people of Nagaland are closely governed by *jhuming* operations. The problem therefore, needs to be tackled at the short-term and long-term basis. Each hillside and slope is to be surveyed and diagnosed on its merit before appropriate steps have to be taken for its utilization. In, a three tier utilization of *jhum* land can go a long way in making the system economically more productive and environmentally sustainable. The gentle slopes, i.e. below 10° with low altitudes should be terraced to developed sedentary agriculture. Efforts should also be made to provide irrigation to the terraced fields. Slopes varying between 10° to 20° should be reserved for orchards, pineapple, fruit trees, nut-trees, beetal-nuts, aricanut and jack-fruits, the slopes over 20° should be exclusively devoted to reserved forests. In the reserved forests, the trees should be allowed to complete their life cycle which shall help in the regeneration of forests by which the bio-diversity shall be maintained.

For the maintenance of resilience character of the ecosystems, efforts should be made to establish more research centres for the development of good seeds for different altitudes which may mature in short duration and could give good returns under the prevailing temperature and moisture conditions. Transformation in technology and cropping structure are also essential. While introducing any innovation in *jhuming* it must be borne in mind that the suggested changes and proposed policies are socially acceptable, economically viable and environmentally sustainable.

REFERENCES

Allen, B.C. (1902). *Gazetteer of Naga and Manipur*. Vol. IX, Shillong.

Christiannsen, C. (1978). *Shifting Cultivation in Bovellia Island*, Copenhagen.

F.A.O. Paper (1967). *Alternative System of Farming for Increasing Productivity in Jhum Lands in North East India*, North East Council of Social Science Research.

Grigg, G.D. (1973). *Agricultural Systems of the World*, London.

Husain, M. (1988). *Nagaland*, New Delhi: Rima Pub. House.

Hutton, J.H. (1921). *The Angani Nagas*, London.

Mills, J.P. (1926). *The Ao Nagas*, London.

20

MEANING OF DEVELOPMENT : THE COMMON MAN'S CONCERN

A Reflection through Participatory Rural Appraisal Methods

AMITAVA MUKHERJEE

Meaning of Development in Eighth Five-Year Plan for India

The Eighth Five-Year Plan has been operationalised from April, 1992 in a more deregulated environment, with a shrinkage in prescriptive planning by the Planning Commission. In the context of a series of economic reforms initiated by the government, and opening up of the Indian economy, the responsibility of the public sector would come down in many areas.[1]

Public sector would make investment only in those areas where investment is mainly infrastructural in nature and would withdraw from other areas, though it would continue to have primary responsibility for investment in social sector such as literacy, health, population control and the environment. A high priority concern of the Government would be to find resources for development of these social sectors.

The Plan sets an average growth target of 5.6 per cent per year for the next five years, taking 1991-92 as the base year, which means there has been a dilution of the growth target considering that the base year experienced a negative growth rate.

A key factor for the success of the Eighth Five-Year Plan is that it would have to be financed in a non-inflationary manner. The Plan projects an external or current account deficit of 1.4 per cent of GDP annually, which would mean an annual net inflow of resources of not more than $ 4 billion. Since assistance from multilateral financing institutions has been running around $ 2.5 billion, another $ 1.5 would have to come in the form of foreign investment and remittances from abroad. But even with this, there would have to be a minimum annual export growth rate of 13.6 per cent by volume.

The clear implication is that if export efforts fall short of the target, either larger resources would have to be mobilised from outside or steps should be taken to reduce the import elasticity currently running around 1.5 per cent. This, in turn, would lower GDP growth.

The Meaning of Development in Eight Five-Year Plan for Uttar Pradesh

The Uttar Pradesh government has proposed an aggregated outlay of Rs. 26,000 crore for the State's Eighth Five-Year Plan which is 154 per cent and 136 per cent higher than the approved outlay and expenditure respectively of its Seventh Five-Year Plan.[2] The proposed outlay indicates that the State's Eighth Five-Year Plan has laid special thrust on dairy development, animal husbandry, rural development, irrigation, energy, village and small industries, roads, education, technical education and social security and welfare.

The goals and objectives of the State's Eighth Five-Year Plan are mainly in consonance with the approach to the Eighth Five-Year Plan at the national level as well as the State's own perception of its needs. Specifically the State's Eighth Five-Year Plan had been designed to:[3]

(i) achieve an average annual growth rate of six per cent against the targeted 5.6 per cent for the country;
(ii) create gainful and self-sustaining employment opportunities for 50 lakh people;
(iii) reduce the percentage of people living below the poverty line from 38.9 per cent in 1991-92 to 24.32 in 1996-97;
(iv) reduce population growth from 2.29 per cent per annum during 1981-91 to 2.2 per cent in the plan period, provide adequate safe drinking water to all villages and achieve literacy rate of 50 per cent and electrification of 91 per cent villages;
(v) raise income of rural poor, improve the quality of life in rural areas, afford reasonable share in public facilities to poor people, maximise productivity in agriculture by diversification and mixed farming in small and marginal holdings and in areas of low productivity; and

(vi) achieve further growth in manufacturing sector and promotion of industries having large potential for employment and anciliarisation.

Three remarks are in order here.

One, the State's economy is essentially agrarian but there has been a substantial decline in the share of agriculture in the state domestic product from about 52 per cent in 1980-81 to 41.5 per cent in 1989-90, showing diversification in economy. The official data shows that the share of secondary sector has moved up from 16.3 per cent in 1980-81 to 20.5 per cent in 1989-90 and that of the tertiary sector from 31.7 per cent in 1980-81 to 38 per cent in 1989-90. These are indicative of the fact that there has been a healthy change in the State's economy as agriculture, mainly limited to small and marginal farmers and confronted by a number of uncertainties like vagaries of weather, could absorb the increase in population.

Two, the disconcerting fact is that after achieving the annual growth rate of 5.7 per cent in the Fifth Five-Year Plan period, it has slid to four per cent in the Sixth Five-Year Plan and 4.8 per cent in the Seventh Five-Year Plan period.

Three, the prime task the State has set before itself is to attack growing poverty as there is likely to be an addition of 54 lakh persons to the labour force during this plan period yielding an annual growth of about 2.4 per cent.[4]

Meaning of Development

Clearly the *meaning of development* emerging from the State's Eighth Five-Year Plan looks like growth in income, increase in employment, reduction in both population growth and in the number of people living below the poverty line. The "strategy" chosen seems to be diversification of agriculture, augmenting that portion of the manufacturing sector which has large potential for employment generation and anciliarisation. These, in fact, are directed toward employment generation and growth in income.

The meaning of development in *India's Eighth Five-Year Plan* seems to be growth in income with attempts at improving the quality of primary health care, basic education, and other social overheads, through non-inflationary sources of finance. The meaning of development in the Eighth Five-Year Plan has seemingly been articulated against the backdrop of the capacity of the country to obtain finances from abroad and generating export earnings.

We are of the view that within an overall meaning of a development adopted for a State's Eighth Five-Year Plan, development ought to understood as articulated by the people's needs and aspirations. If micro-level meanings are not taken into account in formulating the overall concept of development adopted for the State, the chances are that a State's concept of development would, more often than not, be out of tune with what the people actually, at the grassroots level, would like development to be. Where this happens, the entire gamut of planning will be an esoteric exercise, in which the people would not be partners in progress. This is *one* of the surest way to guarantee that planning fails.

Objective of this Study

Against this backdrop and the emerging meaning of development in Uttar Pradesh's Eighth Five-Year Plan, an attempt has been made in this paper to ascertain whether the meaning of development as adopted by the political executive and techno-bureaucratic planning superstructure was reasonably aligned with the meaning of development as understood by the people at large. Obviously it has not been possible to ascertain the meaning of development as accepted by the common man on a one to one basis, except on a sample basis. It was, therefore, necessary to decide upon three aspects:

(a) the area of study,
(b) the sample population whose views on development, perspective were to be ascertained, and
(c) the mechanism through which the views on development perspective of their economy are to be determined.

Area of the Study

Doiwala block in the district of Dehradun (which is one of the Hilly Districts of the State of Uttar Pradesh) was selected as the area for investigation. Doiwala is one of the six blocks in Dehradun, forms the South-Western boundary of Dehradun district, and separates Dehradun and Hardwar districts (See Fig. 20.1). Its economy is a predominantly agricultural one and has a considerable area under forest. It is flushed by the mighty Ganga, along is South Western boundary. It has seventy-eight villages. In order to have a glimpse of the common man's development perspective, eight villages were chosen in the block, which works out to be a little over ten per cent of the villages. The following villages were chosen:

(i) Mohamadpur Barkali
(ii) Bagi
(iii) Majri Grant
(iv) Harrawala
(v) Nagal Jwalapur
(vi) Khadri Kharak Maph
(vii) Balawala
(viii) Ranipokhari

The villages were so selected that they were geographically spread throughout the block and would represent, on the one end, villages which have considerable non-farm activity (Harrawala) and on the other, villages which have no significant activity other than agriculture (Ranipokhari). The sampling technique was clearly purposive.

Since Participatory Rural Appraisal methods (more fully described below) were used to analyse the development perspectives the common men have, no rigid sampling methods was required to sample individuals or individual households, as the methods enjoin as large a participation of the people in general as is possible in the use of these techniques.

Participatory Rural Appraisal (PRA) Methods Used

Participatory Rural Appraisal[5] methods are used to help involve farming households in all stages of development work, from identification of needs to assessment, monitoring and evaluation of completed projects.[6] The methods of investigation available under PRA are many[7] as summarised in Table 20.1. We opted for three methods detailed below:

(a) *First,* Semi-Structured Interview (SSI) or Semi-Structured Learning (SSL), was used, which takes place in informal, guided interview sessions where only some of the questions are pre-determined and new-questions or lines of questioning, arise during the course of the interview, in response to answers elicited from the interviewees. Such semi-structured learning is normally associated with farm, field or village visits and the interviewees could be individual farmers, households, key-informants, village opinion leaders, school teachers of various kinds and senior citizens who are knowledgeable. "Probing questions" are a dominating feature of SSI. Some believe this method to be the most powerful method in the tool kit of PRA.[8]

(b) The *second* key PRA method used lies in the realm of diagrams. For the purposes of this study, resort was taken to Transects and Historical Transects. Transects are diagrams of main landuse zones, which compare the main features, resources, uses and problems of different zones of the area(s) under reference (which in this study are individual villages).[9]

(c) Historical transects are also diagrams of main landuse zones, at *different points in time,* but does not ordinarily contain a comparison of the main features, resources, uses and problems of different zones.

TABLE 20.1: PRA Tool-Kit

Subject	Objective of the Study	Main Techniques Used	Country of Study	References
HEALTH	Assessment of the utilisation ion of rural health	Review of population census and hospital admission data. One-day census at hospitals and health centres	Gambia and Botswana	Walker, G., 1979
SANITATION	Investigation of the need, cultural values, and local	House to house surveys and Village meetings, with: - questionnaires - checklists	Swaziland	Pacey, A., 1979
EMERGENCIES AND DISASTERS	Assessment of extent and impact of refugee influx and proposal of development strategy for their absorption	Visits to villages and refugee camps, with: - Guided interviews	Ethiopia	Ellman, A.O., 1972

Contd.

TABLE 20.1 *Contd.*

Subject	Objective of the Study	Main Techniques Used	Country of Study	References
NON-FORMAL EDUCATION	Assessment of effectiveness of a youth Training scheme and identification of ways of improving it	Surveys in towns of former, present and would be trainees, with: - open-ended questionnaires - 2-6 day visit to check survey findings - informal talks with trainee instructors - informal talks with trainee employers	Sudan	Eyben, R. 1979
AGROFORESTRY	Identification of village agroforestry system and social organisation, and assessment of influence of entrepreneurs on forest land use	SSIs with close observation secondary data, aerial photography analysis. Physical measurement Questionnaires. Group discussion	Thailand	Subhadhira, S. and Apichatvullop, Y., 1987
NATURAL RESOURCE ASSESSMENT	Assessment of soil with regard to possible dam, railway, road construction	Ecological surveys, identifying indicator tree and bush species	Zimbabwe	Stocking, M., and Abel, N., 1981
SOCIOLOGY	Investigation of marriage customs and procedures	Village surveys with: - interviews with households, commune, production brigade and production team cadres. Fixed questionnaire survey of one village.	China	Croll, E.J., 1984

Source: McCracken. Jennifer, et. al. *loc. cit.* pp. 15.

Preparation of Transects involves, walking from one end of the village under study to the other, along with some key informants and record down whatever is observed on the surface, such as trees, forest, settlements/houses/huts, fields, common property resources etc., and find out details about each of these, both with regard to what is seen on the surface and beneath. It naturally involves first finding community members who are knowledgeable and willing to participate in a walk through the village and surrounding areas. The different factors to be included in the Transect (such as crops, land use, trees, soil types etc.) and the route to be taken for walking through the village, are then discussed with the participating community members. The walk is then undertaken, while concurrently observings, asking and listening to the people, *without lecturing them.* The constraints, problems and opportunities are discussed, and the main natural and agricultural zones are then identified. The distinguishing features are sketched for each zone; soil types, crops, trees, livestock, problems, solutions and opportunities are described. The Transact is then drawn up. The picture that then emerges is cross-checked with key informants.

In case of Historical Transect, it is necessary to determine the years in respect of which information is sought. As human memory is short, it is difficult for people to provide details of landuse in relation to exact years. To circumvent this difficulty, it is useful, as a rule of thumb, to request information at points in time, underpinned with reference to special events: floods, earthquakes, wars, major political happenings and so on.

For the purpose of this study, 1900, 1945, 1962, 1965, 1979-80 and 1992 were chosen. To sharpen the "recall response" of the villagers, these years were represented by major events as under:

1900	—	The stories learnt from grand-parents.
1945	—	The end of the Second World War and/or Independence.
1962	—	The Chinese Aggression.
1965	—	The India-Park War.
1979-80	—	Mrs. Gandhi's return to Power: Post-Emergency Era.
1992	—	The Current Scenario.

The choice of wars to represent landmarks in history was expedient for the study, since our Hill people serve the Indian Army valiantly through both the Garhwal and the Kumaon Regiments. Wars are, therefore, remembered very clearly and hence provide extremely good reference points.

Following the above methods, Semi-Structured Interview, Transect and Historical Transect were applied to each of the eight villages during November, 1992. The findings are revealing, to which we may now turn.

Study of the Eight Villages

(i) *Mohamadpur Barkali* village is located in the Ramgarh forest range at the Shiwalik foot hills. It is a semi-forest village inhabited by people of Nepalese origin. It is on the either side of river Suswa, surrounded by reserved forest. A few *Gujjar* (a highly mobile people with large livestock holdings) families have also settled down in the village. Secondary data review reveals that River Suswa has washed and re-washed away the village several times in the past.

The Historical Transect and Transect for village Mohamadpur Barkali are at figures 20.1 and 20.2 respectively. The Historical Transect confirms the secondary data that the village is situated on the banks of a small river, and that the river has changed its course from west to east over approximately the first fifty years of this century. The river then changed its course in the westerly direction, during the sixties tending towards its original course. Towards the beginning of the last decade, the river apparently relocated itself once again to adopt an easterly course. The course of the river has "osccillated" during the last nearly one hundred years.

The Transect in Figure 20.2 indicates that the major problems of Mohamadpur Barkali are erosion, drought and low-fertility. This was rechecked during the course of the semi-structured interviews, and it was clarified that during good monsoon, the surging river water (from the Shiwalik range) brings with it boulders, gravels, pebbles and sand from the upper reaches and dumps them along its banks, whereas alluvial deposits appear on either side, further away from the river course beyond the boulders, pebbles and sand. The problem is accentuated by mining of boulders from Suswa. Under conditions of the Contract that leases out rights to mine boulders in the river, no mining is permissible within 25 feet from the river bank on either side, so that the boulders provide protective cover to embankments. Sadly enough, this is not done and mining of boulders nearer to the banks is the rule rather than the exception. As a result, the centre the of river bed is raised by accumulation of boulders,

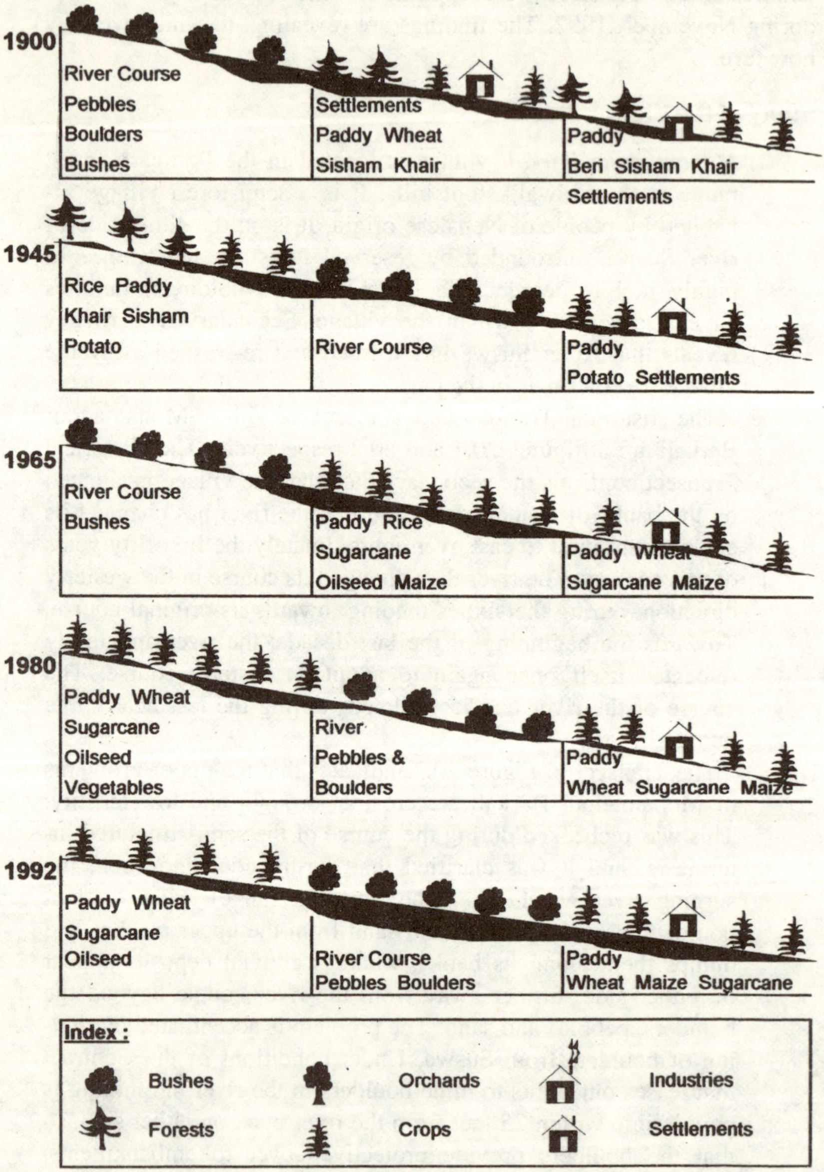

FIG. 20.1: Transect Through Time. Illustration of Landuse Trend in Mohamadpur Barkali — A Semi-Forest Village in Doiwala Block

SOIL	Gravel Clay Sandy Alluvial	Gravel Clay Sandy	Gravel Clay Sandy	Gravel Clay Sandy	Gravel Clay Sandy Alluvial
LANDUSE	Farmland Bushes Settlement	Farmland Barrenland Settlement	Farmland Barrenland watershed	Settlement Barrenland Watershed Farmland	Settlement Watershed Farmland
CROP & VEGETATION	Paddy Maize Wheat Peas Todja	Oilseed Sugarcane	Todia Maize	Wheat Paddy Todia Maize	Wheat Paddy
PROBLEMS	Erosion	Erosion Drought	Erosion Low Fertility	Erosion Drought Pests	Erosion
OPPORTUNITIES	Bushes Check Dams School	Flood Recession Farming Pesticide	Bushes Check Dams	Check Dams	Electricity Irrigation

Index :

Bushes	Orchards	Industries
Forests	Crops	Settlements

FIG. 20.2: Transact Through Mohmadpur Barkali

while the banks are exposed to the onslaught of water currents. In Mohamadpur Barkali, additionally, no conservation measures such as setting up of "spurs" or retention walls has been taken.

The problems of the village inundated at regular intervals by a hill-river are, as the Transect reveals, soil erosion, low-soil fertility and irrigation facilities. The opportunities, therefore, lay according to the common man, in the realm of erecting check dams and in providing irrigation facilities, planting bushes and resorting to such economic practices as would prevent erosion.

There is seemingly a contradiction between what the secondary data reveals and what the people want with regard to irrigation. It appears from the secondary data that the village has 40.47 per cent of its area under cultivation covered by irrigation, yet the cultivators of Mohamadpur Barkali feel that irrigation is an area of major concern. Our Semi-Structured Interview revealed that the area under irrigation is indicative of the command area, but the area that actually receives irrigation water is much less. Hence there is a need to develop irrigation facility, with special emphasis on water harvesting.

(ii) *Bagi village* is located in Mussoorie hills, 10 kms north from Ranipokhari. On the north it is bounded by Nawarkot, on the south by Bhogpur, on the east by Khaldar and on the west by Gadhul village. The village is well drained by Mandir-Ka-Khala, a perennial stream, on east and Chandpather-Ka-Khala on the west. The people are migrants from Bageshwar which is in Almora district.

The Historical Transect and Transect of village Bagi are at Figs. 20.3 and 20.4 respectively.

The village, situated on an elevated stretch of the land surface, slopes downward both towards East and West. The settlement is located obviously at the highest "table" point in the area. It would appear from the Historical Transect that gradually the forest on the Western reaches of the village along Chandpather-Ka-Khala is vanishing with the passage of time, and the once well stocked forests of Sal, Shisham, Kalabansa and Karonda have gradually given way to bushes, shrubs, rice and wheat cultivation. Similarly, on the Eastern segment of the village, along Mandir-Ka-Khala, Sal and Shisham have vanished and Paddy, Wheat and Bushes together with hutments have taken over. The centre of the village continues to be the principal residential area and the location of common property resources.

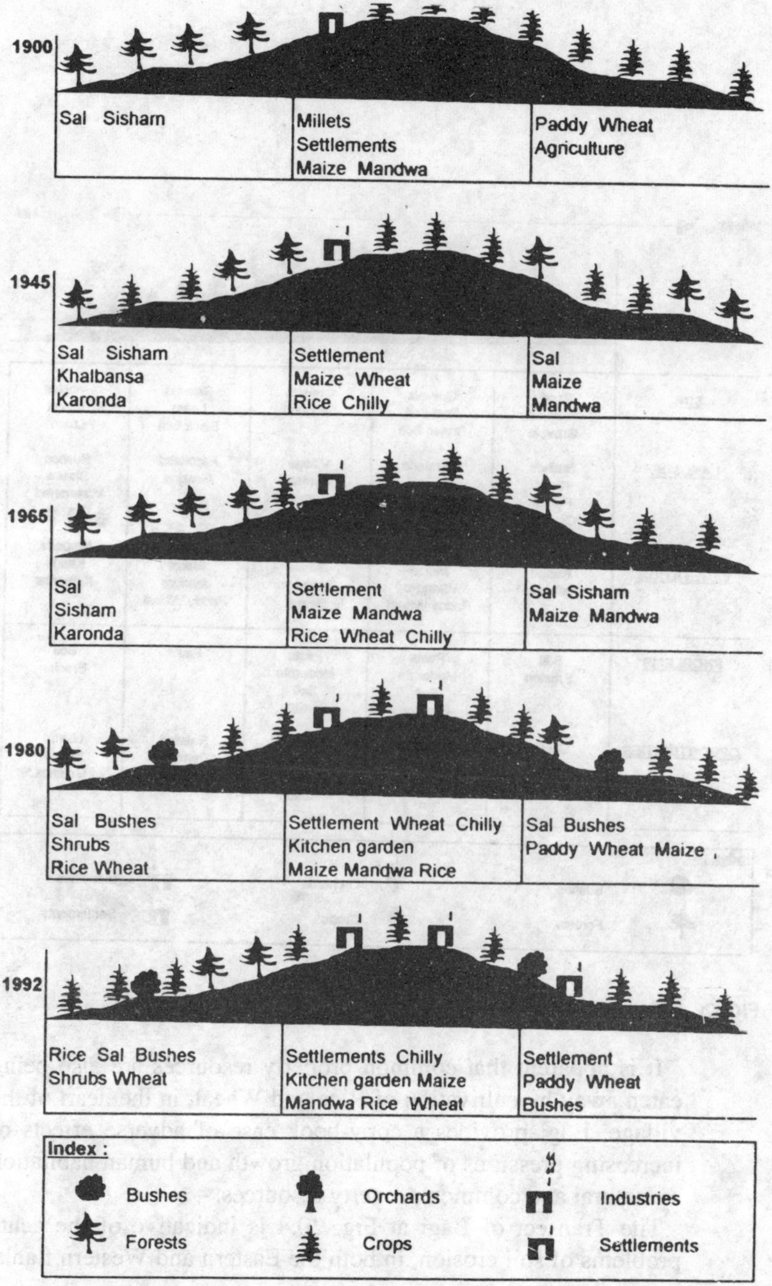

FIG. 20.3: Transect Through Time. Illustration of Landuse Trend in Bagi Village in Doiwala Block

SOIL	Sandy Pebbles Gravels	Gravels Red Soil Brown Soil	Gravels Red Soil	Gravels Loam Black Soil	Pebbles Gravel Loam
LANDSUE	Bushes River Forest Grazing	Farmland	Village Farmland Forest	Farmland Grazing	Bushes Shrubs Watershed Grazing
CROP & VEGETATION	Karonda Kangu Kalbanra	Millets Maize Jhangro Paddy Wheat	Chilly Gagali Turmeric Beans	Millets Maize Jhangro Paddy Wheat	Karonda Kangu Kalbanra
PROBLEMS	Soil Erosion	Pests Moderate Soil Fertility	Pests Moderate Soil Fertility	Pests	Soil Erosion
OPPORTUNITIES	Useful Fodder Grasses	Irrigation	Rainfed Farming Posture Road	Rainfed Farming Pesticides	Useful Fodder Grasses

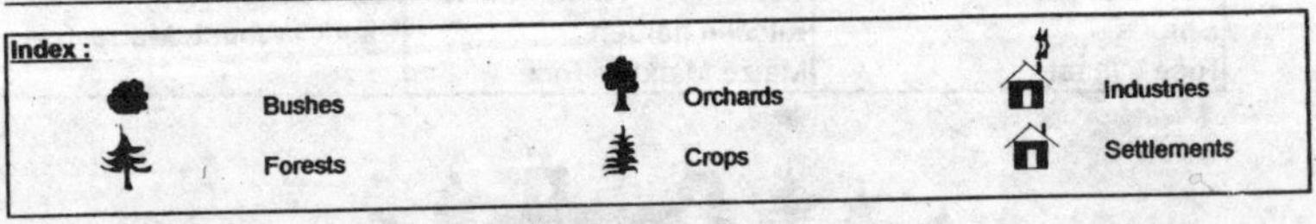

FIG. 20.4: Transect of Bagi Village

It is apparent that common property resources are also being eaten away by cultivation of Rice and Wheat, in the heart of the village. Bagi provides a copy-book case of adverse effects of increasing pressures of population growth and human habitation on natural and common property resources.

The Transect of Bagi at Fig. 20.4 is indicative of the acute problems of soil erosion, in both the Eastern and Western flanks of the village on account of the streams flowing on the two sides. The problem of soil erosion has assumed crisis proportions, on account of vanishing forests and trees. The central portion of the village is affected by low soil fertility and pests (possibly due to reduction in bio-mass availability following deforestation). The development of the village economy, the villagers feel, therefore, largely depends on preventing soil erosion on account of deforestation (for the Eastern and Western flanks of the village); providing irrigation facilities for the central "table", development of pasture land and providing pesticides.

(iii) Village *Majri Grant* is located on the either side of bypass road from Bhaniyawala Atakfarm. It is 12 km due east from Doiwala Block headquarters. On the eastern side, it is bounded by Chiddarwala, on the western side by Bhaniyawala, on the northern side by Jauligrant and on the South by Kansaro Reserve forest. The village is well drained by the Song and the Jakhan Rao rivers. It has very fertile land.

At Figs. 20.5 and 20.6 are Historical Transect and Transect of village Majri Grant.

The village is situated more or less on flat contours. The Historical Transect at Fig. 20.5 indicates that there has been serious depletion of forest resources since the turn of the century. The extremely well endowed forest of Symal, Pipal, Shisham and Haldu have been destroyed both on account of settlement of human beings which has increased very sharply, and on account of extension in agriculture, leading to forests being cleared and used for cultivation, in the main, for Rice and Wheat cultivation. The intrusion of industry has also caused considerable damage to the natural vegetation.

The Transect at Fig. 20.6 indicates that the problems of the area are soil erosion, pest attacks, low soil fertility and drought. A good deal of soil erosion is caused by the rivers that bound the village. As in other villages, which we have mentioned, unscientific mining of river beds for sand, boulders and limestone "chips" have raised the river beds along their central course, while the banks are exposed to the onslaught of swift flowing water during monsoons. This is so despite the Soil Conservation Department, Government of Uttar Pradesh, having built embankments/retention walls and spurs. It is maintained, that

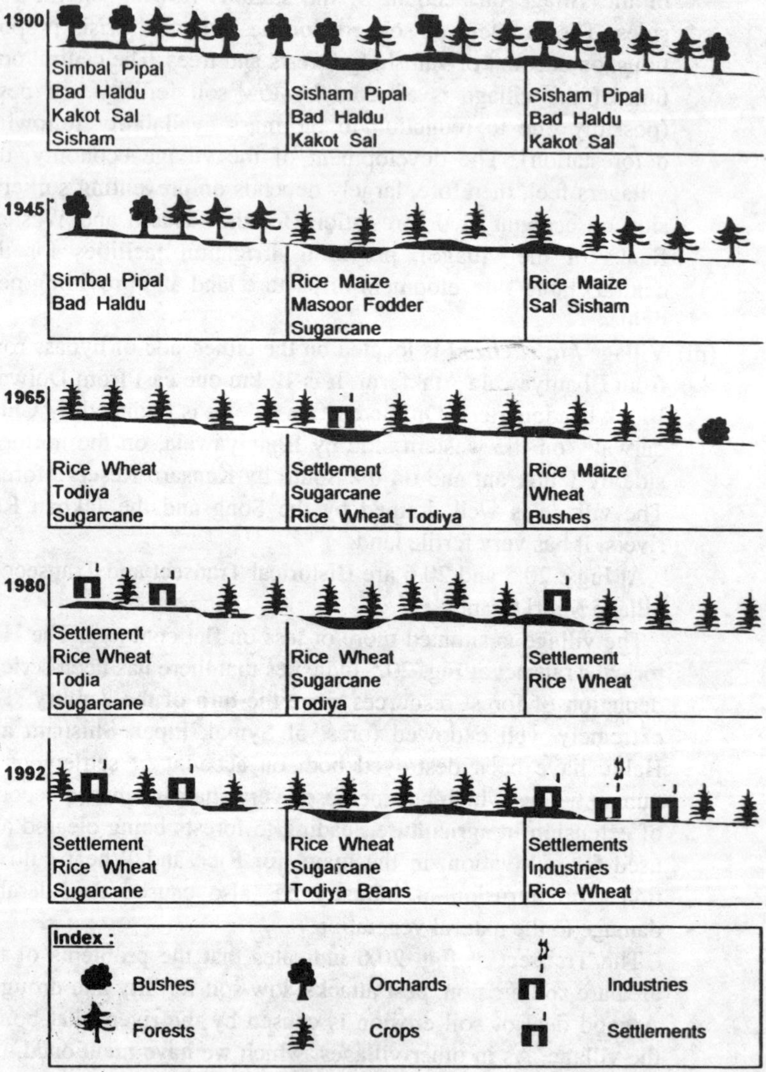

FIG. 20.5: **Transect Through Time. Illustration of Landuse Trend in Majrigrant Village in Doiwala Block**

while the setting up of the Spurs has been technically unsound, these have been accompanied by unscientific mining of river bed resources.

Development of the area, as perceived by the villagers of

Majri Grant, will naturally depend upon providing irrigation facilities, encouraging flood recession-farming, providing fuel-wood in order to preserve whatever little remains of the once rich forest and providing socio-economic infrastructure. The situation not surprisingly in Majri Grant clearly depicts what would normally be expected, namely, problems associated with loss of water aquifers and soil erosion, if forests are recklessly cleared.

SOIL	Sandy	Loam Sandy	Gravel	Loam	Gravel Sandy
LANDSUE	Farmland Village	Farmland village	Watershed Barren Land Forest	Farmland	Farmland Forest Barren land Village
CROP & VEGETATION	Sugarcane Paddy Wheat	Sugarcane Paddy	Sal Sisham	Sugarcane Paddy Wheat	Sugarcane Wheat Todia Maize Oilseed
PROBLEMS	Pests	Pests Erosion	Pests	Erosion	Drought Pests Low Fertility
OPPORTUNITIES	Pesticides	Banks Hospital Co-operative Society	Fuelwood Timber wood	Flood Recession Farming	Irrigation Pesticides

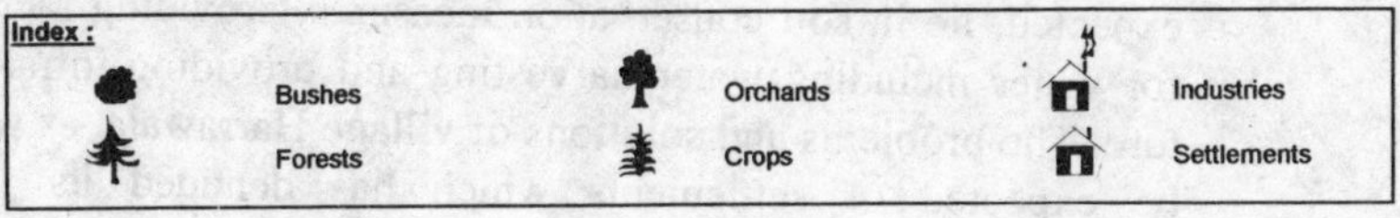

FIG. 20.6: Transect of Majri Grant Village

(iv) Village *Harrawala* is located on both sides of Dehradun Hardwar road. It is 10 km. away from Dehradun city. The village, on the eastern side is bounded by Bakrana, on the west by village Joggiwala and Bulandi Nadi, on the north by Balawala and on the south by Bulandi Nadi.

The village is mainly inhabited by agricultural and other labourers, marginal farmers, and around five big landlords.

Figs. 20.7 and 20.8 relate to village Harrawala. The situation in Harrawala roughly approximates the situation in Majri Grant: what was once a well endowed forest area has been taken away by human settlements and cultivation of commercial crops. The impacts of a growing urban agglomeration in Dehradun are clearly to be seen particularly with regard to a good build up of infrastructural facilities and loss of forest cover to make way for housing etc. The Historical Transect at Fig. 20.7 makes it quite clear that between 1900 and 1992 there has been a steady decline in forest, orchards and tea gardens, and a concurrently steady increase in number of settlements, sugarcane growers and cultivation of paddy. In this case the major problems of the village relate to soil erosion, drought, and low fertility of soil and pests, problems that are invariably associated with reduction in tree cover, on a grand scale. Fortunately, Harrawala is spared of an accentuated problem of soil erosion exerbated by mining of river bed (banks).

The solutions to the problems, suggested by the villagers as is expected, lie in soil conservation measures, providing facilities for water including water harvesting and providing infrastructure. The problems and solutions of village Harrawala, as would be expected of settlements which has denuded its forest resources, and which is near a growing urban agglomeration, have to be tackled both on a short-term and a long-term basis.

Though secondary data reveal that considerable portion of agricultural land has irrigation facilities in terms of tubewells and canals, yet availability of water for irrigation is a problem. This is so because with the population pressure increasing, and with both extensification and intensification of agriculture, the drawal of water has increased several folds, causing the water-table to fall, rendering much of the sources of irrigation dysfunctional at those times of the year when water is needed most.

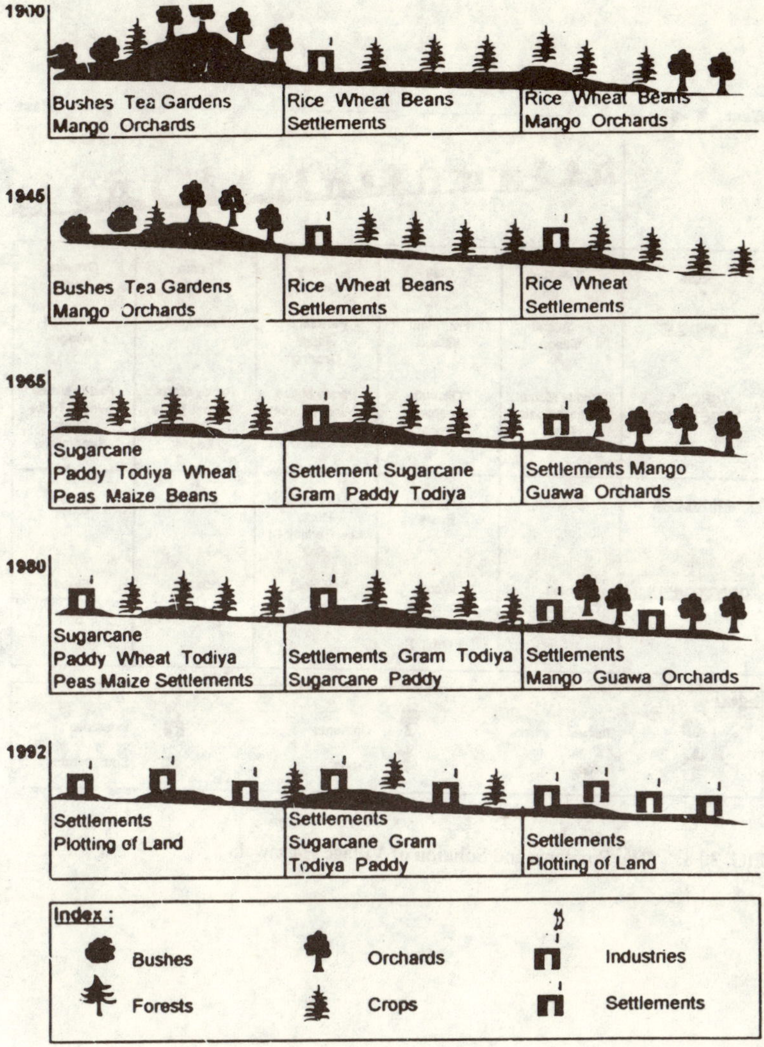

FIG. 20.7: Transect Through Time. Illustration of Landuse Trend in Harrawala Village in Block Doiwala

(v) Village *Nagal Jwalapur* is located 7 km. due west from Doiwala on Doiwala-Dudhali road. It is a forest fringe village originally inhabited by Bogas and Chamars (SC) of plains. Kumaonies from Almora, Pithoragarh and Nainital districts migrated to the village, subsequently, purchased land from

SOIL	Loam	Clay	Sandy Gravel	Loam Clay	Gravrel Clay
LANDSUE	Farmland Village	Farmland Village	Farmland Village Grazing	Farmland	Farmland Village
CROP & VEGETATION	Paddy Maize Wheat Todia Peas	Oilseed Sugarcane Peas	Paddy Maize Wheat Todia Peas	Paddy Maize Wheat Todia Peas Beans	Paddy Maize Wheat Todia Peas Sugarcane
PROBLEMS	Erosion	Drought Pests	Drought Pests Low Fertility Of Soil	Erosion	Drought Pests
OPPORTUN'TIES	Soil Conservation	Water Transport Rainfed Farming	Rainfed Farming	Canal	Flood recession farming Soil Conservation

Index :

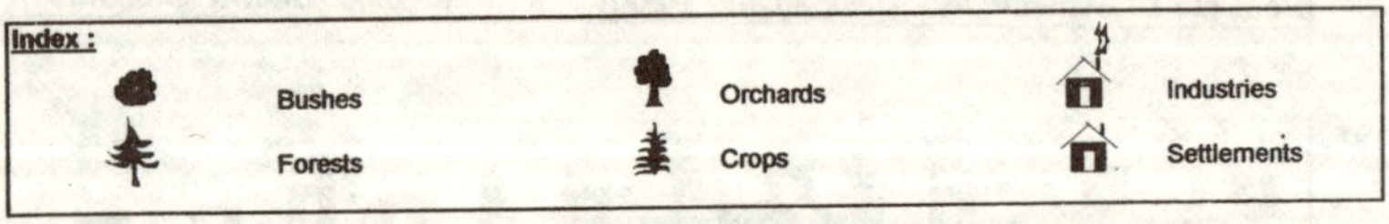

FIG. 20.8: The Problems and Solution of Village Harrawala

Bogas and settled down. At present, around 40 Kumaoni families inhabit the village. The condition of Bogas is miserable, for whatever land they own is mortgaged to the land development bank. There are some big farm houses, where the people belong to SCs apparently work as bonded labourers.

Figures 20.9 and 20.10 provide the Historical Transect and the Transect respectively of this village, Nagal Jwalapur. The history of this village makes an interesting reading. The Historical Transect reveals that at the beginning of the 20th century, this village was situated on the banks of a small river but the river had moved away from the village by the middle of the century. At the turn of century, because of the availability of the river water, this village had orchards, Wheat, Maize and Paddy fields and human settlements. Upto the middle of the sixties there was growth in orchards, but, thereafter, the orchards vanished giving way to cash crop farming which had just began to appear during the 60's by the end of the last decade. Within a period of ten years, orchards which provided valuable nutrition and food to the rural poor particularly during hunger periods, were replaced by cash crops, making in-roads into the food security of the villagers.[10]

The current problems faced by the village, as explained by the villagers of Nagal Jwalapur, are soil erosion on account of the felling of the trees, drought and problems of availability and use of high-yielding variety seeds. Curiously enough the villagers indicated that the wild animals caused extensive damage to their crops and posed a real problem to their livelihood. It was explained during the Semi-Structured Interview, that vanishing orchards provide *one* answer to the problem, for, whereas before and during the 1960's, wild animals could feed on food/fodder provided by the fruit trees, now, with the dwindling area under orchards, the wild animals attack the crops to meet their food requirement.

(vi) *Khadri Kharak Mauf* village is located on the right flank of Rishikesh-Hardwar-Highway. It is on the bank of river Ganga. The village was inhabited by saints and sages. The *Bogas* (a S.C people) worked for these saints and sages, who have now migrated to Hardwar and Rishikesh. The Bogas sold a major portion of their land to the inhabitants of nearby villages.

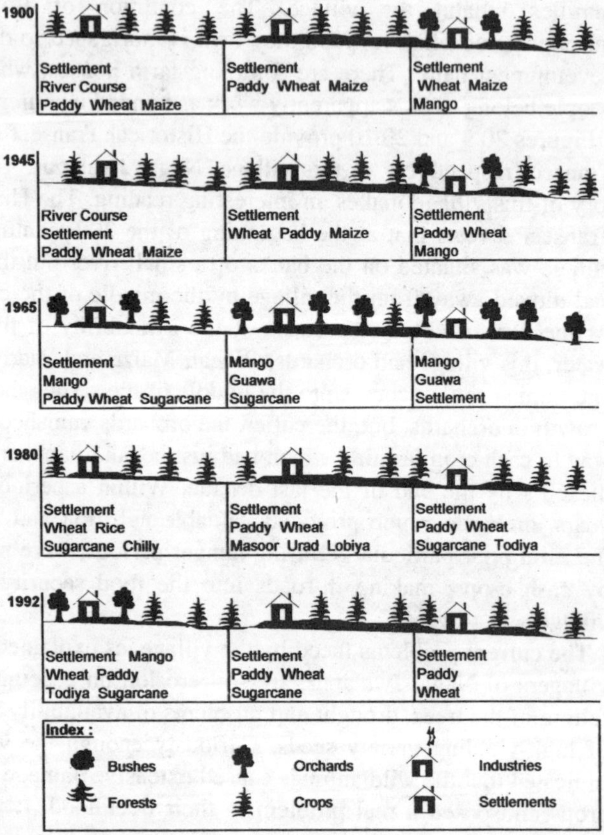

FIG. 20.9: **Transect Through Time. Illustration of Landuse Trend in Nagal Jwalapur Village in Block Doiwala**

Reference is invited to Figures 20.11 and 20.12 provide the Historical Transect and Transect for Village Khadri Kharak Mauf.

The Khadri Kharak Mauf village in Doiwala is another study of human depredation causing extensive damage to well stocked forests that once stood on the land now occupied by huts and settlements. At the beginning of this century most of the settlement was located on the western half of the village, the eastern segment being used for cultivation of food crops such as Paddy

SOIL	Sandy Gravel	Sandy Gravel	Loam	Loam	Loam
LANDSUE	Settlement Orchards Farmland	Settlement Orchards Farmland	Settlement Farmland	Settlement Farmland	Settlement Farmland
CROP & VEGETATION	Paddy Wheat Sugarcane Mango	Paddy Wheat Sugarcane	Paddy Wheat Sugarcane	Paddy Wheat Sugarcane	Paddy Wheat Sugarcane
PROBLEMS	Erosion Low Ferlitity Drought Pest	Erosion Pests HYV seeds Wild Animals	Drought HYV seeds	Drought HYV seeds	Drought HYV seeds
OPPORTUNITIES	Tubewells Seeds to be Available at Proper place	Pesticides Schools Drinking Water	Canal Hospital Road Seeds to be Available at Proper place	Pesticides Check Dams	

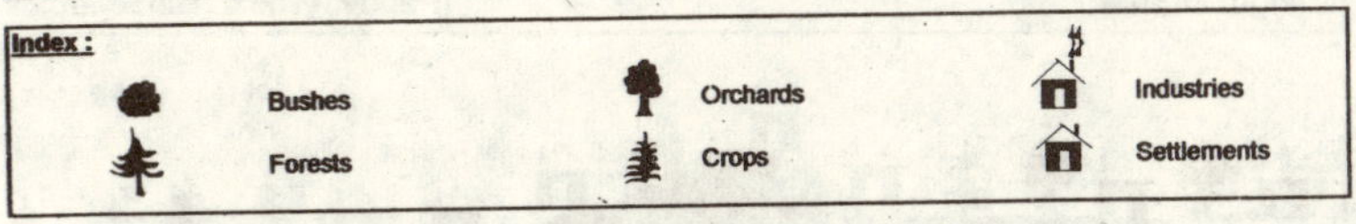

FIG. 20.10: Problems and Solutions of Nagal Jawalapur Village

and Wheat. The central "zone" of the village which is located at an elevation, comprise the core forest area. Some forests were also found on the extreme west. By the 1960's, extension in

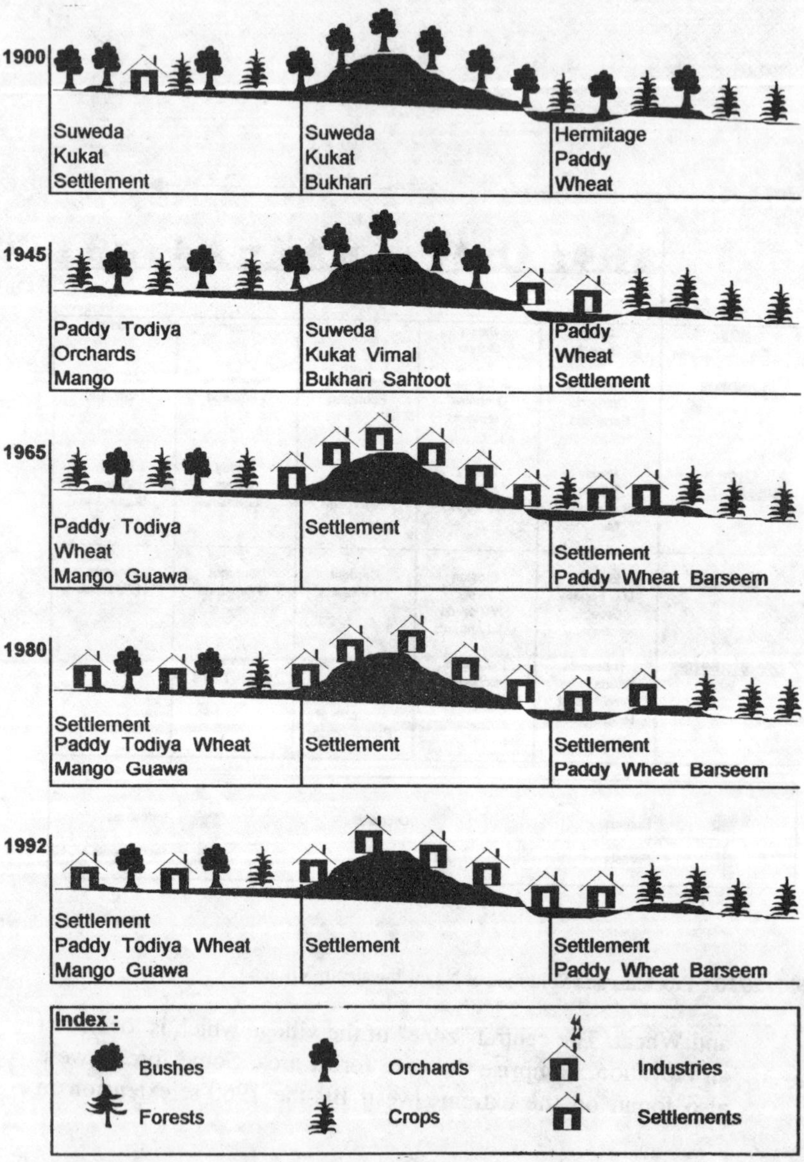

FIG. 20.11: Transect Through Time. Illustration of Landuse Trend in Khadari Kharak Maph Village in Block Doiwala

cultivation made inroads into much of the area where once stood good forest (on the western part of the village). The hutments gradually shifted eastwards over the hillock, concurrently and also encroaching on to the eastern portion. Subsequently, the denudation of forests continued unabated as population pressure took an upturn and the number of human settlements in the village increased markedly.

Contemporaneous scenario obtaining in the village is not something which is not inviting. It would be apparent from Fig. 20.12 that the villagers perceive drought, poor water supply, soil erosion and lack of infrastructure as constituting the core problems. The solutions that people suggested naturally lie in construction of check dams and water chambers on both sides of the hillock that occupies the central stage of the village. It is also necessary to construct canals on both western and eastern portion in order to provide water for cultivation that has since begun on lands previously under forests.

(vii) *Balawala* village is about 15 km. due east of Dehradun city. On the east of village flows river Song, on the west lies Mohakampur; on the north is Nathuwala and on the south it is bordered by Harrawala. The village has plenty of agricultural land. The village is inhabited mainly by the hill people, namely Garhwalis and the people belonging SC of the plains.

Balawala at the turn of the century was a picture of forest, with the little cultivation and very few human settlements, as would be apparent from the Historical Transect of the village at Fig. 20.13. By the end of Second World War, the picture changed where considerable tracts of forest were cleared for extensification of agriculture, particularly of paddy, wheat and cash crops like sugarcane, with human settlements and some forest occupying the central segment/middle of the village and a portion of its Western fringe. By the beginning of last decade much of whatever remained of the vastly depleted forest was cleared. The village now consists of human settlements and arable land under an even larger number of cash crops (such as tomato and sugarcane) and food crops (paddy and wheat).

The Transect of Balawala at Fig. 20.14 reflects the concern of the people for the effects of the denuded forest, namely, pests, lack of fodder and fuel, and lack of water. This implies that the women folk of the village have to put in longer hours of work to

SOIL	Sand	Sand	Gravel	Sandy Loam	Clay
LANDSUE	Settlement Orchards Farmland	Settlement Orchards Farmland	Settlement	Settlement Orchards Farmland	Orchards
CROP & VEGETATION	Paddy Wheat Sugarcane Todia Jawar	Paddy Wheat Sugarcane Mango Todia		Paddy Wheat Fodder Papaya Vegegable Todia	Paddy Wheat Sugarcane Barseem
PROBLEMS	Drought	Drought Poor Water Supply	Road Poor Water Supply Electricity	Drought Erosion	Erosion Road
OPPORTUNITIES	Branch Canal	Water Chamber	Metalled road Canal	Check Dams Canal	Check Dams Canal

Index :

Bushes · Orchards · Industries

Forests · Crops · Settlements

FIG. 20.12: Problems and Solutions of Khadari Kharak Maph Village

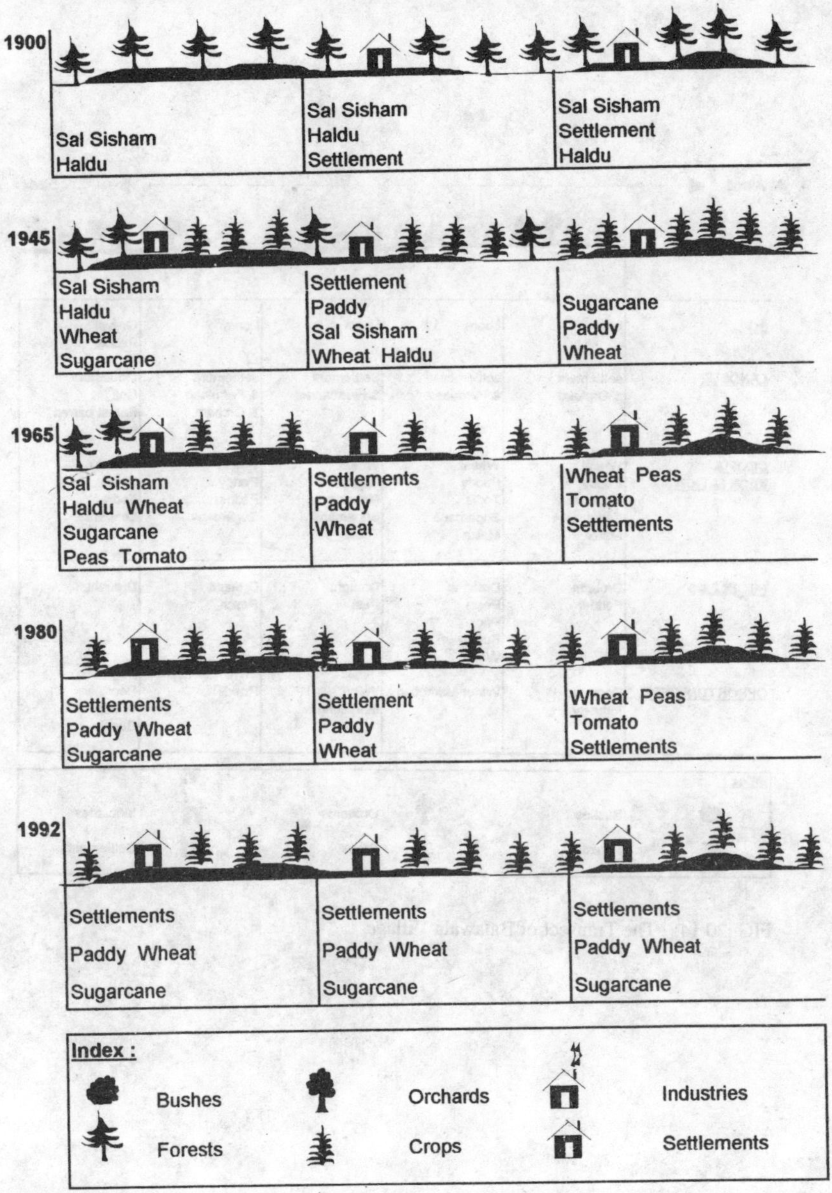

FIG. 20.13: Transect Through Time. Illustration of Landuse Trend in Balawala Village in Doiwala Block

West ← → East

SOIL	Loam	Loam	Loam	Loam	Gravel Pebble
LANDSUE	settlement & Orchard	settlement & Farmland	Settlement & Farmland	settlement & Farmland & Orchard	Industrial Unit Forest barren land
CROP & VEGETATION	Wheat Paddy Sugarcane Todia Maize	Wheat Paddy Todia Sugarcane Maize	Wheat Paddy Maizw Sugarcane Todia	Wheat Paddy Fodder Sugarcane	Factory Wheat Todia Lentana
PROBLEMS	Drought Fodder	Drought Pests Poor Supply of Water	Drought Pest	Drought Pests	Drought
OPPORTUNITIES	Cogttege Industry	Water Marketing	Water Marketing	Road	Poor Water Supply

Index :

Bushes — Orchards — Industries

Forests — Crops — Settlements

FIG. 20.14: The Transect of Balawala Village

collect fuel, fodder and drinking water. The problems in themselves suggest the need for quick solutions, to prevent a collapse of the environmental and eco-system. It is important, the people of the village indicated, to provide irrigation facilities and improve the supply of water for non-agricultural purposes.

The sources of irrigation have a wide command area, but the availability of water is seriously circumscribed by a fall in water-table and poor availability of water during lean seasons when it was required most.

(viii) *Ranipokhari* is a village mainly inhabited by the Garhwalis and people belong to scheduled castes of the plains. It is 10 km. due east of Doiwala on Dehradun-Rishikesh road. The village is rich in agricultural land. A few industries have been set-up in the village over the last decade. Most of the households of the village are in a comfortable position, and are aware of the Government schemes such as Jawahar Rozgar Yojana (JRY) etc.

Most of the land in the village has a steep gradient, and slopes from the east to west. The picture here is a quite similar to what was observed in Balawala, namely, that between the 1900 (approximately) and now, large tracts of forest of sal, toon and shisham were cleared for human habitation, and along with it, for extensification of agriculture. Since the beginning of the last decade small industrial units have come up to further destroy forest, as a result of which, today, the village has a landuse pattern which consists of human settlements and some orchards with cultivation as its central activity. Forests are gone. A disquitening feature in one sense is that considerable amount of land under food crops has been replaced by cash crops, indicating that self-sustaining food-security of the village has been replaced by "exchange entitlement" based food security.

As in case of most other villages under study, villagers of Ranipokhari thought the problems of Ranipokhari were also lack of water, drought and soil erosion. Its development perspective would, therefore, have to be informed, the common people felt, in terms of the need to have check dams, development of water resources for irrigation and pesticides.

Findings and Conclusions

Thus our wanderings through these villages indicate that the meaning of development as understood by the common man lay in the realm of halting the diminution in the availability of bio-mass, prevention of soil erosion, provision of water for cultivation and in one case social/economic overheads. The concern for natural resource management even if implicit, is central to the meaning of development

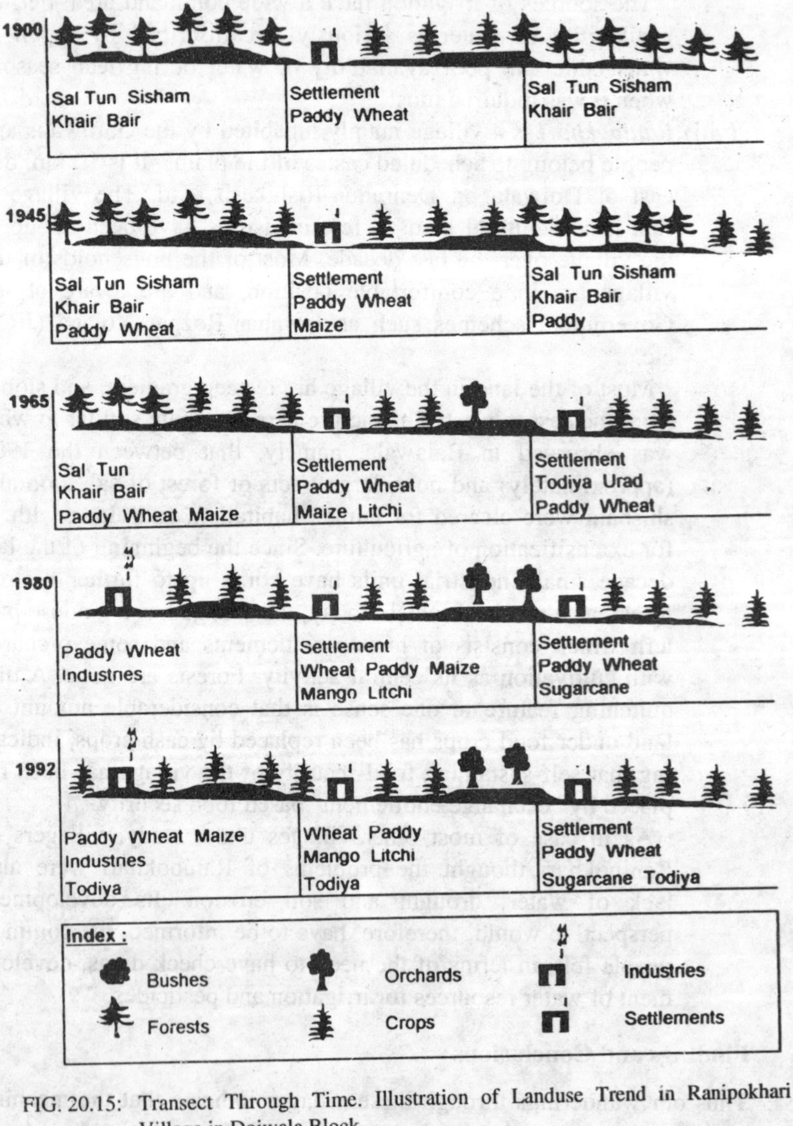

FIG. 20.15: Transect Through Time. Illustration of Landuse Trend in Ranipokhari Village in Doiwala Block

SOIL	Gravel & Clay	Clay	Sand & Gravel	Sand & Gravel	Sand & Gravel
LAND USE	Watershed of Jakhan Rao Forest	Settlement Farmland & Industrial Units	Settlement & Orchards	Farmland & Settlement	Forest Settlement Farmland Orchards
CROP & VEGETATION	Sisham Bair Khair Kikar	Barseem Jai Chari Paddy	Mango & Litchi	Paddy Sugar-Cane Wheat Todiya Tur	Bushes Kikar Bair Paddy Wheat Todiya Mango
PROBLEMS	Erosion	Erosion Drought HYV Seeds	Drought Pest	Low fertility HYV seed Drought pests	Erosion Drought
OPPORTUNITIES	Check Dams Bending	Check Dams &Construction of Canals	Water College Technical Education	Pesticides HYV seeds Irrigation Facility	Check Dams

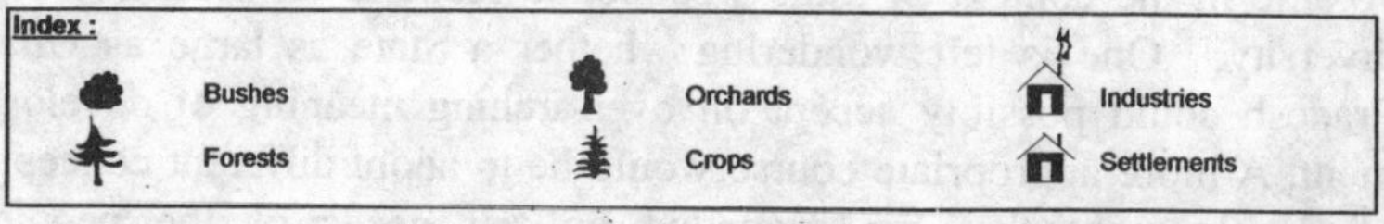

FIG. 20.16: Problems and Solutions of Ranipokhari Village

harboured by the people at the grassroots level. This is so because their understanding of development is based on problems and opportunities at the micro-level as obtaining at the ground condition. Thus development in U.P's Eighth Five-Year Plan based on growth in per capita income or even income per se, reduction in the number of unemployed and population control, would seem to be out of tune, in several cases, with development as is acceptable to the people. Environment has no place the meaning of development thus adopted. The State's Five-Year Plan would have been much better aligned with the hopes and aspirations of the people if it were grounded on availability (and hence growth) of bio-mass per se or availability of bio-mass per capita. Development, so informed, would be much more sound on environmental considerations as well. The following discussion would further clarify the issues.

The meaning of development for the common man is, clearly markedly different from the meaning of development, looked at from "above", because the problems faced by the common man have emerged from causes other than those emanating from low employment, low productivity and minute incremental growth in income. While the concept of development harboured by the experts, technocrats, bureaucrats and the political executive is based on a "bird's eye view" of the economy, far removed from the scene of action, meaning of development for the common man is born out of a "worm's view" generated at the actual scene of action. Small wonder then that there is wide divergence in the meaning of development as accepted by the common man which has environment built into it in terms of prevention of soil erosion and planting of trees *vis-a-vis* the meaning of development in terms of growth in income and employment, expounded by the planners and experts, to whose care the exercise of planning is entrusted.

Even at the cost of suffering the stricture of being repetitive, we reiterate that development is a relative concept and becomes even more volatile in the context of India's economic scenario on account of its diversity.[11] One is left wondering whether a State as large as Uttar Pradesh could possibly accept on over-arching meaning of development. A more appropriate course would be to adopt different concepts of development that are grounded on felt needs of the people, separately for each of the several regions in the State, howsoever, defined: agro-climatic zones or sub-zones, or hills, plains or what have you. The analysis of each Panchayat (or better still each community) within that region may be viewed as representing the micro-view. Then alone can development be achieved by protecting local environment.

To develop, foster, nurture and operationalise such a concept of development, it is no longer possible to conduct a planning exercise in a centralised format. True decentralisation is the only solution: decentralization in planning is necessary upto the smallest level possible. It would only then the possible adopt and understand development which is in tune with what the people want, with what the common man considers his immediate concern, and which articulates people's perception(s). In all other cases probably the meaning of development is a "reflection" of what the technocrats and bureaucrats, based on secondary data and imperfect information, "sell" to their political masters as being development that people want. The Constitution (Seventy Third Amendment) Act 1993, holds some promise of progress in this regard. Hark these words:

Subject to the provisions of this Constitution, the Legislature of a State may, by law, endow the Panchayats with such powers and authority as may be necessary to enable them to function as institutions of self-government and such law may contain provisions for the devolution of powers and responsibilities upon Panchayats at the appropriate level, subject to such condition as may be specified therein, with respect to:

(a) the preparation of plans for economic development and social justice;
(b) the implementation of schemes for economic development and social justice as may be entrusted to them including those in relation to the matters listed in the Eleventh Schedule." (Eleventh Schedule is at Table 20.2).

The extent to which it would be possible to adopt a development paradigm, grounded on collective wisdom of the community will be determined by the sincerity and speed with which the provision of the Seventy Second (Constitution Amendment Bill), 1991 are operationalised. One hastens to add that unless the meaning of development of the State are aligned with the development paradigm articulated by collected wisdom, the likelihood of the State's development energy being lost, looms excessively large. This explains why population control which conditions development efforts of the country and the State, make no headway, because, as is revealed by the Transects, it figures nowhere in the agenda of the common man's primary concern.[12]

TABLE 20.2: Eleventh Schedule (of the Constitution (Seventy Second Amendment Bill, 1991)

1. Agriculture, including agricultural extension.
2. Land improvement and soil conservation.
3. Minor irrigation, water management and watershed development.
4. Animal Husbandry, dairying and poultry.
5. Fisheries.
6. Social forestry and farm forestry.
7. Minor forest produce.
8. Small scale industries, including food processing industries.
9. Khadi, village and cottage industries.
10. Rural housing.
11. Drinking water.
12. Fuel and fodder.
13. Roads, culverts, bridges, ferries, waterways and other means of communication.
14. Rural electrification, including distribution of electricity.
15. Non-conventional energy sources.
16. Poverty alleviation programmes.
17. Education, including primary and secondary schools.
18. Technical training and vocational education.
19. Adult and non-formal education.
20. Libraries.
21. Cultural activities.
22. Markets and fairs.
23. Health and sanitation, including hospitals, primary health centres and dispensaries.
24. Family welfare.
25. Women and child development.
26. Social welfare, including welfare of the handicapped and mentally retarded.
27. Welfare of the weaker sections, and in particular, of the Scheduled Castes and the Scheduled Tribes.
28. Public distribution system.
29. Maintenance of community assets.

TABLE 20.3: Secondary Data About Villages

I. Mohamadpur Barkali

1. Name of the Village : Mohamadpur Barkali;
   Block : Doiwala
   District/State : Dehradun (U.P).
   Area of Village : 140.03 Hectares

Population:	Male	Female	Total	SC	ST
As per 1981 census	52	43	95	0	0

(Contd.)

TABLE 20.3 *(Contd.)*

2. Total No. of Households: 16

3. Landuse pattern:

(i)	Total Geographical Area	140.03 hectares
(ii)	Area not available for Agricultural use	59.09 hectares
(iii)	Other Uncultivable land	8.50 hectares
(iv)	Total area under	
	(a) Net cultivation	31.97 hectares
	(b) Forest	40.47 hectares

4.

(i)	Area under irrigation	40.47 hectares
(ii)	Main source of irrigation	River

5. Basic Amenities:

(i)	Whether village is electrified	Yes
(ii)	Railway Station within 5 kms.	No
(iii)	Metalled road within 2 kms.	Yes
(iv)	Bus stop within 2 kms.	No
(v)	Post office within 2 kms.	No
(vi)	Primary school within 2 kms.	No
(vii)	High/Higher Secondary School within 5 kms.	No
(viii)	Dispensary/PHC within 2 kms.	No
(ix)	Hospital (within 5 kms.)	No
(x)	Safe drinking water source within 1.6 kms. (1 mile)	Yes
(xi)	Fertilizer depot within 5 kms.	No
(xii)	Bank (Cooperative Bank, Gramin Bank) within 5 kms.	No
(xiii)	Seeds store within 5 kms.	No
(xiv)	Veterinary dispensary within 5 kms.	No
(xv)	Fair price shop within 2 kms.	No
(xvi)	Police station within 5 kms.	No
(xvii)	Grain Mandi. *Haat* within 5 kms.	No
(xviii)	Adult literacy centre	No

II. Bagi Village

1. Name of Village : Bagi
Block : Doiwala
District/State : Dehradun, U.P.
Area of Village : 58.68 hectares

Population:	Male	Females	Total	S.C.	S.T.
As per 1981 census	95	85	180	3	1

(Contd.)

TABLE 20.3 *(Contd.)*

2.	Total No. of Households:		34
3.	Landuse Pattern:		
	(i)	Total Geographical Area	58.68 hectares
	(ii)	Area not available for agricultural use	6.47 hectares
	(iii)	Other uncultivable land such permanent pastures, cultivable waste etc.	12.1 hectares
	(iv)	Total area under—	
		(a) Forest	29.95 hectares
		(b) Net cultivation	21.02 hectares
4.	(i)	Area under irrigation	1.62 hectares
	(ii)	Main source of irrigation	Guls
5.	Basic Amenities:		
	(i)	Whether village is electrified	Yes
	(ii)	Railway Station within 5 kms.	No
	(iii)	Metalled road within 2 kms.	Yes
	(iv)	Bus stop within 2 kms.	Yes
	(v)	Post office within 2 kms.	No
	(vi)	Primary school within 2 kms.	Yes
	(vii)	High/Higher Secondary school with 5 kms.	Yes
	(viii)	Dispensary/PHC within 2 kms.	No
	(ix)	Hospital (within 5 kms.)	Yes
	(x)	Safe drinking water source within 1.6 kms. (1 mile)	Yes
	(xi)	Fertilizer depot within 5 kms.	No
	(xii)	Bank (Cooperative Bank, Gramin Bank) with 5 kms.	No
	(xiii)	Seeds store within 5 kms.	No
	(xiv)	Veterinary dispensary within	No
	(xv)	Fair price shop within 2 kms.	Yes
	(xvi)	Police station within 5 kms.	No
	(xvii)	Grain Mandi/*Haat* within 5 kms.	No
	(xviii)	Adult literacy centre	No

III. Majri Grant

1.	Name of the Village	:	Majri Grant
	Block	:	Doiwala
	District/State	:	Dehradun, U.P.
	Area of Village	:	1328.59 hectare

Population:	Males	Females	Total	S.C.	S.T.
As per 1981 census	2752	2297	5049	492	22

(Contd.)

TABLE 20.3 *(Contd.)*

2.Total No. of Households :		802	
3. Landuse pattern			
(i)	Total Geographical Area	1328.59 hectares	
(ii)	Area not available for Agricultural use	286.11 hectares	
(iii)	Other uncultivable land such as permanent pastures, cultivable waste etc.	39.66 hectares	
(iv)	Total area under		
(a)	Forests	21.04 hectares	
(b)	Net cultivation	981.78 hectares	
4. (i)	Area under irrigation	880.61 hectares	
(ii)	Main source of irrigation	Tubewell, canal	
5. Cottage industries if any		None	
(i)	Any other industry	Food Flex, Birla Yamaha	
6. Rural Development IRDP/NREP/RLEGP/DWCRA?TRYSEM/JRY			Yes
7. Basic Amenities			
(i)	Whether village is electrified	Yes	Lal Tappar Hamlet is not electrified
(ii)	Railway station within 5 kms.	Yes	
(iii)	Metalled road within 2 kms.	Yes	
(iv)	Bus stop within 2 kms.	Yes	
(v)	Post office within 2 kms.	Yes	
(vi)	Primary school within 2 kms.	Yes	
(vii)	High/Higher Secondary school within 5 kms.	Yes	
(viii)	Dispensary/PHC within 2 kms.	Yes	
(ix)	Hospital within 5 kms.	No	
(x)	Safe drinking water source	Yes	
(xi)	Fertilizer depot within 5 kms.	No	
(xii)	Bank (Cooperative Bank, Gramin Bank) within 5 kms.	No	
(xiii)	Seeds store within 5 kms.	No	
(xiv)	Veterinary dispensary within 5 kms.	No	
(xv)	Fair price shop within 2 kms.	Yes	
(xvi)	Police Station within 5 kms.	No	
(xvii)	Grain Mandi/*Haat* within 5 kms.	Yes	
(xviii)	Adult Literacy Centre	No	

IV. Harrawala

1. Name of the village	:	Harrawala
Block	:	Doiwala

(Contd.)

TABLE 20.3 *(Contd.)*

	District/State	:	Dehradun/U.P.			
	Area of Village	:	161.87 hectare			
	Population:	Male	Females	Total	SC	ST
	As per 1981 census	858	721	1579	790	0
2.	Total No. of households :		1579			

3.		Landuse pattern	
	(i)	Total Geographical Area	161.87 hectare
	(ii)	Area not available for agricultural use	30.35 hectare
	(iii)	Other uncultivable land such as permanent pastures, cultivable waste etc.	0.41 hectare
	(iv)	Total area under	
		(a) Forest	0.00 hectare
		(b) Net cultivation	13.11 hectare
		(c) Cultivable waste	0.41 hectare
		(d) Not available for cultivation	30.35 hectare
4.	(i)	Area under irrigation	110.48
	(ii)	Main source of irrigation	Tubewell, Canal
5.		Cottage Industries if any :	None
	(i)	Any other industry :	Calcium Industries
6.		Rural Development IRDP/JRY/TRYSEM :	Yes
7.		Basic Amenities	
	(i)	Whether village is electrified	Yes
	(ii)	Railway station within 5 kms.	Yes
	(iii)	Metalled road within 2 kms.	Yes
	(iv)	Bus stop within 2 kms.	Yes
	(v)	Post office within 2 kms.	Yes
	(vi)	Primary school within 2 kms.	Yes
	(vii)	High/Higher Secondary school within 5 kms.	Yes
	(viii)	Dispensary/PHC within 2 kms.	Yes
	(ix)	Hospital (within 5 kms.)	No
	(x)	Safe drinking water source	Yes
	(xi)	Fertilizer depot within 5 kms.	Yes
	(xii)	Bank (Cooperative Bank, Gramin Bank) within 5 kms.	Yes
	(xiii)	Seeds store within 5 kms.	Yes
	(xiv)	Veterinary dispensary within 5 kms.	Yes
	(xv)	Fair price shop within 2 kms.	Yes
	(xvi)	Police station within 5 kms.	Yes
	(xvii)	Grain/*Haat* within 5 kms.	No
	(xviii)	Adult literacy centre	No

(Contd.)

TABLE 20.3 *(Contd.)*

V. Nagal Jwalapur

1.	Name of the Village	:	Nagal Jwalapur			
	Block	:	Doiwala			
	District/State	:	Dehradun, U.P.			
	Area of the village	:	163.49 hectares			
	Population:	Males	Females	Total	SC	ST
	As per 1981 census	388	308	696	390	72
2.	Total No. of Households	:		125		
3.	Landuse pattern:					
	(i) Total Geographical area	:		163.49 hectares		
	(ii) Area not available for agricultural use			13.35 hectares		
	(iii) Other uncultivable land such as permanent pastures cultivable waste			4.85 hectares		
	(iv) Total area under					
	(a) Forests			0.00 hectares		
	(b) Net cultivation			145.29 hectares		
4.	(i) Area under irrigation			144.88 hectares		
	(ii) Main source of irrigation			River		
5.	Cottage Industries if any:					
	(i) Spinning Weaving			Nil		
	(ii) Any other industry			Nil		
6.	Rural Development IRDP/JRY/TRYSEM			Yes		
7.	Basic Amenities					
	(i) Whether village is electrified			Yes		
	(ii) Railway station within 5 kms.			No		
	(iii) Metalled road within 2 kms.			Yes		
	(iv) Bus stop within 2 kms.			Yes		
	(v) Post office within 2 kms.			No		
	(vi) Primary school within 2 kms.			Yes		
	(vii) High/Higher Secondary school within 5 kms.			No		
	(viii) Dispensary/PHC within 2 kms.			No		
	(ix) Hospital (within 5 kms.)			No		
	(x) Safe drinking water source within 1.6 kms. (1 mile)			Yes		
	(xi) Fertilizer depot within 5 kms.			No		
	(xii) Bank (Cooperative Bank, Gramin Bank) within 5 kms.			Yes		
	(xiii) Seeds store within 5 kms.			Yes		

(Contd.)

TABLE 20.3 *(Contd.)*

(xiv)	Veterinary dispensary within 5 kms.	Yes
(xv)	Fair price shop within 2 kms.	Yes
(xvi)	Police station within 5 kms.	Yes
(xvii)	Grain Mandi/*Haat* within 5 kms.	Yes
(xviii)	Adult literacy centre	No

VI. **Balawala**

1. Name of the village : Balawala
   Block : Doiwala
   District/State : Dehradun, U.P.
   Area of village : 1070.03 hectares

Population:	Males	Females	Total	SC	ST
As per 1981 census	1958	1808	3766	287	238

2. No. of Households : 641
3. Landuse pattern:

(i)	Total Geographical area :	1070.03 hectares
(ii)	Area not available for agricultural use	34.81 hectares
(iii)	Other uncultivable land such as permanent pastures, cultivable wastes etc.	1.21 hectares
(iv)	Total area under	
	(a) Forests	414.01 hectares
	(b) Net cultivation	620.00 hectares
4. (i)	Area under irrigation	445.17 hectares
(ii)	Main source of irrigation	Canal, Tubewell
5.	Cottage industries if any	None
(i)	Any other industry	Bengal immunity and Windless industries
6.	Rural Development IRDP/JRY/TRYSEM	Yes
7.	Basic Amenities	
(i)	Whether village is electrified	Yes
(ii)	Railway station within 5 kms.	Yes
(iii)	Metalled road within 2 kms.	Yes
(iv)	Bus stop within 2 kms.	Yes
(v)	Post office within 2 kms.	Yes
(vi)	Primary school within 2 kms.	Yes
(vii)	High/Higher Secondary school within 5 kms.	Yes
(viii)	Dispensary/PHC within 2 kms.	Yes
(ix)	Hospital (within 5 kms.)	Yes

(Contd.)

TABLE 20.3 *(Contd.)*

(x)	Safe drinking water source within 1.6 kms. (1 mile)	Yes
(xi)	Fertilizer depot within 5 kms.	Yes
(xii)	Bank (Cooperative Bank, Gramin Bank) within 5 kms.	Yes
(xiii)	Seeds store within 5 kms.	No
(xiv)	Veterinary dispensary within 5 kms.	Yes
(xv)	Fair price shop within 2 kms.	Yes
(xvi)	Police station within 5 kms.	Yes
(xvii)	Grain Mandi/*Haat* within 5 kms.	Yes
(xviii)	Adult literacy centre	Yes

VII. **Ranipokhari**

1. Name of the Village : Ranipokhari
   Block : Doiwala
   District/State : Dehradun, U.P.
   Area of the Village : 179.27 hectares

Population:	Males	Females	Total	SC	ST
As per 1981 census	491	406	897	53	0

2. Total No. of households : 151
3. Landuse pattern:

(i)	Total Geographical area	179.27 hectares
(ii)	Area not available for agriculture use	27.52 hectares
(iii)	Other uncultivable land such as permanent pastures, cultivable waste etc.	7.68 hectares
(iv)	Total area under	
	(a) Forest	0.00 hectares
	(b) Net cultivation	144.00 hectares

4. (i) Area under irrigation — 132.74 hectares
   (ii) Main source of irrigation — Canal
5. Cottage industries if any — None
   (i) Any other industry — Cement, Polypack Nut, Bolt, Oil etc.
6. Rural Development
   IRDP/JRY/RIEGP/DWCRA/TRYSEM — Yes
7. Basic Amenities

(i)	Whether village is electrified	Yes
(ii)	Railway station within 5 kms.	No
(iii)	Metalled road within 2 kms.	Yes

(Contd.)

TABLE 20.3 *(Contd.)*

(iv)	Bus stop within 2 kms.	Yes
(v)	Post office within 2 kms.	Yes
(vi)	Primary school within 2 kms.	Yes
(vii)	High/Higher Secondary school within 5 kms.	Yes
(viii)	Dispensary/PHC within 2 kms.	Yes
(ix)	Hospital (within 5 kms.)	Yes
(x)	Safe drinking water source within 1.6 kms. (1 mile)	Yes
(xi)	Fertilizer depot within 5 kms.	Yes
(xii)	Bank (Cooperative Bank, Gramin Bank) within 5 kms.	Yes
(xiii)	Seeds store within 5 kms.	No
(xiv)	Veterinary dispensary within 5 kms.	Yes
(xv)	Fair price shop within 2 kms.	Yes
(xvi)	Police station within 5 kms.	Yes
(xvii)	Grain Mandi/*Haat* within 5 kms.	Yes
(xviii)	Adult literacy centre	Yes

VIII. **Khadri Kharak Maph**

1. Name of the Village : Khadri Kharak Maph
   Block : Doiwala
   District/State : Dehradun, U.P.
   Area of the Village : 179.27 hectares

Population: as per 1981 census	Males	Females	Total	SC	ST
	491	406	897	53	0

2.Total No. of Households 151

3.Landuse pattern:

(i)	Total Geographical area	179.27 hectares
(ii)	Area not available for agriculture use	27.52 hectares
(iii)	Other uncultivable land such as permanent pastures, cultivable waste etc.	7.68 hectares
(iv)	Total area under	
	(a) Forest	0.0 hectares
	(b) Net cultivation	144.00 hectares

4.	(i)	Area under irrigation	132.74 hectares
	(ii)	Main source of irrigation	Canal

(Contd.)

TABLE 20.3 *(Contd.)*

5.	Cottage industries if any	None
(i)	Any other industry	Cement, Polypack, Nut, Bolt, Oil etc.
6.	Rural Development IRDP/JRY/RLEGP/DWCRA/TRYSEM	Yes
7.	Basic Amenities	
(i)	Whether village is electrified	Yes
(ii)	Railway station within 5 kms.	No
(iii)	Metalled road within 2 kms.	Yes
(iv)	Bus stop within 2 kms.	Yes
(v)	Post office within 2 kms.	Yes
(vi)	Primary school within 2 kms.	Yes
(vii)	High/Higher Secondary school within 5 kms.	Yes
(viii)	Dispensary/PHC within 2 kms.	Yes
(ix)	Hospital within 5 kms.	Yes
(x)	Safe drinking water source within 1.6 kms. (1 mile)	Yes
(xi)	Fertilizer depot within 5 kms.	Yes
(xii)	Bank (Cooperative Bank, Gramin Bank) within 5 kms.	Yes
(xiii)	Seeds store within 5 kms.	No
(xiv)	Veterinary dispensary within 5 kms.	Yes
(xv)	Fair price shop within 2 kms.	Yes
(xvi)	Police station within 5 kms.	Yes
(xvii)	Grain Mandi/*Haat* within 5 kms.	Yes
(xviii)	Adult literacy centre	Yes

REFERENCES

1. Government of India (1991). *Directional Paper: Objectives, Thrusts and Macro-Dimensions of the Eighth Five-Year Plan 1992-97* (New Delhi: Planning Commission), December.
2. Government of India (1992). *The Eighth Five-Year Plan* (New Delhi: Planning Commission) draft placed before the Forty Fourth Meeting of the National Development Council, held on 22nd and 23rd May.
3. Idem.
4. Idem.
5. Chambers, Robert (1992). *Rural Appraisal: Rapid, Released and Participatory* (Sussex: Institute of Development Studies) Discussion Paper No. 311, October.
6. Mc Cracker, Jennifer; Pretty, Jules and Conway, Gordon (1988). *An Introduction to Rapid Rural Appraisal for Agricultural Development* (London: International Institute for Environment and Development), p. 3.
7. See Khon Kaen University (1985). *Proceedings of the 1985 International Con-*

ference on Rapid Rural Appraisal (Khon Kaen, Thailand: Rural Systems Research and Farming Systems Research Projects, Khon Kaen University), Part III. See also Chambers, Robert, *op. cit.*; and Mukherjee, Neela and Mukherjee, Amitava: *Rural Poverty, Habitat and Environment,* Manuscript.

8. Mc Cracker, Jennifer et al *op. cit.,* p. 20.
9. Theis, Joachim and Grady, Heather, M. (1991). *Participatory Rapid Appraisal for Community Development* London: International Institute for Environment and Development and Save the Children Federation, p. 87.
10. See Sen, A.K. (1981). *Poverty and Famines: Essays in Entitlement and Depravation*, Oxford: The Clarendon Press, and Dreze, Jeane and Sen, Amartya (1989). *Hunger and Public Action*, Oxford: Oxford University Press.
11. Idem.
12. No wonder, according to 1991 Census (provisional) figures the decadal growth in Dehradun population has been over 3 per cent per annum against a national growth of about 2.3 per cent per annum.

21

ECO-DEVELOPMENT:
A Case Study of Haryana

NINA SINGH

Recent thinking on the development process has expressed its great concern for fast depletion of resources and rapid deterioration of environment as a consequence of race for economic growth. Much of agricultural growth is seen as consumptive of minerals and forests. Pollution is the natural outcome. Ecology gets dangerously disturbed.

The paper intends to take a critical view of such ideas with a case study of Haryana. It dwells on the development – ecology question adopting an operational definition. This is followed by (i) a critical appraisal of the ecology of the area in question, and (ii) the concern felt for its maintenance/regulation.

Development – Ecology Nexus

Books such as *Silent Spring* (Carson, 1963), *The Closing Circle* (Commoner, 1972), *Limits to Growth* (Meadows, *et al.*, 1972), and *Mankind at the Turning Point* (Pestel, *et al.*, 1974) voice fears regarding threat to ecology. No wonder that, in the 1980s, a new phrase was added in the development literature: environmentally sound and sustainable development. It is posed as a strategy to meet the present needs without compromising the ability of future generations to meet theirs (World Commission on Environment and Development, 1987, p. 8).

Resources must be used for development but in a manner that these are simultaneously replenished. The gross natural capital must not diminish. A narrow vision of economic growth has been widened to a holistic perspective of environmentally sound and sustainable development.

In point of fact, three schools of though can be identified on the development-ecology question. The first envisages a free use of resources and technology to ensure an accelerated economic growth rate. Environmental considerations are placed subordinate to developmental imperatives. This is deemed as essential when the global population is growing fast and seeking a constant rise in its standard of living. It is argued that advancements in technology will not only provide substitutes to scarce resources but also create a capacity for maintenance of ecology.

The second school represents an opposite viewpoint. It calls for making developmental considerations subordinate to those of environment. Being "eco-fundamentalists" in spirit, it is a vociferous group. It has been successful in thwarting the beginning of new projects at times. A well known case is that of the Silent Valley (Kerala) in India where the construction of the dam and hydro-electric power stations in the Silent Valley of the Kerala state had to be abandoned in response to a grave concern expressed for the loss of the gene pool of some rare tropical plants. The eco-fundamentalists, nay the *Greens* of West Germany, Sweden, the Netherlands, Italy, France and Chile, also make an effective group.

The third group is of the sustainable developmentalists. It believes in blending of the economic objectives with environmental imperatives. It believes that resources have to be used but simultaneously these must be replenished. It insists that the national growth should be calculated in terms of both gross national product and gross natural product. Only the two together can give a correct picture of a nation's wealth and health. For this, resources must be conserved rather than preserved, technology friendly to ecology should be adopted, and all materials should possibly be recycled.

In brief, the first group works against nature, the second group in nature and the third with nature. The last group choose to define regional development as eco-development. It emphasises that the laws of nature not only impose constraints on but also point to the direction of optimal development. Ecology has to be saved from misdirected development no doubt, but development has also to be saved from misdirected ecology (Raza, 1989).

An Operational Definition

In the context of development studies, the kind of which the present one is, we will look at eco-development as representing the degree of concern for conservation of environment. An understanding of the problems with reference to land (soils and minerals), water (surface and underground), air and forests is a must. These individually represent matters relating to lithosphere, hydrology, atmosphere, and biosphere. It is important to make adequate resource provision for tackling their problems. The discussion in the present paper will be guided by these considerations.

It may be pointed out that the prevailing ecological problems are not just the product of development today. These may be inherent in the nature of the area or could have evolved historically over time. Accordingly, the ecological problems of any area can be classified as of three types: (i) which existed from the beginning as a part of the physical set up of the area; (ii) which evolved over time on account of interaction between man and nature; and (iii) which accentuated with an acceleration in the pace of development process.

In effect, it is difficult to distinguish these from another precisely. These pile upon each other. Their specific magnitude can be understood only in a broad sense. As such the ecological problems of Haryana will be discussed as existing today, and their origin will be referred to the varied situations mentioned above.

An Ecological Appraisal

From the viewpoint of ecological setting, Haryana is not much favourably placed. Its basic problems are related to scarcity of fresh water on the surface and abundance of brackish to saline water underground. About two-thirds of the state area is characterised by brackish subsoil water which is unfit for drinking and irrigation (Table 21.1).

Physically, the state is in the nature of a water divide separating the Ganga System to the east and the Indus system to the west. Only the Yamuna is the perennial river making its course on the eastern margins of the state. The Ghaggar stream in the north is dry for most part of the year.

The state is divisible within into three basins, namely the Yamuna basin (16,330 sq. kms), the Ghaggar basin (10,675 sq. kms), and the Internal drainage basin (17,207 sq. kms). Large parts of Haryana are in the form of topographic depression between the Siwalik hills in the northeast and the Aravalli hills to the southeast. Such conditions are generative of both flooding and waterlogging even under a situation of water scarcity.

TABLE 21.1: Haryana: Shallow Ground Water Quality Zones by Their Areal Extent

District	Geographical area (km^2)	Fresh water area (km^2)	Brackish/saline water area (km^2)
Ambala*	3,832	3,168	150
Bhiwani*	5,099	1,942	3,136
Faridabad*	2,150	633	1,422
Gurgaon*	2,716	955	1,500
Hisar	6,315	1,884	4,431
Jind	3,306	934	2,372
Karnal	3,721	3,196	525
Kurukshetra	3,740	2,157	1,583
Mahendragarh*	3,010	1,131	1,817
Rohtak*	3,841	289	3,511
Sirsa	4,276	1,292	2,984
Sonipat	2,206	430	1,776
Haryana	44,212	18,011	25,207

* Excluding the areas occupied by outcrops.

Source: M.C. Gupta (1983): "Groundwater quality", *Use of Saline Water in the Command Areas of Irrigation Projects*, Haryana Working Document 1.7, Haryana State Minor Irrigation Tubewells Corporation.

To compound the matters further, about one-half of the state receives an annual rainfall of less than 50 cms. Even in the rest of the state, variability of rainfall makes the things difficult. Good agriculture is not possible without irrigation in any part of Haryana.

The above physical legacy of Haryana was made worse by events taking place during the historical times. The deforestation of the Siwalik hills leading to soil erosion, overgrazing on the Aravallis causing removal of its soil cover, and spread of Rajasthan desert towards Haryana with gradual deforestation of the former, best describe an evolving scenario.

The initiation of the modern development has further accentuated some environment problems. The rapid extension of canal irrigation, without proper lining of water channels has caused waterlogging in many pockets. The wrong alignment of roads and water drains has given rise to quite frequent floods in some areas. Large scale quarrying and stone crushing, installation of thermal plants, and emergence of a number of industrial units, particularly distilleries, paper mills, and tanneries, is causing both air and water pollution.

Here, it is essential to mention the rapid growth of population as a factor in intensifying pressure on natural resources. Even historically any increase in population numbers led to a greater stress on land resources by way of clearance of forests for extension of cultivable land and for use of wood as fuel and building material. The process has been hastened during the recent decades. The per capita availability of land has declined from 0.96 hectares in 1901 to 0.34 hectares in 1981. Over two-thirds of the rural energy demand is met through the fuel wood (World Bank, 1982).

A note of further caution may be struck here. Haryana has just entered a phase of rapid urbanisation. It would necessitate diversion of additional land for non-agricultural purposes. It calls for a futuristic landuse planning.

Now let us take a look at the main environmental problems of the state and take a stock of the measures taken to ameliorate the situation. As would be seen, most of the state's ecological problems are linked with water, followed by those with soils, forests and pollution (water/air). Recent years have witnessed some efforts toward solution of these problems.

Water

As already noted, Haryana is highly deficit in water. Its average annual rainfall of around 50 cms is less than one-half of the national average of 115 cms. Nor is the surface or underground water adequate in any way. In fact, 18 per cent of the state's area has been notified as a drougnt prone (Government of India, 1972). It covers 13 blocks, namely Nangal Chaudhry, Mahendragarh, Kanina, Narnaul, Ateli of Mahendragarh district; Loharu, Tosham, Badhra, Bhiwani, Dadri I, Dadri II of Bhiwani districts; and Nahar, and Sahlawas of Rohtak district. This tract is located in the state's southwestern part adjoining the Rajasthan desert.

It is ironic that the water scarce state of Haryana suffers from the problem of waterlogging in parts. The National Commission on Agriculture (1976) defined waterlogging as a situation when the water table rises to an extent that the soil pares in the root zone of a crop become saturated resulting in restriction of the normal circulation of air, decline in the level of oxygen and increase in the level of carbon dioxide. The actual depth of water table when it starts affecting the yield adversely may vary from zero for rice to about 1.5 metres for other crops.

The floodplains of the Yamuna, Ghaggar, Markanda, Dohan, and

Sahibi remain waterlogged for varying durations during the rainy season (July to September). The underground acquifers of these river beds contain mostly non-saline/non-sodic fresh water.

The situation in the relect floodplain of the Ghaggar is somewhat different. Here the upstream acquifers contain fresh water but downstream saline or saline-sodic water becomes common.

The lowlying parts of the upland plain in Kurukshetra and Karnal districts also get waterlogged during the rainy season. The underground water is non-saline and seldom rises to depths shallower than 2 metres. This is attributed to large scale tubewell irrigation for rice cultivation.

It is in the lowlying and canal irrigated central part of the state where acute waterlogging conditions are met (Bhargava, 1988). The unlined canals have been responsible for such a situation (Fig. 21.1a). In addition, the underground saline water does not encourage tubewell irrigation which could have otherwise helped in containing the rise of water table.

Likewise, a rising trend in water table is observed in the semi-arid western and southwestern parts of the state. The introduction of canal irrigation through the Bhakra system has rendered some new areas succeptible to waterlogging. Water table has been noted as rising at the annual rate of 0.31 metre in Bhiwani district, 0.52 metre in Hisar district and over 1.00 metres in Sirsa district since 1974 (Tanwar, 1984, pp. 79-80). Here canal irrigation is actively exercised but the groundwater is not acceptable for large scale development of tubewell irrigation.

In the rest of the state, the water table trend is generally neutral but at places it is falling. These are in the form of small pockets in the eastern part (Fig. 21.1b). The Green Revolution beginning in mid-sixties, around the formation of Haryana, generated a big demand for irrigation water. Wherever feasible, it was met through development of tubewell irrigation.

The process accelerated with the provision of electric power to rural areas. Farmers came forward with great enthusiasm in installing private tubewells. As a result, water table declined.

It follows that while waterlogging is a serious problem in canal irrigated parts of the state, the fall in the water table is emerging as a matter of great concern in tubewell irrigated areas. All this calls for a proper water management strategy. Wherever feasible, a complementarity between the canal and tubewell irrigation within the same area needs to be encouraged.

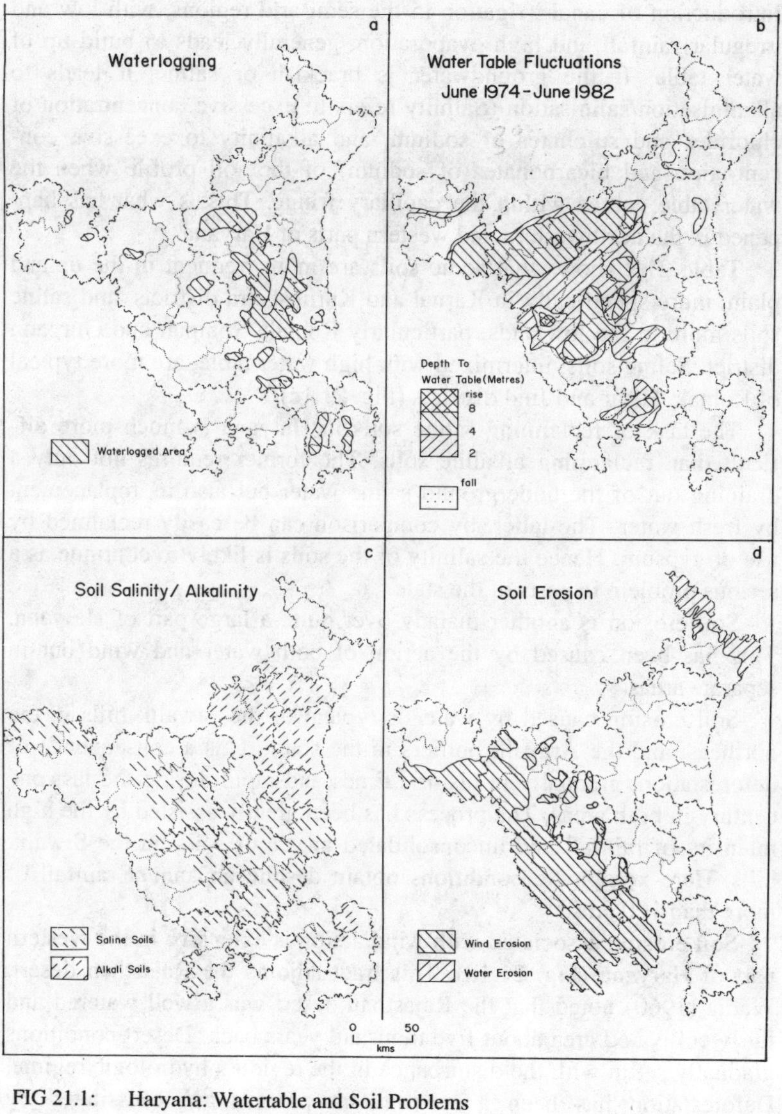

FIG 21.1: Haryana: Watertable and Soil Problems

Soils

Introduction of canal irrigation in the semi-arid regions, with low and irregular rainfall and high evaporation, generally leads to build up of water table. If the groundwater is brackish or saline, it leads to alkalinisation/salinisation (Salinity refers to excessive concentration of chlorides and sulphates of sodium, and alkalinity to excessive concentration and bicarbonates of sodium) of the soil profile when the water table comes within the capillary fringe. This is what has happened in the northwestern and western parts of Haryana.

Table 21.2 shows that sodic soils are more frequent in the upland plain, more specifically in Karnal and Kurukshetra districts, and saline soils more in the lowlands, particularly Rohtak, Sonipat, and Gurgaon district. Saline soils, intermixed with high water table, are more typical of Rohtak, Hisar and Jind districts (Fig. 21.1c).

The task of reclaiming saline soils in Haryana is much more difficult than reclaiming alkaline soils. The former requires not only a draining out of the underground saline water but also its replacement by fresh water. The latter, by comparison can be easily reclaimed by use of gypsum. Hence the salinity of the soils is likely to continue as a serious problem in parts of the state.

Soil erosion is another malady over quite a large part of Haryana. This has been caused by the action of both water and wind but in separate areas.

Soil erosion caused by water is typical of the Siwalik hills in the northeast and the Aravalli outliers in the south. It is a consequence of deforestation, gradually in historic times and rapid during the last one century in both areas. The process has been greatly assisted by the high intensity of rainfall and unconsolidated nature of soils on the Siwalik hills. Here xerophytic conditions obtain despite an annual rainfall of more than 100 cms.

Soil erosion associated with wind action is extensive in the western part of Haryana (Fig. 21.1d). This tract adjoins the Rajasthan desert. Wadia (1960) noted that the Rajasthan desert was a well watered and fairly cultivated area about five thousand years back. Desert conditions gradually set in with the disturbance in the region's hydrologic regime. Deforestation has been a concomitant process as necessitated by increased demand for cultivated land. The result has been an extensive desert which penetrates into Haryana from the west.

TABLE 21.2: Haryana: Salt Affected Soils

(*in hectares*)

District	Upland		Lowland	
	Sodic	Saline	Saline	Saline intermixed with higher water table
Ambala	5,543	3,685	—	—
Bhiwani	—	—	3,533	1,430
Faridabad	7,191	—	—	—
Gurgaon	—	—	10,638	—
Hisar	488	—	8,049	13,215
Karnal	42,605	—	2,035	—
Kurukshetra	21,372	7,660	—	—
Jind	4,220	1,218	9,190	13,026
Mahendragarh	—	—	638	—
Rohtak	—	—	10,762	14,142
Sirsa	N.A.	N.A.	N.A.	N.A.
Sonipat	3,301	—	23,960	9,238
Haryana	84,720	12,563	68,805	51,051

Source: R.C. Sharma and C.P. Bhargava (1987): "Mapping and characterisation of salt affected soils in Haryana using remote sensing", *Annual Report*, Central Soil Salinity Research Institute, Karnal.

Nearly 80 per cent of this arid region is subject to dune formation. These dunes reach a height of 15 to 20 metres at places but generally range from 4 to 8 metres in elevation. Shifting sand dunes have adversely affected the soils of not less than 150,000 hectares (Singh, 1990).

Using the aerial photo mosaics, the area under aeolian cover in the state has been found as 9,820 sq. kms. or 22.81 per cent of the total. Almost the same figure was arrived at by the Landsat Imagery (Singh, *et al.*, 1986). Evidently, one-fifth of Haryana is subject to soil erosion by wind. This is far more extensive than the erosion caused by water action.

Forests

A repeated reference has been made to gradual removal of forest cover in Haryana over the centuries. It was particularly during the British rule that natural resources were opened to rapid exploitation to serve an industrial civilisation. The communal control over the forests was replaced by the state control. The forest wealth was exploited in a non-sustainable manner.

At the time of Independence, 240 sq. kms of land of barely 0.55 per cent of total area was under forests in Haryana. Efforts at afforestation were made after Independence. The forested area increased to 1,339 sq. kms in 1967-68 and further to 1,685 sq. kms in 1985-86. But this accounts for only 3.81 per cent of the total area. This proportion is very low against 2.70 per cent of this country's average and the desired percentage of 33.50 as stipulated by the National Forest Policy.

Pollution

Pollution is the word which represents one of the serious negative fall-outs of the modern process of industrialisation and urbanisation. Both water and air are getting polluted to a greater degree. The public health is being exposed to increasing danger every day.

Since Haryana is not industrialised and urbanised to a very high level, the incidence of pollution is not of a high order and remains localised to some localities. Nevertheless, the situation is gradually deteriorating to cause a serious concern.

Water pollution in the state is primarily an urban phenomenon. About two-thirds of the water pollution has been recorded in its towns and cities. This takes the form of untreated sewerage and industrial wastes disposed of in water bodies.

Notably none of the urban places in Haryana has a plant for treatment of sewage and it is allowed to flow freely through the open drains to the adjoining villages as manure. The use of raw sewerage for agriculture, particularly for cultivation of vegetables, is fraught with health hazards besides causing soil sickness. The fields treated with raws sewage turn into breeding ground of mosquitoes causing malaria and other fevers.

The industrial waste from the distilleries at Yamunanagar, Hisar, Hathin and Panipat and from pulp and paper at Jagadhri, sugarmills at Karnal, Kaithal, Meham, Palwal, Panipat, Rohtak, Shahbad, Sonipat, and fertilizer unit at Panipat cause both air and water pollution. Industrial wastes are also not properly managed and are simply dumped in water bodies causing pollution, as in Yamunanagar, Panipat, and other places.

Air pollution is another emerging problem. About 80 per cent of air pollution in the state is attributed to two thermal plants located at Panipat and Faridabad. An analysis of emission reveals that the suspended particulate matter results in narcosis of lungs; sulphur dioxide emitted causes allergies.

Another source of air pollution is the cement plants located at Dadri and Surajpur. Mineral dust pervades the local atmosphere. Likewise, stone quarries and crushers numbering about 300 are dispersed at places like Panchkula, Bhiwani and around the Delhi-Haryana border, causing serious air pollution. The entire stretch between Faridabad and Badarpur on the Delhi border is covered with a thick layer of silica dust. Visibility is reduced and breathing is difficult. Twenty thousand workers and their families breathe the dust, drink it with water and eat in their food. About 17 per cent of the labourers here are incurable diseased (The State of India's Environment, 1984-85, p. 23).

Some air pollution is associated with the use of rice husk as in the rice bowl of Karnal and Kurukshetra districts, and of coal used in the industrial furnaces as around Delhi. Suspended particulate matter is emitted and air gets affected.

Brick kilns also cause air pollution. Haryana has about 1,430 at present. More than 50 per cent of them are located within a radius of 100 kms from the national capital of Delhi. Since coal is used for baking of bricks, air pollution is common around the kilns.

Thus, water and air pollution is largely an urban phenomenon. The contribution of motor vehicles to air pollution remains small because car ownership is confined to a few people. On the main highways, of course, the trucks and buses do emit obnoxious gases but their effect is felt only along the small stretches passing through the urban places.

Concern for Ecology

Eco-development in an area is to be judged from its concern for ecology. In India, the issue of ecology in the wake of efforts at accelerated development finds a mention in the document relating to Fourth Plan (1969-74, p. 49). It was stated therein: "The physical environment is a dynamic, complex and inter-connected system in which any action in one part affects others. There is also the interdependence of living things and their relationships with land, air and water. Planning for harmonious development recognises this unity of nature and man. Such planning is possible only on the basis of comprehensive appraisal of issues – particularly economic and ecological. . . . It is necessary, therefore, to introduce the environmental aspects into our planning and development".

Following this, the state undertook several programmes related to the promotion of ecology, such as water and soil conservation, afforestation, flood control. A major thrust to this effect is seen during the Fifth Plan (1974-79) when hill and tribal area, desert area and drought prone area programmes were implemented. But it was only in the Seventh Plan (1985-90) when a comprehensive integrated view of environmental protection and improvement with emphasis on the sustainable development was undertaken. A separate Department of Environment has now been established in every state.

In Haryana, the 1970s saw serious efforts at reclamation of alkaline and saline land. The Haryana Land Reclamation and Development Corporation was set up in 1974. By 1989-90 more than 100,000 hectares of land has been reclaimed. The reclamation covered mainly the alkaline soils for which an appropriate technology has been developed at Central Soil Salinity Research Institute, Karnal and the Haryana Agricultural University, Hisar.

Special attention is being devoted to soil conservation and water management on the Siwalik hills and the Aravalli outliers. The 1980s have seen intensive work at the Sukhomajri, Nada and Bunga sites in Ambala district and Bajra-Ganiyar and Siha localities in Mahendragarh district.

Afforestation has been an earnest concern of the state. Forestry in Haryana is connected with the rugged Siwalik hills in the north, barren Aravalli hills in the south, shifting sand dunes in the southwest, and undeveloped wastelands with problem soils in the central parts of the state. Trees are also being systematically planted along the canals, roads and railway lines. The outlay on forestry increased from 0.50 per cent of the total in First Plan (1951-56) to 2.31 per cent during Seventh Plan (1985-90).

The social forestry project was started in Haryana with the assistance of the World Bank in 1982-83. The objective was to increase supplies of fuel, fodder and food through raising of plantations located in all the 12 districts of the state. This took the form of village woodlots, strip plantations, and sand dune stabilisation covers. Agricultural wastelands and alkali tracts were also planted with trees.

Despite all these efforts the area under forests has registered only a marginal increase from 3.10 per cent in 1966-67 to 3.81 per cent in

1985-86. This percentage ranged from 1.26 per cent in Sirsa district to 17.30 in Ambala (Table 21.3). Obviously, the efforts at afforestation did not allow things to worsen.

TABLE 21.3: Haryana: Forests as Per Cent of Total Area

District	1950-51	1967-68	1985-86
Ambala	1.36	22.41	17.30
Bhiwani	—	—	1.86
Faridabad	—	—	2.74
Gurgaon	—	2.16	5.45
Hisar	1.08	0.61	1.57
Jind	—	1.11	2.27
Karnal	0.23	1.50	2.87
Kurukshetra	—	—	2.94
Mahendragarh	—	1.51	3.59
Rohtak	0.33	1.39	2.32
Sirsa	—	—	1.26
Sonipat	—	—	3.54
Haryana	0.55	3.04	3.81

Source: *Statistical Abstracts of Haryana: 1967-68 and 1985-86.*

Total area (in sq. kms) under forests in the state (state forest *plus* private forests:

(i) 1950-51 = 240 sq. kms
(ii) 1966-67 = 1,339 sq. kms
(iii) 1985-86 = 1,685 sq. kms
(iv) (—) means less than 500 hectares.

Another achievement of the state was the establishment of the Haryana State Board for the Prevention and Control of Water Pollution in 1974. According to Sections 24, 25 and 26 of the 1974 Act every industrial unit which is discharging either domestic or trade effluent or both even in the sewer is required to obtain the consent of Board for running his unit.

The Air (Prevention and Control of Pollution) Act, 1981, is more stringent. Section 21 clearly provides that no person shall, without the previous consent of the Board, establish or operate any industrial plant in an air pollution control area. It is important to note that the entire state of Haryana has been declared an Air Pollution Control Area. Till todate about 2,000 industrial units have been covered by the Board and a lot more needs to be done in this regard.

Table 21.4 is a testimony to the concern being felt for ecology in the state plans. The outlays for soil and water conservation, afforestation and flood control have been significantly larger during the post-formation period of Haryana. The allocations for environmental programmes were made only in recent years after 1985.

The philosophy of ecological maintenance also shifted from the curative to preventive medicine style. All this argues well for the welfare of the state.

In brief:

* Ecological problems of Haryana are basically rooted in its geographic setting; scarcity of fresh water sources in general, brackish water underground over a large territory, extension of desert conditions from the neighbouring Rajasthan desert, and a saucer-shaped disposition conducive to drainage problems in the central part.

* These problems aggravated in the process of development during the historical and recent times. Resources were used on a non-sustainable basis. Deforestation in the past and introduction of unlined canal irrigation during the recent decades had the most deleterious effect. The former led to increased aridity and soil erosion and the latter to waterlogging, and soil salinisation.

* Water and air pollution has not assumed big magnitude; this is mainly confined to big cities. With the state gearing towards a rapid pace of urbanisation, situation may become bad if precautionary measures are not taken.

* There is a spatial pattern in ecological problems; deforestation and soil erosion on the Siwalik hills and Aravalli outliers; waterlogging in canal irrigated and lowlying areas in the east-central region and along the streams; a critical fall in water table in the tubewell irrigated area in the northeast; and water/air pollution in industrial centres.

TABLE 21.4: Haryana: Planwise Expenditure on Environmental Parameters

(*Rupees in hundred thousand*)

Plan Period	Soil and water conservation	Forests including wild life preservation	Flood control and waterlogging	Environmental improvement of slums	Integrated rural development programme	Drought prone area programme	Desert development programme	Environmental programme	Total
First Plan (1951-56)	103.04 (0.70)		—	—	—	—	—	—	103.04 (0.70)
Second Plan (1956-61)	188.08 (1.00)		—	—	—	—	—	—	186.08 (1.00)
Third Plan (1961-66)	474.54 (1.82)		2890.71 (11.30)	—	—	—	—	—	3365.25 (13.12)
Fourth Plan (1969-74)	151.55 (0.42)	179.43 (0.50)	847.57 (2.37)	—	—	—	—	—	1178.55 (3.29)
Fifth Plan (1974-79)	171.34 (0.25)	306.37 (0.45)	4145.58 (6.12)	—	—	569.35 (0.84)	12.48 (0.02)	—	5205.12 (7.68)
Sixth Plan (1980-85)	1038.33 (0.65)	2353.88 (1.48)	7726.14 (4.84)	398.00 (0.25)	1650 97 (1.03)	404.15 (0.25)	669.95 (0.42)	8.55 (0.01)	14249.97 (8.93)
Seventh Plan (1985-90)	1725.00 (0.59)	5700.00 (2.31)	7569.00 (2.61)	500.00 (0.17)	1298.00 (0.45)	337.00 (0.12)	*	1569.00 (0.54)	19698.00 (6.79)

Source: Five Year Plan Documents of Punjab and Haryana.

Note:
(i) For the first three plans the data pertains to old Punjab.
(ii) Figures in parentheses indicate percentage to total expenditure.
(iii) Early 1960s witnessed large scale floods in Punjab. Large sums were allocated to tackle the problem. This was an ad-hoc measure.
* Transferred to Central sector completely.

REFERENCES

Bhargava, C.P. (1988). "Salt affected and waterlogged soils of Haryana and their management", in Mahendra Singh et al. (ed.) *Land Use in Haryana*, Land Use Board, Government of Haryana and Haryana Agricultural University, Hisar : 88-97.

Carson, R. (1963). *Silent Spring*, London: Hamish Hamilton.

Commoner, B. (1972). *The Closing Circle-Confronting the Environmental Crisis*, London: Jonathan Cape.

Government of India (1972). *Report of the Irrigation Commission,* Vol. I and II, New Delhi: Ministry of Irrigation and Power.

Government of India (1976). *Report of the National Commission on Agriculture*, New Delhi: Ministry of Agriculture and Irrigation.

Meadows, D.H. et al. (1972). *The Limits to Growth: A Report for the Club of Rome*, New York: Universe.

Pestel, E. et al. (1974). *Mankind at the Turning Point: The Second Report to the Club of Rome*, London: Hutchinson.

Raza, M. (1989). "Regional development as eco-development", *Presidential Address, Eleventh Indian Geographical Congress* held at University of Delhi, Delhi, India.

Singh, M. et al. (1986). "Remote sensing application in the study and mapping of soil problems of Haryana State", *Paper Presented at Workshop on Landuse Planning in Haryana*, Haryana Agricultural University, Hisar.

Singh, P. (1990). "Management of arid wastelands in Haryana through agroforestry", in S.C. Sharma et al. (eds.), *Utilisation of Wastelands for Sustainable Development in India*, New Delhi: Concept.

Tanwar, B.S. (1984). "Haryana's saline groundwater problem and background of the appraisal documents", *Studies for the Use of Saline Water in the Command Areas of Irrigation Projects*, Haryana, Appraisal Document Haryana State Minor Irrigation Tubewell Corporation : 28-92.

Wadia, D.N. (1960). "The post glaciation desiccation of central Asia", *Monograph 10*, National Institute of Science, India, 1-25.

World Bank (1982). *Staff Appraisal Report on Jammu and Kashmir and Haryana Social Forestry Project — A Document.*

World Commission on Environment and Development (1987). *Our Common Future*, Oxford: Oxford University Press.

PART-VII

ENVIRONMENTAL POLICIES (GLOBAL AND NATIONAL)-I

22

URBANISATION, POVERTY AND ENVIRONMENTAL CONSIDERATIONS: A Micro-Level Perspective

PUSHPA PATHAK

It is now university recognised that poor environmental conditions, including lack of potable water, inadequate sanitation, air pollution and land degradation are major risks to health and economic productivity of the people. Increasing concern with human well being as well as with environmental considerations have led to the identification of sustainability and human development as two basic guidelines for the formulation of development strategies in the 1990's. The term 'sustainability' refers to better management of natural resources and environmental protection for meeting the needs of the present and future generations.[1] 'Human development' is defined as a process of development aimed at the ultimate goal of ensuring health, education and economic means for satisfying the basic needs of the people.[2] The human development approach lays considerable emphasis on amenities such as clean water and adequate sanitation.[3] The question of water has special significance for urban areas as it is a scarce and fast depleting natural resources. Therefore, it is all the more important to make optimum use of water, prevent pollution and ensure equitable distribution.

It is also widely held that there exists and interdependence between increasing concentration of urban population, persistence of urban poverty and deteriorating urban environment. Most developing countries following the urbanisation-industrialisation path to\development are faced with the dual problem of increasing population pressure and failure of the trickle-down mechanism. As a result, large proportions of the population continue to be poor and have very low access to basic services, such as, clean drinking water, sanitation, education and health care. The focus on urban environment is all the more important in the case of countries like India which have large concentrations of urban population and industrial activity, limited resource base and poor environmental monitoring system.

It is often stated that the poor are both victims and agents of environmental degradation.[4] The concerned agencies invariably lack resources needed to provide basic amenities to all and poor are generally the victims of unequal distribution of public goods. They do not even have the prerequisite private means to supplement the available amenities to improve the environmental conditions of their habitat and to protect themselves against various environmental hazards. As a result, they are forced to meet their immediate needs by adopting ways which are damaging to their health as well as to the environment. Not having access to treated water supplied by the city government, using poor quality ground or surface water and discharging liquid and solid waste in the same water body is an apt example of the vicious circle of poverty and environmental degradation.

The urban environmental problems can be put in three broad categories. First, micro-level problems pertaining to the immediate working and living conditions at the sub-city level, such as, safe water, inadequate sanitation, and location of hazardous industries or waste disposal sites. Second, macro-level problems affecting the entire city or sub-region, such as, air and water pollution, reduction in open space and green belts and soil erosion. Third, global environmental problems relating to countries and larger regions, such, as deforestation and global warming.

This paper focuses specifically on the micro-level environmental problems associated with the provision of water and sanitation facilities in the low income areas of Indian cities. The paper attempts to examine the interdependence between urban poverty and environment. It focuses on how the urban poor are affected by low access to water and sanitation services as well as the manner in which they add to the deterioration in the urban environment. The paper also attempts to bring out gender specific considerations pertaining to water and sanitation services in low income areas. A larger study of Delhi and Trivandrum, conducted by the author for the World Bank, provides the empirical base for the paper.[5]

The National Scenario

According to the 1991 census, India's urban population was 217 million which accounted for 25.72 per cent of the country's total population. The decennial growth rate of urban population has been well above the estimated rate of natural increase of urban population of about 20 per cent in all the census years since 1941.[6] India's urban population is expected to cross 300 million mark by the year 2001 at the prevailing rate or urban growth.[7]

About 65 per cent of India's urban population resides in 296 class I cities which have a population of over 100,000. India's urban population is becoming increasingly concentrated in a few metropolitan centres which have also been increasing in number over the years. In 1981, there were 12 million plus cities. In 1991, the number of such metropolises increased to 23, which together accounted for one-third of the country's urban population.[8] By the year 2001, the number of metropolitan centres is likely to be 40, which will accommodate nearly 36 per cent of India's urban population.[9]

Taking consumer expenditure required for daily minimum caloric intake of 2,100 per person as an indicator of absolute urban poverty, it was estimated that 28.1 per cent of India's urban population was below the poverty line in 1983-84. Although as per the official statistics, the proportion of urban population below the poverty line declined to 20.1 per cent in 1987-88, the magnitude of urban population living in slums and squatter settlements continues to be high.[10] In 1981, 23 per cent of the total urban population was residing in slums and squatter settlements. In million plus cities, the proportion of slum population was as high as one-third of the total population. According to the projections of the Town and Country Planning Organisation, the proportion of slum population was not likely to change significantly by 1990. In absolute terms, it means that in the year 1990 more than 51 million people were estimated to be living in slums.[11] The proportion of population residing in slums and squatter settlements is generally taken as an indicator of secondary poverty. This means that some of these people may have adequate income for buying the quantity of food that is critical for their survival but they continue to live in extremely poor conditions in terms of the quality of housing and basic services.

An examination of the provision of basic services in India over time shows that an increasingly larger proportion of urban population is being covered. The coverage of safe water in urban India increased from 72.90 per cent in 1985 to 83.80 per cent in 1990. The coverage of sanitation increased from 28.40 per cent in 1985 to 45.93 per cent in 1990.[12] However, these estimates of total coverage are no indication of the quantity, quality and equitable distribution of the available services. For instance, on an average, the water supply in Class I cities is 147 lpcd. as against 157 to 270 lpcd which is the prescribed standard for cities falling in this population size category of 100,000 and above. None of these cities have the luxury of a twenty-four hour water supply. Most cities get water for 2 to 6 hours per day. Moreover, the poor continue to have low access to water even in those cities where the average accessibility to water is improving. A national study on low income households shows that only 44 per cent of the poor have access to tap water while 16 per cent have access to Mark II hand pumps. The poorer areas covered by the public water supply system invariably receive lower quantity of water than the city average. The remaining 40 per cent of the poor depend on other sources of unsafe water.[13] The situation regarding sanitation is even worse. Only 60 of the 296 Class I cities in the country have sewerage systems, which are not connected to all areas of the cities. A large proportion of urban population is still served by septic tanks and service latrines and a significant proportion of the poor (60%) do not have access to any latrine facility.[14] The distribution of urban water and sanitation facilities, although heavily subsidised by the state, is unequal and biased in favour of the rich in general.[15]

It has been observed that less than half of the waste water is collected in most Indian cities and only a part of it goes through primary level of treatment. The disposal of untreated waste water in the water bodies leads to pollution of the sources of water. Solid waste disposal is also a major problem in Indian cities. About 25 per cent of daily waste in Class I cities and about 20 to 40 per cent of the daily waste generated in smaller cities remains uncollected. The low income areas, which do not have proper drainage and solid waste collection suffer from the most unhygienic living conditions. Poor quality of water and inadequate sanitation are the main cause of health hazards, such as, cholera, typhoid, infectious hepatitis, dysentery and diarrhea. The low income areas which lack basic amenities have higher morbidity and mortality rates than those prevailing in other areas of cities.[16]

In spite of the government's efforts to address the urban environmental problems faced by the poor, the water and sanitation situation continues to be dismal in India. The two major government programmes designed to improve the environmental conditions of the low income areas are Environmental Improvement of Urban Slums (EIUS) in operation in the state sector since 1974 and centrally sponsored Urban Basic Services (UBS) programme initiated in 1986. In 1990-91, the two programmes were integrated as Urban Basic Services for the Poor (UBPS) with 100 per cent central funding. It is stated that the widening gap between demand and supply and escalating per capita cost of providing these services are the main reasons for inadequate provision of basic services in urban areas.[17]

Micro-Level Perspective

In this section of the paper, I have made an attempt to present the water and sanitation situation prevailing in low income areas located in two cities of different population sizes, namely, Delhi and Trivandrum. Within these cities, two types of settlements have been identified for observation and analysis, (i) authorised slums which are likely to have better access to water and sanitation services, and (ii) unauthorised squatter settlements which are very poorly served. Such a comparative analysis is expected to help in identifying a number of critical micro-level urban environmental considerations.

Delhi, the national capital and one of the four largest metropolises in the country, presents a picture of extreme inequalities in terms of the distribution of assets, income and access to basic necessities of life. Delhi is a rapidly growing city of approximately 8.4 million inhabitants, of which 35 per cent are estimated to be living in slums and squatter settlements. Delhi has high density of over 10,000 persons per sq. km. However, on an average Delhi Union Territory has better access to services like safe water (91%) and sanitation (73%). The quantity of water supplied in the city is 240 lpcd, which is well above the national average for Class I cities (Tables 22.1 to 22.4).

TABLE 22.1: Population of Delhi and Trivandrum

City	Population (million)			% Decadal growth rate	
	1971	1981	1991	1971-81	1981-91
Delhi U.A.	3.6	5.7	8.5	57.09	46.18
Trivandrum U.A.	0.4	0.5	0.8	26.98	58.75

Source: Census of India, 1981; and Provision Census Tables, 1991.
Note: U.A. = Urban Agglomeration.

TABLE 22.2: Area and Density of Population

City	Area (sq.km.)		Density (persons per sq.km.)	
	1971	1981	1971	1981
Delhi U.A.	446.3	540.9	8172	10599
Trivandrum U.A.	74.9	93.7	5469	5549

Source: Census of India, 1981.

TABLE 22.3: Access to Safe Water and Sanitation Urban Areas of Delhi U.T. and Kerala

State	% of population covered, 1985	
	Safe water	Sanitation
Delhi U.T.	91.1	73.4
Kerala	64.5	28.2
Urban India	72.9	28.4

Source: Mid-term Review of Water, Decade Programme, Ministry of Urban Development, New Delhi, 1985.

TABLE 22.4: Service Level of Water Supply, Delhi and Trivandrum

City	Service level (lpcd) 1985
Delhi U.A.	240
Trivandrum U.A.	150
Average, Class I cities	147

Source: Mid-term Review of Water Decade Programme, Ministry of Urban Development, New Delhi, 1985.

In this broad city level scenario of Delhi, two different types of slums and squatter settlements were selected for empirical investigation. Dakshinapuri located in the southern out-skirts of Delhi is a large resettled slum colony. It is fully authorised with regular land tenure and permanent brick and cement structures. It houses about 36,000 households. Most male residents are engaged in factories, government services, tailoring and trade while women work as domestic maids, sweepers and cleaners, factory workers and tailors. Household income ranges from Rs. 1,500 to 2,500 per month which places these residents at a better position amongst the urban poor.[18] On the other hand, Nizamuddin Bustee is an unauthorised squatter settlement located in the midst of an old middle-class residential area. It contains about 600 households, of which 1/3 are Muslim refugees from Bangladesh. The dwelling units are temporary shacks made of mud, wood, tin, cardboard, and cloth. Men work in rag-picking, construction and as casual labour. Bangladeshi women and children also participate in rag-picking while Indian women work as domestic maids in nearby middle class houses (Table 22.5). The household incomes are also much lower, ranging between Rs. 500 to Rs. 1,500 per month.

Trivandrum is a medium-sized provincial capital with a population of about 0.8 million and does not exhibit as sharp difference in standards of living as observed in Delhi. A much smaller segment (8%) of Trivandrum's population lives in slums and squatter settlements. In Trivandrum, the slums and squatter settlements are of relatively smaller size with larger dwelling units and open-space in and around the settlements. The average density is only 5,549 persons per sq.km., indicating lower pressure on land and resources of the city. But access to safe water (64.5%) and sanitation (28.2%) is not quite commensurate with such favourable conditions in urban areas of Kerala. The average quantity of water supplied in Trivandrum is 150 lpcd, which is considerably lower than what is available to the inhabitants of Delhi.

Four different types of settlements have been identified for field observation in Trivandrum, two of these are unauthorised special slums. Chirakulam located in the city's commercial centre is fully authorised with access to municipal services. Both males and females are engaged as headload workers and government employees. Vadavathu colony at Mattathara is partially authorised settlement located in the outlying residential area, where men are engaged in carrying headload, trade and construction while women work in domestic service, trade and mat-making. Kannanthura is predominantly a Christian fishing settlement located on the sea-shore, where men and women are engaged in fishing and allied activities. Thekkumoodu bund colony located along the banks of a canal, where most men are headload workers and most women are domestic maids. A majority of the dwelling units in all the four settlements have thatched roof made of woven coconut leaves. The range in household income per month is also comparatively wider. Kannathura has the highest average household income, followed by Vadavathu colony and Chirakulam while Thekkmoodu bund colony has the lowest average income level (Table 22.5).

TABLE 22.5: Salient Features: Selected Slums and Squatter Settlements Delhi and Trivandrum, 1990

Name of the locality	Location	Year of establishment	Status	Estimated no. of households	Social background	Major occupation		Range of household income (Rs. per month)	Type of dwelling units	Coverage under slum improvement programme
						Male	Female			
1	2	3	4	5	6	7	8	9	10	11
Delhi										
1. Dakshinapuri	Outskirts of the city	1972	Authorised with 99 year lease to residents	36,000	Migrant of all religions and castes from all over the country, high degree of scheduled caste	Factory labour, sweeping tailoring, trade	Domestic maids, sweeping, factory labour, tailoring	1,500-2,500	Brick and cement pucca 80%, semi-pucca 20%	Yes, 1986
2. Nizamuddin Bustee	Midst of a middle income area in south Delhi	1974	Unauthorised	600	2/3 Indian Muslim from eastern India 1/3 Bangladesh refugee also Muslims	Ragpicking, construction, casual labour	Ragpicking, domestic maids	500-1,500	Temporary shacks, made of mud, wood, tin, cardboard, cloth, etc.	No

Contd.

Contd.

1		2	3	4	5	6	7	8	9	10	11
Trivandrum											
1.	Chirakulam	Close to the city commercial centre	1950	Authorised land allotted to people but belongs to Govt.	250	Mostly Hindus, Christians and Muslims	Headload labour, casual labour, Government jobs	Headload labour, trade, govt. jobs	100-1,000	Semi-pucca with thatch roof or fully thatched	Yes, 1982
2.	Kannanthura	Sea Beach	1950	Unauthorised	750	Mostly Christians, Hindus and Muslims	Fishing casual labour	Fish selling	200-5,000	Mixed, mostly thatched	No
3.	Thekkumoodu Bund Colony	Along a canal in central residential area	1975	Unauthorised	300	Mostly Hindus, Christians and Muslims	Head load labour, trade construction	Domestic maid, trade, mat-making	150-500	Mostly mud and thatch	No
4.	Vadavathu Colony at Mattathara	Outskirts of the city near a sewage farm	1960	Partially authorised	650	Mostly Hindus, Christians, and Muslims	Head load labour, artisans, construction	Domestic maid, head load labour, construction	100-2,500	Mixed, mostly mud and thatch	Yes, 1985, 1987

Access to Water

Only Dakshinapuri in Delhi of the six settlements in the two selected cities, has private water tap connections. This area also has 144 public stand posts and 115 hand pumps. The other settlement in Delhi, Nizamuddin has 4 public stand posts which are illegally connected to the city's main supply line. In case water is not available or is inadequate, the residents resort to fetching water from public taps in the nearby middle-class residential area. Amongst, the settlements in Kerala, Chirakulam has 4 taps, Kannanthura has 8 hand pumps and several wells, Thekkumoodu has one tap, one well and a highly polluted canal, and Vadavathu colony has 15 taps, several wells and a river which is only used for solid and liquid waste disposal. The residents in the two special slums, Kannathura and Thekkumoodu, also use public hydrants along the main street which are far from their houses. Often, the middle class residents prohibit these people from bathing and washing clothes in front of their houses, therefore, the water for all uses has to be carried home. When there is no other option, the residents of Thekkumoodu use the polluted canal water for washing and cleaning. The settlements in Trivandrum with multiple sources of water generally use the tap and hand-pump water for drinking and cooking and saline well water for bathing, washing and cleaning.

Dakshinapuri, which is the only settlement with private water taps gets water supply for 15 to 30 minutes twice a day. But the timing of supply is quite erratic, sometimes it is in the middle of night when residents are unable to store water. Public stand-posts also suffer from short duration of supply and very low pressure, particularly during the summer months. Nizamuddin enjoys 24 hour water supply owing to the illegal state of the connections. All the four settlements in Trivandrum have access to some source of water throughout the day. Owing to the availability of water from multiple sources, the waiting time for water collection at the public stand-posts and hand-pumps is on an average less than half an hour in the selected settlements in both the cities.

The Municipal Corporation of Delhi which is responsible for providing basic services to all regularised residential areas, is not able to provide adequate water to the residents of Dakshinapuri with private connections because there is no overhead storage tank built as yet for this area. The access to safe water through community level supply system also appears to be low in all the six settlements. According to the community-level water supply EIUS norm, there has to be one tap or pump for every 30 households. The number of households served by public taps or pumps is 139 in Dakshinapuri, 150 in Nizamuddin, 63 in Chirakulam, 193 in Kannanthura, 300 in Thekkumoodu and 43 in Vadavathu colony. Moreover, not all the hand-pumps in both the cities are always functioning which further limits people's access to water. In general, the regular slums in Kerala have higher level of service than poorly served special slums. Also, settlements in Delhi get inadequate quantity of better quality treated water while settlements in Trivandrum have access to more water but not all of it is high quality safe water.

Female members of the household are predominantly responsible for fetching water from public sources in all types of settlements, except in Nizamuddin where mostly children are burdened with this responsibility. Children are observed to be helping with water collection, or at least are seen waiting in the queue, in other settlements as well. The quantity of water available for the poor therefore, also depends on the time and energy women and children devote to water collection.

Only those residents with private connections in Dakshinapuri pay a flat rate of Rs. 7.50 per month, the other households in the remaining five settlements do not pay for water at all. There is no incidence of private water vending in the areas under observation (Table 22.6).

Access to Sanitation

Provision of Latrines

The general picture of access of the residents in the selected settlements to sanitation facilities is that of stark deprivation, the degree of deprivation varying marginally from one settlement to another. In Dakshinapuri, a sewerage system for the provision of household level pour-flush latrine was laid-down in 1986 by the Municipal Corporation of Delhi, but it has not become functional as yet due to shortage of water. None of the households have installed private latrines in anticipation of this system's functioning. The residents assign low priority to household level latrines if it involves private cost. Both men and women use community latrines, some men use open space while women defecate along the open drains in the early hours of the morning and late at night.

TABLE 22.6: Access to Water

Name of the locality	% of households with private water connection	Number of Public standpost	Number of Hand-pumps	Other sources of water	Duration of water supply	Waiting time for water collection	Main responsibility of fetching water	Payment for water (Rs.)
Delhi								
1. Dakshinapuri	85	144	115	—	15 to 30 minutes twice a day	10 to 15 minutes	Females children	7.50 per month for private connection
		one per 139 households						
2. Nizamuddin Bustee	0	4 (illegal)	0	—	Throughout the day	Less than 15 minutes	Children, Males, Females	0
		one per 150 households						
Trivandrum								
1. Chirakulam	0	4	0	Well	Throughout the day	Less than 15 minutes	Females	0
		one per 63 households						
2. Kannanthura	0	0	8	Well	Throughout the day	15 to 30 minutes	Females, Males, Children	0
		one per 193 households						
3. Thekkumoodu Bund Colony	0	1	0	Well canal	Throughout the day	15-30 minutes	Females	0
		one for 300 households						
4. Vadavathu Colony at Mattathara	0	15	0	Well river	Throughout the day	Less than 15 minutes	Females	0
		one per 43 households						

Note: The EIUS norm for public supply is one public standpost/hand-pump for 30 households.

Two of the four localities in Trivandrum have shown remarkable private and community initiative for providing some kind of latrines for themselves. In Kannanthura, 71 per cent of the households have access to latrines that are private or are shared by a few neighbours. These are mostly make-shifts enclosures with water-borne single-pit latrines. In the remaining settlements, both males and females use different combinations of community latrines, open spaces and riverside. There is no perceivable difference in their choice of facilities for a simple reason that scope of choices does not exist. Households not having private latrines did not wish to acquire this facility due to high expense involved, lack of space, or both.

Looking at the provision of community latrines alone, one finds that it falls well below the EIUS norm of one seat per 5 households in all the settlements. There are almost equal number of seats for men and women in the two settlements in Delhi, in Chirakulam there are 4 seats for men and 2 seats for women, while there are 2 seats provided for only women in Kannathura (Table 22.7). Moreover, where this facility is available, the residents have complained of not being able to use them regularly because often these are over-crowded, dirty and do not have adequate water all the time.

There is no payment required for the use of municipal latrines in both the cities. In Delhi, men are expected to pay Re. 0.25 per use for using Sulabh facility, while women can use it free of charge.

Both male and female residents seem to be constrained by inadequate provisions of latrines. Children, of course are seen defecating in the streets in all the settlements irrespective of the availability, or non-availability, of private or public latrines. Women seem to be more contained by the lack of this facility, particularly if they have to use open space. Open spaces are fast disappearing due to rapid construction resulting in reduction in privacy and increase in insecurity if they resort to using places far away from their settlements (Table 22.7).

Bathing and Washing Facilities

There are no public bathrooms in any of the selected settlements. Most women bring water to the house, and bathe within their one room dwelling unit, behind the house, or in a make-shift enclosure in the backyard. More men bathe in the open, near a street hydrant or a well than women (Table 22.7). It was also observed that, women bathed less frequently than men due to their inability to fetch adequate water for this purpose.

Washing clothes is predominantly a female chore which requires large quantities of water. Women in Delhi and Trivandrum try to do the laundry close to the source of water, rather than fetch that much more water to their houses for this purpose. But this has its own limitations. There is no proper space for washing near the source of water, there is always a queue of people trying to fill water for other purposes, and as a result at times it leads to compromising on the quality of water used for washing clothes like dirty pooled or ditch water near the main source itself.

Drainage

The two authorised settlements, Dakshinapuri in Delhi and Chirakulam in Trivandrum, have open cemented drains running along the major lanes of the settlements which are connected to the city sewer system. Residents in Nizamuddin have themselves made cemented drains in the Bangladeshi section which takes the waste water to the nearby open space. The other settlements have either mud channels made by the residents or no drains at all. In the sandy area of Kannanthura, the water is absorbed in the ground and in Thekkumoodu and Vadavathu colony the waste water is disposed-off in the canal and the river respectively. It is, however, not uncommon to find pools of waste water collected within the settlements, particularly in the rainy season (Table 22.7)

Garbage Disposal and Street Cleaning

Small quantities of waste is generated at the household level in these slums and squatter settlements. Attempts are made to recover and recycle as much as possible. Generally, vegetable peels and stale food are fed to domestic goats, chickens and pigs. Paper, wood, coconut shells and husk etc. is dried and used as fuel. This is quite a popular practice in slums of Kerala. In Nizamuddin, the materials recovered from garbage dumps while rag-picking, such as, tin, wood and card-board are used as building materials for their huts. Women play an important role in sorting household waste and recycling it as animal-feed, building material or domestic fuel. The remaining garbage is, of course, thrown at the nearest opening in the street, sea, canal or river.

TABLE 22.7: Access to Sanitation Facilities

Name of the locality	Predominant use of				No. of seats in the community latrines		Payment for using community latrines (in Rs.)		Drainage	Garbage disposal	Municipal street sweeping/ garbage collection
	Latrine		Bathing								
	Males	Females	Males	Females	Males	Females	Males	Females			
1	2	3	4	5	6	7	8	9	10	11	12
1. Dakshinapuri	Community open space	Community open space	Own house stand post	House	320 1 per 56 households	320	0.25	—	Open cemented drains	Street, drain	Only on the main street, collection from the main bin 2-3 times a week
2. Nizamuddin Bustee	Open space community	Open space Community	Standpost	Behind the house	14 1 per 21 households	14	0.25	—	Open drains made by residents which led to the nearby open space and waste water keeps collecting there	Street, outside the bustee	No, but the middle class area has garbage bins from where garbage is collected 2-3 times per week

Contd..

TABLE 22.7 *Contd.*

1	2	3	4	5	6	7	8	9	10	11	12
Trivandrum											
1. Chirakulam	Community open space	Community open space	Enclosure house standpost	Enclosure house standpost	4 1 per 41 households	2	—	—	Open cemented drains along the street, some h.h. katcha drains	Street, main road adjacent to the locality	No, garbage is collected from the main road occasionally
2. Kannanthura	Private open space	Private community open space	Enclosure house well	Enclosure house well	— 1 per 41 households	2	—	—	No pucca drains, sandy area absorbs water	Street	No
3. Thekkumoodu Bund Colony	Open space	Open space	House	House	— 0 for 300 households	—	—	—	No pucca drains, water is disposed in the canal by muddy drains	Canal	No
4. Vadavathu Colony at Mattathara	Private river side	Private river side	House enclosure standpost well	House enclosure	— 0 to 215 households	—	—	—	No pucca drains, mud channels leading to river	River	No

Note: The EIUS norms for public latrines is one seat for 5 households.

There is no street cleaning provision in any of the six settlements. In Dakshinapuri only the main streets are cleaned by municipal sweepers. Some of the residents pay Rs. 8 per month to local sweepers for cleaning the street in front of their houses. The municipal cleaners clean the drains whenever they are blocked but not without repeated requests at the local branch office. Dakshinapuri is also the only settlement which has garbage dumps from where the municipality trucks collect the garbage 2-3 times a week. Nizamuddin in Delhi and Chirakulam in Trivandrum have the advantage of being close to middle class area, therefore, the garbage is occasionally collected from the main road in front of the settlement (Table 22.7).

Impact on the Environment

Adverse impact of poor sanitation on environment is visible in all the settlements. Amongst these are water stagnation, bad-smell, mosquitoes and other worms and insects, waterlogging and flooding during the rainy season, and blocked drains. All these lead to further pollution of water sources and poor health of residents, particularly of children.

The two localities which have special environmental problems need to be specifically mentioned here. Piggery is a common practice in Dakshinapuri, which adds to the deterioration of the area's environment. Pigs soak in the drains then walk around the streets spreading garbage, human faces and various infections all over the place. On the other hand, the canal running through Thekkumoodu gets flooded in the monsoons, forcing people to take shelter in the nearby school compound. The residents have to repair their badly damaged huts after every monsoon, which is very expensive. During other seasons also, this canal is highly polluted as a government dairy located on its banks discharges all its waste into the canal.

Conclusion

Three broad conclusions can be drawn from this case study of selected low-income settlements in Delhi and Trivandrum. First, access to safe water and adequate sanitation is very low in all types of slums and squatter settlements. There are, however, a number of settlement-specific environmental considerations which need to be incorporated in the micro-level planning for basic services. Secondly, the low access to water and sanitation has several implications. For instance, in the face of inadequate availability of basic services poor people compromise with the quality of services. It has been observed that when adequate safe water is not available, the poor use untreated water for drinking, bathing and washing which has negative implications for their health. Inadequate provision of sanitation facilities forces poor people to adopt ways of disposing solid and liquid waste which are detrimental to the immediate as well as larger urban environment. This leads to further lowering of the quality of life of the residents in these settlements. Thirdly, the interactive process of poor living conditions and environmental degradation also has wider urban planning implications.

Finally, I would like to emphasise that poor deserve a better deal. They subsidise the cost of urbanisation and development by providing cheep labour and by accepting appalling living conditions. Improving the provision of water and sanitation facilities in slums and squatter settlements will certainly ameliorate the working and living conditions of the poor. The following three sets of considerations have to be taken into account for better planning, implication and management of basic services for the urban poor.

Supply Side Considerations

This includes, increasing the overall supply of service at the city level, reassessing the pricing and cost-recovery of services, finding ways of better management and ensuring more equitable distribution of public services.

Demand Side Considerations

Being aware of the complementarity existing between income-shelter-services priorities of the poor, increasing incomes, shelter upgradation, and imparting hygiene education and increasing awareness of the environment for promoting demand for better basic services should become an integral part of urban planning.

Gender Specified Considerations

It has been observed that women are more adversely affected by poor provision of basic services than men, largely because of the roles they play and partly because of their concern for privacy. Therefore, it is necessary to perceive households as disaggregated units comprising of men, women and children playing different roles and manifesting different needs.[19] This is imperative for taking care of gender determined constraints regarding provision off suitable facilities for bathing, defecating and doing laundry near the source of water, and reducing the burden of women associated with the provision of basic services for the household by appropriate design and siting of these services.

REFERENCES

1. World Commission on Environment and Development (1987). *Our Common Future,* New York: Oxford University Press.
2. United Nations Development Programme (1990). *Human Development Report,* New York: Oxford University Press.
3. Narayan-Parkar, Deepa (1991). Sustainability and the Human Factor (Women, Men and Children), in *Water Supply and Sanitation — Beyond the Decade,* Proceedings of the Asia and Pacific Regional Consultation, 4-8 June 1990, Asian Development Bank, Manila.
4. The World Bank (1992). *World Development Report : Development and the Environment,* New York: Oxford University Press.
5. Pathak, Pushpa (1991). *Women in Development Assessment of Urban Water and Sanitation in India,* Draft Report submitted to the Water and Sanitation Division, the World Bank, Washington D.C.
6. Census of India (1991). *Provisional Population Totals :* Rural-Urban Distribution, Paper-2 of 1991, New Delhi.
7. Government of India (1992). *Eighth Five Year Plan 1992-97.* New Delhi: Planning Commission.
8. Census of India (1991). *op. cit.*
9. Government of India (1992). *op. cit.*
10. Various publications of the Planning Commission.
11. Town and Country Planning Organisation (1985). *A Compendium on Indian Slums,* New Delhi.
12. Government of India (1992). *op. cit.*
13. National Institute of Urban Affairs (1991). *Basic Services and the Urban Poor,* Research Study Series No. 46, New Delhi.
14. *Ibid.*
15. Kundu, Amitabh (1990). "Micro-Environment in Urban Planning — Issues Concerning Access of Poor to Basic Amenities, *Demography India,* Vol. 19, No. 1, pp. 79-91.
16. Raghupathi, Usha P. (1992). State of India's Urban Environment : An Overview, Paper presented at the Green College, 28 December, New Delhi.
17. Government of India (1992). *op. cit.*
18. According to the equivalent monetary value of caloric in take of 2100 per person per day and some non-food items, household expenditure of Rs. 882 per month draws the poverty line in 1989-90.
19. O.N. Moser, Caroline (1989). "Gender Planning in Third World : Meeting Practical and Strategic Gender Needs", *World Development,* Vol. 17, No. 11, pp. 1799-1825.

23

URBANISATION, RURAL ENVIRONMENTAL DEGRADATION AND RESILIENCE IN AFRICA

H.A.C MAIN

Urbanisation embodies many processes that may create and extend environmental degradation. The environmental hazards of residence in Third World cities, and the vulnerability of the urban poor in particular, have been extensively catalogued in recent years (Hardoy & Satterthwaite, 1989; Cairncross, et al., 1990). But "environmental problems in urban areas are often considered in isolation from environmental problems in rural areas, though many rural environmental problems can only be understood (and effectively acted upon) when the rural-urban links are understood" (Satterthwaite, 1991, 122).

As urban populations grow more rapidly than rural populations, especially in the larger cities, a shift is produced in demand for food, water and other provisions. Commoditisation of such goods is strongly encouraged by urbanisation, as urbanites lack access to land to grow their subsistence needs; they are also more likely than their rural counterparts to live in a monetised economy, and to have higher incomes. And the concentration of population in cities implies a tendency towards more intensive production in the immediate rural hinterland than in more distant regions.

It may be difficult or even unhelpful to separate the effects of urbanisation on rural environments from the effects of development in general. But as cities grow, they make additional demands on rural sources for land, energy, food and water, and on rural destinations for waste disposal; and these additional demands are translated into rising pressures on rural environments and societies. Perhaps the most striking thing about such demands is that, broadly, they are met: large cities grow larger, their residents' economic conditions improve overall (but not for many of the poor), and many rural production systems are sustained. But we are now more aware than previously of the price that may be paid for these rural pressures in terms of environmental degradation.

Rural environmental degradation arising from the rapid growth of large cities has become particularly apparent in Africa during the past forty years. Much the same has been happening elsewhere in the South. The North has seen some of these problems during the years of mass urbanisation, but it could compensate its degraded environments by taking more from the South. The South has to bear the brunt of environmental degradation and its economic consequences, whether that derives from its own or from the North's economic development.

The paper's broad aim is to consider why urbanisation produces rural environmental degradation under some circumstances and not others. The first half indicates specific causes of this degradation, and points to some examples in Africa of deforestation, hydrological change and various loss of agricultural land, in order to illustrate what has been happening in recent decades. It is difficult to substantiate links between specific urban processes and particular manifestations of environmental degradation, however, without a fuller understanding of the regional context and other processes in operation. The second half of the paper, therefore, comprises a case study of the Kano region of northern Nigeria, in which a number of urbanisation processes are outlined and their association with rural environments established. This provides the basis for an assessment of the variability in the rural environmental degradation and resilience of recent decades, and from this can be drawn some of the reasons for apparent environmental sustainability in parts of the Kano region.

Negative Environmental Effects of African Cities on their Rural Hinterlands

These negative environmental effects stem mainly from urban demand for land, energy, food and water, and for space to dispose of urban waste. Such demands impact on deforestation and other vegetation loss, soil erosion, altered hydrological conditions and other environmental degradation that culminates in a loss of agricultural land and soil fertility. Each specific environmental effect cannot necessarily be traced to a particular aspect of urban consumption, though in some cases the likely association is apparent.

Land

Consumption of land in the form of construction arises both from the outward expansion of the city's built-up area and from increased transport and other activity generated by urban development. Where fertile agricultural land is in short supply, and large and rapidly-growing urban populations are consuming more and more food, this transformation of rural into urban land is particularly damaging.

Nowhere is this better illustrated than in Cairo, Africa's largest city with a population of about 15 million to which an average of another thousand are added each day. Egyptian agriculture comprises a thin green strip either side of the River Nile, broadening out into the Nile Delta below Cairo. The Delta itself has been shrinking since the Aswan Dam reduced the river's downstream sediment load. The value of fertile farmland adjacent to the River Nile has been recognised for thousands of years. The monuments and temples of ancient Egypt were all built on desert land, in order to conserve precious farmland, and their walls bore advice to those who were to follow that they should never build on green land. But massive urbanisation in the second half of the twentieth century has made such land more valuable (in short-run profit terms) as building-land than as farmland, and between 1950 and 1984 about 12 per cent of this green land was lost to urban development. Government regulations exist to protect farmland from construction, but they are not enforced. A 'Greening of the Desert' project in President Sadat's time was designed to save farmland and encourage people to settle away from the river-banks, but it has not proved popular: a new town in the desert, the Tenth of Ramadan, was planned to house 500,000 people, but so far it has attracted only 15,000. Meanwhile Cairo absorbs that number in a fortnight and sprawls further into the green land. As long as its residents are adequately fed and housed, they are unlikely to see new towns in the desert as attractive alternatives, and demand for accommodation will continue to encourage construction on green land (Nature, 1993).

Similar if less stark consequences of the physical expansion of cities are evident around many African cities. Where cattle are an important element in the urban scene, either en route to urban abattoirs or taken out of the city to pasture daily, growth in their numbers tends to trample increasing areas of land. The cattle market at Omdurman has denuded much of the surrounding land of its grass and shrubs, and this has been a major factor as Khartoum has "greatly increased its impact on the surrounding environment, in fact causing some considerable desertification as it has grown in the last two or three decades" (Lewis & Berry, 1988, 354).

This loss of agricultural land to urban expansion may, however, be overstated. As Satterthwaite (1991, 121) has argued, "in most nations it cannot be ranked as one of the main environmental problems since the proportion of agricultural land lost is so small"; besides, land newly incorporated within the built-up zone often includes important areas of intensive foodcrop production. A greater threat to rural environments is likely to arise from urban demand for energy.

Energy

Urban energy consumption impacts on rural environments in many ways. Electricity may be generated by hydro-electric power, and dams have a wide range of potentiality damaging environmental effects (Goudie, 1990, 158). Like oil- or coal-fired power stations, which emit noxious pollutants into the atmosphere, they may be located at considerable distances from the cities they serve. The most apparent impact of urban energy consumption derives from the major role played by woodfuel (wood and charcoal) in most African cities, especially for domestic energy; woodfuel accounts for something like 80 per cent of total energy consumption in sub-Saharan Africa. Once the urban woodfuel supply system is commoditised, and rising urban demand for woodfuel is generated (though indirectly) by rising urban population, woodfuel traders begin to mine tree stocks in nearby rural supply zones where farmers have previously tended their trees in keeping with their crops. Then two types of woodfuel crisis are likely to emerge: the deforestation of the closest woodfuel supply zones, and expensive energy costs for the urban poor. The environmental crisis of rural deforestation also has social implications for farmers and others in these rural communities, whose livelihoods are certainly subject to major change and may be fundamentally threatened. The problem may be exacerbated as higher urban woodfuel prices give traders the incentive to go further afield in search of tree stocks, while widening deforestation and associated urban woodfuel scarcities make the costs of energy even higher for urban consumers. Many of the urban poor in

Ouagadougou, Niamey and other sahel-savanna cities spend a quarter or more of their monthly income on woodfuel (Eckholm et al., 1984, 13). A theoretical solution to these woodfuel crises is offered by alternative energy sources such as kerosene or gas, when woodfuel costs rise above these alternatives. But the high price of initial outlay on a stove or other equipment, and cultural preferences for food cooked on woodfuel, are likely to delay such a solution; this has happened in Addis Abeba and in some Nigerian cities during the 1980s. And the removal of government subsidies on fossil fuels in oil-producing countries like Nigeria and Algeria, arising from current economic constraints, makes an 'energy transition' away from woodfuel even less likely. Meanwhile, lorries carry woodfuel from tremendous distances to cities like Dakar (over 300 kilometres), Kano (400 kilometres), Khartoum (400 kilometres) and Nairobi (600 kilometres).

Trade in wood and charcoal of this magnitude has a potential for environmental degradation that is plain. More-or-less concentric rings of severe depletion have been reported around sahel-savanna cities such as Dakar, Ouagadougou, Niamey and Kano (Eckholm, et al., 1984, 27-28), Bamako (Baker, 1992, 107) and Khartoum (Lewis & Berry, 1988, 100). But some of these reports are exaggerated: Niamey is not surrounded by a '70 kilometre radius of virtual desert', and in Kano quite the opposite is true, as explained below. Yet it is undeniable that considerable potential for environmental degradation exists in continuing urban woodfuel consumption in at least some of these cities.

Food

Links between urban food consumption and rural degradation are perhaps less easy to demonstrate directly than in the case of urban demand for land and energy. Clearly the requirements of large city populations for food and other farm products place new pressures on agriculture, and contribute in general to the environmental degradation that results from over-intensification of cultivation. But the cost of food for urban consumers is usually subsidised by African governments; and while low staple prices are to be welcomed for city residents, they have tended to depress agricultural productivity through reducing incentives for farmers to invest in their production and their land. Thus rural environmental deterioration may also result from a lack of agricultural intensification (Lewis & Berry, 1988, 386). Food imports of new staples like wheat and rice have done much to form new food consumption patterns, especially for bread as a staple, and thereby undermined internal farm production even further (Andrae & Beckman, 1985).

Many dam and irrigation projects have been justified as producing food for urban markets, either perishable fruit and vegetables or less perishable goods like wheat and rice that can reduce the import bill. But reductions in water and sediment loads available downstream have destabilised existing farming and fishing ecosystems, and in many cases reduced the area of cultivable land more than is compensated by new cultivable land created by the projects. Dam and irrigation projects have made the rural poor especially vulnerable, as they have lost land in the reallocation of plots and been unable to afford the inputs necessary for what plots they have received. Compensation for inundated land is rarely more than a small fraction of market value, so that many peasants have been forced to migrate away from the projects to distant marginal farmland, while others have joined the urban proto-proletariat.

Water

Few large cities have been able to meet their residents' and industries' water needs without large-scale construction projects involving dams, reservoirs and pipelines. Major rivers might be tapped, as at Khartoum, and groundwater supplies might be extensive enough to satisfy a major proportion of demand, as at Kano. But even where groundwater is plentiful, as urban expansion consumes peripheral villages, new wells are dug and existing wells are eventually overused. There is the risk, under certain geological conditions, that urban pollution might get into the groundwater and contaminate the wells of nearby rural as well as urban residents. At Dakar, overpumping has caused the intrusion of salt water into groundwater; as new water supplies for the city are taken from further up Cap Vert, so rural communities' supplies are threatened (White, 1989, 7).

Waste Disposal

Smaller settlements are able to dispose of a proportion of their solid waste by dumping it alongside the road outside the built-up area (or municipal boundary), as in some parts of the Meghreb. This may be a mixed blessing for local farmers, who can extract biodegradable material for fertiliser and as food for goats before the non-recyclable residue is buried. But where the useful content of solid waste has been sorted before it is taken out of the city, peri-urban dumps are at best an eyesore for villagers and probably a health hazard and/or a waste of good land. The large-scale, sanitised waste-disposal facilities that major cities require are absent from most African cities today. Three ultra-modern incinerators were built in Lagos with a European Economic Community grant, at a cost of $30 million: they were never used, and a decade later in 1989 it was decided to dismantle two of them and convert the third into a civic centre (NEST, 1991, 234). Meanwhile residents in and around Lagos, most of whom obtain their drinking water from shallow wells and boreholes in permeable geological conditions, have become increasingly fearful of chemical poisoning as industrial waste pipes empty untreated effluent straight into open drains and gutters (NEST, 1991, 240).

Landfill dumps, located around and beyond the urban periphery, are the standard means of disposal of African cities' solid waste. Fires fed by material in such dumps send noxious palls of smoke over adjacent land and villages. These dumps also carry the risk of groundwater contamination. Almost all Khartoum's industrial waste is disposed of either direct into the River Nile or onto adjacent land, where mounting problems of heavy pollution are compounded by drainage difficulties arising from flat terrain. Sizeable areas of standing water around Khartoum have done much to make malaria common now, where it was rare 25 years ago, and gastro-intestinal and other diseases are also encouraged by the city's poor sanitary controls (Lewis & Berry, 1988, 349-55).

Kano and its Rural Region: Environmental Sustainability, Degradation and Resilience

With a population of may be 1,500,000, Kano is Nigeria's third largest city. It is located in the centre of the most extensive region of dense rural settlement in the west African Savanna, the Kano Close Settled Zone. This comprises an area of about 12,000 square kilometres, with population densities over 400 per square kilometre and rising towards the urban periphery (see Fig. 23.1). These densities reflect a fairly flat terrain of fertile soils, and groundwater close enough to the surface to be tapped by fairly shallow wells. Intensive cultivation has long been sustained in the Close Settled Zone through the application of manure to maintain soil fertility, while effective access to land was encouraged by a complex system of tenure, including loan and hire and pledge as well inheritance, long before the colonial era began in 1903 (Mortimore, 1968). Harrison Church (1980, 453-54) has described the Close Settled Zone as "among the few areas in Africa where indigenous farms have . . . 'humanised' the countryside. . . the impression is that man is dominant, rather than nature. . . . Almost every piece of ground is or has been used. . ."

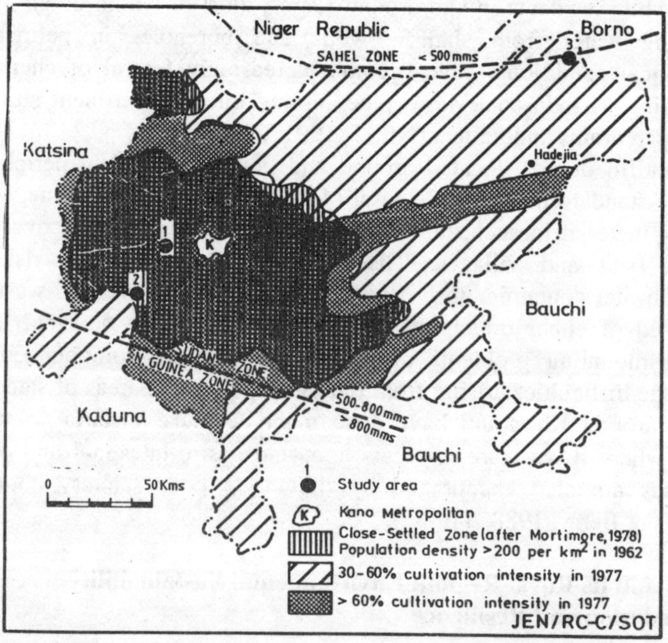

FIG. 23.1: The Kano Region

Source: Cline-Cole, et al., 1990b, 522.

An important centre of administration and trade within West Africa for well over 500 years, Kano has for centuries obtained its energy for cooking and heating and lighting from the trees growing in the inner Close Settled Zone. Fuelwood was carried daily into the city from a distance of up to thirty kilometres by hundreds or even thousands of donkeys, which departed soon afterwards with loads of nightsoil from the city to manure their village fields. This trade, described in detail by Mortimore (1972), performed an array of mutually-reinforcing economic and environmental functions: trade in fuelwood and fertiliser, income generation for donkey owners and drivers as well as traders, urban waste disposal, and the maintenance of rural soil fertility which enabled perennial cultivation on much of the land within the Close Settled Zone.

Donkeys still ply their trade between Kano and surrounding villages, but economic and social developments since the 1960s have reduced their importance in Kano's urban-rural relations. Nigeria's economy boomed with its petroleum exports during the 1970s. Strong urban bias in development policies saw Kano, like other large cities, grow rapidly; and this generated demand for fuelwood that could not be matched by the farmers of the Close Settled Zone, who were unwilling to cut more fuelwood than their farmland trees could sustain. Little bush remained within the Close Settled Zone. So Kano's fuelwood traders looked elsewhere for their fuelwood supplies to meet the burgeoning demand; and they were facilitated in this by ongoing improvements in the region's road network and more widespread vehicle ownership.

Since the 1970s, Kano has obtained a large majority of its fuelwood supply by lorry from a distant supply zone up to 600 kilometres from the city (see Fig. 23.2). Most of these sources are sparsely-populated wooded areas accessible by road. They are increasingly vulnerable to the environmental effects of 'mining' of tree stocks, as fuelwood traders are not concerned with planting new trees and the land is not the responsibility of a local farmer who will tend it.

This potential for deforestation in some of Kano's distant supply zones contrasts sharply with the Close Settled Zone, where farmers are keenly aware of the value of trees on their farmland, and local woodcutters place great emphasis on management of fuelwood offtake as part of a yield-sustaining strategy. Local supply to Kano from the inner Close Settled Zone declined by 1983 to only 19 per cent of its 1969 level, and pickup vehicles were carrying more than half of the local supply in 1983 whereas almost all of it had been carried by donkeys 14 years before (Cline-Cole et al., 1990a, 34-36).

The danger of applying neat models to situations with which one is not familiar is demonstrated by the assertion of Eckholm et al., (1984, 28) that around Kano "over the last 25 years commercial wood demands have led to severe deforestation and the collapse of a sustainable agricultural system. . . rising fuelwood demands in Kano encouraged farmers to overcut trees, selling off their biological capital; now farmland within a 40-kilometre (25-mile) radius of the city has been largely stripped of trees"! In fact it is difficult to walk out of Kano in any direction without being surrounded by hundreds of trees in a radius of a few hundred metres. Indeed a detailed survey of a sample area within the inner Close Settled Zone found that tree numbers had increased by 23 per cent between 1972 and 1981, a finding especially remarkable in the light of the drought of the early 1970s (Cline-Cole et al., 1990a, 55). Thus it is "out of place to diagnose an ecological crisis in the local wood fuel hinterland of Kano, even under present conditions of inflation, recent food shortages, and rising economic expectations. There is no doubt that a system of agro-forestry. . . is still the most rational land use in the Kano Close-Settled Zone" (Cline-Cole et al., 1990a, 43).

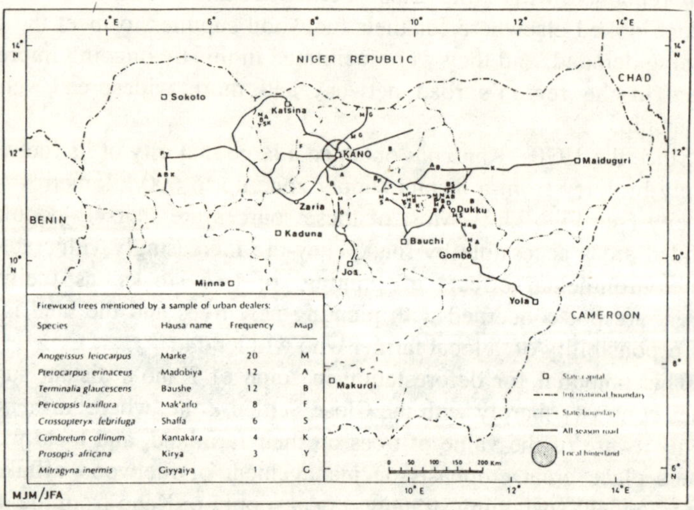

Firewood trees mentioned by a sample of urban dealers:

Species	Hausa name	Frequency	Map
Anogeissus leiocarpus	Marke	20	M
Pterocarpus erinaceus	Madobiya	12	A
Terminalia glaucescens	Baushe	12	B
Pericopsis laxiflora	Mak'arfo	8	F
Crossopteryx febrifuga	Shaffa	6	S
Combretum collinum	Kantakara	4	K
Prosopis africana	Kirya	3	Y
Mitragyna inermis	Giyyaiya	1	G

FIG. 23.2: Major Sources of Fuelwood for Kano, Mid-1980s

Source: Cline-Cole, et al., 1990a, 38.

By the 1970s, the provisioning of Kano's growing population needed a fundamental reshaping in other areas besides fuelwood. Electricity had been supplied since the 1920s to some of the city's better-off residents, and later to its industries, by a coal-fired power station by the railway a few kilometres to the south of Kano, near to where water was pumped from the Challawa River to a low hill inside the city walls. Industrial expansion in the 1970s as well as population growth demanded a new level of supply which the water-pumping station could cope with, but the power station could not. Electricity supply was boosted by the commission in 1969 of Kainji Dam, 600 kilometres away on the River Niger and designed to supply much of Nigeria's electricity, and the subsequent linking of Kano with the dam's hydro-electric generators by 132 kilovolt transmission line.

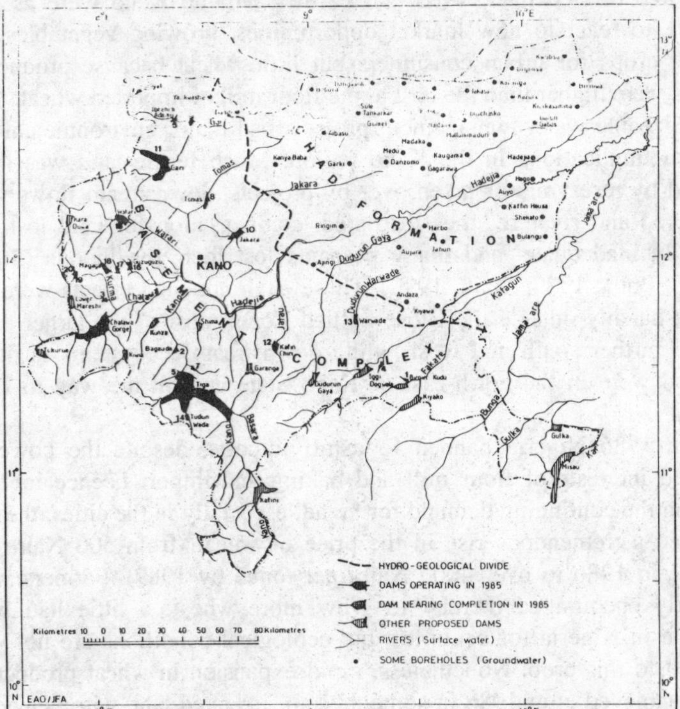

FIG. 23.3: Water Resource Development in the Kano Region, Mid-1980s.

Source: Olofin, 1987, 29.

Nigeria's government approached the question of food supply to major cities as a central component in agricultural development policy, but high levels of profit were to be made from the import economy. Bread and rice to some extent replaced millet and sorghum as urban staple foods, and the value of food imports grew during the 1970s by a factor of 20, rising to 11 per cent of a high import bill in 1980 (Andrae & Beckman, 1985, 9). The oil boom also funded capital-intensive dam and irrigation projects, and twenty zoned earthfill dams had been constructed in the Kano region by 1980 (Fig. 23.3). These dam and irrigation projects were presented by government as investments in food production for urban consumers and, because wheat was to comprise a major part of this additional food production, the projects also supposedly justified interim government support for wheat imports (Andrae & Beckman, 1985, 2). Farmers around Kano were as ever quick to react to new market opportunities, growing vegetables and other crops for urban consumers but little wheat because production costs were higher than the cost at the flour mill of imported wheat.

Sizeable water management projects had major environmental and social implications in the Kano region. Much fertile land was inundated by reservoirs or taken over by projects, downstream flows were reduced and river regimes disrupted, compensation for land lost was wholly inadequate, and many peasants lost their livelihoods (Stock, 1978; Baba, 1989; Main, 1990). These environmental effects were felt most harshly outside the Close Settled Zone: most of the larger dams were further south and west, while downstream ecosystems most affected were in the north-east of Kano State and all the way to Lake Chad.

In 1986 Nigeria banned foodstuff imports, despite the powerful vested interests of flour mill and baking and import licence lobbies. Given the continuing demand for bread, especially in the cities, the ban caused a tremendous rise in the price of wheat (from 500 Naira per tonne in 1986 to over 4000 Naira per tonne by 1989). Farmers were greatly encouraged thereby to grow more wheat: a little had been grown in Nigeria for centuries, but ecological conditions are not well suited to this crop. Nonetheless, rapid expansion in wheat production was achieved after 1986 in some areas of irrigated land with heavy inputs of fertiliser (Kimmage, 1991, 478-79). But soil fertility is not high in these areas, and continuing economic recession meant that commercial fertilisers were increasingly expensive and scarce: during the 1988-89 dry season, only one quarter of the fertilisers required in the wheat-growing areas of northern Nigeria was available. The scramble for new wheat-growing land meant that land was cleared mechanically for extensive cultivation, and this was very damaging to soils in areas like the acacia scrublands of river floodplains north-east of Hadejia

(Kimmage, 1991, 493-94). Soil erosion was accelerated, soil structure broken down, and sheet erosion exacerbated by rainstorms into gullying. A rapid reduction both in soil fertility and in organic matter content resulted. Kimmage's (1991, 495) analysis of this situation saw soil fertility as "likely to disappear entirely. . . . Within five years these cleared areas could become localised dust bowls" unable even to sustain the poor scrub vegetation that had previously been there.

The Nigerian government announced that the ban on wheat imports would be lifted towards the end of 1992, not out of concern for environmental problems in peripheral regions like north-eastern Kano, but in response to pressure from the national bread lobby (and the IMF). What effect this reversal of policy, and the events of the past decade, will have on vulnerable environments has yet to be seen. Remaining subsidies on petroleum-based products are being withdrawn; by making fuelwood more attractive to urban consumers in comparative costs, this represents another new round in the threats of urbanisation to Nigeria's natural environments.

Conclusion

The fertile soils and near-surface water table of the Close Settled Zone have attracted settlement since agriculture was introduced over a thousand years ago, while some irrigable fadama land has encouraged in-migration in more recent years. A long history of intensive cultivation, a high population density, and the development of a complex land tenure system are characteristic of this region; as is the responsiveness of its residents both to market conditions and to the need for environmental sustainability. All this adds up to a resilient society and a resilient environment.

Environmental circumstances beyond the Close Settled Zone are mixed. Less accessible groundwater as a rule combines with much less fertile soils in some areas and lower rainfall in the north to reduce the intensity of agriculture and the density of rural settlement, but extensive fadama especially in the north-east of the Kano region has potential as valuable agricultural land. Land tenure tends to be less developed, and large areas of bush have never been cultivated. Various forms of environmental change are evident in parts of this outer zone, reflecting changes in urban provisioning of fuelwood and food in particular. Some, though not all, of these environmental changes constitute degradation. Deforestation in bush areas will almost certainly enhance soil erosion at least, and may produce severe widespread degradation under some conditions. Severe soil degradation is already apparent in some of the marginal wheat-growing lands. Alterations in river hydrology below dams and irrigation projects may in places be interpreted as environmental change without degradation, as where new channel morphology appears without damaging local production potential (Olofin, 1984); elsewhere, new river hydrology has had a clearly negative impact on the environments of farming-fishing communities. The inundation of good fadama land under reservoirs, and the loss of downstream fadama, have been only partially compensated by the creation of additional land for irrigation; this is environmental degradation by any measure.

An impression of social resilience and environmental sustainability as a rule in the Close Settled Zone, despite its proximity to concentrated demand in Metropolitan Kano, contrasts with greater social vulnerability and environmental degradation in some parts of the wider region. Such a dichotomous interpretation applies, however, less than uniformly. Small upland areas of moderate rill and gully erosion, and some stripping of valley slopes, were identified in a study of the River Tomas catchment in the north of the Close Settled Zone, though no areas of high erosion were found (Ahmed, 1987, 242). Some landlessness has been produced among poorer peasants on the Kano River Irrigation Project, 30 kilometres south of Kano, in much the same way as around the reservoirs outside the Close Settled Zone. Yet the Kano River Irrigation Project's negative environmental effects in altering river regimes mainly affect areas outside the Close Settled Zone some distance downriver.

The more optimistic impression of social and environmental sustainability within the Close Settled Zone does suggest that high rural population densities and rapid rural population growth are strongly beneficial under certain circumstances. In this case such circumstances include changes in social organisation associated with intensification of production on adequate farmland, in which the evolution of a complex land tenure system is central. Opportunities for off-farm income generation supplement agricultural production. Weaving in many of the villages to the north of the city, and dyeing in some of those to the south, helped earn Kano (the market and organising centre) a reputation for textiles in much of West and North Africa over 150 years ago. Daily commuting to employment in urban factories and offices has been important in the past thirty years, and daily market activities like the donkey trade have always provided scope for income supplementation.

Urbanisation does not necessarily, then, imply rural environmental degradation. The urban-rural symbiosis between Kano and its nearby rural hinterland contrasts with a somewhat exploitative relationship with the more distant rural region. But it is important to recognise that neither does environmental sustainability necessarily follow from high rural population densities, intensive south-eastern Nigeria where these features pertain have been degraded by severe sheet erosion and, in places, extensive gullying.

In a country like Nigeria, where the penetration of capitalist relations into rural society is somewhat advanced, capitalisation of land tenure is necessary in order to protect farmers' rights in their land. This has evolved quite effectively in the Close Settled Zone, where it is evident in the heavy investment of time and money in land management (maintenance of soil fertility, hedging etc.) that is encouraged by secure access. Where it has not evolved, as in much of the periphery, peasants are more vulnerable to landlessness either through direct investment by agri-businessmen and speculators, or through government compulsory acquisition for projects. It is not surprising that so many dams were constructed in places like northern Nigeria during the economic boom of the 1970s, given the variety of ways in which they are functional for capitalist development. As receptacles for considerable government expenditure on construction and infrastructure, they involve much contracting and sub-contracting, and scope for enrichment and patronage all the way from central government to village head; compensation exercises provide similar scope. They extract fertile land from the hand of peasants and allocate it into the pockets of capitalist farmers for intensive production to feed urban consumers; and many of those who are made landless around the projects and downriver either migrate to more marginal rural land, or have to offer their labour on the projects or in the cities, thereby adding to the urban labour pool and helping keep urban labour cheap. Dams make very good business sense, despite their considerable potential for social injustice and negative environmental effects.

The State's role under these circumstances should be to cater for the needs of small farmers, rather than those of agribusiness. Small farmers with secure access to their land, like those in the Kano Close Settled Zone, tend to be keenly aware of what is needed to sustain their environments, and to make good use of what is on offer from agricultural extension services. Land tenure change should be encouraged through a proper registration system and a reduction in both the bureaucratic hurdles and the costs involved in formalising ownership. The present muddled tenure situation operates against peasants' interests, making them more vulnerable to the loss of their land to outside interests like agribusiness and compulsory acquisition.

It is important that deforestation and other problems association with urban fuelwood consumption are not left to be resolved by market processes. Fuelwood will indeed eventually become more expensive than alternative fuels like kerosene and gas, but this expense would reflect widespread depletion of fuelwood sources and concomitant environmental degradation. Managed fuelwood offtake from intensively-cultivated areas like the Kano Close Settled Zone can yield a considerably greater volume of fuelwood than unmanaged offtake from bush or reserved natural woodland (Cline-Cole et al., 1990a, 107-08). An increase in the area of intensive cultivation is therefore to be welcomed for the increased fuelwood as well as food supply that it implies, though how far the Close Settled Zone can be extended beyond its present extent is open to debate.

Even if it is inevitable that those evicted by rural projects are not properly compensated at market rates, government must accept responsibility in rehabilitating them in a wider sense: to enable them to find alternative farmland, and to farm their new land effectively, thereby encouraging an increase in sustainable agricultural production, and reducing the numbers migrating into urban poverty.

REFERENCES

Ahmed, K. (1987). Erosion hazard assessment in the Savanna: the Hadejia-Jama are River Basin. In M.J. Mortimore et al., (eds.), *Perspectives on Land Administration and Development in Northern Nigeria*. Bayero University: Kano.

Andrae, G. and Beckman, B. (1985). *The wheat trap*. London: Zed.

Baba, J.M. (1989). The problems of rural inequality on the Kano River Project, Nigeria. In K. Swindell, J.M. Baba & M.J. Mortimore (eds.), *Inequality and Development: Case Studies from the Third World*, 140-57. London: Macmillan.

Baker, K.M. (1992). The changing geography of West Africa. In G.P. Chapman & K.M. Baker (eds.), *The Changing Geography of Africa and the Middle East*, 80-113. London: Routledge.

Cairncross, S., Hardoy, J.E. & Satterthwaite, D. (1990). *The Poor Die Young: Housing and Health in Third World Cities*. London: Earthscan.

Cline-Cole, R.A., Falola, J.A., Main, H.A.C., Mortimore, M.J., Nichol, J.E. & C'Reilly, F.D. (1990a). *Wood fuel in Kano*. Tokyo: United Nations University Press.

Cline-Cole, R.A., Main, H.A.C., & Nichol, J.E. (1990b). On fuelwood consumption, population dynamics and deforestation in Africa, *World Development* 18, 4; 513-27.

Eckholm, E., Foley, G., Barnard, G. & Timberlake, L. (1984). *Fuelwood: the Energy Crisis that won't Go Away*. London: Earthscan.

Goudie, A. (1990). *The Human Impact on the Natural Environment* (third edition). Oxford: Blackwell.

Hardoy, J.E. & Satterthwaite, D. (1989). *Squatter Citizen: Life in the Urban Third World*, London: Earthscan.

Harrison Church, R.J. (1980). *West Africa* (eighth edition). London: Longman.

Kimmane, K. 1991 The evolution of the 'wheat trap': the Nigerian Wheat Boom. *Africa* 61,4; 471-501.

Lewis, L.A. & Berry, L. (1988). *African Environments and Resources*. London: Unwin Hyman.

Main, H.A.C. (1990). Dam projects and urbanization in Kano State, Nigeria. *Singapore Journal of Tropical Geography* 11,2; 87-99.

Mortimore, M.J. (1969). Population distribution, settlement and soils in Kano Province, Northern Nigeria, 1931-62. In J.C. Caldwell & C. Okonjo (eds.), *The Population of Tropical Africa*, London: Longman.

Mortimore, M.J. (1972). Some Aspects of Rural-Urban Relations in Kano, Nigeria. in P. Vennetier (ed.), *La croissance urbaine en Afrique noire et a Madagascar*, 871-78. Centre Nationale de la Recherche.

Nature (1993). *Mother of the Mega-cities*. London: BBC2 Television.

NEST (Nigerian Environmental Study/Action Team) (1991). *Nigeria's Threatened Environment: A National Profile*. Ibadan: NEST.

Olofin, E.A. (1984). Some effects of the Tiga Dam on Valleyside Erosion in Downstream Reaches of the River Kano. *Applied Geography*, 4, 321-32.

Olofin, E.A. (1987). Some Aspects of the Physical Geography of the Kano Region and Related Human Responses. Geography Department Series No. 1, Bayero University: Kano.

Satterthwaite, D. (1991). Urban and Industrial Environmental Policy and Management. in J.T. Winpenny (ed.), *Development Research: The Environmental Challenge*, 119-36. London: Overseas Development Institute.

Stock, R.F. (1978). The Impact of the Decline of the Hadejia River Floods in Hadejia Emirate, in G.J. van Apeldoorn (ed.), *The Aftermath of the 1972-74 Drought in Nigeria*. Centre for Social and Economic Research, Ahmadu Bello University: Zaria.

White, R.R. (1989). "The influence of environmental and economic factors on the urban crisis", in R.E. Stren and R.R. White (eds.), *African Cities in Crisis: Managing Rapid Urban Growth*, 1-19. Boulder: Westview.

24

SUSTAINABLE URBAN ENVIRONMENTS

ALICE COLEMAN

Sustainable development is often regarded as the province of agriculture but it is also an essential concept for urban stability. In the United Kingdom in the second half of the nineteenth-century there have been many new urban developments which were initially acclaimed by design awards but subsequently degenerated into serious problem estates. They proved unable to create and sustain a healthy community spirit based on self-help and neighbour help, and have become foci of crime and social breakdown. They are a heavy charge upon public funds for many different reasons.

The Land-use Research Unit at King's College London has been working since 1979, first to explore what was wrong. Secondly to devise ways of putting it right, and thirdly to engage in practical measures to rectify the problems in specific urban black spots. We are also monitoring the cost and effectiveness of our methods.

Good Intentions

All the problem areas were planned with the best of intentions. Planning machinery was established in Britain by the 1947. Town and Country Planning Act in order to appoint wise and far-sighted planned who would ensure that future development would be an improvement on what have gone before. There were relatively small areas of slums, which were gradually being cleared and replaced, and planning aimed to hasten and complete the process. There were also large areas of semi-detached single family houses build during the first half of the century. These were highly popular and sought after, and also reasonably cheap to rent or buy. They were settled by strangers unknown to each other and were therefore rather impersonal at first, but they lent themselves to a nice balance of privacy and community formation, and came to support law-abiding neighbourhoods. The national crime rate was very low. Planners did not intend to demolish these areas, but they regarded them as inferior to the innovative and imaginative projects which they would devise for the future.

Between the slums and the semis were exclusive streets of 19th-century terrace houses. They were intermediate in price, and suited many people's income. They were not slums and have low crime rates, but planners rated them as even worse than the semis, and scheduled vast number of them for destruction during the 1950s, 1960s and 1970s in order to build idealised modern developments in their place.

These three decades could have been a magnificent period of urban renewal and expansion if the good intentions of planners had produced the ideal environments they envisaged. There is no doubt that they gave a great deal of careful thought to what would, in their opinion, be best for people, and as far as the dwelling interiors were concerned they were often successful.

It is unfortunate that the prevailing, but untested, theory of the time was modernism, which advocated throwing people together in high-rise blocks of flats. This was prosecuted, and accepted, as having multiple advantages and similar principles were later applied, as far as possible to houses as well as flats.

One principle was that if different households shared the same building, it would facilitate community formation. However, this should not be allowed to create high densities, so the building should be separated by generous proportions of open space: principle 2, and also principle 3, as greenery was considered essential for spiritual refreshment. Principle 4 was preoccupied with privacy; one dwelling should not overlook another and this was resolved by Rodburn-type layouts where the front of one house or block looked towards the blind side or end of another.

Principle 5 was the separation of pedestrian and vehicle flows in the interests of road safety. The initial concept of paths leading to one side of the dwelling with vehicle access on the opposite side led to many counter productive knock on effects. For example, drivers had to get from their cars to the block entrances in front, so there had to be alleyways between the blocks, and often at close intervals between houses. Cars were left parked in rear compounds or garage courts, out of sight from their owners' dwellings. Roads were designed as dead-ends to ensure that cars would be slowing down and less lethal as they approached home, and very often there was a fringe of such culs-de-sac nibbling into their periphery of an estate leaving the centre to the traversed by a maze of paths twisting and turning to ensure privacy and often making specific addresses extremely difficult to find. In addition there was the great innovation leap of separating pedestrians from vehicles in the vertical dimension. The footpaths were lifted up to traverse the upper corridors sometimes at several different levels, and the gaps between blocks were bridged by overhead walkways.

Another Modern Movement principle was that the outer form of a building should reflect its function, with no exterior decoration purely for the sake of ornament. This was highly acceptable to planners and architects, as the decorative semis with they bays and gasers had been built to off–the peg designs by small developers, and if they were simply continued, the services of both these professionals might appear unnecessary. Large blocks patently required them and the contrast could be accentuated by stressing the high thinking behind flat roofs, flat facades, raw concrete and shared common areas.

At the same time, architects and planners like to make their mark. They are not content to go on repeating the same big box, so within the constraints imposed by modernist theory they introduced many minor modifications. Our first study surveyed all 4099 blocks in 50 km^2 of inner London, and found hardly two that had exactly the same design in all particulars.

These good intentions were enshrined in official design guides supported by Central government directives and subsidies. There was a general conviction that this new form of built-environment, with its simple aesthetic grace and social engineering through design and layout, was an ideal product, which should be maintained in positive order by council cleanes and groundsmen, while tenants were debarred from any initiatives, such as individual gardens or colour schemes, that would mark perfect picture.

Cracks in the Picture

At first tenants transferred out of older properties were delighted with their new labour-saving flats. In 1971 Pearl Jephcott interviewed people who had moved from Glasgow's worst slum and found 63 per cent were enthusiastic about the dwelling itself, but 59 per cent had complaints about their blocks and estates. Likes and dislikes about the general neighbourhood were every balanced according to whether there was, or was not, satisfactory proximity to shops, schools, bus routes, friends and relatives. On balance most people were glad to be out of the slums, and so the new estates were pronounced generally successful. The complaints were dismissed on the argument that people like to have something to grumble at, a better conclusion would have been that the professionals were getting the dwelling interiors right and the blocks and estates wrong, and that they ought to go back to the drawing board for a better solution.

Oscar Newman's *Defensible Space* (1972) did not rely on what people said but looked at hard data about levels of crime in different types of building used for New York's public housing. From half-a-dozen standard block designs he was able to infer that eight specific types of feature were at fault, and that they created an unsafe environment through three different mechanisms. Where too many people shared the same building, they tended to remain an anonymous crowd who could not all know each other, which made criminals feel that they could safely intrude without being identified. Where large blocks had many inter-accessible lifts, staircases and exits, these encouraged criminals further by providing them with multiple escape routes. And where the principle of ultra-privacy deprives tenants of adequate surveillance over their approaches, criminals know they are unlikely ever to be seen.

As well as establishing that crime levels are related to design, Newman also experimented with modifying a few of the relevant features, which produced a small but noticeable reduction in crime strongly, however, the British Department of the Environment did not use this evidence of reversibility to abandon its counterproductive design guides. The civil servants were unwilling to accept that they had been mistaken, and asserted that Newman's American problem would not apply to Britain. They did, however, stop arguing that their designs would produce utopia and started to blame the "problem people" who lived in the problem estates. Design was declared innocent.

It seemed therefore that a British study was necessary to prove whether Newman's findings would apply this side of the atlantic, and to this end the King's College research team undertook a survey of all 4099 blocks of flats located in a 50 km area of inner London. The results are reported in *Utopia on Trial* (1983).

Test Measures

The influence of design must be judged by means of specific criteria. Newman had excellent crime figures collected by New York's 1600-strong housing police force, but London crime statistics are not broken down on a block by block basis and cannot be related to design. The same is true of most other figures, so it was decided to map our own test measures, consisting of visible signs present in each building. They were litter, graffiti and excrement occurring inside the communal entrances or within a radius of 3m outside them, and types of vandal damage anywhere on the ground floor or the block exterior. These measures are jointly described as *abuse*, and their aggregate record in each block is an *abuse score*.

Types of abuse proved to have unexpected advantages. First, as there were several of them, they could have yielded conflicting evidence, but proved in practice to corroborate each other in indicting the same design features. And secondly, they proved to be early warning signs of social breakdown in a progressive order of seriousness in the breaking of social taboos. Litter-dropping, the mildest breach of taboo, does not occur in the best-designed blocks, and occurs alone in slightly worse ones. Graffiti is more serious and is rarely seen in blocks that do not also have litter. Vandal damage is unlikely unless both litter and graffiti are already present, and pollution by excrement follows where there are all three others. These combinations accounted for 92 per cent of the 4099 blocks. A further 4 per cent had the same combinations minus litter; they had apparently just been swept and the survey followed too quickly for reaccumulation of rubbish to have occurred. Eight more possible but unlikely combinations accounted for the remaining 4 per cent, so the progressive taboo hypothesis seems broadly tenable.

All these test measures proved to be clearly related to design and as a result the Commissioner of the Metropolitan Police at Scotland Yard arranged for two research policemen to assemble a year's crime figures for 729 individual blocks. Nine types of residential crime proved to be related to the same design variables as the abuse measures, further strengthening the evidence that these features are at fault. The crimes concerned were burglary, theft, robbery, criminal damage, theft of vehicles, theft from vehicles (usually with damage as well), bodily harm, sexual assaults and juvenile arrests. The last differed from the others in that the offences were committed off the estate and the offenders were then classified by their home addresses.

A further test measure was family breakdown resulting in children being placed in care. Information was made available for 1955 blocks, and once again the same designs were associated with the social problem.

Design Variables

The design data are more complex to describe. Newman was able to analyse his crime data on a block basis as he was dealing with six standard designs, but this was not possible in London where hardly two blocks were alike. Instead we had to record the individual values of individual design variables, and allow for complete continuance of difference. For example, within the 50 km² there were blocks of every height from two storeys to 27. These fine distinctions allowed more precise analysis.

It proved possible to recognise twice as many influential design variables as Newman's eight, partly because London has additional defects that do not occur in New York, e.g. overhead walkways, blocks raised over concrete silts or garage banks, and maisonettes. All 16 are set out in Table 24.1, where those recognised by Newman are asterisked.

The first group of four are size variables. When the size is too great Newman's anonymity mechanism comes into play. The asterise for dwellings per entrance is bracketed because the variable is surveyed in a different way from that used in New York. In London it is necessary to allow that one entrance may serve dwellings in other blocks via overhead walkways. Our worst estate had 2268 maisonettes accessible from any entry without descending to ground level. This variable is the most powerful factor in the distribution of litter and graffiti.

The second group of four, the circulation of variables, fit Newman's mechanism of escape routes. Overhead walkways cause severe worse nuisance as children and dogs run back and forth and, because of dog dirts, are the strongest factor in the presence of excrement. They also spread crime to smaller blocks that would not have it otherwise. Corridor type is also interesting. Newman found that internal corridors are more dangerous than external, and London tenants in double-loaded blocks say they fear to go out. However, our results reveal that corridor length is even more important than corridor type. If internal corridors accommodate four or fewer dwellings they are the best instead of the worst.

TABLE 24.1: The Influential Design Variables (slightly simplified)

	Harmless values	Harmful values
The Size Variables		
1. Dwellings per block	1 – 12	13 or more
2. Dwellings per entrance(*)	1 – 6	7 or more
3. Number of storeys*	1 – 3	4 or more
4. Flats or maisonettes	Flats	Maisonettes
The Circulation Variables		
5. Overhead walkways	None	1 or more
6. Interconnected exists	1	2 or more
7. Interconnected lifts or staircases*	1 (stair)	2 or more
8. Dwellings per corridor(*)	4	5 or more
The Entrance Variables		
9. Entrance position*	Facing road	Facing interior
10. Entrance type	CG. Co.	C I
11. Doors or open apertures	Doors	Apertures
12. Stilts, garages, etc.	None	Stilts, garages
Characteristics of the Grounds		
13. Blocks per site	1	2 or more
14. Access gates or gaps	1	2 or more
15. Play areas	None	1 or more
16. Spatial organisation(*)	No confused	confused

* given in text 2nd Para.

The third group, the entrance variables, reflect the possibility of surveillance. If they face a road, public surveillance by passing pedestrians can reinforce resident surveillance, and the blocks are safer, and less urine polluted, than those which face the estate interior. The best entrance type has communal entrances for upstairs flats and individual doors with fenced front gardens for ground floor dwellings. The worst type is the same without the fenced front gardens. Communal garages undermine surveillance because the lowest dwellings are raised up and tenants cannot crane their necks down to see who is entering their building underneath them.

The last group of four is related to a new mechanism: control by tenants of their dwelling approaches. The best facilitator of control is the *semi-private* front garden belonging wholly to one household. Next best is *semi-public* space fenced in for the residents of a single block to share. Land that is left open among different blocks, or even to the public at large is termed *confused* space. It robs residents of territorial control and, in spite of the planners' accolade, proves the most powerful factor in the volume of crime. The second most powerful is the presence of access gates or gaps on different sides of the estate, which undermine control by allowing outsiders to take shortcuts across it.

We have also recognised a fifth mechanism, which is an aggregate of the other four. From the design aspect, large size, mazelike circulation, ultra-private layouts and open grounds add up to modernism. On the social side, anonymity, escape rocks, lack of surveillance and lack of control add up to a grave impediment to child-rearing. Parents find it difficult or impossible to integrate their children into the community (which hardly exists anyway), and so the estate not only attracts any pre-existing criminals but also breeds its own. Estate children run a high risk of becoming anti-social, and may graduate to delinquency and crime. Yet another utopia has failed.

Thresholds and Disadvantagement Scores

Table 24.1 divides the values of each design variable into harmless and harmful ranges. These are standards that were established by means of a chi-squared technique as follows. First, the design values were cross-tabulated with values of litter, graffiti, vandal damage and excrement, to give four tables, the cells of which contained the number of relevant blocks. These are observed frequencies. Expected frequencies were then calculated for comparison, and better-than expected cells (i.e. with more abuse-free or fewer abused blocks that the expected frequency) were classified as harmless, leaving the rest as harmful. The four different test measures almost always yielded the same verdict and the worst harmless value has been adopted as a standard *threshold* for future use.

When a block is surveyed the values of its 16 variables are recorded and those that fall within the harmful range are each marked with an asterisk. The asterisks represent design defects and the total number of defects in the same block is termed its *disadvantagement score*. It is a way of looking at all the designs in combination, and it is also possible to characterise a whole estate by reference to the average score of all its blocks.

Public, Private and Housing Association Blocks

The use of the disadvantagement score may be illustrated in the context of block ownership. Newman's study was restricted to public blocks only but the London research included all the blocks in 50 km^2. The majority were publicly owned but over 400 were private and about 100 belonged to housing associations or trusts. The private blocks had least abuse, the association and trust blocks had more, and public blocks most. However, the ownership factor is not significant in itself, but is mediated through design difference.

Crime Related to Disadvantagement Scores

The vertical axis shows percentages and the trend lines reveal what proportion of the blocks with each score have at least one crime. None of the defect-free, zero-scoring blocks reported a single crime of any kind during the year, and as the number of defects increases so does the proportion of blocks with crime. The types of crime also increase. With a score of one, burglary and car theft affect a few blocks. With a score of two, criminal damage makes its appearance. With a score of four violence (bodily harm) emerges and with a score of five, robbery from the person. Bodily harm often springs out of personal grievances, but robbery (mugging) is after a callous attack upon strangers purely for gain. It is the rarest of the residential crimes, although in some areas it is more common as a street crime.

The trend line for total crime crosses the graph diagonally from 0 per cent to 100 per cent of the blocks. This supports the idea that design is a very major factor in total crime. It is not the only factor. However, some people are naturally mere low-abiding than others, so some blocks score better and some worse than the averages shown by the trend lines. The lines are also slightly smoothed, as in order to eliminate irregularities caused where there are few blocks of any individual score, we have recalculated by the method of running means of three values. This is far less smoothing than is involved in a regression line but enough, apparently, to get rid of purely artificial disturbances.

Design disadvantagement is not a determinist theory. At every score, except the first and last, a proportion of blocks are crime free and a proportion have crime. If we had studied just a few blocks they might, by chance, all be in the crime free proportion, or all in the crime-effected proportion. One has to study a large number for the closer pattern to emerge as a trend line. The worse the disadvantagement score the higher the probability of crime. Thus, blocks score to have as 50 per cent probability of crime, a 50 per cent probability of burglary, a 5 per cent probability of robbery, etc.

There are few crimes in the low-scoring blocks and many in the high-scoring ones. If the disadvantagement score is 13 or worse, there was an average of at least one crime for every five dwellings per annum, and in some cases more than one per dwelling. Yet in this same high-crime area the best designed blocks remain crime-free.

The Crime Rate Over Time

My evidence is geographical. The level of social breakdown varies spatially in the same pattern as design variations. But there is also historical corroboration which shows how the low crime rate was very low at the beginning of the century and doubled during the 1930s when some local authorities were beginning to build flats. After planning came in, flats were built on a grand scale, and crime escalated enormously. Younger and younger children were committing crimes, and crime has become much more violent and sadistic.

Even if no more flats are ever built, the crime rate will continue to worsen. Each year the present ones remain, they train another year's age group of children to become criminal, so a progressively greater proportion of the age range belongs to the criminal subculture. The future looks very bleak unless effective action is taken.

The DICE Project

When Mrs. Thatcher was Prime Minister, she read my book, *Utopia on Trial* (1983) which advocated re-design of problem estates as a way of reversing trends in crime and social breakdown. She invited me to Downing Street for a very business like, but also enjoyable discussion, as a result of which I was funded by the Department of the Environment to set up the DICE Project. The acronym stands for Design Improvement Controlled Experiment. It consists of a small research team at King's College, London which surveys and redesigns estates and a government grant of £50 million divided among local authorities willing to co-operate by putting our proposals into action.

The surveys identify 38 defects of design and layout. As well as the 16 influential variables in flats, there are 12 more in houses built according to Modern Movement principles, and 10 related to miscellaneous items such as refuse facilities and car parking. The estate is recorded on a map as well as in tables of design values, and disadvantagement and abuse scores are calculated.

The disadvantagement scores and the values of the individual designs enable us to identify the precise causes of the social breakdown and to target our recommendations to create maximum benefit. The aim is to bring each defective design down to its threshold level, or below it, and for each one that is taken into its harmless range, one point is subtracted from the disadvantagement score. We can therefore, predict what the final score will be, and make an educated estimate as to how far design improvement will be followed by alleviation of social problems.

For example, our Benett Street Estate in Manchester was built with an average disadvantagement score of 13.8 out of a possible 16 for each block. Its social problems were appalling it had had three murder episodes and was infested by drug-pushers. DICE showed how to reduce the score to 1.4. The optimum score of zero is very rarely obtainable, but 1.4 is low enough to be almost problem-free.

DICE aims to make the blocks as much as possible like the houses that dominated the score when the crime rate was very low. This means recreating single households with their own territory, or where different households still have to share the same entrances, stairs and corridors, ensuring that the number is very few, so that they can all know each other.

We begin by demolishing the overhead walkways to leave each block free-standing. This reduces the powerful dwellings-per-entrance variable, and in our first estate it caused an immediate 55 per cent drop in the burglary rate, which has been maintained ever since, even though no locks or other security devices were installed.

Concienge schemes, assisted by security devices such as entryphones and video cameras, can also reduce burglaries by roughly the same amount, but there the burglars simply go elsewhere and crime rises in the surrounding areas. This does not happen with design improvement. On the contrary, the surroundings of our first estate had a drop in the burglary rate. This confirms that design improvement is actually get in to the cause of the problem and influencing the children to behave better.

The next step is to divide each block into smaller self-contained sections. High rise blocks are divided into two layers. The existing lifts and stairs serve only the top half, and a new entrance, lift and stairs are built on the other side to serve the lower part. If more money were available we could divide these towers into three another layers, with no internal connection between them.

Lower-size buildings are partitioned in a different way. The ground floor flats or maisonettes are converted into quasi-houses, each with its own front and back door leading into its own enclosed front and back garden: semi-private space. Quasi-houses have no connection with the rest of the block, except for the fact of being located underneath it.

The upper block above the quasi-houses is now substantially smaller than the original total block, and has to be further divided. This is not done by horizontal layering as in the case of tower blocks, but by creating vertical slices. Walls are built across the corridors at intervals that provide separate sections of not more than six dwellings, and preferably not more than four along the same corridor. Each section would have one entrance and one staircase, with no alternative escape route. The open aperture would be given a door and instead of leading out into confused space, it would open into a front forecourt of semi-public space, with a front wall 900mm high and only one gate. It would face a proper road.

Sub-blocks created to these specifications have final disadvantagement scores of between 0 and 2. They retain one block mark if there are more than 3 storeys and another if they consist of maisonettes rather than flats. Maisonettes are bad because they are larger than flats and usually allocated to families with children. We try to ensure that such families are transferred down to ground level, into the quasi-houses or any existing houses or any new houses then we build as part of the scheme.

Houses

The blocks and houses built by public authorities during the 1950s, 1960s and 1970s were so bad that during the 1980s the government stopped them from building more. This was not due to recognition of the design defects described above, but simply because the money was needed for repairs. Many blocks were badly built, and had leaking roofs, spalling concrete, defective electrical wiring, and loose panels dropping off in addition. They were heavily vandalised, especially the lifts, which were frequently out of action.

However, I explained to Mrs. Thatcher why DICE needed to build new houses, and she agreed that we could. The reasons are as follows.

At present, blocks of flats stand in open confused space, and can be approached by intruders from all four sides. Even if we provide quasi-houses with back gardens, the new walls would still be exposed to greens, alleyways, parking areas, etc., and burglars can easily scramble over. To prevent this we design the back gardens of the flats to about directly upon the back gardens of houses. In fact, we advocate an island-site layout where houses face outward to roads in all four directions and dwellings can be approached only from the front. The sides and backs are secure.

We have also found that houses are safer if they face each other across a road. This allows resident surveillance outward across their front gardens, neighbour surveillance from the houses opposite and public surveillance by passing pedestrians.

It is often thought that if houses could replace flats, all would be well. This is not so. It depends on the design of the houses. Architects have been so saturated in Modernist principles that they have applied them to houses as well. We have identified 12 potentially harmful variables in houses, which can also produce problem estates.

Open-plan space is confused space. Front gardens need to be enclosed behind 900mm front wall with a gate and side fences between neighbours. We have a saying, "Good fences make good neighbours", and it is perfectly true, but officialism was so obsessed with shared grounds that they denied people the right to have their own piece of semi-private space.

Enclosed front gardens are an excellent mechanism for community formation. People are out working in them, to create their own individual mark, and this provides opportunities to chart with passers-by. Resident build up a web off contacts on a ometo-one basis, and they remember people more easily because of their individual settings. This quite difficult from facts where people go in and out too quickly for much in the way of contact, and where it is much less to assess their characters, because they all disappear behind identical doors.

Front gardens provide good social training for children. If a todoller strays inside a neighbour's gate he is taught that he must stay out of his property. This is an easy lesson to learn, as there is a continuous frontage of fences and gates to demarcate forbidden territory, and absorbing respect for gardens seems to preclude the development of a vandalistic attitude.

As well as being less distinctive, house-bred children are less violent. A Japanese study described them as less callous. Flat-bred children do not have the same opportunities to know or be known by neighbours, and to become integrated into a kindly community. They see others as anonymous bodies living in anonymous dwellings and think of them as things rather than people. The rape gang that beat up a jogger in New York felt they were justified because "she was nothing".

We have seen remarkable transformations when front gardens are added. On one estate, the residents described how menacing gangs of youths became polite individuals. Elsewhere, a social worker reported that social harassment had been "killed stone dead". Another estate was being massively abandoned but regained its popularity when the common front lawns were divided up into individual semi-private spaces.

The Complexity of Design Improvement

Design disadvantagement is reversible by means of design improvement, but it is not as simple as it sounds. There are 38 variables to take into account simultaneously and each one has a range of harmful and harmless values, including some weird gimmicks you would never think of. It is all too easy to put one defect right while making of another one worse and blocking all possibility of improving a few others. People send photographs of their efforts without realising they have done just that.

Since every block is different, DICE has to provide custom-made schemes. It is not possible to select an appropriate off-the-pea method and plug it in. We have to explore successive combinations of options to find which one will reduce the disadvantagement score by the maximum amount.

There are many things to be taken into account, such as the location of car-parking in a way that parents children from becoming car thieves and joy-riders, who are increasingly often killing people during high-speed races in stolen vehicles. We have to stop them setting fire to cars and garages, and many other anti-social practices too numerous to mention. It is not just a question of failing young criminals. DICE aims to go back to the causes of decline and eradicate them, so that children grow up naturally non-criminal and would not even entertain the idea of violating the social moves so flagrantly.

It is encouraging to learn from the Department of the Environment that DICE schemes do not cost any more per dwelling that alternatives that do not work as well. Nevertheless, prevention is better than cure, and it grieves me to see new Modern Movement estates still being built, with all their probability of a disastrous future.

Sustainability

What is meant by sustainability in housing and the urban environment? I define the sustainable home as one where individual families–

(a) have autonomous control over their own homes, without having to share their buildings and grounds with others;
(b) have freedom to pursue their chosen lifestyles without fearing that they are creating problems for neighbours;
(c) are responsible for keeping their homes in good order. The buildings should not require frequent repairs beyond their means. Individual self-help is to be encouraged;
(d) have their homes set in a layout that facilitates community formation and mutual help among neighbours; and
(e) feel secure from crime because their kindly social structure does not generate young criminals.

DICE works with estate residents throughout but we do not want them to become dependent on us. We aim to leave them with enhanced ability to manage their own lives instead of being constrained by local authority landlords to the straitjacket of identical homes piled up in crates, and the resulting social breakdown and victimisation by criminals. We believe that design-emancipation is an essential factor in grass-roots democracy.

Mrs. Thatcher tried to introduce grass-roots democracy by means of financial incentives for council tenants to buy their own homes. This was eagerly taken up by house tenants but generally ignored by tenants in flats. Flats were homes they wanted to escape from, and not dig themselves into with ownership and responsibility. She hoped that the DICE Project would make the flats more acceptable, so that more people would exercise the right to buy, and with seems to be happening.

Cross-Cultural Information

Do the housing mistakes of the United Kingdom carry any message for India? I believe they do, but that it may be a difficult message to accept. The Department of Environment in London refused to learn from the American experience, and went on to encumber us with vast social problems. The Japanese were interested in my housing research, but were certain that similar problems could not happen in their country. The Director of Housing in Asahikawa kindly took me to a public estate, where no such difficulties would be found. He was surprised to find litter, graffiti and vandal damage affecting virtually every common entrance. Japan is noted from a low crime level, just as Britain used to be, but as more and bigger blocks of flats are built there, the national crime rate is rising year after year.

The disastrous influence of bad design in houses and flats is a universal problem that affects human nature everywhere. I have seen serious problems in many European countries, in USA, Canada, West Indies, Australia and in China. I have read of it in South America, and people from Singapore, South Africa and other places have visited me to discuss similar issues affecting their own countries. When I was in Delhi in 1987, a taxi-driver explained the anti-social behaviour of the children in a high-size block we saw. I do not believe India is immune.

It saddened me to see almost a forest of tall blocks under construction in the new town of Modinagar. Planners may love them, but they create far more problems than they solve. There are already signs of problems in the vicinity of that town. The low property walls that suffice in law-abiding areas, both in Britain and India were being doubled in height in Modinagar, and rural walls between the road and farm fields had been fortified by barbed wire. The already unsafe situation is bound to grow steadily worse.

Are there any Indian geographers willing to produce scientific evidence like that of USA and the UK, and was it to deflect planners away from modernistic architecture?

It may be argued that flats are needed to create sufficiently high densities. This is not so in Britain. Flats take up space for lifts, corridors, balconies and other items not needed in houses. In one DICE estate we have demolished 128 flats and replaced them with 129 houses with gardens.

India has a remarkable resource for housing. Many people know how to build their own. It might be possible to take sites proposed for flats and divide them into small plots, allowing large numbers of people to exercise self-help simultaneously, instead of waiting helplessly for specialised block builders, and losing their traditional skills. Is it possible for people with a full knowledge of Indian conditions to work out something viable along these lines?

PART-VIII

ENVIRONMENTAL POLICIES (GLOBAL AND NATIONAL)-II

25

URBAN COMMUNITY DEVELOPMENT IN THE THIRD WORLD: Lessons from Visakhapatnam, India

SHEENA ASTHANA

Introduction

Participants at the Rio Earth Summit recently highlighted the growing challenge of urban poverty by calling for a profound change in urban development policies, guaranteeing the right to a healthy environment, education, sanitation, work and popular participation in the decision-making process to eradicate hunger and misery. Despite growing support for *integrated* urban development based on full community participation, such an approach is rarely adopted at the governmental level. However, the Indian experience provides an important exception.

This paper focuses upon the experience of Visakhapatnam Urban Community Development (UCD) Project in Andhra Pradesh, India in order to explore the problems and prospects of programme integration. The UCD Project, which covers the entire slum population of the city, emphasizes the role of community participation, organization and initiative. It undertakes a wide range of activities including environmental improvements, income generation schemes, health and education projects and self-help housing. Particular attention is paid to developing women's organizations and to identifying and training female leaders.

Visakhapatnam's experience provides many positive lessons about improving urban living conditions. However, several problems can also be identified. Firstly, the emphasis on integration is difficult to sustain as 'hard' programmes such as housing and infrastructure, are given grater priority (by project staff and community members alike) than 'soft' project relating to health, education and social development. Secondly, as development activities are carried out at the level of individual settlements, insufficient account is taken of structural influences on participation such as the local and market and the political-administrative system. Thus, tensions exist between the short-term goal of shelter provision and the long-term process of empowerment; between the use value of self-help housing and its status as a potential commodity; and between the Project's commitment to develop female leadership and the tendency for the housing scheme, which provides scope for political patronage and brokerage, to reinforce made dominated leadership structures. The paper concludes by considering ways in which future urban planners can build on the achievements of the UCD Project whilst learning from its failures.

The Growing Challenge of Urban Poverty

In the past forty years the pace of urbanization in less developed countries has been truly dramatic. Between 1950 and 1988 the proportion of the Third World's population living in cities more than doubled from 17 per cent to 43 per cent. Today some 1.3 billion people live in urban centres in the Third World and within the next twenty years this figure is expected to reach 2 billion (Hardoy and Satterthwaite, 1989). The rapid growth in cities has been accompanied by a rapid growth in the number of urban inhabitants living in substandard, overcrowded conditions without the funds for decent housing. It is currently estimated that an average of 50 per cent of the world's urban population live at the level of extreme poverty, with this figure rising as high as 79 per cent in some cities (Harpham et al, 1988).

Despite the scale of urban poverty, much of the literature on health and development has focused upon rural problems. Until recently, conventional wisdom held that there was an *urban bias,* the cities of the Third World benefiting from a disproportionate share of their nations' resources (Lipton, 1977). A reaction against the concentration of productive investment, infrastructure and services in urban centres led many development agencies to explicitly direct their programmes at rural populations. By contrast, the plight of the urban poor received relatively little attention.

In the past decade, the relevance of the concept of urban bias has been called into question. Biases in the allocation of resources, it is argued, work not so much against rural areas as against the poor. Thus, although urban dwellers *appear* to enjoy higher living standards than their rural counterparts, official statistics mask enormous intra-urban inequalities in socio-economic status, environmental conditions and health. It is now widely accepted that the vast majority of urban inhabitants hardly benefit from government investment in industrial development and public services. Much of the labour force is employed in the informal sector which offers minimum wages and minimum job security. Unable to afford 'legal' housing, many inhabitants have no option but to squat on illegal land or inhabit crowded and deteriorating tenements in city centre slums. Concentrated in areas that are geographically discrete to neighbourhoods occupied by high income groups, the urban poor rarely benefit from public works programmes supplying water, electricity, drains, sewers and roads. Health services also fail to reach low-income groups as government facilities are frequently inaccessible, overcrowded and understaffed and private facilities beyond the financial reach of poor patients. As urban bias has neither lessened poverty nor increased basic service provision in low-income areas, poor city dwellers do not enjoy better living standards that their rural counterparts. Indeed, in several countries, higher rates of malnutrition and infectious disease have been recorded in urban slums and squatter settlements than in rural villages (Basta, 1977; Lee and Furst, 1980; Wray, 1986).

Health Problems in Third World Cities

A complex mixture of factors affects health in poor urban environments. In contrast to the urban rich, whose disease profiles increasingly resemble those of the developed world, the urban poor suffer from diseases of poverty, industrialization and social instability (Rossi-Espagnet, 1984; Harpham et al, 1988; Tabibzadeh, 1989). Three groups of health hazards operate on the poor in the cities. The first includes direct problems of poverty such as low income, limited education and insufficient diet. Malnutrition amongst the urban poor is exacerbated by the fact that few urban dwellers have access to a plot of land on which to grow food. In contrast to many rural areas, food intake in the cities depends entirely upon cash income (Nelson and Mandl, 1978). Economic recession and structural adjustment during the 1980s have therefore caused particular hardship for urban dwellers.

At the same time that income and employment opportunities have fallen steeply in the cities, cuts in food subsidies and the removal of price controls on consumer commodities have meant that many households have lost the purchasing power to meet minimum food needs.

The second group of health problems relate to man-made conditions of the urban environment such as overcrowding, poor housing, industrialization, pollution and a generally increased exposure to infectious disease. Housing design, for example, can help spread airborne communicable diseases such as tuberculosis and influenza through poor ventilation. Respiratory illness is exacerbated by indoor air pollution through open fires and disease vectors or parasites have easy access to housing of lacking protected roofs, walls or floors or protected food storage areas (Hardoy and Satterthwaite, 1987; 1989). An inadequate house size may also increase the risk of household accidents as it becomes impossible to safeguard children from open fires, stoves or harmful chemicals and medicines. Problems associated with water and sanitation are often acute in crowded urban settlements, the lack of a clean water supply, sewerage, sanitary facilities and waste control creating favourable conditions for water-borne diseases such as diarrhoea, dysentary and cholera. Pools of standing water provide breeding grounds for vectors of parasitic diseases such as malaria and, where water is scarce, poor personal hygiene can lead to a high incidence of eye and ear infections and skin diseases such as scabies. An additional problem is the lack of rubbish collection in many urban settlements. The accumulation of garbage attracts insects and vermin, many of which carry disease.

Lastly, the urban poor suffer from social and psychological problems associated with the instability and insecurity of life in certain urban areas. These include alcohol and drug abuse, prostitution, venereal disease and child labour. The urban environment can be particularly hostile to children. While children's work in rural areas has traditionally been part of household production, in urban areas it is generally performed under an employer-employee relationship. Hence, the vulnerability of children, deprived of the parental protection they enjoy in agrarian societies, is accentuated (Bequele and Boyden, 1988).

Integrated Urban Community Development

It is clear that the complex mix of factors affecting health in poor urban environments makes integrated development programmes particularly attractive. The impact of nutrition projects, for example, can be undermined if the physical environment remains highly contaminated. A survey in Poona, India found little association between morbidity and income in badly serviced and overcrowded hutments as even better-off households were unable to protect themselves against airborne and waterborne disease (Bapat and Crook, 1984). Conversely, physical upgradation may bring limited benefits when insufficient diets are lowering dwellers' resistance to infectious disease. Malnutrition is a key determinant of ill-health in low-income communities and, even within single slum settlements, rates of morbidity and mortality can vary widely according to nutritional status. Breast-fed infants, for example, have been found to have a significantly lower risk of mortality than infants who are bottle-fed from the first few months of life.

Calls for integrated urban development are receiving growing support and it is possible to discern a shift in policy since the early 1980s from single sector slum upgrading to multisectoral slum improvement (Stephens and Harpham, 1991). In practice, however, programme integration implies intersectoral coordination which can prove difficult to achieve where ministries and departments are competing for resources along sectoral lines. Integrated urban development therefore, has better hopes for success when a special administrative mechanism is set in place to ensure that communication and coordination takes place between different agencies and sectors. True integration also implies that planning is done on an *areal* basis. As health-related problems of poor housing, water and sanitation, poverty and illiteracy tend to be geographically concentrated in the urban environment, it is often argued that urban deprivation does lend itself more easily to integrated solutions than poverty in a rural setting (Tendler, 1982).

Finally, the success of settlement or community-based projects is more likely to be guaranteed if members of the community are fully involved in project planning and implementation. Community participation ensures that project activities and procedures are adapted to serve the specific needs of local groups; it provides a means by which local resources such as knowledge, skills and labour can be harnessed, allowing more people to benefit; it encourages cooperation and solidarity amongst community members and increases their capacity for future participative ventures; and participation can be regarded as an empowering process through which community members achieve greater choice and control in everyday aspects of their lives and learn to collectively withstand manipulation by groups and exploit them (Hollnsteiner, 1982; Oakley, 1989; Moser, 1989).

Despite broad support for integrated urban community development, relatively few governmental agencies address urban health issues in a multi-sectoral way. Indeed, the best examples of integrated projects tend to be run by non-governmental organizations. These are generally much smaller in scale and less bound by red tape and bureaucracy. This allows a greater freedom and flexibility to respond to local needs and initiatives, to coordinate different activities and to experiment with new techniques in order to promote meaningful participation amongst community members. By contrast, state-funded projects often run into difficulties in achieving intersectoral coordination as different departments compete for funds and recognition (Harpham et al, 1988). In several Indian cities, however, this problem has been addressed through the creation of special Urban Community Development Departments (UCDDs) within municipal corporations. In addition to coordinating a range of developmental activities at the community level, UCDDs facilitate linkages between slum dwellers and external organizations including local banks and non-governmental agencies. Thus, with its commitment to inter-sectoral collaboration, integrated development and community participation, the Indian experience of urban community development merits special attention.

This paper focuses upon the activities of the Visakhapatnam Urban Community Development (UCD) Project in Andhra Pradesh, India. It is based upon fieldwork undertaken during a six month period in 1988. Semi-structured interviews were held with Project staff and the community leaders of 33 slum settlements drawn from a cluster sample. Five settlements were then selected for more detailed study. Questionnaires were administered to a systematic sample of 348 households in order to obtain information on dwelling characteristics, socio-economic status, participation in project activities and community-initiated organizations and ventures, morbidity and use of health services, and maternal behaviour with regard to specific aspects of child care. Quantitative data obtained from Project records and the household survey was complemented through the use of qualitative methods including key-informant interviews, focus group discussions and direct observation.

Urban Community Development in Visakhapatnam, India

Situated on the east coast of India, roughly half way between Calcutta and Madras, Visakhapatnam is one of the fastest growing cities in

India. Post-war industrialization, rapid rates of in-migration and an acute shortage of land have limited the housing options of low income groups in the city and slum settlements have proliferated over the past twenty years. In 1986, approximately 25 per cent of the total population of 80,000 resided in 170 officially designated slums in which housing, environmental sanitation and infrastructural provision were grossly inadequate. According to Municipal statistics, 50 per cent of slums lacked a protected water supply and 90 per cent lacked sanitary latrines. The incidence of malnutrition was estimated to be around 20 per cent and the prevalence of communicable diseases (especially respiratory, gastro-enteritic and skin diseases) 25 per cent higher than in non-slum areas in the city.

The Visakhapatnam UCD Project was initiated in 1979 and replicated many of the features of the widely acclaimed UCD Project in Hyderabad. Funded by the State Government and the Municipal Corporation, the Project followed the guidelines first set down by the Rural-Urban Relationship Committee in 1966 (Clinard, 1966). Its objectives include creating a sense of social cohesion on a neighbourhood basis through corporate civic action; developing a sense of belonging to the urban community through increased participation in community affairs and enabling people to solve problems using their own initiatives, organizations, self-help and mutual aid; bringing about a change in consciousness by motivating people to improve their own conditions, particularly those affecting their social and physical environment; developing local initiatives and identifying and training local leaders; and ensuring fuller utilization of technical and welfare services by helping the community to identify what help could be provided by the municipality and other organizations and how to get it.

The activities undertaken in the UCD project fall into five categories: physical infrastructure, housing, community development, economic, educational and social programmes and health. Physical infrastructure includes the provision of dust-proof approach roads; the paving of lanes and walkways; the canalising of runoff and sullage water; and the provision of clean drinking water, community lavatories, street lighting, garbage collection and community halls. Community members are expected to sweep and clear garbage and regularly clean out blockages in storm water drains, to clean and maintain community halls and to undertake simple repairs of borewells, water pipelines and the community latrines. Environmental health is also improved through the 'self-help' housing scheme. Slum dwellers are given legal title to land (*patta*). The layout and design of each settlement's housing scheme are discussed with community members who are issued building materials and housing loans. Households are then expected to undertake construction themselves.

Community development activities seek to enhance the role of community participation, organization and initiative in slum development. Particular attention is paid to identifying and training female leaders. Community Organisers establish personal contact with slum communities and encourage the development of Neighbourhood Committees, the members of which act as representatives for ten to fifteen families. The Committee, which normally comprises women, is expected to meet weekly and is given the responsibility of identifying project beneficiaries for schemes such as income generation loans. Each family pays a membership fee which is placed in a bank account to be used for community such as contributing towards the community creche, the sewing centre or vocational training schemes. Contributions made or raised by community members are often 'matched' by the Project to encourage resource mobilization.

Visakhapatnam UCD Department coordinates a range of economic, educational and social activities through links with local governmental and non-governmental organizations. In 1982, for example, funds in the range of £20,000 were raised from local banks in order to provide loans for income generation. Loans are issued mainly for fruit and vegetable vending, cycle rickshaws, tea shops and small scale craft enterprises. An imaginative series of skill-training programmes have also been arranged for slum dwellers covered by the Project including detergent and tooth powder production, fabric painting, the manufacture of candles, matches and toys and money management. Programmes coordinated by UCDD that are tailored for male slum dwellers include training in masonry, carpentry, brick making and welding.

Educational activities divide into those provided for pre-school children and programmes aimed at improved adult literacy. The former are channelled through *balwadis* (kindergartens) and *anganwadis* (kindergartens run by the Integrated Child Development Services or ICDS). *Balwadis* provide basic education and a useful creche facility and UCDD coordinates short training courses for balwadi teachers in basic health prevention and promotion. *Anganwadis* are funded from Central Government resources and, in addition to providing basic education, anganwadi teachers give supplementary nutrition to and monitor the weights of attending children; identify, monitor and refer pregnant women and treat common ailments (Dayal, 1986; Nutrition Foundation of India, 1988).

The UCD Project has an impressive record with regard to its health programme and has implemented a range of promotive and preventive activities. Mother Leader Training camps, for example, comprise basic health education on immunization, nutrition, pregnancy, family planning and the recognition and treatment of common ailments (including oral rehydration). UCDD works in close liaison with a range of organizations, including Grevaltes, a local NGO working for the detection and cure of leprosy with community participation and Mahila Vikas Sanstha, an NGO for eye screening programmes. Collaboration with the Andhra Medical College and District Medical and Health Officer takes with respect to immunization and family welfare programmes and the College of Nursing has recently become involved in improving community based delivery services. Since 1988, private practitioners have been brought in by the Project to run community clinic sessions. Traditional birth attendants and Community Health Volunteers (CHVs) are also being trained to work in local settlements. The latter carry out a health survey of all dwellers in their community and maintain family health folders which contain the health particulars of individual members of each family. They are also responsible for maintaining the clinic's records.

From its inception, the UCD Project has stressed the importance of programme integration. Until 1987, however, the limited budget available to the UCD Department prevented the widespread implementation of the integrated package. In what is now referred to as the 'UNICEF Phase', emphasis was instead place on community development, socio-economic and health activities which were started in most of the city's slums with financial support from UNICEF. By contrast, housing and infrastructure was provided on a piecemeal basis during the period. In 1987, the Visakhapatnam UCD Project entered into a second phase when it was earmarked for large-scale assistance by the British Overseas Development Administration. Whilst ODA agreed to fund only physical infrastructure and the continued implementation and expansion of socio-economic and health activities, the Municipal Corporation secured funding from the national Housing and Urban Development Corporation (HUDCO) in order to implement the self-help housing scheme concurrently. In the 'ODA Phase', therefore, programme integration has been extended to all of the city's slums.

With its comprehensive approach to talking the problems of urban deprivation, Visakhapatnam UCD Project conforms to the new way of thinking about slum improvement. However, whilst the city's experience provides many positive lessons for urban planners, the goal of programme integration has been difficult to sustain in practice. The following section considers some of the key issues affecting the successful implementation of the integrated development package.

Urban Community Development in Practice: Key Issues

Intersectoral Collaboration

One of the most impressive aspects of the Visakhapatnam UCD Project is the extent to which linkages between different agencies have been successfully established. Some of these linkages have already been described with respect to the Project's health and socio-economic components. However, another notable feature is the fact that the infrastructural works division is housed within the UCD Department itself. Coordination is thus facilitated between the engineering staff (who have little experience of community development) and the community development staff who provide the major point of contact between the Project and its beneficiaries. The Project has therefore, made significant strides in its goal of achieving intersectoral collaboration, a factor that promotes the implementation of urban community development activities in an integrated manner.

Project Content: Priority and Non-Priority Needs

Programme integration, however, depends upon several other factors and whilst considerable attention has been paid to creating a suitable administrative apparatus for urban community development, insufficient account has been taken of the impact of programme *content* and of the *context* within which the Project is implemented. Project documents imply, for example, that there is to be parity between different sectors. In practice, however, the Project's beneficiaries perceive a hierarchy of needs and 'hard' development inputs such as housing and infrastructure generate more community interest than 'soft' projects relating to health, education and social development. As a result, community participation is difficult to sustain after basic services have been provided. This problem is exacerbated by the fact that the physical improvement and housing programmes take up a large proportion of staff members' time, thus diverting resources from the community development component.

Socio-Political Context: The Role of Political Patronage

The tensions that arise between the housing and infrastructural programmes on the one hand and community development on the other are compounded by a socio-political context dominated by political patronage. Clientelism is widespread in Visakhapatnam's slums, vertical links with local politicians being actively sought by slum leaders who promise their dwellers' votes in return for resource provision. As a highly visible resource which has both use and market value, housing is particularly vulnerable to political manipulation. During the UNICEF Phase of the Project, for example, the absence of an established and exclusive link between the UCD Department and HUDCO increased the scope for political patronage as local politicians recognised opportunities for directly negotiating for housing loans on behalf of their client communities. As a result, the distribution of the 5811 loans provided by HUDCO between 1979 and 1985 is highly skewed, 53 per cent being issued in just two wards.

Under the ODA Phase of urban community development, the fact that the housing scheme is being implemented in all of the city's slums would imply that the scope for political patronage has decreased. However, poor dissemination of information about the UCD Department's plan of development perpetuates the view amongst dwellers that political patronage secures resources. Community leaders share this view. According to a 1988 survey of slum leaders, only 15 per cent of respondents believed that links with local politicians offered no advantages. Twenty-seven per cent believed that political affiliation was a prerequisite to receiving the housing scheme (M. Hennion, personal communication). Faith in political patronage increases slum dwellers' vulnerability to exploitation. As one Community Organizer suggested, the 'support' vulnerability to exploitation. As one Community suggested, the 'support' expected by political patrons of their slum communities is not limited to the political kind:

> "In (one slum) the Corporator is collecting 500-1000 rupees per house from all of the loan beneficiaries. The people have no choice. They have been told by their leader that the Corporator sanctioned

their homes and that if they don't give the money, their houses will be taken away from them. I have tried to explain the housing scheme to them, but they won't believe me and follow their leader. If we stayed with community development, there wouldn't be the chance for the corruption that this housing development brings. Urban Community Development Department (UCDD) is step by step losing its community development approach".

The Local Land Market and Gentrification

A third problem associated with the housing scheme is that upgraded property may become a speculative commodity. In Visakhapatnam land is at a premium and demand for middle income housing is unfulfilled. The fact that the city's slums are being comprehensively developed makes them attractive to higher income groups. At the same time, the slum dweller may wish to realise his or her much improved asset. The inadequate size of loans issued to 'self-builders' often necessitates the borrowing of private loans at far higher rates of interest. Renting or selling one's home may therefore become a rational response to mounting debts.

The Project imposes a number of conditions in order to prevent the upward filtering of housing stock. The dwellers are issued with *pattas* or land rights, but not with formally registered deeds and the land is still technically owned by the government. The selling or mortgaging of scheme houses is prohibited and the Project reserves the right to prosecute the offending beneficiary and to reallocate the plot and house to another dweller. The illegality of the deal also implies a risk of eviction for the potential purchaser. However, these disincentives have not prevented illegal sale agreements in settlements that had received the housing scheme. Again, slum leaders play a critical role in property speculation and can profit from it in a number of ways.

Leaders who are officially or unofficially informed that their slums has been earmarked for upgradation may construct huts in vacant plots in order to personally obtain several *pattas* (which tend to be registered in the names of relations). As property speculation is a highly attractive trade in the city, the financial gains to be made from misappropriating plots are considerable. A second way in which leaders can capitalize on their access to information is by exploiting their dwellers' ignorance. A common practice is to preside over the illegal exchange of plots with a cost of Rs. 1000 to the purchaser and Rs. 500 to the vendor. Neither party gains any real protection against eviction or prosecution. However, without access to alternative sources of information about the Municipal Corporation's policy, they are not in a position to object.

Whilst upward filtering as a result of voluntary sales of upgraded property is supported by some workers who suggest that this may be a way by which self-builders can become entrepreneurs (Johnston, 1987), the displacement of the original beneficiaries by higher income groups has a number of negative consequences for integrated urban development. Sustained community participation may be difficult to achieve as incoming families have relatively little to do with community affairs. Where the poorest groups are displaced from their communities, health and other socio-economic inputs are not longer reaching their intended beneficiaries. There are practical problems, too, with achieving total coverage of health interventions such as immunizations as up-to-date health records become very difficult to maintain.

Debt Burdens

It is sometimes suggested that self-help housing schemes fail to accommodate the poorest of the poor, for whom the difficulty of meeting monthly loan repayments is particularly burdensome (Peattie, 1982; Burns, 1983). However, amongst the respondents in this study there was a general feeling that housing loans should be larger. As suggested above, many beneficiaries are forced to take out large private loans in order to complete the construction of their homes. As a result, there is an increase in indebtedness amongst slum families.

According to Stephens and Harpham (1991), increased debt can undermine the impact of integrated development activities in several ways. Nutritional problems may result from families diverting income from food to debt servicing or sending women out to work. Increased maternal labour tends to be associated with a decline in the prevalence and duration of breastfeeding. It may also mean that mothers have inadequate time for child care and food preparation. Children may therefore be withdrawn from school, either too work in paid employment or to help with household tasks including the care of younger children. Female drop-out rates from school remain significantly higher than male and, as the impact of maternal education on child health has been shown to work independently of household income, this has long-term repercussions on child survival.

The Impact on Women's Status

Urban Community Development Department's (UCDD's) commitment to actively involve women in project activities is consistent with an increasing call in the health and development literature for women's empowerment. However, efforts to mobilize women in the studied communities have met with variable success. UCDD's reluctance, or inability, to prevent existing male leaders from dominating negotiations over the housing and infrastructural programmes, and the resulting marginalisation of women into the 'softer' aspects of community development programmes do little to enhance the latter's credibility and potential for leadership. This division of responsibility stems partly from the system of patronage as any leader who participates in the city's patron-clientelist network (from which female leaders are generally excluded) will attempt to take advantage of the power and prestige associated with securing physical improvements. By contrast, the health, education and social development programmes offer little scope for patronage and extortion. They also fail to question the traditional position of women, function without much power in the neighbourhood social system and, although they are normally channelled through Neighbourhood Committees, often have difficulty sustaining the interest of women themselves.

Where male leadership is ineffective or in decline, UCDD involvement has enhanced the credibility of female organizations, enabling women to take primary responsibility for community affairs. Indeed, it would appear to be in the few examples of settlements that are led by women that the rhetoric of urban community development has most closely been translated into reality. The following two case studies, which illustrate a number of the issues raised in this section, provide an interesting contrast in the impact of male and female leadership structures on project implementation.

Urban Community Development in Practice: Two Case Studies

During the 1970s, land in the hillslope to the north west of the central city was made officially available for people evicted from central city slums. However, at a time of rapid growth for Visakhapatnam as a whole, brokerage of plots of families other than the officially rehabilitated was common. The illegal exchange of housing continues to be a problem in this area which, during the early 1980s, benefited disproportionately from the city's UCD programme. The upgraded hillslopes settlements, which are less dense than the inner city slums and more accessible to the central city than the industrial areas, have proved attractive to higher income groups seeking affordable housing.

Beyond their common location, however, the two case study settlements have little in common. 'Ganeshnagar' was one of the first slums in Visakhapatnam to have receive the full complement of UCDD's physical inputs, housing and infrastructure being built in two phases between 1979 and 1982. As a result the settlement, which comprises 502 households, compares favourably with Visakhapatnam's slum communities with regard to environmental indicators. Ninty-nine per cent of households in the questionnaire survey lived in *pucca* or cement built houses, 54 per cent with their own latrines. By contrast, the dwellers of 'Lakshminagar' lived in highly dense conditions at the time of research. Whilst those in the northern half of the settlement were in the process of constructing permanent housing, households in the south occupied rows of small thatched huts, separated by *mud* paths of 3-4 feet in width. With only one functioning borewell in a community of 114 households and no household latrines or electrical connections, this settlement had been earmarked for immediate attention under the ODA Phase of urban community development.

The two settlements also differ greatly with regard to their histories of community organization and leadership. In Ganeshnagar, the frequency and breadth of participation has declined significantly since the settlement was physically upgraded. Leadership in the community is highly polarized, the male leader using his organizational skills and influential political contacts to act as a patron in his own right. By contrast, Lakshminagar has the unusual characteristic (in the context of Visakhapatnam's low income communities) of being led by a woman.

Ganeshnagar

The example of Ganeshnagar raises profound questions about the scope for community development where community relations are characterized by vertical patron-client bonds. Paradoxically, UCDD involvement would appear to have reinforced these unequal relations. According to a number of key informants, including UCD staff, community organization was very lively in the 1970s. As well as petitioning for land tenure, the community members raised 6,500 rupees and built a semi-permanent community hall with tiled roofing, initiated a school to be held in the hall and paid a retired government teacher from the organization's funds. Rupees 3000 were raised by the community to construct a wall on the hillslope border to prevent erosion. Festivals have traditionally been celebrated in style, the dwellers organizing cultural activities, prayer gatherings and free food for the poor. Sports events were also regularly organized during this period.

In the late 1970s, however, a new slum president with links with the local Congress Party took power. At a time when the Congress Party held the balance of power at both the District and State level, Congress Corporators and MLAs (Members of the Legislative Assembly) were in a good position to influence bureaucratic decisions. In 1979 UCDD coordinated the distribution of 2955 housing loans funded by HUDCO and local banks. 1019 were issued to dwellers in this hillslope ward, a reserved Scheduled Caste ward and a Congress stronghold. Although Ganeshnagar did not comprise a large proportion of Scheduled Caste families, it was a sizeable slums in a critical ward for the Congress Party and its organization had already established links with its MLA. The slum was selected for development.

The new leadership which gained legitimation through the housing scheme has had a negative effect on Ganeshnagar's community relations which have since been marked by dissension, a decline in collective mobilization and the polarization of power. From an early stage, dwellers voiced concern that building materials provided by UCDD were not being fairly distributed by the community leader and that influential members of the community had secured themselves larger areas of land at the expense of the poor. Payments were demanded by the leader when households were issued with municipal loans to construct latrines. He also benefits financially from the illegal sale of plots. In order to sustain his reputation as a successful procurer of resources, it is also necessary for the community leader to maintain a monopoly over relations with the Municipal Corporation.

The social cohesion of Ganeshnagar has inevitably been affected by the high turnover of houses since the scheme was implemented. Of the scheme houses in the sample, only 48 per cent were still inhabited by the original beneficiaries of the HUDCO loan (which at the time amounted to Rs. 5,400). 26.5 per cent of houses were rented; 25.5 per cent had been illegally sold. The fact that newcomers to the settlement have a significantly higher income than original residents and are less likely to be employed in the informal sector suggests that upward filtering is taking place. Indebtedness is likely to have been an important factor promoting displacement. Householders in the sample who had received the HUDCO loan were asked to give an estimate of the private loan raised to complete construction. Ninty-two per cent did so, the average amount being Rupees 15,954.

With the influx of new families and the lack of responsibility given to the settlement's Neighbourhood Committee, the level of female participation is very low. Indeed, owing to the difficulties faced by the Committee's office bearers in convening a meeting, the male leader tends to be the community's entry point for information about the social development and health inputs. Whilst attendance of these programmes has been sustained, many women believe that the community development potential of urban community development has been lost. According to one respondent:

> "Since constructing the pucca houses everybody has got too big for their boots and the togetherness we felt has been lost. We used to raise one rupee every month from every household to pay for the school teacher. Now we can't even get that. We have lost the earlier generation who were poor but honest. Now we're just a community of strange faces".

Lakshminagar

Whilst Ganeshnagar had developed an active community organization before UCDD established contact with the community, in Lakshminagar a viable community organization did not emerge until UCD staff encouraged the creation of a Neighbourhood Committee. In this settlement is now the women who receive officials, make representations, collect and account for community funds, disseminate information and organize community labour. Significantly, the women's organization is also the entry point for information about the housing and infrastructural programmes and the focus for discussions about their design and implementation. Land rights, too, are allocated in women's names.

The methods used to create the Neighbourhood Committees in Ganeshnagar and Lakshminagar and the structures and functions given to them were very similar. Indeed, the same Community Organizer worked in both settlements. As the only female leaders encountered during the research period had taken power in communities where male leadership was defunct, it is likely that female organization has been able to emerge as a successful and dominate organization in

Lakshminagar because of the *absence* of effective male leadership in the area. Notwithstanding the unequal relationship between patrons and their clients, the majority of slum dwellers lack the institutional contacts to secure resources individually and as collective organization takes up precious time, relying on a patron can be an efficient and rational way of gaining access to resources. Thus, for the residents themselves, if a pre-existing male leadership structure is successfully securing local improvements, little can be gained by transferring power to women.

Lakshminagar's experience does, however, provide many positive lessons about the rule of female leadership in urban community development. Clientelist links with the partisan political system were not evident in the area, nor did any respondent claim to have paid a client fee for development resources received. The level of awareness about UCD activities was particularly high. This is likely to have been affected by the ongoing housing construction work. However, women interviewed were better informed than men about municipal plans to develop the community. They were also widely acknowledged to be 'responsible' for the settlement's development.

Conclusion

Despite increasing support amongst health and development planners for an integrated approach to urban deprivation, care must be taken in assuming that integration can be easily achieved. The experience of Visakhapatnam suggests that whilst the creation of an umbrella organization for the coordination of different sectors is a prerequisite of successful integration, a number of other factors need to be taken into account. Because of the high priority given to physical improvement programmes, it likely that the urban community development approach has better hopes for success when different project components are phased. Thus, community and social development programmes should provide the entry point for project involvement, housing and infrastructure only being implemented after community organization has been strengthened.

The impact of physical upgradation on indebtedness and gentrification should receive attention. Little is known about the prospects families but it is likely that those who land up on the streets face even greater deprivation. It is important that the system of funding housing construction remains flexible and that sufficient funds are made available to realistically cover the costs of construction. Account needs to be take, too, of households that cannot afford the most competitive loans. Technical considerations regarding the design and implementation of housing and infrastructural programmes often take precedence over the need to respond to local people's circumstances. Thus, the tendency to impose the housing programme in a blanket fashion on a slum as a whole can alienate vulnerable households.

The relationship between male leadership structures, patron-clientelism and the housing programme and the general exclusion of female leaders from systems of political patronage suggests that greater efforts on behalf of UCDD to channel its housing and infrastructural programmes through women's organizations could have two beneficial effects. First, the scope for patronage and extortion would be reduced. Second, the credibility of female leadership and organization would be enhanced by giving women responsibility for 'important' issues that are the traditional domain of male-dominated leadership structures. Giving land rights to women is a step in the right direction. However, as it is in the interests of patrons and brokers to guard their power, the most effective way of developing women's organizations may be to ensure that existing male leaders are by-passed in negotiations over the physical improvement programmes.

Paradoxically, this may be easier to achieve under the ODA Phase of the Project. When housing and infrastructure were implemented on a piecemeal basis, many leaders had vested interests in maintaining a monopoly over the negotiation process. As the pattern of resource distribution evens out throughout the city, claims by patrons that they are responsible for resource provision will sound less and less convincing. The widespread implementation of the housing scheme may also provide a disincentives for leaders who concentrate their power in order to preside over illegal housing exchanges: since upward filtering a result of unsatisfied demand for housing, the very scale of the housing programme may dilute that demand and lower land prices.

REFERENCES

Bapat, M. and Crook, N. (1984). "The environment, health and nutrition: an analysis of interrelations from a case study of hutment settlements in the city of Poona", *Habitat International* 8: 115-26.

Basta, S.S. (1977). "Nutrition and Health in Low Income Urban Areas of the Third World", *Ecology of Food and Nutrition* 6: 113-24.

Bequelle, A. and Boyden, J. (1988). "Working children: current trends and policy responses", *International Labour Review,* 127(2):153-172

Burns, L. (1983). "Self help housing: an evaluation of outcomes", *Urban Studies*

20:299-309.

Clinard, M.B. (1966). *Slums and Community Development. Experiments in Self Help.* London: Collier Macmillan.

Dayal, M.S. (1986). "ICDS - Seventh plan and beyond", *NFI Bulletin*, Vol. 7, No. 3.

Hardoy, J.E. and Satterthwaite, D. (1987). Housing and health. Do architects and planners have a role? *Cities*, 4:221-235.

Hardoy, J.E. and Satterthwaite, D. (1989). *Squatter Citizen: Life in the Urban Third World*. London: Earthscan.

Harpham, T, Lusty, T. and Vaughan, P. eds. (1988). *In the Shadow of the city. Community Health and the Urban Poor*, Oxford: Oxford University Press.

Hollnsteiner, M.R. (1982). "The participatory imperative in primary health care", *Assignment Children*, 59/60:35-56.

Johnson, T.E. (1987). "Upward filtering of housing stock. A study of upward filtering of housing stock as a consequence of informal settlement upgrading in developing countries," *Habitat International* 11(1):173-190.

Lee, O. and Furst, B.B. (1980). *Differential Indicators of Living Conditions in Urban and Rural Places of Selected Countries*, Washington D.C.: Applied Systems Institute.

Lipton, M. (1977). *Why Poor People Stay Poor: Urban Bias in World Development.* London: Maurice Temple Smith.

Moser, C.O.N. (1989). "Community participation in urban projects in the third world", *Progress in Planning* 32(2).

Nelson, V. and Mandl, P.E. (1978). "Peri-Urban Malnutrition. A Neglected Problem", *Assignment Children* 43:25-46.

Nutrition Foundation of India (1988). *Integrated Child Development Services. A Study of Some Aspects of the System*, Scientific Publication No. 7, Nutrition Foundation of India, Delhi.

Oakley, P. (1989). *Community Involvement in Health Development: An Examination of the Critical Issues*, Geneva: World Health Organization.

Peattie, L. (1982). "Some second thoughts on sites and services", *Habitat International*, 6(1/2):131-139.

Rossi-Espagnet, A. (1984). *Primary Health Care in Urban Areas: Reaching the Urban Poor in Developing Countries.* A State of the Art Report by UNICEF and WHO, Report No. 2499 M, Geneva: World Health Organization.

Stephens, C. and Harpham, T. (1991). *Slum Improvement: Health Improvement?* PHP Departmental Publication No. 1, London School of Hygiene and Tropical Medicine.

Tabibzadeh, I., Rossi-Espagnet, A. and Maxwell, R. (1981). *Spotlight on the Cities: Improving Urban Health in Developing Countries*, Geneva: World Health Organization.

Tendler, J. (1982). *Rural Projects through Urban Eyes. An Interpretation of the World Bank's New Style Rural Development Projects*, World Bank Staff Working Papers, No. 532, The World Bank, Washington D.C.

Visakhapatnam Urban Community Development Department. *Visakhapatnam Urban Community Development Project 1987-88 to 1989-90: A Project for Upgradation of 170 Slums in Visakhapatnam.* Undated project document.

Wray, J. (1986). "Child health interventions in urban slums are we neglecting the importance of nutrition?", *Health Policy and Planning*, 1(4):299-308.

26

THE STATE, BUSINESS DIPLOMACY AND THE ENVIRONMENT

CHANDRA PAL SINGH

The state has been as much responsible for environmental problems of today as any other agents. The essence of the state is its ability to mobilize and to exercise power within a defined territory over which it claims sovereignty, and to enter into agreements with other similar sovereign entities. The earth's surface is presently divided into over 170 such units, or containers as Johnston calls them (1992, p. 212), each controlled by an independent sovereign state apparatus, which regulate the behaviour of their residents in all spheres of life. Since the state has the exclusive monopoly over coercive power its overt and covert support for any activities and programmes are backed up by the strongest force that man can collectively generate. This force is equivalent or next to the natural forces that create upheavals and disasters which bring landscape changes. Human force thus channelised through the state apparatus and collective human action on, and in cooperation with, nature is the single most dominant factor which has brought planet earth to its present state. State policies within and without their territorial extents direct and regulate human action for his survival, materialistic attainments and pleasures of life, most of which come from the environment in which he lives on the earth. The magnitude of human action can be seen from the fact that a human force of about 6 billion is at work daily, some of whom have a great capacity of consuming the elements of nature with a rapid speed, while others are clamouring to have such capacity. The earth hurtling through the space is also hurtling towards an ever increasing spiral of consumption which may destroy existing ecological balance of the planet.

Origins of the Spiral and the Role of the State

The origins of the consumption spiral can be traced back to the beginning of the scientific enterprise in Europe about five centuries ago. It started as an innocuous method of satisfying man's curiosity about the universe and the world he lived in. Experimentation, quantification, prediction and control become the paradigm of the new scientific culture for comprehension of the physical universe. A mysterious and capricious universe could now, for the first time in human history, be understood as mechanical and orderly. (Hoodbhoy, 1991, p.3). Initially, the practitioners of science had to face heavy odds against the established beliefs of the priestly class, which was supported by the state.

The birth of modern science coincided with the upheaval during Renaissance when the medieval feudal economy collapsed and gave way to capitalism. The new class of capitalists found in science a means of increasing their productivity and profits on unprecedented scale. To the scientists, the scientific method gave undreamed of power to understand to laws of nature, and subsequently to operate new technologies, to the capitalists science became the weapon with which high productivity and profits could be made much more easily, and with which less technologically developed people around the world could be subdued and their wealth and resources could be controlled for generating more wealth.

The state also realised the immense power that the scientific enterprise gave to its possessors and patrons, and it too joined the scramble for new lands and riches, and supported both the scientists and the capitalists in their respective enterprises. In the process, nature became something which had to be conquered, and so were the original inhabitants of lands in all parts of the world, who also had to be 'civilized'. Baconian science itself proclaimed that nature was there to be conquered, and its conquest was seen as noble inspiration. There is some dispute among historians whether exploitation of nature in medieval Europe was particularly aggressive or that an aggressive attitude might be peculiar to Christianity, or when exactly in the course of the Middle Ages, European Technological prowess came to exceed that of the other complex cultures (Atkinson, 1991, p. 129), the fact remains that a systematic subjugation of people all around the world had exploitation of nature would not have been possible without aggressive attitude and development of complex technology. The following passage from Atkinson (1991, p. 139) describe the situation aptly:

> "the sadistic aggression which Northern European men have meted out on nature, foreign cultures, women and, where they get the chance, their fellow men, and which is reflected also in their 'objective' interpretation of nature: 'red in tooth and claw'."

Science and technology were as important in colonization as the drive of individual initiative and enterprise in capitalism. Without close links between them it would not have been possible for the colonialists to subdue the existing civilizations.

> "Imperialism was complex system - an intricate and well oiled machine whose parts seemed to move with clockwork precision. Modern rifles and canons - as in the battle of Plassey in 1757 - were certainly the most visible manifestations of its strength. But it was the telegraph, steamship, machine produced goods, and modern organizational methods, which were the backbone of the collosus. These elements were alien to the agrarian and pastoral civilization(s). Large local armies, untutored in military techniques, fought valiantly but were decimated by disciplined British and French regiments a tenth of their size." (Hoodbhoy, 1991, .p.3)

The state was on the back of both the scientist and capitalist to ensure peaceful conditions internally at home, where the drive for scientific enquiry and capitalist enterprise with stress on individualism (with concepts like freedom, liberty, justice, equality, autonomy, privacy, dignity were enshrined in statute books), was allowed to flourish, and a stranglehold over the territories for unhindered exploitation of their resources and wealth, and keeping the sealanes free for transportation of raw materials and finished goods. In return, the state received its share of economic growth. With its kitty fattening every year the state could finance its projects to make it more efficient internally, and invest in increasing and improving its arsenal to make it more deadly and effective. It could now finance its research in science and technology in either its own laboratories or universities and other institutions of higher learning and research. The state in west European countries initially, and in other parts of what is termed as the North today subsequently, came to assume coercive and destructive power at a scale where they become capable of destroying the planet earth thousands of times over. Some of the most destructive weapons and technologies got concentrated in the hands of the state in several countries of the North as a result of the scientific enterprise and the accumulation of wealth under the capitalist system.

As against this, the native inhabitants of Asia, Africa and Americas did not have the material means to defend themselves from the physical onslaught, and there was no question of their participating in the scientific enterprise and capitalist accumulation based on it, almost till the end of colonialism which began with the end of Second World War. With traditional economic, social, cultural and political relationships deeply eroded after a series of humiliating defeats at the hands of West Europeans, contact with the alien civilisation left them unsure of themselves. Collateral advantages of colonialism did accrue to them in the form of modern system of medicine, new modes of transport and communication, opportunities of trade, access to western education, etc. But they become available to them in subservient positions in helping the colonialists in exploitation of their own resources, and maintenance if colonial administration over their own people. They were neither capable nor had access to the operation of science and technology, nor did they have sufficient capital to buy technology from Europe. In the case of India, the traditional merchant castes had come capital accumulated with them, and some of the daring entrepreneurs from among them took risks in starting indigenous industrialization based on technology imported from Europe. But for most of the people of the colonized world their contact with Europeans was dazzling and are inspiring because of their material artifacts, work cultures and life styles.

> "The Europeans were, from the standpoint of these natives, certainly peculiar in their ceaseless scurrying about generating new projects and generally new things to keep them occupied well beyond what might be deemed necessary for a comfortable life in such conditions." (Atkinson, 1991, p. 185)

From the very start, people from the colonies were doomed to fall way behind Europeans in science and technology, materialistic possessions and wealth. They were also to be followers in these fields even after becoming independent. But colonialism left a legacy in colonies whereby achievement of wealth and materialistic possessions that go with it in the present century became the ideal to be achieved in the developing countries also. High growth rates became the stated objectives of the states in all the developing countries. This could only be achieved by high production in different sectors of their economies, which could only mean high pressure on the environment. In most cases, these countries of the South, as they are being called now had to sell their resources cheaply inflicting damages to the environment for low returns.

Availability of modern medical facilities had another fall out, unintended through it was, on the environment. Medical facilities, which were the product of the scientific enterprise of Europe, reduced the threat of killer diseases and improved logitivity in developing countries of the South. This has resulted in the steady growth of population in the past half a century. This had two effects on the environment. One, demands on the environment even for sustenance increased steadily and continue to do so. Second, the number of those aspiring for high standards of living, as obtained in the North, is increasing continuously with the rise in absolute numbers of those who can afford it. The very high consumerism in the North is being supplemented with similar levels of demands for consumer goods by an ever enlarging section of population in the South.

As technology transformed the way of producing, consuming, organizing,'living and dying' (Castells, 1985, p. 7), it became a very important agent of regional change, both in the North earlier and in the South now. Technologies altered human societies and gave rise to new centres of power and wealth within them, as well as in relation with others. They resulted in a spatial redistribution of activities, income, wealth and poverty. "The de-industrialization of some cities while others become 'information centres' and the decaying 'sunset' industries in some areas while in other areas 'sunrise' industries are flourishing, have resulted in a spatial shift in centres of economic activities, in wealth, income and therefore power" (Kamann, 1988, p.1). Thus industrial society set in motion a number of other processes, as readjustment to science, technology and mode of production by the society and the state.

There was a fatal deception in Bacon's thinking - and one which has been carefully maintained by the West to this day - concerns the notion that science can and will be used for the benefit of all mankind (Atkinson, 1991, p. 135). But science was from the beginning a tool with which to advance interests of certain individuals, classes and nations, and continues without any deception in the emergent international order (Sethi, 1990, p.). Military strength, political power and economic prosperity have become contingent upon the ability of modern nations to understand, control and create modern science (Hoodbhoy, 1991, p. 2). The North is largely the creator of latest science and technology, with the U.S.A. being one of the major leaders. The disparities among people, regions and nations are only on the increase in most of the cases. Exceptions are very few. Never was there an enterprise like scientific which started with noble intentions but may turn out to be self-destructive ultimately for its creator and practitioner.

With regard to the exploitation of nature and man there was no difference between capitalism and communism. The yardstick of progress under both the systems was the same. The only difference between the two was regarding the ownership of resources, means of production and methods of distribution of profits. The communist system was as exploitative of the nature as its rival system. In the capitalist system individual initiative and drive were considered as the vehicle for growth and development, while in the latter the state was given this role with egalitarian objectives. In practice, both exploited man and nature equally recklessly, basically for, and by, a small number of people in whose hands wealth and power got concentrated (Singh, 1993). The geopolitical dialogues and postures were meant merely to maintain the two systems in their respective areas of control. It was also ironical that the positive intentions of both the systems to provide better living conditions and allround development of man turned out to be injurious to the tender and fragile ecological relationships in the nature, and has created the environmental crisis of today.

The consequences of material growth on the environment become clear by the beginning of the last decade of the twentieth century in the form of apparently unrelated events. Mathews (1991, p. 20) has summarised them as follows:

> "the oil price rise and widespread shortages that opened the decade; the chemical accident of Bhopal; the decimation of European and high altitude U.S. forests from acid rain and other air pollutants; Chernobyl; ozone depletion and the discovery of a "hole" in the ozone layer over Antarctica; drought and famine in Africa; the Rhine River chemical spill; the homeless freighter that sailed the world for two years without finding a place to unload its cargo of toxic ash; steadily rising rates of tropical deforestation and of

> species extinction; closed beaches from Western Europe to the Baltic to New Jersey; the Exxon Valdez oil spill; and as the decade (1980s) closed, an outbreak of freakish weather-drought and record-breaking heat in the U.S., devastating floods in Bangladesh, the most powerful hurricane ever measured, and the warmest winter in Moscow in more than a century - bringing intense new concern to the possibilities of global greenhouse warming."

Several other similar events can now be added to this list, such as the oil tanker disasters off the coasts of Spain, Shetland islands, and Nicobar islands; several nuclear plants in the central Asian republics in very bad state of maintenance; famine and drought in Africa all of which occurred within the last few months.

The Western civilisation based on modern science and technology and capitalism is on more confined to the North only. The South is also clamouring for it to solve its problems compounded by the high growth of its population. This civilization now has global reach and universal appeal. But it has let loose a genie – the vest spiral of consumption devouring materials and living beings, degrading and polluting the land, water and sky. Some of the species have already disappeared under its impact, while others are on the verge of extinction. The spiral can only get more momentum with further advancement in science and still more sophisticated technology, which will be possessed and owned by few, mostly by multinationals, in their well guarded laboratories to prevent secret knowledge of laws and processes of nature from being leaked out or stolen. Besides, recent developments in communication technology has accelerated industrial and business activities to an unprecedented pace. Business transactions which used to take months, even a decade ago, are being conducted within seconds. Goods and raw materials can be received or dispatched, with their inventories properly made and checked at every stage, thereby reducing pilferage and wastage in transit. With the fast movement of raw materials and finished goods their production and consumption have increased. The goal of faster and unlimited growth is being realised. To instill industrial commitment to economic growth among the workers companies are devising new methods of labour efficiency and group psychology, which can best be judged from the Japanese Matsushita (Panasonic) Company an them:

"For the building of a new Japan
Let's put our strengths and minds together
Doing our best to promote production
Sending our goods to the peoples of the world
Endlessly and continuously
Like a water gushing from a fountain
GROW INDUSTRY, Grow, Grow, Grow."

– Herman Arthur quoted in Kassiola (1990, p.44).

This is the aim of modern industrialism, to which and more people from every part of the earth are likely to get committed in the coming years. The spread of democracy will also force leaders not to take unpopular decisions, which may not be in the interest of the environment. The global trend of privatisation and availability of fast global communication are bringing people from all parts of the world closer. Differences between the North and the South in terms of aspirations for a higher standard of living are narrowing, and the Western civilization is truly becoming global civilization.

The State in a New Role of Business Diplomat

The collapse of the Soviet Union, and along with it, the end the Cold War have set in motion processes where capitalist ideology has proved successful. In most of the new countries that have emerged out of the collapse of the Soviet Union, and in Eastern Europe governments have decided to open up their economies for privatisation, and asked their former capitalist adversaries to extend their financial and institutional help and expertise. Even a country like China made a quiet and clever switch over to privatisation with a sugar coating of socialism on it, and opened up coastal areas of China for foreign investment. In the changed global situation the state in India too changed its stance by discarding some of the ideological baggage of socialism and liberalized its economy and removed some of the irritants in industrial licensing. Multinationals which were thrown out of the country once were welcomed again. Suddenly, the investors from North America, Western Europe, Japan, or from countries of the wonder economies of Pacific Asia were is great demand especially in Euresia.

Where political equations and groupings used to dictate trade relations earlier, now trade relations started dictating alliances and groupings at international level. Business interests became primary consideration for political alliances and stances. The North now got an equally potent force, along with supremacy in science and technology and instruments of coercion, in the surplus capital, which could be used as a weapon to bring the world to order to refashion it in its image. That is why the U.S.A. could arm twist Russia not to give oryogenic engines to India for the development of her missile technology, which of course was firmly resisted by Russia. Thus recently business interests have taken precedence in foreign policy over political alliances. Foreign policy has become an instrument to fulfil economic objectives for most of the countries, whether they are from the North or the South.

The importance of business interests in the conduct of international relations today becomes clear from the statement of the U.S. Secretary of State, Warren Christopher, in his confirmation hearings before the Senate foreign relations committee that "economic competition is eclipsing ideological rivalry. We'll not be bashful about linking our high diplomatic goals with our economic goals."[1]

Foreign missions in most of the countries have started playing significant role in bilateral business deals to be in favour of companies of their respective countries. Ambassadors and commercial counsellors based in India, for instance, find it a part of their daily routine to even make public statements to indicate their country's stand on certain key business and economic issues. This new thrust in indian diplomacy is reflected in the appointment of ambassadors in "target" countries like Japan and Germany with the commerce secretary sitting in on panels that decide on postings.[2] Orientation courses for heads of Indian missions abroad held in Indian include subjects ranging from banking and fiscal reforms to the global investment climate and the potential for India. The responsibilities of Indian missions abroad will include acting as sales offices for marketing India's new economic environment as well communicating feedback from the local government and business community. Above all, they should actively seek foreign investment and new markets for Indian exports.[3]

It is becoming a common practice for Heads of States or Governments all over the world to take trade delegations representative of the top industrialists and businessmen of their countries to the country of their visit. The visit which attracted worldwide attention and comment was that of President Bush going to Japan at the head of a trade delegation. The recent visit of the British Prime Minister, followed by that of the Russian President, and later by the Spanish Prime Minister and German Chancellor to India within a short span of about one month are illustrative of this world wide trend. The British Prime Minister John Major brought with him a delegation comprising chief executives and chairmen of multinationals like Guinness, Cadbury, Swepps, Rolls Royce, British Aerospace and British Gas. He described the delegation as the most prestigious group of businessmen ever to accompany a British Prime Minister abroad. The comment of the correspondent of the Guardian, Derek Brown, reflect the globalization of economies and interdependence of business interests between the North and the South, when he said that it was the first time British businessmen were visiting India "without imperial interest or any old strings attached" is a sign of change that has occurred in the Indo-British relations, and is a reflection of global change in which business interest have assumed primacy.[4]

Similarly, the much harassed President Yeltsin by his council of deputies at home for his economic policies, and who was hard pressed for time, made a hurried three-day visit to India. This was dominated by the talks to resolve the Rupee-Rouble dispute, with the new Indo-Russian friendship treaty becoming a secondary subject. His previous visits to West European, American and other Asian capitals were also dominated by economic matters, though super power and strategic relations were also important subjects on the agenda with some countries. The several visits of the Japanese Prime Minister to United States and several capitals of countries of the North also fall in this category.

With substantial cuts in the arsnels of super power and winding up of the Warsaw Pact threat of major global was appears to have receded. But economic wars that will take place in markets, factories and research and development laboratories will be more frequent. All weapons used in economic warfare will be used and new strategies and armament would be devised. It is here that potential for the environmental destruction lies.

The multinationals which have business interest all over the globe are now able to influence formulation of foreign policies of their own countries as well as in the countries of their business interests. Their opinion regarding economic and political situation, at the present and in the future, about a country often becomes an input in foreign policy formulation. Their close relations with the diplomatic missions of their respective countries abroad also influence the policies of diplomats, and through their despatches of their governments. It is becoming increasingly difficult to distinguish between the role of multinationals in diplomacy and of diplomats in business.

The multinationals were responsible for the flow of funds into China even after the events of Tiannenman Square. It was because the Boeing Company, which had obtained an order from China for nearly 200 planes, convinced the U.S. government that despite the massacre, China was a good place to invest in. Once the U.S. investments flowed into China, many european companies which did not want to be left behind in capturing the lucrative Chinese market and wanted a foothold on the Chinese soil, also joined in investment in that country. Now a Clinton administration will find it difficult to tighten the screw on China for its human right record, compelling it to soften Clinton's election promise.

Similarly, the support to Narsimha Rao from President Bush and several European leaders in the aftermath of demolition of the Babri mosque in Ayodhya in December 1992 was to support Rao's economic reforms in India, which were to the liking of the multinationals and multilateral financial institutions of the North. Everyone that mattered in the North rallied behind Narsimha Rao, rather than the Indian government.

Thus the world over, the language of diplomacy is changing. Ideology is no more the guide for diplomats. "Today, the United States 'Primary concern with Germany is the high interest rates, with Japan it is Tokyo's consumer drive, with France it is Paris' agriculture subsidy, and with India it is New Delhi's rigid structures." (Rajghatta and Adhikari, 1993). The mindset of the sixties where East-West and super power relations, anti-colonialism and anti-imperialism, raising tariff walls against the foreign goods, anti-multinational agitations, etc. has begun to change significantly in the South. The collapse of communism, spread of capitalism, quiet marginalization of non-alignment, building bridges with the North, spread of democratic system of government, and the gradual rise of fundamentalism have altered the world already. With this two major issues have become prominent in international discourse – development based on capitalist ideology and the environmental crisis.

Business Diplomacy and Environmental Crisis

As argued above, what began as a disjointed scientific enterprise of

Europe about half a millennium ago to satisfy man's curiosity about the world around him, has blossomed into as instrument of exploitation of nature for profit making. Production, consumption and exchange, accelerated by latest technology, supported by different organs of the state, whether located in the North or the South, have already made excessive demands on the environment. Now the state itself is being marshalled to directly convass and promote business of the capitalist to stimulate growth. Any reduction in growth and any let up in production and sales in the affluent North sends global economy into recession, throwing people into unemployment and related problems with it. The South is struggling to catch up with the advanced developed countries in following the same model of growth, as all others have been either impractical or have failed, to raise the standards of living of its people whose numbers are increasing at frightening rates. These growing demands of the people, both in the North and the South have to be provided by the planet earth. For reasons of accountability, leaders in liberal democracies, whose number is also increasing as compared with a few years ago, can not go against the aspirations of their people, even if it means extorting more from the earth than its systems can afford. The leaders are to be elected on the votes of the human beings who can express their resentment by using the faculty of speech given uniquely to them by nature. The environment, on the other hand, takes a long time to react, often in violent ways, and by that time the leaders are no more on the scene. The present policies of all governments in the world to encourage trade and industrial growth, supported most eloquently by the capitalists, will boost economic growth by increasing the rate of consumption. Latest additions in science and technology contributed laboriously and proudly by scientists working in the universities and laboratories of the multinationals will provide still better competitive to the capitalist enterprise. So growth rates are likely to rise in many new countries which have taken to the capitalist system, along with those countries whose rate of growth has already been high. The end result will be a very heavy demand on the environment in the coming years.

We need not go into the merits and demerits of the limits of growth thesis regarding modern industrialism, as it is already well documented.[5] Our focus is the role that the state is playing in encouraging this industrialism by going out as salesman for the capitalist. Such a role is counter productive to its other responsibility today, namely, protection of the environment. The state has adopted a contradictory policy of promoting growth with environmental protection. There is no problem with it so long as both the objectives are met. But the objective of sustainable development is lost sight of in actual implementation of the stated policy.

First of all, many of the countries of the South which have voiced support for protection of the environment do not have sufficient infrastructural facilities to implement their pro-environment policies. "By the mid-1980s, more than 140 countries – 110 of them in the developing world – had environmental agencies, though many of them remain chronically under-funded, poorly staffed, and near the bottom of the ministerial power hierarchy. The emphasis has shifted from pollution to the management of such resources as forests, fisheries, rangeland, soils, genetic diversity and wetlands." (Mathews, 1991, p. 26). This half-hearted approach to the protection and preservation of environment is no match for the intense desires for high economic growth and materialism.

Secondly, business diplomacy will lead to more business contracts between individuals, companies and governments of both the worlds - the North and the South. The industrialists and capitalists of the North will be too willing to extend their expertise and experience to the South to penetrate the undeveloped markets there which have great potential. The industrial potential of the North has been largely explored, through there is never a limit to it also, and has reached a saturation level in some areas which have witnessed decline in industrial activity. New areas which have potential of further explanation and exploitation have got to be found. The recent inflows of capital and industrial growth in coastal China, South East Asia, with similar possibilities on the horizon in India, as well as the likelihood of investments in Russia and Eastern Europe, are some of the examples in this regard. Investment in these countries, in most cases is not meant to produce goods to be sold in the North, but to tap the lucrative markets right in these countries. The huge populations in several of these countries are big and growing markets which have to be captured at the earliest possible in the competitive spirit of capitalism. The twenty-first century is already being labelled as the Pacific Asia century. When such a large number of people living on such an extensive land mass of Eurasia will become part of the Western civilization the existing environment will not remain unaffected. There are all the signs of this not being sustainable development.

Thirdly, efforts to decelerate growth in the North and accelerate it with great caution in the South are destined to be doomed. Already there is recession in almost all the countries of the North. An American President who could to preside over the end of the the Cold War, and could take credit for the collapse of communism and for victory in the Gulf War, lost election within one year of these epoch marking events, due to being considered to be responsible for recession and unemployment in his country. Deceleration of growth is suicidal politically. The leaders in the South also can not abandon the prospects and plans to improve living standards of their people through increased growth rates of their economies. Going against this would be suicidal for them also politically. Internal politics in countries of both the North and the South will compel political elites there to take the easy path for them, which will higher economic growth with lip service to be paid for the protection and preservation of the environment. The genie created by the scientific enterprise of Europe, nurtured by capitalism and supported by the state in different forms, can not be brought back to the bottle. It is actually growing bigger every day threatening the very existence of its creator and the place in which he lives.

The vigour with which the business deals are advocated, encouraged and supported by the state today is not matched by equal tenacity to control and minimize damage to the environment. Sustainable development is more of a slogan designed to camouflage the real intentions of the capitalist and the state supported by him. Environmental laws enacted by different governments are there more to appease the environmentalists and the greens of different hues. They are not implemented with the same vigour and will as shown in clinching of business deals for, and in co-operation with, the capitalist. The Earth Summit in Rio in 1992 did bring the environment on top of the international agenda, but it was like agreeing to discuss the symptoms of a disease rathering than getting down to the actual treatment with a strong determination. The Earth Summit did not have the strong will and determination of a capitalist or a scientist when he takes up a project with clarity of objectives and approach.

Fourthly, the situation is aggravated by the lack of expertise on environmental matters by the business diplomat. Few political scientists, international lawyers and diplomats, who have wide experience in environmental issues. On the other hand, only a few environmental experts have any experience of diplomacy (Mathews, 1991, p.26). At the present both are misfits and may be doing more harm than good to both the causes.

Finally, there is a lack of supra-national environmental agency which has coercive power to implement environmental laws throughout the world, irrespective of considerations of the North or the South. Environmental systems do not recognize international boundaries and political systems. The environment comprises a single, complexly interacting, three-dimensional system of very many parts, and laws designed by a state to control environmental use in one territory can not prevent action outside that territory from influencing one or more its own parts of the system (Johnston, 1992, p. 212). The spill over effect of unbriddled industrialism in the North, and uncontrolled growth of population in the South along with clamouring the industrialism of Western civilization have already shown the kinds of environmental problems that man and all non-human inhabitants of the earth are going to face. Uncontrolled industrialism, propelled by human greed for unlimited wealth, and supported actively by the scientific enterprise and state power, can lead to only one conclusion - an unprecedented and unimaginable ecological catastrophe, after which new ecological relationships will develop from which Home Sapiens and numerous existing species may be missing altogether.

Can the trajectory that the world has taken since the beginning of the Western civilization be changed to a different course? Can the North and the South refrain or even slow down on industrialism? The helplessness of the situation has been aptly described by Slater (1974, p. 44) in the following words:

> "Western civilization is a man running with increasing speed through an air-sealed tunnel in search of additional oxygen. You can quite reasonably tell him he will survive longer if he slows down but he is not likely to do it."

In the post catastrophic world the states as know it may not be there either.

NOTES

1. Vivek Bharati (1993). "India After the Cold War", *Times of India*, 5 February.
2. Chidananda Rajghatta and Sara Adhikari (1993). "From Talking Shop to Talking Business", *Sunday Times of India*, 7 February.
3. *Ibid.*
4. *Ibid.*
5. See the long list of publications on this theme on Note 5 of Joel Jay Kassiola (1990). *The Death of Industrial Civilization*, Albany.

REFERENCES

Atkinson, Adrian (1991). *Principles of Political Ecology*, London: Belhaven Press.

Castels, M. (Ed.) (1985). *Principles of Political Ecology*, Beverly Hills: Sage.

Hoodbhoy, Pervez (1991). *Islam and Science*, London: Zed Books.

Johnston, R.J. (1992). "Laws. States and Super-States: International Law and the Environment", *Applied Geography*, 12, pp. 211-228.

Kamann, Dirk-Jan F. (1988). *Spatial Differentiation in the Social Impact of Technology*, Aldershot: Avebury.

Mathews, Jessica T. (Ed.) (1991). *Preserving the Global Environment*, New York: W.M. Norton and Co.

Rajghatta, C. and Sara Adhikari (1993). "From Talking Shop to Talking Business", *Sunday Times of India*, 7 February.

Singh, Chandra Pal (1993). "Perspectives in Resource Management and Political Ecology", in B. Thakur (ed.), *Resource Management in Developing Countries*, New Delhi: Concept Publishing Co.

Slater, Philip (1974). *Earthwalk*, Garden City: Anchor Books.

27

URBAN ENVIRONMENTAL MANAGEMENT FOR A SUSTAINABLE QUALITY OF LIFE IN THE METROPOLIS DEVELOPING COUNTRIES:

A Case Study of Madurai Metropolitan, India

K.S. GOPALAKRISHNAN

Introduction

In recent decades India has witnessed a rapid urbanization in which, uncertainty of agriculture, unemployment, lack of amenities etc., have acted as push factors from rural areas, while the intensive development of industries under successive Five-Year Plans in urban centres, especially in large cities acted as a pull factor.

In India, it is estimated that by 2000 A.D. the number of metropolitan cities (more than a million population) may go up to 40 from that of 23 in 1991, with almost doubling the number of people living in such urban settlements. This will aggravate the severe shortage of shelter and basic services and amenities which lead to stress and strains in the political and social fabric of cities.

The perusal of the facts on the nature and type of urbanization in India brings out the following:

1. Rapid urbanization in India is better called as over urbanization or pseudo urbanization.
2. The process of urbanization is not in tune with either industrialisation or modernization.
3. The process is more activated by strong 'push' factor from rela-

tively poor rural areas rather than scope offered for employment from weak urban pull factor.

4. Large scale migration from remote village to large Metropolitan centres has resulted in the lop-sided development of various sizes of urban centres. (Table 27.1)
5. Majority of the work force is absorbed in informal sector with low/nil/technology with limited capital investments naturally puts majority of them under poverty line or slightly above it.

TABLE 27.1 : Urbanization in India

A. Number of Different Classes of Towns

Year	Class I	Class II	Class III	Class IV	Class V	Class VI	All Classes
1901	25	44	144	427	771	503	1971
1911	26	38	158	388	750	546	1909
1921	29	49	172	395	773	626	2047
1931	31	59	218	459	849	580	2219
1941	49	88	273	554	979	478	2424
1951	76	111	374	675	1195	628	3059
1961	107	139	518	820	847	268	2699
1971	151	219	652	987	820	290	3119
1981	216	270	739	1048	742	230	3245
1991	296	341	927	1135	725	185	3609

B. Proportions of Population in Each Size Classes of Towns to Total Urban Population

Year	Class I	Class II	Class III	Class IV	Class V	Class VI
1901	22.02	11.40	16.95	22.62	20.63	6.38
1911	23.63	09.53	18.85	20.75	20.13	7.06
1921	24.45	11.23	18.20	19.21	19.39	7.52
1931	24.41	12.42	19.76	19.61	18.01	5.78
1941	31.84	12.97	18.25	17.47	15.90	3.57
1951	38.00	12.21	17.80	15.02	13.62	3.34
1961	44.50	12.07	19.95	14.32	08.03	1.03
1971	48.93	13.49	18.28	12.80	05.68	0.82
1981	60.37	11.65	14.35	09.52	03.61	0.50
1991	65.20	10.95	13.19	07.77	02.60	0.49

Source : Census of India 1991 General Population Tables

Thus the analysis of the process of urbanization and the spatial pattern of urban population distribution in India has lead to the following environmental problems:

1. Urban poverty
2. Urban land shortage
3. Urban congestion and overcrowding, and limited financial availability.
4. Lack of shelter both quantitatively and qualitatively
5. Transport inadequacy - Linkage as well as modes.
6. Lack of provision of basic civic facilities - provision of drinking water and disposal of urban waste, educational, medical health care and recreation facilities.

All the above facts either independently or interdependently contributed to a law level of life quality in urban center. That is way the investigator has taken up this problem with special reference to Madurai to decompose the elements and their relative degrees of involvement in deciding the Quality of Life.

Quality of Life

Quality of life, is intended to refer either to the conditions of the environment in which people live (air and water pollution or poor housing for example) or to some attitude of people themselves (such as health and educational achievement). Further, Quality of Life is not necessarily a simple function of material health. The search for a broad based definition of life quality has been closely tried to the development of both economic and non-economic, social indicators in an attempt to reflect adequately the overall development of people.

Concept of Sustainable

Sustainable means to consolidate the gains already achieved and to improve/maintain at the set standards forever rather than allow it to deteriorate. The concept of sustainable Quality of Life is both dynamic and relative in nature. Hence, it is very difficult to standardise. A model developed for one urban centre may not be applicable to itself after some time as it is mostly based upon value based judgement rather than objective evaluation at given time.

Urban Environment

Urban is always dynamic in nature both in temporal and spatial context. It is the space over which all economic activities other than primary are carried out predominantly. This functional structure of urban area act as a major attraction of large population and consequently the urban space undergoes a tremendous change both internally and externally.

The transformation of rural cultivated spongy surface to suburban and urban space with highly polluting industrial units with built up area, play a major role in the degradation of urban environment and consequently on Quality of Life. Hence the Diversity of environments make it appropriate to try to devise standard approaches or procedures to monitor and manage environmental systems. One major task of the management effort to ensure that human interference remains less and negligible.

Here an attempt has been made to study the physical, social and economic structure and their interplay with urban environmental quality based on sample survey from Madurai City.

Statement of Problem

It is perceived that with accelerated growth of population in the metropolitan centres the urban environmental Quality of Life is put under tremendous stress and strain leading to its deterioration and thus warrant an immediate strategy to sustain atleast the existing Quality of Life, especially in the developing countries like India.

The 1991 Census of India reveals that about 25.7 per cent of total Indian population are living in 3609 urban centres of various sizes. However, a close examination of this fact brings out the following. (Table 27.2)

1. 296 class I urban centres (8.20%) of the total urban centres of India account for about 65.20% of India's urban population living in them.
2. 23, million cities (0.63%) alone account for 50.57 per cent Nation's urban population
3. 4 megha cities have a little more than one fourth of India's urban population in them. (Table 27.2).

TABLE 27.2: Distribution of Class I Centres India - 1991

Size		No. of Centres	Population	% of U.P. to T.U.P.	Sex Ratio
	Class I	300	139730050		882
M1	Less than 200000	167	22939086	16.42	913
M2	200000 - 400000	40	9606814	6.88	904
M3	400000 - 499999	40	15586157	11.15	906
M4	500000 - 999999	30	20936734	14.98	881
M5	1000000 and above	23	70661259	50.57	864
(i)	1000000 - 1999999	14	17175849	12.29	882
(ii)	2000000 - 4999999	5	16260762	11.64	897
(iii)	5000000 and above	4	37224648	26.64	842

The Quality of Life in large metropolitan centres have been deteriorated considerably due to natural resource depletion, as will as limited resource available at the disposal of civic bodies for development. Thus with in the urban space i.e. in the intra urban, a wide gap on living standards have emerged among the people who are rich, living in sophisticated posh area (in small percentage) and poor, living in congested, ill developed slums/urban blights (inlarge percentage).

Hence the following aspects have been analysed to understand the existing Quality of Life in a urban centre and suitable strategy has been suggested to improve it.

(i) Population distribution pattern - to identify the areas of over-crowding and *vice versa*;
(ii) Distribution pattern of number of households;
(iii) Distribution pattern of number of dwelling units;
iv) Distribution pattern of urban of poor (slums);
(v) Existing transport network pattern; and
(vi) Other Civic facilities/amenities.

Methodology

The first section of the research paper describes the existing conditions of various factors for the city as a whole so as to enable one to understand the problem. The second section of the present work brings out a detailed study carried out in the study area based on systematic random sampling technique encompassing the socio-economic and environmental parameters and their interplay in determining the Quality of Life standards. Quantitatively the relationship between variables of one factor and the other has been related to draw proper conclusions.

Profile of the Study Area

Madurai Metropolitan area is located at 9°55' N latitude and 78°07'E longitude. Madurai urban agglomeration accounts for a population of 1.09 million (1991) which spread over an area of 52.0 sq. km area (Fig. 27.1).

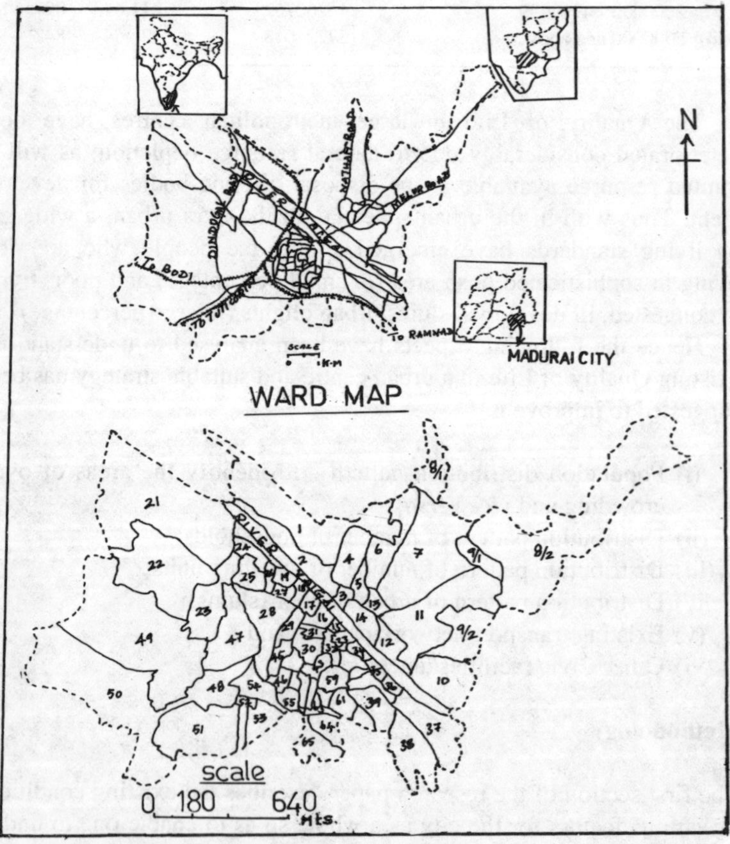

FIG. 27.1: Madurai City: Study Area.

The urban configuration of Madurai Urban Agglomeration can be studied as follows based upon their chronological evolution viz.,

(a) The city core, with temple as nucleus that developed as older part of the city, bounded on the north by river Vaigai, Madurai – Tiruchirapalli railway line in the west and Madurai – Rameswaram line in the south and Anuppanadi road in the east;
(b) The expansion of the city towards north across the river Vaigai by the end of medieval period;
(c) The recent spread of urban development beyond the railway lines which connects Madurai with Tiruchirapalli, Rameswaram and Tirunelveli, and the earlier bounds of the older part of the city on the southern bank of river Vaigai till independence; and
(d) Very recent expansion on western part and the northern part of river Vaigai along the Tiruchirapalli railway line.

Population Growth

The analysis of the growth of population from 1901 to 1991 (Table 27.3) clearly exhibits that the rate of growth is not uniform during the period.

The percentage variation between 1901 to 1911 was about 26.81. However, this has come down to 7.46 per cent in the next decade for Madurai Urban Agglomeration. The low growth is attributed to the out-break of epidemics in 1910 and 1919 in the region. The next two decades i.e. 1921-1941 recorded a moderate growth of population due to industrial development. This moderate growth got accelerated to higher growth during 1941-1951. In the next decade the growth has come down with a net decadal percentage variation of about 23.17 per cent. The decade of 1961-1971 has recorded the highest percentage variation of population of the century and the city got upgraded from the status of a municipality to that of a corporation. About thirteen small settlements with a total population of 101912 (1971) was annexed to the city's administration control. In addition to this the census of India categorised Madurai as Urban Agglomeration for the first time in corporating ten more town and village panchayats with Madurai corporation which made the percentage variation of population between 1961 and 1971 as high as 55.80 per cent. The decadal percentage variation of population has come down to half of the earlier decade (27.26%) during 1971-1981. The percentage variation of population during the decade 1981-1991 has further come down to 17 per cent the second lowest in the century. The shifting of the administrative headquarters of Ramanathapuram and bifurcation of Madurai district have resulted in large scale shifting of various administrative offices from Madurai city was may be the major reasons for the decline in the growth rate of Madurai Urban Agglomeration. Madurai city's population growth is almost identical with that of Madurai Urban Agglomeration except for minor variations. The Madurai Urban Agglomeration has attained the status of a million city with a population of 1093702 in 1991.

TABLE 27.3: Growth of Population (1901-1991)

	Population		% Variation of Urban Population	
Year	Madurai City	M.U.A.	Madurai City	M.U.A.
1901	105984	105984	—	—
1911	134130	134130	26.81	26.81
1921	138894	141448	3.55	7.46
1931	182018	187767	31.06	30.25
1941	239144	244846	31.38	30.29
1951	361781	370791	51.28	51.43
1961	424810	456711	17.71	23.17
1971	651026	711601	53.25	55.80
1981	765120	907732	17.52	27.52
1991	951696	1093702	24.38	17.00

Population Distribution and Density

The population is unevenly distributed in the city. Maximum concentration of population is found around the temple in the old part of the city. Low concentration of population is found in peripheral areas, where new residential colonies were coming up in recent times.

The average density of population in Madurai city is about 16033 persons per sq. km. Highest density of more than 40,000 persons per sq. km. is found in areas of central bus stand, around the temple, Kajimar street, Subramaniyapuram, Kamarajapuram and Madura College. High density of 30000-40000 persons per sq. km. is found in Mahal areas, Panthadi, West veli and West Merret street areas. The concentration of commercial activities, accessibility to all parts of city, and better educational and health facilities have contributed to this concentration. Medium population density of 20000-30000 persons per sq. km. is found in areas like Anna Nagar, Santhai Pettai, Ellis Nagar and Arasaradi. Low density of 10000-20000 persons per sq. km. is found in areas like K. Pudur, Vilangudi, Ponmeni, Madakulam and Palanganatham. The other areas, mostly the peripheral, western and northern parts of the city, register a very low density of less than 1000 persons per sq.km. (Fig. 27.2).

Infrastructural Facilities

Water Supply

Madurai has protected water supply scheme with river Vaigai as the source. An infiltration gallery in the river near Arappalayam was laid in the year 1892 as the yield from this basin was meagre, another infiltration gallery was laid in 1924 at Kochadai, which lies in the western end of the city to supplement the yield from the original Arappalayam headworks.

With the increasing population and excess demand in water supply for the city, further improvements were carried out in the system in the year 1963 by providing another infiltration gallery in the river Vaigai at Melakkal, about 13 km. up stream of Kochadai headworks. The protected water from Melakkal is pumped and collected in the ground level reservoir at Arasaradi and distributed to the city. The city gets protected water supply from the above sources about 6.6 million gallons. (1986)

During summer, the yield from all infiltration galleries is insufficient to meet the demand of the city. To wet the galleries, water is released from Vaigai Dam at frequent intervals.

In order to supply water to the northern part of the city, three overhead service reservoirs have been constructed at Sellur, Rajaji Park and A.R. Lines. These service reservoirs are fed by a pumping station, located near the south end of A.V. Bridge.

The Existing Distribution System

For the distribution of water, the city is divided into seven divisions, with a distribution system having about 23,472 private metred taps and the total length of pipe lines in operation is 1,40,030 metres.

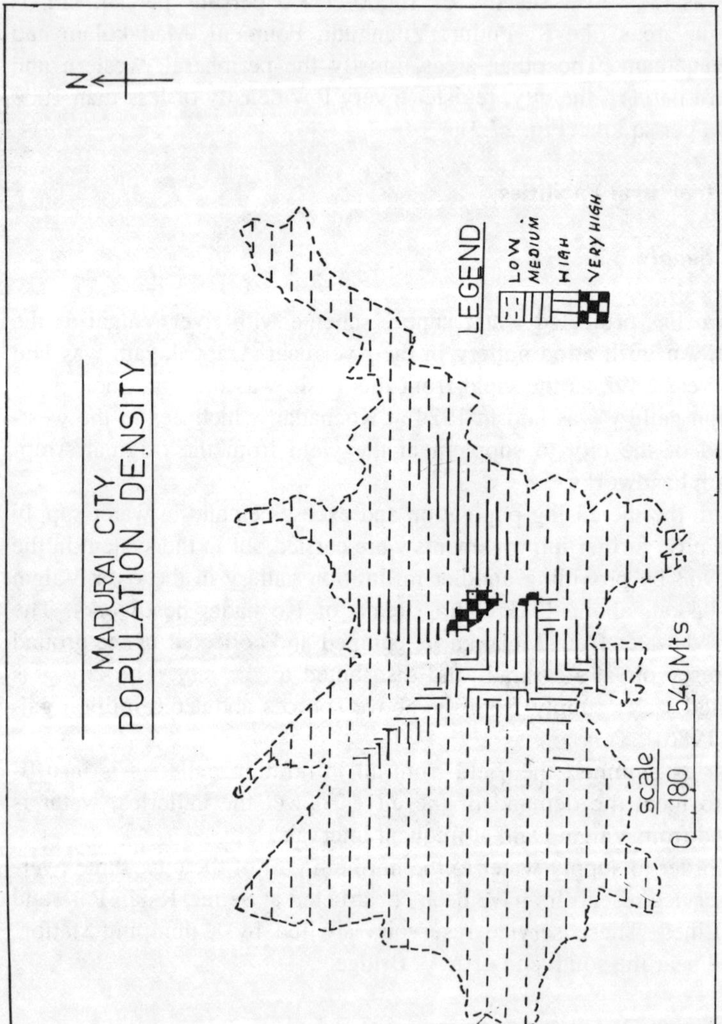

FIG. 27.2: Madurai City: Population Density

In high level areas not covered by the distribution system, the water is supplied by lorries having a capacity of 800 to 1000 gallons. In addition to the protected water supply scheme 964 bore wells and 26 deep bore wells had been dug for supply of water for non-drinking purposes.

The daily requirement of the city is expected to be about 250 lakhs gallons of water at the rate of 25 gallons per person per day. However, at present the city is able to get the supply of water only 130 lakh gallons and even this generally comes down considerably in summer months. Thus the city faces acute water scarcity during dry summer months.

Sewage and Drainage

The underground sewage system of Madurai city has been executed in several stages starting from the year 1924 in the congested portion of the city lying south of the river Vaigai.

About half of the city, mostly on the southern bank of the river Vaigai has been served by the underground drainage system. On the northern bank of the Vaigai such facility was developed mostly on the residential areas developed by Tamil Nadu State Housing Board. (Eastern Side). Rest of the areas is yet to be provided with underground drainage system. In the recently developed residential colonies, sewage disposal is done by septic tank and cess pools.

Storm Water Drainage

No such system is operating in this city. The city is not served with any storm water drain except street drains without any organised system. As the city is almost flat, there is an urgent need for this system. During the rainy days the stagnation of overflow of water in many parts of the city core is a very common sight. Sometimes even 60 to 100 cm. of water stagnates in the main bus stand and the road from Railway junction to the Bus Stand. The recent encroachment on the old irrigation channels, surplus channels and drainage channels due to urbanization worsen the problem to the core. The local body is now taking necessary steps improve the condition by proper storm water drainage system, for which the World Bank has already agreed to provide finance.

Conservancy

The solid waste and garbages are collected in dust bins and removed by trunks to the temporary collecting centres and from these centres, they are carried to the compost yard, located in the northeastern side of the city on the Madurai – Melur Road.

Transport and Communication Facilities

The historical city of Madurai has good transport and communication facilities when compared to the other cities of Tamilnadu. The existing road system of the urban agglomeration area comprises of 2 National Highways (NH 7 and NH 49), one State Highway (SH 5), seven major district roads and several other village roads. The National Highway 7 connecting Madurai with Tirunelveli and Kanyakumari in the south and Salem in the north, and the National Highway 49 connecting Madurai with Manamaduri, Ramanathapuram and Rameswaram in the east and Theni, Cubum and Kottayam in the west are the roads of greater national importance. The others Melur road and Sivaganga road in the north east, Alagar Koil, Natham and Alanganallur roads in the north Arruppukottai road in the south and Theni to Tirumangalam road in the west are the major district roads.

In the city centre the width of many roads are not only inadequate but they also vary in various parts of the same length. Thus these the road bottlenecks cause traffic congestion. Further the situation is complicated by the absence of cycle tracks, pedestrian side walks and parking spaces.

There are 2 over bridges and 2 cause ways existing across the river to connect the northern and southern parts of river Vaigai. The construction of another bridge across the river Vaigai on the eastern side and a proposed ring road and bye-pass development connecting outer area of the city core will help too minimize the traffic congestion problems, in the old city core.

The study area has only metre gauge railway line. At present railways play an important role in making the city as a tourist-cum-service centre. The metre gauge railway line has been functioning from the year 1859. The metre gauge connects Madurai with Tirunelveli, Madras, Coimbatore, Rameswaram and Bodinayakanur. Though Madurai has become an important railway junction in Tamilnadu, now new broad gauge line connecting Salem, Karur and Dindigul is on progress. It is expected that Madurai will be on the broad gauge map in near future.

Regarding Air transport service Madurai has direct air connections with Bangalore, Coimbatore, Madras, Cochin and Trivandrum.

Regarding post and telecommunication facilities Madurai is acting as a regional centre for the southern districts of Tamilnadu. Since independence with all modern telecommunication facilities Madurai is recognized as a telecommunication district and it controls 32 subdivisions.

Growth and Distribution of Slums in Madurai City

The urban poor of Madurai town are spotted in 127 places. There has been a rapid and constant growth of slums in Madurai from 1967. The number of slums found in Madurai were 36 in 1967 (Madurai Master Plan Report 1971) which increased to 92 in 1977, 107 in 1979 and 127 in 1981. Thus there has been nearly three fold increase in the number of slums in Madurai city. The emergence of more industrial units in and round Madurai and brought in the neighbouring districts of Pasumpon Muthuramalingam, Ramanathapuram and Kamaraj districts may be attributed as a causative factor for the rural-urban migration of labourers in large number, thus resulting in the increase of slums in the Madurai city. About 30,000 families are living in slums.

Maximum slums are found distributed along the banks of Vaigai river and Madurai-Rameswaram Railway line (Fig. 27.3).

The slums of Madurai city may be grouped under three zones based on their location location in they city as follows:

Zone I. The slums on the Vaigai river banks
Zone II. The slums on the Madurai-Rameswaram Railway line
Zone III. The slums on the fringe areas of the city.

In the zone I, about 10.2 per cent of the total slum dwellers of Madurai city in the slums situated on the north bank of river Vaigai. In the zone II, about 24.4 per cent of the total slum dwellers of city live in the slums located on the Madurai-Rameswaram Railway line. The remaining slum population 46.4 per cent is found distributed in the fringe areas of the city which constitute the Zone III.

Distribution of Residential Houses

Total number of houses in Madurai city is 1,57,888. They are not evenly distributed throughout the city. The variation is highly noticeable from one part of the city to other and based on this city has been divided into 4 categories, as low, moderate, high and very high areas.

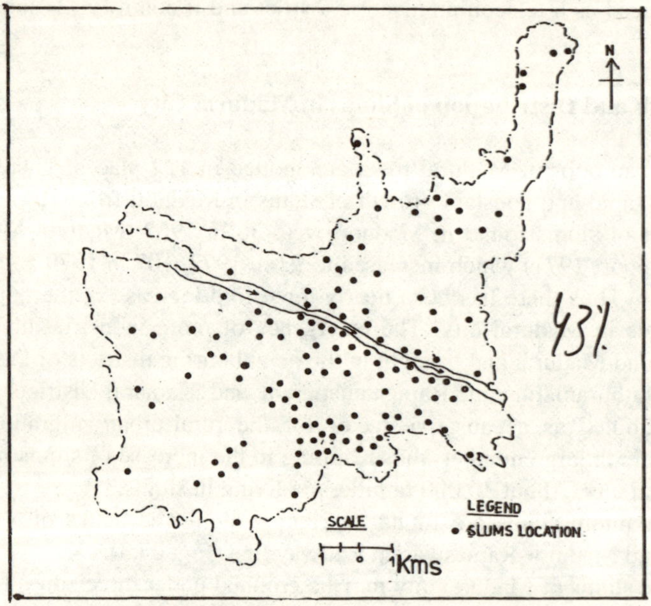

FIG. 27.3: Madurai City: Distribution of Slums

Housing Facilities

Madurai has accounted for 56243 residential units in 1961 and 157888 in 1981. An increase of 280 per cent between 1961-81 may attributed to the following factors.

(i) Establishment of Tamilnadu State Housing Board, Madurai unit;
(ii) Government policy on urban housing, specially for urban poor under slum clearance and improvement board; and
(iii) Liberal financial assistance through urban co-operative

societies.

Even though the overall picture on housing facilities seems to be good in reality it is not so due to its uneven distribution.

The residential dwelling density varies between less than 2000 units/sq.km to more than 4000 units/sq.km within the Madurai city. Hence for better cognition on the residential dwelling units distribution pattern they are classified in to four groups as follows.

1. Low : areas having a residential dwelling units (RDU) of 1000 - 2000/sq.km.
2. Moderate : 20000 - 30000 R.D.U/sq.km
3. High : 30000 - 40000 R.D.U/sq.km
4. Very high : More than 4000 R.D.U./sq.km

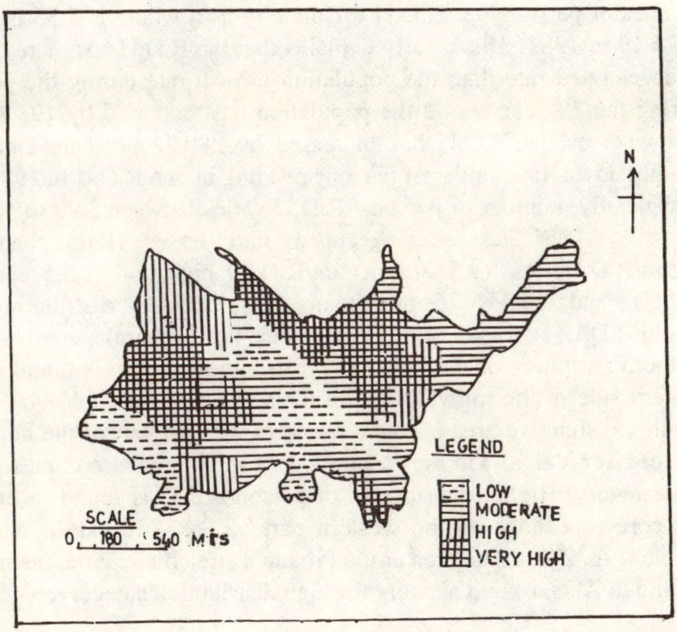

FIG. 27.4: Madurai City: Distribution of Residential Houses

Low R.D.U/sq.km is mostly found in the western and southern periphery of the city and around the city core, where the location of Sri Meenakshi Amman temple accounts for a large area of the particular ward. Otherwise it is comparatively crowded. (Fig. 27.4) Moderate density is found in the areas of North East and north west where the state housing board has developed new residential area in a well planned manner. The north western area, part of southern region and a small patch to the north of the river vaigai account for high density. The very high density of R.D.U is distinctly found in two patches one extending from the city core to the west and another to the north of the river Vaigai excluding the area developed by the state housing board. A small patch of very high density is found in the south eastern part of the city.

Persons per Residential Dwelling Units

Number of persons per R.D.U for the city as a whole is 7.53 in 1961 and 5.19 in 1981. This clearly explains that the R.D.U has increased at an accelerated rate than the population growth rate during the period. During the 20 year period the population has increased by 193.23 per cent whereas the R.D.U has increased by 280.72 per cent and thus brought down the number of persons residing in one R.D.U in 1981.

Spatially, number of persons/ R.D.U varies between 3.99 to 5.98 in the city. This has been grouped into lesser (Less than 4.5 person/R.D.U) less (4.5 – 5 person/R.D.U) high (5.0 – 5.5 persons/ R.D.U) and higher (more than 5.5). Lesser distribution of person/R.D.U is found only in one area i.e. Kamarajapuram on the southern periphery of the city. Less distribution pattern is found in the western side of the railway line on the southern bank of Vaigai river. Another distinctive area is found on north western part of the northern side of river Vaigai. On the eastern side a small area also comes under this category. Higher distribution of person/R.D.U is found in the old city core especially on the western part of Sree Meenakshi Amman temple (Fig. 27.5). The area around it and a stretch along the main road leading to Alagar kovil account for high distribution category.

Number of Households per 1000 R.D.U

In 1961 there were 87904 households in Madurai and it has increased to 1,59,154 in 1981. The number of household/1000 R.D.U. has come down from 1563 in 1961 to 1008 in 1981. This is due to the increase in the number of R.D.U. which has been already explained.

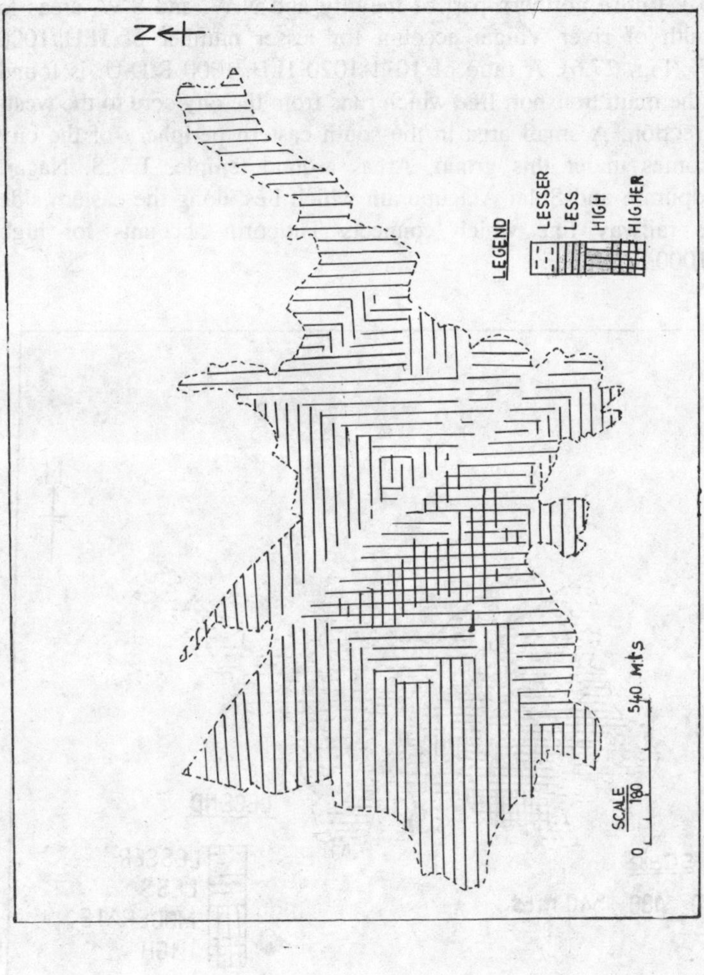

FIG. 27.5: Madurai City: Number of Persons per Residential House

On spatial dimension the number of households/1000 R.D.U. to 1046. This has been grouped into lesser (1000 - 1010 household/1000 R.D.U) less (1011-1020 household/1000 R.D.U) moderate (1021 - 1030 household/1000 R.D.U) and high (more than 1031 H.H/1000 R.D.U.). Entire northern part of the city and N.W. and S.W. areas to the south of river Vaigai account for lesser number of H.H./1000 R.D.U. (Fig. 27.6). A ratio of 1011-1020 H.H./1000 R.D.U. is found along the main transport line which runs from the city core to the western direction. A small area in the south eastern periphery of the city also comes under this group. Areas around temple, T.V.S. Nagar, Jaihindpuram and Solai Alagupuram which lies along the eastern side of the railway line which connects Tuticorin accounts for high H.H./1000 R.D.U.

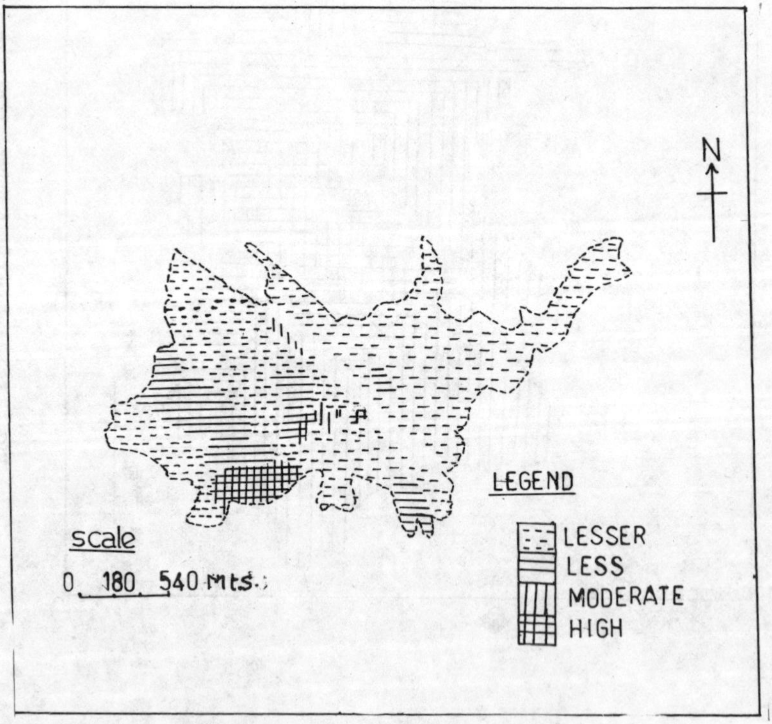

FIG. 27.6: Madurai City: Households per 1000 Residential Houses

Persons per Household

Number of persons per household (Family size) has shown a marginal increase from that of 4.84 persons/H.H. in 1961 to 5.16 persons/H.H in 1981. This may be due to immigration of the family member of already settled persons in Madurai during the period apart the Natural Increase.

Ward number 62, Kamarajapuram is the only area which account for the lesser number of persons/H.H that 3.99 while the ward number 63, Throwpadhiamman Kovil area accounts for more. Here also, the total data is divided into four groups (Fig. 27.7) based on the patterns distribution as follows.

Less than 4.5 persons/H.H	—	Lesser
4.5 - 5.0 persons/H.H	—	Less
5.0 - 5.5 persons/H.H	—	Moderate
5.5 and above persons/H.H	--	Higher

This analysis helps one to identify the actual size of the family and indirectly help to monitor the Residential Environmental Quality.

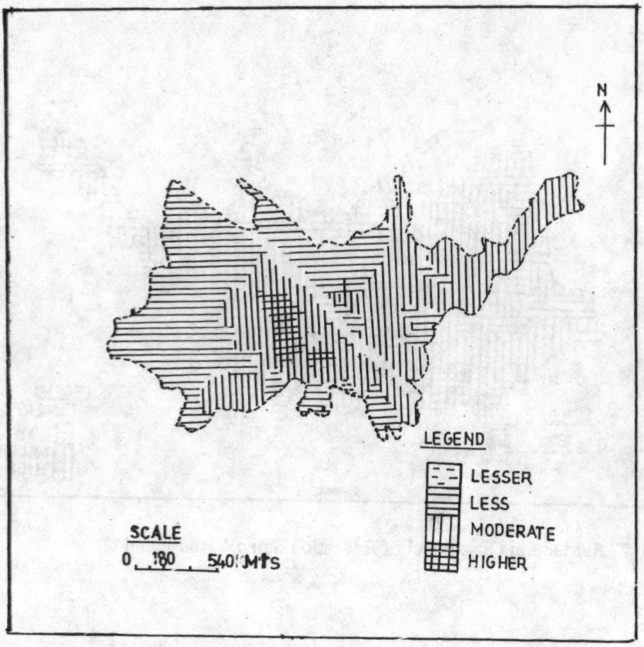

FIG. 27.7: Madurai City: Number of Persons per household

Sample Study

After having a detailed description of various factors, distribution over spatial and temporal dimensions which contribute to overall environmental quality, an attempt is made here study the same at micro level based upon sample studies to understand the Quality of Life with special reference to residential environment.

Based on the systematic random sampling method about 127 sample sites have been identified each at a distance of 90 mts and covering an area of 8100 sq. mts. The social (education level) and economic (income level) indicators have been collected as these two have important influence on the Quality of Life.

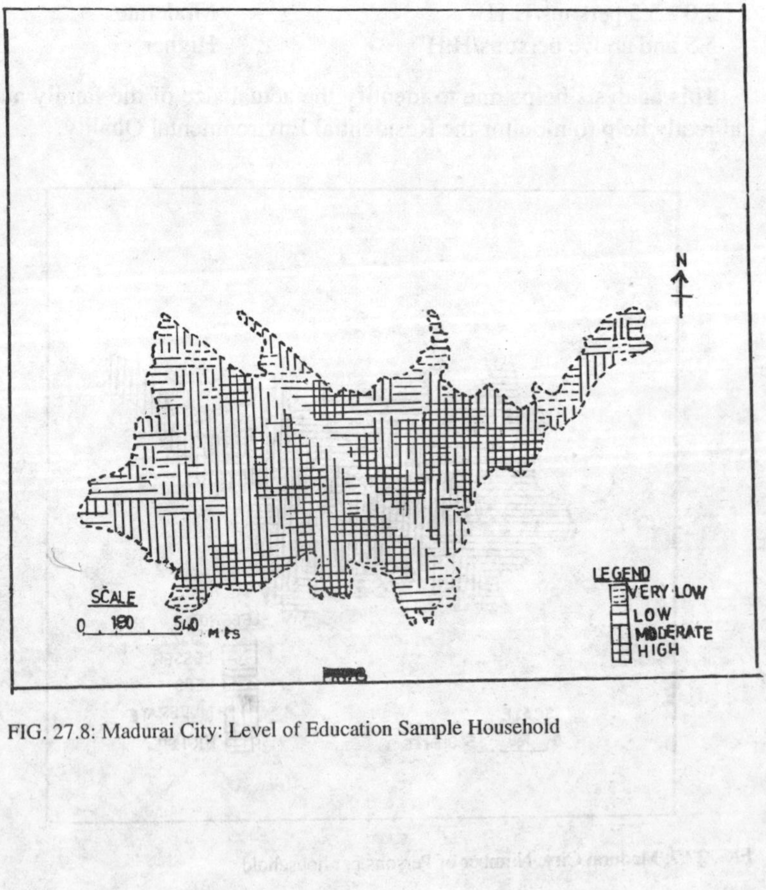

FIG. 27.8: Madurai City: Level of Education Sample Household

Education Level

About 10.1 per cent of the sample households are classified as illiterates (very low) followed by 19.4 per cent with primary education (low). About two fifth of the sample households i.e. about 41.0 per cent has been classified under higher secondary education level (moderate). The remaining 29.5 per cent has been classified with degree level educational standard (high). The spatial distribution of this factor has been clearly brought out in the Fig..27.8.

Income Level

Income is one of the main factors which control the residential quality. So income is considered as a main criteria in the analysis. The surveyed households are divided into four groups based upon their monthly income.

Nearly one fourth of the household surveyed in the city falls in the category of low income of less than Rs. 500 (low). A little over 50 per cent of sample households come under the category of lower middle income groups, having an earning of Rs. 501-2000 per month (medium). About 12.8 per cent having an income of Rs. 2001-4000 in the category of higher middle income group (high) in (Fig. 27.9) Remaining 10.1 per cent of the households fall in the higher income groups with a monthly exceeding Rs.4000 (very high).

Environmental Quality

In order to understand the quality of life with special reference to residential environment an attempt has been made to assess it based upon the primary data. Because of the size of the city systematic random sample method has been applied and about 127 sample locations have been selected each at an average distance of 90 metres so that a comprehensive picture on the quality of life can be better analysed and interpreted.

Score values have been given for the selected variables (Appendix I). Fig. 27.10 brings out the pattern of Quality of Life with special reference to residential environment. Puttuthope along the south bank of river Vaigai almost due north west of the Sree Meenakshi temple is the lone ward to be classified as very bad. Bad category of Quality of Life is found on both banks of the river Vaigai where a major concentration of slum population is found to have concentrated. A small Patch extending in N.W. to S.E. on the western part of the city also comes under this category. Better standard of Quality of Life is found in the Tamilnadu housing board developed residential areas besides T.V.S. Nagar and its adjacent regions. Rest of the area enjoys a good quality of residential environment.

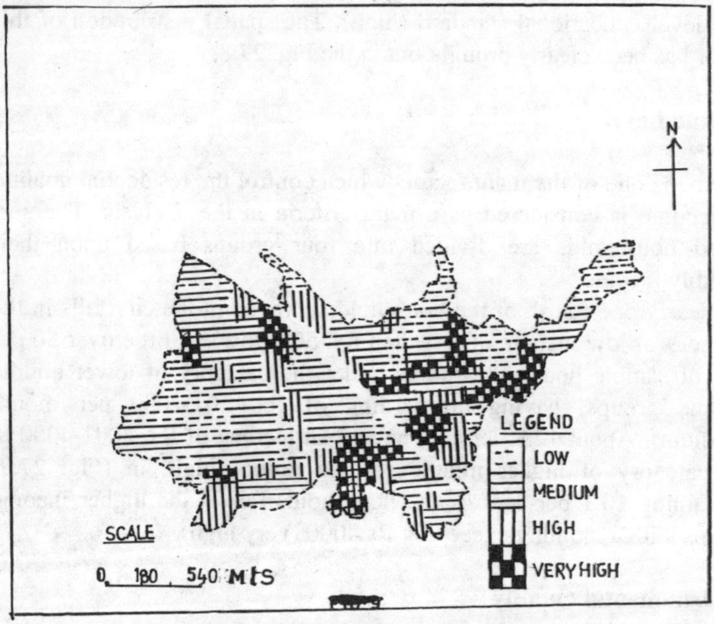

FIG. 27.9: Madurai City: Level of Income Sample Household

Conclusion

The analysis based on primarily data clearly shows there is no immediate possible deterioration in the Quality of Life in Madurai city which is just on the threshold. Hence a proper perspective plan on maintaining the environmental Quality of Life has to be worked out as continuation of this present investigation.

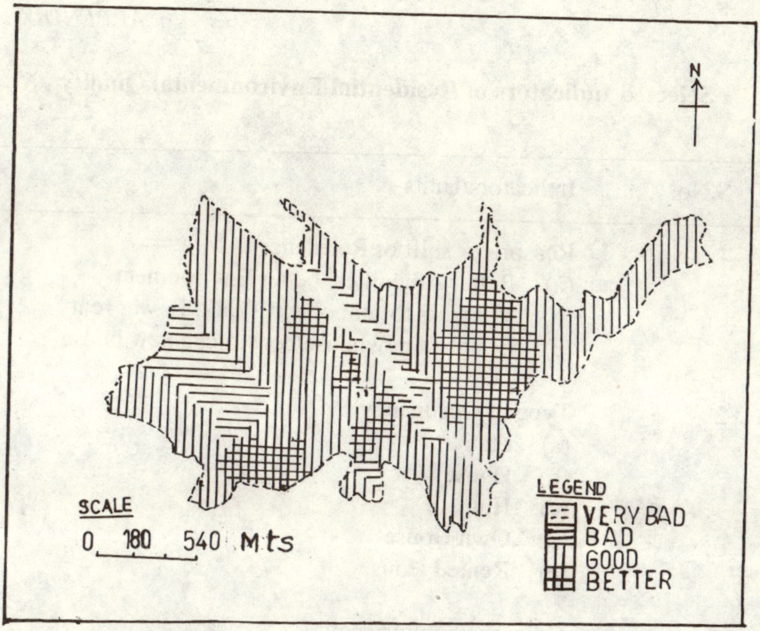

FIG. 27.10: Madurai City: Residential Environmental Quality

REFERENCES

Ramesh, A. & K.S. Gopalakrishnan (1971). "Tamilnadu upland and and South Sahyedri" in *India : A Regional Geography*, R.L. Singh, et al. (ed.), Varanasi: N.G.S.I.

Gopalakrishnan, K.S. (1988). "An integrated Development Model to solve the problem of slums" in *Urban Environment in India: Problems and Prospects*, K.K. Dubey et. al. (eds.), New Delhi: Inter India Publications.

Jaymala Diddee & Vimala Rangaswamy (1993). *Urbanisation Trends, Perspective and Challenges*. Jaymala Diddee & Vimala Rangaswamy (eds.), Jaipur: Rawat Publications.

Reports, (1986). Master Plan of Madurai City. Report of Madurai Local Planning Authority.

Reports (1991). Census of India Primary Abstract, Unpublished M. Phil. dissertation of Madurai Kamaraj University.

Vasantha, R. (1981). *Geographical Study of Urban Environment with Special Reference to Slums : A Case Study of Madurai City.*

Palaniappan, V. (1988). Slum Environment: Issues and Responses. Madurai City: A case study.

Rukmani Devi, D. (1990). Analysis of the Residential Environmental Quality in Madurai city.

APPENDIX I

Selected Indicators of Residential Environmental Quality

S.No.	Indicators/Units
1.	Reason for shift of Residence (a) Better Amenities, better Environment (b) Nearness to school and Work, Lower rent (c) Bought a newhouse/construct a new house
2.	Type of Occupancy (a) Flat (b) House (c) Hut (d) Own House (e) Rented House
3.	Opinion about privacy (a) No Comments (b) Normal (c) Below Normal (d) Adequate
4.	Residential Desirability (a) Satisfied (b) No
5.	Reasons for selection of Area (a) Liked the Area (b) Nearness to market, Shop and Bus Stop (c) Close to work, School for Children
6.	Housing Condition (a) Partial floor occupancy, Street house (b) Full floor occupancy, House with compound wall

(Contd.)

(Contd.)

7.	Nature rooms present (a) Kitchen (b) Bed Room (c) Dinning Room (d) Drawing Room (e) Pooja (f) Guest (g) Office Rooms
8.	Problems faced often (a) Sewage (b) Drainage (c) Noise (d) Beggars (e) Theft
9.	Nature of Residence (a) Pucca Structure (b) Kutcha Structure
10.	Garden Space available (a) Front, Back (b) Both sides
11.	Drinking Water Source (a) Own Tap (b) Hand Pump (c) Others
12.	Sewage and Solid Waste Disposal Facilities I. *Mode of Disposal* (a) Open Drainage (b) Underground II. *Latrines* (a) Separate Latrines (b) Public Latrines (c) Flushed (d) Dry
13.	Satisfied with Shopping Facilities (a) Yes (b) No

28

ETHICAL FOUNDATIONS OF ENVIRONMENTAL AND DEVELOPMENT EDUCATION

R.P. MISRA

Ethics is that branch of philosophy which discriminates between right and wrong and translates values into options for action. From a large number of options open to man, he chooses only a few because of the limitations imposed by a variety external and internal factors. One cannot disobey the laws of nature or the state without retribution. Transgression of ethical principles, however, invites only social disapprovation. It is not always followed by punishment.

This being the nature of ethics, it is never perfectly realized in any society individually or collectively. Yet at the same time no society can claim stability and orderly progress unless its members adhere to ethical provisions which substantially reduce uncertainties in human relations.

Ethical values whose transgression invites social unrest and chaos are usually encoded into formal laws. Laws are formally adopted, institutionalized and specifically sanctioned by the society. There is, however, a vast social space which is not covered by laws. It is the moral and ethical values which guide the people in this space.

Environmental Ethics is an internalized code of behaviour which regulates man's relationship with nature. Moral limitations on human behaviour in relation to the natural environment are needed because some forms of human behaviour are distinctive of the whole or a component of the total environment. Since man is a natural being to begin with and his survival and development is very linked to nature, he should use nature only to the extent that his life is not endangered.

Environmental ethics ensures a healthy man-nature relationship.

People act as they perceive and think. And the perception and thinking of the people is largely determined by the values they cherish. Man's attitude to nature and his habitat is therefore greatly influenced by ethical values. These values however, are not universal, nor are their translation into action universally the same. While looking for national or global code of environmental ethics, one has therefore to begin from local communities. These communities are the building blocks of far larger cultural realms or traditions.

Evolution of Environmental Ethics

Each local community developed a code of environmental ethics most appropriate to its natural conditions and genius. These codes keep a judicious balance between ecology and economy. Many of these communities evolved sustainable agriculture eventhough at a low level of productivity. How can a similar system of agriculture, for example, be developed with a higher level of productivity, is the crux of the problem.

The advent of Industrial Revolution as a driving force of the Cartesian Worldview, set in motion a new pattern of man-nature relationship. From the old pattern of man living in harmony with nature, man tried to control and subdue nature. Nature became a resource for exploitation. The barriers of distance were annihilated, thanks to the steam engine, to lay the foundations of a global society; knowledge of the physical world multiplied fast, thanks to new inventions and discoveries, to capsule time beyond human comprehension; and freedom which Renaissance and Enlightenment promoted to free man of bondage of nature and traditions, triggered off unprecedented exploitation of man by man. The sword and the cross joined hands to create colonial empires of global dimensions.

In due course, the empires died, thanks to the inner contradictions inherent to this predatory concept, but the exploitation of nature to the point of ecodisaster on the one hand and division of world into rich and poor, on the other, continues even today.

The ethical values that once maintained ecological balance and helped people share their joys and sorrows are now thoroughly eroded. Individualism, materialism, and scientism without balancing elements of humanism and spiritualism have given rise to a series of ecological and social problems. Some of these problems are too serious to be ignored or even postponed. They call for the reversal of current trends.

The reversal of trends would not take place in a day. It requires readjustment of all aspects of life – economy, ecology, science, technology and religion. This is, however, not a simple task. Any restructuring is painful; total overhauling means discarding of the Cartesian world view and adoption of a humanistic world view based on scientific knowledge and ethical principles.

Environmental ethics is an integral part of ethics in general. "Clearly an environmental ethic is needed to curb these human abuses of nature now more than ever since the human power to destroy nature is greater than ever. With the emergence of a global industrial human culture, indeed, the human impact on the environment has so increased in force, intensity and ubiquity that under the worse possible scenario imaginable, nuclear holocaust, people may destroy the environment (at least as we know it) along with themselves. Short of this cataclysmic and apocalyptic event, the global ecosystem may gradually be degraded to the extent that the forms of life presently existing (including human beings) are no longer adapted to radically changed conditions.

Rationale of Environmental Ethics

It is now clear that human actions which have direct destructive effects on the environment often have unsuspected deleterious effects on human beings. Deforestation, for example not only destroys the forest ecosystem but also has climatological, hydrological and erosional effects, not only in the area of deforestation but also elsewhere reducing the welfare of people without their concent, and making a few very rich. Deforestation is therefore unethical.

The above approach can be ascribed as secular using the principles of Human Rights. All human beings have right to live as they wish. Any interference without their consent is unethical. These rights can be extended to other forms of life, although with some riders.

The second approach is the moralist one. All human beings are morally accountable for the impact their actions, direct or indirect, have on non-human elements of the environment. While the human rights approach, would not censure man for cutting virgin forests where no human beings live the moralist approach would, because some of the plant and animal species may be extinct because deforestation. Man has no moral right to do that.

Environmental ethics may, therefore, be classified into two: (1) anthropocentric, and (2) biocentric. The former is secular and more acceptable in the West. Judo-Christian tradition gives man the stewardship of the earth. Dominian of man over the rest of the creation forms the basis of a powerful environmental ethic.

According to this tradition, god created a world which he declared to be good. He handed it over in the trust of man, whom alone he created in his own image, to dress and keep. Man, therefore, along among creatures has not only rights to the use of creation but the responsibility to conserve and perhaps even enhance the capacities of other creatures for self-expression.

This concept is specially useful in checking the extinction of plant and animal species for nothing would violate the spirit of stewardship than the wanton and careless destruction of biodiversity.

The biocentric ethics is rooted in Eastern philosophies – Hinduism, Buddhism, Confucianism, and Taoism. In these traditions man was not given the stewardship of the creation. He is an integral element of the 'Life'. All living and even non-living things have equal right to exist. Man being the supreme creation must use his wisdom to ensure that sanctity of nature and life is preserved.

Man has to take a lot from the environment for his survival and development. But this taking must be like taking the milk of the cow. The cow's life is sacred; it must be preserved so that it continues to give milk. Nature is likened to mother, and man-nature relationship as umbilical. Such a concept puts lots of limits on Man's use of nature.

There is an undercurrent of revolt against Western culture in the East. Most of the ills of the society are often ascribed to the western influence. There is an urge to revive the old values – the values which led this part of the world to give rise to some of the greatest civilizations of the world. The mad rush for all that is Western and apparently new is resisted, eventhough unsuccessfully. The chances for the revival of the traditional environmental ethical values are now therefore brighter than ever before.

Another trend that can help revive and review the traditional environmental ethical values, both in the West and the East, in the North and the South is the growing search for identity at the local and regional levels in almost all nation states. This identity in the olden times was based on space bound local communities. Each community and locality was *proud* of its history, its uniqueness, and its traditions. There was a sense of pride in local environmental quality. The new trend towards *communitarianism* within globalism, can be successfully used to rebuilt and preserve the environment.

These traditional values have to be debated in the context of existing scientific knowledge. Whether one likes are not, scientific rationality and scientific knowledge is a great asset of modern society. The revival of traditional environmental values cannot be at the cost of scientific rationality. They must support each other, not work against each other.

Towards Global Environmental Ethic

Can there be global environmental Ethic? Often, the answer is, no. But if the world is becoming a global village, the world must also have a global ethic. Strength of a village is the ethics based community bond. Strength of the global village cannot therefore be without global ethics. Today we are witnessing the merger of nations into a global community of humans. The global village has become an emergent reality because of the United Nations, multinational corporations, growing economic interdependencies, and shortening of distances by new transportation and communication technologies. Environmental problems do not stop at national borders, nor do the natural disasters. There is a growing subscription to the Eastern view, that all living species have right to exist and no nation has the privilege to destroy any of them within or outside its borders. And hence the possibility of a global environmental ethic.

One can look at the global environmental ethic from two interrelated perspectives: (1) people, and (2) government. The people's environmental ethics concentrates on the behaviour of the individuals and small groups like families and communities. The government oriented ethics concerns the behaviour of the governments towards other countries and people. For example, people all over the world, are fighting against any direct or indirect attempt to do violence against any living species. A large number of NGO's are involved in this exercise. They are fighting against the World Banks, national governments and business and industry. Their struggle is not always based on any legal rights; it is based on moral and ethical rights.

The values which form the basis for these struggle have to be strengthened. Incidentally, the people involved in these struggles do not accept national borders in matters of ecology and environment. They are truly global in approach.

There is a need to evolve environmental ethics for the governments. No government should be allowed to take shelter under national sovereignty in matters of ecology and environment. In an inequitous world that we have today, it is not easy to evolve such a global code of conduct, but as a first step, its need must be recognized and efforts must commence to codify them. In fact, in the immediate future, global ethics will have to depend on national governments for adoption and implementation through various laws and statutes.

Unless serious efforts are made both at the NGO level and the government level evolution of environmental ethics at the global level as well as at the local and national levels would take too long a time to avoid and forestall disaster.

Developing Environmental Ethics

Revival and development of environmental ethics at various levels — individual to global calls for two simultaneous steps. The first step involves framing of a series of laws at the global, national and sub-national levels to protect nature from wanton destruction; and second to develop new educational programmes and technologies to sensitise people from the early childhood with environmental and ecological imperatives.

Environmental Laws

Several countries have passed environmental laws to check air, water, land and noise pollution. Some countries have regulations regarding the use of chemical fertilizers, insecticides and pesticides as they have proved to be harmful to human health. Consumer protection laws, food adulteration laws, air, water and noise pollution laws are now almost universal.

These legal measures however suffer from three major infirmities. Firstly, many of the laws go only part way. For example, putting a statutory warning in cigarette packets that 'smoking is harmful to health', does not help much. There has to be restriction on smoking not only in public places but also privately. Society provides medical services in all at subsidized rates. Those who indulge in smoking put undue pressure on this system. They get sick and also induce sickness in others. Smoking should therefore be banned altogether.

Such half hearted measures are found in other environmental areas too. Air pollution caused by motor vehicles, for example, is tolerated almost everywhere either because laws in this respect are weak or because they are not implemented. Take the case of deforestation. There are laws against deforestation in one form or the other almost in every country. Felling of trees, however, continues unabated.

At the global level, there are treaties and agreements which have the force of law, but they leave enough loopholes for powerful nations to violate them. For example, the NPT puts restrictions on non-nuclear states to acquire nuclear capabilities, but leaves the nuclear powers free to test and develop new weapons. One can cite several other international conventions which suffer from similar drawbacks.

The second weakness of the legal approach lies in its negative orientation. Most laws tend to restrict people and organizations from doing something. Laws that encourage and reward people who follow environmentally ethical behaviour are few, if any. For example, it is not enough to curb the tendency of the people to misuse land and destroy soil. Those who use land according to ecological principles are rearly rewarded.

A third weakness of national statutes and international agreements, treaties and conventions is their pro-rich bias. They tend to favour the powerful and rich who also happen to be the polluters. We have cases of NPT, biodiversity, IPR, transfer of technology, international trade, and many other areas where poor nations are being pressurized to accept conditionalities which would not be in their long term interest; while those who are powerful are able to enforce *status quo* or further strengthen their position. The above situation holds good in case of national laws too. Laws against deforestation, poching of wild animals, pollution of rivers and lakes and unscientific use of land etc. are so framed that they affect the poor adversely. While slum clearance is a good idea, where should the slum dwellers go? While check on felling of trees is fine, what should the forest dwellers do for fuel wood, etc.? While large dams and large factories do push up national economic growth, what should the persons displaced by the dams do? These issues have not yet been adequately taken note of by national laws.

This brings us to the gap between state laws and human rights. All human rights cannot be covered by formal laws. And hence everything that is illegal, is not necessarily immoral or unethical. Laws in fact leave a lot of functional space which unless filled by ethics, will create a highly chaotic social situation.

Environmental Education

Education, in its broadest sense is a means to create and inculcate ethics. Environmental education can thus play a very crucial role in evolving, revitalizing, reviving and ensuring environmentally sensitive human behaviour.

Education is a process of learning. It is life long and is not limited to any age group, institution, or aspect of life. The day a child is born, it starts learning. In fact, according to the earliest as well as latest findings, a child learns even when in womb. In the early part of his life, he gets a unified and integrated learning environment. As years pass, the unity of knowledge is fractured and he sees the world in parts and sections. By the time, he enters the high school, he sees no relationship between nature, man and culture. Soon he turns out to be a physicist, an engineer, a historian, or a poet. As a physicist, he sees the nature as matter, as engineer he finds the way to use it; as a historian he studies human progress as record of man's mastery over nature; and as a poet he composes the songs of this victory or laments over what man has done to himself and to the earth he inhabits. Each one sees the world through a tunnel of his own making; and each one tries to make the best by ignoring the legitimate claims of others. The end result is a world full of pollution of air, water, land, mind, and society.

Education from early childhood shapes the personality of man who as a multitude forms the society local, national and global. The current environmental crisis can, to a great extent, be attributed to an educational process which is neglectful of the role natural environment plays in human survival and development.

Three dimensions of environmental education deserve urgent attention. These are formal and informal instruction, cultural diffusion by oral or self-learning process educational mass media, and philosophical and scientific research on human and natural ecology. The three are very closely related. Unless ecology and environment get a right place in world views of various cultures and societies, neither mass media, nor schooling can become instruments of environmental sensivity. This necessitates incorporation of ecological and environmental studies at all levels of education.

University Education

At present universities and other higher educational centres are geared to the Western world view. Analytical approaches require breaking down of the whole into bits. Modern research is engrossed in depth study of parts or segments. It has lead to great scientific discoveries. But the relations of the parts with the whole and among the parts, have not been studied and understood adequately to foresee the injurious effects of new knowledge and discovery.

Here lies one of the basic causes of ecological imbalance and environmental pollution. Analysis without synthesis gives depth of a limited segment of the whole. Application of this knowledge produces lot of unintended side effects. Ecology and environment call for research on interrelations among various forces of nature and human activities as much as in depth analysis of each force and activity. Such approaches are, however, not accepted in discipline based university system. Scientist is not concerned with ethics; and ethics is not concerned with science. Physical sciences and biological sciences did not have a meeting ground until very recently. Biophysics or biochemistry has come to acquire meaning only in recent decades. And hence the question of Science and Religion having a common ground does not arise.

According to Vedic sciences, the functioning an atom is the same as the functioning of the universe and all that comes in between. What in essence it says is that there is a general theory that explains the functioning of all phenomena whether physical, biological or human. Each discipline concerns itself only a part of the totality; it alone cannot produce a general theory and hence is partial and inadequate is a system of knowledge.

Once, the university education gets out of its disciplinary/non-overlapping circles of concern, it will produce knowledge without adverse direct and indirect effects. The beginning has already been made in this direction. Fusing of various physical, biological and human sciences have opened up new opportunities. As this fusing intensifies further, a far more ecology and environment sensitive knowledge would emerge. Environmental impact assessment methodology is still very imperfect. Lot more research is needed within various disciplines and also across disciplines. Training of engineers, scientists and social scientists in EEA is urgently needed. Universities have to be assisted and encouraged take up this work.

Mass Media

Mass media, print or electronic, plays a very important educative role

It carries the message to all those who are neither in universities nor in schools. In fact, they bring to the common man dimensions and implication of various ecological and environmental problems. They are the moulders of public opinion, which in turn moulds the opinion of decision-makers at local, regional, national and global levels. Electronic media (both audio and video) have given new and better opportunities for moulding the public opinion in favour of ecological balance and environmental reconstruction. It is a very powerful tool for it can reach even the remotest corners of the world at a relatively low cost. It can also reach even those are not formally educated.

For the mass media to become an effective channel of environmental education, it needs reorientation from source of mere entertainment of environmental education. It also need adequate number of trained man power not only to handle the gadgets but also and more importantly, to make the software. At present, we do not have enough journalists who take interest in ecology and environment. There are quite many who look for sensational news, but very few who can present a scientific and illustrative document for general readers courses in journalism in the universities do not consider ecology as a major theme. The situation is changing but only slowly.

With the advent of Radio, TV, satellite imageries, computers etc. the situation is a little better in the electronic media, but deep ecology is still at the margin. We have all the means at our disposal, but we do not yet have adequate and appropriate knowledge for presentation, nor we have enough people who can handle environmental issues and create programmes for various target groups such as children, students in junior highs, colleges and universities, adults, professionals, businessmen, politicians, etc.

The use of mass media and various educational technologies in much of the world, particularly the developing world is extremely limited. Not even 0.001 per cent of the primary schools in India, for example, have television sets. How can the children watch these programmes. This applies to adults too to a great extent.

The developed world can help countries like India in the field of electronic media, both on the hardware and software sides. What we need is a massive environmental education programmes through mass media all over the world. People are too ignorant about the critical man-nature relationship in the North because of ignorance and arrogance in the North and because of ignorance and poverty in the South. While it will take time to remove arrogance and poverty, something can be done to remove ignorance sooner than later. Mass media is an important means to active this goal.

Primary and Secondary Education

School provides the first opportunity for a child to come out of the influence of the family fold and influence of parents, and to learn about the world beyond through other children and through teachers. What the child learns has much to do with school environment and the quality of teacher. The curriculum is important but far more important is what the teacher does and the image of the teacher that child fixes in his mind.

At this level students must be taught about ecology and role of each individual and group in maintaining ecological balance. They should be taught about environmental pollution and the cause there of. They should be taken to factory sites; areas with soil erosion, deforestation, polluted rivers, etc. so that they can feel and experience what they read in books and hear from teachers. The extracurricular activities must include trecking in hilly, forested, and water front areas. Students should be enabled to appreciate nature and healthy environment. Field work to collect local plant specimens and classroom study of each specituen community must form part of instruction.

Each discipline has its own environmental and ecological dimension. Course outline and details of each subject must end up with environmental implications.

Teacher education therefore needs reorientation. Ethical and environmental dimensions have to be brought in forcefully in teacher education.

Early Childhood Education

What a child learns during the first five years of his life is most crucial for its personality as an adult. In this period, the parents, particularly the mother, are the teachers and home and its surroundings, the environment. In a society where parents have no time to show their love and affection to children; where they are too busy in mundane affairs to spend time with them; where child is trained to consume milk and bread produced in refrigerators, people cannot be environment friendly. Similarly, children brought in poverty and pestilence; in disharmony and conflict situation cannot be environment friendly.

Children in the developed countries are brought up in a culture which takes pride in anihilating nature; in cutting trees, in hunting wild life; in the banality of individualism, and in equating life with matter. And those in poor developing countries are brought up in a culture which preys on all that nature provides, physical or biological, to meet the basic human needs. These children, when they grow up, have no compunction in destroying nature for short-term gains

Only such persons would be sensitive in ecology and environment and would be guided by ethical values which protect, conserve, and enrich nature while taking life supporting elements from it, who are brought up in an environment which is wholesome; which is not marked by deprivation or and consumerism, which is sensitive and sympathetic to nature and fellow human beings.

Perhaps the most important element of this environment is the mother. She is the best teacher one can think of. The love and affection, the mother, has for her children is unparalleled. None else can match her. Hence, the education of the mother with respect to ecology and environment is a crucial factor in child's upbringing.

The condition of women in general and mothers in particular is not good at all in the developing countries. Illiteracy, ignorance, poor or no maternal care, poverty and deprivation haunt them day and night. Very few women are lucky enough to lead a decent life. This situation has serious implications for children. Most of them grow under utter neglect. Many of them do not survive infancy. To expect these children in adulthood to be humane and sensitive to ecology and environment to expect too much.

In the developed parts of the world lot of children grow up in the care of single parents. Those who are brought up in healthy homes, are never given the knowledge and experience of how the other half of the world lives and what role nature plays in their life. They obsessed by consumerist culture.

All those children brought up in broken homes and in poor homes often turn out to be violent towards nature and as well as fellow beings. Any meaningful environmental education programme must therefore be integrated with overall socio-economic development programmes with a thrust on women's development and women's education. This naturally takes us beyond the purview of environmental education *per se*, but then that is the way things are and should be. Education and development have too close relationship to be treated independently when it comes to man-nature relationship.

INDEX

Abbas, B.M., 240
Açu valley, 188
Adult literacy, 512
Africa, resilience in, 469-72
Afforestation, 75, 213, 220, 442
Agro-alpine, 189
Agenda for research, 83
Agglomeration, footloose industries, 111
Agnihotri, Y., 200
Agrawal, S.C., 141
Agreement, 242, 350, 363
Agriculture, 99
  diversification of, 132-33
  industrialisation in, 107-10
  integration of horticulture, 133
Agricultural areas, 107
  labourers, 116
  operation, 145
  pollution, 79
  production system, 257
Agro-economic setting, 269
Agro-forestry, 129, 188
  system, 135, 137
Air pollution, 22, 59, 63, 120, 298, 441
Air (Prevention and Control of Pollution) Act, 443
Amte, B., 210
Anderson, Francis Philip, 254
Anderson, M., 297
Anganwadis, 512
Animal husbandry, 54
Animal liberation front, 282
Asian Development Bank, 74
Asthana, Sheena, 505
Atkins, P.J., 309
Atkinson, Adrian, 526, 528
Ayodhya, 535

Baba, J.M., 480
Babri mosque, 535
Bagasse, 116
Bagi village, 398
  transact of, 400
Balasubramian, R., 283
Balawala village, 411
Balwadis, 512
Bandyopadhyay, J., 209
Bangladesh, 249
  border, 224
  environmental problems, 224-25
  cereal production, 240
  flood disasters, 244
Barrages, 242
Basic Minimum Needs Approach (BMNA), 71
Basta, S.S., 507
Bathing and washing facilities, 461
Bengal delta,
  floods in, 237
  formation of, 223
  problem of, 228
Bergen conference, 351
Bhakra Dam, 209
Bhattacharya, Vidyadhar, 91
Bhopal tragedy, 34
Biodiversity, 66
Biological pedoturbation, 172
  resources, 355
Biomasses, problem of, 155
Biophysical condition, 41
Biosphere reserves, 220
Bioturbation, 172
Blowers, A., 285, 349, 365
Bookchin, Murray, 282
Bosnia, 367
Boswell, 339
Bremmer, H., 232, 238, 244
Brazil, 32, 181, 185, 357

Brahmaputra valley, 243
augmentation, 243
Brennan, A., 279
Bretton woods institutions, 32
British administration, 191
British culture, remoteness in, 333
British General Election, 367
Brookfield, H., 191
Brown, P.J., 40
Brown, S., 281
Bruntland Commission, 72, 73
Budapest, 295, 304
Buddhism, 285, 287
Bulla, M., 299, 300
Burgen, J., 225
Business diplomacy, 525, 532, 535
transactions, 531

Cairncross, S., 469
Canal irrigation, 259, 263, 266, 273, 438
Capistrano, A.D., 29
Carpenter, R.A., 40
Carrying Capacity (CC), 43, 45
Cash crops, 411, 415
Cauvery Delta system, 257
Central Ganga Authority (CGA), 64
Central Water Pollution Control Board (CWPCB), 63
Centre for Earth Science Studies (CESS),48
Challenges, 354
Chandigarh, 200
Chandrashekhar, C.S., 72
Chapman, Graham P., 223
Chattopaddyay, Srikumar, 39
Checkdams, construction of, 202
Chemicalization, 317
Chernobyl, 349
Childhood education, 577
Chimneys, distribution of, 114
China, 357, 532
Chinese land mass, 228
Chipko movement, 284
Chittaurgarh, 141
Chokaris, 91
Clark, J., 364
Clean technology, 33
Climate changes, 164-65
Clinton administration, 535
Close settled zone, 477, 482, 483
Club of Rome, 72
Coal subsidies, 301
Cocoyok declaration, 39
Cold War, 309, 349, 532, 538
Coleman, Alice, 487
Coleridge, 335
Colonial administration, 185
Colonization, 527
Commercial crops, 404
Common property, 34
Communication facilities, 552
Community Health Volunteers (CHVs), 513
Complex slope sequences, 171
Constraints, 317, 319
Crime rate overtime, 496
Criticism, 33, 286, 309
Crops, 380
management approach, 135
productivity, 273
rotation, 377, 381
types grown, 186
Crop and water management agencies, 130
Cropping patterns, 131, 213, 259, 269, 271
Cross cultural information, 501
Crow, B., 242, 249
Cruz, O., 167
Cultivating techniques, 188
Cyclones, 234, 250

Daly, H.E., 40
Dambos, 173
Damuth, J.E., 163
Dardis, G.r., 162
Davidson, Ogundade R., 141
Decolonisation, 69
Deforestation, 29, 32, 134, 136, 213, 217, 223, 225, 249, 259, 349, 401, 444, 470
De-industrialization, 529
Dehradun, 390
Democracy, 148
Democratic People's Republic of Korea (DPRK), 310

Deploey, J., 167
De Oliveira, M.A.T., 169
Desertification, 224, 226, 349, 352
Development planning, organisational
structure of, 77
Dhar, S.K., 204
Dharmadhikari, S., 210
DICE schemes, 500
Dietrich, W.E., 169
Disadvantagement scores, 494, 495
Disciplines, 85
Diseases, 267
Dixon, J.A., 209
Dogra, B., 209
Doiwala village, 390
Domestic fuel, 301
Drainage, 462
Dry evergreen forest, 182
Dry season, 238
Dulcherra, 232

Earthquake, 228, 232, 233, 234
Eckholm, E., 223, 477
Eco-development, 431
operational definition, 432
Ecology nexus, 431
Ecological appraisal, 433
factors, 43, 209
management, 197-200
problems, 197, 444
Economic colonialism, 70
growth, 69
Economies, globalization of, 535
Educational activities, 512
development, 567
level, 561
Eighth Five Year Plan, 387
development in, 388
Employment, 340, 418, 517
Energy use models, 149
dynamics of, 146
pattern of, 141
resources, 139
sector, 301
sectoral flow of, 142-43
Environmental,
agendas, 372
appraisal, 43
challenges, 107, 120
claims making, 225
consequences for, 112-13
considerations, 449
crisis, 313, 472, 535
degradation, 44, 81, 85, 91, 353, 356, 360, 450, 469
disturbances, 326
eastern values, 282-83
education, 574
ethics, 567, 572
evolution of, 560
rationale of, 569
towards global, 571
factors, 258
global values, 285-86
hazards, 469
inequalities, 352
issues, 24
key elements, 24
laws, 572
management, 21, 25, 367
manifestation, 282, 470
multi-dimensional problems, 13
movement, 364
myth, 223-26
obstacles, 25
orientation, 76
perspectives of, 59-64
planning system, 368
policy, 23, 197, 279, 301, 365
pollution, 71
problems, 22, 27, 28, 135, 197, 209-12, 215, 224, 259, 317, 367, 465, 543
protection, 26, 300, 304, 306
quality, 561
sustainability, 475
tropical, 181
values, 23, 279-84
western values, 280-81
Environmental Impact Assessment (EIA), 75
Environmental Improvement of Urban Slums (EIUS), 453
Erosional *rampas,* 169
Etching, 172
Ethical foundations, 567

Ethiopia, 190
Exploitation, 21, 82, 285
Export crops, 31

Fairbridge, R.W., 163
False Colour Composite (FCC), 94
Family planning, 513
FAO dismisses, 225
Farakka, 249
barrage, 240
dispute, 241, 242
Fatherland liberation war, 324
Ferreira, R.C., 169
Fifth Five Year Plan, 389
Fleischer, T., 299
Floods, 237
control, 209
crops, 415
human response to, 244
plain, 173
protection levees, 237
Flue-gas desulphurisation, 301
Food consumption, 473
Forecasting impacts, problem of, 355
Forests, 439
development initiatives, 137
Fuelwood, 467
Fulani Community, 187

Gabcikovo Hydropower Dam Project, 294
Gadgil, M., 284
Ganeshnagar, 519
Ganga, 3
system, 433
Ganges-Brahmaputra plains, 229
Garbage disposal, 462
Garhwal, 394
General Agreement on Tariffs and Trade (GATT), 365
Gentrification, 516
Global Environmental Facility (GEF), 363, 371
Global pollution, 360
system, 65
Globalisation, 363-64
Gobar gas plants, installation of, 203
Godavari delta system, 257, 260
Gopalakrishnan, K.S., 541
Gopalan, C., 141
Gondwana land, 185
Goodland, R., 209
Gorz, A., 366
Graffiti, 491
Greenhouse gasses, 65, 360
Grande Carajas Project, 32
Green Revolution, 108, 131, 319
Greene, O., 353
Grewal, S.S., 200
Growing environmental awareness, 73
Gross National Product (GNP), 70
Gulf war, 349, 538

Hardwar and Rishikesh, 407
Haryana, 130, 434
saline soils in, 438
salt affected soils, 439
Harrawala village, 391, 404
Hazardous wastes, 356
Health hazards, 452
Highlands and Islands Development Board, 341
Hillslope colluvium, 168
Himachal Pradesh, 130, 134
Himalayan deforestation, 225
Hirakud dams, 209
Hollows, 169
Hong Kong, 169
Hoodbhog, Pervez, 526, 526
Horticultural activities, 133-34
Housing facilities, 554
Housing Association Blocks, 494
Housing and Urban Development Corporation (HUDCO), 513, 520
Hungary, current problems, 292
future improvement, 303
water quality, 295-96
Hungarian environment, 291
political structure, 297-98
Husain, Majid, 377

Income level, 561
India's urban population, 451
Indigenous Technical Knowledge (ITK), 186
Indo-British Seminar, 35
Indonesia, 32

Industrial agglomerations, 115
corridors, 1112
wastes, 356, 440
Industrialisation, 60, 93, 108, 280, 284, 528, 541
choosing new direction, 123-24
environmental consequences, 112-13
process, 111
Indus valley, 184
Infrastructural facilities, 549
Integrated Mapping Unit (IMU), 44
Integrated Rural Development Programmes (IRDP), 71
Integrated Rural Technology Centre (IRTC), 48
Integrated Urban Community Development (IUCD), 508
Inter-cropping, 270
International Geosphere Biosphere Programme (IGBP), 65
Intrinsic landscape, 182
Irrigation, 213, 257
canal, 115, 263, 266
facilities, 272-73, 397, 403, 405
impact of, 261
settlements, 194
surface, 263
Islam, N., 223
Ives, Jack D., 223, 229

Jackson, J.B., 314
Jacobs, M., 368, 369
Jaipur, forest area, 98
industrial area, 99
land transformation, 97
changes, 100
population growth, 97
Jamuna river, 232
Japan, 532
Jawahar Rozgar Yojana (JRY), 415
Jay, M., 313
Jephcott, Pearl, 489
Jammu & Kashmir, 130, 1134
Jhum cycle, 382
Jhum land, 380
Jhumias, 380, 383
Jhuming (shifting cultivation), 377
Jodha, N.S., 80
Joggiwala village, 404
John Major (British Prime Minister), 534
Johnson, B.L.C., 234, 339
Jones, F.O., 167

Kainji dam, 479
Kalliassery Panchayat, 52
Kandati river, 215
Kano close settled zone, 475
Karl Marx, 281
Khadri Kharak Mauf village, 407
Kiker, C.F., 29
Kimilsungism, 309
Kim Jong II, 316, 318, 324, 327
Kimmane, K., 480
Korea, landscape as political project, 314
nature and nation, 310
Korean crop varieties, 319
war, 310
Kosi river, 229
Koyna catchment, 209
demographic characteristics of, 212-15
Krishan, Gopal, 197
Krishna delta-system, 257
Kumaon regiments, 394
Kurukshetra, 436
Kwon, J.G., 317

Land alleviation, 213
degradation, 23, 59
families, 201
Landscapes, 182, 316, 338
dynamics, 164
Land Information System (LIS), 137
Landslides, 167
scars, 168
Landsurface downwasting, 172
stability, 174
Land transformation, 91
changes, 100-101
Landuse change, 129, 131
Land and water resources, 41
Late quaternary environmental change, 163
Lee, O., 507
Lele, S.M., 40
Link Road Plan, 108, 120, 122

Liton, M., 506
Little water, problem of, 238
Loans, 512
Local land market, 516
Local level planning, 44
Localisation schemes, 274
Lovelock, J., 286, 358
Lower colluvium, 169, 171
Lundquist, A., 243, 249

Maastricht Treaty, 367
MacGill, S.M., 144
Madurai, growth and distribution of
slums, 553-54
metropolitan area, 546
urban agglomeration, 548
Mahabaleshwar,
demographic characteristics, 213-14
plateau, 210
Mahatir (Prime Minister of Malaysia), 352
Mahila Vikas Sanstha, 513
Main, H.A.C., 469, 480
Maisonettes, 498
Majri Grant village, 401
Malaria, incidence of, 267
Malnutrition, 507
Mass media, 575
Mathews, Jessica T., 530, 538
Max Weber, 2280
McCully, P., 357
McDonald, Flora, 339, 344
McFarlone, M.J., 172
Meadows, D.H., 123
Mechanization, 317
Messerli, Bruno, 229
Metropolis developing countries, 541
Micro-level, perspectives, 453
projects, 204
Misra, R.P., 200
Mittal, J.P., 200
Modern agricultural practices, 257
irrigation programmes, 258
medical facilities, 529
Modernisation, 304, 541
Mogulpet village, 260
Mohallas, 91
Mohamedpur Barkali, 395, 397
Mohnen, V.A., 62
Monoculture,
patterns, 270
trends, 187
Mortimore, M.J., 477
Morgan, W.T.W., 181, 182, 191, 193
Mukherjee, Amitava, 387
Multiple cropping, 270
Murra, J.V., 190
Murray, L.M., 169
Musslewhite, Benton, 29
Mussoorie, 398
Muzaffarnagar, 108

Nagal Jwalapur, 407
Nagaland, *jhuming* in, 378
sustainable development, 377
Nakamura, H., 284, 310
Narasimha Rao, 535
Nash, R.F., 281
National conservation plan, 129
National Front policy, 440
National malaria eradication programme, 268
Nature conservation club, 305
Nathawat, M.S., 91
Nepal, 242
New environment policy, 303
New Guinea, narrow cordillera of, 191
New York, 334
New Zealand, 337
Nigeria, 181, 186, 480
Nile Valley, 163, 471
Nizamuddin *Bustee*, 455
Non-Governmental Organisations (NGOs), 363
Nutritional problems, 517

Odum, H.T., 144
Olofin, E.A., 482
Olsen, M.T., 169
Open-plan space, 499
Optical Reflecting Projector (ORP), 94
Ozone depletion, 23
layer, 65

Pakistan, 240, 241
Panchayat, 418

programmes, 53
Panchayat Development Society (PDS), 55
Pandeya, R.C., 283
Pant, C., 210
Participatory Rural Appraisal (PRA), 391
Passmore, J., 280
Pathak, Pushpa, 449
Pattas, 516
Pavich, M.J., 166
Pedisediment, 168-69
Pepper, D., 281
Pezzey, J., 40
Phadke, V.S., 209
Place-work-folk, interrelationships, 86
Plassey, battle of, 527
Polarization, 520
Polger, J., 305
Political structure, 297
Polonoreste projects, 32
Pollution, 93, 285, 341, 367, 370, 431, 440
control, 292
costs in, 33
levels, 25
Population,
control, 30, 387
displacement and rehabilitation, 215-16
distribution and diversity, 548-49
growth, 547
control, 30
Postmodern culture, 336
Postscript, 372
Post-war industrialisation, 511
Poverty, 22, 30, 39, 71, 73, 352, 449
problems, 22, 82
Primary and secondary education, 577
Privatisation, 295
Public sector, 27, 387
Public water supply system, 452
Punjab, 130, 204, 243
Pyongan province, 327

Quality of Life, 543, 544, 545, 560
Quasi-houses, 498
Quarternary deposits, 174
geomorphology, 161

Rajasthan desert, 435
Ranade, Francois, 149
Rampa complexes, 169
Ranipokhari, 341
Rao, K.V.S., 209
Rao, N. Ram Mohan, 257
Rao, R. Ram Mohan, 257
Rashmi tehsil, 140
Ravindra, R., 283
Rawat, D.S., 107, 110
Raza, M., 432
Redclift, M., 312, 359, 366
Rees, W.E., 43
Reeves, Alison D., 291
Refugee, 191
Relict discontinuities, 167-68
Regression coefficients, 151-52
Rehabilitation, 210, 213, 215, 217, 220
Residential dwelling units, 555-56
Rupee-Rouble dispute, 534
Rio conference, 59, 66
declaration, 370
Rio de Janeiro, 349
Rio Earth Summit, 29, 367, 372, 505, 538
Rio São Francisco, 185
River valley development, 257, 266
Romanticism, 281
Rural energy system, 140
dynamics of, 139-42
policy implication, 153-54
Rural environment degradation, 469
policy, 25
Rural hinterlands, 470
Rural landscapes, 316

Sailab irrigation, 257
Sanitation, 93, 459
São Francisco valley, 187
Saprolite profiles, 166
Sarin, Madhu, 204
Sarre, Philip, 279
Satellite remote sensing data, 94-95
Satterthwaite D., 469
Scarce pubic funds, 24
Schwarz, M., 225
Schedule caste syndrome, 33
Second World War, 411
Seismic (earthquake), 228

Semi-public space, 493
Seventh Five Year Plan, 389
Sewage and drainage, 551
Shafi, M., 59
Sharma, H.S., 91
Shifting cultivation, 217, 220, 377, 378, 379
Shurmer-Smith, Pamela, 333
Silent valley, 432
Singh, Chandra Pal, 525
Singh, Mehar, 197
Singh, Nina, 431
Singh, R.B., 129
Single cropping, 270
Sita, K., 209
Sixth Five Year Plan, 289
Skye, population of, 342
Smith, P., 281
Slums and squatter settlements, 456
Small drainage basins, 1161
Soils, 438
    conditions, 261
    erosion, 262, 438
    pollution, 298
    salinity, 263
Speth, J., 362
Sriramsagar command area, 260, 269
Steep slopes, 213
Stephens, C., 517
Stock, R.F., 480
Stocking, M.A., 172
Stockholm, 71
Stone line complexes, 171
    progress, 172
Stoops, G., 162
Storm water drainage, 551
Subsidiarity, 364
Suez canal, 185
Sukhomajri project, 198, 202
Sundaram, K.V., 69, 72
Surface irrigation, 263
Sustainable Development (SD), 40, 41, 72, 129, 349, 350, 358, 377, 384
    concept, 197
    natural resources, 86
    political implications, 358
    programmes, 49, 360
    urban environment, 487
Tabibzadeh, I., 507
Tamil Nadu, 181
Tanzania, 181
Tapponnier, P., 228
Technology transfer scheme, 201
Tendler, J., 509
Third world cities, health problems, 507
Thomas, Michael, F., 161, 172
Thompson, M., 225
Thorp, M.B., 174
Thresholds, 494
Tisza river, 3303
Tokar, B., 282
Town and County Planning Act, 487
Transect reveals, 397
Transport, 552
Trewartha, G.T., 188
Trickle-down mechanism, 449
    process, 70
Trivandrum, 435
Tropical environment, contrasts in, 181-86
Tropical forests, 34
    hydromorphic podzols, 174
    uplands, 185
Tucurui dam, 32
Tuan, Yi Fu, 282

Uloor Panchayat, 46
Umitsu, Masatoma, 234
Unemployment, 60, 71, 293, 536, 541
UNCD Conference, 283
UNICEF phase, 513
United Nations Conference, 71, 226
United Nations Environment Programme, 59
Upper colluvium, 169, 171
Upper corridors, 489
Upper Ganga plain, 108
Urban Basic Services (UBS), 453
Urban Community Development (UCD), 505, 510, 514, 518
Urban energy consumption, 472
    environment, 544
        management, 541
        problems, 450
    pollution, 62
    poverty, growing challenges, 506

villages, 102
Urbanisation, 449, 469, 542
process, 543
Urry, John, 342
Uruguay Round, 365
Utilitarianism, 281
Uttar Pradesh, 388, 418
five year plans, 390

Vaigai Dam, 549
Valley sediments, 173
Varga, P., 295
Vedas, 126
Velbel, M.A., 166
Venezuela, 189
Visakhapatnam Urban Community Development, 505, 510, 515
Vyas, N.S., 139

Warbandi, 274
Waste disposal, 474
Wastelands, 99
Waste management, 75, 220, 302
Water, access to, 458-59
distribution system, 549-51
pollution, 63, 446
quality, 295-96, 302
supply, 549
Water-borne diseases, 267, 508-09
Waterlogging, 259, 263-64, 433
causes of, 265
West Germany, 432
Wet paddy system, 320
White, F., 182
White, G., 306
White, R.R., 474
White highland policy, 193
White sands, 173-74
Whitlow, J.R., 173
Wilson, A.G., 144
Williams, Raymond, 333
Womens' status, 518
Workers' Party of Korea (WPK), 310, 323
World Bank, 33, 73, 79, 139, 241, 306, 442, 450
World Commission, 285, 350, 359
World Summit, 32
Wray, J., 507

Yamuna river, 118, 473
Yamunanagar, 440
Yearley, S., 358
Yeltsin (President), 534
Yulli reservoir, 323

Zimbabwe, 172